Understanding International Law

Understanding International Law

Conway W. Henderson

A John Wiley & Sons, Ltd., Publication

Blackwell Publishing was acquired by John Wiley & Sons in February 2007. Blackwell's publishing program has been merged with Wiley's global Scientific, Technical, and Medical business to form Wiley-Blackwell.

Registered Office
John Wiley & Sons Ltd, The Atrium, Southern Gate, Chichester, West Sussex, PO19 8SQ, United Kingdom

Editorial Offices
350 Main Street, Malden, MA 02148–5020, USA
9600 Garsington Road, Oxford, OX4 2DQ, UK
The Atrium, Southern Gate, Chichester, West Sussex, PO19 8SQ, UK

For details of our global editorial offices, for customer services, and for information about how to apply for permission to reuse the copyright material in this book please see our website at www.wiley.com/wiley-blackwell.

Library of Congress Cataloging-in-Publication Data

Henderson, Conway W.
    Understanding international law / Conway W. Henderson.
        p.   cm.
    Includes bibliographical references and index.
    ISBN 978-1-4051-9764-9 (hardcover : alk. paper) – ISBN 978-1-4051-9765-6 (pbk. : alk. paper) 1.   International law. I.   Title.
    KZ3410.H46 2010
    341–dc22

                                                                2009033118

A catalogue record for this book is available from the British Library.

Set in 10.5/13pt Minion by SPi Publisher Services, Pondicherry, India
Printed and bound in Singapore by Ho Printing Singapore Pte Ltd

1   2010

This book is dedicated to Victoria, my bride of twenty-five years,
on our Silver Wedding Anniversary

Contents

Boxes

Preface

This textbook has been written by a political scientist with many years of experience in the classroom. I have tried to write the book that students need but will enjoy reading. Much attention has been given to making this text accessible and interesting to students new to this field. Other textbooks in international law have been written, but they tend to be either thick tomes of technical case law or thin volumes with some political perspective. This textbook aims to give proper coverage to the scope of international law with appropriate length, but also to better balance political and legal perspectives. The legal emphasis in this text favors treaty law because it is the primary source of international law today. Not only is it listed first in the hierarchy of sources in the *Statute of the International Court of Justice*, but treaty-making has risen to a quasi-legislative status in an age of multilateral conference diplomacy. Case law is also important, and there are turning-point cases decided by judges which can influence the direction that international rules take. The findings of international criminal tribunals that widespread rape is a war and humanitarian crime, and not just the wrong-doing of individual persons, is a good example. Court cases are referred to in the text but are also available in the website accompanying this textbook.

The list of persons for whom an author should be grateful is always a lengthy one, and only some can be mentioned here. My wife, Victoria, has had to contend with my focus on this writing project on a daily basis. Her patience and support have been invaluable. I have two colleagues who have read and critiqued every page. These are Joyce Wiley and Richard Combes. Their friendship and collegiality go far beyond any reasonable expectation. I should also like to thank the Interlibrary Loan Specialist of my university, Mary Kaye Gault, for her considerable help and cheerful courtesy. The Acquisitions Editor, Nick Bellorini, has been kind and patient throughout. Others have contributed their skills with tireless efforts and refreshing civility. These include Liz Cremona, Senior Production Editor, Ben Thatcher, Senior Publishing Coordinator, and Graeme Leonard, Project Manager. Without qualification, all faults and shortcomings belong to the author alone.

Finally, I am very open to comments, suggestions, and criticisms. I am available at chenderson@uscupstate.edu or 800 University Way, 136 Media Building, USC Upstate, Spartanburg, SC, 29302, United States.

Abbreviations

ABMs	Agreements on Anti-Ballistic Missiles
ACHPR	African Court on Human and Peoples' Rights
ACHR	American Convention on Human Rights
ACJ	Andean Court of Justice
ADZ	air defense zone
AEPS	Arctic Environmental Protection Strategy
AL	League of Arab States
ANC	African National Congress
AOSIS	Alliance of Small Island States
APC	Asian, Pacific, and Caribbean Countries
APEC	Asia Pacific Economic Cooperation
ASEAN	Association of South East Asian Nations
ASIL	American Society of International Law
ATA	Arms Trade Agreement
ATCP	Arctic Treaty Consulting Parties
ATILO	Administrative Tribunal for the International Labor Organization
ATS	Arctic Treaty System
AU	African Union
BCE	Before the Common Era
BITs	bilateral investment treaties
BTU	British thermal unit
BWC	Biological Weapons Convention
CAFETA	Central American Free Trade Agreement
CAS	Court of Arbitration for Sport
CAT	Convention against Torture
CBD	Convention on Biological Diversity
CCAT	Criminal Campaign against Terrorists

CCC	Clean Clothes Campaign
CCCW	Convention on Certain Conventional Weapons
CE	Common Era
CEDAW	Convention on the Elimination of all Forms of Discrimination against Women
CFE	Treaty on Conventional Forces in Europe
CFCs	chlorofluorocarbons
CITES	Convention to Regulate International Trade in Endangered Species of Flora and Fauna
COE	Council of Europe
COMESA	Common Market for Eastern and Southern Africa
COP	Conference of Parties
COPUOS	Commission on the Peaceful Uses on Outer Space
CSA	Confederate States of America
CSD	Commission on Sustainable Development
CTBT	Comprehensive Nuclear Test Ban Treaty
CTOC	Convention against Transnational Organized Crime
CWC	Chemical Weapons Convention
DSB	Dispute Settlement Body
DSD	Department of Sustainable Development
ECHR	European Convention on Human Rights
ECHR	European Court of Human Rights
ECJ	European Court of Justice
ECOSOC	Economic and Social Council
ECOWAS	Economic Community of West African States
EEA	European Environmental Agency
EEZ	Exclusive Economic Zone
EP	European Parliament
ESA	European Space Agency
EU	European Union
Europol	European Police Office
FAO	Food and Agricultural Organization
FDI	foreign direct investment
FGM	female genital mutilation
FLN	National Liberation Front
FMCT	Fissile Material Cut-off Treaty
FSIA	Foreign Service Immunities Act
FSO	Foreign Service Officer
GATS	General Agreement on Trade Services
GATT	General Agreement on Tariffs and Trade
GDP	gross domestic product
GEF	Global Environmental Facility
GEMS	Global Environmental Monitoring System
GLBTs	gay, lesbian, bi-sexual, and transgender persons
GSP	generalized system of preferences

GSTP	global system of trade preferences among developing countries
G-8	Group of Eight Top Economic States
G-20	Group of Twenty Top Economic States
G-77	Group of Seventy-seven Developing States
HCA	High Court of Australia
HDI	Human Development Index
HIPC	Heavily Indebted Poor Countries
HRE	Holy Roman Empire
IACHR	Inter-American Court of Human Rights
IAEA	International Atomic Energy Agency
IANSA	International Action Network on Small Arms
IBRD	International Bank for Reconstruction and Development
ICANN	Internet Corporation for Assigned Names and Numbers
ICAO	International Civil Aviation Organization
ICBL	International Campaign to Ban Landmines
ICBMs	intercontinental ballistic missiles
ICC	International Criminal Court
ICCPR	International Convention on Civil and Political Rights
ICESCR	International Convention on Economic, Social and Cultural Rights
ICJ	International Court of Justice
ICRC	International Committee of the Red Cross
ICSID	International Center for the Settlement of Disputes
ICTR	International Criminal Tribunal for Rwanda
ICTY	International Criminal Tribunal for Yugoslavia
IDA	International Development Association
IFC	International Finance Corporation
IGOs	International Government Organizations
ILC	International Law Commission
ILO	International Labor Organization
IMF	International Monetary Fund
IMTs	International Military Tribunals (Nuremberg and Tokyo)
INF	intermediate nuclear forces
Interpol	International Police Organization
IPCC	Intergovernmental Panel on Climate Change
IPR	intellectual property rights
ISAF	International Security Assistance Force
ISO	International Standardization Organization
ISP	Internet service provider
ITLOS	International Tribunal for the Law of the Sea
ITU	International Telecommunications Union
IWC	International Whaling Commission
LBMP	land based marine pollution
LRTAP	Long-Range Transnational Air Pollution (Geneva Convention)
MAD	mutually assured destruction

MARPOL	Marine Pollution Convention
MDG	Millennium Development Goal
MFN	most favored nation
MIGA	Multilateral Investment Guarantee Agency
MIRVs	multiple independently targetable re-entry vehicles
MNCs	multinational corporations
MTCR	Missile Technology Control Regime
NAFTA	North American Free Trade Association (Agreement)
NATO	North Atlantic Treaty Organization
NGOs	non-government organizations
NICs	newly industrializing countries
NIEO	new international economic order
NLM	National Liberation Movement
NPT	Nuclear Non-Proliferation Treaty
NSG	Nuclear Suppliers Group
NWFZ	Nuclear Weapons Free Zone
OAS	Organization of American States
OAU	Organization of African Unity
OECD	Organization for Economic Cooperation and Development
OPCW	Organization for the Prohibition of Chemical Weapons
OPEC	Organization of Petroleum Exporting Countries
OSCE	Organization for Security and Cooperation in Europe
Oxfam	Oxford Committee for Famine Relief
PAP	Pan-African Parliament
PCA	Permanent Court of Arbitration
PCIJ	Permanent Court of International Justice
PICT	Project on International Courts and Tribunals
PLO	Palestinian Liberation Organization
PMCs	private military companies
POPS	Protocol on Persistent Organic Pollutants
POWs	prisoners of war
PSI	Proliferation Security Initiative
RCC	Roman Catholic Church
RPG	rocket propelled grenade
RTAs	Rocket Trade Agreements
SALT	Strategic Arms Limitation Talks
SLV	space launched vehicles
SORT	Strategic Offensive Reduction Treaty
START	Strategic Arms Reductions Talks (Treaty)
TBT	technical barriers to trade
TEDs	turtle exit devices
TI	Transparency International
TNC	transnational corporation
TOC	Transnational Organized Crime (Convention)

TRIPS	(Agreement on) Trade Related Aspects of Intellectual Property Rights
UDHR	Universal Declaration of Rights
UNAT	United National Administrative Tribunal
UNCCD	UN Convention to Combat Desertification
UNCITRAL	UN Commission on International Trade Law
UNCTAD	UN Conference on Trade and Development
UNDP	UN Development Program
UNEF	UN Emergency Force
UNEP	UN Environmental Program
UNESCO	UN Educational, Scientific, and Cultural Organization
UNFCCC	UN Framework Convention on Climate Control
UNICEF	UN International Children's Fund
UNLOS	UN Law of the Sea Convention
UPU	Universal Postal Union
WB	World Bank
WEDO	Women's Environmental and Development Organization
WEF	World Economic Forum
WHO	World Health Organization
WIPO	World Intellectual Property Organization
WMD	weapons of mass destruction
WOMP	World Orders Model Project
WOT	war on terror
WTO	World Trade Organization
WWF	World Wildlife Fund
ZPG	zero population growth

Part I

Making the World More Lawful

Law is a major force in international affairs; nations rely on it, invoke it, observe and are influenced by it in every aspect of their foreign relations. (Professor Louis Henkin)

International law is that law which the wicked do not obey and the righteous do not enforce. (Abba Eden, past Israeli ambassador to the United States)

1

The Rise of International Law

Contents

The discipline of political science failed for decades to give international law its due as a framework for constraining and channeling politics at the international level. The competitive, and sometimes conflictual, interactions among states over "who gets what, when, and how" has prevented many international specialists from imagining that international law could perform a role similar to law inside countries (Ku & Diehl 1991: 3–5). These political scientists, known as *realists* with a focus on power-driven international politics, either ignore international law or place it on an idealistic plane with limited prospects for taming ungoverned international politics. E. H. Carr once observed that many scholars could only hope to "transfer our differences from the turbulent political atmosphere of self-interest to the purer, serener air of impartial justice" (Carr 1946: 170; Hsiung 1997). Yet, as Carr went on to point out, "In practice, law and politics may be different but are indissolubly intertwined." An interplay between politics and law at the international level is an ongoing process, with each shaping the meaning of the other. Bearing in mind that the two fit closely together, like a hand in a glove, *studying international law in its political setting is the guiding perspective of this textbook*. Fortunately, international specialists have recently taken international law more seriously. They are no longer dismissive of it simply because this law lacks a central authority with strong enforcement powers.

The following chapter sections should help the reader form a clear picture of the evolution and status of international law. This chapter begins with a discussion of international law as to whether it is real law followed by a section on the roles international law can play to serve international society. Then, a section on the early history of international law appears with sections on the views of early legal philosophers and current approaches to this law coming next. The favorable and unfavorable conditions operating around international law is the last chapter section before the chapter summary.

The Nature of International Law

Anne-Marie Slaughter says that professors of international law have long known that international law can constrain and channel conflictual politics into cooperative patterns, but she thinks political scientists in the international relations field need to catch up to this thinking and believes they began to do so in the 1970s through their study of **regimes**. These entities are sets of rules and norms that states converge around and usually obey. For instance, the rules of the International Whaling Commission against hunting whales amount to the *whaling regime*. Slaughter claims that international relations specialists have rediscovered international law and are simply giving it a different name (Slaughter Burley 1993: 205–39; see also Slaughter, Talumello, & Wood 1998: 367–97). Luckily, there is now an ongoing dialogue between law and political science professors (Arend 1999: 6). The belated appreciation for world law may have been due to the absence of a world government to generate and enforce this law. For decades, many international relations scholars and the informed public regarded international law as a marginal specialty, well meaning but naïve and mostly irrelevant (p. 4).

Yet, it is the workability of international law in **anarchy**, that is, in a system without a centralized government, which makes this subject so fascinating. A full appreciation and understanding of international relations is not possible without recognizing that international rules do exist and are very much needed. Louis Henkin has argued persuasively that law is a major force in international affairs since states rely on it, invoke it, and observe it in all aspects of their foreign relations (Henkin 1979). Argentina's invasion of the Falkland Islands in 1982 and Iraq's aggression against Kuwait in 1990 were defeated, in part, because most states saw these acts of force as illegal. Throughout most of the twentieth century and continuing into the twenty-first, aggressive behavior has been seen as a violation of *jus cogens*. This concept involves a peremptory norm so fundamental that its transgression is always unacceptable. Nevertheless, major powers, and sometimes lesser powers, still choose to use force, posing a tough problem for international law. At least when states rely on force, they are put on the legal defensive as they struggle to rationalize their actions as "self-defense," the sole allowable justification in the UN Charter for the independent use of force. International law may be weak and imperfect compared to some national legal systems, but its several hundred years of development and influence are incontestable. This law, as with other human institutions, survives, and even flourishes, because it is functionally useful.

A clear definition of the core concept is necessary. **International law** is the collection of rules and norms that states and other actors feel an obligation to obey in their mutual relations and commonly do obey. In international relations, **actors** are simply the individuals and collective entities, such as states and international organizations, which can make behavioral choices, whether lawful or unlawful. **Rules** are formal, often written, expectations for behavior, while **norms** are less formal customary expectations about appropriate behavior that are frequently unwritten. Diplomats receive immunity from their host states as a clear treaty *rule*, while a diplomatic *norm* requires spoken and written correspondence to be very polite.

Is international law really law? This question is an enduring one for many scholars and leaders. The observable behavior of states and other actors, as well as their frequent references to law in communications and documents, demonstrate the law's reality. Perhaps a more suitable question is whether international law can be viable without emanating from a world government. Some theorists look down their noses at international law, regarding it as primitive, because this law lacks a *command* feature. Effective sanctions are not readily available to punish transgressors, as is possible inside countries (Bull 1995: 124). Countries cannot be arrested and simply put in jail. Nor does this law have a *vertical* structure involving an authority operating over the heads of the states. Thomas Hobbes, a seventeenth-century English philosopher, is often quoted for having said, "where there is no common power, there is no law" (p. 124). Theorists of this persuasion view international law as little more than international morality easily ignored in an anarchical world where naked power tends to prevail.

Actually, compelling reasons do exist for reaching the conclusion that international law is true law. International law is not based on commands backed by sanctions but instead rests on *voluntary compliance*. As a matter of fact, **municipal law**, or domestic national law, from Afghanistan to Zimbabwe counts heavily on the cooperation of the various citizenries. If a national government had to force every citizen to obey every law, that government would need to hire mercenary police officers equal in number to that country's citizens. Although there are enough law-breakers in every country to justify a prison system, people usually obey the law because they believe it is in their enlightened self-interest to do so. Drivers halt at stop signs because they do not want to die in a car wreck or, less severe, receive a ticket. Paying taxes, serving on juries, and respecting the rights of other citizens is fairly natural to most citizens because they understand this kind of behavior creates a more wholesome society for everyone. Consequently, law does not succeed or fail depending on enforcement alone.

This observation applies equally well to a horizontal authority system in which the "citizens" (primarily the states) are **sovereign**, meaning they are legal equals and free of any central authority operating over their heads. States obey the law because it is usually in their interests to do so, and a legal structure makes international life less dangerous and costly. Because of international law, states have confidence that they can safely send their ambassadors to foreign soil; they can ship goods across borders and expect payment; their ships on the high seas will not be interfered with; or, in the case of a breakdown in relations that leads to war, refugees and POWs will be repatriated. The reason this decentralized legal system is able to work does not depend on the few risky sanctions available to states, such as war or retaliation including breaking off trade or diplomatic contact. States hang together within a legal system due to a relationship of **reciprocity.** This relationship is one of give and take, with states returning in like kind the privileges and services they receive from other states.

The energy propelling international law is positive, not negative. Of course, the degree of cultural consensus, shared material interests, and the growing sense of global interdependence says a lot about how well this relatively non-coercive, non-centralized, legal system can work. Most diplomatic and economic exchanges move along smoothly, and to mutual advantage, although general world public opinion might have a hard time realizing the everyday usefulness of international law. The pervasive global media of today stress violent conflict, much like local news programs choose to show the wreck and carnage on our highways rather than steady flows of traffic moving safely to their destinations. The regular practice of international law by most actors results in a more orderly and predictable world, which goes unappreciated by a CNN world addicted to news of suicide-bombers and bloody ethnic civil war.

Fully appreciating the nature of international law is possible only by recognizing that international law is built into the **order** of international relations. An order is an enduring pattern of values and behaviors which structures the relationships of actors over time, usually decades or even centuries. Today's order includes democratic, human rights, and capitalist values rising to primacy with the major states striving to get along and trying to persuade lesser states to accept more fully the same order, with its decidedly Western character. The rules of international law help to establish and perpetuate a particular world order.

States vary greatly in size and power, but all try to shape the international order by influencing the content of international law. Since the end of the Second World War, the United States, with its power growing to **hegemon** status, or the world's most powerful state, has tried to secure its vision of world order through international organizations and international law. The creation of the UN, the World Bank, the World Trade Organization (WTO), the promotion of human rights treaties, and much else of the post-Second World War structure have come about in large part due to US influence. In the past, some observers claimed that the world order had begun to resemble not just a Western but a *Pax Americana*, an American designed peace in particular. Any lasting American imprint on the global order may be in question since the United States has become hesitant to support important treaties, and its vaunted military and economic prowess are undermined by the seemingly endless Afghanistan and Iraq wars plus the sharp downward turn in the US economy in 2008–9.

The Roles of International Law

The first role of international law is *to arrange for the cooperation most actors wish to have most of the time.* Try to imagine a world with global trade grinding to a halt, diplomats unable to represent their governments to other states, radio and television signals jamming each other across borders, students unable to study or go backpacking in other countries because they cannot acquire visas, health and economic development programs in poor countries screeching to a halt because the UN ceases to exist, or the degradation of the oceans, outer space, and Antarctica because these common heritage spaces no longer enjoy the protection of treaties. Modern international life, as we know it today with its pervasive and predicable patterns of cooperation, would be impossible without the rules and understandings bound up in international law. Without rules to develop and sustain multiple kinds of positive interactions, international relations would be little more than a set of states co-existing in an atmosphere of constant worry over security threats. The "law of nations," as these rules are sometimes called, is at least a cornerstone, if not the foundation, of modern international relations.

Another essential role is that international law *identifies the membership of an international society* of sovereign states (Bull 1995). Under law, states are granted formal recognition as members of the international society, and given rights and duties within this society. Enjoying membership, states can engage other states over competitive as well as mutual interests through diplomacy and at the forums of numerous organizations and international conferences. Additionally, there are non-state actors as well participating in international society, such as the United Nations, revolutionary movements, and even individuals in some circumstances. Non-state actors have a lesser degree of legal standing reflecting the continued primacy of the state over other actors sharing international society.

The law is also a mechanism *to regulate the competing interests of the various actors and to carry their agreements into the future.* Any place where people intermingle in patterns of cooperation or conflict can be called a "political space" (Rochester 2000: 43; Lung-ch Chen 2000: 410). The world political space contains nearly two hundred states with several other kinds of actors, with most of these wanting to believe that what has been arranged today will still be in place tomorrow (Starr 1995: 302). When a challenge to the *status quo* does occur between those wanting change and those who do not, international law helps constrain the ensuing political struggle by providing diplomatic and judicial options such as arbitration (Carr 1946: 179–80). States mostly accept international society, underpinned by a legal system, because they see the possibility of protecting what they have or making some gains with minimum costs (Hurrell 2000: 328). The law can be a means to a political end (Ku & Diel 1991: 6). This role of international law has been summed up in one sentence of Christopher C. Joyner's that "International law codifies ongoing solutions for persistent problems" (Joyner 1998: 263).

International law as well *empowers weaker countries as they press for change against the will of the powerful.* In diplomatic conferences and international organizations, where strength is partly measured in votes, small and medium-sized states have sometimes won the day. For instance, at the Law of the Seas Conference, 1958–82, the majority of states successfully pressed for a 12-mile offshore territorial jurisdiction to replace the traditional three-mile limit. The Soviet Union and the United States, despite being Cold War adversaries, wanted the three-mile jurisdiction to remain in place as an international rule. This traditional rule, dating back to the seventeenth century would leave them with a greater expanse of ocean for their powerful blue water navies. Superpowers on occasion have had to bend their knees

Box 1.1 Community or Society?

American specialists in international relations are prone to use *international community* and *international society* as if they are interchangeable synonyms, but it is useful to distinguish the two. Both call for a degree of cohesion and inter-dependence among the actors associating in some sort of group affiliation. The difference in degree between the two, however, is great. A *community* has more solidarity, as in the cases of the family, a village, a church, or a small ethnic group where personal interaction is possible. The identity with and loyalty to the group are strong. A *society*, in contrast, is always busy adjusting significant differences among a loose association of actors. The actors of the society relate to one another within a shared group in meaningful ways but lack a strong sense of common identity and loyalty. Examples might be a joint stock company or today's international relations among a core of Western states. A society is less likely to withstand internal conflict since it must regularly deal with the centrifugal force of self-interest by the members. International law is important because it provides the platform for the adjustments necessary to keep the society whole. The best hope for a society to continue its life is that members will focus on the common interest to a society-sustaining degree.

It is possible to think of a society evolving into a community, or a community deteriorating into a society. The nascent international society has a long wait before turning into a community, if it ever does. If there is an international community today, it might be in the limited sense that many people around the world hold a cosmopolitan belief in the oneness of humanity. For instance, people on one side of the globe deserve to be treated as well as people on the other side; after all, humankind is one great family of individuals with all deserving to enjoy a full range of human rights.

Sources: Main source is George Keeton and Georg Scharzenberger, *Making International Law Work* (New York: Garland Publishing, Inc., 1972; originally published in 1939 and a second edn. in 1946). Other sources are Mathias Albert, Lothar Brock, and Klaus Dieter Wolf (eds.), *Civilizing World Politics: Society and Community Beyond the State* (Lanham, MD: Rowman & Littlefield, 2000); and Robert Jackson, *The Global Covenant: Human Conduct in a World of States* (New York: Oxford University Press, 2000).

in a world conditioned by the existing law as well as by a majority of states pressing for new law. This situation did not change when the United States held sway as a lone superpower in the 1990s. David J. Bederman put the matter poignantly when he said, "It is patently false to believe that one state – even a superpower – can unilaterally captain the course of international law" (Bederman 2001b: 10).

As international law channels and controls the push and pull of politics, it can sometimes serve as an instrument *to promote justice*. Decades ago, Gerard Mangone wrote, "The functions of international law, as in any system of law, are to assist in the maintenance of order and in the administration of justice" (Mangone 1967: 1). Hedley

Bull believed if an international order were to endure, it not only needed the support of major powers, but this legal system must also provide justice for the international society as a whole (Bull 1995: 74–94). Bull recognized this role of international law concerning such matters as improving human rights and promoting economic development for the less advantaged states. At the same time, Bull cautioned about going too far, too fast with "social engineering" by means of law. Demands for radical change can be disruptive to an international order, he stated, since international law has always depended on a large degree of consensus (1995: 136–55).

Finally, the most interesting and ambitious role of international law is the *outlawry of war*. Historically, leaders regarded war as the *ultima ratio Regis* (or the ultimate means of a king), but in the twenthieth century, a sea change occurred when war ceased being a legitimate option of foreign policy. Eliminating war as a normal means of international politics were core elements of the League of Nations' Covenant and the UN's Charter. Should war break out anyway, international law is sufficiently prepared so that if *jus ad bellum* (law to begin war, but often understood as war for a just cause) is violated, *jus in bello* (law of war) goes into effect. The intent of this momentous reform was to move political conflict into diplomatic and judicial channels. Toward this end, international law offers many options for conflict resolution short of war (Starr 1995: 307–8). Admittedly, however, international law has a more successful record regulating trade, international electronic communications and airline travel, as well as many other subjects, than is the case when national leaders perceive and react to security threats against their states (Brierly 1963: 77–8; Wilson 1990: 292).

The Early Beginnings of International Law

Scholars interested in international law seem to enjoy a game of one upmanship as they try to pinpoint the earliest possible beginnings of international law. Some scholars draw attention to the rules of the ancient civilizations of China, the Greek city-states, the Indian states, and Persia in the dealings of these entities with outsiders. A favorite point of other writers is that the Mesopotamian communities concluded treaties as early as 3100 BCE. Still other scholars prefer to begin with Roman law. The elaborate code law of the Romans heavily influenced continental Europe long after the collapse of the Roman Empire, and the study and use of Roman law exposed Europeans to the notion of natural law that the Romans had earlier borrowed from the ancient Greeks. Roman law also had a nice distinction between *jus civile* (civil law for Roman citizens) and *jus gentium* (law of nations). The latter governed the relations of Romans and non-Romans, although not on a basis of equality.[1] In the centuries after Rome's collapse, law among separate entities would be known as the "law of nations" until Jeremy Bentham introduced the term "international law" in 1780. In some languages, the law of nations is still preferred, as in the cases of Dutch and German speakers who use *völkerrecht* (Malanczuk 1997: 1).

Martin Wight once argued that international law began with the sixteenth-century debate in Spain over the status of "Indians" in the Americas. Did Spain have the right to absorb much of the Americas in the western hemisphere into their empire by refusing to recognize any rights on the part of the indigenous peoples to their own lands? (Epp 1998: 56–7). The Spanish and other Europeans came to view the Americas as *terra nullius*, that is, land belonging to no one and subject to European conquest. The interests of the indigenous peoples were simply brushed aside. Many scholars, as a convenience, date the beginning of international law, along with the sovereign state system, from the 1648 *Treaty of Westphalia*.

This textbook operates from the assumption that to understand the beginnings of international law, investigation must start with the collapse of the Roman Empire in the West in 478 CE and the Byzantine half of the empire not long afterward. The epochal recession of the Roman Empire left in its wake the Medieval Age (476–1350 CE) with its mishmash of entities, including manor estates, duchies, walled cities, monasteries, and fiefdoms ruled by kings. As for unity, there existed only a loose order of overlapping authorities, the *Roman Catholic Church* (RCC) and the *Holy Roman Empire* (HRE). Together, these overlapping authorities headed a ramshackle society in Western Europe known as *Christendom*. With the disappearance of Roman rule, Europe lost its unity under an effective central authority. Rome did leave behind the important legacy of the *Justinian Code*, the apex of Roman law compiled between 528 and 534 CE. Not only did this law, when rediscovered by Europeans centuries later, set the basis for the code laws of European states (with the notable exception of England's customary or common law), it also allowed the notion of law among separate peoples to survive. Europeans were able to conceptualize that if Rome could have special law governing relations with the peoples living on the periphery of their empire, then Europeans might have law among independent kings. **Jus gentium** no longer applied to the inferior barbarians outside the boundaries of the Roman Empire but to the rudimentary states of Europe.

If the Church offered spiritual authority, the HRE tried to offer temporal authority. The HRE built on Charlemagne's (742–814 CE) effort to establish a Christian kingdom in Western Europe. About 150 years after Charlemagne's death, the HRE tried to pull his empire back together. Usually governed by a German emperor, with the approval of a RCC pope, the HRE existed from 962 until 1806. Over its history, the HRE tended to recede in territory rather than expand until Napoleon Bonaparte dissolved it in 1806 after the HRE had become hardly more than a whimper. Voltaire (1694–1778), the famous French philosopher, denouncing the HRE as an artifice, reportedly said that it was "neither Holy, Roman, nor an Empire."

The two overlapping but weak vertical authorities of Christendom, a kind of rule that P. E. Corbett once called a "thin film over political anarchy" (1951: 6). exerted little effort to develop a full body of international law in medieval Europe. In time, powerful historical forces undermined the semblance of *vertical* law and created a strong functional need for a *horizontal* legal system appropriate for a set of independent kingdoms.

The Reformation devastated the Catholic religious monopoly over Europe. This period started in 1517 with a demand for religious reform. Martin Luther, a Professor of Theology, nailed his 95 Theses on a door at the University of Wittenberg and triggered a widespread debate over the corruption and doctrine of the RCC. With the aid of the relatively new technology of the printing press, the debate spread rapidly across

Europe until protest against the RCC led to the creation of various sects of the Protestant faith. The Reformation eventually divided Europe into Catholic and Protestant states, a situation that contributed heavily to the Thirty Year War (1618–48).

The Renaissance also contributed to the making of strong kings and countries. This period began in the late fourtheenth century in Italian cities and in the fifteenth century in the cities of Holland. In this era, there was a great flowering of new ideas in art, science, and even politics. A new merchant class, or *bourgeoisie*, arose because of inventiveness in technology, and the belief that people should fulfill themselves in all their creative and economic potentials. This thinking spurred on the *Protestant Ethic* of the Reformation which called for people to work hard and sacrifice now in order to enjoy economic success later, an approach to life believed pleasing to God. The new bourgeoisie class could provide loans and taxes for kings who, in turn, could develop professional armies equipped with cannon capable of knocking down castle walls. Recalcitrant nobles could no longer resist the will of their king by holding up in impregnable castles. In time, the kings of Europe developed unqualified control in their realms and needed to doff their crowns neither to the Pope nor to the Emperor of the HRE. Except for the cataclysm of the Thirty Years War, the stage was now set for the emergence of modern international law to govern public affairs. Private business law, known as merchant law, was already underway.

Many scholars nonchalantly refer to the cause of the Thirty Years War as rivalry between the Protestant and Catholic states. The religious cause was, indeed, a major one, but the war was more complex. Protestant Sweden and Catholic France feared that the Hapsburgs would dominate Europe much as Napoleon and Hitler would try to do later in history. Although of different religious persuasions, France and Sweden fought as allies to block the expansion of the Hapsburg alliance that included, among others, Austria, the Netherlands, Northern Italy, and Spain. For the times, the war was fought with great intensity, leaving much of central Europe (chiefly the German princely states) in devastation (Kegley & Raymond 2002).

The principal outcome of the 1648 *Peace of Westphalia*, ending the Thirty Year War, was the acceptance of the thinking of Jean Bodin (1530–1596) that kings and their states should enjoy their sovereignty as legal equals and able to act independently of each other. A critical rule that emerged was that states could not interfere with one another in internal matters for religious or other reasons. After Westphalia, with a group of independent states in place, a strong functional need arose for a set of horizontally based rules. Without the guidance of a superior authority, such as a pope or emperor, sovereign kings would need new rules on how to deal with one another (Malenczuk 1997: 10).

These rules would have to emerge from the customary practices of states and the writings of philosophers. After all, there was no world parliament or other overarching authority to perform the task of making rules. The Peace of Westphalia was the first explicit expression of a nascent European society, a society that had been forming before 1648 and continues to develop today, but now on a global scale (Jackson 2001: 42–6). Following from the Enlightenment Age (1648–1789), the seedtime of progressive views, the acceptance of democracy and human rights would eventually characterize most of the states of the European state society. Through exploration by

---

Box 1.2 Merchant Law

During the Renaissance period, rising numbers of towns and cities in Europe became centers for fairs, markets, and banks. These centers drew merchants from other countries as maritime and land travel improved. Since Roman and early medieval law did not contain concepts that supported sufficiently the expanding business enterprises of the day, merchant organizations and crafts- man guilds began to develop their own rules and regulations. Usually regarded as fair, private merchant law and courts were accepted in many countries to handle business issues. Government and church courts came to use *lex merca- toria*, or merchant law, as well.

Merchant law provided a smooth surface for trade that transcended the local and national peculiarities that otherwise would have obstructed business among merchants of different countries. This law came to full-bloom under the guidance of the Hanseatic League (1241–1669), which began as a merchant guild in the German states and reached outward to include 85 cities across northern Europe. Agents of the League were very useful for enforcing mer- chant law at large annual trade fairs in various countries.

This area of law continued into modern times and is known today as com- mercial law. Originally it was thought of as *private law* because business people are private actors. However, in modern times, with powerful multinational corporations tangling with host governments in the latters' courts, commercial law has edged into the *public law* category. Today, national courts in many countries recognize a growing *corpus* of commercial law that has roots in the merchant courts of the medieval age.

Sources: Ana Mercedes López Rodríguez, "Lex Mercatoria," School of Law, Department of Private Law, University of Aarhus, Aarhus, Denmark (written as a PhD student); Helen West Bradlee, "History of the Law Merchant," found at http://szabo.best.vwh. net/lex.html.

---

sailing ships, colonization, and international trade, European states gradually carried the Westphalian system out into the world with transforming effects.

By the nineteenth century, the European states began to insist on a "civilized stand- ard" that non-European states would have to meet before they could participate in the international society Europeans had created. Europeans expected non-Europeans to accept international law, to practice diplomacy in the European way, to have an integrated and efficient government bureaucracy, to practice a form of justice in their countries suitable for European visitors, and to accept the European views opposed to polygamy, suttee, and slavery as legitimate moral norms (Sørensen 2001: 50ff.). It would be unusual in history if the militarily strong and rich peoples did not think they were also culturally superior to others.

Ironically, before the nineteenth century, European statesmen did not think of international society as belonging to Europeans alone. In fact, natural law theorists from the sixteenth through the eighteenth century viewed international society as global. Hedley Bull states the irony aptly, "There is … an element of absurdity in the claim that states such as China, Egypt, or Persia, which existed thousands of years before states came into existence in Europe, achieved rights to full independence only when they came to pass a test devised by nineteenth century Europeans" (Bull 1984: 123).

Turkey, located at the geographical intersection of Europe and Asia, would become the first non-Christian state accepted fully by Europeans, but it was as the Ottoman Empire that this entity took a seat at the diplomatic table at the 1856 Concert of Europe (Melanczuk 1997: 12). With the collapse of European empires after the Second World War, the newly independent peoples readily accepted the Westphalian system (Watson 1992: 275–6, 299), and helped quadruple the number of states in the international society. Interestingly, the European colonizers helped sow the seeds of their own demise by inadvertently inculcating in their colonial peoples the emotional appeal of nationalism and the strong ambition for sovereign independence.

Dueling Philosophies

The international legal system had developed a life before the Westphalia system crystallized into place; however, the emergence of territorial states in the sixteenth and seventeenth centuries required a more pronounced set of rules to coordinate the relationships among these states. To fill this void, **publicists**, or legal commentators, stepped forward to offer recommendations. The earliest legal writers had philosophical or theological backgrounds since law professors in universities did not come on the scene until the late sixteenth century (Brierly 1963: 25). During the Renaissance, publicists tried to offer reasoned tracts on what they thought the law should be; they hoped the kings of Europe would observe these suggested rules in peace and in war. For sources, the publicists drew on the Bible, Canon Law, Greek and Roman literature, and various treaties that reached back into antiquity (Corbett 1951: 7–8).

Two legal philosophies dueled for supremacy, with first **natural law** and later **positivism** holding sway. Natural law originated in ancient Greece and centered on the idea that laws of divine origin governed human affairs much as laws of nature ruled in the physical world. These rules inherent in nature supposedly could be deduced by insightful minds, but goods minds often reached markedly different conclusions. Natural law was so broad it was difficult to employ for solving practical problems, and leaders of countries could easily stretch natural law's moral norms to fit their own selfish interests. At the very least, it was available as a source sort of some legal structure when little else existed (Carr 1946: 173; Charlesworth & Chinkin 2000: 25). On this matter, Sir Henry Maine once said, "The grandest function of the law of nature was discharged in giving birth to modern international law" (Brierly 1963: 24). By the seventeenth century, most publicists accepted natural law philosophy as the basis of international law, as did many political leaders.

After a long intellectual struggle lasting through the seventeenth and eighteenth centuries, positivism ultimately mounted a strong and successful challenge to the dominance of natural law. Positivism argued that international law could be no more than what states were willing to accept as obligations, especially in written treaty form. Positivism was realistic since it placed emphasis on "what is" and not "what ought to be." This simple but practical approach blended well with the modern state and its emphasis on sovereign independence. The operation of power politics in Europe was comfortable with a philosophy that permitted states to shape rules to their liking. Although positivism ascended to a superior position in the nineteenth century, natural law was not entirely eclipsed. Natural law made an important comeback in the post-Second World War period with the birth of the modern human rights movement and later, as a *just war* rationale, at least as rhetoric, when the UN approved a coalition in 1990 to undo Iraq's invasion of Kuwait. More specific justification favored the positive law of the UN Charter. A brief look at the positions of some of the publicists will help clarify the two philosophies. This task is a difficult one because some writers do not fit neatly in one camp or the other.

Francisco de Vitoria (1480–1546), a Dominican professor of theology at the University of Salamanca in Spain, argued that state obligations depended on the principles of natural law. He was a humanist who concerned himself mostly with Spain's brutal treatment of indigenous peoples (Indians) in the Americas, but Vitoria also lectured on just wars, among other subjects. A Spanish Jesuit professor of theology at the University of Coimbra in Portugal, *Franciso Suárez* (1548–1617) worked on the *duality of law* concept, trying to find the appropriate relationship between natural law and human-made law. He wanted to go beyond the metaphysics of natural law. Suárez believed *jus naturale* mandated observance by all, whereas, *jus gentium* required the consent of all. For him, natural law was universal and immutable while the law of states could change over time. Suárez is a writer that some authorities might classify as an *eclectic*, or a writer able to derive international law from more than one source.

If there has been a purist natural law advocate, that writer would be *Samuel von Pufendorf* (1632–1694). He was a German professor of law at the University of Heidelberg and later at Lund, Sweden. Pufendorf asserted that eternal truths, founded upon the laws of God and reason, were the basis of international law. Consequently, he disapproved of treaties derived from human experience and custom. For him, a superior source of authority, higher than the subjects of law, must supply the law, and this point applied to sovereign states as well as to individuals. Thus, consent among kings was insufficient as a basis of law. Pufendorf is better known for the purity of his views than for producing a legal legacy. *Emerich de Vattel* (1714–1769), a Swiss who worked in the diplomatic service of the German state of Saxony, published his *Le Droit des Gens* (*The Law of Nations*) in 1758, a work that had influence on other theorists through the nineteenth century and was cited by judges into the twentieth century. Vattel is another thinker called an eclectic; in fact; some scholars call him the originator of the eclectic approach to international law. To him, the law of nature applied to all people and, since states are made up of people, states too must obey this higher law. Vattel saw two levels of law:

God-given *jus naturale* and the other human-made *jus gentium voluntarium* that states voluntarily accept. The latter forms as leaders try to understand and apply natural law to state affairs.

As states grew confident in their legal independence but paradoxically found their relationships more interdependent with economic and diplomatic ties, their leaders grew receptive to a more practical law. They wanted a law that would accommodate their respective interests but with attention to the common good of all (Carr 1946: 177). The positivist philosophy increasingly seemed well-suited to a system of sovereign states. *Alberico Gentili* (1552–1608), an Italian protestant who fled to England and became a professor of civil law at Oxford University, often receives credit for separating international law from theology and ethics, as well as for initiating the positivist approach. Although Gentili recognized natural law of divine origin, he preferred to look at treaties and the practice of states for the content of law. *Richard Zouche* (1590–1660), an Englishman, replaced Gentili after his death at Oxford and also became a forceful advocate of the positivist school of thought. He too recognized the existence of natural law, but thought that the behavior of states was based on reason that could be drawn from principles of nature.

Cornelius van Bynkershoek (1673–1743), a Dutch judge, strongly recommended the central idea of the positivists, that states must give their consent before they can be bound by law. Additionally, he preferred that recent precedents receive emphasis over ancient ones so that international law could adjust to newly arising needs. Bynkershoek specialized in commercial and maritime law. He is best remembered for suggesting that a state's territorial sea extends three miles from shore. Among positivists, the purist would be German professor *Johann Jakob Moser* (1701–1785), who led a vigorous intellectual revolt against the use of natural law as opposed to relying on the customary conduct of states. He thought of natural law as metaphysical, and as such unobservable. Natural law was little more than what any person thought was right or wrong. A prolific writer, Moser broke a path for positivism that allowed it to arrive in the nineteenth century as the dominant philosophy in the field of international law.

One publicist stands out from the rest, in the opinion of many modern international law specialists. He offered an eclectic approach but with a clarity that had special impact in the foreign ministries and courts of Europe. This Dutch writer, as well as a diplomat and lawyer, was *Hugo Grotius* (1583–1645). He built a bridge between natural law and positivism by arguing that the two were compatible and that states should obey both. Grotius wanted states to develop the law of nations through custom and treaties and, as they did so, to take into account the basic principles of natural law. Grotius further argued that natural law must be separated from theology and given a rational basis. Moreover, his writings recognized the presence of an embryonic international society emerging from the old medieval order and in need of rules to govern the growing interactions of the states.

The best-known work by the prolific Grotius is *De Jure Belli Ac Pacis* (1625) (*On the Law of War and Peace*), which offered a general system of law suitable for both Catholic and Protestant states. As with other publicists, he was keenly interested in determining when war is just or unjust. Another special interest of Grotius was freedom of the seas, discussed in his *Mare Liberum* (1609). Grotius audaciously challenged the closed-sea doctrine of Spain and Portugal, the leading sea powers of the day, by arguing for open seas. All sea-going states, he argued, could then travel freely and trade with each other for mutual economic benefit. For his notable contributions, Grotius is frequently called the "Father of International Law." This honor may be excessive, for even Grotius acknowledged his debt to other writers (Corbett 1951: ch. 1; Brierly 1963: 25–40; Bledsoe & Boczek 1987: 20–5). Probably scholars today should speak of "*Fathers* of International Law."

Contending Modern Approaches

During the Renaissance, publicists debated over the source and nature of international law, a debate that contributed many rules for the *corpus*, or body, of international law. Modern-day scholars' contentions are more critical in the sense that they argue over whether international law has any real importance. Two main camps of theorists exist today, although there are numerous strands of thought within each camp. The **realists** are skeptical of international law and focus instead on power. Scholars who credit international law with providing some order to the world, and who believe this law will play an increasing role in an interdependent and globalizing world, are **liberals**. Most theorists fit in one of these camps.

The realists have a strong intellectual tradition stretching back across the centuries, including the thinking of Thucydides in the fourth century (BCE) Athens, Machiavelli in early sixteenth-century Florence, and Thomas Hobbes in seventeenth-century England.

Realists rose to prominence in America after the disillusionment with the League of Nations (1919–39) and the UN's (founded in 1945) inability to check national power and to prevent wars in an anarchic world. These world bodies came to life through international treaty arrangements and operated on the belief that sovereign states would comply with world rules even in matters of national security. The thinking of realists became the paradigm of international relations studies in the United States in the 1950s and 1960s and had influence in other countries as well.

Realism is a parsimonious approach that tries to account for much that happens in the world by focusing on power. In realist thinking, states are unitary actors that behave rationally over their chief concerns, namely security and power. States focus on pursuing power so they can use it as means of defense or to expand their influence and control over other territories and peoples. States have little other choice because of the dangerous anarchy that is the world, and they do not expect conditions to improve. Realists can see nothing but a dark, hostile future because history is an endless cycle of warfare. After all, the lust for power that drives states into conflict is rooted in unchangeable human nature. The attitude of realists is reflected in some of the truisms that have flowed from realist pens: "states are always getting ready for war, fighting wars, or getting over wars;" "the strong do as they please, and the weak suffer what they must;" "the enemy of my enemy is my friend;"

Box 1.3 The Career of Hugo Grotius

Hugo Grotius was born in Delft, Holland, in 1583 and died in 1645. This noted lawyer, poet, theologian, and scholar wrote and published in Latin, as did many of his contemporaries, and even changed his Dutch name, Huigh de Groot, to the better-known Latin version. Grotius entered the University of Leiden at age 11 and graduated at age 15 as a lawyer. His involvement in Dutch politics landed him in prison for life in 1619, but he escaped two years later with the aid of his wife. She hid him in a large box intended for transporting books to and from his cell.

After his famous escape from prison in 1621, he fled to Paris where he wrote his classic *De Jure Belli ac Pacis* in 1625, which many legal scholars regard as the first definitive text of international law. Earlier Grotius had published *Mare Liberum* (1609).

This book may be the first call for the free use of the seas by all states, a practice that greatly benefited oceanic trade. Only in 1864, with the discovery of *De Jure Praedae* (*The Law of Prizes*) written in 1604, did later generations of scholars realize that *Mare Liberum* was all along Chapter 12 of *De Jure Praedae*. Grotius, one of the most prolific of writers among the Renaissance publicists, also wrote on contemporary Dutch affairs. Grotius finished his career as an ambassador representing the Swedish king to the French court from 1635 to 1645, the year of his death. On his deathbed, his last words were, "By undertaking many things, I have accomplished nothing" (Dumbauld 1969: 18). His inventory of his own life was a gross understatement.

Sources: Edward Dumbauld, *The Life and Legal Writings of Hugo Grotius* (Norman, OK: University of Oklahoma Press, 1969); the ideas and impact of Grotius are well presented in Hedley Bull, Benedict Kingsbury, and Adam Roberts (eds.), *Hugo Grotius and International Relations* (Oxford: Clarendon Press, 1992).

"if you want peace, prepare for war;" and "might makes right." Not surprisingly, realists denigrate the role of international law, if they mention it at all. They view international law as but an epiphenomenon of power, or, put another way, the rules of the strong states.[2]

Among the modern realists, E. H. Carr, in his 1939 *The Twenty Years Crisis* sounded the warning about counting heavily on legal structures, such as the League of Nations, for this organization had been too idealistically contrived, he thought, to blunt the power urges of the aggressors of the 1930s (Carr 1946). Although trained in international law, Hans Morgenthau, the best known modern realist, concluded after the Second World War that while international law existed, it was an ineffective tool for restraining power. His masterpiece, *Politics Among Nations*,[3] published originally in 1948, had a tremendous impact on generations of American political scientists. Generally, they accepted Morgenthau's observation that international law is weak and primitive. His one chapter on this subject focused mainly on the problems of international law, not its effectiveness or promise. The thrust of his book is that international politics is a struggle for power, largely unaffected by law. So impressive was Morgenthau's work that some realists believed the prototype of a true political theory was at hand, a theory built on power that could afford to give short shrift to international law.

Liberal thinkers, as supporters of international law, did not surrender or retreat to an academic wilderness as realism ascended in prominence. They continued to speak, though with a weak voice, until dramatic historical forces intruded on the realist conceptualization of the world. Global interdependence intensified so that by the 1970s and 1980s, especially in the world economy, strong patterns of cooperation were taking place. Also, international government organizations (IGOs) exploded in growth after the Second World War magnifying cooperation to new historical levels. The European Union (EU), in particular, has been successful, attracting 27 member-states with others eagerly waiting in line to join and enjoy a bundle of economic benefits. Normative goals of non-government organizations (NGOs), such as Amnesty International in the human rights field and Greenpeace in the environmental area, also influence the world agenda.

Liberals believe that human nature is essentially good and that people are improvable. They doubt wars have to happen in recurring cycles; rather, humans can strike out on a linear path toward progress (Kelgley, Jr 1995: 1–24). Liberals also view the world as more than a system of states focused only on their mutual fears and security calculations. Liberals see a *social* nature inherent to the character of international relations, with states able to carry on a social life despite the absence of a world government (Hurrell 2000: 330). Harkening back to the publicists such as Grotius, modern liberals also believe that social interaction leads to rules despite the absence of a world government. As some of the medieval publicists would say, "*ubi societas ibi jus,*" or, where there is society, there is law (Corbett 1951: 39–40).

Liberals live under a "big tent" containing multiple strands of thought. A modern strand of liberal thinking that has much to say about international law is the *English School*. Non-English scholars have also participated in this approach, but it is so-named because the founding thinkers met at Cambridge and Oxford Universities.[4] These meetings began in the 1950s, the period when realism ascended to prominence in the United States At the time, few American scholars thought about the world in societal terms.

If the English School had a single "founding father," that scholar would be Martin Wight. Strongly influenced by the work of Hugo Grotius, he reminded modern scholars that there was a "middle way" between the warring anarchy assumed by the realists and some sort of world government preferred by the idealists. Wight is important because he renewed the insight that the social nature of humans was ultimately the glue that holds a society of states together. He asked the critical question for the English School: "What is international society?" Wight observed that states form a society through commerce, diplomacy, and especially international law.[5]

If one name stands out prominently among English School thinkers today, it is that of Hedley Bull. He thought that a society of states formed out of functional need similar to the development of national and local societies. The main functions he identified are: the control violence, the protection of property, and the enforcement of agreements. To international law, he assigned the grand task, "to identify, as the supreme normative principle of the political organization of mankind, the idea of a society of sovereign states" (Bull 1995: 134).

As if playing off Wight's question about "what is international society," Bull wanted to know "how much international society is there." In time, Bull became interested in thinking about an "international society" that would take into account a variety of actors besides the states, such as IGOs and NGOs. Also, Bull eventually moved past thinking about international society as merely an *order of peace* because he thought this society could also be an *order of justice*. Not long before Bull's death, his 1983 Hagey Lectures reflected a growing concern among English School thinkers about the conditions of humanity as well as the health of the society of states. These lectures addressed human rights, the environment, and especially the unjust economic disparity between peoples of the rich and poor states.[6]

Finally, Bull and other English School scholars worried much over the quality of international society following the break up of European Empires. Would the explosion in the numbers of new states in Africa and Asia, with their myriad cultures, cause a dilution and disruption of international society, or would they fit in comfortably? (Buzan 1991: 166–74) Bull and his co-editor, Adam Watson, concluded in 1984 *The Expansion of International Society* that the international society developed in Europe might possibly absorb a wide-range of new states, but these new states could also dilute this society. The new states recognized that *sovereignty* meant replacing colonial status with independence and legal equality with their old colonizers; *international organizations* provided a platform for collectively addressing the rich, powerful states with their grievances; *diplomacy* offered the chance to advance the interests of new states in both bilateral and multilateral contexts; and *international law* presented the opportunity to make new rules that might restructure the world in a more favorable way for deprived states.[7]

At about the time of the Cold War's end, a seemingly new approach appeared on the theoretical scene called *constructivism*. It is a direct heir of *social constructivists'* thinking from the sociology departments of American and English universities and, as a result, constructivism has a strong societal bent. The English School has had a considerable influence on constructivism, although not all constructivists will agree. John Gerhard Ruggie has claimed constructivism is *sui generis*, although he leaves room for a slight influence by the English School (Ruggie 1998: 11). Timothy Dunne, in contrast, believes there is a strong affinity between the approaches (Dunne 1995: 384).

Adherents of constructivism believe people make, or "construct," the world through a social process of generating and sharing ideas. The world ultimately hangs together, according to this approach, through rules and norms produced by social interaction, a process that can happen successfully in spite of anarchy. As the rules and norms stabilize into persistent patterns, the order, or *social structure*, of international society takes shape. International law contains many of the more important rules that have been constructed (Onuf 1989; Wendt 1992: 424–5). Some constructivists speak of a special identity involving masses of people around the world, the **global civil society**. This society involves a mix of private persons, and their organizations, which link up across national borders, usually through NGOs, to pursue a common agenda for the good of humankind, including working on human rights, disarmament, and the environment. The depth of commitment to a civil society on a global scale is difficult to know especially since national outlooks, particularly the nationalistic affection that people hold for their respective countries, are still strong.

Closely tied to the rise of a global civil society is the role of **global governance**, another concept supported by constructivists. A loose array of states, IGOs, and NGOs exercise a weak *supranational* authority to influence global policy and global law in various issue-areas. The actors taking part and the level of success varies with each issue (Hewson & Sinclair 1999: 6–11). For instance, a well-known example of an NGO affecting global policy is the case of Amnesty International leading a moral crusade to persuade states and the UN to accept first the 1975 *Declaration on Torture* and then the 1984 *Convention on Torture*. This convention received numerous ratifications and helped dampen the heinous practice of torture. Global governance is now sufficiently established that some scholars have turned their attention to making global governance more democratic and transparent (Held 1995). The general notion that human progress is possible and that international law can help make for a better international society inspirits this textbook.

Operating Conditions: What Helps and What Hinders?

Every individual and institution is environed in some manner. The institution of international law, at the core of international society, operates within a mixture of conditions that sometimes enhance this law's prospects and at other times undermine its usefulness. On balance, conditions in the world are pushing international law forward more than holding it back.

The historical process of **globalization** has intensified in the last quarter of a century to an unparalleled degree. A cause that begins in one part of the world can quickly resonate in other places, even throughout the world. Commercial air travel, economic exchanges, violations of human rights, terrorist attacks, transnational crime, arms races and sales, and much else produce widespread, troublesome effects that require global cooperation. The role of international law will almost certainly expand with the globalization process. More human activities and interactions will require more regulation. So close has today's international society pulled together that it has long been known as a "global village."

This interconnected nature of the world has been greatly facilitated by the nearly instantaneous modern communication grid that encircles the globe with satellites, cell phones, computers, and optic fiber lines, all enmeshed together to provide an electronic highway that binds the world together to a degree unimaginable by earlier generations. The use of English as the global *lingua franca*, providing a common language for diplomacy and business, further streamlines global communication and, potentially, cooperation.

Regional identities and activities cannot be lightly dismissed, however. **Regionalism** refers to an identity among a sub-set of states linked together through a shared culture, history, and geographical proximity. States sharing regional identities often endeavor to promote common interests with treaties and organizations to that group of states.[8] The existence of the African Union, the European Union, the League of Arab States, and the Organization of American States, among many others, bear testimony to faith in regional arrangements. Often both global and regional efforts are both needed. In truth, global and regional orders are mostly compatible and even reinforce one another.

Closely related to regionalism are cultural differences. There are myriad distinctions among the peoples of the world, distinctions relating to history, languages, religions, and outlook on law, among others. Writing several decades ago, Abba Bozeman saw a fundamental incongruence between a culturally diverse world and an international law drawn form the Western experience. She advocated accepting the world for what it is, a world of vigorous power politics and feeble international law (Bozeman 1971: esp. 186; 1984: 387–406). In contrast Werner Levi thought it is erroneous to claim, for international law to work, there must be substantial agreement among legal cultures. He believes it is clashing national interests, and not cultures, that tear at international law. Levi insists that common norms and rules of international law will evolve and grow strong as all parties work through their disagreements and conflicts (Levi 1974: 417–49; 1976: 135–50).

A powerful force binding the world together is the global market. An integrating world economy requires constant negotiation and reworking of the many rules and regulations that allow the world's gigantic economic machine to operate. The world is increasingly aware of its economic interdependence. The United States needs China as a source to borrow huge amounts to cover its budget deficits, and China requires the large consumer market of the United States to keep its factories busy. Not everyone is equally happy with the global economy, however. The world remains divided between the "haves" and "have nots." The poorer states are in the majority, but have not been able to "reform" the world economy and its supporting legal regime in substantial ways. Despite some economic progress by the poorer states, Joseph S. Nye, Jr. has had to offer the opinion that the poor states may be doing better but, because the rich states are advancing at an even greater pace, the gap between the two is still widening (Nye, Jr 2002: 133).

Many scholars, especially the realists, place a great deal of attention on the distribution of power to explain international outcomes. One might think power spread among several or more major states would be the preferred power distribution. The reasoning goes, since no one state can dominate, states are more willing to cooperate and develop rules for their interaction. History suggests, however, that a hegemon, or dominant power, often has controlled ideas and values that pervade international society, such as the rules of international law. The decades-old, classic study of Wilhelm G. Grewe, *The Epochs of International Law*, identifies a series of hegemons that impacted on the rules of their eras: Spain 1494–1648, France 1648–1815, and Great Britain 1815–1919 (Grewe 2000).

After the Second World War, did the United States take up a similar mantle and manage global affairs in a way that promoted international law? Following this war, the United States appeared to be on such a mission with its efforts to rebuild the world's shattered economy. Unfortunately, the United States has established a mixed record at best regarding international law. In recent times, the United States has failed to ratify multiple treaties world opinion considers of the highest importance. Some examples are the 1982 *Law of the Sea Convention*, the 1996 *Comprehensive Test Ban Treaty*, and the 1998 *Statue for the International Criminal Court*.

Grewe, in an epilogue to the 1998 edition of his magisterial work, taking note of disappointment in the United States' record, suggested international society as a whole might be able to shape international law in the global interest without the driving force of a great power (2000). He is probably correct. Since Grewe first published *The Epochs of International Law*, conference diplomacy has changed from the meeting of the few to a meeting of the many. Some modern conferences have had 180 or more states in attendance, and the weight of the majority has been able to trump the will of major powers.

All worthwhile endeavors meet with challenges, and so it is with the promotion of international law. Yet, this law has proven very successful in its service to international society, enjoying more help than hindrance.

Chapter Summary

- International law emerged as a functional necessity, as a set of rules for the Westphalia state system.
- International law spread from its Eurocentric base to become a global framework, especially after the break-up of colonial empires and the creation of numerous new states.
- The chief role of international law is to accommodate mutual interests and allow for peaceful change.
- Among the earliest sources of international law were ethical principles and the writings of publicists.
- Realist thinking in modern political science gave international law short shrift but constructivists, since the 1990s, have recognized its power to help structure an international society.
- International law is inchoate as a legal system and far from the level of accomplishment found in a well-governed state.
- The future of international law is promising but not guaranteed.

Discussion Questions

1   Is international law really law given that it has a horizontal structure within an anarchical world?
2   Some scholars distinguish between an *international society* and *international community*. What is the difference between the two?
3   International law performs several roles. Which one do you think is the most important and why?
4   Who is Hugo Grotius? Should he be called the "father of international law?"
5   Who are the realists and what is their view of international law?

Useful Weblinks

http://www.washlaw.edu/forint/
Website of Washburn University School of Law Library. Basically an easy to use search engine arranged alphabetically. It includes subjects, authors, countries, and occasional titles.

http://www.globalpolicy.org/ go to "International Justice"
Website of a study group that focuses on the UN System. First page offers many very accessible links to such topics as sanctions, globalization, 9/11, and the Secretary-General.

http://www.etown.edu/vl/
Included are many options such as legal dictionaries, search engines, and directories. The first page contains a wide range of links to multiple subjects in international relations, including "International and National Law."

http://www.asil.org/
Website of the American Society of International Law. It is an authoritative source for almost every imaginable subject in international law.

http://www.un.org/en/law
The section of the UN website devoted to international law. This site covers the international law bodies of the UN, treaties, and courts and tribunals.

Further Reading

Albert, Mathias, Brock, Lothar, and Wolf, Klaus Dieter (eds.) (2000) *Civilizing World Politics: Society and Community Beyond the State*. Lanham, MD: Rowman & Littlefield.
Anghie, Antony (2000) *Imperialism, Sovereignty and the Making of International Law*. New York: Cambridge University Press.
Bederman, David J. (2001) *International Law in Antiquity*. New York: Cambridge University Press.

Biersteker, Thomas, J. (2007) *International Law and International Relations: Bridging Theory and Practice.* New York: Routledge.

Buzan, Barry (2004) *From International to World Society? English School Theory and the Social Structure of Globalization.* New York: Cambridge University Press.

Byers, Michael and Nolte, George (eds.) (2003) *United States Hegemony and the Foundations of International Law.* New York: Cambridge University Press.

Century of International Law: American Journal of International Law Centennial Essays, 1906–2006 (2007) Washington, DC: American Society of International Law.

Chieh Hsiung, James (1997) *Anarchy and Order: The Interplay of Politics and Law in International Relations.* Boulder, CO: Lynne Rienner.

Clark, Ian (2005) *Legitimacy in International Society.* New York: Oxford University Press.

Covell, Charles (2004) *Hobbes, Realism and the Tradition of International Law.* New York: Palgrave Macmillan.

Craven, Matthew C. R., Fitzmaurice, M., and Vogiatzi, Maria (2007) *Time, History and International Law.* Boston, MA: Martinus Nijhoff Publishers.

International Law: 100 Ways It Shapes Our Lives (2006) Washington, DC: American Society of International Law.

Kaikobad, Kaiyan Homi and Bohlander, Michael (eds.) *International Law and Power: Perspectives on Legal Order and Justice.* Boston, MA: Martinus Nijhoff.

Koskenniemi, Martti (2002) *The Gentle Civilizer of Nations: The Rise and Fall of International Law, 1870–1960.* New York: Cambridge University Press.

Müllerson, Rein (2000) *Ordering Anarchy: International Law in International Society.* Boston, MA, Martinus Nijhoff.

Sands, Philippe (2005) *Lawless World: America and the Making and Breaking of Global Rules from FDR's Atlantic Charter to George W. Bush's Illegal War.* New York: Viking.

Simpson, Gerry (ed.) (2001) *The Nature of International Law.* Burlington, VT: Ashgate/Dartmouth.

Slaughter, Anne-Marie (2004) *A New World Order.* Princeton, NJ: Princeton University Press.

Notes

1 Shaw 1994: 15. For a general work on ancient roots of international law, see Bederman 2001.

2 For some of the most interesting literature on realism, see Donnelly 2000; Mastanduno 1999; Legro & Moravcsik 1999: 5–55; Kegley, Jr. 1995; Baldwin 1993.

3 Morgenthau 1978. This is the last edition handled entirely by Morgenthau.

4 Dunne 1998. Another interesting work on this approach is Buzan 2004.

5 Wight 1992). G. Wight and Porter assembled writings and notes by M. Wight to produce this work.

6 For an assessment of Bull's writings, see the review article by Henderson 2001: 415–23.

7 Bull & Watson 1984. Also, refer to Dunne 1995: 381.

8 Recent efforts to define and assess the importance of regionalism are Mansfield & Milner 1999: 589–627; Väyrynen 2003: 25–51; and Fawcett & Hurrell 1995.

Never doubt that a small group of thoughtful, committed citizens can change the world. (Margaret Mead)

National interests aren't what they used to be. Our Survival requires global solutions. (Jeffrey D. Sachs)

2

A World of Actors
A Question of Legal Standing

Contents

Traditionally, the study of international law focused on the state as the dominant actor and paid passing attention only to international organizations such as the UN. Today there is a general awareness of the multiple kinds of actors that populate the world and must be taken into account because their behaviors and resulting consequences are important. The state remains primary, but IGOs, NGOs, MNCs, insurgency groups, individuals, and churches, among others, may have a measure of legal standing in some circumstances. The organization of this chapter is a straightforward one. Each actor will be identified and its role and legal status elaborated.

Actors

All legal systems recognize specific actors that must comply with the rules of that system or face some form of sanction. For instance, US law not only holds individuals accountable but treats business corporations as if they were individuals. Usually, actors in a system possess both *rights* and *duties* in some manner. Actors so constituted are said to enjoy **legal personality**. Of course the only real, or natural, actor is the individual person, but individuals can organize into a variety of institutional arrangements as the international relations of today richly illustrate. The degree of legal personality these actors possess varies considerably, with the state alone possessing full legal personality. In fact, some actors are merely **objects** of international law rather than **subjects**. As objects, actors can receive the effects of international law including both benefits and sanctions. Subjects have duties and rights including the capacity to appear before a panel of arbiters or an international court. The state monopoly over legal personality lasted for several centuries, with only one significant exception. Pirates, known as the scourge of humankind, were subject to international law as individuals, and any state's navy could capture and try them.

The State

Law professors use the term "state" while many political scientists refer to the "nation-state." Since "nation" can have a sociological implication, referring to ethnic groups as in the case of the French-speaking minority in Canada, the choice of law professors will be applied here. The **state** is a sovereign actor with a central government that rules over a population and territory and protects and represents that population in international politics. Despite myriad differences among states in physical size, wealth, and military clout, as sovereign entities they are legal equals and, according to the positivist legal philosophy, states are independent of any vertical authority over their heads. This definition of the state is essentially the same as offered in the 1933 *Montevideo Convention on the Rights and Duties of States*.[1] This treaty is frequently cited for its definition of statehood even though it originated as a regional treaty set among Latin American countries.

The Montevideo Convention also called on states to enter into relations with other states, implying that states will normally carry on diplomatic intercourse with each other by offering **recognition** through the exchange of ambassadors. Unfortunately, state practice has never clarified whether recognition by other states is a firm requirement of statehood, and so the necessity of recognition remains controversial today. States have generally rejected the 1930 *Estrada Doctrine* of Mexico, which called for recognition to be automatic instead of a subjective decision of policy by other states. Mexican officials could remember when President Woodrow Wilson withheld recognition of the military dictatorship of Victoriano Huerta in 1913, a repressive regime that came to power through revolution instead of democratic elections.

The question of recognition has sometimes taken the form of **collective recognition** as by the European Union (EU), the UN, or, earlier the League of Nations. This type of recognition can be understood as an action taken together by a sub-set of states usually belonging to an IGO. These governments voice an opinion about what behavior is acceptable and what is not, as criteria for recognition. The League recommended against recognition of the puppet-regime of Manchukuo, which Japan set up after seizing Manchuria from China in 1931. When Rhodesia, under the control of a minority white-regime, broke away from Great Britain in 1965, the UN Security Council, in 1970, ordered all member-states of the UN to withhold recognition of the Rhodesian government because it obviously had denied governing power to the large majority of black citizens. At the end of the Cold War, the EU held a meeting in 1991 to discuss a common recognition policy regarding the new states splintering off from the Soviet Union and Yugoslavia. The EU let it be known that the formation of democratic governments would weigh heavily in the decision to grant or withhold recognition of the new states.

Besides a formal definition of statehood, states also have duties and rights that guide their treatment of one another. These duties and rights provide a social lubricant for the mutual interactions of states that makes for a more convivial international society than otherwise would be the case. States, for example, are to act in good faith in their dealings with other states, and, very importantly, they must respect the principle of **pacta sunt servanda.** This hallowed legal principle requires that states respect and obey all treaty obligations. Additionally, states can expect to benefit from rights based on **state immunity**, which means that normal *acts of state* should be free from interference. Most importantly, a state's government cannot be taken to court in another country without that state's permission.

Among a world of diverse states, irresponsible behavior can and does happen, sometimes shaking the system of duties and rights, but there have been important efforts to strengthen the system of rights and duties with written understandings. The 1970 *Declaration on Principles of International Law Concerning Friendly Relations and Co-operation Among States in Accordance with the Charter of the United Nations* calls on states to refrain from the use of force, intervention, or other harmful acts toward other states and to act in good faith according to the UN Charter.[2] This declaration is often cited in UN General Assembly resolutions, court decisions, and diplomatic communiqués. Also, the UN International Law Commission labored for decades on revisions before adopting the *Draft Articles on the Responsibility of States for Internationally Wrongful Acts*. In 2001, the General Assembly commended the Draft Articles to states for adoption as treaty law.[3] States have been slow to warm to this proposed treaty.

The international law on **state responsibility** involves the circumstances under which a state is held responsible for a breach of an international obligation. Historically, this concept focused on the way a state dealt with *aliens*, or foreigners, on its territory. Fair and civilized treatment was expected at a minimum. Certainly an alien was not to encounter a lesser treatment than a citizen of the state in question. Under the UN International Law Commission's handling of the Draft Articles on the Responsibility of States, the concept now seems more open-ended. These articles could cover state obligations about very controversial subjects such as peace, human rights, and the environment. Conceivably, if the proposed treaty had been in force in 1986, the Soviet Union might have been held liable under treaty law, rather than a

---

Box 2.1 Selected Duties and Rights of States

1 *State Doctrine*, a court in one state will not sit in judgment on the act of another state carried out on its own territory.
2 *Pacta Sunt Servanda*, states are obligated to obey treaties and international law in general.
3 States must not intervene in the affairs of other states or attack them militarily.
4 States must not allow their territory to be used to harm other states by counterfeiters, revolutionaries, terrorists, or even commercial operations that may cause pollution to reach the territory of another country.
5 States have an obligation to compensate other states and their citizens in cases of material harms that include, for example, shipwrecks, the fall of space vehicle debris, and the nationalization of private property belonging citizens of another country.
6 States have a duty to protect foreign nationals and their property and to treat them as well as their own citizens with a few exceptions, mainly, regarding matters of voting and holding political office.

1 States have a right to self-preservation including self-defense.
2 States enjoy a right to legal equality and sovereign independence including control over their domestic affairs.
3 States have a right to recognize one another and to participate in diplomatic intercourse including joining international organizations.
4 States can exercise the right to sue other states in the International Court of Justice and other courts if they have ratified the treaty creating these courts.
5 States possess the right of immunity for acts of state, for their diplomats, and for vehicles of war including ships and planes.
6 States expect other states to reciprocate acts of good faith and comity.

---

general principle, for the nuclear disaster in Chernobyl that cast radiation across northern Europe. The society of states has long embraced the principle that one state's territory and activities should not be allowed to harm another state. Under the concept of state responsibility, an offending state is expected take compensating steps ranging from an apology to reparation payments for damages depending on the nature and extent of damage (Brownlie 2002; Caron 2002: 857–73).

An area of legal obligation that remains ill-defined concerns **state succession**. When a state breaks up into two or more new countries, what becomes of the treaty obligations, national debts, and the original state's property and government archives? Occasionally states do fragment, and recent history bears witness to several prominent cases. The Soviet Union, in 1991, dissolved into 15 separate states, and Yugoslavia quickly divided into 5 and now 6 states with Kosovo. About the same time, Czechoslovakia, in "a velvet divorce," became the Czech Republic and

Republic of Slovakia. With the meltdown of communist suzerainty emanating from Moscow, these countries could pursue new political forms more to their liking. The troublesome fragmentation of states has been handled on a case-by-case basis and without enough consistency to establish clear rules, but two treaties are available to help despite a small number of ratifications. These are the 1978 *Vienna Convention on the Succession of States in Respect of Treaties* and the 1983 *Vienna Convention of States in Respect of State Property, Archives, and Debts.*[4] Five states, emerging from the Yugoslavian federation, accepted the 2001 *Agreement on Succession Issues* to cover their specific situation.[5] Succession remains highly political, with states insisting on leaving their options open. Ample political will must always precede successful law.

Some states have moved in the opposite direction by forming voluntary mergers. With the retreat of British colonialism, Tanganyika and Zanzibar became Tanzania in 1964. More recently in 1990, East and West Germany, having been divided into two states by the Cold War, began a merger when the citizens of both Germanys, acting with dramatic spontaneity, tore down the infamous Berlin Wall. In 1975, North Vietnam, never having accepted South Vietnam as a legal state, conquered the south and simply ignored all the international obligations of South Vietnam. A state completely absorbed in this manner is regarded as *extinct* (Papenfuß 1988: 469–88). Mergers generally are much easier to complete than a division of a country into two or more states. German diplomat Dieter Papenfuß insightfully offers the metaphor that mergers are like marriages and are easy to enter into, while breaking up a country is similar to divorce, with the experience painful and expensive (1998: 488).

Offering a legal definition of the state as an actor with duties and rights is relatively easy. States as actors, however, are caught up in forces of change that can create a new environment for state interaction and potentially even the meaning and importance of statehood itself. In the last decade, a veritable cottage-industry of scholarship has raised questions about the viability of the state and its future as the primary actor. So far, the state has held on for several centuries, while rivals, such as city-states, empires, and tribes, among others, have dwindled in importance and landed in the dustbin of history (Finnemore 1996: 332). The gist of concern is that forces below and above the state are whittling away at its importance. Ethnic groups in many countries wish to break away and form their own states. Cities and provinces of different countries ignore their national governments and use "telephone diplomacy" to iron out transborder problems on their own. States appear more vulnerable as illegal immigrants, illicit drugs, terrorists, cultural forces, and, above all, the tightening grip of a globalizing economy, demonstrate convincingly the permeability of national borders. Not all writers have joined this cottage-industry, however. Anne-Marie Slaughter refers to the state as not *disappearing*, after being battered by various forces, but *adjusting*. Slaughter rightly points out that the state is fine-tuning itself, not to create a "hermetically sealed sphere," but to intensify state power for more effective participation in the world (Slaughter 1997: 83ff.; 2000: 177–205). Despite country name changes and shifting borders over time, the population of states in the world is at the healthy number of about two hundred, the largest count in history.

While all states share the same legal characteristics of statehood, the reality of the state appears in myriad variety. It is important to be aware of the kinds of differences that exist among states because these differences often shape the policy choices of the states including their position in a legal dispute. Traditionally, professors of international relations have given much attention to the *military power* of states. The range is from the United States, widely acknowledged as the world's unrivaled military titan, to numerous small states that simply cannot defend themselves at all. An example would be Comoros consisting of three impoverished islands with a half million population located off the southeastern coast Africa. In 1995, this tiny country was seized by mercenaries until French soldiers charitably came to the rescue. Charles de Gaulle once called these scattered island states "the dust of empires" (Watson 1992: 300).

The states of the world can be divided at times by *political ideology* and always by *culture*. Differences among fascists, communists, and democratic states led to the Second World War. Now the world copes with radical terrorists, many of whom are from fundamentalist Muslim sects. When deep political and cultural fissures divide states, the chances of peacefully guiding relations by rules of law are bound to decline markedly. *Economic differences* among states are huge, and the disparity between rich and poor states is also a source of one the world's great simmering conflicts.

The *physical differences* among states are so great that it is hard to imagine that they can all be fitted into a common category, even if it is based on a legal definition. There is gigantic Russia covering the Eurasian heartland, which contrasts sharply with the minuscule Pacific island countries of Kiribati, Nauru, and Palau, and with every imaginable size existing in between. Disparities in *population size* are even more striking, with China and India leading the way at over a billion people each out of the world's total of 6.6 billion people. Numerous countries have fewer than a million people, and some of the tiny states, such as Liechtenstein, Monaco, and San Marino, have only 30,000 to 50,000 people. Countries also vary tremendously over the extent of their *ethnic heterogeneity* and the problems that arise from these cultural differences. Religious, racial, language, tribal, and other cultural differences can cause serious difficulties. Many states face disintegration by ethnic secessionist movements or turn to political repression to hold their minorities in line (Groarke 2004; Beck & Ambrosio 2002).

Two special types of states that have bedeviled international society in recent years are *failed states* and *rogue states*. As Stanley Hoffman pointed out several years ago, the chief problem facing the world today is not finding a way to establish a world government or fending off an ambitious strong state wanting to dominate the others, but finding a way to deal with the many weak states that are wracked by ethnic conflict and poverty until they just seem to fall apart creating "nobody-in-charge" states (Hoffman 1995: xi). Somalia, for instance, has been in turmoil since the 1980s and now plagues international shipping in the Red Sea with a serious outbreak of piracy that has drawn the attention of the UN Security Council.

The other type of bedeviling state is that of the rogue state. The US State Department maintains a list of states that it perceives as harmful to the peace and security of international society. This list of the notorious has included Cuba, Iran, Iraq, Libya, North Korea, Serbia, Somalia, Syria, and the Sudan. Robert Harvey offers three criteria of roguery: (1) the act of unprovoked aggression, (2) the sponsorship and direction of terrorism toward other state, and (3) a refusal to respect international law (2003: 188–97). In addition to the United States, other actors of international society often regard the same states as problems, although they may not apply the pejorative term of "rogue state." These rogues have scoffed at international law and fervently resisted an international order that they are unable to overturn.

International Government Organizations

It is states that create IGOs, but IGOs frequently take on an independent life of their own and redound on states with suggested policy changes that states sometimes accept. IGOs can become teachers of norms in policy areas such as human rights, science, culture, and much else (Finnemore 1993: 565–97). IGOs have a history reaching back to the river commissions and international conferences of nineteenth-century Europe, but their numbers rose sharply in the twentieth century, especially after the Second World War. Following this war, Western democracies pressed for a new world order friendly to free trade and human rights and one that would banish war as a legitimate policy option, an order pursued mainly through the panoply of IGOs making up the UN system. Above all else, IGOs exist to help states deal with problems that they cannot handle alone. Performing this role, IGOs have become indispensable as they spin webs of cooperation among states (Coicaud & Heiskanen 2001).

IGOs exist at the global level, examples being the *World Trade Organization* (WTO) and the *World Health Organization* (WHO), but five-fold more IGOs operate at the regional level, to name a few, the *Organization of American States* (OAS), the *African Union* (AU), the *Commonwealth of States*, the *Council of Europe* (COE), and the *League of Arab States* (AL). Most IGOs focus on one major purpose and are referred to as *unifunctional*. Of these, economically focused IGOs have the most pronounced growth rate. These include, for example, the European Union (EU), the *North American Free Trade Agreement* (NAFTA), and the *Association of South East Asian Nations* (ASEAN), all designed to increase the economic prosperity of their member-states. Some IGOs are *multifunctional* as is the case of the UN and some of the major regional organizations, such as the OAS and the AU, which busy themselves with maintaining peace, promoting human rights, and raising living standards, among other worthwhile objectives.

Approximately 400 IGOs exist in the world and have a measure of legal personality which is determined by the exact set of duties and rights assigned to each organization by its member-states through the treaties that create these organizations. IGOs can send and receive ambassadors, who enjoy immunity, as well as make treaties with states and with other IGOs. IGOs and treaties have gone together for a long time, but this kind of cooperation became more formally managed by the 1986 *Vienna Convention on the Law of Treaties between States and International Organizations or Between International Organizations.*[6]

A typical treaty between IGOs and states concerns *host agreements* that lay out the privileges and immunities of the IGOs while they conduct international business on the soil of a sovereign state. IGOs have to have headquarters on one state or another's territory, and they require protection for their properties and personnel. The principal headquarters of the UN, for example, is in New York City, although major activities of the UN are also carried out in Geneva, Switzerland. The UN took over the old facilities of the defunct League of Nations. The UN has a goodly number of its specialized programs spread out in other cities and countries as well, for instance, the *UN Environmental Program* in Nairobi, Kenya and the *UN High Commissioner for Refugees* in Vienna, Austria. Each requires a headquarters agreement with its host country. Good examples of IGO-to-IGO treaties can be found in the UN System. *The International Labor Organization* (ILO), the *Universal Postal Union* (UPU), and the *International Atomic Energy Agency* (IAEA), among many others, are specialized, autonomous organizations melded into the UN system by treaty arrangements.

Among the many IGOs, the UN is paramount. The UN is the inheritor of the League of the Nations, carrying on the traditions of the sovereign equality of states and respect for diplomacy and international law. The UN continues today as the best chance for replacing violent conflict in the world with the peaceful settlement of disputes (Buzan 1991: 170). UN membership is now at 192, almost the entire population of states. A few tiny states cannot afford to maintain a diplomatic delegation at the UN. Although these states are the legal parents of the UN, the UN symbolically represents humankind as well as the states. The Preamble of the UN Charter begins with, "We the peoples of the United Nations," and then offers a grand litany of worthy goals ranging from promoting human rights to establishing world peace and security. The Secretary-General, as the chief executive, is commonly viewed as a world spokesperson, able to take an enlightened view about all interests involving the global good.

Although the various treaties and agreements between the UN and states suffice to create a legal personality for this IGO, the defining historical moment of UN legal personality is the well-known 1949 *Reparations for Injuries Suffered in the Services of the United Nations* case, an **advisory opinion** of the International Court of Justice (ICJ), one of the six principal organs of the UN. The ICJ, unlike many national or municipal courts, can and does render some of its most important decisions as advisory opinions. Without litigants bringing a case before the court, the ICJ offers an opinion on what the legal outcome would have been if an actual case were being decided. In this case, fighting erupted between Jewish settlers, struggling to create the state of Israel, and the Palestinians in the UN Trust territory of Palestine. The UN sent into the dispute its diplomatic agent, Swedish Count Folke Bernadotte, to mediate a settlement. Jewish militants assassinated Count Bernadotte in 1948, as they had earlier assassinated British Army officers when they tried to supervise the Palestinian Trust territory. Did the UN have the legal standing to bring a case that would hold Israel responsible? In the 1949 Reparation Case, the ICJ answered in the affirmative, even though the UN lacked the full set of duties and rights of states. Israel paid damages to the UN all the while denying that it had a legal obligation to do so. The UN's considerable legal personality would not again be in question.[7]

Another important problem the UN has had regarding its legal personality has been raised by the United States, its major host and the country that provides the largest single amount of membership dues, close to one-fourth of the total. Amidst an anti-communist crusade in the early 1950s, the US government pressured the first UN Secretary-General, Trygve Lie of Norway, into dismissing 18 UN employees of US citizenship who could not pass US security clearances. The central question concerned the competence of an international body to determine its own requirements for civil service personnel. The next Secretary-General, Dag Hammarskjöld of Sweden, acted quickly to retrieve lost ground by asserting it would finally rest with him and not with any state, to determine who was a suitable employee of the UN, no matter how important that particular member-state was. Articles 100 and 101 of the UN Charter clearly intend that the UN is to have an independent and loyal civil service.

A more severe form of disrespect for the UN's rights and role has come from terrorists. The UN suffered a terrible blow in 2003 when a truck, laden with a large bomb, was driven into the UN Headquarters in Baghdad, killing several top UN diplomats and wounding others. The Security Council called for Secretary-General Kofi Annan to alert host states of any UN bodies, in this case the ruling council of Iraq operating under the US occupation authority, to pay attention to key provisions of the 1994 *Convention on the Safety of UN and Associated Personnel*. These provisions call for those harming UN personnel to be considered war criminals and required that they either be prosecuted or extradited to a country that is willing to prosecute them. The hackles of the US government were immediately raised when Secretary-General Annan asserted that the United States was responsible for UN Headquarters security. The United States responded that it had offered protection but was turned down by UN officials who were trying to protect the UN's image of neutrality. Still early in Secretary-General Ban Ki-moon's tenure, another terrorist suicide mission using a bomb-laden truck caused the destruction of UN offices in Algiers, Algeria, in 2007.

Another prominent IGO is the *North Atlantic Treaty Organization* (NATO) created in 1949 by Canada, Iceland, the United States, and Western European states to defend themselves against the rising specter of the Soviet Union and its communist allies. NATO was billed as a regional collective security organization, meaning that if any member were attacked by an outside source, the other states would come to the attacked member's aid and defense. It was implicitly understood that the aggression would almost certainly come from the Soviet Union and its *Warsaw Pact* allies, after this pact was formed in 1955. Since no war occurred between the two Cold War camps, the NATO alliance has been called a success story in terms of deterrence. As ex-Warsaw Pact member-states have joined NATO, its membership has risen to 26 states.

Although never tangling with the Warsaw Pact in a significant military way, NATO did step up to serve in the mid-1990s as the muscle of a grateful UN since the global body had struggled without success to halt the bloody ethnic fighting in Bosnia, a former province of Yugoslavia. Then, in 1999, without UN approval, NATO planes attacked Serbia, another part of fragmented Yugoslavia, forcing Serbian leaders to retreat from their depredations against their Albanian minority living in the province of Kosovo.

Article 5 of the NATO treaty, providing for the collective defense of any member-state, was never invoked until after the infamous terrorist attack on the United States in 2001, now known as the "9/11" crisis, a full decade after the collapse of the Soviet

Union and the Warsaw Pact. This devastating terrorist attack aroused unmatched sympathy for the United States and was widely perceived as an attack on the West in general. The terrorists that carried out 9/11 were linked to al-Qaida, the terrorist organization based in Afghanistan under the protection of the radical Islamist Taliban regime. NATO members activated Article Five by cooperating to track terrorist networks and set up the *International Security Assistance Force* (ISAF). NATO Forces were still operating in Afghanistan in 2009 but with some strain on the alliance. Over half the forces there are from the United States, and US Defense Secretary Robert Gates, in early 2008, complained that only a few NATO members will risk troops in combat, preferring to occupy relatively safe areas.

The most developed IGO in the world is the EU. After facing the massive destruction of the Second World War, a handful of European states began a cooperative venture on free trade in coal and steel that eventually grew into an impressive **supranational** body of 27 states. These states pool their respective sovereignties creating a quasi-authority above the state level to make more effective policy decisions for the common good. The institutional structure of the EU includes a European parliament, court, and executive bodies. The EU also has its own flag and anthem as well as the Euro currency shared by 16 of the member-states. Some of the most impressive cooperative ventures of these states include *Europol* for tracking terrorists and criminals, *Eurojust* that helps with extradition and cross-border prosecutions, and the *Shengen Agreement* that monitors outsiders entering the EU states to watch for terrorists and criminals.

By 2003, the EU began to process of adopting a constitution providing for more consolidation that ultimately failed when several states, including the important leader of France, rejected it. The 2001 *Treaty of Nice* had already proven inadequate for the complexities of an expanding organization. The EU leadership next tried to accomplish the goal of consolidation with the 2007 *Treaty of Lisbon*, which would add more transparency and democracy as well as consolidating power.[8] The aim was to have this treaty in force by the summer of 2009, but an Irish referendum has turned the treaty down. Its future is now in jeopardy since all 27 EU members must to approve.

If the EU can create a more elaborate governance structure and draw more authority to its center, it will generate a more evolved legal personality. The EU is not of course a *super state*. The IGO has not forged the sovereignty of its member-states into an alloyed regional government, reducing its national governments to mere minions. Despite an impressive record of integration, the EU still has a long way to go before it can become the "United States of Europe," as envisioned by some European intellectuals several decades ago.

Non-government Organizations

Because of the combined forces of democracy, advanced communication systems, and strong moral awareness by a world citizenry, a veritable global civil society has emerged into place, ready to tackle a wide range of issues. Individuals and private groups that once only lobbied national governments at home now also lobby IGOs, attend annual conferences at the regional and global levels, and hold demonstrations at summit conferences attended by executives of the leading states. A sense of global awareness appears through activists from around the world networking together as their NGOs form alliances with like-thinking IGOs and states friendly to a given cause.

A prime example of the effectiveness of an NGO is that of the *International Campaign to Ban Landmines* (ICBL). This organization formed in 1992 as a coalition of 1,000 national and international NGOs operating from a base of 55 countries. The movement was helmed by Jody Williams, an American housewife. The ICBL received the support of a few countries, mainly Canada, and, in 1997, the Canadian government hosted a conference in Ottawa that resulted in 120 state signatures approving the *Treaty to Ban Anti-Personnel Landmines*. In 1999, after 40 states completed the ratification process, this ban on landmines became part of international law. Today, over 100 countries have ratified this treaty prohibiting the millions of landmines now seeded in the soil of many countries or stacked on the shelves of national armories awaiting use. In place of the usual famous statesmen and IGOs, Jody Williams and the ICBL were chosen to receive the 1997 Nobel Peace Prize. Unfortunately, China, Russia, and the United States, the top military powers, have not accepted this treaty.

NGOs are now commonly seen as playing a role in global governance because they feed ideas and norms into global policy contributing to the rules of international law. Since NGOs frequently speak for people at the grassroots level, the policy-making process, once dominated by states and later influenced by their IGOs, has made global governance more democratic (Keck & Sikkink 1998; Slaughter 2000: 193; Brown, Khagram, Moore, & Frumkin 2003: 271–96). Obviously, NGOs cannot participate directly in law-making in the sense of signing and ratifying treaties, but they do sometimes voice an original idea that becomes widely accepted as seen in the example of the ICBL. Two other good examples of NGO input on treaty formation are the roles of the *World Wildlife Fund* (WWF), promoting the 1973 *International Convention on Trade in Endangered Species*, and *Amnesty International*, proposing the 1980 *Declaration Against Torture*, which later was converted into the 1984 *Convention Against Torture*.

NGOs are not always puny organizations hoping they may get lucky and spark a moral response from the more powerful entities of states and IGOs. They can be very influential at times because of considerable resources, including millions of dues-paying members who may be divided among fifty or more national chapters. Any given NGO typically links to other like-thinking NGOs, as a force-multiplier, allowing their combined organizations to quickly rally for a cause. NGO campaigns involve lobbyists visiting government offices, pressuring corporations with publicized campaigns, their lawyers filing legal briefs in national and even international courts, and attending international conferences on matters such as human rights, the environment, trade, urbanization, and population issues, among many others. NGO representatives at international conferences usually outnumber state representatives by far and push their views at every opportunity. For instance, at the 1992 Earth Summit on environmental problems, 1,400 NGO representatives were present to influence 150 state delegations, which included nearly 100 heads of state.[9] Estimates on the number of NGOs vary widely. One source claims there are about 100,000 NGOs of every imaginable kind, counting both national and international NGOs. Of these, perhaps 5,000 are fundamentally international in nature and organizational structure (Dierks 2001: 135).

NGOs contribute importantly to democratizing today's global governance by bringing the interests of ordinary citizens to the fore when world agendas are set and by insisting persistently that policy-making reflect *transparency*. NGO activists want a full disclosure of accurate information from governments, corporations, international banks, IGOs, and by NGOs themselves, for that matter. The transparency movement in today's global governance is illustrated by the role of the widely respected German NGO, *Transparency International*, making assessments of national government's corruption; *One World Trust* for evaluating the accountability of NGOs, IGOs, and business corporations; and *Corporate Watch* specializing in tracking business corporations.[10]

The legal personality of NGOs is limited and probably lags behind their mounting importance in international affairs as doers of good deeds and inspirers of new rules. NGOs commonly have some sort of legal standing in the country where they are based. Municipal, or domestic, laws usually classify them as non-profit organizations for tax purposes and allow them to sue and be sued in civil court actions. At the international level, many NGOs receive *consultative status* with the Economic and Social Council of the UN under Article 71 of the UN Charter. This status enables an NGO to submit information relevant to an issue and even offer expert testimony. Being granted consultation status in the UN Charter, perhaps the world's most important treaty, demonstrates that NGOs can have appreciable legal standing. Early in the twenty-first century, 1,700 NGOs have UN consultative status.[11]

A few prominent NGOs have advanced consultative status such as the *American Society of International Law* (ASIL), and the *International Committee of the Red Cross* (ICRC). Of special interest is the *Palestinian Liberation Organization* (PLO). The PLO status is referred to as the "Permanent Observer Mission of Palestine." The PLO status was upgraded in 1998 to include speech-making before the UN General Assembly, the capacity to raise new issues, and the ability to co-sponsor resolutions. Undoubtedly, this improvement in status represents overwhelming world opinion that the PLO should be allowed to govern an independent state of Palestine. The UN treats the PLO as if it were the government of a state-in-waiting.

The regional IGO of the *Council of Europe* (COE) goes even further than the UN by covering the role of NGOs in a special treaty. The COE created the *European Convention on the Recognition of the Legal Personality of International Non-Governmental Organizations*, which assigns duties and rights to NGOs. This convention entered into force in 1991, and about one-fourth of the COE has ratified this convention.[12]

Other strong evidence that NGOs enjoy a degree of legal personality is the arbitration case of 1987 between the French government and *Greenpeace*, the prominent environmental NGO. In 1985, French agents blew up the *Rainbow Warrior* in the harbor of Auckland, New Zealand, sinking the ship that Greenpeace had used to protest and block the testing of atomic bombs in French Polynesia. A crewman died in the bombing. The Secretary-General of the UN and an arbitration tribunal reached a decision punitive to France. The very fact that Greenpeace, as an NGO, was a party in an arbitration proceeding with a state suggests Greenpeace benefited from a worthy legal personality.

The outstanding case of a relatively strong legal personality afforded an NGO belongs to the ICRC. Not only does Swiss civil law recognize the famous Red Cross, but internationally the ICRC holds a unique status because the 1949 *Geneva Conventions* recognize the ICRC and provides for its important role during wartime. Actually, the ICRC's role in taking care of civilians, the wounded, and POWs goes back to the latter part of the nineteenth century. The 1949 Geneva Conventions, and their 1977 Protocol, are updates on a treaty process that began in 1864 and included a role for the ICRC (Finnemore 1999: 149–65; Forsyth & Riefer-Flanagan 2007).

Multinational Corporations

Multinational corporations (MNCs) are a special case of the NGO actor, one that has risen to a height of power and influence beyond that of other NGOs in general. MNCs are economic actors in pursuit of profits, and they operate at the heart of the economic globalization process. They are business enterprises with ownership, management, production, and sales activities located in several or more countries. As in the case of BMW, the headquarters is in Bavaria, Germany, manufacturing takes place in Austria, Germany, and the United States, and sales occur in 100 other countries. Hundreds of MNCs, such as GMC, Coca Cola, Nestle, Michelin, Sony, Pfizer, McDonald's, Toys-R-Us, Boeing, and Citicorp, relentlessly pursue efficiency by acquiring material resources, cheaper labor, and bigger yields on investments in as many national markets as possible.

There are an estimated 38,000 MNCs along with their 250,000 affiliates, or subsidiaries spread out in numerous host countries, helping to knit together the complex, interdependent world economy.[13] Through their exponential growth, MNCs now hold in their hands the bulk of world trade in goods and services, technology transfers, patent ownership, and capital investment.

The economic clout of the MNCs, and the political influence that extends from it, are incontestable. Writers interested in the role of MNCs in the global economy are fond of ranking the top 50 or 100 economic entities of the world so they can show that MNCs occupy some of the higher slots in the ranking, well ahead of many small states (e.g. Love & Love 2003: 95–118, esp. 98). MNCs often have more money, expertise, personnel, technology, and access to world leaders, including the Secretary-General of the UN, than do the governments of many states.

The facts about MNCs invite widely different interpretations about their role in the world economy and their impact on national economies, especially their effects on weaker states. The Western, or capitalist view, is that MNCs are helping build a burgeoning world economy that will advantage all states and peoples.

The other interpretation, one associated with socialism and many Third World leaders and economists, is that MNCs are further enriching the already rich states at the expense of the poor states and are even causing human rights and environmental harms along the way. Many interested NGOs and Third World governments would like to see MNCs regulated in a way that would protect human rights, preserve the physical environment of a country, and produce economic benefits for the general population. International law that can offer such guarantees does not exist. The powerful MNCs have kept regulation restricted to *Codes of Conduct*, which are ethical guidelines. Corporations essentially remain free to concentrate on profits that will reward their shareholders (Artz & Lukashuk 1995: 70–1).

The most important effort to rein in corporate power is probably the *UN Center on Transnational Corporations* (or TNCs – a synonym for MNCs). This Center tried to create an effective, comprehensive *UN Code of Conduct on TNCS*. Unfortunately for the critics of MNCs, this effort faltered in 1993, leaving a mish-mash of organizations and NGOs to carry on the cause in specialized industrial sectors. By 1999, the UN could only produce an ethical code for MNCs known as the *Global Compact*. MNCs have never objected completely to international regulation, especially if those regulations would harmonize multiple national laws and thereby reduce transactional costs across borders (1995: 78). What MNCs have objected to are rules that would require corporations to share their wealth to pay for peoples' wants and needs, since corporations generally believe it is the states' responsibility to do so (Love & Love 2003: 212).

From this description, the economic power of MNCs cannot be in doubt, but can MNCs be said to have an appreciable legal personality? Most regulation of MNCs has come from their home countries where they are headquartered and are usually treated under law as legal persons, or "citizens." Efforts at international regulation, described earlier, were attempts to treat the MNC as an "object" of ethically based codes of conduct. Most discussion of MNCs' international legal status has had to do with corporate nationality that involves deciding which state speaks for a corporation when it has problems in another country. Is it the state where the MNC is registered as a corporation, or is a corporation's nationality reflective of its stockholders' nationality? The often cited *Barcelona Traction* case of 1970 helps answer these questions. Barcelona Traction was identified by the ICJ as a Canadian company since it was registered in Toronto. The fact that the primary stockholders were Belgium citizens did not make Barcelona Traction a Belgium enterprise. For Barcelona Traction's stockholders to receive help dealing with Spain as the host country, they would have to turn to Canada, and not Belgium.[14]

Noted legal scholar Louis Henkin is sanguine about the chances of MNCs moving beyond their status as entities holding economic power and possessing the nationality of their home state. With the capitalist market economy in full ascendancy over the old communist sphere of the world, he believes the MNC is poised for a momentous change. In time, the MNC may no longer have to operate in the shadow of the state, where it must be registered, but may act on its own as a new actor with duties and rights before international tribunals (Henkin 1995: 24; see also Zerk 2006: ch. 2). Opposition to this change would no doubt include Third World states which

---

Box 2.2 The Barcelona Traction Case

Barcelona Traction, Light and Power Company, Ltd, formed as a registered corporation in Toronto, Canada in 1911. Barcelona Traction then set up a number of subsidiary companies, which supplied the major part of the electricity used in the Catalonian Province of Spain with its operations directed from the city of Barcelona. Shortly after the First World War, Barcelona Traction's capital shares came to be held by Belgium nationals. Following the Spanish Civil War in the mid-1930s, Barcelona Traction's sterling bonds were suspended because the Spanish exchange-control authorities refused to authorize the transfer of the foreign currency necessary to resume servicing the bonds. In 1948, a Spanish court declared Barcelona Traction bankrupt, which was followed by the executive branch of the Spanish government expropriating the company.

This case bounced around in the Spanish court system for years until Canada finally dropped all *espousal* efforts on behalf of Barcelona Traction in 1955. The Belgian government grasped the baton for another run at the Spanish court system but to no avail.

The Spanish government viewed Belgium as lacking *jus standi*, or legal standing, despite the fact that Belgian citizens owned the lion's share of Barcelona Traction's stock. Once Belgium and Spain agreed to have this case placed before the International Court of Justice, this court's justices rejected Belgium's right to espouse for Barcelona Traction by a vote of 15 to 1 in 1970. Although it was in vogue between the world wars to determine the nationality of a corporation by a majority of its stockholders, the *Barcelona Traction* case confirmed the clear shift to assigning nationality to the country where the corporation was originally registered.

Sources: Refer to: http://www.lawschool.cornell.edu/library/ > Int Ct of Justice > Decisions of the ICJ > Second Phase-Judgment of 5 Feb 1970.

---

would not care to see MNCs acquire legal personality on top of their considerable economic power (Artz & Lukashuk 1995: 82).

Europe, always a leader in international law and institutional development, has provided MNCs some basis for legal personality. The EU's *Corporate Social Responsibility* requirements appear to be so clear and firm that compliance by corporations is generally expected, as if they were "subjects" of law.[15] Also, the 2003 *Criminal Law Convention on Corruption*, sponsored by the COE, aims to harmonize multiple states' regulation of corruption and bribery. Subject to the 2003 Convention would be individuals in their own right and individuals acting as corporate agents, making MNCs directly liable. Apparently, corporations in Europe are subjects with an appreciable legal personality.[16] Finally, the *European Court of Justice* of the EU, arguably the most developed international court in existence, has been settling legal disputes since 1952 among member-states, EU institutions, and individuals living under the EU arrangement, but has also been hearing cases involving corporations. MNCs, in this instance, have legal personality because they are subjects of the Court of Justice's jurisdiction.[17]

In another important case, the legal personality of the MNC was particularly pronounced. After the egregious seizure of the American embassy in Tehran, Iran, in 1979, coupled with Iran's holding of US State Department employees for 444 days, Algeria mediated an agreement between Iran and the United States, known as the *Algeria Declaration*. By this agreement, the United States would get its people back and Iran would regain control over its $5 billion in gold in American banks. As part of the settlement, citizens of both countries could bring claims before the *1981 Iran–US Claims Tribunal* that had been set up for this purpose. Moreover, the Claims Tribunal went well beyond the old **espousal doctrine** that requires the government of a state to speak for individual or corporate citizens in international matters, as happened in the Barcelona Traction case. Both individuals and corporations were allowed to act in their own capacity as legal persons before an international tribunal with binding outcomes (Artz & Lukashuk 1995: 75–6).

Incidentally, the *Algeria Declaration* defined a company as a US corporation if 50 percent or more of its capital stock was owned by American citizens.[18] This definition of the nationality of a corporation flies in the face of the major precedent recorded with the *Barcelona Traction* case, which bases nationality on where the corporation is registered as a business enterprise. Only time will tell if the Claims Tribunal's definition will challenge the *Barcelona Traction* precedent, or have meaning just for the Claims Tribunal's limited purposes.

Individuals

Since the individual human being is the only natural person, one would think the legal personality of individuals might have a long, impressive history. A distinguished record of this kind does not exist, however. Only during the early history of the Westphalian system, in the seventeenth century, when the natural law tradition prevailed, was it assumed that the individual had a legal personality of duties and rights. By the nineteenth century, the positive philosophy clearly won out over natural law, a development that placed the state at the center of international law and left the individual mostly out of considersation (O'Brien 2001: 153; Melanczuk 1997: 100). With the exception of pirates, who have long been regarded as the enemy of humankind, international law for centuries was almost hidebound as a legal system of states. States were the *subjects* of international law, and individuals figured in only as *objects* of states. Individuals received either benefits or restrictions, as the case might be.

This traditional view of the individual as object was sustained in the 1928 Danzig Railway case that occurred between Germany and Poland. The *Permanent Court of Justice* of the League of Nations (the precursor to the ICJ of the UN) offered the advisory opinion that the treaty between the two countries could not create duties and rights for individuals but only benefits (Cassese 2000: 78–9; Higgins 1985: 476–94).

Box 2.3 The Danzig Railway Officials Case

One of the outcomes of the First World War was the creation of the Free City of Danzig (now the city of Gdansk, Poland) as an entity separate from Germany and Poland and administered by a High Commissioner answerable to the League of Nations. Article 104 of the 1919 Treaty of Versailles, which ended the First World War, called for a treaty between Danzig and Poland that would transfer the railway system serving Danzig to the Polish Railway Administration. The 1921 Danzig–Polish Agreement left the Danzig railway officials unhappy with their new employers over the issues of pay and pensions and they sued in Danzig civil courts. Poland's government objected to the use of Danzig courts to the High Commissioner who finally ruled in 1927 in Poland's favor. The Free City of Danzig appealed over the head of the High Commissioner to the Council of the League, which in turn asked for an advisory opinion from the Permanent Court of Justice (PCJ).

In its 1928 advisory opinion, the PCJ viewed the 1921 Danzig–Polish Agreement as an international treaty and, in keeping with legal views of the day, observed that there was a well-established principle of international law which precluded *international agreements from creating duties and rights for individuals.* However, the justices of the PCJ found that an international agreement can create rules enforceable in national courts that involve duties and rights for individuals, as in "contracts of service." This advisory opinion overruled the High Commissioner. Danzig and Poland had previously agreed to abide by the advisory opinion.

Source: Advisory opinion 15, March 3, 1928 found in Manley O. Hudson (ed.), *World Court Reports* vol. II, 1927–32 (Dobbs Ferry, NY: Oceana Publications, Inc., 1969), pp. 236–67. See especially pp. 246–7.

Immediately following the Second World War, the Nuremberg Military Tribunal probably changed the status of the individual's role in international law forever. This terrible war took well over 40 million combat deaths, with millions more dying in concentration camps simply because they were Jews, Roma (Gypsies), or members of some other ethnic group the Nazi leaders of Germany wanted eradicated. The Nuremberg trials handed down long sentences and even the death penalty to German civilian and military leaders, whose charges included waging a "war of aggression," and "crimes against humanity." The "badge of state," that is, acting in the name of the state, could no longer protect individual violators. The claim that an individual was "only obeying a superior's orders" would at most a mitigating circumstance. At the Nuremberg Tribunal, the American Chief Prosecutor, Justice Robert Jackson, in his opening statement, declared "Crimes against international law are committed by men, not by abstract entities, and only by punishing individuals who commit such crimes can the provisions of international law be enforced."[19] A parallel tribunal in Tokyo brought charges against Japanese leaders for similar crimes.

Individual responsibility before the bar of international justice continues today with the UN tribunals for Cambodia, Rwanda, Sierra Leone, and Yugoslavia. In 1998, many states took the bold step of creating a permanent *International Criminal Court* at The Hague in the Netherlands that can try individuals for a range of serious crimes, a significant institutional improvement over *ad hoc,* or temporary, tribunals.

In addition to punishing individuals for war and humanitarian crimes, the status of the individual in international law took a strong, positive turn when the UN produced the 1948 *Universal Declaration of Human Rights.* This litany of rights, morally powerful and broad in scope, became the progenitor of numerous human rights treaties that greatly benefit individuals. The 1976 *Covenant on Civil and Political Rights,* for instance, offers an optional protocol that allows individuals to petition a *Human Rights Committee* concerning their treatment at the hands of their government. The *European Court of Human Rights* cannot only receive an individual's appeal from the highest court of a state, but can also overrule the decision of that state court. Today, human rights are no longer viewed as the good fortune of the few, those lucky enough to be born in say England or Switzerland, as was the case only a century or two ago. Rather, rights belong to everyone as a matter of birth and are inalienable. That is, rights can be violated but cannot be taken away legally. Universal rights are the main vestige remaining of the natural law tradition in international law.

In some instances, individuals also have been able to advance material claims in their own right without the espousal of a state. Individuals, like MNCs, were able to present claims before the Iran–US Claims Tribunal. Also, when the *UN Compensation Commission* was set up after the 1990–1 Persian Gulf War, individual claims were actually given priority (O'Brien 2001: 155).

Insurgents

Insurgents are groups of citizens waging revolution against the central government of their state. They usually have *de facto* control over part of the territory of the state and may enjoy popular support among the people under their rule. Insurgents are either fighting to create a breakaway state of their own or, more ambitiously, to take complete control of the country. The large majority of wars today involve internal warfare. Insurgents are involved in an action much more prolonged than a riot or a brief rebellion that can be quickly quashed by the central government's police or army. Because the insurgents are able to persist over time, they take on the character of a *quasi-international person,* that is, they can enjoy a provisional legal personality. Insurgents possess both duties and rights involving diplomatic intercourse with states, although their status as a state-in-waiting does not give them a full legal personality comparable to that of a central government.

The fate of insurgents, however, does not depend so much on a temporary legal standing as it does on the outcome of military engagement. If the insurgents are militarily successful, they can form a new state, as happened in Bangladesh in 1971, when it broke away from Pakistan with India's help. Or, if the military effort fails, as was the case for insurgents in the western Sahara in 1991, then they must submit to the government of an unwanted state, in this case, Morocco. If the insurgency should show a promise of success, some states may decide to offer **belligerent recognition** conferring some duties and rights on the insurgents for the time being. To be given belligerent status, there must be a general state of war between the central government and the insurgents, and the interests of the recognizing states must be involved. A state granting belligerent recognition, for instance, may be worried about its citizens and property located on the territory held by the insurgents. The leadership of the insurgency bears responsibility for aliens and their property wherever the insurgent forces exercise *de facto* control; in fact, the insurgent forces, once so recognized, must operate under the laws of war.

The recognition of an insurgency by another state almost certainly will be viewed as an *unfriendly act* by the central government as it tries to avoid territorial dismemberment, or even its own extinction. When the Ibo people tried to secede from Nigeria in 1968 and form a new state called Biafra, the premature recognition by several African states caused hard feelings between these countries and the Nigerian government, a diplomatic problem that lingered well after the Ibo rebellion was crushed. This case was especially sensitive since African states have borders mostly set by European colonial powers in a by-gone era, with boundaries both enclosing old enemies within the same territorial state and dividing tribal peoples in two or more countries. The potential for serious political mischief over the territorial bases of states was enormous. For this reason, the OAU, early in its history, established the strong norm of leaving boundary issues alone.

Antonio Cassese identifies a **National Liberation Movement** (NLM) as a special case of insurgency. NLMs are implicitly interested in gaining territory, but are mostly interested in pursuing international acceptance and legitimacy based on what they see as a rightful claim to **self-determination**. Legally, self-determination applies to a people wanting to be free of (1) colonial rule, (2) a racist regime, or (3) an alien occupation (2001: 75–7). A NLM will likely oppose one of these three kinds of rule. The *National Liberation Front* (FLN) wished to end French colonial rule in Algeria in the 1950s. South Africa's white regime faced a relentless demand by the *African National Congress* (ANC) to turn government over to the Black majority. And, for decades, the *Palestinian Liberation Organization* (PLO) has wanted the occupation forces of Israel out of the Palestinian territories. The most strident Palestinians want Israelis completely out of all of Palestine, which, before 1948, reached from the borders of Jordan to the Mediterranean Sea to the west. The FLN and the ANC have succeeded in taking control of their own states while the PLO remains a state-in-waiting.

Besides the actors possessing varying measures of legal personality, covered so far, there are several others that can complicate international relations without holding appreciable legal personality, if any at all. It is a daunting task in international relations studies to keep up with the growing cast of actors that can play a meaningful role in international politics and, in some way, relate to international law as either a subject or object of law. Deserving special attention are ethnic groups, terrorists, and private military companies.

Box 2.4 Belligerent Recognition: Great Britain and the South

With the outbreak of the American Civil War (1861–5), the government of Great Britain faced a quandary: a humanitarian option versus a power opportunity. Great Britain could ignore the new Confederate States of America (CSA) yearning for recognition as a new state and, thus, preserve a good relationship with Abraham Lincoln's government with its anti-slavery cause. Or, the British government could militarily intervene, permanently dividing and weakening the growing rivalry of a young United States. Britain opted for a middle choice by offering the South *belligerent recognition* while continuing full recognition with the US government in Washington, DC. Although feigning neutrality, Britain sold armed ships, including the storied cruiser the *Alabama*, to the South and supplied most of the South's infantry with the Enfield musket-rifle. Any temptation by the British to intervene further, say by extending full recognition to the CSA government in Richmond or landing troops to assist Southern independence was stifled by the 1863 Emancipation Proclamation of President Lincoln, which freed all slaves and firmed British public opinion's support of the Union cause. The stalemate at the 1862 Battle of Antitem and the decisive defeat of the South at the 1863 Battle of Gettysburg doomed any chance that the South might receive Britain's full recognition as a permanent state. Great Britain also had to worry about its power calculations in Europe, involving especially the rise to great-power status by Prussia.

The conditional belligerent recognition of the South, as a state-in-waiting, allowed the British government to back out of a policy that was hurting their relationship with the Lincoln government, increasingly victorious and certain to reunite the country. Full recognition of the South would very likely have led to war between the United States and Great Britain.

Ethnic Groups

Sometimes scholars speak prematurely of the demise of the state, but one actor that does, on occasion, tear at the fabric of the state is the **ethnic group.** This group is a collective of people who share a special and enduring sense of identity based on a common history and shared culture. Cultural identification with the group may depend on language, religion, tribal status, and racial characteristics such as skin color and facial markers, or any combination of these. Equally important is the group's self-perception that its members are different from other peoples around them. The group may, in fact, feel that it is at risk from one or more other ethnic groups sharing the same country. The world of states has been hectored by the nearly complete lack of congruence between states and ethnic groups. The large majority of states are ethnically heterogeneous, forced to deal with some stress caused by persistent ethnic animosities that involve disputes ranging from how to spend government budgets to outright civil war. Ethnic minorities often pursue secessionist causes to form their own country, or at least insist on a degree of autonomy to protect their culture.

Tragically, conflict between ethnic groups can even reach genocidal proportions as happened in Rwanda in 1994, when the Hutu people went on a rampage and killed hundreds of thousands of Tutsi, among them women and children. It is ethnic group discontent that is frequently behind insurgencies and secessionist efforts, rioting, and acts of terrorism. Even if none of these dramatic events occur, central governments often view their ethnic minorities as troublemakers and target them with political repression that may involve torture and political murder. Before the defeat of Saddam Hussein's Sunni-controlled government in Iraq in 2003, being a Marsh Arab or a Kurd meant second-class citizenship status in Iraq at best.

Lucky are the multi-ethnic states that can live by what French historian and sociologist Ernest Renan (1823–1892) called the "spiritual principle." He reviewed geography, religion, language, race, and other potential common denominators but found none sufficient to meld a diverse people together. Renan decided that an ethnically varied state can only achieve an appreciable solidarity if its members have a strong sense of a shared past and expect to share a future, whether it is one of glory or of grief (1971: 82–90). Australia, Canada, the United States, and many European countries enjoy a sense of nationalism, or "spiritual principle," that bonds their peoples together with a strong sense of national identity despite their ethnic diversity. For these states, nationalism is a psychological sense of belonging that bridges over ethnic fissures. During the Second World War, for example, African–Americans, Italian–Americans, Japanese–Americans, and other American ethnic communities fought bravely for the United States despite the fact that these minorities had experienced long histories of discrimination.

Since time immemorial, ethnic groups have had to share a territory and government with peoples unlike themselves and perhaps with inimical feelings shared by all. Salvation seemed at hand, however, when President Woodrow Wilson announced his famous Fourteen Points, which were America's war aims for the First World War. Especially important was the principle of *self-determination*, mentioned earlier, that later would be stretched in meaning to suit different goals and situations. President Wilson wanted to break up the German, Austro-Hungarian, and Ottoman–Turkish Empires and create democratic states in their stead, a major step that Wilson thought would contribute to lasting peace. Wilson's approach seemed modest and reasonable at first glance but, unfortunately, the ambition for statehood held by many groups, some of them quite small, soared (O'Brien 2001: ch. 5). Wilson's Secretary of State, Robert Lansing, wrote insightfully about the new principle of self-determination when he said, "The phrase is simply loaded with dynamite…what misery it will cause."[20] Since the end of the First World War, the problem of deciding which territories and peoples should have the coveted status of "sovereign state" remains an issue today.

The concept of self-determination entered the UN Charter in 1945, in Article 1 (2) and Article 55, in a moderately expressed form, when read in context. Several years later, in 1948, the writers of the *Universal Declaration of Human Rights* (UDHR) saw no urgency to include references to minority rights or self-determination. This situation changed dramatically, however, when anti-colonial forces in the UN made self-determination a sacrosanct principle. In 1960, the *Declaration on the Granting of Independence to Colonial Countries and Territories* expressed a strong moral demand that peoples in Africa and Asia be allowed to rule themselves instead of continuing to bear the rule of Europeans. Then, in 1966, self-determination appeared as a right in the very first articles, respectively, of the twin *Covenants on Civil and Political Rights* and *Economic, Social and Cultural Rights*. It is ethnic groups that usually express a demand for self-determination, sometimes expressed through a NLM. Ethnic groups may not confine themselves to the legitimate rationales for expressing self-determination, namely, objection to colonial rule, racist government, and military occupation (Cassese 1995: 319). These groups may simply want to secede and from their own country, even when they are governed by democracies willing to grant a significant measure of democracy. The Basque people in Spain and, in the 1960s, the French-speakers in Canada are prime examples.

Box 2.5 The Special Case of Kosovo

Kosovo was legally a province of Serbia (aka Yugoslavia) but had a *de facto* independence from Serbian rule that became permanent. The attempts by Slobodan Milošević to create a "Greater Serbia," as the old Federal Republic of Yugoslavia broke up, included not only ethnic cleansing in Bosnia and Crotia but in Kosovo as well. In 1999, the Serbian army attacked the Albanian ethnic community, who made up the large majority of the citizens of Kosovo, driving them toward the country of Albania or into the mountains to live a meager existence. As news of depredations, that included the rape of Albanian women and the shooting of men of military age, reached Western Europe, NATO organized a form of humanitarian intervention that consisted mainly of aerial bombardment directed at the Serbian military and political infrastructure, all without UN authorization. Serbia finally capitulated.

Following NATO and Russian occupation of Kosovo, the UN set up the Interim Administration Mission to Kosovo in June 1999. The UN, the EU, and other international organizations shared nation-building duties to improve social, economic, and political conditions in Kosovo. The United States and European states mulled over whether Kosovo was to remain a province of Serbia or become an independent country, Kosovarian leaders declared the country's independence in February 2008. The United States and the EU states quickly recognized the new country. While the Kosovo case does not meet the legal criteria for self-determination based on either colonial status, racist rule, or foreign occupation, Kosovarian leaders could at least make the moral claim that they were ruled badly and undemocratically by the Serbs.

The dynamic force of self-determination barreled across the twentieth century mostly knocking the props of legitimacy out from under colonial empires. This force still rambles about unspent in the twenty-first century, with numerous minorities taking on strong governments in a bid for independence, whether they can lay claim to an argument of international law or not. Probably most disgruntled ethnic groups, set on creating their own country, will pay little heed to legal niceties. The break-up of states is certainly not encouraged by international society, but human rights concerns may still be at stake. When the Russians attempted to crush the Chechens near the Caspian Sea, China its Muslim minority, or Turkey its Kurdish population, the world accepts the prerogative of these states to remain whole, yet some states and human rights NGOs do not hesitate to aim human rights criticisms at the central governments because of their ruthlessness.

When an ethnic group succeeds with secession to form its own country, the success often involves outside intervention by an IGO or a powerful state. NATO's military strike on Serbia in 1999 set the stage of Kosovo to become independent. Russia's defeat of the Georgian Army in 2008 gave hope to South Ossetia and Abkhazia that these areas could permanently break away from Georgia. If all the restive ethnic minorities of the world managed statehood status, there would be a complexity of unmanageable numbers of states. A state society of two hundred states would transform into two or three thousand states very quickly.

Terrorists

Terrorists are private actors that use or threaten violence calculated to create an atmosphere of fear and alarm. This atmosphere is designed to break down the willpower and morale of a target, usually one or more governments and their citizens, so the agents of violence can push forward some sort of political agenda. Kidnapping, assassination, hijacking aircraft, sabotage, and, above all, setting off bombs are the typical actions of terrorists. Terrorists have a strong sense of injustice but an equally strong sense of military weakness, hence the need for them to resort to hit and run tactics. Today's terrorists seek modern weapons so they can escalate death and mayhem on an unprecedented scale. The 9/11 incident involving the hijacking of commercial airliners and flying them into the Pentagon and the World Trade Towers in 2001 constitutes the worst case of terrorism in history.

Often dedicated "true-believers," terrorists kill a few to frighten the many and frequently suffer the fate of death themselves.[21] While most terrorists focus on one country and its government, terrorist groups may operate internationally in the sense that they recruit supporters, weapons and money across borders and use several countries as places to train, hide, and rest. The infamous al-Qaida is international in every way. Its recruits come from several dozen countries, mostly Islamic states, and usually target the Western world, whether the object of attack is the World Trade Towers in New York City or American military personnel serving in Iraq.

International law concedes to states a monopoly on violence, although in modern times, under the UN Charter, that monopoly is restricted to self-defense and multinational operations to stop aggression and restore peace approved by the UN Security Council. The laws of war currently cover states but can drop down to the level of an insurgency, a revolutionary group that might possibly become a state.[22] Terrorists generally fall beneath this level and hence do not have international legal personality. For increasing numbers of people, there may be little hesitation to call terrorists "outlaws" and to regard them as the enemy of humankind, along with pirates, slavers, war criminals, and those guilty of genocide. A consensus is not present, and one can still hear the refrain, "one person's terrorist is another's freedom fighter."[23] At least there is a tightening noose of UN-sponsored treaties to criminalize various aspects of terrorism.

Mercenaries and Private Military Companies

The status of the **mercenary** appears to be in a state of flux. A mercenary is an economically motivated volunteer participating in military engagements in service to a government or some other entity. Usually a mercenary is an individual from a state that is uninvolved in a given conflict. Mercenaries have a storied history, but their various names of "soldiers of fortune," "dogs of war," or "sword-sellers" reveal a generally negative image of their activities.

Mercenaries have often appeared in the wars of Europe and received the same treatment as any other combatants so long as they obeyed the laws of war. Their legal status was verified by the 1949 *Geneva Conventions* covering the laws of war. A fundamental change occurred, however, with the 1977 Protocol I, an add-on to the Geneva Conventions. Protocol I declared that mercenaries no longer enjoyed the right to be a combatant and were not entitled to POW status. After 1977, mercenaries could be treated as objects of international law and prosecuted for criminality. This reversal of fortune came about mostly at the insistence of Third World states, particularly the African countries.

Some of the blame for the bloody internal conflicts in Africa has been attributed to the interfering role of white mercenaries. One of the first steps taken by the UN Peacekeeping force in the Congo, in the early 1960s, was to arrest Dutch and South African mercenaries. Also, in 1977, the Organization of African Unity (OAU) – now the African Union (AU) – drafted the *Convention for the Elimination of Mercenaries in Africa*. Later, responding to the many Third World states, the UN General Assembly adopted the 1989 *International Convention against the Recruitment, Use, Financing and Training of Mercenaries*, which still needs additional ratifications to enter into effect (Morton & Jones 2002: 638).

The matter of the legality of mercenaries would appear settled were it not for the regular appearance in the 1990s, often much ballyhooed by the media, of **Private Military Companies** (PMCs). These military companies are usually led by retired military officers from various countries, including especially Great Britain and the United States Legally, PMCs are registered in a given country as corporations and operate under the contract law of that state. Operating from Great Britain, Sandline International tried to involve itself in Papua New Guinea in 1997. Apparently,

Sandline International was under contract to protect a private corporation's interests in a copper mine by preventing its takeover by a rebel force. And in 1998, this same PMC gave advisory and logistical support to Nigerian troops when they ousted the oppressive government of Sierra Leone. In doing so, Sandline International violated a UN embargo on arms shipments to the area just to protect corporate interests in the area's diamond trade.

Better known among PMCs is Dynacorp, which is registered as a US corporation in Reston, Virginia. This PMC has a history reaching back to 1946. Contracting with the US government, Dynacorp has supplied police officers for Bosnian and Iraqi nation-building missions and bodyguards for the president of Afghanistan, and has flown defoliation missions over Colombia to thwart the illicit cocaine trade. Dynacorp is the 13th largest military contractor in the United States and has annual revenue of $2.3 billion.[24] Another PMC, Blackwater USA, employed armed guards that fired on a crowd in Baghdad in 2007. These employees were placed on trial for murder under US *extraterritoriality laws*. These laws govern a state's citizens while they are away from the territory of the state.

The actual legal standing of PMCs is murky, except for the guidance national contract and extraterritorial law offers. International law developments appear to run against PMCs, if they are counted as mercenaries, but states, including the United States, employ them to supplement overstretched militaries. A special concern about PMCs has to be the treatment of their employees if captured during a conflict. In Colombia, Marxist insurgents have on occasion shot Dynacorp employees and other times held them for ransom. It is unclear whether the Colombian insurgents gave any particular attention to these persons. Did they treat them merely as corporate employees, or more ominously, as mercenaries? PMCs probably have a better chance of being seen in a positive light if they are taking part in a multinational effort at nation-building, working as police officers or protecting humanitarian workers. As for taking part in an open conflict, PMC employees are probably at greater risk if captured than the uniformed military personnel of a state. In their careful study of mercenaries, Jeffrey S. Morton and Presley Jones, in the spirit of transparency, conclude that international law should recognize mercenaries as legal combatants, as in the 1949 Geneva Conventions, so their role in conflicts can be properly regulated (2004: 625, 630).

Domestic Actors

Besides ethnic groups, terrorists, and mercenaries, there are other actors, essentially domestically situated, but sometimes extend themselves into the international arena and may, at some point, require the attention of international law. Religious organizations increasingly want a transnational presence. The Roman Catholic Church already has a long history that predates the Westphalian state system and, in some respects, is treated as a state. In recent decades, Protestant churches, through the World Council of Churches and evangelical missionary work, are having a large impact on Third World countries. Islamic groups have helped each other across national boundaries in efforts ranging from economic development to supporting terrorism. Mafias, or internationally organized criminal associations, have become commonplace, whether they are smuggling people, cars, arms, or drugs from country to country and continent to continent. All too easily, they operate along the edges of national law enforcement jurisdictions. Then, there are the activities of cities, states, and the provinces of some countries. Often local governments have practiced "foreign policy" by passing resolutions on such matters as human rights and environmental practices in other countries. On occasion, local governments of two or more countries work out transborder agreements for their mutual advantage while by-passing their foreign ministries.[25]

Especially notable are twenty or so prominent cities, such as Frankfort, London, New York City, Paris, and Tokyo, which are frequently called "global cities." These cities have developed a pronounced international outlook as they have burgeoned into centers of international transportation, communication, finance and banking, and serve as the headquarters of MNCs and the loci of cultural centers and world-class universities and research centers. A super-stratum of cosmopolitan leaders and world-wise citizens populate these global cities (Sassen 2002; Neyer 2000: 179–97).

Chapter Summary

- Traditionally, international law has focused on the state as an actor but gradually other actors have taken the international stage with a degree of legal personality.
- The international society of today would be unimaginable without IGOs such as the UN or NGOs like Amnesty International or Greenpeace.
- The MNC is a special case of the NGO and together hundreds of these account for most of the world's trade and investment.
- Mercenaries' status is highly controversial, and today's PMCs may or may not be mercenaries depending on the choice of definitions.
- The only real persons are individuals but surprisingly it has taken several centuries before the individual person developed a significant legal personality based on duties and rights.

Discussion Questions

1   The state has the clearest legal personality. Why is this so?
2   What is the difference between *subjects* and *objects* of international law?
3   Should private military companies be regarded as mercenaries?
4   What is the status of terrorists as an actor under international law?
5   Why have MNCs become so important in international relations and law?

Useful Weblinks

http://www.corpwatch.org/
A website aimed at holding corporations accountable. This site offers an internal search engine and additional research tools. Reports on current corporate misdeeds and is regularly updated.

http://www.transparency.org/
Formed in 1993 and headquartered in Germany, Transparency International has gained respect for its carefully done corruption surveys of many countries around the world.

http://www.uia.org/
The website of the Union of International Associations offers numerous publications online including *Who's Who in International Organizations* and provides links to thousands of IGOs organized alphabetically, statistics on IGOs, and the *Yearbook of International Organizations.*

http://www.gdrc.org//ngo/index.html
The website of The Global Development Research Center offers the NGO Café which lead to thousands of NGOs organized by subject-matter.

http://www.mitpress.mit.edu/journals/INOR/deibert-guide/TOC.html
Among many other useful options, Professor Ronald J. Deibert of the University of Toronto offers "Countries, Regions, Governments." This option lead to government sites as well as academic studies of countries and regions.

http://www.globalpolicy.org/nations/index.htm
This website offers articles on states and their future. One special set of articles deal with the forces challenging the state and which threaten to usurp this actor as the primary actor.

Further Reading

Allman, T. D. (2004) *Rogue State: America at War with the World.* New York: Nation Books.

Beck, Robert J. and Ambrosio, Thomas (eds.) (2002) *International Law and the Rise of Nations: The State System and the Challenge of Ethnic Groups.* Washington, DC: Congressional Quarterly Press.

Bianchi, Andrea (2009) *Non-State Actors and International Law.* Burlington, VT: Ashgate.

Brownlie, Ian (1983) *State Responsibility.* Oxford: Clarendon.

Brownlie, Ian and Brookfield, F. M. (1992) *Treaties and Indigenous Peoples.* New York: Oxford University Press.

Danspeckgruber, Wolfgang (ed.) (2002) *Self-Determination of Peoples: Community, Nation, and State in an Interdependent World.* Boulder, CO: Lynne Rienner.

Dupuy, Pierre-Marie and Vierucci, Luisa (eds.) (2008) *NGOs in International Law: Efficiency in Flexibility?* Northampton, MA: Edward Elgar.

Fassbender, Barbo (2009) *The United Nations Charter as the Constitution of the International Community.* Boston, MA: Martinus Nijhoff.

Fernández-Sànchez, Pablo Antonio (ed.) (2009) *International Legal Dimension of Terrorism.* Boston, MA: Martinus Nijhoff.

Grant, Thomas D. (2000) *The Recognition of States: Law and Practice in Debate and Evolution.* Westport, CT: Praeger.

Klabbers, Jan (2002) *An Introduction to International Institutional Law.* New York: Cambridge University Press.

Klabbers, Jan (2005) *International Organizations.* Burlington, VT: Ashgate/Dartmouth.

Leonard, Mark (2005). *Why Europe Will Run the 21st Century.* New York: Public Affairs.

McCorquodale, Robert (2000) *Self-Determination in International Law.* Burlington, VT: Ashgate.

Paul, T. V., Ikenberry, G. John, and Hall, John A. Hall (eds.) (2003) *The Nation-State in Question.* Princeton, NJ: Princeton University Press.

Peters, Anne (ed.) (2009) *Non-State Actors as Standard Setters.* New York, NY: Cambridge University Press.

Prestowitz, Clyde V. (2003) *Rogue Nation: American Unilateralism and the Failure of Good Intentions.* New York, NY: Basic Books.

Provost, René (ed.) (2002) *State Responsibility in International Law.* Burlington, VT: Ashgate.

Simpson, Gerry (2004) *Great Powers and Outlaw States: Unequal Sovereigns in the International Legal Order.* New York: Cambridge University Press.

Notes

1   The 1933 Montevideo Convention can be accessed at http://avalon.law.yale.edu/ enter "1933 Montevideo Convention" in the website search engine.

2   The 1970 Declaration can be found at http://www.un.org/documents/ga/res/25/ares25. htm > Resolution 2625 (xxv) 24 October 1970.

3   The 2001 Draft Articles on Responsibility of States, with commentary, can be located at http://untreaty.un.org/ilc/texts/instruments/english /commentaries/9_6_2001.pdf.

4   The 1978 Vienna Convention can be found at http://treaties.un.org/Pages/ParticipationStatus. aspx, see Chapter XXIII; and the 1983 Vienna Convention is available in Chapter III.

5   The Agreement on Succession Issues is at http://treaties.un.org/Pages/ParticipationStatus. aspx, Chapter XXIX.

6   The 1986 Vienna Convention can be located at http://treaties.un.org/Pages/Participation Status.aspx, Chapter XXIII.

7   This 1949 advisory opinion can be accessed at http://www.icj-cij.org/ > Cases > Advisory Proceedings > 1948 reparation for injuries (note: proceedings began in 1948 but it is usually referred to as a 1949 case).

8   These treaties can be viewed at http://europa.eu/abc/treaties/index_en.htm.

9   For an estimate of attendance numbers at world conferences, see Kegley and Raymond 2001: 166.

10   See the following websites: http://www.transparency.org/; http://www.oneworldtrust. org/; and http://www.corpwatch.org/.

11   This paragraph draws in part from Malanczuk 1997: 98; Chinkin 2001: 135–40.

12   http://www.coe.int/T/E/NGO/public/consultative_status/_summary.asp/.

13   Although some sources cite much larger estimates, the number of MNCs given here are an estimate from Kegley and Raymond 2001: 174.

14 Abi-Saab 1987: 549–76; http://www.icj-cij.org/ > cases > Contentions cases > 1962 Barcelona Traction. (Note: The case began in 1962 and was decided in 1970.)
15 http://europa.eu.int/eur-lex/en/com/gpr/2001/com2001_0366en01.pdf/.
16 http://conventions.coe.int/ > Search > Criminal Law Convention on Corruption.
17 http://europa.eu.int/ > institutions > Court of Justice.
18 http://www.iusct.org/background-english.html/.
19 Quoted from Artz and Lukashuk 1995: 67.
20 Quoted in Grant 1999: 85.
21 A brief but excellent description of current terrorism is in Laqueur 2002: 1–13.
22 Frederic L. Kirgis, "Terrorist Attacks on the World Trade Center and the Pentagon," (September 2001), http://www.asil.org/ > Publications > ASIL Insights > 2001.
23 An interesting discussion about moral subjectivism and terrorism is found in Graham 1997: 115–31.
24 Pratap Chatterjee, "Dynacorp Rent-a-Cops May Head to Post-Saddam Iraq," found at http://www.corpwatch.org/ pp. 1–3.
25 Interesting accounts of domestic actors are found in Fry 1998.

The element of power is inherent in every political treaty. The contents of such a treaty reflect in some degree the relative strength of the contracting parties ... Respect for law and treaties will be maintained only in so far as the law recognizes effective political machinery through which it can itself be modified and superseded. (E. H. Carr 1939)

It is not a single world state, but a system in which states are increasingly hemmed in by a set of agreements, treaties and rules of a transnational character. Increasingly, these rules are not based just on agreement between states but on public support generated through global civil society. (Mary Kaldor 2003)

3

The Sources of International Law
Creating Law without Government

Contents

People living in the world's democracies are accustomed to legislative bodies generating a steady flow of laws to serve the needs and wants of their populations. At the same time, the many authoritarian governments that continue to exist impose rules by whim and often enforce these rules through repression. Whether democratic or authoritarian, a hierarchical legal system is in place. An entirely different situation exists at the international level. It is a horizontal legal system. No world parliament is available to produce rules or a global dictator to provide enforcement. A large number of diverse, sovereign states create their own laws for their common needs. Given the experiences most people have had with law at the domestic level, comprehending the method of creating law at the international level can be somewhat baffling. A close look at the sources of international law will offer clarification.

Imposition of law by some sort of world government appears to be unnecessary since states are motivated to develop and comply with rules to gain the benefits of international trade, arms control, restraints on war, safer and more convenient international travel, and an improved environment, just to name a few of the worthwhile rewards accruing through international law. Although some idealists have proposed a world government, as if it might be a panacea for global troubles, such a proposal remains anathema to most states. Joining IGOs and obeying most law most of the time, with the concomitant reduction of some sovereignty, is about as far as states will go in the present age. Once states are moved to promote their common interests through shared rules, it only remains to find a way to create these rules.

The procedure of this chapter is to identify and describe the various sources of international law. To avoid a rule-less vacuum, states over the centuries have relied heavily on customary law that emerged from common practice as well as written treaties when agreement is fairly close. States also have put principles of law to good use whenever international law begins to regulate a new international activity, before customs and treaties have taken firm control. And, as subsidiary sources for filling in gaps in the law, judicial precedents and the teachings of publicists have been helpful. The rapid expansion of the scope of international law is also covered.

Customary Law

These sources span the history of international law and are authoritatively recognized in Article 38 of the *Statute of the International Court of Justice*. Customary law has historically come first in many areas of law and will be discussed first. Treaty law often follows and confirms long-standing custom-written rules. It is true, however, that some treaties do produce norms that become customary law for states that have not ratified a given treaty. **Customary law** consists of the rules that emerge from the experiences of states over time as they try to resolve interstate problems. As the international society of states has built up, older states have socialized newer states with the rules already developed. For most states of international society, their official statements, court decisions, legislative acts, and diplomatic behavior will reflect that these states do, indeed, accept international society's customs.

Customary rules became law when there was a conviction that the expected behavior is *opinio juris sive necessitates* (often shortened to *opinio juris*), a legal rule that it is necessary to obey. A brief definition is that a customary rule is a general practice accepted as law. Customary law is still important today especially in the areas of state duties and rights, state immunity, and state succession. These areas have been slow to give way to written treaties that a large number of states are willing to ratify. In some areas, states are reluctant to give up the latitude of choice customary law gives them and that the written rules of treaties might take away (Byers 1999: 4).

Faith in customary law remains strong to a degree that states will sometimes challenge the written law, even the UN Charter, with arguments drawn from customary law. During Ronald Reagan's tenure as president, the United States attacked Libya in 1986 with Air Force and Navy bombers as an act of *reprisal* for Libyan terrorist attacks against US service personnel in Germany. While the Security Council of the UN is supposed to approve the use of force, reprisal, as an act of national self-enforcement, has a long history in customary law. To the Reagan administration, the customary rules on reprisal appeared to have legitimacy on a par with the written law of the UN Charter. However, if one predominate trend stands out concerning customary law, it is that many areas of international law – including the laws of the sea, war, and diplomacy – have gone through a **codification process**, becoming the written law of

---

Box 3.1 Article 38 of the Statute of the International Court of Justice

1   The Court, whose function is to decide in accordance with international law such disputes as are submitted to it, shall apply:

    a   international conventions, whether general or particular, establishing rules expressly recognized by the contesting states;

    b   international custom, as evidence of a general practice accepted as law;

    c   the general principles of law recognized by civilized nations;

    d   subject to the provisions of Article 59, judicial decisions and the teachings of the most highly qualified publicists of the various nations, as subsidiary means for the determination of rules of law.

2   This provision shall not prejudice the power of the court to decide a case *ex aequo et bono*, if the parties agree thereto.

Source: This Statute can be read at http://treaties.un.org/Pages/ParticipationStatus. aspx > Chapter I.

---

treaties. An appreciable degree of legal consensus within international society must exist before it is possible to codify a customary rule into a written one. Even in the areas of state immunity, responsibility, succession, and rights and duties, where countries are especially cautious, some treaties and declarations have at least been promoted.

There is a solid reason why much of customary law has been codified. Christine Gray has observed that as non-European states, for instance Ethiopia, Japan, and Turkey, entered the Eurocentric international legal system, it became difficult to create new customary law satisfactory to the growing diversity of states (1983: 280). New states want new rules, and as Sir Arthur Watts has observed, customary law often lacks precision and is a slow vehicle for change (2000: 15). This problem was magnified after the Second World War when a large number of socialist and Third World states encountered the Europeanized legal system. The pressure of absorbing all these states led to multilateral conferences and the UN International Law Commission producing a considerable number of treaties for states to consider ratifying. Helping generate new treaties gave non-European states a sense of meaningful participation, insuring their support for international society in the future. Antonio Cassese is almost certainly correct in claiming that the high-water mark of customary law was the nineteenth century when about 40 European and European-settled states on other continents, such as Australia and Canada, could work out legal rules through shared experiences (2001b: 124–5).

Although international "legislating" may have shifted from customary law to an emphasis on treaty writing, customary law remains important and is often central to some important international court cases. For customary law to be seen as clearly established, several important questions are at stake: how many states must adhere, over what period of time, and with how much consistency before a custom is a firm rule of international law?

The number of states question

The 1969 *North Sea Continental Shelf* case that came before the UN's International Court of Justice (ICJ) is instructive regarding the number of states and even the amount of time needed to bolster customary law. Denmark, Germany, and the Netherlands, as adjacent countries, share the North Sea continental shelf, but there was a question as to how these three countries would divide their continental shelf into three national jurisdictions. The 1958 *Geneva Convention on the Continental Shelf*, one of four new sea treaties proposed at the time by the UN's International Law Commission, might have given guidance. Unfortunately, Germany had signed but not ratified the 1958 Geneva Convention. Germany also took note of the fact that the treaty called for a settlement based on the *equidistant principle*. Since Germany's coast is concave while Denmark and the Netherlands have moderately convex coastlines, Germany would receive a much smaller share of the shelf than if the division was simply based on shares more or less in proportion to the length of their sea coasts. The ICJ did not agree with Denmark and the Netherlands that the 1958 Geneva Convention should control the outcome. The Court recognized that the 1958 convention had come into force only in 1964 with the requisite 22 ratifications, and, by 1969, the convention could still just claim 39 state ratifications. The Court failed to agree that the 1958 convention had sufficient standing to imply a customary rule with *opinio juris* on non-participating states, namely Germany. Presumably, there was an insufficient number of states and time involved to create a customary rule for a non-adhering state. The ICJ, did, however, for the first time, substantiate the thesis that provisions in treaties can sometimes generate new norms as customary law for non-treaty states, only not in this case.[1] A treaty should have the support of a strong majority of states before the claim is made that a given treaty can imply norms applicable to the non-treaty states. For example, no one questions that the UN Charter, ratified by the vast majority of states, applies as customary law for the few states which have not joined the world body.

Since the ICJ could not find that the equidistant principle was a customary rule for Germany, the court decided that the three parties should use the *equitable principle* to divide the shelf, a legal principle drawn from many domestic practices. This principle gave Germany a larger share of the continental shelf of the North Sea than otherwise would have been the case. Interestingly, when the four 1958 conventions of the sea, recommended by the International Law Commission, were updated and integrated into the 1982 UN *Convention on the Law of the Sea* (LOS), Article 83 of the continental shelf section of the LOS called for equitable solutions and not the equidistant principle. The large majority of states have ratified the LOS with a few notable exceptions.

The time question

The traditional approach requiring a long period of time for a customary rule to take hold is underscored by the *Paquette Habana* and *Lola* case. Usually decades, if

Box 3.2 The *Paquette Habana* and the *Lola* Case

Judgment delivered 1900 by the US Supreme Court (Summary and Commentary)

The *Paquette Habana* and the *Lola* were coastal fishing boats operating near the Cuban coast while flying the Spanish flag. When the Spanish–American war began in 1898, a US naval squadron intercepted and took the two fishing vessels as prizes of war. Usually a "prize" is suspected of serving the enemy in some capacity. The appropriate federal district and circuit courts upheld the seizure as a legal act of war.

The Supreme Court reversed the lower courts and returned the two fishing vessels to their owners. The majority opinion of the court included an extensive review of various states' practices regarding the status of fishing boats going back to the policy of Henry IV of England in the early fifteenth century. Over the centuries, numerous states made an exception for fishing vessels in their prize courts; thus, customary law on the matter appeared clear. Moreover, this case resorted to customary law as a source because the US Constitution, treaties, and federal law failed to address the issue at hand.

Once wireless codes could be transmitted ship to ship and ship to land, the status of fishing craft began to change. This technology was available before the First World War, although it was usually found only on major ships. In 1912, the *Titanic* teletyped for help after it struck an iceberg. By the time of the Second World War, even small fishing craft would likely have voice radio and, thus, could serve as spies for the naval forces of their country. When the famous Jimmy Doolittle mission of 1942 was approaching Japan, the American carrier equipped with B-25 medium bombers was spotted by Japanese fishing craft. The Americans sank the fishing boats as quickly as possible but had to assume the Japanese fishermen sent a radio message to Japan. For this reason, the raid was launched several hundred miles ahead of the planned launch point. The raid was an overall success, but several planes, due to the early launch, ran out of fuel and had to ditch in the sea near the coast of China, their destination.

Source: This case can be read at http://caselaw.lp.findlaw.com/scripts/getcase. pl?court=US&vol=175&invol=677, pp. 1–24.

not centuries, may be involved (Malone 1998: 30). As William W. Bishop, Jr. points out, it is difficult to say exactly how much time must pass for a custom to become customary law (1989: 470).

Louis Henkin speaks of "instant" customary law and cites the well-known example of President Harry Truman's Proclamation of 1945 (1999: 470). President Truman said the United States would claim the continental shelves adjacent to the US coastlines up to a distance of 200 nautical miles and the resources these shelves might provide. President Truman did point out that the use of the sea above the shelf by other states would operate unaffected. Many other states in rapid succession made similar claims. Instead of objecting to the instantaneous nature of the Truman Proclamation or its content, states were all too willing to monopolize a set of nearby resources that could eventually include off-shore oil-drilling. Almost overnight a new customary law was in place. The Truman Proclamation is an extraordinary exception to the time rule in the area of customary law. Moreover, his proclamation led to efforts to put this custom into treaty form, first in the 1958 *Geneva Convention on the Continental Shelf* and then in the much broader 1982 LOS. Interestingly, the Truman Proclamation also called for use of the equitable principle instead of the equidistant principle to divide a continental shelf among adjoining states. The LOS convention finally confirmed the use of the equitable principle for dividing continental shelves as the written law of nations.

Professor Henkin also observes that when states want to change the rules quickly, rather than go through the lengthy treaty-making process, they may press for a special resolution from the UN General Assembly, known as a *declaration*. This type of resolution is designed to create new norms to guide states, as when Third World states wanted new trade rules in the 1970s. Declarations usually carry moral weight and may represent a large step toward a convention in the future. Henkin calls this process a radical innovation because it involves the purposive creation of a new norm to stand in place of a customary rule evolved through practice.[2] In the final analysis, a specific time frame for a custom to ripen into law is difficult to ascertain, but the longer the period of time, the better the chances of establishing the custom's legitimacy.

Making the same point in stronger terms, Anthony D'Amato, in an article with the title "Trashing Customary International Law," sharply criticizes the ICJ's use of a declaration to impute customary law. In the 1986 Nicaraguan case, the court made reference to the 1970 *Declaration on Principles of International Law Concerning Friendly Relations and Co-operation Among States In Accordance with the Charter of the United Nations*. He objects to this "instant" or modern form of determining customary law as opposed to the traditional method of relying on long-term practice.[3] Another interpretation is that the court merely wanted to show that the 1970 declaration reflected the 1945 Charter prohibition against intervention and the use of force by one state against another. The United States was supporting an insurgency movement trying to overthrow a Marxist government in Nicaragua. In fact, the 1970 declaration refers to principles that have been developing for decades and are now foundational to international society and its law.

The consistency in practice question

Besides the number of states supporting a custom and the length of time in development, the consistency of state practice regarding a customary rule is important. The traditional view is that customary law is universal with all states expected to obey it. A violation now and then probably will not undermine the custom, however. Some

---

Box 3.3 The Asylum Case Judgments in 1950 and 1951 by the ICJ (Summary)

The Colombian ambassador in Lima, Peru, granted asylum to M. Victor Raúl Haya de la Torre, head of a political party in Peru. The ambassador allowed him to enter the Colombian embassy in 1949 following a military rebellion that the Peruvian government claimed Hoya de la Torre instigated in 1948. Asylum is recognized as regional Latin American international law, and so all that seemed to remain was for the Peruvian government to grant a safe conduct pass to Hoya de la Torre so he could leave the country.

However, the ICJ declared that Colombia was not qualified to decide unilaterally that the offense was a political one as opposed to a common crime. Thus, Peru was not obliged to regard Hoya de la Torre as a political refugee and Colombia could not under any treaty bind Peru to do so. The 1911 *Bolivarian Agreement* and the 1928 *Havana Convention on Political Asylum* did not permit unilateral assignment of refugee status. Furthermore, the 1933 *Montevideo Convention on Asylum* had not been ratified by Peru and so could not be invoked against that country. The court ruled Colombia was unable to demonstrate a constant and uniform practice of asylum as *customary American international law*. The ICJ found too many inconsistencies in asylum practices.

The ICJ was asked in what manner the issue could be resolved. The court only replied it was not part of its judicial function to end what was in effect a political situation, but did allow that Colombia was under no obligation to surrender Hoya de la Torre to Peruvian authorities. Hoya de la Torre finally left the Colombian embassy and Peru in 1954, basically as a political outcome rather than a legal one.

Source: This case can be read at http://www.icj-cij.org/ > cases > contentious cases > 1949 Asylum Case.

---

states have even tried to argue that a principle of *persistent objector* is valid. As a new custom is forming, some states might make a point of objecting to the rule year after year, with the intent that they are exempt from compliance with the rule. Actually, there is no solid support for the principle of persistent objector in case law or practice (Cassese 2001b: 123).

The classic case on consistency is the well-known 1950 asylum issue between Colombia and Peru. Not only does Latin America have treaties on asylum but some customary practices too. Asylum in Latin America is an excellent example of what is known as *regional international law*. Most countries around the world do not wish to to embrace asylum practices that would encourage political refugees to seek shelter in their embassies and thus stir up trouble with the countries hosting foreign embassies. Colombia tried to argue before the ICJ that even if Peru had not ratified the 1933 *Monteveido Convention on Political Asylum*, customary practice in Latin

America should control the outcome. The Court, however, found too many inconsistencies in practice to conclude that there was a clear customary law on asylum that could be applied to Peru.

A modern use for customary law

Customary law has further proven its staying power by coming to the aid of the human rights movement. Following the 1945 UN Charter's commitment to the goal of improving human rights, a spate of declarations and treaties quickly emerged, but unfortunately a sizable gap has always existed between the written rule and the actual human condition. Promoting and enforcing human rights standards in a world of sovereign states, with governments historically accustomed to treating their populations as they saw fit, is a major undertaking.

Box 3.4 The *Filartiga v. Peña-Irala* Case

Appearing in US Federal District of Eastern New York and the Second Circuit Court of Appeals, 1979–1980 (Summary and Commentary)

Seventeen-year-old Joelito Filartiga was tortured to death in 1976 at the hands of Americo Norberto Peña-Irala, the Inspector-General of Police in Ascension, Paraguay. This cruel act was aimed as a punishment for Joelito's father who opposed the government of Paraguay. Joelito's sister, Dolly Filartiga, sought asylum in the United States in 1978, only to discover Inspector Peña-Irala was living in the United States on an expired visitor's visa.

Ms Filartiga filed a civil suit for the torture and wrongful death of her brother under the 1789 *Alien Tort Claims Act*. The Federal District Court of Eastern New York refused to hear such a novel case, but on appeal to the Second Circuit Court of Appeals, the case was heard in 1979 and the decision rendered in 1980. Since Peña-Irala had been deported for overstaying his visa, a default judgment of over $10 million was awarded to Dolly Filartiga.

Awards of this kind are easier to make than to collect, and of course a criminal charge that might place Peña-Irala in prison was not at stake. At least the wall of national sovereignty was breached with the message that the way individuals are treated by their governments can be a concern elsewhere.

Sources: To read this case and interesting commentary, enter "Diana Online Human Rights Archive" in a search engine and select "cases" and then "Filartiga" ; also go to: http://www.pbs.org/wnet/justice/law_background_filartiga.html; http://www.womenon theborder.org/alien_tort.htm.

In the famous US case of *Filartiga v. Peña-Irala*, appearing in US federal courts during 1979–80, a small step was taken to protect human rights, namely, opposing the odious practice of torture through the use of customary law. This protection became possible because of something that happened almost two hundred years earlier. The first US Congress enacted the 1789 *Alien Torts Claim Act* as part of a broader judiciary act. This law allowed aliens on US soil to sue one another in a civil action for a *tort,* that is, a damage committed in violation of either the "law of nations" or a US treaty. This law probably was intended to help aliens use US courts to recover damages incurred in international waters, especially for an act of piracy. The Filartiga case argued that, by 1979, torture was as much prohibited by customary law as piracy was in 1789. The US federal courts delved into the weighty evidence of declarations, treaties, and national constitutions and reached the conclusion that a customary international law of human rights does exist, at least for the most heinous of crimes.

Moreover, following the Filartiga case, the United States confirmed jurisdiction over suits by aliens alleging torture, by passing the 1991 *Torture Victims Protection Act*. In fact, this act covers any individual victim including citizens of the United States. The United States further shored up its anti-torture stance in 1994 by ratifying the 1984 *Convention against Torture and Other Cruel, Inhuman or Degrading Treatment or Punishment*. Unfortunately, the mistreatment of terrorist suspects during President George W. Bush's tenure undermined an enviable human rights record of opposition to torture.

Treaty Law

The 1969 *Vienna Convention on the Law of Treaties* defines a **treaty** as "an international agreement concluded between states in written form and governed by international law." The 1986 *Vienna Convention on the Law of Treaties between States and International Organizations or between International Organizations* extends the same definition to agreements between IGOs and states or other IGOs.[4] Although the 1986 Vienna Convention awaits a few more ratifications before entering into force, IGOs have been participating in the treaty-making process for decades. The term "treaty" is usually thought of in a generic sense and so covers all agreements, whether they are called accords, conventions, charters, covenants, pacts, protocols, or statutes, along with other terms in use. These terms are synonymous with "treaty."[5]

Patterns in the use of terms

There are some interesting patterns in the use of the various terms referring to agreements but none displace the generic meaning of treaty. "Agreement" is often used to refer to regional economic trade treaties, for instance, the *North American Free Trade Agreement*. "Convention" has come into use for multilateral treaties when a large number of states, either at the regional or global level, generate treaty law. Conventions often enjoy the sponsorship of the UN or one of the specialized IGOs within the UN System.

Well-known examples are the 1969 *Vienna Convention of the Law of Treaties*, the 1982 *Convention on the Law of the Sea*, and the 1989 *Convention on the Rights of the Child*.

For founding instruments that create IGOs, "Charter" is often preferred, for example, the 1945 UN Charter and the 1952 *Charter of the Organization of American States*. However, the League of Nations, the precursor to the UN, preferred to call its foundational document the League "Covenant." Finally, a "protocol" can have several slightly different meanings but usually appears in the form of an "optional protocol," which is an add-on agreement to an existing treaty. Treaties sometimes begin as **framework treaties** with add-ons at a later date expected. Such a treaty covers the general subject-matter, which can then be elaborated with optional protocols. These protocols have a sufficiently independent character to require their own ratifications. The 1966 *Covenant on Civil and Political Rights* now has two optional protocols, which allow a sub-set of ratifying states to make deeper commitments regarding the enforcement of human rights.

The relationship of treaties and customary law

Before continuing on to other interesting aspects of treaties, some further comment on the interplay between treaties and customary law is in order. It has been mentioned before that customary law is often codified into treaty law. And reference has been made to treaties, if widely accepted, giving rise to a customary expectation for non-signatories. The most insightful observation about the treaty–custom relationship, however, may have been made by John King Gamble, Jr. About any given area of international law, he thinks there is often a long causal chain with customs and treaties alternating in a process of creating a body of law. Gamble believes the two generate each other (1998: 86–7).

Traditionally, a hierarchical difference between treaty and custom has not existed. If the two should be in conflict, the "time-rule" applies. The most recently developed rule of law prevails. The shift to an emphasis on treaty law is explained by its political popularity, not the inadequacy of customary law. At one time, customary law was general law for a Eurocentric world, while treaties were for bilateral arrangements between two states requiring a specific rule, say, for a border agreement. As mentioned before, since the Second World War, there has been a sharp rise in the population of new states wanting treaty-making conferences that can provide these states with greater influence than otherwise would be the case. Gradually, treaties have come to be seen as more definite law and, when in conflict with customary law, are usually seen as possessing more authority.

History and purpose of treaties

The history of treaties has covered three millennia, and the purpose of treaties has remained essentially the same. During the 400-year-old history of the society of states, treaties have allowed states to cooperate over an ever expanding list of subjects, including security, trade, health, the environment, terrorism, telecommunications, and much else. Philip Allott believes states were always conscious of operating within an international society, one that was well defined by the early nineteenth century. For the benefit of this society, Allott thinks treaties performed a social function analogous to legislation in national systems (2000: 80–1). In the current time of rapid globalization, with its tightening interdependence among actors, the reliance on treaties to guide deepening patterns of cooperation has grown in importance.

Anthony D'Amato asks the interesting question of whether international law is just a grab-bag of treaties, customs, court decisions, and writings of publicists and, thereby so ramshackle as to be chaotic (1995: vii). True, international law, with treaties particularly in mind, cannot match the carefully constructed Justinian Codes of Roman times or the modern code law of present-day Germany, with their almost seamless and systematic coverage of every governable subject and issue. Nonetheless, an impressive *corpus* of international law has evolved. In every area of this law, whether concerning human rights, terrorism, diplomacy, intellectual property rights, or specialized issues of maritime law, treaties exist that constitute the basis of written law for that area. If needed, further reference can be made to customary law, principles, and court decisions when treaty law falls short. The Foreign Offices of governments and some scholars have made considerable efforts to pull together multiple volumes of *digests* of all relevant documents, involving all sources, relating to specialized areas of international law.[6]

Treaties are not just instruments for cooperation but can be tools for progress. Although law can be a conservative force and used to protect the *status quo*, reform can be the purpose of treaties. There is a growing list of conventions that call for bold change and reform. By accepting these conventions, states have been willing to provide better human rights practices, cleaner environments, and to reject weapons ranging from landmines to atomic bombs, all aimed at making a safer world for human living.

Unequal treaties

Although cooperation and progress have been the purposes of treaties, sometimes in history treaties have been used to freeze a power relationship of the strong over the weak. Treaties made in this fashion have come to be called *unequal treaties*. This term is essentially a political one and not a legal concept. The sense of injustice caused by unequal treaties, however, stings no less. At the conclusion of great wars, such as at the end of the Napoleonic Wars and the First and Second World Wars, when the dust settled and the winners and losers became clear, the treaties ending the wars appear to have confirmed new international orders (Gilpin 1984). When wars were seen as normal and as legal policy options, treaties that confirmed the loser's position seemed appropriate and were a natural element of a war-making system. A major drawback is that treaties accepted under duress may set the stage for later problems. E. H. Carr, on the eve of the Second World War, looked back at the 1919 *Versailles Treaty* forced on Germany and concluded that this unwise act contributed to German rearmament and its repudiation of the Versailles Treaty (1966: 187–8).

Few historians fail to point out that the unfairness of the Versailles Treaty was one of the major causes of the Second World War.

Unequal treaties go back to the earliest history of the state system. They were common between Europeans and indigenous peoples in the new world of the Americas, and established "spheres of influence" over the Chinese, Persian, and the Ottoman Turkish Empires. The apex of these unequal treaties might be the 1901 *Boxer Protocol* imposed after the Boxer Rebellion. European governments felt this rebellion endangered their diplomats and families living in the diplomatic quarter of Beijing, the Chinese capital. Under this humiliating protocol, the Chinese government was forced to cede full authority to foreign governments in the diplomatic section of Beijing.[7]

Since the Second World War, Third World and communist states have brought up the subject of unequal treaties at international fora, but to little avail. Western states have insisted that this problem is political in nature, and not legal. The 1969 Vienna Convention on the Law of Treaties seems to reflect the Western point of view because it omits the subject of unequal treaties. Consequently, there is no clear legal redress as in municipal law where a private contract can be invalidated if signed under duress. J. L. Brierly calls this situation a grave defect of international law and advocates full consent by all parties to a treaty (1963: 317–18).

Unequal treaties have not been a prominent issue in recent years. This good result may have come about in part because of the accumulated wisdom that unfair terms will lead to instability in the future. Also, war is no longer a legal policy option under the UN Charter, except in self-defense, so the opportunity to impose asymmetrical terms in a treaty is less available. For this reason, Louis Henkin believes the UN Charter leans toward requiring the full consent of all parties signing a treaty (1995: 29). Finally, the trend toward multi-state conference diplomacy, with a large number of states taking part, allows weaker states to use their numbers to offset the major powers' influence, including that of the United States as the world's only remaining superpower.

The breadth of treaties

Treaties, like other sources of international law, can be conceptualized as *universal*, *general*, and *particular*. *Universal* obligations involve fundamental norms or principles that are binding rules for all states, whether a given state has ratified a universal type of treaty or not. The UN Charter has universal character. For instance, the deeply invested norm of non-aggression applies to every state, and the UN Charter embodies rules about force that reflect this norm of non-aggression. The Charter applies not only to its 192 ratifying states but is also valid as customary law for the handful of small states that have not joined, as already mentioned. Further bolstering the universality of the Charter is its Article 103, which makes clear that if a treaty of any kind conflicts with the Charter, the latter prevails.

General treaties

General treaties are multi-party treaties usually involving a large number of states drawn from all regions of the world. A general treaty is likely the product of a conference attended by diplomats from a wide range of countries and even the representatives of IGOs and NGOs. Such a conference is more democratic than a process that allows great powers to dictate rules within a small pool of states. In practice, general treaties sometimes move toward universal status. Additional states may accede to the treaty or its terms may extend to non-ratifying states as customary rules. Conventions dealing with the law of treaties, the law of the seas, genocide, and racial discrimination have arguably achieved universal status. *Particular* treaties apply to only a few states, often just two. Typical examples would be treaties calling for sharing the waters of a river as it passes through a limited number of states, regional trade agreements, or border arrangements.

Stages of treaties

A formal process exists for creating the written law of treaties, a process that may take many years. Almost a decade was needed before the 1982 UN LOS was ready for ratification, and it was 1994 before enough states ratified so the treaty could enter into force. The first stage is **negotiation.** This step is essentially a political bargaining process, whether two foreign offices are constructing a bilateral treaty or an international conference is turning out a multilateral convention. Sometimes states exchange *travaux préparatories*, or working papers that will establish each side's position and help set an agenda before a meeting takes place.

The **signature** stage requires that diplomatic representatives sign the text of the treaty as an expression of provisional consent, but the treaty is still subject to the approval of the representatives' governments. **Ratification** is the stage when the government of a state agrees to be bound by the treaty as a lawful obligation, and becomes a *party* to the treaty. The procedure for ratification can range from the signature of the country's chief executive to a more complex process involving the national legislature. Sometimes a president and prime minister, after toiling long and hard for a treaty, may face serious disappointment. President Woodrow Wilson, often called the "Father of the League of Nations," campaigned vigorously to persuade public opinion, and indirectly the Republican-controlled Senate, to accept the 1919 Versailles Treaty. President Wilson needed a two-thirds approval vote by the Senate to complete the ratification process for a treaty that would formally end the First World War and provide for the League's creation. Campaigning for the Versailles Treaty on an extensive tour by train, Wilson suffered a stroke in Oklahoma and later died. The Senate never approved the Versailles Treaty, leaving the United States outside the League. When a treaty is ratified, a state sends its *instrument of ratification* to the state serving as the *depositary*, or "keeper of records." Treaties also have to be registered with the UN, and at an earlier time, with the League of Nations.

At the time of signature or ratification, states may insist on a **reservation** about one or more articles of a treaty. In such a case, a state is saying it will be bound by all articles of the treaty except for those articles it finds objectionable. Some treaties might not ever go into force if reservations were not allowed, and yet enough reservations by a lot of states could easily vitiate the purpose of a treaty. Numerous states insisted on reservations to the *Statute of the International Court of Justice* because they wanted to limit the situations and issues that could draw them before the world court. Compulsory jurisdiction is a jolting notion to a sovereign state, especially considering the long history of states' independence from higher authority. When reservations are allowed by the other signatories, the rule followed is that the reservation must not mitigate the fundamental purpose of the treaty. The rule derives principally from the advisory opinion of the ICJ in a case involving the 1948 *Convention on Genocide*. In their 1951, ruling, the justices allowed for reservations, but only if they were compatible with the basic purposes of the treaty.[8]

A modern trend has been for treaty-creating conferences to be cautious about allowing reservations or sometimes to prohibit them altogether. The 1966 *Convention on the Elimination of All Forms of Racial Discrimination* provided that a reservation would be unacceptable if two-thirds of the ratifying states objected to it. The United States has experienced several diplomatic defeats because of its pursuit of reservations.[9] The United States has failed to ratify the 1982 LOS, the 1997 landmine treaty, and the 1998 statute creating the International Criminal Court because its proposed reservations were seen as undermining the basic purposes of these treaties. The World Health Organization's (WHO) 2003 *Framework Convention on Tobacco Control* is an example of a multilateral treaty prohibiting all reservations without exception.

Entry into Force is the next stage of treaty-making, and it is ordinarily without controversy. Treaties normally make clear the conditions under which they enter into force as international law for the ratifying states. Usually a prescribed minimum number of ratifications are needed to make the treaty lawful. The 1948 Genocide Convention specified 20 state ratifications, the 1982 LOS required 60 ratifications, and the 1969 Vienna Convention on the Law of Treaties needed 35 ratifications.

The last major stage for a treaty is **registration**. Although states can still choose one of their ranks as *depositary*, Article 102 of the Charter requires additionally that all treaties be registered with the UN and made public. This practice started with Article 18 of the League's Covenant, which says no treaty can be considered binding until registration with the League takes place. The Charter requirement is not as strict since it permits a non-registered treaty to apply its rules without registration, but such a treaty cannot be used before any agency of the UN, including the ICJ. Both the League and UN requirements reflect the influence of President Wilson who called for treaties to be arrived at openly, believing that such public diplomacy would contribute to peace. His call for openness was an early example of transparency, which the global governance process of today tries to apply as a standard. Finally, the stages of treaty-making presented here are the bare bones of what can be a much more complex and formal process. A UN source lists 23 separate treaty actions, or stages, and makes no promise that its list is exhaustive.[10]

The hard work of negotiating treaties is basic to the problem of creating law without a central government, or world government. The story of treaties does not end with their creation, however. After a treaty enters into force, additional states, through an act of **accession,** can sign and ratify the treaty at a later date. Most members of the UN obviously have ratified the UN Charter long after its founding date of 1945 in San Francisco. Treaties often provide for an **amendment**, which might call for a general revision of a treaty or a change in only one or two articles. Another post-ratification development is the **invalidity** of treaties which can occur but is rare. The *Vienna Convention on the Law of Treaties* provides that a treaty may become invalid for one or more signatories if a state's *internal law* for approving treaties was not followed, if a state representative *exceeded authority* in committing the state to the agreement, if an *error* occurred, as when an incorrect map is used to set a boundary line, if one state tricks another into ratifying by *fraud* or persuades by *bribes*, or if the representative of his or her state is threatened with *force*.

Interruption of treaty obligations

A more serious problem is the refusal of a state to abide by a treaty or one of its critical provisions, or unilaterally terminates its role in the treaty altogether. Trust in that particular state is gravely undermined so far as future relations are concerned on the part of other states and important IGOs like the UN. When a state performs in such a maverick manner, its action is called a **material breach**. If one state suspends or terminates a bilateral treaty, the other party is free to withdraw from the treaty if the material breach is serious. Obviously, if a multilateral treaty is at stake, the legal outcome is more complicated. After a breach by one state, the other parties to the treaty may terminate the treaty altogether or suspend treaty obligations with only the offending state. For example, if a state were to back out of an arms treaty and create a weapon of mass destruction (WMD), the remaining parties might rush to create a similar weapon for deterrence purposes. However, if a trade treaty were breached by one state, the remaining signatories would probably support the treaty as long as it helped them to prosper.

A rarely used rationale for derogation from a treaty obligation involves the legal phrase **rebus sic stantibus**, literally meaning as long as conditions remain the same. In this situation, one party attempts to derogate by claiming a major change in the conditions on which the treaty was originally founded. The *Vienna Convention on the Law of Treaties* imposes tough standards for a country to be able to withdraw from a treaty on these grounds. One of the few cases that can be cited is the Iceland fishing case involving Great Britain. In 1961, Iceland and Britain exchanged diplomatic notes containing an agreement between the two countries that allowed Iceland to extend its territorial fishing waters beyond the traditional 3-mile territorial limit of that period to 12 miles. It is important to bear in mind that both countries count heavily on the fishing industry and have for a long time fished in much of the same waters of the North Atlantic. After agreeing to the new 12-mile limit, Britain wanted, in return, a promise that if any question arose between the two, the case would go to the ICJ. When Iceland decided unilaterally to extend its exclusive fishing jurisdiction to 50 miles, Great Britain objected and placed the case on the docket of the ICJ. Iceland asserted its action was justified by claiming substantial change in *rebus sic stantibus*. The government of Iceland maintained that more intense fishing with modern technology warranted its decision. In its 1973 ruling, the court found that it did have jurisdiction and ruled against Iceland.[11] A few years later, the British-Iceland argument over 12- versus a 50-mile fishing jurisdiction lost its relevance when the 1982 LOS allowed for a 200-mile Exclusive Economic Zone, which covers fishing.

The Vienna Convention on treaties also recognizes **supervening impossibility of performance**, although an instance of derogation of this kind is unlikely to arise very often. If a treaty depended on a river as a boundary line but the river dried up, or an island shared by two countries' fishermen under a bilateral agreement permanently became submerged, then terms of the relevant treaty would no longer make sense and thus it could be terminated. Lastly, war can interfere with a wide-range of treaties covering the relations of two or more states at war. Most publicists have long argued, that during war, treaties are only suspended and that their terms resume once hostilities cease.

The UN and treaties

The UN, through the roles of the Sixth Committee (the legal committee), its International Law Commission, and General Assembly declarations, have helped blanket the world in international law. The UN role has been to support law that bolsters peace and strives to advance the human condition of the over six billion people sharing the planet. The last decade of the twentieth century was declared by the UN to be the *Decade of International Law*. Perhaps the best service of all the UN's efforts is the UN Treaty Collection, which has registered over 40,000 treaties. As referred to earlier, all treaties currently in force around the world are required to be in registered with the UN.[12]

Another important service came directly from the Secretary-General's office. Secretary-General Kofi Annan, beginning in 2000, in anticipation of the *Millennium Assembly for Heads of State or Government*, urged every willing state to engage more effectively in support of international law and to ratify what he called the 25 core treaties Most of these treaties were human rights-related treaties, but the list also included disarmament and environmental treaties as well. In each subsequent year of Annan's tenure, a specialized category, such as treaties on women's rights or terrorism, received priority.

The Role of Principles

A **principle** of international law is an accepted rule followed by judges, arbiters, and the diplomatic representatives of states when customs and treaties are unclear or when these two sources of laws appear to be in conflict. Principles fill in gaps left by these firmer sources of law. The formal status of principles is found in Article 38 of the *Statute of the International Court of Justice* which lists, among other sources, "principles of law recognized by civilized nations." Within the hierarchy of these sources, most legal authorities view principles as a subsidiary source, along with judicial decisions and the writings of publicists. Undoubtedly principles are expected to continue in importance as a source since they are referred to in Article 21 of the 1998 *Statute of the International Criminal Court*.

In the early development of international law, publicists had little choice but to use principles extensively, but in modern times they receive less attention due to the emergence of a substantial *corpus* of widely agreed-upon customary and treaty law. In fact, the most relied- upon principles have sometimes evolved into customary law or found a place in treaties (Cassese 2001a: 499–501). Principles are likely to be reprised whenever international society experiences a new development that requires regulation, and before firm law is in place. A poignant example involves the UN's *International Criminal Tribunal for Yugoslavia* (ICTY) which has drawn on the penal laws of the major legal systems around the world for guidance. Common usage of a legal practice in many countries has proven to be a ready source for principles accepted at the international level. For instance, the ICTY has acted more decisively on charges of rape that involved the forcible entry of the vagina or anus, but less so in cases of forced oral sex because the handling of the latter crime lacks uniformity in national legislation (2001: 48).

Principles of international law can be placed in three categories as to their origins, although these categories can overlap to some extent. First there are the principles commonly used domestically in the major legal systems of the world. The meaning accorded to the crime of rape mentioned earlier is a good example. These principles are well known and accepted by leaders and judges at the international level. As John O'Brien has observed, judges deciding international law issues have often served previously in the municipal context, and they bring their national experiences with them to the international level (O'Brien 2000: 87). The municipal, or domestic, con-text provides most of the principles in use at the international level. *Estoppel* is a doctrine that prevents an actor from discontinuing an established practice on which other parties have become reliant Parties should act in *good faith* concerning their promises or compliance with the law. Another domestic principle used internation-ally is *neo iudex in sua causa* (one should not be a judge in his or her own case). Already mentioned earlier in an international setting is *rebus sic standibus*, which refers to a possible change in conditions underpinning an agreement. To get out of the agreement, one party must demonstrate a drastic alteration of the conditions. *Res judicata* (a matter already adjudicated) is a stand most courts will take by refus-ing to hear a case for a second time.

Second are the principles that arise at the international level itself instead of being borrowed from municipal systems. These principles are sometimes referred to as general principles. One principle cited as an example above all others is *pacta sunt servanda*, which means that agreements must be observed. This principle is the singularly most important because the international legal system would be nearly meaningless without it. This principle's great importance is illustrated by its appearance in the preambles of both the UN Charter and 1969 Vienna Convention on the Law of Treaties. Other examples of general or international level principles are found in the 1970 Declaration on Principles of International Law Concerning Friendly Relations and Co-operation among States In Accordance With the Charter of the United Nations.[13] This declaration is intended to elaborate the Charter by identifying principles that states have agreed to use in their mutual relationships. These principles include refraining from the use or threat of force, settling disputes peacefully, avoiding intervention in the affairs of other states, respecting other states' sovereign equality, and fulfilling all Charter obligations (O'Brien 2001: 91–2).

The third and final source of principles is natural law. The best-known examples are principles of equity and humanity. Equity calls for a fair settlement and can be identified with the jurisprudence of common law countries but also placed in the natural law tradition. Judges at the national and international levels have used equity decisions to prevent an injustice that might otherwise occur if laws were slavishly applied in a technical way. Judges have applied equity mostly to handle boundary and maritime issues, as in the North Seas Continental Shelf case of the ICJ. Equity decisions can be a potentially serious problem if the parties at issue, or the judges in a case, represent sharply differing political and legal cultures. Although judges of the ICJ and arbiters have on occasion used equity law, neither the ICJ nor its predecessor the Permanent Court of Justice, have applied *ex aequo et bono* (what is just and fair) provided in Article 38. This principle is similar to equity but is much more general. For this source of law to apply, both parties in a dispute must agree to its use. While there is no bright line between the two, equity calls for fairness but is rooted in norms of law and precedent. *Ex aequo et bono* is free of legal moorings (Franck 1995: 54–6).

A sense of humanity, as a social and political force, no doubt helps explain the laws of war that protect POWs and the outpouring of human rights treaties since the Second World War. Humanity considerations have also appeared in case law. The 1949 *Corfu Channel* case involved two British destroyers damaged by mines, with a heavy loss of life, off the coast of Albania in 1946 during peacetime. The destroyers should have been able to enjoy the right of "innocent passage" through the Corfu Channel, from one part of the high seas to another. The ICJ decided that Albania had an obligation to notify other countries of the minefield or at least give immediate warning to the British warships as they approached. Since the incident happened in peacetime, the court concluded, among other factors, that "elementary considerations of humanity, even more exacting in peace than in war" applied. The ICJ found Albania responsible for the damage done to the two destroyers and reserved for further deliberation the amount of compensation Albania would have to pay Great Britain.[14]

One special principle in the natural law category that deserves to be revisited is *jus cogens*, an inviolable norm states must adhere to without exception. Treaties and customary law are rendered invalid if they support or condone genocide, slavery, a war of aggression, torture, or any other reprehensible acts. The exact source of *jus cogens* is not completely clear. Most authorities discuss *jus cogens* as a development since the mid-twentieth century based on core norms representing supreme, unbreakable law (e.g. Henkin 1995: 38). Li Haopei takes note of this principle's recent attention, including its appearance in Article 53 of the Vienna Convention dealing with treaties; however, he claims it originated in the municipal law of Rome and finally reached many municipal systems of today through the writings of publicists of the seventeenth and eighteenth centuries (2001: 499–501).

Judges and Publicists

For the citizens of Australia, Great Britain, the United States, and other English-speaking countries, judges making decisions that serve as precedents is a normal expression of the *common law* tradition. The foundation of common law is **stare decisis** (to stand by a decision). Lower-court judges in this system would fail to receive a promotion to a higher bench if they were unable to bear in mind a long line of precedents and logically apply these precedents to a case before their bench. Sometimes the more activist judges of common law countries are accused of *making* law instead of *declaring* the meaning and application of the existing law for a given case based on a legislature's intent. Judges in the United States can even practice *judicial review*, which is a great power on the part of a court for declaring a law null and void because it conflicts with the US Constitution. Common law countries are in the minority among the world's two hundred or so states.

Most countries of the world have *civil law* systems, usually based on a heritage originating with Rome, traveling over time to the rest of Europe, and from there to other parts of the world via colonial rule. Civil law involves lengthy and elaborate codes of law similar to the Justinian Codes of Roman times. The job of civil law judges is more straight-forward than that of common law judges. These judges apply a large body of explicit law based on detailed codes to the facts of the case before them. While common law judges can reshape the meaning of legislative statutes and create case-derived precedents, civil law judges assume they have a complete body of law on hand provided by a legislative body.

The role of judges and arbiters dealing with international law does not match exactly either the work of common or civil law judges; rather, judicial decision-making at the international level is *sui generis* (of its own kind). Article 59 of the *Statute of the International Court of Justice* appears to repudiate completely *stare decisis* of the common law tradition when it states, "The decision of the Court has no binding force except between the parties and in respect of that particular case." And certainly no elaborate codes associated with civil law are on hand for the justices of the ICJ. They are left to search among treaties, customs, and principles of law to find a basis for a sound decision. The justices do not always succeed at this task, however.

When a dispute arises or a crime has been committed, any court is loath to admit it cannot find appropriate law, but in at least one case the ICJ had trouble determining the law. In a 1996 case about the legitimacy of nuclear weapons, the UN General Assembly asked the ICJ for an advisory opinion on the following question: "Is the threat or use of nuclear weapons in any circumstance permitted under international law?" The ICJ searched through the areas of human rights, environmental, and armed conflict law, but still could not provide a definitive answer, not even on the question of nuclear weapons' use in self-defense. The Court appeared hamstrung on this issue, unable to be decisive after reviewing a wide assortment of legal sources. The ICJ had to turn to a series of UN General Assembly resolutions which "declared that the use of nuclear weapons would be a violation of the Charter and a crime against humanity."[15]

In practice, the ICJ, as well as other international courts, does pay some attention to their own prior decisions and the judgments of other international and, even national, courts. Richard B. Lillich and Daniel B. Magraw claim that trying to block out precedents in international law is like trying to stop the wind (1998: 36–7). When the ICJ, for instance, offered an advisory opinion in the 1949 Reparations for Injuries case, it established the precedent that IGOs can empower themselves sufficiently enough to fulfill the goals of their treaties of creation, a precedent that from then on would be available to other courts and international organizations besides the UN. Other examples of ICJ precedent-setting decisions easily come to mind. The 1951 genocide case helped clarify how reservations to treaties would be handled in the future. And the 1970 *Barcelona Traction* case largely defined the nationality of corporations, while the 1950 asylum and 1969 North Sea Continental Shelf cases contributed some understanding to the relationship between customary and treaty law. Finally, the UN International Tribunal for Rwanda in 1998 established the precedent that rape can be construed as a war crime rather than merely an ordinary criminal act committed by an individual. History contains many examples of the systematic use of rape as an adjunct to waging war, but, until recently, has been a neglected prosecutorial issue.

Bing Bing Jia offers a clear-eyed perspective about international courts and precedents. Writing about judicial decisions in the context of international criminal tribunals, he sees precedents as "persuasive" to judges rather than serving as "binding authority." He notes that Article 21 of the 1998 *Statute of the International Criminal Court of Justice* allows justices of this court to look at previous decisions, but that the same article regards judicial decisions as subsidiary (Bing Bing Jia 2001: 83–95). John O'Brien offers an interesting insight about the *Statute of the International Court of Justice,* which downplays the use of precedents. He opines that judicial decisions have had more influence on the evolution of international law than the creators of the Statute in 1921 could have ever imagined (O'Brien 2001: 94). The Statute served the Permanent Court of Justice, associated with the League of Nations, before coming into use by the ICJ as a major organ of the UN. Amidst a proliferation of international courts and tribunals in recent years, judges undoubtedly are aware of prior decisions by their own court as well as the judgments handed down by other judicial bodies. However, as Anne-Marie Slaughter goes on to point out, the world falls far short of a unified legal system headed by a top world court that can impose global uniformity on lower-levels of courts (Slaughter 1997: 186–9).

In addition to principles and judicial decisions, publicists' writings are another source clearly identified as a subsidiary source of international law. The years of profound dependence on publicists coincide with the lives of such noteworthy writers as Grotius, Pufendorf, and Vattel. Although burgeoning customary and treaty law have mostly eclipsed the role of publicists, they are still useful today. Publicists delve into subjects at great depth and pull together all the fragments of treaty law, customs, and court decisions into a meaningful whole. Gerhard von Glahn cites Ramphaël Lemkin's *Axis Rule in Occupied Europe* (1944) as contributing materially to the framing of the UN *Convention on Genocide* in the aftermath of the Second World War. Lemkin even coined the term "genocide," meaning the killing of a tribe or nation of people, as Adolf Hitler's Nazi Germany attempted to do to the Jewish community of Europe.[16]

Another way publicists provide a service to international law today is to take on **moot issues**, or theoretical questions, and offer suggestions as to how the law can deal effectively with a problem. Much of outer space law had been written, partly under the influence of publicists, before many states could even clear the Earth's atmosphere with their rockets, satellites, and crewed vehicles. Only the Soviet Union and the United States had the rockets to place a small number of satellites into orbit when the core space law, the 1967 *Outer Space Treaty*, was offered for ratification.

The academic spade work of publicists may happen as the result of individual efforts, like that of Lemkin's work on genocide, or it may be the product of a body of scholars. Several well-known academies of international law publicists exist, including the American Law Institute, *L'Institut de Droit International*, the Hague Academy of International Law, and the International Law Association, which has 50 national branches. Deserving special attention is the UN International Law Commission (ILC). While the other academies are private, the ILC is a public body since it is an organ of an IGO. The ILC has helped propose a number of conventions opened for ratification by states.

Other Sources

The formal sources of Article 38 have been covered, but it is necessary to identify a few less explicit ones. These sources do not have the binding nature of *opinio juris*, nonetheless, states are inclined to respect them. One such source is **comity**, which consists mainly of courtesies that surround diplomatic intercourse. If one side offers supporting evidence to clarify a position before negotiation begins, then the other side can be expected to reciprocate. Or, if one state sends a diplomatic note to another, the sending state should not make its contents public until the receiving state has had a chance to read it. Then there are *memoranda of understanding*, which are usually technical rules produced by two states' bureaucracies to handle common interests regarding commodity trades, antitrust laws, or such concerns as environmental damages and health issues (Slaughter 1997: 189–92). More broadly, the 1975 *Helsinki Agreements* provided a basis of understanding on how the East and West would deal with each other during the great Cold War divide.

There are several instances of *unilateral pronouncements* by a state serving as binding law. The best known is the 1973 announcement by France that it was going to conduct nuclear atmospheric tests in 1974 in French Polynesia, but after that date would cease such tests altogether. The ICJ regarded as binding France's unilateral pronouncement in the 1974 *Nuclear Tests Cases*. Australia and New Zealand brought the case in objection to nuclear radiation in proximity of their countries.

Even a famous case of a binding *oral agreement* has occurred. Denmark and Norway have disputed over the possession of Greenland, especially the more habitable eastern coast, since 1819. In 1919, the Norwegian Minister of Foreign affairs asserted to a Danish diplomat that Norway would no longer object if Denmark claimed all of Greenland. The dispute, nonetheless, arose once more, going before the Permanent Court of International Justice in 1933. The Permanent Court found in Denmark's favor. A written record of the conversation between the Norwegian foreign minister and the Danish diplomat proved to be Norway's undoing.

Finally, there is a source some scholars speak of as *soft law*, which essentially refers to resolutions or declarations of intended policies by a body of states. Declarations are resolutions that carry considerable moral weight and may call for bold policy changes. The Third World tried to change the world economy to their liking with UN General Assembly declarations. These declarations are neither lawful nor mere political statements, but something in between. The UN General Assembly has issued a goodly number of declarations in different policy areas. Multilateral conferences sometimes turn out declarations as well as treaties, usually because the politics surrounding the conference will permit only this lower level of agreement. Then, there are policy agendas for states to follow that emerge from multilateral conferences. A well-known example is *Agenda 21* for promoting the health of the planet that stemmed from the 1992 *Earth Summit*.[17] *Codes of conduct*, encouraged by the UN and NGOs for MNCs to follow as ethical guidelines, are another variant of soft law. Soft law is sometimes referred to as **lex ferenda**, as "law in the making" or "law as it should be." This law is usually contrasted with **lex lata**, or law as it exists.

The Scope of International Law

The **scope** of international law is the range of subjects regulated by international rules. The simplest way to indicate the breadth of this scope is to point out that virtually every issue that receives the attention of municipal law sooner or later is regulated at the international level. The fast pace of globalization has left international law scrambling to catch up with all sorts of new human activities spilling across borders.

A traditional way of analyzing the scope of international law is to distinguish between **public international law** and **private international law**. The public side of international law primarily deals with the duties and rights of states and IGOs. Typical public laws are found in the areas of diplomacy, state succession, war, intervention, and various issues of jurisdiction relating to air space, territorial waters, and land territory. Private international law focuses on private individuals and groups as their activities cross national boundary lines, producing effects on two or more countries. The distinction between public and private international law is gradually blurring. As early as 1963, Wolfgang Friedmann claimed that many activities once taken to belong to the private sphere have become a matter of public concern, drawing the attention of governments and IGOs. Friedmann stated that, "There is today [1963] hardly any field of private law which could be adequately understood without a strong and often decisive admixture of public law" (1963: 279–99). Treaties as public law are increasingly absorbing private activities for regulation on everything from transnational business to the protection of children in custody and adoption cases (Bozeman 1994: 206). One of Hilary Clinton's early tasks in 2009, as Secretary of State, has been to champion the cause of an American father who has for several years sought his son's return from Brazil.

There are ongoing meetings from time to time of the Hague Conference on Private International Law that has held sessions since 1893. Numerous conventions among states regulating private lives on a transnational basis have been produced by the Hague Conference, for instance, the 1980 *Convention on the Civil Aspects of International Child Abduction* and the 1993 *Convention on Protection of Children and Cooperation in Respect of Inter-Country Adoption*.[18]

Another broad division made in international law is *global* versus *regional* law. The UN Charter, numerous other multilateral treaties, declarations, principles such as *jus cogens*, and other types of rules have multiplied rapidly at the global level, especially since the Second World War. Additionally, developments at the regional level have been equally robust. Africa, the Middle East, Europe, Latin America, and Southeast Asia, among other regions, have designed treaties, as well as IGOs, they believe meet their special needs.

A third and final broad distinction is between the *laws of war* and the *laws of peace*, with the *laws of neutrality* closely involved. For once war has begun, the relations of two or more states change dramatically. For example, foreign nationals belonging to enemy countries can be interned, members of the other side's military can be shot on sight or held as POWs until hostilities cease, and foreign property of the enemy, such as ships, can be seized and employed in the war effort. Trade, foreign assets in banks, and other economic properties become frozen until the war is over. Neutrals should have complete freedom to move cargo ships and planes in and out of warring parties' harbors and skies, but the practicality of entering a zone of conflict has always been a treacherous undertaking. The traditional night and day difference between war and peace has broken down in recent times since security issues often turn on terrorist activities. This kind of conflict operates in twilight of neither peace nor war, as traditionally understood.

Since the end of the Second World War, the focus of international law has been on a spate of issues that requires the world to busy itself with more regulation for the good of all. Challenging international law's capacity to keep up with the demand load, among a growing list of concerns, are outer space, intellectual property theft, transnational drug gangs, corruption in business, the regulation of telecommunications, a rising level of travel by ships and planes, the protection of human rights and the environment, health issues, the spread of missiles and weapons of mass destruction, and even the development of international sports law. The scope of international law can be regarded as boundless. This law will probably expand on a parallel course with the most modern countries as the two levels cope with many of the same problems.

Chapter Summary

- Since the earliest state system development, customary rules emerged among states as these actors worked through problems and established solutions as precedents.
- Treaties are agreements, usually written, that date from ancient times but have grown in importance as products of modern multilateral conferences, which are made possible by rapid travel and communication.

- Principles of law are used to fill in when customs or treaties do not provide sufficient rules and are often drawn from the domestic experiences of states.
- Formally the decisions of judges rank at the bottom rung of the hierarchy of sources of law, but the growth of courts and tribunals can only highlight the importance of judicial decision-making.
- The writings of publicists have lost ground as a source of law, but their research and writing still have some influence as new problems in law are encountered.
- The scope of international law covers almost every subject that states deal with in their municipal or domestic context.

Discussion Questions

1 Based on Article 38 of the Statute of the International Court of Justice, what are the four levels/sources of international law?
2 Despite considerable emphasis by some international law scholars on court cases and precedents, can an argument be made that treaty law is the most important source of international law?
3 What are unequal treaties and are they as likely to occur in modern times as they have in the past?
4 When principles of international law are emphasized from what sources are they drawn and what is their role?
5 Within the scope of international law, what is meant by private international law and is it diminishing or increasing in importance? Why?

Useful Weblinks

http://untreaty.un.org/
The official site of the UN Treaty Series (UNTS) contains over 40,000 treaties. This site has many offerings, including "Photographs of Signature Ceremonies," a "United Nations Treaty Series Index," and "Treaty Reference Guid," with an overview of key terms related to treaties. Access to the treaties can require a subscription.

http://www.state.gov/www/global/legal_affairs/tifindex.html
This is a site of the US Department of State. Available is a list of the treaties and other agreements of the United States that are in force as of January 1, 2000. The index is alphabetized based on the country or IGO name.

http://www.questia.com/popularSearches/customary_law.jsp
This site offers online books and journal, magazine and newspaper articles. One section available is on customary law. A "search tool" for the library is offered. Reading the material is by subscription.

http://repositories.cdlib.org/blewp/art96/
A site provided by the University of California, Berkeley, offering free the paper, "Stability and Change in International Customary Law" by Vincy Fon and Francesco Parisi. The paper is a PDF file, 154k.

http://www.un.org/law/ilc/index.htm
This site is the homepage of the International Law Commission, a public body of publicists. This site offers information on "Membership," "Program of Work," "Conventions and Other Texts," as well as other options, including related web sites.

Further Reading

Aust, Anthony (2007) *Modern Treaty Law and Practice*. New York: Cambridge University Press.

Byers, Michael (1999) *Custom, Power, and the Power of Rules: International Relations and Customary Law*. New York: Cambridge University Press.

Byers, Michael and Nolte, Georg (2003) *United States Hegemony and the Foundations of International Law*. New York: Cambridge University Press.

Davidson, Scott (ed.), *The Law of Treaties*. Burlington, VT: Ashgate.

Dekker, Ige F. and Post, Harry H. G. (ed.) (2003) *On the Foundations and Sources of International Law*. New York: Cambridge University Press.

Evans, Malcolm D. (ed.) (2006) *International Law*, 2nd edn. New York: Oxford University Press.

Kelsen, Hans (1966) *Principles of International Law*, 2nd edn. Revised and edited by Robert W. Tucker. New York: Holt, Rinehart, and Winston.

Klabbers, Jan and Sellers, M. N. S. (2008) *The Internationalization of Law and Legal Education*. London: Springer.

Koskenniemi, Martti (ed.) (2000) *Sources of International Law*. Burlington, VT: Ashgate/ Dartmouth.

Treaty Handbook (2008) New York: United Nations Publications (available as a PDF file at http://treaties.org/ > Publications > Treaty Handbook).

Notes

1 D'Amato 1970: 894–5. The North Sea Continental Shelf case can be read at http://www. icj-cij.org/ > cases > contentious cases > 1967 North Sea Continental Shelf.

2 Henkin 1995: 37. Also see Presidential Proclamation No. 2667 issued September 28, 1945 at http://www.oceanlaw.net/texts/truman1.htm

3 D'Amato 1987: 101–5. The Declaration can be read in Brownlie 1995: 36–45. Or refer to http://www.un.org/ > main bodies > General Assembly > Quick Links > Resolutions > Archives > Resolutions > 25th – 1970.

4 Both conventions on treaties can be found at http://treaties.un.org/Pages/ PartyicipationStatus.aspx > Chapter XXIII.

5 These specialized examples of "treaty" and other terms are found at http://untreaty. un.org/english/guide.asp, pp. 3–12.

6 On this point, see Joyner 1998: 259–60. A good example is Weston 2000.

7   "Unequal Treaties," *Encyclopedia of Public International Law* 1984: vol. 7, 514–

8   http://www.icj-cij.org/ > cases > advisory proceedings > 1950 Reservations to the Convention on Genocide.

9   For an interesting article on the United States and treaty reservations, see Frederic L. Kirgis, "Reservations to Treaties and United States Practice," American Society of International Law (May 2003) http://www.asil.org/insights/ pp. 1–3.

10   See, http://untreaty.un.org/english/guide.asp pp. 6–12.

11   This case can be found at http://icj-cij.org/ cases > contentious cases > 1972 Fisheries Jurisdiction.

12   The treaty collection homepage is at http://untreaty.un.org/.

13   This Declaration can be read by using the citations in note 3.

14   This case can be read at http://www.icj.org/ > cases > contentious cases > 1947 Corfu Channel Case.

15   To read this case, see http://www.icj.org/ > Cases > Advisory proceedings > 1996 Legality of the Threat or Use of Nuclear Weapons.

16   von Glahn 1996: 20. See note 13 for a reference to Raphaël Lemkin's work.

17   An interesting article on "soft law" is by Chinkin 1989: 850–66.

18   This conference's activities can be found at http://www.hcch.net/index_en.php?act=home. splash > conventions.

For Centuries the defining feature of international law has been the lack of central and comprehensive law creation, enforcement, and judicial mechanisms. (Georg Nolte)

The United Nations surely will maintain its impressive record as a seedbed for developing new rules and norms of international law. (Christopher C. Joyner)

4

The Efficacy of International Law

Contents

For international law to have efficacy, it must carry out three classic legal functions found in every society in some form, including international society: rule-making, rule enforcement, and rule adjudication. In a primitive society, all three functions might be in the hands of a tribal chief, but in a complex, modern government there can be specialized branches dedicated to each function, as is the case with the United States The critical question here is whether these functions perform adequately at the international level. Another concern about international law's effectiveness is whether states are willing to integrate relevant international rules into their municipal legal systems. International rules are increasingly affecting the domestic laws and policies of states as a growing number of treaties require national governments to bring about changes at home. As well, if international law is performing effectively as a legal system, might the evolution of international law be headed toward a world government? Such a grand vision of international law's future may be unrealizable, or perhaps even undesirable for that matter.

The first task of this chapter is to assess the effectiveness of the legislation function followed by sections on how well enforcement of international law and adjudication functions are carried out. An evaluation of bringing relevant international law to bear in domestic jurisdictions comes next. Finally, some insight about the prospects of world government emerging from the international legal process is offered.

Legislating International Law

All societies have some way of producing rules for their constituents, whether individuals or states. This process of rule-making can range from the informal socialization of norms within a small group of people to a congress or parliament turning out hundreds of complex, written rules for national societies. Rule-making for international society is at best quasi-legislative, that is, this process may happen in an international conference or the UN General Assembly. It only resembles the deliberative procedures of a parliament enacting law but, in fact, falls short of such legal power.

Today's global governance offers many opportunities for diverse actors, including NGOs and IGOs as well as states, to help form new rules. The relatively new international conventions against torture and landmines, for instance, reflect NGO input indicative of a more democratic kind of global governance, one ready to improve the world for people rather than promote only the interests of states. Yet proposed international law, regardless of which kind of actor recommends it, is unlikely to gain much traction without states deciding a given rule is acceptable to them. The shadow of the positivist tradition, with its premise that states must approve of a rule before they are bound by it, still lingers over the quasi-legislative process at the international level.

States developing the UN Charter during the Second World War were overwhelmingly opposed to conferring true legislative powers on the UN.[1] The UN, however, has been able to approach a legislative function in a roundabout way. As mentioned in the previous chapter on sources of law, UN General Assembly declarations can become international law if states choose to ratify them as multilateral treaties. Reliance on the slow customary law process among consensus-oriented European states had to give way increasingly to the varied demands of a worldwide society of states reflecting different moral attitudes about justice and struggling with an interdependent global economy. A quasi-legislative process managed to arise within the UN, based on a role of suggesting law to the states so they can better cope with the discordant demands of an expanding international society.[2]

The Preamble to the UN Charter and Article 13 (1) of this Charter call on the UN to promote the development of international law, but no one in 1945 could have imagined the outpouring of declarations and conventions from the UN that have enriched the body of international law. As Christopher C. Joyner once pointed out, the UN has emerged as the pre-eminent institutional source of international law (1997: 432). The UN General Assembly closely mirrors the world, represents almost all the states, and is open to the entreaties of several thousand NGOs and several hundred other IGOs. The General Assembly is the natural political space for placing issues on the international agenda and winning a legitimizing endorsement for a given position. From the deliberations of the UN have come hundreds of treaties, many of them narrowly focused on technical matters such as food hygiene or aircraft safety, while others splash across the news when they involve human rights or arms limitations. Whatever the attention received by a proposed treaty, it must be remembered that national interests and power are always lurking in the background. Ultimately all the hard work of UN bodies and NGOs pushing for reforms depends on the endorsement of sovereign states (Schechter 1994: 1–23).

The General Assembly can pass hundreds of resolutions per year, but only a few of them stand out as declarations marking a potentially significant change in policy. And not all declarations evolve into treaty law, a distinction discussed in the last chapter. It can be remembered these declarations are "soft law," representing a climate of political, and sometimes moral, opinion that occasionally transforms into the legal obligations of conventions, if support for a declaration gathers into a strong force.

For example, there is the famous 1948 Universal Declaration of Human Rights that grew into two distinct treaties in 1966, the *Covenant on Civil and Political Rights* and the *Covenant on Economic, Social and Cultural Rights.* The 1961 and 1963 Declarations on Principles of Outer Space led to the 1967 *Outer Space Treaty.* A 1975 declaration opposing torture became the 1984 *Convention against Torture.* Important declarations that did not become treaties but helped change policies of states and influenced International Court of Justice decisions are, respectively, the 1960 Declaration on the Granting of Independence of Colonial Countries and Peoples and the 1970 Declaration on Principles of International Law Concerning Friendly Relations and Cooperation among States. A resolution about "common heritage" helped Third World states stake a claim to whatever the technologically advanced countries might find of value in the seabed of the oceans or outer space, a provision that did make its way into the 1982 *Law of the Sea Convention.* And the General Assembly has helped define war crimes with its formulation of the Nuremberg Principles that guided the prosecution of Nazi war criminals at the end of the Second World War and with its 1974 Declaration on Aggression.

Other proposals the General Assembly intended from the beginning to be treaties are the 1948 *Convention on the Prevention and Punishment of the Crime of Genocide,* the 1961 and 1963 *Conventions on Diplomatic Relations and Consular Affairs,* the 1968 *Nuclear Non-Proliferation Convention,* the 1982 *Convention on the Law of the Sea,* the 1990 *Convention on the Rights of the Child,* the 1998 *Statute of the International Criminal Court,* and the 2000 *Convention Against Transnational Organized Crime.* The list of declarations and conventions could be considerably longer, but the ones offered here show that the quasi-legislative process of the UN General Assembly is a robust one.

The General Assembly appears to resemble a legislative process even more because of its specialized committees. For purposes here, the legal committee, or Sixth Committee, has special relevance, but there are other committees dealing with economics and finances, politics and security, humanitarian and cultural issues, administration and bureaucracy, and decolonization and trusteeship. These committees can meet as "committees of the whole," with every General Assembly member-state attending but, in practice, many small states do not have the personnel in their UN delegations to cover all the meetings and gatherings of the complexly organized UN System.

The most often cited accomplishment of the Sixth Committee is the development of the 1948 Convention on Genocide before the International Law Commission (ILC) was up and running. Very shortly thereafter, the ILC took on the chief responsibility for codifying and developing international law but with the Sixth

Committee serving as its review body on behalf of the General Assembly. As the world entered the twenty-first century, some of the interesting work of the Sixth Committee involved reviewing reports from the ILC on subjects including the responsibility of international organizations, regional economic organizations, shared natural resources involving ground water and aquifers, transboundary harms from hazardous activities, and reservations to treaties. The Sixth Committee has also worked on terrorist conventions trying to distinguish terrorists from revolutionaries, and the Committee set up a Working Group to study the "Scope of Legal Protection" under the 1994 *Convention on the Safety of the United Nations and Associated Personnel* in light of the bombing of the UN offices in Baghdad in August 2003. The Sixth Committee can report on its work to the General Assembly or send a legal task onto the ILC for fuller development.[3]

The UN Charter's call for expanding international law in Article 13 resulted in the 1947 *Statute of the International Law Commission*. The ILC's job is to craft carefully proposals for law, subject to the advice of the Sixth Committee and the approval of the General Assembly. And the Commissioners of the ILC must always keep in mind that state approval will be required. The Commissioners are elected by the General Assembly to serve in their individual capacity for 5-year terms. The ILC started with 15 Commissioners serving at the first meeting in New York City but gradually expanded to 34 legal experts to accommodate the UN's growing and diverse membership. With rare exception, the 3-month-long meetings of the ILC have been held in Geneva, Switzerland.

The 1947 Statute commits the ILC to the dual task of both *codifying* and *progressively developing* international law, as called for in Article 13 of the UN Charter. The Statute of the ILC, in Article 15, conceptualizes the two tasks as if they can be meaningfully distinguished. Codification refers to the more precise formulation and systemization of rules of international law in fields where extensive state practice, precedent and doctrine already exist. Changing customary law into treaty law is the most obvious kind of codification. Progressive development calls for the preparation of draft conventions on subjects which have not been regulated by international law or in cases where the law has not been sufficiently developed in the practice of states.[4] When an international body like the ILC advances new rules, as in the cases of state responsibility and succession, states may resist these additional rules either because they do not like them or did not have a full role in negotiating their creation. Conceptual purity does not always hold up when concepts are put to work, and, in practice, the ILC usually blends the two tasks during its meetings. In its first session, ILC reviewed 25 possible topics and settled on a working list of 11 of these. Best known among the ILC's accomplishments are the preparations on conventions regarding the law of the sea, treaties, and diplomacy; its summary of the Nuremberg Principles; work on the draft declaration regarding the rights and duties of states; and the attempt at defining the will-of-the-wisp concept of aggression.[5]

The ILC has given meticulous care to most of the conventions and declarations emanating from the UN but its record is still somewhat mixed. The most common complaint concerns the slow, ponderous work style of the ILC. Taking a decade or more for its work is basic to the nature of the ILC. The Commissioners tend to focus on narrow issues with an eye on quality instead of quantity. A point Leo Gross made years ago is still true. He averred that the ILC takes cautious steps rather than writing and rewriting law in bold, sweeping strokes (1971: 344–5). Moreover, Oscar Schachter has criticized the ILC because the eminent scholars serving as Commissioners have given way to diplomats and government officials, rendering this body more political in its character (1994: 4–5). Finally, not all of the projects of the ILC are a success story. Some projects are never finished and reported out while others, such as the conventions on state responsibility and succession, are not ratified by many states.

As in national legislatures, politics can never be completely separated from the law since each helps create the other. All aspects of law creation by UN bodies operate under the watchful eye of the states with their governments playing an important role at every stage of legal development. The ILC consults regularly with state representatives at the outset of discussion, during the process, and definitely over the final outcome.[6] Law-making for international society is much more complex and nuanced with the advent of the UN, but the process is still an *intergovernmental* matter ultimately resting on the will of sovereign states.

Other elements of the UN System also help develop law on occasion. A few examples can be offered. The UN Human Rights Commission assisted with the Universal Human Rights Declaration from which a variety of conventions have sprung. Since 1919, the International Labor Organization has promoted over 180 conventions to protect the rights of millions of laborers around the world. The UN Commission on International Trade Law has developed several conventions dealing with contract law on trade goods and their shipment by sea. A convention to discourage tobacco use has emanated from the World Health Organization. Over 140 international airlaw conventions have been sponsored by the International Civil Aviation Organization. The Legal Affairs office of the UN Secretariat has contributed ideas to legal developments, including the drafting of the convention covering the privileges and immunities of the UN.

One of the most interesting developments in "UN law-making" concerns the specific rules and regulations that technical bodies impose on countries with some regularity. The International Civil Aviation Organization, the World Health Organization, the International Telecommunications Union, the Universal Postal Union, and the Food and Agricultural Organization, among others, set numerous practical rules that states frequently accept as binding without their prior approval. This development relaxes considerably the strong tradition of states' sovereign independence entrenched in the positivist approach. For example, the World Health Organization and the Food and Agricultural Organization have developed hygiene codes for handling foods and treat these as firm rules. Without objection, many states simply adopt these codes into their national law (Schacter 1994: 5–6).

Another example of international quasi-legislation deserves attention. The EU offers a virtually unique legislative body known as the European Parliament (EP). Its parliamentarians do not sit in national delegations, but according to ideological and political-party alignments. The EP can recommend changes in laws and review the

EU budget, yet it does not regularly initiate and pass bills or raise revenue. Any legislative role on the part of the EP is squeezed in between the Council of Ministers (now called the Council of the EU) and the European Commission. The Council, made up of the top executive leadership of the member-states, including presidents and prime ministers, decides the basic rules and policy directions as well as which states can join the EU. It falls to the Commission to issue hundreds of specific regulations to implement general policy and to direct the EU civil service. Perhaps the finest moment of the EP came in 1999 when its investigation and criticism of European Commissioners over corruption charges forced them to resign.[7] The parliamentarians themselves came under attack in 2004 for their generous use of expense accounts and for hiring family members as staff. In regard to the EP's legislative prowess, while it looks and quacks like a duck, it does not quite walk like one.

One other international regional body aspires to be a regional legislature. After the African Union succeeded the OAU in 2002, one of its principal organs became the Pan-African Parliament (PAP). Holding its first session in 2004, the PAP is designed to act as an advisory and consultative body for its first five years. Drawing inspiration from the EU, the plan is to allow the PAP to mature into the legislative arm of the AU with delegations popularly elected instead of being selected by their national parliaments. The parliament's inaugural meeting promised to push Africa toward democracy and sound human rights practices as well as monitor African countries' progress in these areas. These goals are proving highly ambitions within the African context.[8]

Enforcing International Law

The enforcement of law can be troublesome in any legal system but, in the absence of a world government, is enforcement at all plausible at the international level? The very notion of enforcement implies that some measure of coercion may be necessary to make a legal system work properly. States vary considerably in their need and ability to use coercion in their municipal legal systems. Strong, successful states use force with their citizens only on some occasions because their populations are, as a rule, loyal to the government and habituated to obey the law. Weak or failing states, in contrast, frequently rely heavily on force since their governments often face restive or rebellious populations.

Because it is a horizontal legal system, the enforcement of international law is problematical whenever voluntary compliance fails. Muscular force cannot easily be dispatched to bring recalcitrant states and other actors into line with the law. Nonetheless, just as international society has managed to operate a quasi-legislative process, so too has international society contrived methods of rule-enforcement from its earliest history.

The story of international law enforcement begins with **self-help**, the only method that was available in the highly decentralized Westphalian state system. Self-help is a customary law practice that allows a state to enforce international law at its own volition, within certain limits. The kings of Europe could turn to tools of enforcement that states sometimes still rely on today. States have used **retorsion**, which is a legal act by one state to protest a wrongful act by another state. Retorsion does not involve armed force, but it is regarded as an unfriendly act. The best known instance is the withdrawal of an ambassador for a time as when the United States recalled its ambassador from Syria in 2005 because of that country's interference in Lebanese affairs. Much more serious is the severance of diplomatic relations altogether. In addition to other responses, the United States broke diplomatic relations with Iran in 1979 when its citizens seized the US Embassy in Tehran and then held the embassy staff as hostages for 444 days. US–Iranian diplomatic relations have yet to be repaired. Acts of retorsion are acts any state can commit at any time at its own discretion.

Another tool of self-help enforcement is **reprisal**, a punitive act that is normally illegal but considered justified under customary law because of another state's prior offense. The punishment chosen by the offended state can be nonviolent, such as the US seizure of Iranian gold in American banks in 1979. Opting for a military punishment, however, is likely to be seen as excessive and illegal. The UN Charter prohibits force except in self-defense, and the 1970 Declaration on Principles of International Law Concerning Friendly Relations and Cooperation among States affirms that states have a duty to refrain from military acts. President Ronald Reagan's 1986 bombing attack against Libya, in response to that state's suspected terrorist attacks on American military personnel in Germany, received widespread criticism not only for its military nature but also because the aerial attack on Libya exceeded the *proportionality rule* of reprisal. The punishment must be balanced and similar to the harm experienced.

Other acts states can use for muscle-flexing to enforce law are **demonstrations** and **interventions**. A demonstration is a display of military force to indicate a state is serious about its rights being respected. One country blockading the ports of another to encourage debt repayment and sailing ships along the coastline of another country to show concern over the treatment of its citizens and business interests are acts of enforcement that mostly belong to a by-gone era. Intervention still occurs with some frequency and can take several different forms. It is a vague political concept rather than a legal one. Essentially, intervention is the dictatorial interference by one state in the affairs of another, sometimes involving the illegal use of force on the territory of another state. Some instances of intervention are nothing more than "quick-in, quick-out" operations to rescue a country's citizens when the host government is unable to protect them. Host governments may even cooperate in these operations because they want the foreigners out of the way when they quash a rebellion or battle with a revolutionary army.

More controversial are interventions that mix state interests and ambitions with humanitarian rationales. In 1979, Tanzanian troops, provoked by a Ugandan border incursion, entered Uganda to remove the cruel despot Idi Amin. Few, if any, governments complained. In 1989, President George H. W. Bush ordered American paratroopers into Panama and arrested the unelected but *de facto* leader Manuel Noriega. The US government accused Noriega of facilitating drug smuggling to the United States and harassing American service personnel and their families. Panama's democratic government was then restored. Although popular in the United States, the "insertion" of troops in Panama was criticized by many countries, including US allies.

In addition to unilateral measures, multilateral interventions can also be controversial even if they are conducted under the auspices of an IGO. In 1999, NATO planes attacked Serbian targets with telling effect as a response to Serbia's "ethnic cleansing" policy directed at its Albanian minority living in Kosovo Province. This attack did not have the UN Security Council's approval and consequently violated the UN Charter; nevertheless, this attack gave relief to the Albanian minority and was widely accepted by world opinion. Michael Byers appropriately asks, is there to be a "humanitarian exception" to international law that protects the sovereignty of states? (Byers 2000: 1).

Traditionally, before the twentieth-century legal restraints of the League of Nations and then the UN, states were free to go to **war** as they saw fit to protect their rights or to advance their interests. War is a belligerent struggle involving armed groups operating across borders or within a state as civil war or revolution. A well-accepted definition of *war* requires such a conflict to involve 1,000 battle deaths or more and to last for several weeks or months.[9] Historically, war has been viewed as the *ultimo ratio*, or legitimate means of last resort, by the kings of Europe. The only limitations on war were the king's treasury and wisdom about the dangers of warring with another state.

Overall, forceful measures are usually viewed as the "rule of the strong" instead of the "rule of the law," unless sanctioned by the UN Security Council. While the occasional military action may find approval in some quarters, the use of force threatens the harmony of a nascent international society. Today, demonstrations, interventions, and state-initiated wars are questionable tools for enforcement since they will likely violate one set of rules as they try to impose another.

Creating the world bodies of the League and the UN was supposed to mean that states would have something more than self-help tools to provide security and enforce international law. The assumption was that these bodies could marshal sufficient enforcement power to handle transgressors, especially when states threaten or breach the peace. First the League's Council and then the UN's Security Council were assigned the task of coordinating enforcement. With enforcement powers thus centralized at the international level, states were expected to accept the rule that their individual use of force would be restricted to the immediate needs of self-defense.

For a variety of reasons, the UN's collective efforts have been uneven in outcome when dealing with the most serious breaches of international law. To the credit of the UN, it did stanch aggression in the Korean War (1950–3) and the Persian Gulf War (1990–1). Both successes, however, depended heavily on the United States taking a vested interest and deploying massive forces to back up the UN cause. And the UN has tried, again with mixed results, peacekeeping operations among numerous Third World countries as well as recently coordinating global anti-terrorist policies. Unable to count completely on the UN, however, states are still partly dependent on the self-help concept of the past. The UN Charter does allow states the right to act in self-defense until the UN can bring a crisis under control, but some states have given the concept of self-defense a mighty stretch to cover a wide range of military activities. Israel has even used a pre-emptive self-defense rationale to justify delivering the first blow to an opponent.

In addition to self-help measures and UN efforts at securing peace, some enforcement can be quite mundane. Many agencies of the UN system quietly go about their business of administering technical rules and regulations to help states and other actors cooperate with one another more effectively. When it comes to the management of food hygiene, airline routes, transportation of toxic wastes, postal regulations, and containment of contagious diseases, among many other problems, an individual state cannot handle such matters without assistance from other states. It is much more efficient to allow an IGO, with its trained experts, to set, monitor, and enforce specialized rules. This area of enforcement is analogous to "administrative law" as used by almost all states. Many legislative bodies around the world commonly empower specialized agencies to make and apply appropriate rules as changes arise. The US Congress, for example, allows the Environmental Protection Agency to determine the average fuel mileage for a fleet of cars and how to measure compliance.

From the complexity of UN agencies, a few examples will have to do. The International Monetary Fund (IMF), sometimes called the "debt police," has considerable enforcement powers for its currency exchange and banking rules. Without the IMF's stamp of approval, states find it harder to engage in trade on credit and borrow money. The International Civil Aviation Organization (ICAO) can set rules for its own enforcement in such matters as airline safety unless a majority of the member-states object to the proposed rules within three months. Lastly, the more developed regional organizations also have some form of "administrative law" activities. The European Commission of the EU, unsurprisingly, leads the way in making and enforcing regulations to carry out broad policy decisions made elsewhere. While the Security Council's role in securing the peace among states represents the "high politics" of international relations, specialized agencies of the UN and some regional organizations deal with the less controversial "low politics" of administering technical rules.

Despite the presence of some self-help tools and institutions with limited enforcement powers, widespread compliance with international law rests on a basis other than strong-armed means. Louis Henkin has observed that at the international level a "culture of compliance" exists which leads states to cooperate. Most states recognize that it is in their interest to obey the laws of international society, and the governments of these states value a reputation for compliance (1995: 48–9). In a careful study of the IMF, Beth A. Simmons concluded that states complied with the IMF more from a concern over their reputation with regional neighbors than because IMF sanctions were dangling over their heads. Simmons wrote that "Legal commitments can push a country onto a behavioral trajectory of compliance from which it is decreasingly likely to deviate" (Simmons 2000: 832). Compliance basically occurs because the international legal system is based on a tireless replication of reciprocal acts among states. If a state wants other states to obey international law, it must do so as well. A state that commonly flouts international law cannot expect the trust or cooperation of others. In theory, should enough states fail to meet their obligations regarding reciprocation, the entire international legal system could begin to unravel.

Realists are wrong to assert that international law cannot be real law since it is not *command law*, which requires that sanctions are sure and swift for non-compliance. They consign international law to an underdeveloped, primitive category, if they pay it any attention at all. Actually, few legal systems work as command law but instead depend on much voluntary cooperation. Hans Morgenthau, a prominent realist, but with a legal background, had to concede "that during four hundred years of its exist-ence international law has in most instances been scrupulously observed" (1978: 281). John H.E. Fried even takes note of a special advantage international law enjoys over municipal systems. While governments and constitutions of states can be overthrown, international law, in contrast, cannot be usurped by a few scofflaws (Fried 1998: 25–51). The turmoil wrought by dictators and revolutions may come and go in numer-ous states, but international law has always survived, waiting patiently for the Soviet Unions, Libyas, and North Koreas of the world, as revolutionary states, to come around and accept the well-entrenched ways of international law and international society.

Adjudicating International Law

In addition to methods of legislating and enforcing international law, international society has found ways to resolve issues by adjudicating them, that is, by using judi-cial means. In a general sense, **adjudication** refers to all forms of legally binding third-party settlements, including **arbitration**. More formally, adjudication involves a permanent court while arbitration is set up on an *ad hoc* basis for a one-time use. In arbitration, disputing parties can often choose the arbitrators and the law and procedure that will apply to the case at hand. While arbitration dates back to ancient Greece, adjudication, based on an established court at the international level, is a twentieth-century phenomenon that continues today with the acceptance of inter-national courts growing with each passing decade.

Adjudication

Taking the bold step toward adjudication carries sovereign states well past the polit-ical process of diplomatic negotiation or the use of force. Turning to courts and arbitration tribunals reflects great hopes about what is achievable in a world still troubled by violence and war. As E. H. Carr observed decades ago, judicial procedures rise dramatically above the political context because they exclude a role for power and instead rely on facts and law to determine an outcome (1966: 205). Writing in 1939, Carr, however, found the notion of an international court to be a little idealis-tic for the political order of his day (pp. 193–207). He published his *The Twenty Years' Crisis* on the brink of the Second World War.

The judicial advancements that began in the nineteenth century and continue to the present have been impressive. The NGO Project on International Courts and Tribunals (PICT) counts more than 20 international courts and tribunals set up as permanent bodies and at least 70 other international institutions exercising judicial or quasi-judicial functions on an *ad hoc* basis.[10] Besides the ICJ, there are regional courts, mostly dealing with economic and human rights issues, specialized criminal courts and tribunals, and a large number of arbitration panels for handling border and trade issues. Does this plethora of judicial arrangements constitute an international judicial system? There is no system in the sense that a recognized hierarchy ties these varied judicial institutions together with a single court, at the apex of the hierarchy, able to unite all lower courts around one understanding of firm law. National court systems are designed to work in this manner, but not the highly disaggregated international level.

Arbitration

The use of arbitration in modern international law dates from the 1795 Jay Treaty between Great Britain and the United States that called for disputes over property and territory to be resolved by arbitration. The success of this arbitration process encouraged states to turn increasingly to arbitration throughout the nineteenth century. The most famous instance of nineteenth-century arbitration concerns the *Alabama Claims* of 1872 between Great Britain and the United States. The cruiser *Alabama* was built and armed by the British for the use of the Confederate Navy during the American Civil War. This cruiser assaulted US shipping with great loss of ships and cargo, and led the United States government to charge Britain with violating the laws of neutrality. A board of arbiters assembled at Geneva, Switzerland and rendered a binding verdict, or "award," as a decision of arbitration is usually called. The award required Britain to pay the United States $15.5 million, a sum commensurate with the damages inflicted by the *Alabama*.[11]

Although originally designed for *ad hoc* use, arbitration achieved a measure of permanency at the turn of the twentieth century. The 1899 and 1907 Hague Conventions provided for the Permanent Court of Arbitration (PCA). The features that were to be permanent were the staff and rules of arbitration plus lists of publicists that could be selected as arbiters as cases arose. An established bench of judges operating in regular sessions month after month and year after year was not intended. The PCA became the first global mechanism for the judicial settlement of international disputes. Only a trickle of arbitration cases came before the PCA, especially after the League of Nations created a permanent court in 1921 which stole the thunder of the PCA. The PCA began to experience a revival in the 1990s, however. It found a niche for itself hearing half a dozen cases a year on specialized issues regarding trade, boundary, and environmental issues. Today, 101 countries, as parties to the PCA, in addition to other actors, can ask for an *ad hoc* arbitration panel. In sum, the PCA is not a permanent court in the sense of regular sessions, but its machinery for arbitration is always available when requested.[12]

Another arbitration process that relies on an ongoing mechanism is the Court of Arbitration for Sport (CAS) that has been operational since 1986 as a body of the International Olympic Committee. The CAS can draw on 60 lawyers with expertise in the sports field to form arbitration panels. These sports arbiters can make binding and final awards. The CAS normally meets *in camera* in Lausanne, Switzerland (Ettinger 1992: 97–121). In a celebrated case that made headlines following the Summer Olympics of 2004 in Greece, the CAS ruled that American gymnast Paul Hamm could keep his gold medal in the face of a challenge by South Korean gymnast Yang Tae-young, who unfairly had been docked a tenth of a point. Protest by the South Korean had not been entered within the allotted time for appeals, so the panel ruled.

Numerous tribunals have been set up to arbitrate for a limited time over a specific set of issues. Only a few examples can be given. The Marshall Islands Nuclear Claims Tribunal was established to make awards over a 15-year period beginning in 1988, drawing on a $150 million fund to cover medical costs resulting in harms done by 67 nuclear tests in these islands from 1946 to 1958.[13] There is the Iran–US Claims Tribunal, established in 1981, which allowed for arbitrated claims brought by either of the two governments as well as corporations and citizens of both countries after the breach in diplomatic relations following the Iranian seizure of the American embassy in 1979 (Lillich & Magraw 1998). After Eritrea seceded from Ethiopia in 1993, years of border hostilities followed and led to arbitration through the Eritrea-Ethiopian Claims and Boundary Commissions, beginning in the year 2000. The International Bureau of the PCA at The Hague lends its help to these two countries to facilitate their arbitration.[14]

Probably the most frequent use of international arbitration is found in commercial activities employing both IGO and private mechanisms. Instead of hundreds of small disputes languishing unsettled in the corridors of state diplomacy, arbitration brings matters to a close, helping trade and investment to flourish. A near universal

---

Box 4.1 Administrative Tribunals

It is not unusual for some prominent IGOs to have administrative tribunals to arbitrate personnel grievances. The UN Administrative Tribunal (UNAT), formed in 1949, hears cases involving contract disputes between employees and the UN Secretariat. The seven members of the tribunal can also hear cases from much of the UN System, including the independent agencies with their own funding, for instance, UNICEF, the UN Development Program, and the staffs of the Registries of the International Criminal Court and the International Tribunal for the Law of the Sea.

Another prominent example is the Administrative Tribunal for the International Labor Organization (ATILO), which also has seven members. This tribunal can hear complaints from employees of the International Labor Office and many other IGOs that recognize this tribunal's jurisdiction, for example, employees of WHO, WTO, WIPO, the European Free Trade Association, and INTERPOL.

Sources: See the home websites of these tribunals at http://www.ilo.org/public/ English/tribunal.

practice now exists for states to include arbitration provisions in their commercial agreements. The World Bank's International Center for the Settlement of Investment Disputes (ICSID), in operation since 1966, has arbitrated numerous cases, usually concerning MNCs involved in contract disputes with a host country or because corporations resist expropriation by the government of that country. There are hundreds of bilateral investment treaties (BITs) calling for reliance on the International Center should disputes arise. Without the assurance that this arbitration provides, billions of dollars of corporate capital investment would not flow from one country to another, causing a giant loss of jobs and needed technology for poorer states.[15] The ICSID is part of the UN System and so is the Commission on International Trade Law (UNCITRAL), also formed in 1966. The Commission provides widely used comprehensive procedural rules concerning arbitration.[16]

Also found within the UN System is the World Intellectual Property Organization (WIPO) organized in Geneva, Switzerland, in 1974. The WIPO is the inheritor of protective efforts begun in the late nineteenth century concerning respect for copyrights, patents, and trademarks. Intellectual theft of pharmaceutical formulas, machinery innovations, and entire books would be far more common without the WIPO. The WIPO maintains an Arbitration and Mediation Center that has been especially useful in the age of the Internet, with many disputes arising over domain names. The WIPO can draw on a thousand arbiters and mediators from 70 countries called the "WIPO List of Neutrals" to help resolve issues.[17]

The best known overseer of commercial activities and the only global organization focused on exchange in trade goods is the World Trade Organization (WTO). Formed in Geneva, Switzerland in 1995 as the successor to the General Agreement on Tariffs and Trade (GATT) and presently with 153 member-states, it too is associated with the UN system. Not unlike American regulatory commissions, the WTO tends to merge executive and judicial functions. The WTO can determine that an unfair trade practice has occurred against a state and allow the injured party to use commensurate trade sanctions against the offending state, usually in the form of higher tariffs for specified imports.[18]

Private NGOs also regularly assist with binding arbitration in business matters. Best known is the International Chamber of Commerce's International Court of Arbitration, formed in 1923, which hears as many as 500 cases a year.[19] Then there is the London Court of International Arbitration, organized in 1892, and the Stockholm Chamber of Commerce's Arbitration Institute that got its start in 1977. Arbitration awards can be enforced through the 1958 *UN Convention on the Recognition and Enforcement of Foreign Arbitral Awards* (also called the New York Convention). As of 2009, 144 signatory states to this convention had promised to do what they could to help enforce awards.[20]

World courts

With arbitration regarded as a major nineteenth-century success, the next logical step after the PCA would be a permanent world court. When the harsh realities of the First World War spurred national leaders into action to found a deliberative world body, the writers of the League of Nations' Covenant, in Article 14, called upon the League's Council to formulate plans for the Permanent Court of International Justice (PCIJ). This court would hear contentious cases between states and offer advisory opinions on legal questions put to it by the League Council and Assembly. The PCIJ handed down decisions in 29 contentious cases and produced 27 advisory opinions. The PCIJ, like the PCA, used the Peace Palace at The Hague, Netherlands as its seat. Formally, the PCIJ operated from 1922 until 1946, but the actual work of the PCIJ shut-down in 1940 with the German invasion of the Netherlands. Although the PCIJ had no enforcement machinery, compliance with its decisions was generally good (Meyer 2002: 88). The PCIJ probably had an easier time as a world court than its successor, the International Court of Justice (ICJ). While the PCIJ worked within a Eurocentric legal culture, the ICJ began its life soon to encounter a mixed world of Western democracies, communist states, and the Third World (Abi-Saab 1996: 3–5).

The new court, the ICJ, was essentially a change in name only. The PCI's judges met briefly in 1946 to resign and turn over the archives, case records, and library of

---

Box 4.2 Tribunal for the Law of the Sea

Another important court that is a world court of sorts is the International Tribunal for the Law of the Sea created in 1996 and located in the Baltic sea-port of Hamburg, Germany. The Tribunal has its own special bureaucracy known as the Registry. The ITLOS judicially oversees the application of the UN Convention on the Law of the Sea promulgated in 1982 and entered into force in 1994, once there were enough signatories. Most countries of the world have both direct and indirect interests in the seas and oceans of the world. The UNLOS stands as the longest and largest diplomatic undertaking as far as UN-sponsored conventions are concerned.

The ITLOS has 21 independent members to adjudicate the LOS convention, a body which usually breaks up into Chambers on "summary procedures," "fisheries disputes," "marine environment disputes," and a special chamber on "swordfish stocks" created in 2000. The tribunal can hear cases involving states, private companies, and the *International Seabed Authority* that administers the sharing of the seabed's resources under the principle of the "common heritage of humankind." The ITLOS exercises compulsory jurisdiction and can offer advisory opinions. As of 2004, this tribunal has heard 12 cases, issued 6 judgments and issued 26 orders. Seventeen states have been before the Tribunal. A typical case has involved one state's flagged fishing vessel violating the fishing jurisdiction of another state.

Source: See, http://www.itlos.org/ and http://www.pict-pcti.org/courts/ITLOS.html.

the Peace Palace to the incoming judges of the ICJ. The ICJ was based on the same statute, or treaty, with only a few changes, and continuity was further enhanced with the election of several PCIJ judges to the new court. While the PCIJ had a more consensual legal environment, with most judges drawn from Europe, the ICJ at least had the advantage of following in the wake of a proven court (Meyer 2002: 91–8). Because of the similarity and continuity between the two courts, together they are sometimes referred to as the "world court" or "world court system."

The importance ascribed to the ICJ is suggested by the fact that it is one of the original six organs of the UN System and not a later creation, as was the PCIJ for the League. The ICJ is the principal judicial body of the UN and is intended to be the premier court in the service of international law and the world. The ICJ is composed of 15 judges elected to 9-year terms by both the Security Council and the General Assembly. The judges serve in their personal capacities and not as state representatives, but their selection is designed to reflect the variety of legal cultures in the world. No two judges can be from the same country. All 192 member-states of the UN are automatically members of the ICJ's *Statute of the International Court of Justice,* or treaty-of-creation, although states can ultimately control whether the court's jurisdiction applies to them. States accept the court's jurisdiction by: (1) accepting the "optional clause" of Article 36 of the Statute committing states to compulsory jurisdiction, with which 64 states presently comply; (2) making a prior arrangement on a bilateral basis to take a specific issue before the court; or (3) placing a provision within a treaty resolving that questions of interpretation of that treaty will be referred to the ICJ. Only states can bring cases before the ICJ, and the few states that are not members of the UN can still ratify the ICJ's Statute.

The ICJ got off to a slow start with only a case or two each year until the 1990s, when use of the court increased noticeably. Since 1946, the ICJ has handed down about 100 judgments on such issues as boundary disputes, the use of force, the right of asylum, nationality, the right of passage at sea, and diplomatic relations. As for advisory opinions, approximately thirty have been handed down on subjects including the status of Southwest Africa (Namibia), assessments of dues for UN operations, the terms of the UN Headquarters Agreement, the legality of nuclear weapons, and reparations for injuries suffered while in UN service, among other questions.[21] These judgments and advisory opinions, as well as numerous pending cases, suggest that the world is finding this court useful.

However, some of the most critical issues of international society will not find their way into the ICJ. Possessing sovereignty allows states to choose whether or not they will accept a court's jurisdiction. Many states live with security threats and other concerns that impinge on important interests. As a result, states are often reluctant to trust these interests to binding judicial settlement. Of the five veto-wielding states on the UN Security Council, only the United Kingdom (Great Britain plus Northern Ireland, and the country name used before international bodies) embraces a version of compulsory jurisdiction before the ICJ. The issues with the best chance of judicial resolution are those in which both parties can stand to lose the case, hence the reason the large majority of ICJ cases turn on such matters as demarcating continental shelf boundaries or dividing fisheries.

While respect for the ICJ is on the rise, the court has had to overcome several negative experiences. The ICJ possesses neither purse nor sword, but Article 94 of the UN Charter asserts that states have a duty to comply with court decisions and allows the Security Council to enforce court decisions. This article, however, has never been implemented. In its first decision, the court found Albania responsible for leaving mines in the Corfu Channel, adjacent to its coast, which damaged British destroyers in 1946. The court ordered Albania to pay Great Britain one million pounds in damages, but the payment was slow in coming. In several instances, states have failed to respond when they were obliged to do so or deserted the proceedings when legal developments began to turn against them.

Box 4.3 The Southwest Africa Cases

Southwest Africa, a former German colony, became a Mandate territory under the auspices of the League of Nations following the First World War and was placed under the stewardship of South Africa, a country controlled by white elites operating a strictly segregated society. When the League was replaced by the UN in 1945, South Africa argued that it did not have to place Southwest Africa in the new UN Trusteeship program. In 1949, the UN General Assembly requested an advisory opinion from the ICJ. The court ruled in 1950 that South Africa's Mandate obligations were still in force and that South Africa could not unilaterally alter Southwest African status, but that South Africa did not have to move Southwest Africa into the Trusteeship system.

South Africa ignored the court's opinion, and in 1960 Ethiopia and Liberia, as former members of the League, began proceedings against South Africa, mainly charging that South Africa was practicing *Apartheid* (a strict form of race segregation) in South-West Africa and preventing this territory from making progress toward self-government. In an 8–7 preliminary decision of 1962, the court ruled the Mandate obligations continued and that Ethiopia and Liberia could rightfully bring a case against South Africa.

A final judgment, in another close vote, by the ICJ came in 1966 focused on the standing of Ethiopia and Liberia. The court ruled that only League organs could bring a case and, with the League now defunct, no basis for enforcement against South Africa existed. The upshot was utter dismay by all the Third World countries, which were intensely committed to ending all vestiges of racism and colonialism in the world. Disillusionment with the ICJ was the paramount view for many years on the part of many countries. After years of a bloody insurgency, Southwest Africa became the country of Namibia in 1990 and joined the UN in the same year.

Source: See, www.icj-cij.org/ > cases > see under 1949 "Advisory Opinion of 11 July 1950," and under contentious cases, see "Preliminary Objections 1961" and "Merits 1963."

The British government held onto Albanian gold in its banks until well after the Cold War ended when, in 1996, Albania paid $2,000,000 in reparations and Britain returned the gold. Iran refused to enter proceedings when the United States brought a case over Iran's failure to protect the US embassy in Tehran in 1979. In a different matter, the United States ended its acceptance of the court's compulsory jurisdiction in 1985 over the Nicaragua case. The United States became disenchanted with the world court after it took up the issue of US force against Nicaragua. The court ruled against the United States for supplying an insurgency fighting the Nicaraguan government. Probably most damaging to the ICJ was the series of cases dealing with South African rule over southwest Africa, cases that began in 1949 and lasted into the 1960s. Third World countries were especially disappointed that the court did not condemn South Africa's racist, colonial-style rule in forthright terms.

Regional courts

Perhaps inspired by impressive integration efforts in Europe, a proliferation of regional courts has taken place in recent decades. The most important court developments have been in the fields of economic relations and human rights. The main instances of such courts are located in Europe, Latin America, and Africa. Some examples will help clarify the role of regional courts.

The most remarkable regional court is unquestionably the *European Court of Justice* (ECJ), located in Luxembourg, which serves as the constitutional court for the 27 states of the EU. The ECJ, founded in 1952, has steadfastly dismantled national barriers to regional economic integration and has established EU law as supreme over national laws. In addition to states, individuals, MNCs, and IGOs can be parties to court proceedings. Its numerous decisions can affect everything from the manufacture of German beer to French hunting laws. Considering the ECJ's impact on the EU's legal and political setting, it is no exaggeration to say it is the most powerful international court in the world.[22]

Another regional economic court is the *Court of Justice of the Andean Community*, or more commonly, the Andean Court of Justice (ACJ). The 1969 *Andean Pact* set in motion a process to develop an economic union for Bolivia, Colombia, Ecuador, Peru, and Venezuela, which was modeled to some extent on European success with economic integration. The ACJ was proposed in 1979 and established its bench in 1983 at Quito, Ecuador. The ACJ has had limited use, however, and will become more important only if a deeper pattern of economic integration among the Andean states calls for a bigger judicial role.[23]

The *Court of Justice of the Common Market for Eastern and Southern Africa* (COMESA) was established in 1994 and since 2003 sits at Khartoum, Sudan. It too takes its lead from the European model and on paper is a powerful court calling for its rulings to take precedence over national courts. This Court of Justice for COMESA has heard only a handful of cases and awaits further economic developments in its region to become a significant court.[24]

The emergence of human rights courts is a spectacular development when it is remembered how guarded states have been historically over their sovereignty, especially when sovereignty let leaders treat their citizens virtually as they saw fit. At least in theory, the existence of such a court suggests that individuals and groups can appeal to a court at the international level for protection from their own national governments. As with economic courts, it is in Europe where the most pronounced example of a human rights court can be found.

The *European Court of Human Rights* (ECHR) operates within the organizational setting of the Council of Europe (COE), which contains 47 member-states. These countries span the vast Eurasian continent, reaching from the Atlantic Ocean eastward to the Pacific Ocean, once Russia had joined the COE in 1998. The ECHR maintains its bench in Strasbourg, France, and began its work there in 1959, implementing the 1950 *European Convention for the Protection of Human Rights and Fundamental Freedoms* as the rule of law for Europe. With a large number of member-states and because of the work of human rights NGOs, the ECHR is a very busy judicial body. The cases coming before this court are as varied as family relationships, caning as corporal punishment, property rights, and the rights of homosexuals to enter military service. This court's jurisdiction is regarded as compulsory, and its decisions are almost always accepted by the responding states. Dozens of times, states of the COE have changed their national laws to comply with ECHR rulings.[25]

The Latin American human rights arrangements are promising but not as developed as those in Europe. This region began with the 1948 *American Declaration of the Rights and Duties of Man*, which was upgraded to the 1969 *American Convention on Human Rights*. In 1979, the Organization of American States (OAS) created the *Inter-American Court of Human Rights* (IACHR) to oversee human rights protection based on the 1969 convention that went into force in 1978. The seven judges of the court constitute a part-time court that has its bench in San José, Costa Rica. An Inter-American Commission as well as states can bring cases before the IACHR, but the governments of member-states must agree before their citizens can appeal to this court. The court has had several contentious cases and offered a number of advisory opinions.[26] Regrettably, the cultural climate has not been as friendly to human rights in Latin America as in Europe. The years of military rule and political repression in many countries of this region during the 1970s and 1980s were especially detrimental to human rights development.

The *African Court on Human and Peoples' Rights* (ACHPR) is the third regional human rights court in existence. This court was proposed in a 1998 protocol to the 1981 *African Charter on Human and Peoples' Rights*. Enough ratifications occurred by 2004 for the ACHPR to get its start. Judges must now be selected and a place for the seat of this court established. Thus far, Burkina Faso alone has presented a declaration allowing a citizen to appeal a case to the ACHPR. Africa's generally poor human rights record will provide ample opportunity for an active human rights court, if it is allowed to function in a meaningful way. One asset in the ACHPR's favor is that it can adjudicate not only the African Charter but any human rights treaty a responding state has ratified.[27]

Box 4.4 The Lori Berenson Case

American citizen Lori Berenson was originally convicted of high treason in Peru in 1996 by a secretive military tribunal and sentenced to life without parole. Then, under strong US diplomatic pressure, Peru tried her a second time in 2000–1 in a civilian criminal court. The second trial found her guilty of collaborating with terrorists and reduced her sentence to 20 years. Berenson's managed to appeal her case to the Inter-American Court of Human Rights. In 2004, the Inter-American Court upheld the 20-year sentence but did at least order Peru to cancel Berenson's $30,300 fine and to provide Berenson with medical and psychological treatment as well more humane prison conditions.

Her defense, led by former US Attorney-General Ramsey Clark, argued that she was tried under draconian anti-terrorist laws and by hostile judges who accepted coerced testimony and tainted evidence. Her defense was supported by the Inter-American Human Rights Commission which voted sympathetically 7–0 in 2002 to condemn the legal system used to convict Berenson.

The Peruvian government rejoiced over the Inter-American Court of Human Rights' decision to uphold the 20-year sentence. They were convinced that Berenson was at least a collaborator with the terrorist group, Tupac Amaru Revolutionary Movement, helping them prepare for an attempt at seizing the Peruvian Congress.

Source: For a website friendly to Lori Berenson but also providing additional information, see http://www.freelori.org/whoislori.html.

Criminal courts

Interest in an international criminal court has risen and fallen over time as the following brief narrative indicates. At the time of the 1864 Geneva Conventions, an unrealized proposal was made that a criminal court be established to adjudicate the laws of war. At least after the Second World War, *ad hoc* tribunals were established in 1945 in Nuremberg and Tokyo to try German and Japanese civilian and military leaders for crimes committed during the war. Although these tribunals were somewhat tainted as exercises in "victors' justice," they stamped history indelibly with the notion that individuals cannot hide behind the "badge of state" but instead held accountable for their crimes. A typical response by those accused at these tribunals was, "I was only obeying orders."

While the victorious states of France, Great Britain, the Soviet Union, and the United States showed little interest in turning the Nuremberg experience into a permanent court, the shock over the horror of "ethnic cleansing" practices decades later in the former Yugoslavia and Rwanda led the UN Security Council to create an *ad hoc* war crimes tribunal for each area, the *International Criminal Tribunal for the Former Yugoslavia* (ICTY) (1993) and the *International Criminal Tribunal for Rwanda* (ICTR) (1994).

The tribunals for Yugoslavia and Rwanda are temporary in time and place, but their creation acknowledges a growing concern in the world that heinous crimes must not go unpunished. The fact that countries will not, or cannot, punish their own criminals is the driving impetus behind the formation of international judicial bodies. The two tribunals, created by the UN Security Council in the wake of horrific ethnic conflicts, have struggled with overcoming limited budgets, a mix of languages, differing legal cultures, and long drawn-out trials that in some cases have lasted for years. The success of these tribunals, however, far outweighs their practical difficulties as they attend to justice. In addition to encouraging international society to create a permanent international criminal court in 1998, the tribunals have had two other notable effects: one is that top leaders can be held accountable and the other is that systematic rape is now recognized as a war crime.

The ICTFY, from its seat at The Hague, has managed to try and sentence more than forty individuals. Many others await trial while about twenty wanted persons are still at large. Security Council resolution 1503 calls for all the tribunal's work to be completed by 2010, but this date may be optimistic. Trials are lengthy and some cases have to be reexamined by the Appeals Chamber that also serves the Rwanda tribunal. The trial of Slobodan Milosevic proved particularly vexing. Stemming from the bloody ethnic conflict among Bosnians, Croatians, and Serbs of the former Yugoslavia, Milosevic was charged with several counts of war and humanitarian crimes. Initially indicted in 1999 for crimes in Kosovo Province and later for crimes against Bosnians and Croatians dating back to 1991, Milosevic was surrendered to the ICTFY in 2001 after having recently resigned the Yugoslavian (Serbian) presidency. Milosevic regularly took advantage of his right to serve as his own attorney to launch into numerous, hours-long diatribes against the legitimacy of the tribunal, NATO, and the UN, helping to prolong his trial for several years. He died in 2006 during the trial. Much attention will now be on two major leaders of the Bosnian Serbs accused of atrocities from the early 1990s. Radovan Karadzic, a civilian leader, was captured in 2008 and is now in jail at The Hague. Ratko Mladic, a military leader, is still at large and possibly protected in a Serbian stronghold surrounded by well-armed militia.[28]

The ICTR got off to a very slow start but began trying and convicting people by the middle of the last decade of the twentieth century. This tribunal had to deal with the aftermath of Hutu depredations against the Tutsi people when the former came to power. Hundreds of thousands were raped and killed. This tribunal, located in Arusha, Tanzania, broke new ground by operating the first UN detention center and a witness protection program for some of those testifying before the tribunal. The most notable successes have been the conviction of Jean Kambanda, the former Prime Minister of Rwanda, for genocide and a radio journalist for fomenting genocide over the airwaves. This tribunal, in 1998, was also the first judicial body to define rape as a war crime and held that widespread rape can contribute to genocide. Thousands more Hutu languish in Rwandan jails where they await trials in national courts. In a rather paradoxical development, the lesser perpetrators of terrible crimes can face capital punishment in Rwanda's national court, while the major criminals tried by the ICTR cannot. Neither of the two tribunals can give the death penalty. Finally, the ICTR experience reflects widespread cooperation by African states, as well as states outside Africa. Various countries offered prison facilities for those convicted and helped track down both the accused and witnesses and then returned them to the tribunal in Arusha.[29]

These two tribunals have inspired the creation of *hybrid criminal courts*, or mixed courts. The Special Court for Sierra Leone, for instance, is based on a treaty between the UN and Sierra Leone. This tribunal uses a mixture of international and national law and has judges provided by both the UN and Sierra Leone. One of the most important acts by the Sierra Leone tribunal has been to seal an indictment in 2003 against Charles Taylor, once the leadear of Liberia, for humanitarian crimes and to issue an international arrest warrant in June 2004. Unfortunately, he escaped into exile in Nigeria for a time but was captured in 2006. He is undergoing trial before the Special Court of Sierra Leone, but at The Hague for security reasons. The grave, unspeakable crimes against innocent civilians that have characterized the diamond wars of West Africa have also occurred in some form in other places in the world, leading to calls for more hybrid courts. Cambodia, after years of waiting since the Khmer Rouge horrors, is ready to put a mixed court to good use (Drumbl 2002: 252–8). Hybrid courts are being considered for East Timor and Kosovo as well.

With interest in punishing war crimes at a peak, the experience with the Rwandan and Yugoslav tribunals led to a strong interest in a permanent International Criminal Court (ICC). As these tribunals were getting underway, the ILC developed a draft for a permanent world criminal court and reported on it to the UN General Assembly in 1994. The draft for this court traveled through two General Assembly committees before finally arriving at Rome in 1998 to be crafted into a convention by an international conference.

At Rome, 120 states participated in producing the 1998 *Statute of the International Criminal Court*, with 60 state ratifications required for the court to become a reality. The Statute of the ICC entered into force on July 1, 2002, and, in early 2003, 18 judges were installed in the temporary quarters of the ICC at The Hague, Netherlands. The court will have its own permanent quarters at The Hague in a few years. This judicial body is funded by assessed dues of the states participating and by voluntary contributors. The jurisdiction of the court covers crimes committed only after its creation in 2002. The crimes the ICC will try are acts of genocide (the deliberate killing of a particular ethnic group's members intending to eliminate that group), humanitarian crimes (including widespread murder, enslavement, forced transfers of population, and torture), and war crimes covered by the Geneva Conventions. Countries have the option of trying citizens accused of these crimes themselves instead of turning them over to the court. As in the case of the tribunals, the ICC cannot use to death penalty.

Aggression, which Nigel White has called the core crime of the international system, is referred to as a crime that might be prosecutable in the future (2002: 200). Extensive efforts to define aggression legally have not been entirely successful. The Assembly of States party to the Statute will revisit aggression for review and could add it to the list of crimes, with two-thirds approval. The Assembly of States could also consider terrorism and drug smuggling as international crimes at some future time.

The creation of the ICC was impeded somewhat by US resistance. President Bill Clinton signed the Statute of the ICC in December 2000, although he expressed some doubts about it. Then, President George W. Bush became obstructionist in attitude and made strong demands when he learned the United States could not override ICC decisions with its veto power in the UN Security Council. Shortly afterward, for two years in a row, 2002–4, the United States won guarantees from the Security Council that US peacekeepers in any UN mission would be exempt from prosecution. After the Abu Ghraib prison scandal in Iraq shocked the world in 2004, embarrassing the United States over its harsh treatment of prisoners, the Bush administration recognized the folly of any further requests for exemptions. Instead, President Bush's administration instigated at least 90 bilateral agreements with other states that they would not surrender American citizens to the ICC.[30] The ICC has handed down several indictments, including one in 2009 against Omar al-Bashir, the President of the Sudan, for war crimes in the Darfur region.

The Incorporation of International Law

Incorporation is the process of applying the rules of international law within national jurisdictions, or municipal systems. Despite impressive growth in the three traditional governmental functions at the international level, the efficacy of international law still depends heavily on the governments of states enforcing this law within their domestic contexts. True, some strictly international jurisdictions exist, as in the areas of the international seas, the seabed, international airspace, and outer space, but a large portion of international law is aimed at municipal systems. The rise of globalization, with its tightening interdependence, has only intensified the incorporation process as thousands of treaties and agreements perforate the once nearly solid walls of national sovereignty. The harmonization of banking and currency rules, the application of most environmental treaties, the use of the same traffic signs by adjoining states, the protection of foreign embassies and aliens, the respect for headquarter agreements for IGOs, the standardization of passports, and tracking terrorists and criminals are all examples of international agreements calling for enforcement inside national jurisdictions. The most radical qualification of sovereignty through incorporation involves human rights treaties because states are obliged to treat their citizens according to international standards. The plight of millions of people, however, demonstrates that half or more countries of the world are not enforcing human rights standards properly.

Two broadly different views of incorporation have long co-existed. **Dualism** holds that international law and municipal law are two separate legal domains which operate independently of one another. **Monism**, in contrast, asserts that international and national law systems share the same legal order, whether in a hierarchical or a compatible arrangement.[31] In practice, no state adheres in pure fashion to one or the other; in fact, publicists and foreign ministries do not any longer argue much about preferring one view over the other. All states must regularly make internal adjustments to accommodate their international legal commitments. Some treaties are explicit on this point. As an example, the Genocide Convention requires signatories to have in place national law prohibiting genocidal acts on their territory (Henkin 1995: 65–7). If a state does forthrightly embrace dualism, it still faces the revered principle of *pacta sunt servanda* reinforced by Article 26 of the 1969 *Vienna Convention on the Law of Treaties*. Then there is Article 27 of the same convention that disallows states from using domestic law as an excuse for failing to carry out treaty obligations.

The United States is oriented toward the dualist view more so than most states. Only a few cases can be cited here from the rich constitutional law history of the United States. The US government has always recognized that its constitution is the supreme law of the land. The constitution is placed hierarchically above treaties as well as national law. The superiority of the constitution also applies to *executive agreements* (presidential agreements with foreign countries), which are regarded as equivalent to treaties. In the 1957 *Reed v. Covert* case, the Supreme Court struck down an executive agreement with another country that authorized military trials without full protection of constitutional rights; thus the executive agreement was in conflict with the constitution. Generally speaking, the executive tries to avoid embracing international obligations that conflict with the Constitution, but sometimes the US courts find that the executive branch has not succeeded.

Treaties are at least equal to national law, with the "time-rule" normally followed. If in conflict, the one coming last prevails. In practice, the time-rule does not come up often as an issue. One important case in which the time-rule was side-stepped illustrates how hard the US courts work to avoid conflicts between treaties and national laws.

Congress's 1987 *Anti-Terrorist Act*, calling for the closing of PLO offices in the United States, came long after the 1947 *UN Headquarters Agreement* and should have prevailed under the time-rule. This 1987 act conflicted with the US Headquarters Agreement providing immunity for the UN as an IGO on US soil. Under this agreement, the UN is clearly empowered to receive the PLO Observer Mission and has done so since 1974. A federal district judge ruled in 1988, on a technicality, that the Anti-Terrorist Act could not be enforced since it did not specify the New York PLO offices. The judge opined that Congress probably had no desire to violate the UN Headquarters Agreement, and that the PLO's acceptability was better handled by the executive branch (Higgins 2002: 160–1).

Another issue is whether treaties are **self-executing**, a question reoccurring in the United States since the early nineteenth century. A self-executing treaty does not require enabling legislation for it to be implemented. The language of a treaty should indicate if it is self-executing or not, but this point is not always clear. In the 1952 *Fujii v. State of California* case, the plaintiff invoked UN Charter Articles 55 and 56 dealing with human rights protection, but the Supreme Court of California ruled these articles are not automatically self-executing and require expression through national legislation.

Federal systems can pose special problems as well. The 10th amendment of the Bill of Rights of the US Constitution reserves considerable policy control for the states of the federal system. Yet, treaties, as with national laws, prevail over state laws. Conflict arising between US treaty obligations and the exercise of authority by a federal state is not difficult to imagine. In the 1920 *Missouri v. Holland* case, the US

Supreme Court ruled a migratory bird treaty with Canada (acting in its dominion status under Great Britain) allowed US national policy to govern the conservation of migratory birds. Otherwise, the conservation of wildlife would be reserved to the states. Also, in the 1924 *Asakura v. Seattle* case, a treaty with Japan calling for the protection of its citizens on US territory was used to override discriminatory law and practice against Japanese persons in Seattle, Washington.[32]

Great Britain's practice on incorporation leads the way for other common law states, such as Australia, Canada, and New Zealand, which Britain strongly influenced during its colonial history. Under the "English Rule," as Linda Malone calls it, international law is part of English Common Law but cannot be implemented without enabling legislation from Parliament (Malone 1998: 42). Parliament is supreme, so treaties cannot apply until they are expressed in parliamentary law. The United States, as a common law country, is an exception since it does accept some treaties as directly self-executing. If parliamentary legislation is inconsistent with international law then Britain and other Common Law countries violate international law until these countries pass a new act. In a well-known case from British history, the 1906 *Mortensen v. Peters* case, the British Parliament passed an act disallowing the harvesting of sea otters in the Moray Firth of Scotland, even though this law might affect foreigners outside Britain's three-mile territorial limit used at the time. In the effort to protect the sea otters, a Danish boat captain was arrested and fined (Brierly 1963: 86–93). More in keeping with Britain's good record of compliance with international law are the 1969 parliamentary act implementing the 1948 *Genocide Convention*, a 1988 act to put the 1984 *Convention Against Torture* into force, and its 2000 incorporation of the 1950 *European Convention on Human Rights* providing Britain, in effect, with a modern-day bill of rights. Some years may pass between a British prime minister signing a treaty and parliament passing legislation to implement a treaty, but such a hiatus is not particularly unusual for many countries.

Civil law countries, and they are the large majority, are inclined to accept international law for direct incorporation without enabling legislation. A growing number, like France, place treaties at the apex of domestic law in national constitutions (Frowein 1997: 87). Besides the patterns of the common law and civil law countries, some countries have not established a clear path for incorporation and so fitting treaties into their national systems is *ad hoc* from one treaty to the next. The most thorough-going incorporation on the planet is among the EU states. The ECJ has ruled that EU law is superior to national law and must be incorporated into the 27 national systems. Even Great Britain's common law system must accept EU law, although enabling parliamentary acts must play a role. All of the states of the EU seem agreeable to a regular and deep pattern of incorporation because of the advantages that accrue to them.

More important than specific procedures of incorporation is the acceptance that global interdependence, with all the attending advantages of mutual cooperation, is driving the legal penetration of national systems. Values and rules agreed upon in world conferences and at the UN must reappear as national laws if human rights standards, environmental protection, reliable business practices, removal of landmines, and much else are to benefit humankind. Across the second half of the twentieth century and continuing into the twenty-first, the doors of sovereignty have graciously opened to allow in the necessary rules of a burgeoning international society. Perhaps

---

Box 4.5 Treaties as Superior Law

The most avid supporter of the dualist approach cannot escape the ultimate requirement of complying with international law. Even if a powerful political force builds up in a country and demands a new policy direction, the proposed change can be trumped by a treaty obligation.

A recent case between the former Czechoslovakia and Hungary illustrates the power of treaty law. The two states entered into a 1977 treaty to create the *Gabcikovo-Nagimaros* system of dams on the Danube River. After Czechoslovakia experienced its "friendly divorce" and became the Republics of Czech and Slovakia, due to the geography of the situation, the issue then existed between Slovakia and Hungary. Hungary, responding to its rising environmentalist movement, wanted out of the treaty obligation, but the new Republic of Slovakia would not agree. In a 1997 decision, the ICJ ruled the agreement to build the system of dams would have to stand unless both countries agreed to terminate the treaty. Neither the momentous change of both countries converting from communism to democracy nor the break up of Czechoslovakia reduced the treaty obligation in any way.

Sources: See, Eyal Benvenisti, "Domestic Politics and International Resources: What Role for International Law?" in Michael Byers (ed.), *The Role of Law in International Politics* (New York: Oxford University Press, 2000), pp. 107–29; see also www.icj-cij. org/ > cases > contentious cases > 1993 Hungary-Slovakia.

such ready acceptance worldwide is part and parcel of a new international legal culture now being forged. When countries choose not to incorporate an important treaty or protocol, such as the environmental rules of the Kyoto agreement, they risk damage to their international reputation as has happened to the United States

Can There Be a Future World Government?

Some impressive but inchoate legislative, executive, and judicial steps have been taken at the international level in the service of international law despite confronting several serious challenges. That service is further enhanced by international law's regular and effective penetration of municipal legal systems. Are these developments so far-reaching and promising that they can be imagined as part of an evolutionary process sure to end in world government? Idealists have long wanted to convert the world from the conditions of anarchy, power, and war to an orderly, disarmed world with a central government dedicated to human betterment and justice. World government advocates claim that peace is possible only through centralized authority at the global level and that attending to the many problems that transcend national jurisdictions – such as terrorism, environmental issues, and international crime – can be dealt with effectively at the global level alone.

For instance, the World Federalist Movement formed in 1946 and claims a 25,000 membership spread across 40 countries. As this movement has become a little more realistic about the chances of world reform, it has changed from a maximalist position of advocating a fully-developed world state to a minimalist one of strengthening UN law enforcement.[33] Two scholars, Glenville Clark and Louis B. Sohn, rewrote the UN Charter in the 1960s offering a stronger role for the UN if the world chose to accept their extensive modifications, which it did not (1985: 73–99). Less ambitious is the World Orders Models Project (WOMP), also begun by scholars in the 1960s. Whether world government is possible or not, WOMP has at least sought a world guided by the priorities of humane governance as championed by the emerging global civil society. Ending poverty, promoting the rule of law, bettering human rights practices, raising environmental standards, and ending warfare have been among the long-sought after goals of WOMP. It has much in common with today's thousands of NGOs that are active in global governance.

World government schemes now seem clearly out of fashion, although supporters for this kind of bold transformation are unlikely to disappear altogether.[34] What dooms idealistic schemes is that they ignore significant problems which can easily undermine such schemes. States' fears and power ambitions, ideological and cultural differences, gross inequality in wealth, and other harsh realities causing friction and conflict are expected, in some way, to melt away once a benevolent world government takes charge. As Inis Claude once insightfully noted, the political process and its inherent obstacles are played down as world government advocates imagine "that somehow *law*, in all its purity, can displace the soiled devices of politics." He further observed that world government would prove to be no magic wand and that the UN may be as ambitious a structure as world politics can support in this age.[35]

If the world order of today is less than what idealists want, it is certainly more than a clashing anarchy of hostile states. The world is, in fact, what liberals, as opposed to realists, would tell us: an international society of multiple actors sharing many of the same interests and goals and working hard to build lasting progress through the guidance of international law. The international quasi-legislative, executive, and judicial activities building up international law, though weak compared with many national legal systems, are no small accomplishment in a complex and still dangerous world.

Chapter Summary

- Although a horizontal system in terms of authority, international law still functions effectively.
- The role and scope of international law is expanding as a response to the forces of globalization and interdependence.
- Rule-making is carried out in quasi-legislative fashion through IGOs such as the UN and multilateral conferences.
- Rule-enforcement can be haphazard, especially in security matters, but collectively and individually states have enforcement options.

- Rule-adjudication is impressive with the use of arbitration and the recent growth in courts and tribunals.
- States vary in the pace and manner of incorporating relevant international rules into their domestic context but generally comply with this obligation.
- The vitality of international law suggests that world government is not necessary for an effective global legal system.

Discussion Questions

1   In the absence of a world government, in what way can the legislative function be carried out at the international level?
2   What are the options available for enforcement of international law?
3   International courts are growing in number, but there is no clear hierarchy among them as in national legal systems. Explain why this is so.
4   What is the difference between *monism* and *dualism* incorporation methods?
5   Is a world government likely to form in the future using international law as a foundation?

Useful Weblinks

http://www.pict-pcti.org/courts/
All courts of international character can be accessed from this web page as well as tribunals. This site also offers a list of the latest news items on courts by date.

http://www.pca-cpa.org/
The Permanent Court of Arbitration has an interesting web page with lists of recent and pending cases and general information on its background. This page contains a useful search engine.

http://www.icj-cij.org/
This is the home page of the International Court of Justice containing easily accessible links to all its contentious cases and advisory opinions. Go to "Decisions." Some cases have to be found by going first to "Decisions" and then "Contentious Cases Listed in Alphabetical Order by Country."

http://curia.europa.eu/jcms/jcms/j_6/home
This is the website of the European Court of Justice of the EU.

http://www.oas.org/oaspage/humanrights.htm
The Inter-American Court of Human Rights home page and that of the Inter-American Commission of Human Rights are located at this site and contain option about jurisprudence, publications, general information, among other links.

Further Reading

Alvarez, José E. (2005) *International Organizations as Law-Makers*. New York: Oxford University Press.

Bederman, David J. (2008) *Globalization and International Law*. New York: Palgrave Macmillan.

Bekou, Olympia and Cryer, Robert (eds.) (2004) *The International Criminal Court*. Burlington, VT: Ashgate/Dartmouth.

Benvenisti, Eyal and Hirsch, Moshe (eds.) (2004) *The Impact of International Law on International Cooperation*. New York: Cambridge University Press.

Birdsall, Andrea (2008) *The International Politics of Judicial Intervention*. New York: Routledge.

Broomhall, Bruce (2003) *International Justice and the International Criminal Court: Between Sovereignty and the Rule of Law*. New York: Oxford University Press.

Charlesworth, Hilary and Coicaud, Jean-Marc (eds.) (2009) New York: Cambridge University Press.

Delsol, Chantal (2008) *Unjust Justice: Against the Tyranny of International Law*. Wilmington, DE: ISI Books.

Dunoff, Jeffrey L. and Trachtman, Joel P. (2009) *Ruling the World? Constitutionalism, International Law, and Global Governance*. New York: Cambridge University Press.

Goldsmith, Jack L. and Posner, Eri A. (2005) *The Limits of International Law*. New York: Oxford University Press.

Goldstone, Richard J. and Smith, Adam M. (2008) *International Judicial Institutions: The Architecture of International Justice at Home and Abroad*. New York: Routledge.

Jinks, Derek and Sloss, David (eds.) (2009) *The Role of Domestic Courts in Treaty Enforcement: A Comparative Study*. New York: Cambridge University Press.

Kaikobad, Kaiyan Homi (2000) *The International Court of Justice and Judicial Review: A Study of the Court's Powers with Respect to Judgments of the ILO and UN Administrative Tribunals*. The Hague: Kluwer Law International.

Mandelbaum, Michael (2006) *The Case for Goliath: How America Acts as the World's Government in the 21st Century*. Boulder, CO: Public Affairs.

Muller, A. S. and Loth, M.A. (eds.) (2009) *Highest Courts and the Internationalization of Law Challenges and Changes*. New York: Cambridge University Press.

Pauwelyn, Joost (2008) *Optimal Protection of International Law: Navigating between European Absolutism and American Volunteerism*. New York: Cambridge University Press.

Ralph, Jason (2007) *Defending the Society of States: Why America Opposes the International Criminal Court and Its Vision of World Society*. New York: Oxford University Press.

Ratner, Steven R. and Slaughter, Anne-Marie (2004) *Methods of International Law*. Washington, DC: American Society of International Law.

Romano, Cesare, Nolkaemper, André, and Kleffner, Jann K. (eds.) (2004) *Internationalized Criminal Courts: Sierra Leone, East Timor, Kosovo, and Cambodia*. New York: Oxford University Press.

United Nations [1997] (2008) *International Law on the Eve of the Twenty-First Century: Views from the International Law Commission*. New York: United Nations Publications.

van Krieken, Peter J. and McKay, David (eds.) (2005) *The Hague: Legal Capital of the World*. New York: Cambridge University Press.

Notes

1 Go to http://www.un.org/ > International Law > International Law Commission.
2 This paragraph is influenced in part by Schachter 1994: 2–4.
3 For a description of recent work by the Sixth Committee, see http://www.un.org/> International Law > Sixth Committee.
4 The Statute of the ILC can be found at http://www.untreaty.un.org/ilc/texts/instruments/english/statute/statute_e.pdf.
5 See note 1.
6 See note 1.
7 The EP can be read about in Tsoukalis, *What Kind of Europe?*
8 Follow PAP developments at http://www.africa-union.org/> AU Organs > PAP.
9 A widely used definition of war is that of Singer and Small 1972: 19–22.
10 Refer to http://www.pict-pcti.org/courts/.
11 A fuller account of the *Alabama Claims* can be read in Meyer 2002: 1–2.
12 The court can be read about at http://www.pca-cpa.org/ and http://www.pict-cti.org/courts/PCS.html.
13 Information about this tribunal is available at http://www.nuclearclaimstribunal.com/text.htm.
14 Refer to http://www.pca-cpa.org/ > Eritrea-Ethiopia Boundary Commission and Eritrea-Ethiopia Claims Commission.
15 This investment-dispute body can be found at http://www.worldbank.org/icsid/treaties/intro.htm; and http://www.pict-pcti.org/courts/ICSID.html.
16 Refer to http://www.uncitral.org/en-index.html.
17 Use http://arbiter.wipo.int/domain/index.html.
18 Access at http://www.wto.org/.
19 Available at www.iccwbo.org/home/menu_what_is_icc.asp, pp. 1–6.
20 Locate at http://www.wipo.int/amc/en/arbitration/ny-convention/.
21 The ICJ can be read about at www.icj-cij.org/; The Statute of the ICJ can be located at www.icj-cij.org/ > Basic Documents > Statute of the Court.
22 Alter 2001; and see http://curia.europa.eu/en/instit/presentationfr/cje.html.
23 This court is at http://www.pict-pcti.org/courts/TJAC.html.
24 This African court is at http://www.african-union.org/root/AU/recs/comesa.html.
25 Go to http://www.coe.int/ > European Court of Human Rights; and see Bernhardt 2001: 387–97; MacDonald 2001: 409–22.
26 Refer to http://www.oas.org/oaspage/humanrights.htmm.
27 Find at http://www.pict-pcti.org/courts/ACHPR.html.
28 Read about at http://www.icty.org/.
29 This tribunal is at http://www.ictr.org/.
30 Additional reading about the ICC is available in Sewall and Kaysen 2000; and Tochilovsky 2003: 291–300.
31 Higgins 1994: 205.
32 Good overviews of international law's application to the US national system are Trimble 2002; and Malone 1998.
33 Dover 2003: 117. And see the website at www.lwfa.org/about/.
34 For instance, see Gulick 1999); and Taylor 2002.
35 For the best brief analysis of the prospects for world government, see Claude, Jr. 1971: 411–33.

With ever-increasing interstate intercourse and ever-growing complexity of activities involving or affecting more than one state, the traditional simple pattern of exclusive territorial government has become archaic. (Louis Henkin)

Borders are more permeable, and threats are decentralized, fast, fungible, and fluid. How can transovereign issues be tackled in a system that is based on sovereignty? (Maryann Cusimano) Love

5

Jurisdiction
Domain over Places and Persons

Contents

The governments of the approximately two hundred states enjoy a legal monopoly over their territories and are entitled to control who and what crosses their territorial borders. Over time, additional places have attracted the attention of states as jurisdictional concerns. From the fifteenth through the seventeenth centuries, European states contended with the issue of whether the oceans would be owned by a few or shared by the many. By the early twentieth century, the age of the airplane was born and a new concern immediately arose over rules for the airspace above the territories of the states. Then, in the midst of Cold War rivalry, the Soviet Union rocketed a satellite into orbit in 1957, creating another jurisdictional area of outer space that quickly captured the attention of a growing number of states. Finally, the Antarctic and Arctic areas attracted strong international interest in the post-Second World War period after the polar regions had been mostly neglected due to their harsh climates and near-inaccessibility.

States, of course, are concerned with more than the physical spaces of the world. Over six billion people live as citizens spread out among the states, and states regulate their citizens and others in some circumstances. In a globalizing, interconnected world, millions of people travel to other countries as tourists, students, business people, and, unfortunately, as terrorists and drug traffickers. Some visitors reside for a time in a foreign state or may even wish to change their nationality. States have the sovereign authority to regulate many human choices that affect a state's territory and population, even when those activities, such as terrorism or counterfeiting, may originate in another state.

This chapter will identify and appraise the rules that states have created for managing the physical spaces of the world, the activities of their citizens and foreigners, and extraterritorial jurisdiction when states and their citizens are involved beyond a state's territory. Have the evolving rules of international law provided a more orderly world that is moving deeper into a formative international society, or are there large, unsettled issues causing conflict and encouraging centripetal tendencies among the 200 states and their peoples?

Territorial Jurisdiction

Jurisdiction is a domain for making and enforcing rules over *places* and the *activities of persons*. The place with the clearest jurisdiction is the territorial base of the sovereign state, whether it is the tiny 109 acres of the Vatican or the gigantic expanse of Russia stretching across Eurasia. Since the 1648 *Peace of Westphalia*, it is axiomatic that a state's government exercises exclusive authority over its territory and citizens and also applies its rules to foreign business people, corporations, tourists, and others who are located there. States jealously guard their prerogatives over internal affairs and rarely relinquish them. Whether a military intrusion, the abduction of a person by a foreign state, or criticism of a government's human rights record, the leaders of a state usually resent anything perceived to be an unwarranted interference from the outside. The sovereignty of states appears sacrosanct with state rights and duties fairly well agreed upon, including especially the duty requiring states not to interfere in one another's affairs. Moreover, even the UN Charter prohibits the UN from intervening in states' domestic jurisdictions.

All the landed territory of the planet is claimed by one state or another, mostly as the domestic territory of states but a few instances of overseas territories and colonies still remain. The only exception of unclaimed land is a sliver of territory in the southwestern part of Antarctica. With the land masses of the world now delineated by national borders, one might be tempted to think territorial issues and conflicts belong to a by-gone era. It is true that the race by Europeans to colonize the world from the sixteenth to the late nineteenth century and two world wars fought over the extension of great empires have passed into history, but some problems still remain.

While states generally have been successful in recent decades at extending their territorial control seaward and skyward, arguments over boundary lines are still common. Contention seems without end over specific territories such as Kashmir, which is located between India and Pakistan, and about ownership of continental shelves, islands, islets, and reefs. Disputes over some of these minute places might at first appear petty, but their possession can greatly enlarge a state's claim to fisheries, and oil and natural gas deposits in the seabed.

Not uncommonly, boundary issues can be part of a colonial legacy. A British colonial treaty set in motion a boundary dispute between Belize and Guatemala that lasted 143 years. Boundaries originally marked out on a map in the comfort of a foreign minister's office may never have been properly surveyed through a jungle or across a desert. In time, Belize granted maritime concessions to Guatemala in exchange for the latter dropping its land claims against Belize, and then the Inter-American Development Bank provided $200 million to demarcate an accurate boundary between the two. Boundary disputes of one kind or another are frequently at the center of cases before arbitration panels or the ICJ. At the end of the twentieth century, 38 percent of maritime boundaries and 17 percent of land boundaries were tangled up in some form of disagreement.[1]

On occasion, territorial jurisdiction may be decided in favor of the state that demonstrates effective administration over time in at least one policy area. In the eastern Greenland case in 1933, the PCIJ decided in favor of Denmark over Norway's claim because Denmark had exerted the intention and will to act as sovereign over eastern Greenland for an extended period of time. The world court went on to say that even a minimal policy in an inhospitable Arctic region would be sufficient for establishing sovereignty. Another example is a decision in 2002 by the ICJ awarding two small islands off the northeast coast of Borneo to Malaysia rather than Indonesia. Neither country had a treaty-based title to the islands but at least Malaysia had set up turtle and bird preserves on them. These modest acts demonstrated to the ICJ a pattern of administrative policy by Malaysia.[2]

Good fences make for good neighbors among farmers and so too do well-marked, agreed upon borders among states help keep the peace and promote comity among states. Fortunately, most states do not currently have serious territorial issues that can lead to war. There are some notable exceptions, however. Iraq and Iran contested bitterly from 1980 to 1988, in part over their joint border, islands in the Persian Gulf, and control of the confluence of the Euphrates and Tigris Rivers; India and Pakistan have fought three wars, and almost a fourth involving nuclear weapons, with the possession of Kashmir as a principal issue. The Iraq War of 1990–1 began with Iraq seizing neighboring Kuwait claiming that it had always been Province 19 of Iraq.

Law of the Sea

It is almost impossible to overestimate the value of the vast bodies of salt water that covers about 71 percent of the Earth's surface since these waters provide food, recreation, oil and natural gas from continental shelves, and, most importantly, a liquid highway for most of the world's commerce carried by today's container-ships (Juda 1996: 1–2). These bodies of water can be referred to as either oceans or seas, but common practice calls the largest bodies "oceans," such as the Atlantic and Pacific Oceans and lesser bodies "seas," such as the Bering Sea or North Sea. In modern times, the oceans and seas are **res communis**, or a commons available for the use of all states. In the latter half of the twentieth century, international society undertook a major diplomatic campaign through a series of multilateral conferences to better manage and protect these waters.

A sharing policy, however, was not the first approach taken in the early history of the state system. Portugal and Spain became the dominant seafaring states in the 1400s and 1500s and arranged for a **mare clausum**, or closed sea, to restrict the development of rising trade competitors like England and Holland. Pope Alexander VI graced Portugal and Spain with a papal bull legitimizing their 1494 *Treaty of Tordesillas*, which divided the oceans between the two states. A line of demarcation was drawn north to south that crossed through the western part of today's Brazil. Everything to the east of the line was Portugal's and to the west all belonged to Spain. Presumably these states could "own" thousands of miles of ocean expanse. The "closed sea" approach reached its heyday by the 1600s when this concept was critically evaluated by the great intellect of Hugo Grotius, sometimes called the father of international law. This Dutch lawyer and diplomat argued persuasively in his 1609 **Mare Liberum** (Free Sea) that enormity of oceans could not, by their very nature, be owned as could land, and that all states would benefit commercially if the seas were open to the merchant vessels of all (Galdorisi & Vienna 1997).

After this shift in ocean policy, European states relied for five hundred years largely on customary law to provide rules for managing their interactions on the seas. However, when many new states joined international society following the breakup of colonial empires, the mounting number of new states proved to be a disruptive force. Ambitious states clamored to control more of the sea and the continental shelf to enrich themselves with the bounties of fish and oil. Consequently, an important series of conferences was held to codify and progressively develop the rules of the sea into written treaty law.

The third and final conference started its meetings in New York City in 1973 and concluded them in Montego Bay, Jamaica, in late 1982. It remains today as one of the world's largest conferences, with 160 states in attendance, and also one of the most successful in history. This conference did not even have a working document at the outset, yet it rolled out a 200-plus page proposed convention that contained 320 articles before reaching the annexes of the treaty. Some authorities have complimented this accomplishment by calling the 1982 *Law of the Sea Convention* (LOS convention) "a constitution for the oceans."[3]

The LOS convention offers numerous rules. Several seaward jurisdictions start with the **baseline** of a coastal state, which is the land-water demarcation marked at low tide. The seaward jurisdications are indicated in Figure 5.1. If a state's coastline has significant indentures or a fringe of island, that state is allowed to draw a reasonable *straight baseline* along the outermost islands. This rule was first recognized in the well-known 1951 *Anglo-Norwegian Fisheries* case.[4] Norway had used its fringe of islands to establish its baseline since the early nineteenth century.

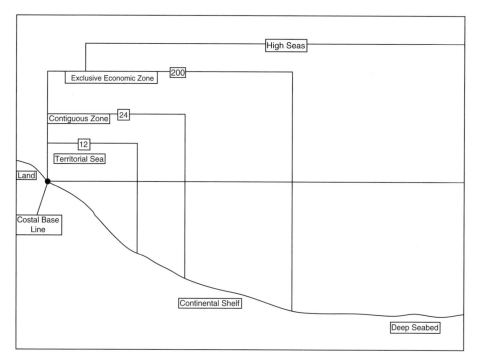

Figure 5.1   Seaward jurisdictions
Source: Figure made by Justin A. Brown.

One innovation of the LOS convention assisted the **archipelago states,** which are states with a territorial base consisting of a set of islands recognized as geographical and political entities. Close to 35 states, such as Indonesia and the Philippines, are allowed to draw their baselines around the outermost islands, giving these states sovereignty over the waters within the encircling baselines.[5]

States have complete sovereignty over their **internal waters,** which are rivers, lakes, ports, bays and the like, generally on the landward side of the baseline. The LOS convention briefly mentions internal waters but customary law mostly controls this jurisdiction. For instance, a foreign ship moored in a state's harbor can manage its own affairs unless that ship in some way impacts on the peace and good order of the harbor. Bays, as an internal water area, can sometimes be particularly trouble-some. Canada claims the large Hudson Bay as part of its internal waters, but the United States has objected in the past on the grounds that the mouth of this bay, at fifty miles wide, far exceeds Canada's territorial sea jurisdiction measured from either side of the bay's mouth. The United States has argued international waters must surely lie in the middle of the bay's entrance and much of the center of the bay, making this bay available to all ships. Canada rejects the width-of-mouth argument, insisting that the Hudson Bay is a *historical bay* that Canada has governed in all respects for a lengthy period of time.

The **territorial sea** is the band of water along a state's coast under the state's exclu-sive sovereignty, including the airspace above and the seabed below. From the early

---

Box 5.1 A Foreign Merchant Ship in Port

*Mali v. Keeper of the Common Jail of Hudson Country, U.S. Supreme Court 1887,
120 U.S. 1*

While the Belgian merchant ship the *Noordland* was in the port of Jersey City,
NJ, a fight broke out below decks with Belgian Joseph Wildenhaus stabbing
and killing a fellow seaman. Under customary law, if incidents on board a ship
in port do not disturb the *peace and tranquility* of the port, the officers of the
ship handle discipline and exercise the law of their flag. This practice was reinforced by the Belgium–US Consular Convention of 1880.

When Wildenhaus and witnesses from the ship were incarcerated in the
local Hudson Country Jail, Belgian Consul M. Charles Mali sued for their release
to his custody. The case rose to the US Supreme Court, which ruled murder
was of such gravity that the port tranquility exception to Belgium's jurisdiction
could be invoked. Wildenhaus remained in jail to face local charges.

Source: This case can be accessed at http://supreme.justia.com/us/120/1/case.html.

1700s on, most states were content to use the traditional 3-mile width, but exceptions
persisted right up to the eve of the LOS conference. Several Latin American states
even claimed a 200-mile territorial sea while other states have for years claimed a
12-mile territorial sea. As it happened, the LOS conference agreed on 12-miles of
territorial sea extending outward from the baseline. (This measure and other
seaward jurisdictions are stated in nautical miles, with one nautical mile equal to
1.15 land miles.)

Understandably, the United States, with several hundred naval vessels sailing every
ocean and sea, argued for the 3-mile limit at the LOS conference so its ships would
have more ocean to sail and have greater proximity to other states' coastlines.

Broadening the territorial sea from 3 to 12 miles also brought heightened concern
over the long-established principle of **innocent passage**, the continuous and expeditious voyage of a foreign ship through the territorial waters of a coastal state as long
as there were no harmful effects to that state. Obviously, much more of the sea would
be enclosed as territorial sea with the change to a 12-mile width so the innocent passage rule now comes into play much more frequently. Warships and innocent passage have been a special issue. Except for the LOS convention requirement that
submarines surface en route and show their flag, warships are not discussed. China,
among other states, insists warships are a special category of ship that must have
prior approval before sailing under the innocent passage rule through another state's
waters.

A specialized version of innocent passage is **transit passage** through one of the
many **straits** that may fall within the territorial jurisdiction of one or two states. There
is a firm expectation that ships and aircraft of all kinds are not to be impeded as they

follow a strait. A strait is a narrow sea passage connecting two bodies of open sea. A strait can exist between an island and the coast of a single state, as in the case of the Corfu Channel in the Adriatic Sea formed by an island off the coast of Albania, or between two states such as the Malaccan Straits lying between Malaysia and Indonesia. After a careful study, Bing Bing Jia believes that international law covers 116 relevant straits, while other writers identify up to 250 straits as important (1998).

Although rapid travel and instantaneous communications have shrunk the world in some ways, critical "choke-points" of the world demonstrate the long-lasting importance of geography. Along with important human-made canals (counting among them the Kiel, Panama, and Suez Canals) connecting large bodies of the oceans and seas, straits provide economic lifelines supporting the world's economy. Much of the oil that fuels the world's machines and generators leaves the Persian Gulf through the Hormuz Strait, and the prodigious trade between Asia and the West passes through the Malaccan Straits. It is no surprise that straits would receive serious attention at the LOS conference.

In addition to a territorial sea, a coastal state possesses a **contiguous zone** that extends 24 miles from the baseline and overlaps the territorial sea. This type of juris-diction traces back to English "hovering acts" of the eighteenth century allowing English authorities to police smuggling. The United States used a similar law during the Prohibition Era (1919–33) to prevent "mother ships" from hovering beyond the 3-mile territorial seas of the time and then off-loading illegal whisky onto small speed boats for a quick run past Coast Guard cutters. With an extra 12 miles of jurisdiction, states can police all manner of smuggling, such as trafficking in drugs and they can also better enforce their immigration and environmental laws.

Moreover, states can now claim a jurisdiction of 200 miles of the seabed from their baseline, and in some special geographical cases 350 miles depending on the natural prolongation of its territory known as the **continental shelf**. With this new jurisdiction, coastal states could latch onto a new dividend of natural gas, oil, and minerals located in their adjacent shelves. This opportunity of state enrichment, however, has caused many a dispute to arise among adjoining states over the point where one state's continental shelf begins and another's ends. Another jurisdiction that states have found attractive is the **exclusive economic zone** (EEZ) of 200 miles of sea measured from the baseline and overlapping other jurisdictions. With the EEZ, coastal states acquired sovereign rights to conserve and exploit all living and non-living resources in the waters and seabed. The chief advantage is exclusive fish-ing rights in a world relying more and more on fishing to help feed a burgeoning global population (now at 6.6 billion and estimated to reach 9.5 billion by the 2050s.) Since edible fish stocks mostly range inside this jurisdiction, it is safe to say that almost all the important fisheries of the world fall under the sway of one coastal state or another.

Interestingly, *landlocked* and *geographically disadvantaged* states (the latter are coastal states bordering enclosed or semi-enclosed seas with limited opportunities for living resources) are provided for in the LOS convention. Basically, the fortunate coastal states are called upon to share with the less fortunate countries but can do so on their terms. As it happens, a handful of countries still catch most of the world's fish by paying licensing fees to use the EEZs of other states and by operating high-tech factory ships and fishing boats. With the expanding world population pressuring the world's fisheries, it is no wonder that much of the business of the International Tribunal for the Law of the Sea (ITLOS) involves violations of fishing rights.

After these several overlapping jurisdictions are taken into account, what is left of the ocean is known as the **high seas.** These great bodies of water are a *res communis* open to all states for unimpeded navigation, fishing, over-flight by aircraft, and the laying of cables and pipelines. The extension of several types of seaward jurisdictions under the LOS convention of course has reduced the size of the open seas.

The LOS convention has been widely accepted, either through ratification or by treating its rules as customary law, and yet several prominent problems remain unresolved. The first concerns the nationality of a ship on the high seas. Every ship must fly the flag of its nationality, determined by where the ship is registered. According to Article 91 of the LOS convention, "There must be a genuine link between the State and the ship." A greater incongruence between a stated rule and the actual practice can hardly be imagined where **flags of convenience** are concerned. For an ample fee, any ship can be registered in Liberia or Panama, the primary purveyors of this practice, which permit low standards for a ship's safety, maintenance, and crew conditions, thus saving ship-owners considerable money. The upshot is that many ships in poor condition sail the seas. More Third World states are joining the lucrative business of providing flags of convenience, further jeopardizing international navigation (Langwiesche 2004).

A second problem is the historical scourge of piracy. The LOS convention clearly addresses this issue and defines piracy in its Article 101. Any private act of violence or depredation against passengers or crew and their ships or planes on or above the high seas is piracy. The problem is not with the law but its level of enforcement. Unlike Blackbeard and other swashbucklers of legend, modern-day pirates use cell phones, speed boats, and grenade launchers to assist in overhauling the largest of vessels. Pirates frequently rob a ship's safe and crew and sometimes take both the ship and cargo.

Hundreds of piracy acts have occurred in recent years. Until recently, most pirate activity has been in the South China Sea, especially in the 550-mile long Malaccan Straits (2004: 54–6). Other piracy "hot-spots" have been off the coasts of Nigeria and Somalia and in the Caribbean Sea, where drug smugglers are known to seize private yachts for transporting their illicit cargo. Lately, a spike in piracy has happened off the Horn of Africa with Somalian pirates seizing dozens of ships, including a Saudi Arabian oil tanker in 2008, and holding the ships and crews for ransom. The problem is so severe that the UN Security Council has authorized several navies to patrol the area, but this step is only partly successful. In the past, enforcement has probably been no better than it is because insurance companies replace owner losses and most of the 40,000 ships at sea are flagged by Third World countries without strong navies. The intense campaigns of the United States against terrorism and drug-smuggling now must be matched by a more effective anti-piracy campaign. In April 2009, the US Navy rescued a kidnapped American captain taken hostage from a US-flagged freighter by Somalian pirates. This was the first time the United States

---

Box 5.2 Piracy against the *Alondra Rainbow*

The *Alondra Rainbow* was attacked and seized off the coast of Indonesia in 1999. It was of Panamanian registry, owned by a Japanese corporation, and crewed mostly by Filipinos. Based on a reported sighting at sea in 2000, the Indian Navy gave chase, although India had no connection to the ship. Indian planes and ships fired on the repainted and renamed ship for 35 hours as it made for Pakistani waters.

India captured and tried 14 pirates in 2001, and they were sentenced to 7 years of "rigorous imprisonment." India could have claimed to exercise universal jurisdiction under long-standing customary law treating pirates as a scourge of humankind or applied the 1982 LOS Convention's articles on piracy. Yet, when filing charges against the captured pirates, India used its own national laws on armed robbery, attempted murder, theft, and forgery of ship's documents. India chose this legal path because it had no assigned penalties in its laws for piracy. As a British-influenced common-law country, India normally converts international rules into national law before exercising authority. According to William Langewiesche, more interesting is the fact that India's prosecution of these pirates, as an exercise of universal jurisdiction, is the first case in history of prosecuting pirates that had nothing to do with the prosecuting state.

Source: William Langewiesche, *The Outlaw Sea: A World of Freedom, Chaos, and Crime* (New York: North Point Press, 2004), pp. 71–80.

---

has tangled with pirates since raiding Barbary Coast pirate strongholds on the southern rim of the Mediterranean Sea in the early nineteenth century.

The last, and at one time the most controversial, issue centers on the provision of a Seabed Mining Authority for licensing mining activities and ensuring that profits are shared by all states. The name seems innocuous enough, but this Authority, beginning its operations in Kingston, Jamaica, in 1996, became caught in a crossfire of ideologies. In 1970, Third World states, with a socialist orientation of sharing the world's wealth, won approval for a UN General Assembly declaration to apply the principle of "common heritage of humankind" to the expected wealth of poly-metallic nodules on the floor of the seas. These states secured the same principle in Part XI of the LOS convention dealing with the seabed of the ocean. The Western, industrialized states had accepted the 1970 declaration yet, by the 1980s, led by President Ronald Reagan, these states took a strong capitalist view that seabed mining should be a matter of private enterprise, a position obviously privileging the advanced Western countries with the technology to mine the nodules at great ocean depths. It was anathema to capitalist states that countries without any investment in the enterprise should reap a dividend.

At first it appeared that the LOS convention would be embraced by only the Third World countries. However, between 1990 and 1994, the UN Secretary-General negotiated a more capitalist-friendly compromise that amended the convention, satisfying most parties, especially on the matter of having to share technology with less fortunate states. After all the heat and flash of this ideological collision, market forces and a sufficiency of minerals within national jurisdictions have largely weakened the importance of the Seabed Mining Authority as an issue (Swing 2003: 332).

The LOS convention entered into force in 1994 with the necessary 60 ratifications and has since been ratified by 157 states as of early 2009, with the important exception of the United States. The United States did finally sign the convention in 1994 but has yet to ratify it, even though President George W. Bush, in early 2002, supported ratification and the US Senate Foreign Relations Committee in 2004 unanimously recommended the same. Pro-convention interests have yet to marshal a Senate two-thirds majority needed to complete the ratification process. Nevertheless, the United States generally follows the LOS Convention rules.

Airspace

The Wright brothers' plane had barely landed after its brief flight in 1903 when geographers and military people began speculating about the implications of flight in heavier-than-air vehicles. Notions of using the column of air above countries as a *res communis*, similar to the high seas, evaporated completely with the air combat over Europe during the First World War. Planes, first flown on reconnaissance missions, were soon armed with machine guns and small bombs. The fear of sudden attack from above, heightened by the attack on Pearl Harbor and later the role of strategic bombers and intercontinental missiles, set the tone for international law covering airspace.

Immediately following the First World War, the 1919 *Paris Convention for the Regulation of Aerial Navigation* gave states exclusive sovereignty, or jurisdiction, for the column of air above a state's landed territory and territorial sea. The 1944 *Chicago Convention on International Civil Aviation* further confirmed exclusive state control over airspace and also laid down many specific rules, including assigning nationality to planes according to their country of registration. The Chicago Convention is the framework treaty for airspace as the LOS convention is for ocean law.[6]

Perhaps the Chicago Convention's most important contribution was the creation of the International Civil Aviation Organization (ICAO), which became a specialized agency of the UN System in 1947. The ICAO's Executive Council has recommended numerous rules for international navigation and safety that are regularly accepted. This oversight function is critical since countries have organized international air travel through a vast web of bilateral treaties, an arrangement that might be anarchical without the ICAO. Air flights were a luxury for a privileged few from the 1930s to 1950s, but, since then, travel by commercial airliners has increasingly become routine for millions of people, both domestically and internationally.

The violation of a country's airspace is a very serious and sensitive issue. Most countries have means for intercepting violators of their airspace, either by jet fighters, ground-to-air missile, or both. The history of the Cold War is replete with cases of military planes and helicopters straying past the "iron curtain" dividing Europe and being shot down or forced to land. A diplomatic crisis erupted in 1960, canceling a summit conference, when the Soviet Union shot down an American U-2 spy plane with a ground-to-air missile. Tragically, several civilian airliners have been brought down over the years as well. The most infamous instance was the shocking attack on a South Korean airliner in 1983 by a Soviet fighter, with all 269 people on board perishing. The plane was flying slightly north of its usual route and edged into Soviet airspace. The ICAO quickly amended the Chicago Convention by calling on all states to refrain from using weapons on civilian aircraft in cases of violated airspace.

The crisis now known as the 9/11 attack raises a new scenario. On September 11, 2001, hijackers flew America's own commercial aircraft into the twin towers of the World Trade Center in New York City and reduced them to rubble with over 3,000 lost lives. Another hijacked plane was flown into the Pentagon adjacent to Washington, DC. What should the rules of international law be in cases of terrorists hijacking planes and flying them into population centers or critically important buildings like the Pentagon? The 9/11 emergency involved domestic flights, but international flights could be put into play by terrorists just as easily. Few can doubt that any state would hesitate to shoot down such planes, even with innocent passengers on board, justifying it as an act of self-defense.

A dangerous incident happened in 2001 that raises other interesting questions about international law governing airspace. A US Navy turboprop reconnaissance plane was flying about 50 miles off the Chinese coast when it collided with a Chinese fighter that had been harassing it, causing the loss of the fighter and its pilot. Both sides blamed the other. The American plane, barely airworthy, struggled to an emergency landing on Hainan Island, which is Chinese territory. After tense negotiations and an apology by the US government, the plane and crew were allowed to leave China. Can a plane in distress land at the closest airport, just as a ship can seek any port in an emergency? Should China have to respect the plane and its equipment as it would the sovereignty of a foreign warship? Can China assert an air defense zone (ADZ) of 50 miles or more out to sea? A few other states have also created such zones. Most legal authorities would probably answer the first and second questions in the affirmative, but clearly there is no basis in international law for China to award itself a generous ADZ unless it is at war.[7]

In addition to the Paris and Chicago conventions, several other treaties contribute to airspace law. All three have been promoted by the ICAO. The 1963 *Tokyo Convention on Offenses and Certain Other Acts Committed On Board Aircraft* affirms that for any commission of a crime the state of the aircraft's registration has jurisdiction, not unlike exercising national jurisdiction on board a ship at sea. However, this convention does not directly address hijacking. A rash of hijackings that began in the 1960s, and still happens on occasion despite enormous security precautions, led to the 1970 *Hague Convention for the Suppression of Unlawful Seizures of Aircraft* concerning individuals hijacking planes in flight. Any state party to this convention must try the hijackers or extradite them to another country with jurisdiction. Providing security for civilian aircraft, once a tempting and highly vulnerable target, has cost billions of dollars for states and logistical aggravation to millions of passengers.

Then, there is the 1971 *Montreal Convention for the Suppression of Unlawful Acts against the Safety of Civil Aviation* that deals with sabotage. This convention covers harming persons on board planes, damaging the aircraft in flight, placing explosives on the plane, or interfering with navigation facilities. As with the Hague Convention, contracting parties are expected to try or extradite an accused person. These three conventions on aircraft are also frequently mentioned among the growing list of conventions aimed at suppressing terrorism.[8]

Outer Space

Concern with outer space and the need for law in this area started with the first Soviet satellite in 1957. The United States soon joined the race to put the first astronaut in outer space and the first man on the Moon. These two Cold War rivals eventually developed space stations and space shuttles, and sent aloft hundreds of satellites dedicated to a variety of purposes. Other scientifically advanced states, including China, France, Great Britain, and Japan, have at least produced rockets that can propel satellites into orbit. Unlike the several hundred years of development in the law of the sea or the several decades of air law evolution, much of space law has made a rapid entrance into the body of international law (Lyall 1996: 531).

Unquestionably, the UN has been the leading actor to create space law. A UN Committee on the Peaceful Uses on Outer Space (COPUOS) was formed in 1959 and then drafted the treaties and proposed additional principles that add up to the specialized body of space law (Steinhardt 1997: 338–40). Moreover, three specialized agencies of the UN have had notable input. The International Telecommunications Union (ITU) has regulated the location of communication satellites, while the UN Education, Scientific, and Cultural Organization (UNESCO) has argued for the interests of developing states of the Third World in the field of telecommunications. The ICAO has been concerned with falling space debris affecting aircraft and the demarcation line between airspace and outer space (1997: 342–3). Also, worthy of mention is the European Space Agency (ESA), headquartered in Paris with 17 member-states sharing expenses to maintain a rocket-launching facility in French Guiana. The ESA studies outer space and the Earth's environment, and services a multi-tasked network of satellites. Nowadays, China, India, and Japan, among others, can send satellites to orbit in outer space.

Finally, private actors are scratching at the boundary of space and will have to be taken into account as they are in airspace and on the high seas. In early 2005, Richard Branson of Virgin Airlines and Paul Allen, a Microsoft co-founder, teamed up with the money and technology to launch a private spacecraft which twice reached a 62-mile altitude, the edge of outer space, and then returned safely to Earth, earning these men the $10 million Ansari X Prize. Other entrepreneurs are promising to join this private enterprise and develop a tourist industry for outer space.

The first decision about space law concerned which model would guide this law's development. Would space-faring states attempt to colonize heavenly bodies and claim portions of outer space above their respective airspaces? Or would they view outer space as they did the seabed, and increasingly the Antarctica region, as the "common heritage of humankind," a vast place where states would serve as stewards for the good of all? (Peterson 1997: 245–75).

Early in the space age, several UN General Assembly resolutions pertained to outer space, the most important being the 1963 *Declaration of Legal Principles Governing The Activities of States in the Exploration and Use of Outer Space*, which led, in turn, to a framework treaty, the 1967 *Treaty on Principles Governing the Activities of States in the Exploration and Use of Outer Space, Including the Moon and Other Celestial Bodies*. Basically, this treaty allows for scientific exploration but forbids sovereign ownership of space and heavenly bodies; moreover, it prohibits placing weapons of mass destruction (WMD) in space. It also calls upon all states to assist any astronauts and treat them as the "envoys of humankind," and to bear responsibility for any damage their space vehicles cause.

One important, but unresolved, issue is the location in space of weapons of a lesser grade than WMD. President Ronald Reagan's grandiose "Star Wars" scheme in the 1980s, for shielding Americans from Chinese and Soviet intercontinental ballistic missiles, called for placing several kinds of "defensive weapons" in outer space. More recently, President George W. Bush's administration assumed *anti-missile missiles* could be placed in orbit. Others have argued that the spirit of the 1967 Outer Space Treaty precludes all weapons.

The 1967 Outer Space Treaty has been elaborated further by four additional treaties. These are the 1968 *Agreement on the Rescue of Astronauts, the Return of Astronauts and the Return of Objects Launched into Outer Space*; the 1972 *Convention on International Liability for Damage Caused by Space Objects*; the 1976 *Convention on Registration of Objects Launched into Outer Space*; and the 1984 *Agreement Governing the Activities of States on the Moon and Other Celestial Bodies*. The last, the Moon Agreement, has not been well received by the space-faring states. Similar to the argument over seabed mining, these states want to reserve the right to mine for profit on the Moon without sharing finds with others. Any showdown on this issue is probably in the distant future.[9]

Of special interest are the 1972 Convention on Liability and the 1976 Convention on the Registration of Objects. Several large human-made objects have exploded or disintegrated with parts reaching Earth, including a US space station impacting a remote area of Australia and the break-up of two US space shuttles over US territory. The only case brought under the 1972 Convention on Liability involved the Soviet nuclear-powered *Cosmos 954* crash in 1978 in northwest Canada near Great Slave Lake. The Canadians asked for $6 million Canadian in damages but settled for $3 million in 1981 (Stenihardt 1997: 351–2). This experience led to the 1992 UN General Assembly resolution known as *Principles Relevant to the Use of Nuclear Power Sources in Outer Space*, intended to promote the safer use of nuclear power in space.

The 1976 Convention on the Registration of Objects calls on states to carefully mark all parts of space vehicles so they can be identified later and to report all objects to a registry kept by the Secretary-General of the UN. An identification system helps point the finger of blame in cases of legal liability and allows dangerous objects to space travel to be checked-off from the registry if they are known to have re-entered the Earth's atmosphere and burned up. Over 9,000 human-made objects that are large enough to endanger space vehicles – including defunct satellites, rocket engines, gloves, lens covers, and paint chips – float about in space. The Inter-Agency Space Debris Coordination Committee, an inter-government forum of space-faring states, also tries to keep up with the "junkyard" in space.[10] In 2007, Russian cosmonauts had to install protective panels on the international space station. Even so, the space station has to alter course to avoid the larger debris, such as a "dead" satellite.

An issue that remains unsettled as written law is the absence of a clear demarcation line between airspace and outer space. Any jurisdictional area of a physical kind needs known boundaries. None of the treaties and principles governing space provides law on this point. Should the demarcation between the two areas be marked by the perigee, or low orbit, of satellites as they pass overhead, or should it be the altitude at which a plane loses "lift" under its wings and begins to operate entirely from the thrust of its engines and becomes a rocket? Most discussion of this problem centers on a past Soviet Union proposal that outer space would begin at 100 to 110 kilometers (62.1 to 68.3 miles) above Earth (Grove & Kamenetskaya 1995: 244–7).

Satellites

One special dimension of outer space concerns the role of satellites. At least three jurisdictional issues arise regarding the constellation of hundreds of satellites hovering in orbit above Earth.

The first issue concerns the sensing capability of satellites. Satellites are useful in all manner of ways, including weather and environmental research, navigation, and the transmission of massive amounts of data and news to all points on the globe. Satellites also have remote sensing functions such as high-resolution photography and imaging radar that allows one country to scoop up important information that another country, under the electronic "footprint" of the satellite, may not wish to share. Satellite sensing has been the most effective means by which the United States has gathered intelligence on the North Korean atomic weapons program. The critical role of satellites, in tracking the Iraqi Army and guiding smart-bombs to target, led Steven Lambakis to designate the Persian Gulf War of 1990–1 as the first "space war" (Lambakis 1995: 417–34).

The use of satellite sensing has remained controversial even though there is supposedly guidance from the UN's 1986 *Principles Relating to Remote Sensing of the Earth from Outer Space*. These principles seem to tilt in favor of protecting the sovereignty of states from surveillance by other states. However, as Ralph G. Steinhardt points out, the sensing does not have to have the explicit permission of the sensed state (Steinhardt 1997: 356), and so states with a sensing capability collect at will whatever data matches their interests. Since outer space is a "common heritage," activities there by one state do not violate any of the jurisdictions of another state.

The second issue concerns **geostationary satellites** located at about 22,000 miles above Earth, which allows them to synchronize with the Earth's rotation. A satellite so placed can continuously broadcast its "footprint" to the same region on Earth. The problem is that the more advanced states have enjoyed a near-monopoly over the slots in the geostationary orbit, and combined with their powerful news services, such as CNN, BBC, or the German Wave, thereby control news and its interpretation for the world. One major exception is *Al Jazeera*, a privately owned station located in Qatar, which can speak for an Arab point of view. Contention over geostationary satellites, and the near-monopolization of world news coverage, is another example of the long-running conflict between the rich, industrialized countries and the Third World (Krasner 1991: 336–66).

One group of eight states of the South, located around the Equator, took the forward-leaning step of claiming national sovereignty over the geostationary orbit above their countries. This radical assertion of sovereignty was expressed in the 1976 *Bogotá Declaration*. This declaration was in direct contradiction of the practice of treating outer space as a *res communis* unavailable for territorial claims (Grove & Kamenetskaya 1995: 263). Under diplomatic pressure, these eight states had to retreat and settle for a promise that the ITU would reserve geostationary slots for states of the Third World for their future use.

A related matter is whether these geostationary satellites can broadcast any message anywhere their owners wish. Just as principles on sensing exist, there is also the 1982 *Principles Governing the Use by States of Artificial Satellites for International Direct Television Broadcasting*. Steinhardt believes that while there is no clear norm requiring prior consent before broadcasting to other states, there is more support for this norm than in the case of prior approval for intelligence gathering by satellites (Steinhardt 1997: 357). In regard to the 1982 Principles, a number of the more advanced states voted against these principles because their governments believed prior consent would be tantamount to censorship. Principles on sensing and broadcasting are, in any case, the soft law of UN General Assembly resolutions and not the strong law of a treaty.

The third issue is determining jurisdiction when something unwanted or harmful passes through the Internet. The Internet depends, in large part, on communications satellites and provides millions of web sites with specific addresses for sales of merchandise, email addresses, news blogs, chat rooms, research data, and multiple other uses.[11] This cyberspace arrangement is a virtual reality inclined to treat the world as if it were borderless. With some frequency, serious objections to information flows across borders do occur. The French government stopped the sale of Nazi memorabilia to French citizens posted on an American web site. The Attorney-General of the state of Minnesota, as a component part of the US federal system, announced that any transmission of data via the Internet, accessible in Minnesota, would be subject to Minnesota law. A court in Munich, Germany fined Compu-Serve, an Internet Service Provider (ISP), for allowing pornography to be transmitted into Germany. Some authoritarian governments, especially China, go so far as to "firewall" their countries from much of the Internet and create national *intra*nets (Banisar 2003: 24–6; Kalathil 2003: 43–9; Kalathil & Boas 2003).

What should determine jurisdiction? Is it appropriate to use the territory where the transmission began, the nationality of the Internet user, or the place where an effect is felt? (Franda 2001: 149–53). Consensus on this question has yet to form, but a 2002 Australian case may have considerable impact on the outcome. A Mr Joseph Gutnick, an Australian businessman, felt he had been defamed by the electronic publication of *Barron's Online*, owned by Dow–Jones & Co., Inc., a publisher located in the state of New Jersey of the United States. The article in question accused Mr Gutnick of participating in a money-laundering scheme. Gutnick fought his case all the way to the High Court of Australia (HCA) winning at each level, as Dow–Jones kept appealing. Dow-Jones persisted that the case should be heard in New Jersey where the transmission of the article originated. Gutnick prevailed, however, because the HCA ruled that defamation occurs where the "infliction of damage" is comprehended and, in this case, it was comprehended by Gutnick's business associates in Australia.[12]

The Polar Regions

The Antarctic region is the circumpolar area that begins at the 60 degrees south latitude. This region contains the ice-covered land of the Antarctica continent and much of the surrounding oceans extending beyond the Antarctic Circle. The fifth-largest continent at over five and half million square miles, Antarctica is a frozen land with a treasure-trove of oil, minerals, and much of the world's fresh water. Antarctica lacks terrestrial animals but is home to bird and marine life on its coast and in its adjacent waters, including seals, penguins, and whales. The Antarctic region is a very fragile but relatively pristine ecosystem. Because of its formidable cold weather, this region was never involved with human settlement, but today there are over three dozen scientific stations on the Antarctic continent representing many countries.

One of the great success stories of international law is the evolution of this region as a "common heritage of humankind." As the world settled in to live with the tensions of the Cold War, the United States led in organizing a diplomatic conference that produced the 1959 *Antarctic Treaty* (also known as the Treaty of Washington), a framework treaty for the region, ratified by the Soviet Union, the United States, the seven states with territorial claims, and several others with scientific interests in the area. Essentially, the treaty demilitarized the region and dedicated it to scientific research, a remarkable achievement considering that the seven states of Argentina, Australia, Chile, France, New Zealand, Norway and the United Kingdom had territorial claims to most of the Antarctic continent. Several of these states have overlapping claims. Only Ellsworth Land and Marie Byrd Land in the southwest have gone unclaimed; in fact, these are the last landed territory in the world unclaimed by a state. The territorial claims of the seven states were placed in abeyance by the 1959 treaty.[13]

The Antarctic Treaty set the stage for additional agreements aimed at environmental protection covering fauna and flora, seals and other marine living resources, and eventually saving Antarctica from the despoliation of mining operations. In 1988, a

Convention on the Regulation of Antarctic Mineral Resource Activities was negotiated allowing limited mining, but it was met with an outcry of world opinion. A 1991 protocol to the 1959 treaty suspended mining operations, a fortunate development for such a pristine environment. Sufficient productive commercial mining elsewhere allowed for this positive outcome. Taken together, the several treaties on the Antarctic are known as the Antarctic Treaty System (ATS), and, as other states have taken interest, a total of 26 states now belong to the Antarctic Treaty Consultative Parties (ATCP) arrangement to regulate the Antarctic region. The ATCP has added about 200 "Recommendations" to the ATS that are generally followed by the states.[14]

In direct contrast to Antarctica, the Arctic is not a continent but an ocean surrounded by Asian, European, and North American land masses that encompass part or all of the territory of eight states. The Arctic has been referred to as an ice mass floating on an ocean. Because there are two major inlets (or outlets), the Bering Strait above the North Pacific Ocean and the Denmark Strait over the North Atlantic Ocean, the Arctic Ocean has been called the "Polar Mediterranean." The Arctic region is usually demarcated by the 60 degree north latitude, an area that is inclusive of but greater than the Arctic Circle. All of Finland, Iceland, and Denmark's Greenland fall within the region, while only the northern areas of Canada, Norway, Russia, Sweden, and the United States's Alaska do so. Together these national territories form the coastline of the Arctic Ocean, a body of water amounting to a little more than five million square miles.[15]

Unlike Antarctica, the Arctic region does have terrestrial animals, such as polar bears, wolves, foxes, musk-ox, reindeer, as well as both a rich bird life and marine animals including seals and whales. Another strong contrast with the Antarctic region is the presence of human inhabitants. Many of the Arctic's peoples are indigenous, or the original inhabitants, including the Inuit (Eskimo) of Alaska, Canada, and Greenland, and there are also the Sámi (Laplanders) of northern Scandinavia and Finland, and several similar peoples in the upper Siberian regions of Russia (Kelleher & Klein 2005: 51–4).

Territorial claims in the Arctic have arisen mostly over competition for natural resources, but two instances in this area are worthy of mention. The 1920 *Treaty of the Archipelago of Spitsbergen (Svalband)* resolved competitive claims over a small chain of islands. Norway was given sovereignty, but with the understanding that other states would enjoy mining rights. These islands are located about half way between Norway and the North Pole (Rothwell 2001: 160). More contentious, at least since the LOS Convention, are conflicting claims about continental shelves and EEZs. The wealth involved in fisheries, oil, gas, and minerals tempt the eight states of the region to maximize their maritime claims. In 2007, Russia sent a small submersible down two and a half miles to plant a Russian flag, made of titanium, on the seabed beneath the North Pole as a symbolic claim to minerals and oil that might be there. The Russian government, however, will have to make a strong geographical case before the UN that is convincing to other states. Due to this type of competition, plus the long years of division created by the Cold War, the concerned states were slow to conceptualize the Circumpolar North as a special region needing collaborative policy (Young 1993).

Nevertheless, environmental awareness for this region is just as critical as it is for the Antarctic, and at least some progress can be reported. Positive developments began as early as the 1911 treaty to protect seals in the Bering Sea and then, much later, five states in the region agreed to a 1973 treaty for the protection of polar bears. More recently, Finland took the lead to draw the other countries into the 1991 Arctic Environmental Protection Strategy (AEPS), and Canada urged Arctic states in 1996 to participate in the Arctic Council to promote policy consultation. Eight governments must agree on environmental measures while, at the same time, contending with special interests at home that are constantly making demands for access to the Arctic's natural wealth. Consequently, converting the Arctic to a "common heritage of humankind" is a worthy goal but one difficult to achieve. The eight countries have a consulting body known as the Arctic Council.

Moreover, multiple articles of the LOS convention have relevance for both Polar Regions. There are articles that call for conserving fish stocks and marine animals, and other articles that regulate pollution due to the ecological fragility of these regions.[16] Article 234 specifically calls upon coastal states to protect the ice covered areas of the world from marine pollution.

One essentially territorial issue involves Canada and the United States arguing over Canada's sovereignty claim to a waterway known as the Northwest Passage located above the Arctic Circle that would allow ships to move back and forth between the North Atlantic and the North Pacific Oceans. This difference between good neighbors is hardly more than a trifle since the route is nearly impassable for most ships during much of the year. Part of the issue, under international law, is whether a country can claim a wide expanse of an uninhabited polar area. It can be recalled from the Greenland case of 1933 that the standard for an administered policy in an inhospitable climate is not very high. Canada does, in fact, patrol the Passage, and with ice breakers if necessary. In any case, Canada and the United States decided to agree to disagree and set the matter aside with the 1988 *Arctic Cooperation Agreement* (Rothwell 2001: 432). If global warming melts this passageway, making it more available to shipping, this argument may renew.

Nationality

Jurisdictional matters are not just about places but involve people, their interests, and their actions. Not only is the landed territory of the world appropriated to about 200 states, but so are the over six billion people who live under the jurisdiction of one state or another. People, with rare exception, possess a **nationality,** which is the legal identification of a person with a state, based on owing allegiance and performing duties in exchange for the enjoyment of rights and privileges of citizenship plus the diplomatic protection of a state.

Some countries distinguish between *citizens* and *nationals.* Citizens enjoy a full set of rights while nationals may have only obligations of allegiance. Nationals usually lived in colonies and overseas territories, but the historical shift away from these dependencies has eroded the need for the status of national. Although each state can define nationality in its municipal laws, the 1948 *Universal Declaration of Human Rights* insists in Article 15 that every person is to have a nationality, and the 1966 *International Covenant on Civil and Political Rights* asserts in Article 24 that every child has a legal right to a nationality. Movement across borders, whether as a tourist, the representative of an NGO, a business person, exchange student, or even a diplomat, usually requires that a person possess a nationality and a passport to prove it.

The nationality of a person is determined either by *jus soli* (law of the soil) *or jus sanguinis* (law of blood). Some of the Western Hemispheric countries, including the United States and Mexico, apply the *jus soli*, or "birthright citizenship," rule meaning that any person born in a country can be a citizen. Exceptions are often made for children born to diplomats, parents temporarily in another country, or parents stationed abroad in the military service. The trend among states is moving away from *jus soli*. While a constitutional issue, some members of Congress have wanted to depart this approach because newborns of illegal immigrants automatically become citizens. Other states use the *jus sanguinis* rule, with the nationality of the parents passing to their children regardless of where births occur. If a child is born to parents of differing nationalities, many states have accorded the nationality of the father to the offspring, a practice women's groups have understandably opposed. For the large majority of people, the distinction between *jus soli* and *jus sanguinis* is not important because they are usually born on the territory where both parents are citizens. Most people readily meet both criteria (Aleinikoff & Klusmeyer 2002: 7; see also Castles & Davidson 2000).

Box 5.3 The United States as a *Jus Soli* State

U.S. v. Wong Kim Ark, U.S. Supreme Court 1898, 169 U.S. 649

As a 21-year-old, Wong Kim Ark left the United States for China in 1894 and when he returned in 1895 was refused entrance by customs. He had been born in San Francisco in 1873 to Chinese parents still possessing Chinese nationality. At the time, naturalization for Chinese as American citizens was not allowed, and Chinese persons entered the United States as laborers at the US government's discretion.

Wong Kim Ark sued, insisting he was an American citizen by reason of birth on US soil. The case reached the US Supreme Court, which cited the 14th Amendment to the US Constitution: "All persons born or naturalized in the United States and subject to the jurisdiction thereof, are citizens of the United States." The case affirms the status of the United States as a *jus soli* state.

Source: Further reading on this case is available at http://supreme.justia.com/us/169/649/case.html.

Individuals can change nationality and millions have. Some countries, including Australia, Canada, the United States, as well as Western European countries, are "immigrant-magnet" states because millions around the world wish to emigrate from their countries to the more desirable ones. This situation allows the magnet states to be picky about who becomes a citizen. These countries are often accused of "brain-draining" the best and brightest for their own purposes when Third World states need these people at home. A challenging law-enforcement problem for the much sought after countries, however, is the arrival of thousands of illegal migrants all too willing to by-pass legal processes.

A variety of interesting problems have arisen over **naturalization**, the legal process of changing from one nationality to another. Traditionally, a naturalized citizen is expected to swear allegiance to the new state and renounce ties to the old one. This process can be discriminatory. In the past, women were not allowed, in many instances, to naturalize on their own but had to follow their husband's nationality. For some states, reform came through the 1933 *Montevideo Convention on the Nationality of Women* and the 1957 *Convention on the Nationality of Married Women*. Under these conventions, women can freely choose their nationality. Ethnic and racial preferences have also affected immigration and citizenship.[17]

In the past and sometimes even today, a few states have followed a policy of "perpetual" or "indelible allegiance," meaning a country will not allow its citizens to take up nationality elsewhere. One historical case helped cause a war. The war of 1812 was largely caused by Great Britain's naval officers boarding American ships and forcing thousands of seamen from these ships to serve in the British Royal Navy. Britain claimed these men were Britons and "deserters" instead of "new Americans" who had properly immigrated to the United States. No doubt the British Navy scooped up native-born Americans as well. Basically, the British Admiralty needed manpower and pressed anyone available into service (Thomson 1994: 31).

Some individuals have had the opposite problem by being *expatriated*, or relieved of their citizenship, by their governments. In 1974, the Soviet Union expelled famous novelist and critic Alexander Solzhenitsyn, winner of the 1970 Nobel Prize for Literature. The Soviet government charged him with treason and stripped him of his citizenship in a very questionable manner so far as human rights are concerned. This radical step was, in fact, an act of repression designed to silence critics of the Soviet government. The 1966 *International Covenant on Civil and Political Rights* is not explicit on this point, but it does refer to a right to leave and return to one's country in Article 12. After the fall of communism, Solzhenitsyn's citizenship was restored, and he was able to return to Russia in 1994 to celebrity status in his homeland. He died there in 2008.

On occasion, individuals have denaturalized themselves by renouncing their citizenship before acquiring a new nationality or, through no fault of their own, by becoming refugees. In either case, they are **stateless persons.** Such individuals often do not have documentation for international travel and nor do they enjoy the diplomatic protection of a state's diplomatic service. Stateless persons can easily find themselves held in detention by the customs officials of one country or another. Chess Champion Bobby Fischer renounced US citizenship in 2004 and spent a year in a Japanese customs detention center until Iceland granted him citizenship and travel documents. Additionally, millions of people become refugees, uprooted by war and revolution, forced to flee, sometimes with only the clothes on their backs, to refugee camps located in other countries. As many as 25 million people are currently refugees.

Dual Nationality

International law has traditionally assumed that people would have a single national identity, nationality being taken very seriously by governments. Nationality was not an identity to be shed easily if it posed an inconvenience. The often-cited *Nottebohn* case before the ICJ in the 1950s illustrates this strong view of citizenship, calling for a "genuine link" between persons and their countries, a view that lasted until the latter part of the twentieth century. By this time, a clear trend toward accepting, if reluctantly, **dual nationality** was underway. Basically, dual nationality means a person is a citizen of two countries at the same time. Hostility toward such a status died a slow death, however. President Teddy Roosevelt called dual nationality a "self-evident absurdity."[18] George Bancroft, an American ambassador in the nineteenth century, said a man should not have two countries any more than two wives (Koslowski 2003: 158). The 1930 *Hague Convention on Certain Questions Relating to the Conflict of Nationality Laws* contains in its preamble the much-quoted phrase, "[E]very person should have a nationality and should have one nationality only" (Aleinikoff & Klusmeyer 2002: 158).

Box 5.4 "Genuine Link" and Citizenship

Friedrich Nottebohm was born a German national in 1881 but spent most of his life in Guatemala as a rich landowner. Given the looming outbreak of the Second World War and Guatemala's likely alliance with the United States, Nottebohm anticipated being interned with loss of property for being a citizen of an enemy state. To avoid an ill fate, Nottebohm managed to acquire citizenship in the neutral country of Liechtenstein, even having the usual three-year waiting period waived. Upon returning to Guatemala with Liechtenstein passport in hand, he was nonetheless interned and lands seized. After the war, Liechtenstein brought a case against Guatemala, under the compulsory jurisdiction of the ICJ, to assert Nottebohm's citizenship status.

The ICJ ruled against Liechtenstein, noting that Nottebohm's new citizenship was a matter of convenience and not a "genuine link" to a country where he had no intention of living. Guatemala was under no obligation to accept a citizenship of contrivance.

Source: This case can be read at http://www.icj-cij.org/ > cases > contentious cases > 1951 Nottebohm.

Against this bedrock of resistance, a new climate about nationality gradually evolved. The way many people live today no longer comports well with a single national identity. Millions of people migrate as "guest-workers," transnational marriages are commonplace, people have business interests in more than one country, and inexpensive travel and communication allow people to carry on lives in more than one country.[19]

Dual nationality status typically originates from being born in a *jus soli* country to parents who have emigrated from a *jus sanguinis* state. An individual has a citizenship because of where he or she is born and a second through the bloodline of parents. As David A. Martin has observed, it just so happens that the most common migration pattern of the world involves people going to *jus soli* countries while leaving those that are *jus sanguinnis* (Martin & Hailbronner 2003: 5–12).

An estimated 500,000 children born each year in the United States could potentially acquire dual nationality. The United States reluctantly began accepting dual nationality based on federal court decisions beginning in the 1960s, despite the retention of a citizen-naturalization oath that calls on a new citizen to renounce past

---

Box 5.5 Citizenship and Treason

Kawakita v. U.S., United States Supreme Court 1952, 343 U.S. 717

Choosing to switch allegiances in time of war can be a very risky decision, sometimes resulting in a charge of treason. Although the definition and punishment for this crime varies, treason generally means giving aid and comfort to the enemy of one's country, in an effort to defeat said country or to overthrow its government. The death penalty has been a common punishment in time of war.

Japanese–American Tomoya Kawakita, born in the United States, left America in 1939 at age 18 to study in Japan. Living there as the Second World War began, he registered as a Japanese citizen and acquired a Japanese passport. His specific crime was to work for Japanese authorities, primarily as a translator, supervising American POWs in a cruel slave-labor system that cost many Americans their lives.

Justice William O. Douglas referred to Kawakita's "fair-weather citizenship" as he voted with the majority in 1952 to confirm a lower federal court's conviction and sentence of death. Later, President Dwight Eisenhower commuted his sentence to life in prison, followed by President John Kennedy's decision a decade later to free and deport him to Japan.

Sources: Also, see Thomas M. Franck, "Clan and Super-clan: Loyalty, Identify and Community in Law and Practice," *American Journal of International Law* (1996) 90 (3), p. 378, see footnote 67. Further reading on this case is available at http://supreme.justia.com/us/343/717/case.html.

allegiances.[20] Many other countries have also accepted dual nationality. European states have made a policy shift from the conservative 1963 *Convention on the Reduction of Cases of Multiple Nationality and on Military Obligations in Cases of Multiple Nationality* to the reformative 1997 *European Convention on Nationality* that readily accepts citizenship in two countries and tries to regulate any associated problems. For business and other advantages, a prized dual citizenship involves a combination of US citizenship and citizenship in one of the EU countries. China is one of the countries remaining adamantly opposed to dual citizenship. Once a person naturalizes in another state, that individual is automatically stripped of Chinese citizenship.

Conscripted into two different armies, double-taxation, accusation of disloyalty in time of war, transnational fights over child custody, and eased travel by criminals and terrorists are some of the concerns that have arisen over dual nationality. Serious problems can occur but countries are learning how to manage these. Stefan Oeter recommends that international law place more emphasis on habitual residency in cases of conflicting nationalities. One nationality, he suggests, would be the *active nationality* while the other would be regarded as the *dormant nationality* (Oeter 2003: 55–77, esp. 77).

Alien Status

States not only exercise their prerogative in rule-making and enforcement over their native-born and naturalized citizens, but also expect anyone on their soil to be mindful of their laws. A non-citizen located on the territory of a state is an **alien**. Most countries are easy to enter for business, tourism, education, family visit, or other reasons. Presenting a passport and checking through customs may be all that is necessary. While the sojourn of most aliens is temporary, some countries will grant *permanent residency* status to an alien. However, a few countries can be very restrictive about who enters their jurisdiction as is the case for isolated, communist North Korea. Even countries with relatively open doors may put considerable emphasis on the country from which a visitor originates. Receiving states can require of aliens from at least some countries a *visa stamp* on a passport, a proof of prior approval for the visit. The United States screens aliens from Islamic countries, for instance, far more carefully than it does Canadians, who traditionally have been able to cross the US border by showing a driver's license as they embarked on a day of shopping. Since the 9/11 attack, Canadian–US border crossings are now more carefully scrutinized.

Any state can remove an alien or an entire group of aliens as an act of **expulsion** if the government of that state determines security, health, or public order justifies such a step. Sometimes expulsion is abused and turned into a serious human rights matter. Idi Amin, dictator of Uganda in the early 1970s, forced thousands of Indians out of Uganda with only 24 hours notice and gave permission for each person to take only one or two suitcases with them. The **deportation** of aliens can occur whether they are in the immigration process or have completed the naturalization process. Grounds for deportation often include lying about their past identity or activities, as well as involvement in criminal behavior in their adoptive country. If a state goes to war, its government can place aliens from an enemy state in **internment** (temporary detention) status and use their property for the duration of the war. The laws of war require humane conditions for internees but serious violations have sometimes occurred. During the Second World War, Japan's horrid treatment of European and American colonial administrators, captured in the Asian and the Pacific regions, was exceeded only by Japanese barbarity toward allied POWs.

The saga of John Demjanjuk, a Ukrainian immigrant with citizenship, is a particularly interesting one. A retired auto-factory worker from Cleveland, Ohio, in the United States, he was accused in 1977 of being the notorious guard "Ivan the Terrible" of the Treblinka concentration camp run by Nazis in the Second World War. Deportation proceeding were begun resulting in his loss of citizenship in 1981 for hiding his past on his citizenship application, and he then found himself on trial in Israel in 1986–8 resulting in a death sentence. When new evidence strongly questioned the Treblinka connection, he was freed, returned to the United States, and his citizenship restored in 1998. With further evidence suggesting he was a guard at another concentration camp, Demjanjuk once again lost his citizenship in 2002 and faced deportation, with a legal battle ensuing for years. In 2008–9, Germany pursued the extradition of the 88-year-old man accusing him of being an accessory to 29,000 murders.

Of course alien status is a two-sided coin. As well as scrutinizing foreigners for state reasons, governments of states also have important obligations to aliens. While the host state can expect aliens to obey local laws and keep state authorities informed of their whereabouts, international law requires that *state responsibility* be exercised to see to it that aliens receive full and fair treatment and that they experience no denial of justice in the national court system. State responsibility also calls for exercising **due diligence** to protect aliens from **delicts** (or wrongs), including violence by both government officials and private citizens. Punishment of wrong-doers and compensation for property losses is expected if wrongful acts or omissions of duty by officials are **imputable** (attributable) to the state. Efforts by the International Law Commission over several decades to codify this area of law have produced most recently the 2001 *Draft Articles on Responsibility of International Wrongful Acts*. States have proven sensitive about issues related to state responsibility and state succession and thus have not ratified the relevant treaties in large numbers.

The **Calvo Doctrine**, named after the nineteenth-century Argentine jurist and diplomat Carlos Calvo, attempted to place a restriction on state responsibility by claiming that damage done during revolutions to aliens, as well as citizens, is often beyond state control. Thus, aliens should not expect compensation over citizens. Latin American countries have been sympathetic to this doctrine, while the richer, industrialized states want their citizens and businesses compensated. This doctrine has never been accepted in general international law.

Another issue that has strained relations between Western democracies and Third World states is whether an *international standard of justice* can supplant the older rule of treating aliens and nationals on an equal footing. This problem occurs

---

Box 5.6 The *Ehime Maru* and State Responsibility

On February 9, 2001, the nuclear submarine *USS Greenville*, while practicing an emergency surfacing drill, struck and sank the *Ehime Maru* 9 miles from the Hawaiian Island of Oahu. This vessel was a Japanese fishing-training vessel 180 feet in length and with 830 tons displacement. The *Ehime Maru* went down in 10 minutes with 26 people rescued and 9 lost, including 4 teenagers.

Responsibility of the United States was undisputed. The case could have been settled by American Admiralty Law, since the wreck occurred in US territorial waters, or by rules of international law. International law would require an award for replacement costs only. The Japanese government, however, wanted the raising of the fishing vessel so the bodies could be recovered for proper burial, a very important practice in Japanese culture. By November 2002, an agreement was reached with $11.47 million given to replace the boat and for other associated costs. The United States additionally spent millions more to drag the vessel to a depth that allowed for the recovery of all the bodies save one, and then the United States made an official apology to Japan.

Source: The information presented here depends in part on Thomas J. Schoebaum, "The Ehime Maru Incident and the Law," http://www.asil.org/ > Publications > Insights > ASIL Insights > *2001*.

---

because of a large gap in views among states about such matters as a speedy and fair trial, appropriate punishments, and the quality of prison conditions. The Third World sees the international standards position as a way to insist that foreigners receive special treatment, but the West counters that justice anywhere should be applied according to a minimal standard derived from universal human rights.

More alien issues have probably arisen over foreign business enterprises, or MNCs, than individuals. Communist and Third World countries for decades tended to be unfriendly toward MNCs, which were viewed as exploiters. Their capitalist enterprises resulted in profit-making that was wealth sent back home instead of re-invested in Third World national economies. This interpretation caused foreign corporations to be viewed as candidates for **expropriation.** This is a seizure of foreign-held property and its transfer to the control of the government of the seizing state. The Western states, as the home-states of most MNCs, expected prompt compensation but payment was not always forthcoming. Investment agreements and arbitration have helped relieve this problem.

When business and other contract disputes have surfaced involving aliens, Latin American and other Third World countries have tried in the past to apply the **Calvo Clause** (not to be confused with the Calvo Doctrine), which requires aliens to rely on local remedies instead of turning to the diplomatic services of their countries. To a Third World country, the Calvo Clause puts home-grown and foreign businesses on an equal footing and therefore seems fair. To a foreign government, however, its right to intercede diplomatically on behalf of its citizens is improperly nullified by the Calvo Clause. Relief for this issue has not come through new developments in international law so much as it has sprung from a new attitude about foreign businesses. Third World states today are more receptive to MNC investments and technological know-how.

Sovereign Immunity and Act of State

Sovereign immunity is the exemption of one state's public acts and property from the court cases of another state. It is an act of comity. In a friendly way, one state keeps the business of another out of its courts. An American court might tell a party wishing to bring a case involving another government that the American court is *forum non conveniens*, or an inappropriate court for the case at hand. Until the mid-twentieth century, the immunity of another state was seen in nearly absolute terms, as indicated in the classic case of *Schooner Exchange v. McFadden*, decided by Chief Justice John Marshall's Supreme Court in 1812. This privately owned, US-flagged schooner was seized by the French Navy during its hostilities with Great Britain, ostensibly for blockade-running, and then armed as the warship *Balaou*. When this ship was forced into the port of Philadelphia during a storm, McFadden recognized his ship and sought relief in American courts. The Supreme Court, however, ruled that the *Balaou*, as a warship, fell under the sovereign immunity of France. McFadden did finally receive some compensation from France through diplomatic entreaties.[21]

After the Second World War, national governments were increasingly involved in a variety of businesses, such as banking, insurance, and transportation, leading more and more countries to adopt a policy of **restrictive immunity**. If state acts were of the traditional kind, *acta imperii*, involving such matters as security or diplomacy then absolute sovereign immunity was respected. If state activity, however, concerned commercial acts, *acta gestionis*, then the doctrine of restrictive immunity applied and a state's commercial business could wind-up in another state's courts. The United States moved in this direction with the 1952 "Tate letter," announcing it would follow several European states' practice of recognizing restrictive immunity where appropriate. (Jack Tate was the acting legal advisor to the US Justice Department.) Restrictive immunity was further secured as policy for the United States with the passing of the 1976 *Foreign Sovereign Immunities Act* (FSIA). This law placed the question of whether a state would receive immunity in a particular instance in the US courts instead of leaving it to the discretion of the executive branch.

Internationally, there is no uniformity among judges and countries as to when and how to apply sovereign immunity. The states of international society can be placed on a continuum ranging from absolute immunity to relative immunity allowing for various exceptions, or restrictive immunity. The Council of Europe attempted to harmonize practices of its membership with the 1972 *European Convention on State Immunity* and set a low bar by requiring only three ratifications for the treaty to go into effect. Eight of 47 states have so far ratified. The UN also made an effort at harmonization with its 2004 *Convention on Jurisdictional Immunities of States and Their Properties* that basically allows cases against states to go forward in court when commercial transactions are involved. With a mere six ratifications, this convention is well short of the necessary 30 ratifications needed to enter into force. Harmony among states over their immunity remains a distant goal.

Often mentioned in almost the same breath with state immunity is the **act of state** doctrine. Like state immunity, deference is given to the sovereignty of another state, but here emphasis is on *acts of a government on its own territory*. Carefully followed, this doctrine means decisions made by a government within its national context, that affects another state's citizens in a negative way, will be given full respect as a sovereign act. The act of state doctrine is by no means widely followed. Great Britain and the United States probably give this doctrine the most attention. As with sovereign immunity, the act of state doctrine found its limits. In the 1964 *Banco Nacional de Cuba v. Sabbatino* case, the US Supreme Court ruled that the new communist government of Cuba could keep profits from selling the sugar of an American company recently expropriated in Cuba. Congress was extremely upset with this decision and passed a law known as the Second Hickenlooper Amendment, named after an outraged Iowa Senator Bourke Hickenlooper. This law prohibited US courts from applying the act of state doctrine when the illegal expropriation of American private property is involved.[22]

Extraterritoriality

The monopoly over authority by a state on its own territory is clear-cut and fundamental to the state system, but states can sometimes exert their authority beyond their borders according to several jurisdictional principles. Together these principles are known as **extraterritorial jurisdiction**.

First is the *nationality principle* that allows the government of a country to prosecute one of its citizens or corporations for violating its law, even though the criminal act may have taken place in another country or in an international space. Several states have prosecuted their citizens for taking part in overseas sex tours exploiting children and fined corporations for bribing officials in other countries.

Second is *passive personality*, which involves a criminal act against a state's citizen while abroad. The assumption behind this principle is that the state's own legal personality is affected indirectly, or passively, when one of its citizens is the target of an illegal act. In the much-studied SS *Lotus* case, the PCIJ ruled that Turkey had jurisdiction to try a French officer for allowing his ship to collide with a Turkish ship on the high seas, killing some of the crew. The PCIJ reflected on passive personality, in consideration of the Turkish loss of life, but stopped short of applying this form of jurisdiction. The modern age of terrorism and the human rights movement, however, have breathed new life in the relevance of the passive personality principle. With extensive global patterns of travel on the part of millions of people, any country's

Box 5.7 The S.S. *Lotus* Case

September 7, 1927

On August 2, 1926, the French-flagged SS *Lotus* wrecked with the Turkish coal-carrier *Boz-Kourt*, causing the latter to sink with a loss of eight lives. The *Lotus* picked up the survivors and the next day docked in Constantinople. The Turkish government began prosecution against both Lt Demons, the deck officer of the *Lotus* and the Turkish captain of the *Boz-Kourt*, finding them both culpable. A Turkish court sentenced Demons to 80 days confinement and a 22-pound fine, with the Turkish captain receiving a slightly more severe punishment.

France objected and demanded an indemnity of 6,000 Turkish pounds for what the French government regarded as the wrongful arrest and conviction of Lt Demons. However, the PCIJ ruled in favor of Turkey on the grounds that the Turkish vessel assimilates to Turkish territory allowing the application of Turkish criminal law.

This precedent was overturned later by the 1958 Convention on the High Seas and the 1982 LOS Convention. If a similar incident occurred today, jurisdiction would belong to the French under the nationality principle based on the nationality of Lt Demons and that of the *S.S. Lotus*. This position is exactly the one the French government took in 1927. The Permanent Court of International Justice (PCIJ) merely reflected on the passive personality principle where Turkish loss of life was concerned, but did not grant jurisdiction to Turkey on this basis.

Source: This case can be read in Manley O. Hudson (ed.), *World Court Reports*, vol. II, 1927–32 (Dobbs Ferry, NY: Oceana Publications, 1969).

citizens could randomly or deliberately become the victims of terrorist attack anywhere or political repression in many countries.

The third and fourth principles of extraterritorial jurisdiction involve the *effects* and *protective* principles. Some legal writers collapse the two together, but that is not the choice here. Both involve wrongful acts that begin outside a country but, nonetheless, impact that country in some way. The effects principle applies to non-security issues such as environmental damage that begins in one country but affects another as happened in the *Trail Smelter* case between Canada and the United States, when the territory of the United States was harmed environmentally by a smelting process in Canada. When security threats arise outside a country, the perpetrators, whether they are citizens of the threatened country or foreigners, may find themselves sought under the protective principle. Acts to overthrow the government, commit espionage, carry on smuggling, and print counterfeit currency often begin beyond the borders of a state and thus bring to bear this jurisdictional principle.

The final extraterritorial principle is *universal jurisdiction*. This jurisdiction covers international crimes so heinous that the perpetrators are considered **humani generi hostis,** or the enemy of all humankind as in the case of pirates. Any state capturing such an individual can try that person regardless of where the crime was committed, the nationality of the victim(s), or the nationality of the accused. Each crime within this jurisdiction has its own special mix of history, precedents, customary and treaty law, and degree of support by states. Fortunately, a panel of over 20 scholars, working for a year at Princeton University, produced the first systematic effort to bring order to this rather disjointed area of international law. Their important contribution was published as the *Princeton Principles on Universal Jurisdiction* in 2001 (Macedo 2001).[23]

These scholars included the following international crimes as falling under universal jurisdiction: piracy, slavery and slave trafficking, war crimes, crimes against humanity, genocide, and torture. Terrorism was not on this list, but a spate of anti-terrorist treaties lean terrorism toward universal jurisdiction. In addition to identifying appropriate crimes, the Princeton panel offered 14 *operating principles* to guide enforcement. Chief among these are that leaders are not immune from prosecution, no statute of limitations or amnesty can apply, and, as a major operating principle, these crimes require a state to **aut judicare aut dedere** (either try or extradite) (Macedo 2001: 28–46).

Extradition

Governments naturally prefer law and order within their territories, but cannot always enforce their laws without the help of other states. With growing frequency, governments must rely on an international process of reciprocal cooperation known as **extradition,** by which one state requests a wanted person from another state. At one time, states cooperated in returning those wanted as an act of comity but, by the late nineteenth century, extradition more and more came under the control of bilateral treaties. When states make extradition requests, it may be that one of the extraterritoriality jurisdictions described earlier is at stake. More likely, laws at home are broken involving such common crimes as murder, bank fraud, or prison escape, but the wanted person has relocated to another country.

Today, hundreds of bilateral extradition treaties are in place and typically share several elements: (1) the crime must be couched in law; (2) sufficient evidence to suggest a trial can go forward must be available; (3) double criminality must exist, meaning the sending and receiving states recognize the same crime; and (4) the specialty rule applies requiring that the wanted person cannot be extradited on one charge but then tried on another.[24] Requests for extradition are usually sent to a foreign ministry (or US State Department), which asks an attorney-general to seek a warrant from a judge. The judge, in turn, then holds a hearing to look at the evidence against the accused. Some states are willing to hold a wanted person in detention for a specified time, often 30 days, so the requesting state has time to accumulate *prima facie* evidence.

In an age of global patterns of rapid travel, the movement of wanted persons can be difficult to trace as they shift from one national jurisdiction to another. Since all states must sooner or later experience a need for extradition, it is surprising that they rely so much on bilateral treaties rather than create a global convention for extradition. The UN General Assembly in 1990 did adopt the *Model Treaty on Extradition* to promote commonality among bilateral treaties and to give more priority to international crimes.

At least several regional extradition treaties have been ratified, including, among others, the 1933 *Montevideo Convention on Extradition* for Latin America and the 1957 *European Convention on Extradition*.

What should be an orderly legal process serving justice is not without problems, however. One of the first issues concerned the meaning of a **political offense.** In modern history, countries have been disinclined to extradite on this basis, but just what is a political offense? Political acts have traditionally been associated with a rebellion to take power from the existing government. Failed rebellions often put rebels in flight to other countries and leads to governments seeking their return for punishment. For most states, the question of extradition turns on the exact methods of the rebels. Late nineteenth-century European practice still provides guidance. Political offense status was accorded to those who attacked police and military personnel and was not an extraditable offense, but indiscriminate bombings that randomly took civilian lives were terrorist acts and considered to be extraditable offenses. After assassination attempts on the life of Napoleon III of France in 1855 and 1858, European extradition treaties treated attacks on heads of state and their families as criminal, rather than political, and thereby extraditable.

Another issue is whether deportation of an alien should be allowed to circumvent extradition. Expelling aliens is legal and a fairly common practice that can place them in the hands of a state wishing to prosecute them for an earlier crime. Reasons for deportation can involve crimes committed in the state of residence or concealing an unsavory past upon application to reside in a new country. If an alien does achieve citizenship through a naturalization process, this citizenship can be revoked if that person has covered up something serious in their past, such as war crimes or murder.

The abduction of wanted persons across borders has been an additional issue, and one that sometimes causes prickly relations among states. Only the state where an individual is located can legitimately take that person into custody. For another state to have agents seize a person and carry him or her across a border is a serious violation of customary international law. Some legal authorities speak of such acts as violation of *international due process*. Yet a number of states have ignored extradition treaties in preference for abduction. Courts of the United States and of some other countries have accepted *male captus bene detentus* (bad capture is still good detention.)

The United States has a history of practicing such abductions, the best known case involving the 1990 abduction from Mexico of Dr Alvárez-Machaín, wanted for involvement in the 1985 torture and slaying of an American drug agent. Abduction by the United States has been an element of "extraordinary rendition," the highly questionable practice of sending individuals suspected of terrorism to countries known to practice torture. In 2005, an Italian judge issued arrest warrants for 13 US CIA agents for allegedly kidnapping Hassan Nasr in Italy and sending him to Egypt for questioning. The world's most famous case of abduction occurred many years earlier when Adolf Eichmann, a principal agent in Nazi Germany's campaign to eradicate the Jewish people of Europe in the early 1940s, was abducted by Israeli agents from Argentina in 1960 and tried in Israel in 1961. He was hanged there in 1962 for humanitarian crimes, in particular, for genocide waged against Jews.

The use of the death penalty is an issue that has also complicated extradition. Within the US federal system, 37 component states and the national government, for some crimes such as terrorism, can apply the death penalty. The state of New Jersey ended its death penalty in early 2009. Most European states, plus Canada and Mexico, will not extradite unless the requesting government takes the death penalty off the table.

One of the most interesting recent developments in extradition has been a flurry of efforts to extradite military and political leaders by applying universal jurisdiction. Not since the worldwide effort to bring Nazis to justice after the Second World War has there been an international campaign like this in the name of justice. It seems to have started when Spanish Judge Baltazar Garson sent an extradition warrant to Great Britain in 1999 for General Augusto Pinochet of Chile, who was in Great Britain for medical treatment. Other states have sought similar extraditions. The two criminal tribunals for Yugoslavia and Rwanda and the ICC also seek extraditions for persons charged with humanitarian and war crimes.

Chapter Summary

- Numerous jurisdictions exist permitting states to exercise authority over various spaces and persons.
- States exercise strong control over their air space, landed territory, and various seaward jurisdictions such as the 12-mile territorial sea along their coasts.
- Outer space, the high seas, and the polar regions, especially Antarctica, are governed under treaty arrangements and are considered "common heritages of humankind."
- States acknowledge their citizens as having nationality and issue passports recognizing this status for international travel purposes; some states reluctantly accept dual nationality.
- Many states exercise extraterritorial (outside their territory) jurisdiction mainly for state security reasons and to protect their citizens while they are located outside a state's territory.
- States generally respect the sovereign acts of other states but, when another state government is involved in a business enterprise, states may apply a qualified version of state immunity.
- States commonly have extradition treaties with other states to return a criminal suspect into the custody of the aggrieved state; the use of capital punishment has complicated the extradition process especially for the United States.

Discussion Questions

1   Why do states strongly assert claims to islands, reefs, and continental shelves?
2   What are the jurisdictions coastal states possess that extend seaward from the baseline of a state?
3   Why do many ships fly "flags of convenience" on cargo vessels?
4   Why are countries so sensitive about their air space? Was China justified in asserting a fifty-mile Air Defense Zone in 2001 against a US reconnaissance aircraft?
5   All three can remove a person from a state, but what are the differences among extradition, deportation, and expulsion?

Useful Weblinks

http://www.un.org/Depts/los/index.html
UN's web page for "Oceans and Law of the Sea." Links are directly accessible for the LOS Convention, the compromise on the seabed mining regime, the Seabed Mining Authority, reports of the Secretary-General on ocean matters, the settlement of disputes, and many other valuable links.

http://www.oosa.unvienna.org/oosa/en/COPUOS/copuos.html
Web page of the UN Committee on the Peaceful Uses of Outer Space. Offers many links including those to a Register of Space Objects, Space Activities of Member States, and Space Activities of the UN System.

http://www.itu.int/home/
Home page of the International Telecommunications Union with links to ITU publications, ITU meetings and conferences, the ITU and Internet Governance, as well as many other links

http://www.smartraveller.gov.au/tips/dualnat.html
http://travel.state.gov/travel/cis_pa_tw/cis/cis_1753.html
These websites on dual nationality provide useful information on defining dual nationality, choice of passports, liability for military service, consular assistance, child abduction, renunciation of a citizenship, and much else.

http://www.globalpolicy.org/intljustice/universal/univindex.html
A web page devoted to recent developments on the role of universal jurisdiction. Links exist to an archive of articles and direct links are available for the current year and two-years past.

http://www.geocities.com/cdelegas/PIRACYWEBSITE_legal.html
For a report about international efforts to control piracy go to this website of the International Chamber of Commerce.

Further Reading

Caminos, Hugo (ed.) (2001) *Law of the Sea*. Burlington, VT: Ashgate.

Fidler, David (1999) *International Law and Infectious Diseases*. New York: Oxford University Press.

Franda, Marcus (2002) *Launching Into Cyberspace: Internet Development and Politics in Five World Regions*. Boulder, CO: Lynne Rienner.

Goldsmith, Jack and Wu, Tim (2008) *Who Controls the Internet? Illusions of a Borderless World*. New York: Oxford University Press.

Guilfoyle, Douglas (2009) *Shipping Interdiction and the Law of the Sea*. New York: Cambridge University Press.

Lehr, Peter (2006) *Piracy in the Age of Global Terrorism*. New York: Routledge.

Lyall, Francis and Larsen, Paul B. (2009) *Space Law: A Treatise*. Burlington, VT: Ashgate.

Reisman, W. Michael (1999) *Jurisdiction in International Law*. Brookfield, VT: Ashgate/Dartmouth.

Tanaka, Yoshifumi (2009) *A Dual Approach to Ocean Governance: The Cases of Zonal and Integrated Management in International Law of the Sea*. Burlington, VT: Ashgate.

Viikari, Lotta (2008) *The Environmental Element in Space Law: Assessing the Present and Charting the Future*. Boston, MA: Martinus Nijhoff.

Warner, Robert (2009) *Protecting the Oceans Beyond National Jurisdiction: Strengthening the International Law Framework*. Boston, MA: Martinus Nijhoff.

Notes

1　Percentages cited in "Peace in Our Time," *Foreign Policy* (November/December 2002), 19.

2　http://www.icj-cij.org/ > cases > Contentious Cases ordered by countries involved > Malaysia.

3　For example, see Oxman 1997: 309–335. The LOS can be read at http:///www.un.org/law/ > Law of the Sea.

4　The Anglo-Norwegian case is found at http://www.icj-cij.org/ > cases > Contentious Cases ordered by countries involved > Norway.

5　*The Law of the Sea: Archipelagic States Legislative History of Part IV of the UN Convention of the Law of the Sea* (New York: United Nations, 1990).

6　See the website of the International Civil Aviation Organization at http://www.icao.org/ > About > Chicago Convention.

7　This paragraph draws on Frederic L. Kirgis, "United States Reconnaissance Aircraft Collision with Chinese Jet," found at http://www.asil.org/ > Publication > Insights > ASIL Insights > 2001.

8　These three conventions are on the UN's anti-terrorist list of treaties at http://untreaty.un.org/English/Terrorism.asp.

9　The latter two conventions can be read at http://Treaties.un.org/Pages/Participation Status/aspx ; a site for outer space treaties in general is the UN Office of Outer Space Affairs at http://www.oosa.unvienna.org/ > space law.

10　Leonard Davis, "Tossed in Space," *Foreign Policy* (May/June 2003), pp. 68–69; also see http://space.com/spacewatch/space_junk.html.

11　A good overview of the Internet is by Franda 2001.

12   *Dow Jones & Company, Inc. v. Gutnick* HCA 56 (December 10, 2002). This decision can be read about at http://www.rogerclarkecom/II/Gutnick.html. The transcript of case proceedings is at http://www.auslii.edu.au/au/other/hca/transcripts/2002/M3/2.html.

13   This treaty can be read at http://www.ecoearth.org/article/Antarctic_Treaty_System > Treaty of Antarctic.

14   Other treaties and agreements about Antarctica can be found at the site provided in note 13, and at http://www.polarlaw.org/Treaty.html.

15   Rothwell 1996; Elferink and Rothwell 2001); and Bobo, "Antarctic Treaty Papers: A Brief History of the Antarctic Treaty System," pp. 1–4 at http://www.polarlaw.org/History.html.

16   A good overview on cooperation in the Arctic Region is Verhaag: 555–79.

17   The 1957 Convention can be read at http://treaties.un.org/Pages/Treaties.aspx > Chapter XVI.

18   Quoted from Martin and Aleinikoff 2002: 80.

19   Koslowski 2003: 158; many interesting points about identity are made in Franck 1996: 359–83.

20   Martin and Aleinikoff 2002: 80–1. The US "Oath of Allegiance" for new citizens can be read at http://uscis.gov/graphics/services/natz/oath.html.

21   The case Schooner Exchange is discussed in the article, "A Primer on Foreign Sovereign Immunity" at http://www.hg.org/articles/article_223.html; and a useful compendium on state immunity on the UK and the United States, as well as several other countries, is Dickinson, Lindsay, and Loonam: 2004.

22   The National Bank of Cuba case can be explored at http://supreme.justia.com/us/376/398/case.html.

23   Stephen Macedo, *The Princeton Principles* 2001. The checkered history of universal jurisdictional crimes is aptly described by Bassiouni 2004: 39–63. A good review of international crimes and enforcement is John F. Murphy, "International Crimes," in Joyner 1997: 362–81; and see Cassese 2003.

24   Pyle 2001: 323–325; also, a brief summary of American extradition policy can be found in this work.

Part II

Making the World Safer

The principles and rules of diplomatic privileges and immunities are not – and this cannot be overstressed – the invention or device of one group of nations, of one continent or one circle of culture, but have been established for centuries and are shared by nations of all races and all civilizations. (Judge Manfred Lachs of the ICJ)

Diplomacy is an essentially political activity and, well resourced and skillful, a major ingredient of power. (G. R. Berridge)

6

Diplomacy in Pursuit of Peace

Contents

Diplomacy offers an opportunity to avoid conflict or at least minimize it. The value of diplomacy rests on its cost-effectiveness by defusing situations before they can grow into trade disruptions or outbreaks of war. If international politics consisted of total conflict or complete cooperation, diplomacy would be ineffective or unnecessary. Since the reality of the world operates mostly in the middle, diplomacy has evolved into a major tool of states' foreign policies. More than any other form of politics, diplomacy is the art of the possible and is practiced according to fairly well-known rules.

Diplomacy does more than contain conflicts between countries; it also contributes to a burgeoning international society by spreading values and building consensus over global issues and the policies to deal with them. The peace that might come from diplomacy is no longer seen by today's international society as merely the absence of war but is conceptualized as *positive peace*: an overarching value that encompasses democracy, human rights, economic and social development, environmental improvements, and a general sense of justice shared by humankind.

Diplomacy, at its best, especially at the forum of the UN, reflects a towering ambition to do good deeds for the world.

This chapter begins with a brief history of diplomacy and continues with sections on international rules regarding diplomatic and consular relations. Then, the formal functions of diplomats and the real-world conditions they encounter are covered. Finally, there is a section on diplomatic law concerning IGOs, with special attention on the UN.

A Brief History of Diplomacy

Diplomacy is a process of communication and negotiation among official representatives of approximately 200 states and about 450 IGOs for the purposes of maximizing cooperation and minimizing conflict. Diplomacy has a long and interesting history. Its beginnings probably were in prehistoric times when cave dwellers discovered they could bargain over hunting grounds and other issues rather than fight. Every known civilization, including the Chinese, Indian, and Persian societies, has conducted a version of diplomacy. Today's diplomacy is traceable to ancient Greece and Rome, but it is mainly based on modern European experience that influenced the rest of the world with its diplomatic rules and practices during the colonization era (Watson 1992a: 160; White 2002: 48–51, 54–5, 72, 161–5, 177, 297–8). By the late eighteenth century, the English government began referring to its envoys sent to other countries as diplomats (Nicolson 1964: 10–12).

The Romans first placed diplomacy under law using their *jus gentium* to prescribe rules for dealing with tribes on the periphery of their empire, but the form of diplomacy recognizable today had its start within the Italian city-state system. These cities had begun sending professional diplomats to one another by the fourteenth century, and a permanent mission, or **embassy**, could be found in some Italian cities in the fifteenth century. After the 1648 Peace of Westphalia, which left at least a dozen independent states in place and in need of a way to communicate with one another, other European capitals soon followed the Italian precedents. At the important Congress of Vienna in 1815, marking the end of the Napoleonic Age and a clear return to independent states governed by kings, the ranks and privileges of diplomats were established and further refined three years later at the Conference of Aix-la-Chappelle (Muldroon 1999: 1–5; Aviel 1999: 8–14).

The culmination of permanent embassies, proper diplomatic procedures, and the development of professionalism within the diplomatic corps crystallized into the so-called "French system of diplomacy" in the early nineteenth century, so-named because French had come to replace Latin as the language of diplomatic intercourse (Berridge 2005: 108–15). By the Versailles Conference in 1919, following the First World War, English had come to rival French in diplomacy and is today's *lingua franca*, not only in diplomacy but also in business and academic circles. The ascendancy of English, however, does not preclude multiple language translations at the UN, at the fora of other IGOs, and at various international conferences.

In time, European influences in international law would spread to other parts of the world. In the seventeenth and eighteenth centuries, European states sent envoys to far-flung kingdoms and empires in search of trade opportunities, but these diplomatic contacts frequently led to the colonial subjugation of peoples on other continents. The result was mostly hierarchical and administrative communications instead of diplomatic exchanges among legal equals. Only with the breakup of colonial empires in the Americas in the eighteenth and nineteenth centuries, and in Africa and Asia after the Second World War, were the non-European areas able to participate in diplomacy. The 50 states at the UN Conference in San Francisco in 1945 dramatically increased to an international society of nearly 180 states before the end of the Cold War. The dissolution of European communism, beginning in 1989, raised the total number of states to about 200, requiring a parallel increase in embassies and diplomatic personnel.

James P. Muldroon, Jr. usefully distinguishes between an "old diplomacy" that reached its zenith in the early nineteenth century and then transitioned to a "new diplomacy" (1999: 5–7). Old diplomacy was the French system emphasizing mostly *bilateral* relations handled by ambassadors who often had more in common with diplomats from other countries than with the general population of their own state. Diplomats serving in this period were almost by default invested with **plenipotentiary powers**, meaning their kings had to give them wide latitude for decisions and actions due to the poor communication and transportation of their era.

The shift to new diplomacy had its beginnings in the two dozen *multilateral* conferences of the nineteenth century that brought most of the European states to the same table and encouraged a budding sense of shared international society. The development of steam locomotives, steamships, and telegraph lines connecting European capitals increasingly made conference diplomacy more feasible. Gradually multilateral diplomacy included not only conferences but expanded into full-time IGOs created by states to manage their common interests. The river commissions for the Danube and Rhine Rivers, the 1865 International Telegraphic Union, and the 1874 Universal Postal Union are the best known examples. These IGOs are the forerunners to the more complex twentieth century League of Nations and its successor, the United Nations, with each in its turn serving as the "meeting hall" of the world.

After the Second World War, the practice of diplomacy came to involve several well-known diplomatic strategies. These strategies are not prescribed by international law but are not incompatible with it either. **Summit diplomacy** is a face-to-face meeting of leaders for direct negotiations, facilitated by the age of jet aircraft. Summit meetings offer the opportunity for major breakthroughs regarding stubborn problems, but they can also raise grand expectations on the part of watchful publics which may have to deal with sharp disappointment on occasion (Dunn 1996: 3–22). **Shuttle diplomacy** is fairly new and also depends on rapid travel by air. This diplomacy involves travel back and forth between or among disputing states by an important envoy such as a US Secretary of State. This diplomacy may or may not bring the parties closer to terms, but it will certainly wear out the envoy. In both summit and shuttle diplomacy, communications take place above the heads of ambassadors and, thus, fail to utilize their expertise and skill that might be better suited for handling complex issues.

Preventive diplomacy derives from UN experience and aims at stopping an escalating situation from reaching a violent climax. UN Secretary-General Dag Hammarskjöld initiated this strategy early in the Cold War to prevent a nuclear holocaust between the superpowers. The trick is to interrupt the momentum toward conflict early enough. As Bruce W. Jentleson puts the matter, "preventive diplomacy deals with today's problems before they become tomorrow's crises" (Jentleson 2000: 3; Zartman 2001: 1–18; Boutros-Gali 1995). If preventive diplomacy fails, a country or the UN Security Council can ramp up to **coercive diplomacy**, a mix of diplomacy and force aimed at persuading a state, perceived as aggressive, to halt further action or even to back down. Frederick the Great of Prussia reputedly once said, "Diplomacy without armaments is like music without instruments." This diplomacy requires considerable

---

Box 6.1 The Roman Catholic Church

The Roman Catholic Church exists primarily to nourish one of the world's great religions but the Church also has legal personality as a state. The Papal state was once a large district in central Italy, but its territory was incorporated by Italy in 1870. The Papal state reappeared in 1929 as the Vatican or Vatican City, set aside within Rome, as a tiny enclave of 109 acres (44 hectares). Occasionally the Papal state is referred to as the Holy See, which is actually the chancellery or the administrative offices of the Vatican.

The Papal state territory of course contains St Peter's Cathedral and the Sistine Chapel but also a library, an art museum, a post office, and the Vatican Bank. Its army, since medieval times, is the Swiss Guard costumed in medieval uniforms, and the Vatican is served in foreign relations by papal (or apostolic) nuncios (ambassadors) who operate the nunciatures (embassies) in the countries recognizing the Vatican. At times, the Church has served as a mediator in disputes, as it did between Argentina and Chile in their conflict over the possession of the Beagle Channel and Islands, finally bringing this conflict to a conclusion in 1984.

The Vatican can enter into agreements known as *concordats* with states when Catholic matters are at stake and has ratified a few humanitarian conventions. The Church holds observer status at the UN and also sends representatives to the Council of Europe, the OAS, and the EU, among others, and to a handful of NGOs.

The Church, as of 2007, has not recognized the rising power of China because this state will not clear the way for the Vatican to freely appoint bishops without China's approval

---

Source: See, "Vatican Diplomacy," at http://www.catholic-pages.com/vatican/diplomacy.asp.

skill, for otherwise serious miscalculations can occur (e.g. Lawen, Carig, & George 1995; Nathan 2002; Alterman 2003: 274–303). A successful example is President John F. Kennedy's handling of the 1962 Cuban Missile Crisis. He "quarantined" Cuba with the US Navy and offered Premier Nikita Khrushchev of the Soviet Union a face-saving arrangement that called for the United States to remove its missiles from Turkey as the Soviet Union withdrew theirs from Cuba (George 1991: 19–23, 31–71).

A final strategy associated with today's diplomacy is **track-two diplomacy**, which involves *private parties* addressing the issues between disputing parties. The private parties can be scholars, journalists, or representatives of advocacy groups who hope they can shed new light on the issues and recommend new ways to solve them. Private parties have met on behalf of the United States and North Korea, Israel and the Palestinians, and the Catholics and Protestants of Northern Ireland, among other disputants. Thousands of NGOs in the human rights, environmental, and disarmament fields crowd international conferences and the fora of the UN, the EU, and other IGOs trying to persuade IGO leaders to change or intensify their policy agendas.[1]

There are several non-state actors that do take part in formal diplomacy, however. The Roman Catholic Church has for centuries assisted states with their relations and today maintains mutual recognition and exchanges representatives with over 160 states. The Knights of Malta, a charitable group that offers aid to the sick and wounded of war, maintains diplomatic relationships with more than 90 states, has permanent observer status at the UN, and sends representatives to several organizations including the Council of Europe, and the International Committee of the Red Cross with its special humanitarian role recognized in the 1949 Geneva Conventions.

The Rules of Diplomacy for States

After several hundred years of European development of customary diplomatic law, the growing society of states embraced two conventions that transformed these customs into written law and produced one of the better defined areas of international law. These conventions are the 1961 *Vienna Convention on Diplomatic Relations* (Diplomatic Convention) and the 1963 *Vienna Convention on Consular Relations* (Consular Convention), both well received by the large majority of states. *Codification* from unwritten to written law went smoothly with *progressive development*, or added changes, amounting only to some efforts at reducing immunity for private acts and lower ranks of diplomats.[2]

Putting the rules of diplomacy into the written law of conventions was sought in the early 1960s because of a rise in violence against diplomats and due to the growing number of states. The older states feared that the newer states leaving colonialism might mount a challenge to the rules of diplomacy if they were left in the fluid state of customary law. The acceptance of embassies, ambassadors, and diplomatic law, all developed in Europe, by new countries in Africa and Asia is one of the clearest indications that a worldwide international society is in place (Bull 1995: 269).

The 1961 Diplomatic Convention provides generous **privileges and immunities** so diplomats and embassies can efficiently carry on their necessary functions to serve their respective states and the general good of international society. The privileges and immunities are not "to benefit individuals." The preamble of the Diplomatic Convention makes this point, and Article 41, moreover, makes clear that persons enjoying such privileges and immunities have a duty to respect the laws and regulations of the states where diplomats are in residence.

The enjoyment of privileges and immunities means that diplomats are to be free of any threat or harm and they are not to be arrested or incarcerated. Their residences, baggage, and correspondence are inviolable, and diplomats are free of most taxes. The staffs and families of diplomats also enjoy most of the same privileges and immunities. Even in cases of armed conflict, the host state has to help diplomats and their families to leave the country if they so desire. After the Japanese attacked Pearl Harbor in 1941, in the midst of shock and great anger, the American government correctly assisted the departure of Japanese diplomats from Washington, DC.

The Diplomatic Convention's Article 14 recognizes three classes of diplomats who can serve as heads of a diplomatic mission. These are ambassadors, ministers, and *charges d'affaires*. Almost always the highest rank of **ambassador** is sent by one state to another in modern times as head of mission and as the agent in charge of a country's foreign affairs in the host state. The exchange of ambassadors between two countries accomplishes their formal recognition of each other. A newly appointed ambassador presents his or her **letter of credence**, or credentials, to the head of state of the host government, usually a president or a constitutional monarch. The host is under no obligation under Article 4 to accept the new ambassador or to explain a refusal, but usually an **agrément,** or formal acceptance, is issued to accredit the ambassador in the host's capital.

The rank of **minister** can do everything that an ambassador can do but is a lower rank. This rank has almost passed into a by-gone age. Sending a minister today would be like sending a colonel to negotiate with generals. The United States used this rank commonly in the nineteenth century but, with growing power and influence, wanted to symbolize its status as a front-rank state by sending ambassadors. A *chargé d'affaires* usually runs much of the day-to-day business of an embassy and can stand in for the ambassador on an interim basis when the ambassador is absent. The foreign minister of a country, or the Secretary of State in the case of the United States, appoints the *chargé d'affaires* who is accredited to the foreign minister of the host state. Another important official assigned to an embassy is the *attaché*, who works under the direction of the ambassador but represents a government department other than the foreign ministry. Depending on the interests of the sending state, military, cultural, agricultural, immigration, and tourism *attachés* may be assigned to a diplomatic mission.

Article 9 of the Diplomatic Convention places an interesting power in the hands of the receiving state. Regardless of the role or rank of a diplomat, the host government may, without explanation and at any time, declare that diplomat *persona non grata*, or unwanted person, forcing the sending country to recall its diplomat. Otherwise, a diplomat may assume that he or she is *persona grata*, or acceptable. The principal reasons why the receiving state might declare a diplomat *persona non grata* are personal misconduct, espionage, and retaliation by a state that has had one of its own diplomats found unacceptable.[3] During the Cold War, it was a common occurrence for diplomats to be declared *persona non grata*.

Collectively, the ambassadors of various countries gathered in a capital city are known as the **diplomatic corps.** These diplomats usually view themselves as a micro-community sharing common interests. To promote the comity of this community, **protocol** is used. Protocol in this context refers to established practices and courtesies that allow diplomats to focus on the substance of negotiation; otherwise, diplomats would haggle endlessly over their status and the prestige of their state, trying to maximize their influence with the host state. Protocol is governed more by custom than formal law, but the 1815 Congress of Vienna did adopt a principle of seniority based on the dates of accreditation of ambassadors in a given capital. From that time on, seniority would control position on formal occasions such as dinners or reception lines. Many capitals employ a chief of protocol officer to see that proper procedures are followed. If problems do arise within the diplomatic corps, the **dean** (known in French as *doyen*), the ambassador with the longest tenure in a capital, can often reconcile disputes (Thayer 1959). An exception to the seniority rule occurs in predominately Catholic countries where the *papal nuncio* (or ambassador) of the Vatican is normally accorded the status of dean of diplomats (Rana 2004: 52–3).

Another important role in the field of diplomacy is that of the **diplomatic courier**, a role given appreciable attention in the Diplomatic Convention. Couriers carry important documents from their home state to a foreign diplomatic mission or from one embassy to another. Their person is inviolable, meaning they cannot be detained or arrested. The documents they carry will be in a **diplomatic bag** (also called a diplomatic pouch). Couriers can also escort large cargoes, a radio transmitter for instance, which will be under diplomatic seal. One of the most controversial issues in diplomacy concerns the diplomatic bag. They have been misused for smuggling weapons, drugs, counterfeit money, and even kidnapped and drugged persons. Since the 1970s, the International Law Commission has been studying proposals for rectifying abuses of the diplomatic bag, and their efforts may someday lead to an optional protocol to the Diplomatic Convention with new rules on how to handle the diplomatic bag.[4]

In addition to the immunities of diplomats, protection of the physical properties of a diplomatic mission is also covered in the Diplomatic Convention. Most countries house their diplomatic missions in an embassy following the Italian practice. The grounds around embassies are referred to as the **premises** and, in some cases, may contain, besides embassy offices, living quarters, a parking garage, and even a swimming pool. Typically, embassies of many countries cluster together in one part of the capital city, often called the "diplomatic quarter," or along an avenue known as "embassy row." The Diplomatic Convention states forthrightly that premises are inviolable and that the agents of the host country may not enter without permission. And it gives special protection to the archives and documents of the embassy when they are being transported. Moreover, the private residence and correspondence of a diplomat are to be safeguarded equal to the embassy premises. Finally, Diplomatic Convention calls for the host state to respect another state's embassy and its archives even if diplomatic relations are severed due to armed conflict, or for some other reason, and to allow the sending state to arrange for a third state to take charge of its embassy.

While most states comply assiduously with these well-established diplomatic rules, violations still happen and on occasion they can be violent. During the Chinese "Cultural Revolution" of the late 1960s, several Western embassies in Beijing were ransacked by radical students. Perhaps the most egregious violation to an embassy in history is the seizure of the US embassy in Tehran, Iran in 1979 by a student militia. Although African–Americans and women were released, this seizure resulted in the rest of the embassy personnel being held as hostages for 444 days. Other violations may not involve violence but are invasive, surreptitious acts. In the Cold War, the Soviet Union and the United States frequently complained about the other side "bugging" their embassies and embassy cars with listening devices. Discovering a "bug infestation" in the unfinished new American embassy in Moscow in 1985, the United States halted construction and started over with a completely new building in 1992.

Two Special Issues concerning Embassies

Two issues in the field of diplomatic law have caused considerable confusion, especially on the part of the general public. The first involves a questionable exercise of *extraterritoriality*, which is the exercise of a state's sovereign authority outside its boundaries. This exercise of authority could conceivably occur not only in international spaces but possibly on the territory of another state. Many people wrongly assume that an embassy and its premises are actually small pieces of national territory of Brazil, France, or the United States, or whatever country has its flag over the embassy. If extraterritorial authority was ever exercised at embassies in the past, it is definitely an anachronism today. Any attempt by one state to push for extraterritorial authority on another's territory, even inside an embassy, will smack of imperialism. Embassies and diplomats have full immunity for the sake of diplomatic business, but diplomats are not free to do anything they wish within their premises. They may not commit murder, practice slavery, or to do anything else that would be in conflict with the host's laws.

In one exceptional case, an American *chargé d'affaires* killed another American diplomat in Equatorial Guinea in 1973, but the US government was allowed to try the *chargé d'affaires* in a US federal court. The United States wanted jurisdiction and apparently the government of Equatorial Guinea saw no impact on its interest, by not trying to enforce its homicide laws (Blakesley, Firmage, Scott, & Williams 2001: 794–5). In recent years, some Western states have taken a more circumspect view of immunity for embassies if private activity is at stake. Embassies have been taken to court if they do not pay their bills to a local merchant, meaning restrictive sovereign immunity is being used. If an embassy car not on official business is guilty of causing a traffic accident, the matter might be treated as an ordinary misdemeanor. Immunity for private activities is being narrowed but practice in this area is not yet sufficiently uniform and consistent as to create a new rule.

The other issue is the controversial practice of *diplomatic asylum*. Many countries allow *territorial asylum*, accepting refugees who wish to escape from an oppressive homeland. Letting individuals enter diplomatic posts to evade local authorities, however, is a very different situation. Granting diplomatic asylum can lead to serious clashes with the host government, undermining the essential reason for an embassy to exist in the first place, which is to foster good relations between states. Countries in general do not recognize diplomatic asylum as a part of the law on diplomacy, but sometimes a state will make an exception. The views on the subject are so mixed and uneven that the 1961 Vienna Conference did not try to address diplomatic asylum, and it remains unrecognized as worldwide law (Denza 1998: 357).

When countries make exceptions it is usually on humanitarian grounds, especially if a person is threatened by mob violence.[5] During the French Revolution of 1789, the US embassy in Paris became overcrowded with French noblemen fleeing angry peasants and the guillotine. Other kinds of exceptions can occur as well. In a well-known case of asylum in US experience, Cardinal Josef Mindszenty, during the 1956 Hungarian Revolution, sought refuge in the US embassy in Budapest after serving eight years in a communist prison. The revolution set him free but, once the communist regime returned to power, he had to live in the embassy for 15 years before the Hungarian government would allow him safe passage out of the country (Riveles 1989: 157).

Only in Latin America is diplomatic asylum recognized. The practice of allowing asylum in embassies in this region is one of the foremost examples of regional international law. This law derives from the 1928 *Havana Convention on Asylum*, the 1933 *Montevideo Convention on Political Asylum*, and the 1954 OAS-sponsored *Caracas Convention on Diplomatic Asylum*. These conventions allow individuals who are in political trouble, and not wanted for common crimes, to find refuge in a diplomatic post, warship, military aircraft, or camp and to seek safe passage to the country whose flag covers these objects of refuge. A 1950 ruling by the ICJ in a Colombia-Peru case observed that Peru had not, at the time, ratified the Montevideo Convention and that asylum practices were not sufficiently constant and uniform to obligate Peru through customary law.[6]

The most interesting case, however, goes back to 1989 when the United States "inserted" paratroopers into the country of Panama and arrested Manuel Noriega, the dictator of Panama. He fled to the Vatican's papal nunciature (or embassy), knowing the United States would be in hot pursuit because of allegations that he had mistreated American citizens and was complicit in smuggling drugs to the United States. The United States surrounded the nunciature as well as several other embassies and even searched the Nicaraguan embassy, an action that President H. W. Bush later admitted was a mistake. The Vatican, under strong US pressure, turned Noriega over to the United States, more or less accepting the US argument that he was a common criminal and not protected by immunity. The United States gave no credence to Noriega's position as *de facto* head of state and thus someone exempt from prosecution while in office (Blakesley, Firmage, Scott, & Williams 784: 817–19). Noriega was tried and sentenced in a US federal court. It is hard to know what Noriega thought about all of this, but he probably expected safe-passage from the papal nunciature to another country, a feat some of his associates managed in good Latin American fashion.

Rules for the Consular Relations of States

While ambassadors receive most of the attention in the media since they concentrate on major policy problems at the intergovernmental level, a lower rank of diplomat performs numerous services helpful to both individual citizens and foreigners. This diplomat is known as a **consul,** a rank covered by the 1963 Consular Convention. A consul is an agent, with a lower level of immunity than an ambassador, who promotes commercial interests and protects fellow nationals. Consuls are usually located in the major cities and ports of other states. Consuls are issued a **commission** by their own foreign minister (Secretary of State for the United States) and are accepted by the foreign minister of the host state. The acceptance of the consul is expressed by a certificate of **exequatur** as opposed to the *agrément* that an ambassador receives. A consul's offices are known as a **consulate,** and there can be several of these offices spread out in different cities of a country, depending on the amount of interaction between any two countries. Some countries still separate diplomatic and consular staffs, but most countries today, including the United States since 1924, combine the staffs into a single Foreign Service. A new US Foreign Service Officer (FSO) can

---

Box 6.2 Consular Immunity Has Limits

In 1926, a Princess Zizianoff, originally of Russia, sued Consul Bigelow for defamation of character in a French court. Mr Bigelow was an American official working for the American Consulate General in Paris and in charge of passports and visas. After turning down the Princess for a visa to enter the United States, he shared his rationale for the visa denial with the press, including the accusation that Princess Zizianoff was an international spy. Bigelow, along with persons associated with the Paris office of the *Boston Sunday Post*, was successfully sued by the Princess in 1927 at the bar of the Conventional Tribunal of the Seine.

On Bigelow's appeal, the case made its way to the Court of Appeal of Paris in 1928. The court ruled that the 1853 Consular Convention did not protect him from what the court called a "private act," providing negative information about the Princess to the public via the public press. The question for the court was whether Bigelow's action fell outside the purview of his official duties, and it ruled that his action did so. Undoubtedly, the 1963 Consular Convention would not protect a consular officer performing an injurious private act.

Sources: This case was reprinted as "Princess Zizianoff v. Kahn and Bigelow," *AJIL*, 21 (4) (1927), pp. 811–15; and see the case as appealed, "Bigelow v. Princess Zizianoff et al.," *American Journal of International Law*, 23 (1) (1929), pp. 172–9.

expect to serve interchangeably between diplomatic and consular missions (Thayer 1959: 130). The Consular Convention provides for several consular ranks depending on the level of responsibility.

Consuls and consulates operate with lesser levels of immunities and inviolabilities than those of ambassadors and embassies as provided under the Consular Convention. Consuls can be tried for common crimes and civil offenses and called upon to serve as witnesses. Local authorities can enter a consulate in case of fire or other emergencies, but the work space of the consul cannot be entered nor the archives or documents touched.

In other respects, the consul and consulate's statuses are about the same as for ambassador and embassies. The protection of these diplomats and their offices during conflict, as a responsibility of the host state, is equivalent. The *consular bag* and the consul's baggage also operate under equal protection as that accorded to ambassadors. Moreover, consuls live under the dangling sword of *persona non grata* as much as ambassadors. Despite the creation of two separate conventions, one for diplomats and the other for consuls, the privileges and immunities of the two have drawn closer together over the years through customary developments and bilateral treaties. Interestingly, however, a severance of diplomatic relations does not necessarily require the end of consular relations as noted in Article 2(3) of the Consular Convention. States may break-off relations at the ambassadorial level over a security issue, but may still want to trade and allow their citizens to travel back and forth between the two countries. For these commercial and private activities, consuls will be useful.

Article 5 of the Consular Convention provides a lengthy and explicit list of duties. Consuls' work mostly relates to the nitty-gritty tasks of helping businessmen from their home state, aiding stranded fellow citizens, acquiring lawyers and translators for citizens in foreign courts, serving as a notary public for births, weddings, and death, and inspecting ships and aircraft from the consul's country as well as seeing to the needs of the crews. Consuls even arrange for **letters rogatory**. These letters are sworn statements that are made before judicial authorities in one country to be used as evidence in the courts of another state. A consul can stay quite busy serving a virtual "colony" of fellow citizens living in the same foreign city. As well, there will likely be a steady flow of temporary visits by tourists, students, athletes, journalists, and businesspeople from the consul's home country often requiring time and attention.[7]

A responsibility of the consul, once considered part of the humdrum of every day work, is now on the frontlines of the campaign to check terrorism. Many countries' consuls are involved in the issuing and handling of **passports** and **visas**. A passport is an internationally recognizable travel document that verifies the identity and nationality of the bearer, while a visa, usually in the form of a stamp on a passport, is a prearranged permission for a foreigner to enter a country.[8] Tens of thousands of passports are lost or stolen every year and become available for terrorist use to penetrate the domestic space of a target state (Slater 2003: 150). The 19 hijackers that were responsible for the 9/11terrorist attack on the World Trade Center in New York City in 2001 had suspicious passports and yet 15 of the terrorists received visa stamps from a US consulate in Saudi Arabia. Obviously fraud-proof passports and better screening of visa applicants are in order. Interpol tries to track missing passports in a

Box 6.3 *Radwan v. Radwan*

England, Family Division, 1972, 3 W.L.R. 735

Although there may be in the public mind an image of embassies and consulates representing foreign soil as an exercise of extraterritorial jurisdiction, modern international law does not support this position, as the Radwan case demonstrates. Mary Isobel Radwan filed for divorce in 1970 in English courts and at the same time argued that her husband's effort at a Muslim divorce earlier that same year be set aside.

Mr Radwan, a Muslim and citizen of Egypt, had married Mary Radwan as his second wife in a Egyptian consulate in Paris, France. He sought to divorce her by exercising *Talaq* rules in the Egyptian Consulate-General's offices in London. He decreed three times before two witnesses, "I divorce you" in reference to Mary Radwan. In 90 days the divorce would then be final.

The question for the English judge was whether this divorce was an Egyptian divorce on Egyptian soil. Or, put another way, are the premises of an embassy or consulate part of the territory of the sending state or of the receiving state?

While embassies and consulates have considerable immunities for diplomatic business, they are not foreign soil with all sorts of foreign law applying within them. Mrs Radwan acquired an English divorce on the grounds of cruelty.

Sources: Portions of the case are quoted in Christopher L. Blakesley, *International Legal System: Cases and Materials*, 5th edn. (New York: Foundation Press, 2001), pp. 792–4.

Box 6.4 Beyond the Call of Duty

Japanese Consul Chiune Sugihara, assigned to Kaunas, Lithuania, on the eve of the Second World War, defied his orders by working 18–20 hours per day to handwrite over 2,000 visas allowing Jewish refugees to flee Europe early in the Second World War and find sanctuary in Japan. The refugees traveled by the Trans-Siberian Railway across much of the Soviet Union, finally arriving in Japan and staying there for most of the war. Although the refugees were eventually sent to a Jewish ghetto in Shanghai, China, Japan did resist its German ally's pressures to turn the refugees over to them. Sugihara had quit his prior post in Manchuria in protest of the Japanese Army's mistreatment of the local population. Given Japan's egregious human rights and humanitarian record during the war, this generous act of Consul Sugihara stands out as an extraordinary exception.

Source: Reported in *U.S. News and World Report* (May 9, 2005), p. 72.

computer program based on each passport's serial number but not nearly enough countries cooperate. Another more promising step is to change to "bio-passports." Passports of this kind can be based on one or more biometric identities such as fingerprints and eye retina scans in addition to a picture of the passport bearer.[9]

One role of consuls has been particularly troublesome for the United States because of the use of the death penalty by at least 35 of the US 50-state federal system. Article 36 calls for notification of consuls if their citizens are arrested and are to be tried for any crime. This notification allows a consul to visit a prisoner, provide mail from home, or find a lawyer and interpreter for an incarcerated citizen. Hundreds of foreigners are in American prisons and several dozen are likely to be on death row at any given time. The notification obligation appears to have fallen between the cracks of the American federal system. Opposed as they are to the death penalty, Canada, Mexico, and some European governments have carried their concerns to the ICJ and asked for provisional measures to cause a review of the cases of their condemned citizens. Mexico has had as many as 50 of its citizens on death row in the United States. The legal basis for such a review by the ICJ is contained in the *Optional Protocol of the Vienna Convention on Consular Relations Concerning the Compulsory Settlement of Disputes*. Under this optional protocol, states can bring cases to the ICJ over the interpretation of the Consular Convention.[10]

Prosecutors at the state level argue that consular notification would have made no difference in the outcomes of these capital cases, and the US Supreme Court has not supported the ICJ provisional rulings calling for delay of execution and review. The position of the US Supreme Court is that the consular notification issue must be brought up earlier in the original state trial.[11] While it should be easy for the United States to comply with the consular notification requirement, what these cases are really about was aptly expressed by Judge Shigeru Oda in a 2003 ICJ case. He said these cases concerned the abhorrence by Mexico and other states of capital punishment.[12]

Weary of the challenges to the death penalty in the United States, Secretary of State Condoleeza Rice informed UN Secretary-General Kofi Annan, in early 2005, that the United States "hereby withdraws" from the Optional Protocol dealing with dispute settlement over consular matters. The United States will continue to be bound by all the terms of the Consular Convention, including consular notification, but disagreements over the interpretation of this convention can no longer be used to bring the United States before the bar of the ICJ. Ironically, in the fall of 2007, President George W. Bush, who as governor of Texas oversaw 152 executions, wanted to honor the ICJ decision and halt the Texas execution of Jose Ernesto Medellin, who was sentenced to die in 1994, on the grounds that Medellin did not have access to his Mexican consul. The state of Texas went ahead on its on schedule, and Medellin was executed in 2008.

The Peaceful Settlement of Disputes

If there is a paramount function of diplomats it is to reduce conflict and head-off war. The simple statement made in Article 3 (1–C) of the Diplomatic Convention, "negotiating with the Government of the receiving State," scarcely begins to suggest the importance of this function. Spanning the twentieth century was a clarion call, enshrined in declarations, customary law, and treaties, to the effect that states are to avoid the use of force and instead peacefully settle disputes by either negotiation or adjudication.[13]

The 1899 *Hague Convention for the Pacific Settlement of Disputes* called for the friendly resolution of disputes through third-party political assistance with negotiation or by arbitration, in particular, taking disputes to the Permanent Court of Arbitration created by the 1899 convention. The 1907 *Hague Convention for the Pacific Settlement of Disputes*, in effect, incorporated the 1899 Convention but elaborated upon the procedures of settlement by employing over 30 more articles than the 1899 version. The 1907 Hague Conference also attracted more states, including a number of non-European countries, thereby better representing international society.

The creation of the League of Nations (1919–39) marks the first effort to establish a permanent global institution to channel states toward peaceful resolution of differences and away from reliance on force. The members of the League's Assembly and Council were special ambassadors of the states that they represented. Article 12 of the League's Covenant places priority on arbitration and judicial settlement, and Articles 13 and 14 call for the establishment of the Permanent Court of International Justice, the forerunner to the ICJ. Failing resolution by adjudication, members of the League were to refer an issue to the League Council under Article 15. Interestingly, the Covenant does not categorically forbid war but only requires that states wait for three months after peaceful resolution efforts have been attempted before turning to force.

An effort to tighten the prohibition against force appeared in the form of the 1928 *Kellogg–Briand Pact* (or Pact of Paris). Rather idealistically, it sought to outlaw war altogether. Obviously, it failed to stop major acts of aggression in the 1930s, but it was invoked after the Second World War in the trials of war criminals accused of violating international peace. The 1945 UN Charter superseded the Pact. Article 2 of the Charter requires that states find a peaceful end to disputes and that they refrain from threats or use of force. This obligation is echoed in the important UN General Assembly 1970 *Declaration on Principles of International Law Concerning Friendly Relations and Cooperation Among States in Accordance with the Charter of the United Nations* as well as the 1982 UN General Assembly *Manila Declaration on the Peaceful Settlement of International Disputes*. Finally, regional IGOs, such as the Organization of American States and the African Union, reinforce the twin tenets of peaceful settlement and prohibition of force.

The UN Charter's Article 33 briefly identifies several *political instruments* of pacific resolution as well as *adjudication* through arbitration or the judicial settlement of an established court. The political instruments are mentioned in other treaties and declarations and, in fact, some are traceable to antiquity. First is **negotiation**, involving bargaining with offers and counter-offers until some sort of compromise is reached. Negotiations sometimes fail because both sides strive to maximize their gains while making the fewest concessions possible. When negotiations succeed, it is because the states involved can afford to make concessions and they prefer settlement to continued contention or a resort to armed force. Negotiations are more often than not bilateral, but multilateral negotiations occur with some frequency, as in the case of the six-sided talks (including China, Japan, North Korea, Russia, South Korea, and the United States) over North Korea's nuclear program. Within IGOs and conferences, complex patterns of bi-lateral and multilateral negotiations often take place before a treaty or a policy can be concluded and implemented.

In his widely read book *How Nations Negotiate*, Fred Charles Iklé recommends rules for facilitating successful negotiations, beginning with both parties engaging in the negotiating process in good faith. Iklé also calls for avoiding disputes over the status of diplomats and their states, following the agenda agreed upon, honoring agreements, staying flexible and reciprocating favors (Iklé 1964).

Other political measures involve intermediaries, or third parties. The minimal role played by a third party is offering **good offices** by passing information back and forth between the two parties in dispute. As if an oversight, the Charter's Article 33 does not specify this third-party technique, but it is recognized as early as the Hague Conventions at the turn into the twentieth century. Not only states, but IGOs, NGOs, and individuals can perform this service. Swiss diplomats, because of their country's assiduous attention to neutrality, have often been called upon to offer their "good offices."

At a somewhat higher level of involvement is **inquiry** (spelled "enquiry" in the Charter's Article 33). This act of assistance refers to a helpful state ascertaining the facts behind a dispute and possibly clarifying some points of international law. In some cases a *commission of inquiry* is formed that can include both disputants' representatives and neutral experts. The League, the UN, and regional IGOs have used these commissions.

The next step up in the role of the intermediary is **mediation**. The third party becomes an active participant by making substantive suggestions for a settlement. Closely related is **conciliation** which usually involves a commission empowered to discover the facts and issue a final report with concrete proposals to end the dispute. If a commission is formed, the members serve in their own right as experts and not as representatives answerable to states. Mediation can drag on indefinitely while conciliation is thought of as occurring within a known time-frame.

If negotiation and third-party assistance are attractive alternatives to conflict and war, why do states often hesitate about taking the next big step to arbitration or judicial settlement in a permanent court? The answer is simple and understandable. If states choose one of the political methods of dispute settlement, they retain more control over the final outcome. Whatever the terms offered, a state's government can ultimately reject any proposal at any time even though that state may face negative world opinion. Once the issue goes to any form of adjudication, however, the states in dispute must accept the binding judgment as a matter of international law.

As Chapter 4 on the efficacy of international law demonstrates, the creation and use of tribunals and courts are definitely on the rise; yet, the simple truth about international politics is that the bulk of disputes are still handled by traditional negotiation, sometimes with third party assistance. To many, judicial settlement seems to be the next logical step when negotiations fail but, in fact, going to court at the international level is the least used mechanism for dispute settlement. The international level does not parallel the domestic situation where national courts are often accorded a pre-eminent status as final arbiters. Even in the domestic context, parties at dispute frequently prefer to settle out of court to save money and avoid the risk of losing (Caron & Shinkaretskaya 1995: 317; Collier 1996: 364–72, esp. 365; Bilder 1998: 234–5; Peters 2003: 12–15).

The Operating Conditions of Diplomacy

No matter how much good faith diplomats display, how many rules of protocol they obey, or how willing they are to compromise, many non-diplomatic factors shape the environment of the best intended diplomatic efforts. The *economic costs* of diplomacy are a serious matter from the smallest to the largest states. Many small states, such as Bhutan, Comoros, Monaco, Nauru, Vanuatu, or Western Samoa, send out few diplomatic missions and may count on larger, friendly states for help in this area. Even countries larger than these may expect an ambassador to attend to business in two or more capitals in adjoining states (Berridge 1985: 178–80). The UN is beneficial to small states since each ambassador to the UN can easily contact the ambassadors of 191 other states, all conveniently located in New York City.

The *changes in technology*, including jet aircraft that make summit and shuttle diplomacy possible and modern telecommunication hook-ups that permit direct conversations between leaders on different continents, have allowed ambassadors to be by-passed. Noted realist Hans Morgenthau once suggested that the decline of diplomacy became noticeable after the First World War when the telegraph, and gradually the telephone, tightened the control and authority over the diplomat. Professor Morgenthau observed that diplomacy only arose in the first place because of a lack of speedy communication (1978: 536).

Another change after the First World War that may have diminished the influence of diplomats was the changeover from *secret to open diplomacy*. Acting on the assumption that secret treaties contributed to a widening circle of First World War participants, President Woodrow Wilson called for treaties and diplomacy to be made more public. Consequently, the League of Nations, like the UN today, required that countries publish every treaty and register it with the League. This step is mostly to the good, but open diplomacy, operating beneath the spotlight of modern media, can create a "fishbowl environment" in which diplomats either make empty gestures or feel pressured to take rigid positions.

All states practice diplomacy not only in accordance with the rules of international law but with different *styles* rooted in their national cultures. National cultures hold different prescriptions for attitudes and behavior, sometimes causing diplomats to encounter "cultural static" as they meet across the bargaining table. Americans like to get right down to business, speak with candor, and take at face value what they are told. Some Presidents, including Lyndon Johnson of the 1960s and today's George W. Bush, have been prone to take their foreign counterparts into their homes where they hope the casual hospitality will lead to "straight talk." The Chinese prefer to cultivate a sense of friendship and obligation and then manipulate these to achieve their goals. Russians can be confrontational and blunt, putting diplomatic counterparts on the defensive. Japanese are uncomfortable with negotiations because they seem inherently confrontational. They tend to agree with the other side out of politeness but do not feel committed to the terms discussed. Raymond Cohen, in his *Negotiating Across Cultures*, concludes that if cross-cultural ignorance hurts negotiation, then it must be cross-cultural knowledge and appreciation that facilitates negotiation.[14]

Whatever the obstacles faced, *diplomatic skill* will enhance the prospects for success. Michael Watkins and Susan Rosegrant's *Breakthrough International Negotiation: How Great Negotiators Transformed the World's Toughest Post Cold War Conflicts* testifies to the value of skilled individual diplomats (Watson & Rosegrant 2001). European states are widely thought of as maintaining high standards for their diplomatic services. Excellent diplomats have also come from Third World countries, but many are political appointees without formal training. They may be relatives of rulers or appointments made to get opponents and troublemakers sent out of the country.

The United States is the object of much criticism for the numerous political appointments to diplomatic service. Typically one-third of the ambassadors of the United States receive appointments through presidential patronage. It is astounding that the world's only superpower uses so-many inexperienced diplomats, a situation that portends problems and could easily be put right. These appointees often lack knowledge as to how embassies function, they do not know the language and culture of the host state, and they cause a low morale to develop among foreign service officers because many of these professionals are denied a deserved ambassadorship as the capstone of a long, dedicated career.

The *extent of agreement* between countries can make the diplomat's task relatively easy. If countries have a similar culture, many common interests, and a history uncluttered with serious disputes, the diplomats for both sides can usually resolve most problems in a spirit of friendship. The United States and Canada, with the longest demilitarized border in the world, share this good fortune. In contrast, China and Russia have a historical dispute over territory and long-running fears of the other's intentions. Not even the presence of communist governments in both capitals assuaged these fears very much.

Power distribution, if it is particularly uneven or asymmetrical, may limit a useful role for diplomats. If a substantial power asymmetry operates between two states, one side may virtually set aside diplomacy and choose to bully the other. Adolf Hitler demanded and got the Sudetenland from Czechoslovakia in 1938 because Germany's power was overwhelming and the Czechs dared not fight.

If *wars* break out between or among states, mutually felt antipathy may render negotiations nearly impossible. The use of military force implies that the goals of the warring states are irreconcilable. And once the fighting starts, each side may continue fighting hoping to score a major victory on the battlefield to bolster the most favorable settlement terms. Only when one or both sides are exhausted, either psychologically, materially, or both, can serious negotiations can get underway. The Vietnam War dragged on for a decade before the North Vietnamese and the United States could finally come to terms. The United States wanted to end this war after the

American public grew restive over the casualty rates and the plight of American POWs. North Vietnam, for its part, had suffered massive American bombing strikes.

Exercising *retorsion*, a legal but unfriendly act, through diplomacy can have an obvious and direct impact on the prospects for diplomacy being helpful. Perhaps the favorite expression of retorsion by a state is to either withdraw an ambassador temporarily or break off diplomatic relations altogether. In either case, a helpful role by either country's diplomatic cadre will be greatly constrained. Because Iran and the United States have not recognized each other since 1979, EU countries have had to take the lead to persuade Iran to back away from its nuclear program.

Finally, the *terrorism* has had serious consequences for diplomacy undermining its effectiveness. Terrorists have existed probably as long as governments have, but they have been especially active since the 1960s. Terrorists use violent acts to force governments to pay attention to their grievances, including attacks on aircraft, ships, trains, and buildings of all sorts. It was only a question of time before terrorists would turn their attention to diplomats since their traditional peaceful and often public role makes them easy prey for people with violent intent. Assassinating or kidnapping diplomats and bombing embassies have occurred with some frequency.

By the 1980s, many countries, including the United States, began to upgrade the security of their embassies, turning them into fortresses with steel doors, surveillance cameras, and barbed wire as well as conducing extensive searches on all persons entering embassy premises. Because security upgrades focused on Europe and the Middle East, al-Qaida then turned to softer targets in Africa. The US embassies in Nairobi, Kenya and Dar es Salaam, Tanzania, were struck minutes apart on August 7, 1998 with car bombs killing 224 people, including 12 Americans, and wounding thousands more. Now these embassies have been rebuilt with bomb-blast walls and bullet-proof glass. They are set back from public streets with barriers to block vehicles from reaching them.

Having finished the $0.5 billion embassy in Beijing, China during 2008, the United States is completing the largest embassy in the world in Baghdad, Iraq that will cost about $0.75 billion and employ 1,700 people. Its premises contain 104 acres, over 20 buildings, and it is outfitted with the services of a small town. The US Baghdad embassy will have the most extensive security arrangements of any embassy in history. These embassy personnel must take the State Department's "Diplomatic Security Anti-terrorism Course" to learn about firearms, bombs, and prearranged "signal words" to use if kidnapped. They will no doubt receive the danger pay, like combat soldiers, that the Department of State offers to those who serve in perilous posts. In 2008, the State Department requested over $8 billion for new buildings and upgrades to make more secure the approximately 265 embassies and consulates around the world. Such is diplomacy in much of the world today.

The Rules of Diplomacy for IGOs

The development of IGOs is traceable to the nineteenth century, and they continue to grow in prominence as they set much of the agenda and priorities involved in the tasks of global governance. Although IGOs are created by states, today's 450 IGOs both help states to cooperate and often influence their governments on policy choices. IGOs, especially the UN, sponsor conferences that can have a quasi-legislative function and provide opportunities for the thousands of human rights, environmental, and disarmament NGOs to have a say in global governance. Whether it is the World Health Organization containing a potential pandemic, the Universal Postal Union arranging the delivery of global mail, the International Monetary Fund stabilizing countries' currencies, the International Civil Aviation Organization and the International Maritime Organization promoting safe travel, or the Council of Europe regulating human rights, states and millions of their citizens have come to count on the myriad services of IGOs. Despite having a legal personality secondary to states, the headquarters and diplomats of IGOs have come to enjoy a set of privileges and immunities not unlike the embassies and ambassadors of states.

At the turn into the twentieth century, privileges and immunities for IGOs held the promise of replicating those enjoyed in state to state relations. Officials associated with the Permanent Court of Arbitration, the League of Nations, the Permanent Court of Justice, and the International Labor Organization seemed slated to enjoy generous diplomatic privileges. Article 7(4) of the League Covenant, for example, stipulates "Representatives of the Members of the League and officials of the League when engaged in the business of the League shall enjoy diplomatic privileges and immunities." And Article 7(5) states "The buildings and other property occupied by the League or its officials or by Representatives attending its meetings shall be inviolable."

Only the language of Article 7(4), "when engaged in the business of the League," hints at a more restrictive immunity usually referred to as **functional immunity**. This immunity is not full-time nor does it cover all circumstances, but, rather, provides sufficient privileges and immunities to perform required tasks but no more. The issue over the exact extent of immunity did not come into focus for the League because it employed only a few hundred people, and the diplomatic missions of the member-states were by-passed in policy-making by their own capitals and were largely ignored by the League's Secretariat in Geneva. The question of a more restricted immunity began to come to the fore after the Second World War with the exponential growth of IGOs in their number, size, and influence.

Articles 104 and 105 of the UN Charter appeared to embrace functional immunity more clearly. Article 104 permits the UN to exercise authority on the territory of member-states "as may be necessary," while Article 105 states that the UN officials and state representatives to the UN shall have privileges and immunities "as are necessary" for the exercise of their functions.

The preamble to the 1946 *Convention on the Privileges and Immunities of the United Nations* repeats what can be called the functional immunity of the Charter, but then lays out specific rules similar to the 1961 Diplomatic Convention for states regarding such matters as the inviolability of UN archives and premises, exemption from direct taxes, and the immunity of couriers and diplomatic bags. The 1946 Convention also seems to provide traditional immunities for the officials of the UN and the state representatives to the UN. Because of somewhat contradictory language in conventions, some contention over the exact immunities to be allotted to the UN and its personnel is not surprising.

The 1947 *UN Convention on the Privileges and Immunities of the Specialized Agencies* was also to reflect functional immunity as it aimed at unifying privileges and immunities enjoyed by the UN and its Specialized Agencies. The UN is often referred to as the UN system because of the plethora of bodies associated with the UN, not the least of which are the approximately 20 specialized agencies tied to the UN by IGO-to-IGO treaties. The International Labor Organization, the World Health Organization, the International Telecommunications Union, and the Universal Postal Union are among some of the best known specialized agencies. Basically, officials of the Specialized Agencies and state representatives to them appear to be treated in practice like UN officials and state diplomats of comparable rank.

The issue of functional immunity reappeared with the 1975 *Vienna Convention on the Representation of States in their Relations with International Organizations of a Universal Character*. Its purpose was to shore up the status of state representatives to IGOs, but it quickly became controversial among states. Western states, where most of the headquarters of IGOs are located, and non-Western states, which send most of the diplomatic representatives, have come down on opposing sides in the debate about whether officials of IGOs, and state representatives to them, should receive full privileges and immunities or be restricted to functional immunity. Especially vexing to the Western states was Article 66, extending privileges and immunities even to administrative and technical staff.[15]

The Western states have long worried about the "elephantiasis" of a diplomatic corps, a large concentration of people in one city hosting an IGO who enjoy extensive immunity. In New York City, there are 192 diplomatic missions to the UN, all with accompanying staff. There are also several thousand protected UN officials. Misbehavior has not been uncommon, ranging from flagrant disregard of parking tickets to serious crimes of rape, murder, and espionage. In the early 1980s, a series of rapes implicated the son of the Ghanaian ambassador to the UN, but he had to be released. Members of the Cuban mission to the UN in 1994 brawled with demonstrators and the New York police, leading the US government to ask Cuba to withdraw those involved. Although most diplomats comport themselves in a professional manner, the host countries of the 450 or so IGOs have had to deal with undiplomatic behavior at some level.

Because of disagreement among the Western and non-Western states, the 1975 convention has not been able to reach fruition. All states were invited to the 1975 conference but only 81 states accepted, with just 60 participating regularly. The 1975 convention has had a few recent ratifications but, after several decades, it is still several ratifications short of the 35 necessary to put it into play. The ratifying states are mostly Third World countries, plus a few ex-communist European states. Consequently, diplomatic immunity for IGOs today depends on their various headquarters agreements with host states instead of a general treaty covering all IGOs.

The push for functional immunity by many Western states is somewhat offset by the competition among states to serve as hosts of IGOs. These states want the political and prestige benefits plus the influx of money that comes with hosting.

Thus, what host states resist in an international convention they tend to extend as privileges and immunities through individual host agreements that will attract the IGOs.[16] The upshot is that it is increasingly difficult to draw a distinction between immunities in state-to-state diplomacy and diplomacy associated with IGOs.

Overall, the post-Second World War effort to check the expanding IGOs with the restrictions of functional immunity has largely failed. The Western states, usually the hosts of IGOs, have found themselves fighting a rearguard action. The large majority of states have pressed persistently over the years for a fuller set of privileges and immunities until a clear line of distinction between the respective rules for IGO diplomacy and state diplomacy has become blurred.

The Special Case of the UN

A primary example of a headquarters agreement between an IGO and a state is the 1947 *US–UN Headquarters Agreement*. In anticipation that the United States would become the host of the UN and other IGOs, the US Congress passed the 1945 *International Organizations Immunities Act* only months after the close of the Second World War. This act recognized the legal personality of IGOs and accorded to them similar privileges and immunities enjoyed by embassies and diplomats of foreign governments. Besides the UN in New York City, NAFTA, the OAS, and the World Bank system operate from Washington, DC.

Although serving as host for the UN, the United States did not ratify the 1946 Convention dealing with UN privileges and immunities until 1970, but its relationship with the UN was secured with the US–UN Headquarters Agreement of 1947, which was also incorporated into US law (Public Law 357–80th Congress). The agreement calls for a headquarters district specified as bounded by particular streets in Manhattan, a district that would have inviolable premises. The UN was allowed its own telecommunications system and could arrange with its host a separate post office and even its own aerodrome (a small airport) if it wished. The United States was to permit easy transit to the UN district by providing the necessary visas for UN officials, state representatives, and accredited foreign media reporters. Public services such as water, electricity, and telephone services were to be guaranteed, as was police protection. The UN Headquarters District could not be used as a refuge for those fleeing law enforcement or facing extradition. In cases of disagreement, the United States and the UN were to turn to arbitration. Within a year, there was an add-on agreement for the US government to provide a loan of up to $65 million for the construction of the UN's facilities.[17]

The governments of states ultimately define their powers not only through their constitutions but by their experiences under these constitutions. Similarly, the UN's legal personality has likewise been shaped by its life as an IGO in addition to its Charter and headquarters agreement with the United States. A few examples will help make this point clear. In a landmark decision for the UN, the ICJ ruled in a 1949 advisory opinion that the UN could sue for reparations when UN mediator

Count Folke Bernadotte was assassinated by Jewish terrorists in 1948. Israel, as a *de facto* state, had failed in its duty to protect his life as he tried to resolve territorial disputes between the Israelis and Palestinians.[18] This case made clear that the UN has sufficient legal personality to sue a state.

In another matter, the UN suffered a temporary setback. The first Secretary-General of the UN, Trygve Lie of Norway, gave in to US pressures in the brief period of 1952–3 and fired 18 American employees of the UN Secretariat. The United States suspected numerous UN civil servants of being communists. The early 1950s was the infamous "McCarthy Era" when anti-communism in the United States reached fever-pitch. Senator Joe McCarthy led this anti-communist hysteria and often made out-landish charges about communist infiltration in the US government as well as the UN. The presence of the UN headquarters in one of the Cold War's chief protagonists was clearly a disadvantage at the time. Eleven of those fired appealed to the UN Administrative Tribunal and won awards totaling $179,420 to compensate for their wrongful firing. A 1954 advisory opinion of the ICJ confirmed both the Administrative Tribunal's authority to make such a decision and the UN General Assembly's obligation to pay the award.[19] When the next Secretary-General, Dag Hammarskjöld of Sweden, came into office in 1953, he made it clear that the United States was not to undermine the UN's independence in the future by screening its employees.

The UN managed to protect its independence in another case by having the final word on whether the Palestinian Liberation Organization (PLO) could continue its diplomatic mission at the UN. The UN had extended Observer Status to the PLO in 1974 but, in 1987, the US Congress amended the US State Department's budget bill to the effect that all PLO offices were to be closed in 1988 because it was believed the PLO sponsored terrorism. This law would clearly violate the Headquarters Agreement since it impinged on the UN's capacity to control the diplomatic missions attending its sessions. The ICJ ruled in a 1988 advisory opinion that the United States was obliged to arbitrate the issue with the UN based on the US–UN Headquarters Agreement.[20] Arbitration was only averted when a US federal court ruled that it was up to the executive branch to decide the status of the PLO and not Congress. The State Department was only too happy to avoid a collision course with the UN by leaving the PLO mission in place, including its offices in New York City outside the UN Headquarters District. A decade later, the observer status of the PLO was upgraded even further by the UN to that of a non-voting member of the UN General Assembly.

Transit to and from the UN Headquarters across US territory has caused a few problems as well. Based on the headquarters agreement, the United States is expected to cooperate in a reasonable way to facilitate transit through New York City airports and across the city to reach the Headquarters District. The United States's own special political outlook has colored the process, however. In 1960, the United States permitted Premier Nikita Khrushchev to attend a session of the UN but he could not leave Manhattan Island where the UN Headquarters is located. Later in 1988, the United States refused Yasir Arafat, leader of the PLO, an entrance visa to the United States altogether. At great expense, the UN reconvened in the old League Headquarters in Geneva, Switzerland, to hear Arafat's address.[21]

Maintaining the integrity and independence of the UN has involved challenges by other states besides the United States as the host state. In two fairly similar cases, the ICJ issued advisory opinions protecting the privileges and immunities of two UN experts from the authority of the countries of their respective nationalities. In 1989, the ICJ ruled that Mr Dumitru Mazilu, a Special Rapporteur of the UN Sub-Commission on Prevention of Discrimination and Protection of Minorities, could not be retired from UN Service by his government of Romania for health or any other reason. Romania's communist government denied Mr Mazilu a travel permit, violating Article 6, Section 22 of the 1946 *Convention on the Privileges and Immunities of the United Nations*. This article provides that "Experts on Mission for the United Nations" with the same protection as diplomats.[22] Then in 1999, the ICJ, citing the same convention and article, ruled that Malaysia could not charge Dató Param Cumaraswamy, the UN Commission of Human Rights Special Rapporteur on the Independence of Judges and Lawyers, with libel. He had criticized his own country's courts and, in response, the Malaysian officials wanted to take him before their civil courts.[23]

Much more serious are physical attacks that can threaten the diplomats involved with IGOs; these representatives are just as vulnerable as those of states. Reflecting the fact that most attacks on diplomats today are by various terrorist groups, international bodies have produced conventions to help suppress behavior that harms diplomacy as a fundamental institution of international society. Two well-known examples are the OAS 1971 *Convention to Prevent and Punish the Acts of Terrorism Taking the Form of Crimes against Persons and Related Extortion that are of International Significance* and the UN-sponsored 1973 *Convention For the Prevention and Punishment of Crimes Against Internationally Protected Persons, Including Diplomatic Agents*. The UN convention went into effect in 1977 and has been widely ratified. Although it focuses on diplomacy, this convention is usually listed among a dozen or so conventions aimed at the general suppression of terrorism. The conventions protecting diplomats also cover heads of state, foreign ministers, and their families against such crimes as assault, kidnapping, and murder. States are called upon to either try perpetrators or extradite them to a state that will.[24]

States frequently incorporate the terms of these conventions into their national laws, as does the United States, to further add to the protection of those enjoying diplomatic immunity. What is all too clear, however, is that terrorists, as outlaws, operate beyond the pale of civilized standards ensconced in law. Many terrorists sacrifice their lives willingly for a cause often opaque to others; they do not care a whit about the terms of conventions and laws protecting diplomacy. They rationalize that, without armies and air forces, unorthodox methods are all that is available them. The only actors responsive to the rules of international law are those states willing to cooperate in the common cause of providing security for the world's diplomats.

More recent is the 1994 *Convention on the Safety of United Nations and Associated Personnel* that followed on the heels of numerous attacks made on UN Peacekeepers in Bosnia and Somalia. The 1994 Convention calls for the protection of peacekeepers, usually military people contributed by various member-states. Also covered by this convention are both UN officials and experts on mission who enjoy diplomatic status and UN offices located in the countries receiving help. While these conventions may not impress terrorists and lawless militias fomenting attacks, they do include the familiar "prosecute or extradite" rule that encourages states to punish wrong-doers. After the 1994 UN Safety Convention entered into force in 1999, the Commission on Human Rights expressed concern that too few countries assisted by UN peacekeeping missions were ratifying this convention. These countries obviously are the ones which must respect UN personnel and offices.[25]

The urgent need for respecting the 1994 UN Safety Convention became clear when UN offices in Baghdad were attacked by a truck-bomb in August 2003, killing 23 people. Among the casualties was UN Special Envoy Sergio Vieira de Mello, a distinguished diplomat from Brazil working for the UN and a friend of Secretary-General Kofi Annan. Since this terrible attack, the UN presence and ability to help this troubled state have been minimal. The UN mission in Iraq was downgraded to a small staff helping to organize elections. In 2007, another truck-bomb was rammed into UN offices in Algiers, Algeria.

Chapter Summary

- Diplomacy exists to permit useful communications among states and IGOs to minimize conflict and maximize cooperation.
- Diplomacy is one of the oldest areas of international law evolving under customary rules which culminated into written conventions by the early 1960s.
- Diplomacy often relies on the help of third parties recognized in the UN Charter such as mediation and conciliation.
- Diplomacy's operating conditions include modern travel and communication that allow ambassadors to be by-passed.
- Embassies and consulates both enjoy immunities, but the latter have somewhat less protection.
- The headquarters of IGOs also possess immunities as do states' ambassadors to these IGOs.
- Calling ambassadors home or closing embassies is a favorite act of retorsion by an unhappy state.

Discussion Questions

1 What are summit and shuttle diplomacy, and how has modern travel made these possible?
2 What are the differences in immunity for ambassadors and their embassies and consuls and their consulates?
3 *Persona non grata* is a term frequently appearing in the news about international relations. What does it mean and how is it used?

4   Are embassies purposively used for asylum? Explain. Is there a region of the world that follows a pattern of exception to the embassy/asylum nexus?
5   Can the United Sates control persons' travel to the UN Headquarters in New York City since this headquarters is an enclave within US territory? Explain.

Useful Weblinks

http://www.diplomacy.edu
DiploFoundation promotes research in the field of diplomacy and offers books and other publications in the field. Updates can be received by subscribing with an email address.

http://www.yale.edu/lawweb/avalon/avalon.html
The Avalon Project at Yale University offers numerous documents for the eighteenth to twenty-first centuries relating to law and diplomacy.

http://www.state.gov/
The web site of the US Department of State offers press releases, audio and video releases, travel warning and much else in addition to information about passports and visas.

http://www.emb.com/
An interesting web site that allows access to the web sites of all the embassies located in Washington, D.C. as well as a worldwide directory on embassies. Anyone can submit their email address to join the "Embassy Network e-list" for updates.

http://www.cartercenter.org/
The website of ex-President Jimmy Carter is an excellent example of Track II diplomacy. Emphasis is on promoting human rights and fighting disease.

Further Reading

Barker, J. Craig Barker (2006) *The Protection of Diplomatic Personnel*. Burlington, VT: Ashgate.
Barston, R. P. (2006) *Modern Diplomacy*. New York: Pearson Longman.
Berridge, G. R. (2005) *Diplomacy, Theory and Practice*, 2nd edn. New York: Palgrave Macmillan.
Bolewski, Wilfried (2007) *Diplomacy and International Law in Globalized Relations*. New York: Springer.
Carter, Jimmy (2009) *We Can Have Peace in the Holy Land: A Plan That Will Work*. New York: Simon & Schuster.
Chatterjee, Charles (2007) *International Law and Diplomacy*. New York: Routledge.
Dizard, Wilson, Jr (2001) *Digital Diplomacy: U.S. Foreign Policy in the Information Age*. Westport, CT: Praeger.
Kissinger, Henry (1994) *Diplomacy*. New York: Simon & Schuster.

Merrills, J. G. (2005) *International Dispute Settlement*, 4th edn. New York: Cambridge University Press.

Muldoon, James P., Jr., Aviel, JoAnn Fagot, Reitano, Richard and Sullivan, Earl (2005) *Multilateral Diplomacy and the United Nations Today*. Boulder, CO: Westview.

Zartman, I. William (2005) *Cowardly Lions: Missed Opportunities to Prevent Deadly Conflict and State Collapse*. Boulder, CO: Lynne Rienner.

Notes

1 Agha, Feldman, Khadlidi, and Schiff 2003: 1–3. A good example of such an NGO is the Carter Center. Its website is http://www.cartercenter.org > "Peaceprograms." Along the same line of Track II diplomacy, see a more complex version in Diamond and McDonald 1996.

2 Denza 1976: 1–15. The conventions on diplomacy and consular arrangements can be read at http://treaties.un.org/Pages/ParticipationStatus.aspx > Chapter III.

3 The above paragraphs draw on Thayer 1959; Feltham 1980.

4 This subject can be read about at http://www.un.org/law/ilc/guide/9_5.html.

5 See note 3.

6 This ICJ case is at http://www.icj-cij.org/icjwww/decisions/isummaries/ > cases > contentious cases > 1950 Columbia/Peru.

7 For an interesting description of a consul's life, see Thayer 1959: 130–8.

8 For definitions on "passports" and "visas" go to http://state.gov/ > Travel > Passports (and) > Visas.

9 Regarding this symposium, see http://www.icao.int/mrtd/biometrics/intro.cfm; and see Torpey 2000: esp. 3, 9, and 17.

10 A brief but useful article on this problem is by Pieter H.F. Bekker, "Consular Notification and the Death Penalty," http://www.asil.org/ Publications > Insights > ASIL Insights 2003.

11 The US Supreme Court has cited the 1996 *Antiterrorism and Effective Death Penalty Act* in pointing out that US law requires a petitioner to the court to have raised the consular notification matter during the state-level trial.

12 "Declaration of Judge Oda," (February 5, 2003) can be found at http://www.icj-cij.org/ > cases > Contentions Cases > 2003 Avena and other Mexican Nationals > Order > Declaration of Judge Oda.

13 On this point, see Peters 2003: 1–34.

14 See primarily Cohen 1997; also refer to Nicolson 1964: ch. 6; Binnendijk 1987; Fisher 1988; Hopkins 1992.

15 The three conventions relating to the status of the UN and its Specialized Agencies are available at http://treaties.un.org/Pages/ParticipationStatus.aspx > Chapter III.

16 The above paragraphs draw in part on Frey and Frey 1999: ch. 13).

17 The headquarters agreement can be found at http://avalon.law.yale.edu/20th_century/decad036.asp.

18 This case can be accessed at http://www.icj-cij.org/ > cases > Advisory proceedings > 1948 Reparations for injuries.

19 http://www.icj-cij.org/ > cases > Advisory proceedings > 1953 Effect of Awards Compensation.

20 http://www.icj-cij.org/ > cases > Advisory proceedings > 1988 Applicability of the Obligation to Arbitrate; see also Blakesley, Firmage, Scott, and Williams 2001: 849–53.

21 Examples of problems are found in Frey and Frey 199: 563–73; also see, Blakesley, Firmage, Scott, and Williams 2001: 786–91, 842–8.

22 http://www.icj-cij.org > cases > Advisory Proceedings > 1989 Applicability of Article VI.

23 http://www.icj-cij.org > cases > Advisory proceedings > 1998 Difference Relating to Immunity.

24 This convention is available at http://treaties.un.org/Pages/ParticipationStatus.aspx > Chapter XVIII.

25 This convention can be read at the same site as note 24.

From the dawn of consciousness until August 6, 1945, man had to live with the prospects of his death as an individual; since that day when the first bomb outshone the sun over Hiroshima, mankind as a whole has had to live with the prospect of its extinction as a species. (Arthur Koestler)

Every gun that is made, every warship launched, every rocket fired signifies, in a final sense, a theft from those who hunger and are not fed, those who are cold and are not clothed. This world in arms is not spending money alone. It is spending the sweat of its laborers, the genius of its scientists, the hopes of its children. (President Dwight D. Eisenhower)

7

Arms Limitations for a Less Violent World

Contents

Over the millennia, tribes, city-states, empires, and modern states fought and conquered one another, with the better armed groups usually prevailing in battles and wars. Iron swords prevailed over bronze swords. Cannon and gunpowder smashed the walls of the strongest castles. Small European armies, with breech-loading rifles, easily overwhelmed large indigenous forces equipped with spears and bows and arrows. And the allies, in the Second World War, won largely because they had clear superiority in strategic bombers.

With the evolution of the modern state in Europe, the power and status of kings and the fates of their countries in warfare largely depended on the armaments of their military forces. Caught up in an environment of anarchy and hostility, European states often lived in fear of one another, a fear that would take on a global pattern as the European state system reached all corners of a post-colonial world. Besides the dangers brought by well-armed states, large amounts of lethal tools have fallen into the hands of revolutionaries, guerrilla bands, transnational criminal gangs, private military companies that often work under contract with governments, and terrorists.

If one fear captures the attention of the world today, it is that a nuclear weapon might fall into the hands of an aggressive state or a terrorist group with an apocalyptic vision of the near future. Understandably, many leaders of states, IGOs, and NGOs have worked to constrain the spread of many types of weapons.

This chapter begins with a brief history of arms limitations followed by chapter sections on the worthy objectives of arms limitations and the obstacles that stand in the way of these agreements. Nuclear, biological, chemical, missile, and conventional weapons *regimes* are then discussed. It can be remembered that a regime is the accumulated norms and rules that states converge around and usually obey for a given policy area. These norms and rules of treaties restrict or outlaw particular arms. An effort will be made to appraise the strength of the various regimes to restrain some weapons and eliminate others. The regimes aim at making a safer world and, if quarrels turn to violent conflict, rule out some of the most heinous weapons ranging from dum-dum bullets to atom bombs.

A Brief History of Arms Limitations

It is safe to say that across history peoples have spent much more time and energy developing weapons than trying to get rid of them, but the effort to limit weapons is about as old as warfare itself (Wheeler 2002: 19–39). Dating as far back as 5000 years, various civilizations, including the Assyrian-Babylonian, Chinese, Egyptian, Indian, Muslim, and Persian, have all designed rules for war and sometimes for specific weapons.

After the seventh century CE, it was mostly Europeans that shaped today's norms and laws governing weapons, although it was a spotty record for centuries. A well-known example is the Second Lateran Council of 1139 CE that prohibited the use of the crossbow and the harquebus, a primitive firearm. Much later, in North America, American and British negotiators agreed to demilitarize the Great Lakes region under the 1817 *Rush–Bagot Agreement*, an understanding that would later follow the Canadian–US boundary line all the way to the Pacific Ocean. Another example is the 1869 *St Petersburg Declaration,* which renounced the use of explosive projectiles weighing less than 400 grams (14 ounces).

Concern over war and weapons eventually came to be expressed through the rules of manuals or declarations that would foreshadow the modern weapons conventions of international law. Some of these include Swedish King Gustavus Adolphus' 1621 *Articles of Military Laws to be Observed in the Wars*, the 1863 Francis Lieber Codes that covered rules of land warfare for the Union Army during the American civil war, the European 1874 *International Declaration Concerning the Laws and Customs of War*, and the 1880 *Oxford Manual on the Laws and Customs of War on Land*.

Around the turn into the twentieth century, several important arms limitations agreements appeared. The 1899 Hague Conference, attended by 28 mostly European states, came up with a convention prohibiting explosives dropped from balloons, projectiles containing asphyxiating gases, and dum-dum bullets that expanded and fragmented when striking the human body. The 1907 Hague Conference, attended by 44 states including more non-European states than at the 1899 conference, added the additional rules that sea mines must be anchored and become harmless if they break loose from their moorings. The 1913 *Manual on the Laws of Naval Warfare* required the same for torpedoes, that they become harmless if they missed their target.

Other developments between the two world wars include the 1921–2 Washington Naval Conference, which, among other important decisions, established a ratio among the major naval powers as to how many battleships each could have. Then, the 1930 London Naval Conference set limits for Great Britain, the United States, and Japan on the number of cruisers, destroyers, and submarines that each might possess, with Japan only allowed two-thirds as many as the other two naval powers. In 1936, Japan abrogated its naval agreements and built up a powerful navy, possibly to prepare for a contest with the United States for control of the Pacific Ocean. Another important inter-World War agreement was the 1925 *Geneva Protocol* prohibiting the use of gas and germ weapons in wartime.[1]

The inter-war years would witness a contest between the competing strategies of **disarmament** and **arms control** on how to handle arms limitations. Disarmament calls for the complete or partial elimination of weapons while arms control, more modestly, refers to limitations or caps on the numbers of existing weapons. Disarmament gained a strong footing in the 1919 Covenant of the League of Nations and was reaffirmed in the UN Charter in 1945 (Claude, Jr 1971: 294–300). Disarmament had an idealist bent that reached its high-water mark at the League-sponsored 1932 World Disarmament Conference held in Geneva. The 1925 Geneva Protocol had called for a conference like this, which meant at least getting rid of offensive weapons enabling aggression. This ambitious conference floundered over the great power struggles that set the stage for the Second World War, including Germany's departure from both the conference and the League.

Realist Hans Morgenthau never held a sanguine view of disarmament's prospects. He saw disarmament efforts as a story of many failures, with success realized only under extraordinary circumstances. Morgenthau has famously observed that, "Men do not fight because they have arms. They have arms because they deem it necessary to fight." Morgenthau regarded the possession of arms as symptomatic of outstanding political issues that require settlement before disarmament can be addressed (1973: 394, 410, 416). By the early 1960s, security specialists, much to the chagrin of disarmament advocates, began to speak of arms control as a more practical strategy than idealistic disarmament (Larsen 2002: 3). For much of the Cold War, the strained Soviet–US relationship would permit only arms control to limit weapons.

The issue that overshadowed all others was what to do about the nuclear arms race. The United States, as the first state to possess the atomic bomb, made some efforts to put the nuclear genie back into the bottle. President Harry Truman's administration offered to the world the 1946 *Baruch Plan*, named after diplomat Bernard Baruch. Under this plan, the United States would destroy its nuclear weapons and place all nuclear knowledge under the control of an IGO empowered to restrict nuclear energy to peaceful uses. Joseph Stalin's Soviet Union rejected the plan outright, claiming that the United States could secretively store away a few atomic bombs and would probably do so (Waller 2002: 102). Then in 1953, President Dwight Eisenhower proposed the *Atoms for Peace* program in a speech before the UN General Assembly. He offered to deflect nuclear energy from further weapons development and to focus on nuclear plants for generating electricity (Davis 1998: 137). Unfortunately, by this time, the proliferation of nuclear weapons was underway.

Joining the United States in possession of nuclear bombs were the Soviet Union (1949), the United Kingdom (1952), France (1960), China (1964), Israel (probably 1968), India (1974), and Pakistan (1989). The latter two weaponized their nuclear devices in 1998. South Africa developed atomic weapons in 1979, but voluntarily relinquished them in 1991. North Korea may have had an atomic bomb since 1994, but is not believed to have exploded a bomb until 2006 in a possible underground test. Until fairly recently, Iraq and Libya had nuclear weapons programs. Iraq's program ended as an outcome of the 1990–1 Persian Gulf War, and Libya, long under international pressure for its international pressure for its WMDs and state-sponsored terrorism, gave up its ambitions for atomic weapons in 2003. Iran may currently seek an atomic bomb, but the Iranian government has steadfastly claimed its nuclear developments were for peaceful purposes only (Spector 2002: 119–41). It is no wonder that in the early 1960s, President John Kennedy, among other observers, had a profound fear that nuclear proliferation was unstoppable (Kile 2003: 577–609, esp. 609).

The Soviet Union and the United States developed nuclear arsenals that made other nuclear powers look puny. The United States, with its long-range bombers and missiles, held a strategic edge over the Soviet Union until the 1970s, when both sides found themselves caught in an arrangement of *mutually assured destruction* (MAD). If one side attacked, the other would have enough nuclear might left over to retaliate, leaving both sides destroyed in a nuclear holocaust. So great were the number of missiles and warheads on both sides that some scientists hypothesized that an all-out nuclear war would cause a *nuclear winter*. According to this hypothesis, a full nuclear exchange would envelop the Earth with enough dust to block out the sun for months, finally killing off all life (e.g. Hewell 1984).

Unlike many who viewed the nuclear balance of power, or *balance of terror* as Winston Churchill once called it, with dread, realist Kenneth Waltz embraced the bi-polar world structure favorably. He thought it provided a high degree of international management and stability as it allowed for a long, if cold, peace during the last half of the twentieth century (1979).

For several decades, any stability achieved during the Cold War was underpinned, in large part, through arms control agreements. The 1962 Cuban missile crisis, that brought the Soviet Union and the United States to the brink of nuclear war, set these agreements in motion. Soon after this crisis the 1963 *hotline agreement* allowing rapid, direct communication between Moscow and Washington, the 1963 *Limited Test Ban Treaty* that would restrict American, British, and Soviet nuclear testing to underground sites, the 1971 *Seabed Treaty* prohibiting the launching of nuclear weapons from the ocean floor, and the 1974 *Threshold Nuclear Test Ban Treaty* reducing the size of nuclear underground explosions to 150 kilotons (1 kiloton explosive equals a 1,000 tons of TNT). Years later, a complete nuclear test ban treaty would receive widespread support, but this 1996 agreement has not yet gone into force.

The centerpiece of nuclear arms control is the 1968 *Nuclear Non-Proliferation Treaty*, which aims to include all states. The original five nuclear powers (China, France, the Soviet Union, the United Kingdom, and the United States), known as the "Nuclear Club," were allowed to keep their nuclear weapons for an unspecified time but were barred from sharing nuclear weapons with other states. All non-Nuclear Club states would refrain from using nuclear materials and technology except for producing energy.

In the early 1970s, during a period of *détente* of relaxed relations, the two super-powers moved toward arms control agreements that would place ceilings on the number of their most valued weapons, intercontinental ballistic missiles (ICBMs) armed with multiple nuclear warheads. These were known as the *Strategic Arms Limitation Talks* (SALT) agreements of 1972 and 1977. SALT I placed a cap on ICBMs, and SALT II was intended to limit multiple independently targeted re-entry vehicles (MIRVs) that could involve as many as ten warheads per missile. Unfortunately, the US Senate delayed on the ratification of SALT II and, when the Soviets invaded Afghanistan, President Jimmy Carter withdrew SALT II from further consideration by the Senate.

In 1972, the superpowers wanted to further stabilize their relationship and head off a costly arms race in the area of defensive missiles. Negotiated at the time of SALT I, the *Agreement on Anti-Ballistic Missiles* (ABMs), designed to shoot down incoming ICBMs, would allow the two Cold War antagonists two fields of defensive missiles each but changed this to one each. This agreement saved both sides a vast investment in defensive missiles for numerous cities and military installations. This type of missile was ineffective then and still does not operate reliably today.

There were other important arms control agreements known as *Confidence Building Measures* that applied to states in the respective alliance systems of the Soviet Union and the United States. The 1975 *Conference on Security and Cooperation in Europe* called for Warsaw Pact and NATO states to give warning before practicing maneuvers, and the 1986 *Stockholm Agreement* allowed observers from each alliance to watch the other's maneuvers. Later, negotiations for the *Open Skies Agreement* began in 1990 and formally entered into force in 2002, when the agreement received a sufficient number of ratifications. This accord permitted countries in both alliances to fly over each other's territory with aircraft equipped with several kinds of sensing devices. The idea for the Open Skies Agreement originated from a proposal made by President Dwight Eisenhower to Soviet Premier Nikita Khrushchev at the 1955 Geneva Summit, but, because of historical Russian paranoia about inspections from outsiders, the plan was rejected at that time. These flights are routine today.

Important conventional weapons agreements were made as well. A 1980 convention focused on several kinds of inhumane weapons such as blinding laser weapons and incendiary devices. In 1990, the Soviet Union and the United States managed a drawdown of their tanks, artillery, and combat aircraft. Then in 1996, a worldwide organization of NGOs produced the Ottawa Convention calling for a complete ban on anti-personnel landmines. Although receiving much less dramatic attention than nuclear, biological, and chemical weapons, conventional weapons, in practice, have killed far more people than the three most dreaded weapons combined.

As if to prove that disarmament as a strategy was not completely lost from the lexicon of arms limitations, a complete prohibition of biological weapons was accepted in a 1972 convention ratified by many states. This convention was the first to ban an entire category of weapons. Also widely accepted by numerous states, a 1993 convention eliminated chemical weapons and went even further than the biological convention by providing for an IGO that would exercise inspection and verification duties. Then, as if to amaze the world, the Soviet Union and the United States agreed in 1987 to destroy a class of intermediate-range missiles with nuclear warheads that were positioned on both sides of the Iron Curtain in Europe. Nuclear disarmament had been regarded as next to impossible.

Between 1989 and 1991, the Soviet Union and the Warsaw Pact collapsed raising hopes for a more general nuclear disarmament breakthrough. In the midst of this huge change, a series of *Strategic Arms Reduction Talks* (START) got underway. These three agreements called, not for ceiling levels, but actual reductions in missiles and warheads. While the first two were ratified, the START process began to unravel by 2002 (Roberts 2002: 181; Wittner 2003: 447–8; Levi & O'Hanlon 2005: x–xi).

Objectives of Arms Limitations

States want arms for a variety of reasons, ranging from prestige to security, but they also have strong motives for pursuing arms limitations. Basically, the objectives of arms limitation agreements are to save blood and treasure. Most states and their peoples want peace, and their governments often use arms treaties as one means to bolster peaceful relations. Arms limitations between adversaries can tacitly signal desires for reduced tensions and a relationship that stops short of violent conflict. Even if fighting does break out, weapons restrictions, such as the outlawry of lethal gas, will reduce the suffering in war.

The massive amount of destruction wrought by two world wars, followed by decades of living under the shadow of nuclear war, have sensitized those living in the early twenty-first century to put peace at a premium. Over 20 million died in the First World War and more than 50 million lost their lives in the Second World War. The First World War killed more people than all the nineteenth century wars put together, and the Second World War accounted for deaths amounting to more than half the war deaths over the past two millennia (Russell 2001: 10). After these world wars, the further loss of more than 40 million lives through 250 wars and conflicts in the Third World has also been sobering (Ball 1994: 216). The enormity of human costs in war is difficult to fathom, but certainly the "butcher's bill of combat" is always a high price to pay.

Another kind of cost is in economic wealth. Arms limitations can save billions of dollars, leaving monies available for homes, schools, hospitals, and medicines which all humankind requires. The Cold War's decline provided some relief. Between 1987 and 1997, Warsaw Pact expenditures fell by one-third, mostly affecting the Soviet Union/Russian budget, while the NATO states' costs dropped by one-fourth (Burroughs 2002: 11). Unfortunately, the war on terrorism has caused costs to rise once again, especially for the United States, which alone accounts for nearly half of the world' military expenditures. Under President George W. Bush, annual military budgets have risen sharply to cover wars in Afghanistan and Iraq. In 2009, the war is winding down in Iraq, but President Barack Obama has raised the US military commitment in Afghanistan. For the entire world, military expenditures for the entire world are close to $1 trillion per year.[2] Moreover, numerous internal conflicts, ranging from 20 to 40 each year in as many as several dozen Third World countries, has made for a lively global arms bazaar. The much ballyhooed *peace dividend* talked about at the end of the Cold War, allowing old military money to become new benefits for human needs, has not been fully realized (Renner 1994).

Obstacles to Arms Limitations

The appealing goals of saving lives and money encourage arms limitations, but serious obstacles also stand in the way of their success. Obstacles are at least two-fold. The main obstacle is the mutually felt fear states have of one another's intentions in an anarchic world. True, the budding international society does share international law and much of the same global agenda, ranging from airport security to a more prosperous world economy; nonetheless, dangerous actors such as weapons-hungry states and terrorists still inhabit the world and threaten its order. A second and lesser obstacle, but one that sometimes hobbles potential arms treaties, involves the technical problems that arise during arms negotiations.

In compliance with the UN Charter that eliminates the offensive option as normal state policy, many states today are committed to a defensive stance, but they can still be caught up in a vexing security dilemma. Efforts by one state to enhance its security for defensive reasons can easily cause fear and uncertainty on the part of other states. One state's security is another state's insecurity.

States so entwined may be drawn into an arms race. Leaders may try to match or surpass the armaments of a potential adversary, and then the adversary responds in similar fashion, forcing arms acquisition into an upward spiral. The tensions endemic to an arms race might well contribute to the outbreak of war. It is equally true that weapons agreements can check arms races and help avert war (Wesson 1990: 63; O'Connell 1989: 301).

Today, the political and security environment for many states has improved substantially. The Western European states, after suffering the devastation of two World Wars, have for decades had an informal understanding that it is inconceivable that one state would attack another. Gradually most of the Eastern European states are being drawn into this community as is evidenced by their inclusion in NATO, the Council of Europe with its human rights program, and the EU with its economic criteria for membership. As for Russia, it is a member only of the Council of Europe. This new environment is promising but not completely assured. Russia's resentment of the eastward expansion of NATO and its questionable commitment to democracy are particularly troublesome.

Many other states around the world have minimal military forces and do not seem to be lured toward expensive weapons programs, despite the realists' past assertion that states are caught up in a lust for power (Morgenthau 1973: 29–41). For instance, Costa Rica got rid of its army in 1954, and Iceland manages with a small coast guard. New Zealand gives as much priority to its Disarmament Agency as it does defense arrangements (Renner 1994: 59, fn. 13).

Yet, there are some states, the *rogues* as they are called by some leaders in the West, which seem unwilling to fit into the international order of peace and economic prosperity pursued by the majority of states. States like Iran and North Korea seem intent on nuclear weapons programs with their ultimate purposes for nuclear weapons unclear. Before President George W. Bush sent American military forces into Iraq in 2003, he referred to Iran, Iraq, and North Korea as the "axis of evil" because of their presumed dangerous ambitions for weapons with catastrophic consequences. Whether a state deserves rogue status is ultimately a matter of perspective.

Should the United States be put in this category of dangerous states, instead of being regarded as a benevolent hegemon? In the opinion of some, the willingness of the United States to use "shock and awe" pre-emptive military strikes, the ongoing upgrade of its nuclear program, and the US determination to maintain unchallengeable military supremacy qualify the United States as the "rogue superpower" (MccGwire 2005: 115–40). These Bush policies might still prove to be an aberration to the US historical record of emphasizing disarmament, peace, diplomacy, and international law. In 2009, President Obama faces a challenging domestic agenda that may force the United States to downsize militarily.

Even if states can move past their fears and political ambitions to negotiate arms limitations, they still face several technical problems that can disrupt arms treaties. *Power ratios* require measuring the military power of one country against another. Specifically, this measure can mean deciding how many of a particular weapon each country will be allotted. Since states have military forces and weapons configured in different ways, calculating ratios among their weapons can be taxing. Perhaps the best known treaty using a ratio arrangement was the 1922 *Washington Naval Treaty*. This treaty dealt with the battleships of five countries that promised to arrive at the following ratio over a 20-year period: Great Britain (5), the United States (5), Japan (3), France (1.67), and Italy (1.67).

In weapons negotiations, states also disagree about the *orientation* of weapons, basically whether they are *offensive* or *defensive* weapons. Usually, military forces use offensive weapons when on the attack and defensive weapons to repel an attack. In practice, a theoretically clear distinction can blur. In ancient Greece, Sparta objected to the Athenians building a wall around their city, which to the Athenians seemed purely defensive. The Spartans worried that Athens, as a naval power, could attack Sparta with near impunity since the Athenian wall would blunt the effectiveness of Sparta's famed infantry. The defensive wall allowed Athens to go on the offensive elsewhere.

Arguments can also arise over a *strategic weapon* as distinguished from a *theater weapon*. Long-range bombers and ICBMs that can strike from one point to the other side of the world are strategic while a theater weapon operates within a geographical region such as North America or East Asia. The United States insisted that the Soviet "backfire" bomber, which could be refueled in mid-air and reach the United States, had to be counted as a strategic weapon. The Soviets then countered that cruise missiles, attached to the wings of a B-52 long-range bomber, were also strategic weapons.

Verification refers to the inspection of weapons systems, or of sites to guarantee that agreements about weapons are indeed being kept. The inspectors can be from an adversary state or an IGO. Security rests not only with a country's armaments but on the sure knowledge that an opponent is not cheating on an arms agreement. The maximum achievements countries might hope to accomplish through arms negotiations rest largely on verification possibilities. Verification can include aerial surveillance, spy satellites, on-site inspections by arms experts, and monitoring devices such as cameras placed in sealed lock-boxes at nuclear facilities.

Russia, since at least the time of Peter the Great, has been highly suspicious of outsiders so verification arrangements were slow to develop in the Soviet-American relationship. The Soviets turned down Truman's Baruch Plan and Eisenhower's Open Skies proposal. Spy satellites did offer some inspection opportunities by both sides and helped SALT I become a reality. The first true inspections on the territories of the two superpowers came about through the 1987 INF treaty, with American and Russian observers watching the other side destroy the rockets for medium-range missiles. Today, inspections are considered to have paramount importance for the success of weapons treaties but, unfortunately, some treaties fail to include such safeguards. Traditionally, countries have jealously guarded their sovereignty and are inclined to see inspections as unwanted intrusions.

The Nuclear Regime

The next several sections focus on the norms and rules that states agree to as they develop a regime for a particular weapons category and the effectiveness of that regime. The weapons' profiles of selected states appear in Table 7.1. Nuclear weapons, along with biological and chemical weapons, are together known as *Weapons of Mass Destruction* (WMDs), although there is no customary or treaty law that authoritatively defines this set of weapons.[3] The WMD concept is widely understood, however, and is used by military experts, journalists, and scholars. For instance, the UN Security Council in 2004, acting under its enforcement powers, required that all states take measures to prevent the proliferation of WMDs and their means of delivery.

The first atomic bombs, including those used at Hiroshima and Nagasaki, were fission bombs, meaning they release an enormous explosive energy when a chain reaction of enriched uranium or plutonium atoms is set off in all directions. By the early 1950s, the American and Soviet bomb-makers turned to hydrogen bombs, sometimes called thermonuclear weapons because these weapons need a high degree of heat and pressure to trigger the explosive energy in a fusion process. Hydrogen bombs draw atoms together instead of driving them apart in a chain reaction. These bombs are many times more powerful than the atomic bombs dropped on Japan in 1945.

Radioactive, or "dirty bombs," can also be placed in the nuclear category. A dirty bomb is nothing more than radioactive materials, perhaps gathered from a nuclear

Table 7.1 Weapons profile of selected states

Nuclear club	Nuclear	Biological	Chemical	Missile	NPT	BWC	CWC
China	Over 100 warheads	Some	Advanced	Short-range to ICBMS	Acceded 1992[a]	Acceded 1984	Ratified 1997
France	300 strategic warheads	Program ended	Possibly some stocks	Short-range to ICBMS	Acceded 1992	Acceded 1984	Ratified 1995
Russia	4,978 strategic warheads; 3,500 tactical	Huge stocks under destruction	World's biggest stock pile under destruction	Short-range to ICBMS	Ratified 1970	Ratified 1975	Ratified 1997
UK	Fewer than 200 warheads	Program ended	Possibly some gas stocks	Short-range to ICBMS	Ratified 1968	Ratified 1975	Ratified 1996
US	5,968 strategic warheads; 1,000 tactical	Unilaterally destroyed stocks in 1969	Stocks being destroyed	Short-range to ICBMS	Ratified 1970	Ratified 1975	Ratified 197
"Axis of evil"							
Iran	Program in development	Probably	Several types	Short to medium range	Ratified 1970	Ratified 1973	Ratified 1997
Iraq	Program quashed	Program quashed	Program quashed	Short to medium range but destroyed	Ratified 1969	Ratified 1991	Not signed
North Korea	Up to 6 untested bombs	Probably	Sizeable stockpile	Short to medium range; ICBM in development	Acceded in 1985 but withdrew	Acceded 1987	Not signed
Troubling states							
India	45–95 nuclear weapons	Biodefense program	Destroying stock	Short to medium range; ICBM in development	Not ratified	Ratified 1974	Ratified 1996
Israel	75–200 nuclear warheads	Probably	Probably	Short to medium range	Not ratified	Not ratified	Signed in 1993 but not ratified
Pakistan	30–50 nuclear weapons	Limited research	Possibly a small stock	Short to medium range	Not ratified	Ratified 1974	Ratified 1997

[a] Acceding (an act of accession) to a treaty refers to a ratification by a state that did not take part in the original negotiation of the treaty.

N = Nuclear weapons; B = Biological weapons; C = Chemical weapons; M = Missiles; NPT = Nuclear Non-proliferation Treaty; BWC = Biological Weapons Convention; CWC = Chemical Weapons Convention.

Sources: http://armscontrol.org. See, "Nuclear Weapons: Who Has What at a Glance," "Chemical and Biological Weapons Proliferation at a Glance," and "Worldwide Ballistic Missile Inventories." NPT ratifications are from the Monterey Institute of International Studies at http://cns.miis.edu/pubs/inven/index.htm > Inventory > nuclear weapons and energy > number of parties.

energy reactor, and attached to a conventional explosion such as dynamite or C-4 plastic. A radioactive bomb of this type is the one most accessible by terrorists to use in crowded cities for making thousands of people sick with radiation effects. Chechen rebels placed a container of cesium 137 in a Moscow park in 1996, but did not set it off. Perhaps they just wanted to show Russian authorities they could carry out such a deed. US authorities arrested Jose Padilla in 2002 and held him in detention for over three years as an "illegal non-combatant" for plotting to bring a dirty bomb into the United States. He was never convicted on this charge. A former street-gang member from Chicago who had converted to the Muslim faith, Padilla eventually had federal charges filed against him and, in early 2008, he was sentenced to 17 years for criminal conspiracy concerning overseas terrorism.

Nuclear Non-Proliferation Treaty (NPT)

Since entering into force in 1970, the 1968 NPT has anchored a fairly strong and successful regime for stopping the spread of nuclear weapons. Despite dire predictions in the 1960s that dozens of countries might have atomic weapons in a few decades, the number of nuclear weapons states has remained relatively stable. Currently no more than 10 states have nuclear weapons or programs dedicated to building an atomic bomb in contrast to 16 in the 1980s and 21 in the 1960s.[4] At the end of the Cold War, Belarus, Kazakhstan, and the Ukraine, former Soviet republics, turned over their nuclear warheads and missiles to Russia for disposal, and South Africa voluntarily destroyed its atomic bombs in 1991 and joined the NPT. Argentina, Brazil, Libya, Sweden, Taiwan, and South Korea are among the states that suspended their nuclear weapons programs altogether before making an actual bomb.

Without a doubt, the NPT has helped contain runaway proliferation. Its considerable success has not only come about through the legal mechanism of a treaty binding about 190 states, but also by promoting a strong global norm, a taboo against nuclear weapons of all kinds.

All the news is not good, however. India and Pakistan have never joined the NPT and now have atomic weapons. Israel probably acquired its first atomic bomb in the late 1960s, and their arsenal today could contain as many as 200 atomic bombs, although the Israeli government will not confirm or deny possession of such weapons. North Korea withdrew from the NPT in 2003 and claims to have had an atomic bomb since 1994, which it probably tested in 2006. President George W. Bush took North Korea off its state-terrorist list in 2008 as it dismantled its nuclear weapons facilities, but North Korea has long waged off-and-on-again weapons programs. Iran has resisted the monitoring efforts of the UN's International Atomic Energy Agency (IAEA) and has been reported by the IAEA to the UN Security Council. As for Iraq, its WMD program ended with the Persian Gulf War of 1990–1 and the subsequent UN arms inspections.

Not only does the NPT curtail the expansion of nuclear weapons, but it points the way one day toward a world free of nuclear weapons. The original five nuclear powers, or the "Nuclear Club," were acknowledged by the treaty as legitimate possessors

---

Box 7.1 The IAEA

The International Atomic Energy Agency (IAEA) is a specialized, autonomous agency within the UN System that performs the tasks of regulating safety measures for nuclear energy reactors and, increasingly, since the 1990s, enforces safeguards against the misuse of nuclear technology and materials that would violate the 1968 Nuclear Non-Proliferation Treaty. In 1993, the IAEA offered the *Additional Protocol* to states for ratification that strengthened its safeguards against inappropriate use. The IAEA is known as the world' "nuclear watchdog."

The IAEA began in 1957 as the international body envisioned by President Dwight Eisenhower in his "Atoms for Peace" speech before the UN General Assembly in 1953. The IAEA has 35 member-states on its board of governors and is headquartered in Vienna, Austria. The IAEA and its Director General, Egyptian Mohamed El Baradei, are well-respected, having jointly won the 2005 Nobel Peace Prize.

The most troublesome state the IAEA has had to contend with currently is Iran. Despite its protestations to the contrary, Iran is under suspicion for pursuing a covert nuclear weapons program. Finally, in early 2006, the IAEA reported Iran to the UN Security as being uncooperative. It is unclear whether the Security Council will sanction Iran. Either China or Russia might veto an enforcement step.

Sources: The homepage of the IAEA is http://www.iaea.org/. Additional reading is Ko Colijn, "Non-proliferation: Reinforcing the IAEA Nuclear Safeguards Regime in the 1990s," in Bob Reinalda and Bertjan Verbeek (eds.), *Autonomous Policy Making by International Organizations* (New York: Routledge, 1998), pp. 93–107.

---

of nuclear weapons because their possession of these weapons predated the 1968 NPT. Naturally, this arrangement created a system of nuclear "haves" and "have nots" with the would-be nuclear weapons states, in particular, finding this arrangement hypocritical.

During the 2000 review of the NPT, numerous states, still chafing over the two-class system of "haves" and "have nots," reminded the privileged five of their obligations, under Article 6 of the NPT, to move toward their own nuclear disarmament, a commitment they accepted (Perkovich 2003: 2–14, esp. 2). Presumably, India and Pakistan, and any other nuclear state, would be expected to do the same if they were parties to the NPT.

Comprehensive Nuclear Test-Ban Treaty (CTBT)

Another major arms control development was the move toward a moratorium on testing nuclear explosions. A comprehensive test ban was mentioned as a future goal in the 1963 Partial Test Ban Treaty and was restated as a goal in the preamble of the 1968 NPT. The UN Conference on Disarmament in Geneva produced the 1996 CTBT, after working on the project for over two years. It was hoped the CTBT would slow down nuclear arms competition and block further nuclear weapons proliferation. When the CTBT enters into force, it will have a verification feature, a Comprehensive Test Ban Treaty Organization that will monitor treaty parties' compliance (Cirincione 2002: 142–3).

The CTBT faces a high hurdle before it can be implemented, however. All 44 states in possession of nuclear reactors, whether for weapons or energy, must ratify the treaty before it goes into force. A total of 148 countries have ratified but not all those states with nuclear reactors have made this commitment.[5] Of the Nuclear Club, France, Russia, and the United Kingdom have ratified the CTBT but not China and the United States. President Bill Clinton signed the CTBT in 1996 but the US Senate has not completed ratification process. The United States has so far respected the moratorium against testing nuclear weapons, nonetheless. India, North Korea, and Pakistan have not even signed the CTBT, and India and Pakistan, so far, are the only states breaking the test-ban taboo by exploding nuclear weapons underground in 1998. Despite these exceptions, a strong international norm against testing is firmly in place.

The Intermediate Nuclear Force Treaty (INF)

In 1987, the INF required the destruction of a class of intermediate-range missiles in Europe and their warheads shelved in an arsenal. Not only did the INF involve partial disarmament, this treaty also created the first major inspection and verification arrangement on weapons between the Soviet Union and the United States. The INF was very likely made possible because the Soviet leader and reformer, Mikhail Gorbachev, needed relief from weapons competition with the United States to concentrate on his pressing economic problems at home.[6]

The Strategic Arms Reduction (Talks) Treaties (START)

The START process built on the SALT process of the 1970s. An era of improving relations at the Cold War's twilight led to START I, signed in 1991 and entered into force in 1993. This treaty called for a limit of 1,600 delivery vehicles (missiles and bombers) and 6,000 warheads and bombs apiece, down from over 10,000 possessed by each side. Taking 9 years to negotiate, this treaty offered multiple types of inspection in its 400 pages, making it the longest and most complex of arms treaties.

Continuing this favorable momentum, START II was signed in 1993 with the United States ratifying in 1996 and Russia in 2000. This agreement would take the old adversaries through two phases of nuclear downsizing before finally reaching a limit of 3,000 to 3,500 nuclear weapons on all delivery systems by 2007. START II would also prohibit MIRVED systems, or ICBMs equipped with multiple warheads. Unfortunately for this treaty, when President George W. Bush announced the US withdrawal from the ABM treaty in late 2001, President Vladimir Putin of Russia refused to implement START II. Another unavoidable consequence was that plans for a START III had to be scrapped. This agreement would have cut nuclear weapons to a range of 1,500 to 2,000 for each side.[7]

As a fallback agreement, and mostly to please President Putin, President Bush agreed to meet in Moscow and sign the 2002 *Strategic Offensive Reduction Treaty* (SORT), a treaty that entered into force the next year. President Bush made it clear, however, that he wanted no further nuclear weapons agreements.[8] Better known as the Moscow Treaty, SORT requires a reduction in strategic nuclear weapons to range of 1,700 to 2,200 deployed weapons by December 31, 2012, when the agreement can be renewed or allowed to expire. What the Moscow treaty does not do is eliminate MIRV systems, tactical warheads, and the large stock of thousands of warheads that can be kept in storage. In April 2009, President Barack Obama and Russian President Dmitri Medvedev met in person for the first time and announced a desire to return to the START process.

Nuclear Weapons Free Zones (NWFZs)

The treaties discussed so far try to limit or discard nuclear weapons that already exist. A very different approach to proliferation is the NWFZs. A NWFZ is a specific region where the states of that region, say Africa or Latin America, agree that they will not acquire, make, test, or deploy nuclear weapons in any form. Article Seven of the NPT provides for these zones, which complement and reinforce the NPT by adding one more way to check nuclear proliferation. Essentially NWFZs are *preclusion arrangements*. Countries can much more easily agree to preclude nuclear weapons than get rid of them once they count on these weapons for their national security. Other regions wish to avoid the South Asian experience in which India developed a nuclear weapon partly because China, next door, had one, and then Pakistan followed suit because India, their adversary in three wars, had built one. Preclusion arrangements throttle an arms race before it can get underway.

NWFZs have helped keep the entire southern hemisphere of the planet free of nuclear weapons. These zones include Latin America under the 1967 *Treaty of Tlatelolco*, the South Pacific guided by the 1985 *Treaty of Rarotonga*, Southeast Asia with the 1995 *Treaty of Bangkok*, and Africa will be governed by the 1996 *Treaty of Pelindaba* when it goes into force. Similarly, the 1959 Antarctica Treaty, the 1967 Outer Space Treaty, the 1971 Seabed Treaty, and the 1979 Moon Treaty ban nuclear weapons and WMDs in general. Other proposed NWFZs include the Korean peninsula, Central Asia based on five former Soviet Republics in that area, and the Baltic Sea region.[9]

The legality of nuclear weapons

If major regions have turned their backs on nuclear weapons, why not rid the entire world of these weapons, perhaps by means of international law? The obvious answer is a political – military one: nuclear armed states view their security and status as dependent on these weapons and take a stern view of their sovereign right to possess them. Nevertheless, an effort to have these weapons declared illegal has, in fact, taken place. As early as 1961, the UN General Assembly passed a resolution stating that any state using nuclear weapons would be violating the UN Charter and humanitarian law.[10]

In 1993, the World Health Organization (WHO) asked for an advisory opinion from the ICJ about the legality of nuclear weapons but was denied standing before the court in a 11–3 ruling. The ICJ said WHO could only bring questions about health effects once a nuclear weapon has been detonated.[11]

The issue was more seriously engaged in 1994 when the UN General Assembly sought an advisory opinion on the question, "Is the threat or use of nuclear weapons in any circumstance permitted under international law?" In 1996, the ICJ ruled unanimously that neither customary nor treaty law specifically authorizes the threat or use of nuclear weapons, but in an 11–3 vote it also said no law prohibits these weapons either. In the narrowest vote possible, a tie-vote of seven to seven broken by the President of the court, the ICJ concluded that the threat or use of nuclear weapons would be contrary to the rules of international law, with the possible exception of a state facing a desperate need for self-defense.

The chief concern of the court was that any use of nuclear weapons would obliterate the distinction between non-combatants and combatants. This distinction is one of the oldest principles behind the laws of war. Yet, the "block-buster" and napalm bombs of the Second World War had already erased the line between civilian and military persons before the two atomic bombs were dropped on Japanese cities in 1945. Fortunately, the Second World War practice of bombing cities into rubble did not establish customary law allowing such acts. Finally, the ICJ issued a unanimous opinion reconfirming the obligation under Article Six of the NPT that nuclear powers must disarm these weapons. This case was reported in several hundred pages and includes numerous declarations and separate assenting and dissenting opinions by the 15 judges of the ICJ. Perhaps the safest conclusion is that this 1996 advisory decision by the ICJ falls short of an unequivocal outlawry of nuclear weapons but, even so, the thrust of the decision is toward the general illegality of nuclear weapons and supports the growing taboo of international society against nuclear armaments.[12]

Export-control groups

Not all support for an arms limitation regime operates through treaties or norms generated by international society. There are several groups of states within international society that have set up voluntary export controls to reinforce treaty prohibitions. These export-control states are usually called *suppliers groups*, and they reinforce nuclear, biological, chemical, missile, and conventional weapons regimes. In the case of the nuclear regime, two suppliers groups are at work (Gualtieri 2000: 467–86).

The *Zangger Committee*, named after the first chairman, Dr. Claude Zangger of Switzerland, is formerly known as the NPT Exporters Committee and began meeting with ten states in 1971 and now has grown to 35. This suppliers group meets in Vienna twice a year, the host city of IAEA. The Zangger Committee restricts exports of materials and technology that would violate the Safeguards Program of the IAEA and might eventually contribute to the development of a nuclear weapon.[13] The *Nuclear Suppliers Group* (NSG) began meeting in 1975 and its 39 members overlap with the membership of the Zangger Committee and largely duplicates its function. The two groups took steps to harmonize their export-control list in 1992, but with the NSG using somewhat tougher standards on the production and use of fissile materials, namely, enriched uranium and plutonium.[14] Despite some duplication, operating with both groups means more states are brought on board to help.

The business-oriented Bush administration apparently flouted a bedrock principle of export controls by selling nuclear technology and fissile material to India, a state that is not a member of the NPT and whose nuclear reactors were not inspected by the IAEA. In the 2005 Indo-US Nuclear Agreement, many of India's nuclear reactors were designated civilian in purpose, and the others military, with IAEA's inspectors allowed to visit the civilian reactors. The IAEA gave its approval for the agreement, probably hoping India can be gradually drawn into the nuclear nonproliferation regime.

An old idea that would assist the supplier groups and the nuclear regime in general is the proposed *Fissile Materials Cut-off Treaty* (FMCT) to ban fissile materials for making nuclear weapons. The UN General Assembly called for such a treaty in 1993, and UN Conference on Disarmament considered the FMCT for over a decade. President Bill Clinton offered his support in 1996, but President George W. Bush objected on the grounds that the FMCT would not be verifiable.[15] This treaty has not come to fruition. Since the major nuclear powers have stopped producing fissile materials, this treaty would mainly affect new nuclear weapons states such as India, North Korea, and Pakistan and possibly Iran, assuming it wants weapons-grade fissile materials.

Also, other policies are designed to prevent fissile materials or technology from reaching the wrong hands. In 2003, the United States began an innovative policy that has received support from an increasing list of states, accumulating to as many as 60 cooperating at various levels. Known as the *Proliferation Security Initiative* (PSI), the United States and cooperating states have begun interdicting suspicious cargoes by land, sea, and air that might involve the proliferation of WMDs. The first line of defense calls for states to monitor carefully their ports and customs facilities. Many states are also willing to search ships within their territorial waters regarding suspicious cargoes. The boldest part of PSI is the bilateral arrangements that allow participating states to board the ships of other states on the high seas. The United States has boarding agreements with Liberia and Panama, among other states, which are notorious for "selling" flags of convenience and whose ships carry a large portion of the world's cargo (Squassoni 2005: 1–6; Levi & O'Hanlon 2005: 70–1).

Another US policy has eliminated fissile material from the territory of the old Soviet Union. The 1991 *Soviet Nuclear Threat Reduction Act*, better known as the Nunn – Lugar Act, provided for the *Cooperative Threat Reduction Program* which got underway in 1993. This program has disposed of thousands of nuclear weapons, leaving the ex-Soviet states of Kazakhstan nuclear free in 1995 and Belarus and the Ukraine in 1996.

A danger existed that fissile materials, and even completed nuclear weapons, could reach rogue states and terrorists. In 2002, the G-8 (the leading industrial democracies of Canada, France, Germany, Italy, Japan, the United Kingdom, and the United States plus Russia) began helping with the costs in a program known as the *Global Partnership against the Spread of Weapons and Materials of Mass Destruction* (Campbell & Einhorn 2004: 340–1; Roberts 2002: 183ff.).

The utility of nuclear weapons

Perhaps the ultimate danger threatening the nuclear regime is that some states may actually believe nuclear weapons have utility. Not everyone left the Cold War behind convinced that using nuclear weapons would be an irrational act, which assumes that

---

Box 7.2 A. Q. Khan

Abdul Qadeer Khan has been at the nexus of a black market trade in nuclear weapons and missiles since the early 1990s. A PhD in metallurgical engineering, but not a nuclear physicist, Khan still learned enough while working for a Dutch nuclear facility to help his country, Pakistan, to develop the first and, so far, only nuclear bomb in the Islamic world. He is a great hero in his country and is called the "father of Pakistan's atomic bomb." Khan has also been referred to as the "Johnny Appleseed of centrifuges" because he has helped several or more states acquire this special equipment needed to enrich uranium for an atomic bomb. His major trade partners were Iran, Libya, and North Korea. By trading with other states, Khan accumulated all that Pakistan required including a blueprint for a Chinese atomic bomb in the 1980s and missile technology from North Korea after 1992. Along the way, he enriched himself and his associates.

Suspicious of Khan's activities as early as 2001, the United States pressured Pakistan to halt this trade. Pakistan's President Pervez Musharraf placed Khan under house arrest in 2004, but he was released from house arrest in early 2009. Khan is unlikely to face charges in a court due to an insufficiency of evidence. The position of the Pakistani government has always been that Khan's activities were unknown to government leaders, a position that strains belief.

Sources: More can be read about A. Q. Khan in Michael Laufer, "A. Q. Khan Nuclear Chronology," http://www.carnegiendowment.org/publications/; *World Press Review* (April 2004), pp. 7–12. Many of Khan's specific activities are reported in Jim A. Davis and Barry R. Schneider (eds.), *Avoiding the Abyss: Progress, Shortfalls, and the Way Ahead in Combating the WMD Threat* (Maxwell Air Force Base, Alabama: USAF Counter-proliferation Center, 2005); see also "Khan" in the index of this work.

no goal is worthy of employing nuclear weapons. Each member of the Nuclear Club has commented on the circumstances that might justify the use of these weapons. The United States, for instance, has the largest and most sophisticated arsenal of these weapons and has considered some nuclear options. President George W. Bush's *Nuclear Policy Review* of 2002 strongly suggested that his administration thought about practical applications of nuclear weapons in today's world. Under President Bush, the United States upgraded its nuclear arsenal, at least qualitatively, while opposing the proliferation of these weapons elsewhere (Deller, Makhijani, & Burroughs 2003: 139–40; Campbell & Einhorn 2004: 322–3; Lieber & Press 2006: 42–54). In particular, the Bush administration wanted a "Robust Nuclear Earth Penetrator," a bunker-buster that could be used to knock out underground WMD facilities in rogue states through pre-emptive strikes. This administration also desired a weapon about half the size of the Hiroshima bomb so it would be more "usable" to retaliate against biological or chemical attacks. As long as nuclear weapons states find these useful, some non-nuclear states will attempt to follow their example.

The Biological Weapons Regime

Biological weapons are based on living organisms, mostly bacteria and viruses. Anthrax has been used as a bacterial weapon while smallpox could be used as a viral weapon, and then there are toxins such as ricin. The dangers of rogue states or terrorists using these agents are very real. In 1984, a religious cult, Bhagwen Shree Rajneesh, made 750 people in the state of Oregon ill with the bacteria salmonella, but fortunately without any deaths occurring. Shortly after the 9/11 terrorist attack in 2001, an unknown party sent letters contaminated with anthrax to members of the US Congress and members of the media, killing 5 and making 18 other people ill. This anthrax incident caused widespread panic and billions of dollars in security and de-contamination costs (Cirincione 2002: 11). In early 2004, ricin was found in US Senate Majority Leader Bill Frist's office, but no one was harmed.

The biological weapons regime began with a treaty that covered both gas and germ warfare, as these categories of weapons have been called in the past. The 1925 *Protocol for the Prohibition of the Use in War of Asphyxiating, Poisonous, or Other Gases, and of Bacteriological Methods* (Geneva Protocol) entered into force in 1928 and today has over 130 ratifications.[16] This protocol does not prohibit stockpiles of these weapons but only their use in wartime. The victors of the First World War, having witnessed thousands die or become injured by mustard and chlorine gas, wanted to be sure these heinous weapons would never be used again, and outlawed germ warfare for good measure. This treaty was mostly honored in the Second World War, although Japan is known to have set up a germ warfare facility in northern China and may have killed thousands of Chinese with this weapon.

Many years would pass before another important development in the biological regime would occur. The 1972 *Convention on the Prohibition of the Development, Production, and Stockpiling of Bacteriological (Biological) and Toxin Weapons and on Their Destruction* is usually cited as the Biological Weapons Convention (BWC).

This convention entered into force in 1975 and has more than 160 ratifications.[17] It imposes a complete ban on possession and use of biological weapons and is the first treaty to call for the elimination of an entire category of weapons.

As in the case of nuclear weapons, the biological regime has an export-control suppliers group for screening all exports, including dual-use materials and technology. Something that might start out for normal civilian use could be diverted to a weapons program. Assuming this important responsibility is the *Australia Group*, which formed in 1985 and today has 39 members.[18] It monitors chemical exports as well. Members are required to have ratified both the 1972 BWC and the chemical weapons convention that appeared later in 1992. Because of so many dual-use problems, the Australia Group has a complex and difficult job, but one made somewhat easier by being able to focus on a dozen or so roguish states that are thought to have or are pursuing biological and chemical weapons programs. Sometimes these states are referred to as the "dirty dozen."

Although the BWC and the Australia Group are in place, the world is not completely free of biological weapons. Usually placed on the list of suspect states for possessing these weapons are China, India, Iran, Libya, North Korea, Pakistan, Russia, Sudan, and Syria.[19] Iraq supposedly has none since at least the time of the US intervention in 2003 and probably disposed of its biological weapons even earlier. For Third World states the temptation for cheap easy-to-make biological and chemical weapons is understandable since the technology behind atomic weapons is out of the reach of most.

The Soviet Union in the 1970s and 1980s maintained a huge biological weapons program and, thus, violated the BWC on a massive scale. After the Cold War ended, Russia continued a clandestine biological weapons program into the early 1990s. Russia had 60,000 employees working in 18 facilities set up to look like pharmaceutical companies (Wright 2002: 13; Ainscough 2004: 166). If states keep biological weapons, especially if they are unstable and under poor security, the additional danger exists that these nefarious weapons will fall into the hands of bio-terrorists. The program for dismantling nuclear weapons is also supposed to help Russia dispose of biological and chemical weapons.

The US record on biological weapons is mostly a good one but does not go as far as arms limitations advocates would like to see. In 1943 during the Second World War, President Franklin D. Roosevelt said the United States would not be the first to use biological and chemical weapons and would abide by the 1925 Geneva Protocol. The United States, however, did not ratify the Geneva Protocol until 1975 (Graham, Jr 2002: 22). The United States had stockpiled biological weapons from 1942 to 1969, permissible under the Geneva Protocol, when President Richard Nixon announced the United States would destroy these stockpiles. President Nixon's announcement helped set the stage for the United States's 1975 ratification of the 1972 BWC, which called for exactly this act of destruction.

While the BWC was the first post-Second World War weapons agreement to call for the elimination of an entire class of weapons, it has no verification and compliance mechanism (Guthrie, Hart, & Kuhlau 2005: 603–28, esp. 604). Often the ratifying states do not even turn in their voluntary reports. A protocol calling for on-site inspections has been proposed for the BWC for some time. While President Bill Clinton said he was for it, President George W. Bush, in 2001, opposed an inspections capability citing as his reasons that such inspections would threaten US bio-defense plans and US proprietary interests (Chevrier 2002: 153). As a consequence, global inspections for biological weapons are not in place.

At least Russia, the United Kingdom, and the United States set-up a trilateral inspections arrangement after the bio-weapons program of Russia was discovered in the early 1990s. This arrangement permitted inspections by the three states of each other's biological facilities to make sure they were for peaceful purposes. Unfortunately, the trilateral inspections stalled when Russia refused inspectors entry to facilities controlled by their Ministry of Defense (2002: 146–7).

Finally, although the United States is very alert to the continued presence of bio-weapons in other countries, it has had at least one very serious allegation leveled against its practices. One source claims that the United States, in the late 1990s, built an anthrax weapon and did so in secrecy, clearly violating the 1972 BWC (Deller, Makhijani, & Burroughs 2003: xiii).

The Chemical Weapons Regime

Unlike biological weapons, chemical weapons are made from non-living materials. This category includes the mustard and chlorine gases used in the trench warfare of the First World War, and nerve gases that were first developed in Germany in the 1930s. Nerve gases block enzymes in the human body causing loss of muscle control, respiratory failure, and then death. Sarin and VX nerve agents are well-known examples (Cirincione 2002: 5–6).

While biological weapons are regarded as poor battlefield weapons, chemical weapons have worked all too well. In addition to the gas attacks of the First World War, Egyptian troops used gas warfare in Yemen in the 1960s. Iraq, in a much better known case, used lethal gas in the 1980s against Iranian troops, with Iran retaliating in like kind. Iraq also gassed Kurdish villagers in 1988 because Saddam Hussein accused them of disloyalty in wartime. The United States received considerable criticism during the Vietnam War for using tear gas to drive the Viet Cong out of their tunnels and a defoliate, known as Agent Orange, to destroy many square miles of plants and trees, so guerrilla soldiers would have fewer places to hide.

Probably the greatest fear about chemical weapons today is that terrorists will acquire them. Already the terrible incident of the Japanese cult, Aum Shinrikyo, releasing sarin gas in the Tokyo subway system in 1995 has taken place. Twelve people died and hundreds were injured as a mass panic took place. Until this episode of terrorism occurred, Japan was regarded of as one of the safest countries in the world (Russell 2001: 231; Couch 2003: 4–5). Al-Qaida, the terrorist organization behind the 9/11 attack, has made it clear that it seeks a WMD to greatly strengthen its striking power (Couch 2003: 6–7). If an atomic device is out of reach, a chemical weapon would be the terrorist's next best choice because it is more deadly and controllable than biological agents. Chemical weapons have been called the "poor man's atomic bomb."

Construction of a chemical weapons regime began in the nineteenth century at the 1899 Hague Convention with a protocol banning projectiles designed to spread asphyxiating gases. Later the 1925 Geneva Protocol then prohibited the use of gas and germ agents in war, but not the making and stockpiling of these weapons. Negotiations for a comprehensive chemical convention began in the 1980s because of a worldwide concern over the use of lethal gas in the Iran–Iraq war of that decade.

The result of these negotiations was the 1992 *Convention on the Prohibition of the Development, Production, Stockpiling, and Use of Chemical Weapons and on Their Destruction*, better known as the Chemical Weapons Convention (CWC).[20] The CWC went into force in 1997 and has 187 state parties. This convention not only prohibits an entire category of weapons, but goes the BWC one better by having enforcement powers requiring transparency in countries' chemical industries. Enforcement is through the *Organization for the Prohibition of Chemical Weapons* (OPCW) with its headquarters at the Hague staffed by 500 employees. Any member of the CWC can ask for verification on short notice regarding another member's activities. The CWC is the closest arrangement yet to a WMD treaty with teeth.[21]

With over 70,000 tons of declared chemical weapons in the world, their destruction is a big job, but based on the CWC, this task was supposed to have been accomplished by 2007. Many countries could not meet this deadline, especially Russia with its huge stockpile of more than half the world's total plus limited funds and technology for this task (Guthrie, Hart, & Kuhlau 2005: 611–13). As in the case of nuclear and biological weapons, the Cooperative Threat Reduction Program, initiated by the United States, is helping Russia to destroy its gas stocks. The US record on the CWC has been a good one. The United States led in negotiating the CWC from the outset and has made better progress than most at destroying its gas stocks.

As with the biological regime, the Australia Group reinforces the chemical weapons regime through voluntary export controls; in fact, the Australia Group arose first as a concern with chemical weapons proliferation and added biological export controls in 1990. The 38 members monitor over 50 chemicals and specific kinds of equipment (Gualtieri 2000: 475–7). The dual-use nature of chemicals is as much a problem as it is for biological materials and technologies. The gas Iraq's Saddam Hussein used against Iranian soldiers was supposedly made with insecticide-making equipment bought from West Germany years before. Even the solvent in ballpoint pens can help make mustard gas (Cirincione 2002: 396). At least the Australia Group, as with biological exports, can focus on monitoring chemicals exported to the "usual suspects," a dozen or more countries with possible clandestine chemical weapons programs.

The Missile Control Regime

The missile control regime is the only one without a treaty to ground the regime. The main line of defense against further proliferation of missiles is the *Missile Technology Control Regime* (MTCR), a voluntary export-control arrangement. The basic idea behind the MTCR is to limit the danger of WMDs by controlling a major delivery system that can easily carry these weapons to target.[22]

The MTCR was established in 1987 largely at the urging of the United States and other leading industrial powers and presently has 34 members. The missiles at concern are non-crewed air-vehicle systems with the minimum capabilities of carrying a payload of 500 kilograms (1,100 pounds) and traveling a distance of 300 kilometers (186.2 miles). Missiles usually fall in one of three categories according to their range: short-range of 300–500 kilometers (186.2 to 310.5 miles), medium-range of 1,000–2,000 kilometers (621 to 1,242 miles), and long-range ICBMs that can successfully launch from one site, travel through outer space, and then strike a target in a country on the other side of the planet. These missiles are often called "ballistic missiles" because they involve the science of being designed for maximum flight performance.

Ballistic missiles are a special threat because they can strike very fast, with the longest flight of ICBMs measured in minutes, and there is no really effective defense against them at this point in time. They are a particularly frightening weapon capable of carrying biological, chemical, and nuclear warheads (Husbands 2002: 172). The MTCR works to minimize this danger by requiring export limitations on complete rockets and the various parts and technologies necessary to construct missiles, including propellant fuels, gyroscopes, special metals, heat shields, electronic guidance systems and much else. Undelivered, one critical part can stop or undermine the development of a missile.

More than 25 states have short-range missiles, and at least five regional powers (India, Israel, Iran, North Korea, and Pakistan) possess intermediate range-missiles. Five states (China, France, Russia, the United Kingdom, and the United States) have ICBMs, although China's 18–20 ICBMS operate with a lower-level of technology than the other ICBM states, and Russia's strategic capability is widely perceived to be much degraded since the end of the Cold War. Only the United States has ICBMS in large numbers and in a state of high readiness. And very importantly, many of the US ICBMs can be sea-launched from nuclear powered submarines (Mistry 2003: 8). One US Trident submarine alone can carries 24 ICBMs with multiple warheads and can deliver these nuclear weapons to any point on the globe. It can be argued that the US Trident submarines are the singularly most powerful weapon in the history of humankind.

The chief concern over missile proliferation has been the sale of missiles or related equipment and technical know-how by China, North Korea, and Russia to other states. Supposedly China and Russia have suspended sales of this kind and cooperate with the MTCR despite lacking membership in this supplier's group. China made this commitment in 2000 after the United States agreed to allow American industries to send their satellites aloft on Chinese rockets.

The focus today is on North Korea, which shocked the world with a three-stage rocket launch in 1998. The Taepo Dong I splashed into the Pacific Ocean instead of sending aloft a satellite, but still galvanized the attention of missile experts around the world. North Korea's missiles use liquid fuel instead of the more sophisticated solid-fuel propulsion system, but can easily reach Japan and may have greater range in the future. An effort in 2006 with a Taepo Dong II did not fare well, but led to the UN Security Council forbidding further ballistic missile tests by North Korea. In direct violation of the Security Council, North Korea fired another three-stage Taepo Dong II rocket in April 2009 that may have traveled 1,900 miles before falling harmlessly in the Sea of Japan. A nightmarish scenario for Washington planners is that North Korea does have a nuclear weapon and may some day be able to fashion it as a warhead on the Taepo Dong II still in development. Moreover, North Korea is known to have helped Iran and Pakistan with their single-stage rockets, allowing these states to reach intermediate-range by 1998.

Another problem that might frustrate the work of the MTCR is the ABM system under development in the United States. If this defensive missile system becomes truly workable, it may trigger a new missile arms race. A reliable defensive missile will frighten other states because it will help neutralize their retaliatory capability. China and Russia might then develop many more ICBMs to saturate US defenses and perhaps make their own ABM systems (Larsen 2001: 294).

Confronting the dangers of missile proliferation, the MTCR has performed reasonably well, even without the support of a treaty, by reducing the proliferation problem to a few hard cases, mainly India, Iran, North Korea, and Pakistan that not only are pursuing better missiles but either have or want nuclear weapons. At least Argentina, Brazil, Egypt, South Africa, South Korea, and Taiwan have been persuaded to give up their missile programs and of course Iraq is no longer a player in this field since being occupied by the United States in 2003. Libya terminated its missile and WMD programs in 2003, but it is difficult to say whether it was the MTCR and other weapons regimes or the US intervention in Iraq that persuaded the mercurial leader Moammar Gadhafi to change course.

The MTCR seeks to be a stronger regime by inviting the widest participation possible by states, even if they do not choose to be members. In 2002, the MTCR offered to non-members the *International Code of Conduct against Missile Proliferation* (also known as the Hague Code of Conduct). If states subscribe to this code, they make a political commitment to refrain from developing missile programs. Well over one hundred states have taken what amounts to a pledge to comply. This code was endorsed by the UN General Assembly in 2004, helping to firm up the international norm against the spread of missiles to more countries.[23]

If the MTCR has a serious short-coming, it is its failure to cover space-launched-vehicles (SLV). Already there are eight countries (Brazil, China, India, Israel, Japan, Russia, the Ukraine, and the United States) plus the European Space Agency that build rockets for sending satellites into space (Mistry 2003: 168). Rockets for launching missiles equipped with warheads could easily be built under the cover of a space program (Speier 2000: 205–6). Dinshaw Mistry offers an appropriate and succinct evaluation of the MTCR. He says it is "partly effective, and generally necessary but rarely sufficient, as a non-proliferation tool" (Mistry 2003).

The Conventional Weapons Regime

In recent years, the high drama in the arms limitations field has concerned the dual danger of rogue states or terrorists gaining control of WMDs. The reality is that most casualties, both military and civilian, result from conventional arms, everything from assault rifles to battle tanks. While several significant wars have occurred among states since the Second World War, like the three India–Pakistan wars and the Iran–Iraq war, most conflicts have been internal civil wars and revolutions fought in Third Word countries. Since most of these states do not have significant arms industries, import-ing or smuggling weapons is necessary to supply Third World fighting. This fact high-lights the need for export restraint and control by arms suppliers, both on the part of arms industries and the governments of countries where these weapons are made.

The supply of conventional weapons to the world is no longer structured by the Cold War, with the Soviet Union and the United States offering an abundance of arms to client-states as rewards for their loyalty. In recent years, the arms trade has been more market-driven (Cornish 1996: 5–6). The five vetoed-empowered states of the UN Security Council, the same states as the Nuclear Club, account for nearly 80 percent of the conventional arms that find their way to Third World states, with Russia and the United States far outpacing the other three in arms exports. By itself, the United States accounts for more than half of all conventional arms sales. All together, arms suppliers of this type of weapon have left the world awash in conventional arms.[24]

Why would poor, underdeveloped countries, with so many pressing needs in health care, education, housing, and economic infrastructure, want to spend pre-cious dollars on killing tools? The settlement of political arguments by violence has been ubiquitous in time and place, and certainly Third World countries, troubled by ethnic strife and scarcity, have not escaped politics by means of bloodshed.

Driving the sale and purchase of arms are several forces. Arms suppliers naturally want the profits that arms sales bring. Governments of many countries use weapons to stay in power, relying on everything from pistols to gunship helicopters, as well as torture devices, to carry out acts of political repression. In many failing, or failed, states the government is weak or has collapsed altogether leaving various militias vying with each other for control. In some Third World countries, guerrillas and revolutionary forces "tax" the trade in oil, diamonds, and illicit drugs to raise money for an ample supply of arms. The three Marxist revolutionary armies in Colombia, drawing hefty profits from cocaine trafficking, purchase first-quality weapons and out-gun the Colombian army until the United States supplied this army with heli-copters and machine guns, among other armaments.

As a "term of industry" conventional weapons include the *large arms* of attack helicopters, battle tanks, artillery, warships, jet fighters, and some missiles such as ground-to-air missiles, and *small arms* that usually can be carried by one soldier. These weapons include pistols, assault rifles, and rocket propelled grenades (RPGs). Landmines are also conventional weapons and received a great deal of attention in the 1980s and 1990s.

Several important treaties have helped create a conventional weapons regime. Often overlooked for helping end of the Cold War, with so much focus on WMDs, is the 1990 *Treaty on Conventional Forces in Europe* (CFE), which went into force in 1992 and now has 30 parties. At the Cold War's close, this treaty helped reduce the large Soviet advantage in armor, artillery, combat aircraft, and helicopters, providing equal strength on the part of NATO and the Warsaw Pact (Graham 2002: 185–90). Importantly, this treaty permits inspection and verification. A noteworthy change was arranged in 1999 to allow these weapons to be designated for each country instead of along the lines of the two alliances since the Warsaw Pact dissolved after the breakup of the Soviet Union. However, the United States and a number of

Western European states have not been willing to ratify the changed treaty until Russia removes weapons it has placed in Moldova and breakaway regions of Georgia. Russia, for its part, suspended participation in the CFE in 2007 because of the United States's plans to place defensive missiles in the Republic of Czech and Poland, not far from the western border of Russia.

Another support for the conventional weapons regime is the 1980 *Convention on Prohibitions or Restrictions on the Use of Certain Conventional Weapons which May Be Deemed to Be Excessively Injurious or to Have Indiscriminate Effects.*[25] This convention went into force in 1983 and has 109 states that have ratified. This lengthy title is usually cited as the Convention on Certain Conventional Weapons (CCCW). Operating without a verification system, this convention is based on four protocols with signatories required to accept at least two. The first prohibits fragmentary weapons that cannot be detected by x-ray. The second regulates landmines. While landmines can be deployed under this convention, anti-personnel mines (as opposed to those targeting armored vehicles) must be in mapped fields, detectable by de-mining equipment, and self-deactivating over time. Mines or booby-traps cannot be used against civilians. The third protocol forbids the use of flamethrowers and incendiary devices against civilians. Following rocket attacks by Palestinians in the Gaza strip, Israeli forces attacked in January 2009, using phosphorous artillery shells to create smoke screens for their infantry. Because some Palestinians were burned by these shells, the Palestinians accused Israel of being in violation of the laws of war. Blinding laser weapons are banned by the fourth protocol. Finally, a fifth protocol calls for the clean-up of old munitions. The first three protocols are in force.

In a storied mobilization of the international civil society, hundreds of NGOs formed the *International Campaign to Ban Landmines* in 1992, instead of waiting on states to come up with a convention banning all anti-personnel landmines. In record time, a conference was organized in Ottawa, Canada in 1996 and lasted into the fall of 1997, producing a convention ready for ratification. The 1996 *Convention on the Prohibition of the Use, Stockpiling, Production, and Transfer of Anti-Personal Mines and on Their Destruction* (Ottawa Convention) was the result and it goes much further than the landmine protocol of the CCCW.[26] That is fortunate. There are today tens of millions of landmines still in the ground, often waiting for years after a war is over to kill or maim civilian and wildlife. Millions of more mines remain on shelves of national armories. This convention requires a total ban on anti-personnel mines. The Ottawa Convention entered into force in 1999, and 156 states are parties so far. There is no verification process, but states are to report their progress on the demobilization of mines, both in the ground and on shelves, to the UN. Although China, India, Israel, Pakistan, Russia, and the United States have ratified the CCCW, they have not done so in the case of the Ottawa Convention.

A recent addition to checking conventional weapons is the 2008 *Convention on Cluster Munitions*. There are presently five ratifications, but 30 must occur for this convention to enter into force.[27] This convention prohibits the making or use of cluster bombs which scatters "bomblets" over a wide area. These sub-munitions, about the size of a flashlight battery, can have differently timed fuses set to explode minutes or hours later. They are particularly dangerous to civilians, especially curi-

---

Box 7.3 The Ottawa Convention

The creation of the Ottawa Convention to ban anti-personnel landmines is a phenomenal story of grassroots activism on a global scale. This "citizens' campaign" may be the high-water mark, thus far, of success within the emerging global civil society, which is based on networks of private citizens from many countries working through NGOs. These NGOs are often impatient with the slow pace of sovereign states and their IGOs when it comes to getting results. The International Campaign to Ban Landmines (ICBL) coordinated over a thousand NGOs in more than 60 countries to finally produce a treaty in Ottawa, Canada in 1996.

At the apex of the ICBL was Jody Williams, a citizen of Putney, Vermont who performed much of her leadership duties from her home via the internet. The ICBL and Williams shared the 1997 Nobel Peace Prize.

The broad base of support quickly brought the necessary 40 ratifications required to bring the Ottawa Convention into force with many more ratifications to follow. The US government withheld ratification because it was not allowed a treaty reservation that would leave in place their extensive minefields along the DMZ between North and South Korea. The United States, however, has for years banned the export of landmines and has given millions of dollars to help countries de-mine minefields left over from many wars.

Source: More can be read about the ICBL at its website, http://www.icbl.org/

---

ous children who discover them. During the summer war of 2006, waged against Hezbollah in southern Lebanon, Israel was sharply criticized for dropping hundreds of thousands of these bomblets.

The conventional weapons regime is one where more effective export-controls are needed. Many states can make conventional weapons, and there are many customers, thus, a complex market has emerged and is difficult to monitor. Given the turgid river of weapons flowing into areas of conflict, the record of export-controls, at best, is a mixed one (Husbands 2002: 178). Although a good many states and several IGOs work diligently to stem the weapons flow, their efforts are often undone by secretive activities on the part of weapons companies. One source ranks the weapons industry as the second most corrupt; it is only surpassed in corruption by public works and construction.[28] Questionable practices by arms manufacturers are called the "gray market" while outright illegal sales and smuggling are known as the "black market."

A multilayered regime of export-import controls based on global, regional, and national efforts must build-up to a level of effectiveness. In 1991, the UN General Assembly asked the Secretary-General to set up the *UN Register of Conventional Arms* to bolster transparency in the arms field that would result in more trust and restraint. The weapons covered are the large arms of artillery, battle tanks and other armored vehicles, combat aircraft, helicopters, warships, and certain missiles such as the ground-to-air type. The major arms exporters have responded reasonably well, but many states fail to submit their voluntary annual report on arms transfers.[29]

At the regional level, the EU adopted a 1998 Code of Conduct to set rigorous standards on the sale of arms. The EU has tended to focus on arms shipments to Africa where numerous countries have been or are embroiled in civil strife (Boutwel & Klare 1999: 220). The EU has also adopted the *Program for Prevention and Combating Illicit Trafficking in Conventional Arms* to better monitor black market arms transfers (Husbands 2002: 176). Another regional arrangement is the OAS, which produced the 2002 *Inter-American Convention on Transparency in Conventional Weapons Acquisitions*. It operates in a similar way as the UN Register and covers the same categories of large arms (McShane 1999: 173–8).

The role of governments at the national level is of course to license carefully all weapons sales, check every shipment through customs, and prevent smuggling. Assisting a number of major arms exporters is the *Wassenaar Arrangement* proposed in 1995 in Wassenaar, a town in the Netherlands. Today, 44 member-states maintain export controls over conventional weapons and related dual-use equipment to avoid contributing to ongoing conflicts. Mostly North American and European countries as well as Argentina and Japan participate. Unfortunately, the important arms exporters of Belarus, China, Israel and South Africa do not take part. The Wassenaar Arrangement is voluntary and without an enforcement mechanism. It does have a secretariat in Vienna, Austria, and meets annually to update its export-control lists, and the members exchange reports on what arms they have sold. All decisions are made by consensus. And finally, a "best practices" policy on small arms was agreed to in 2002.[30]

If conventional weapons can be said to have killed far greater numbers than WMDs, it is equally true that the sub-category of hand-held small arms has been chiefly responsible for the high-rate of casualties in the numerous internal conflicts that have cropped up in Third World countries during the 1990s. Amidst these conflicts are a stewpot of militia, rebels, ethnic clans, child soldiers, criminal gangs, and mercenaries, as well as some regular military forces, all well armed. Some fight for economic gain, some for power and turf control, and some for both of these reasons.[31]

Small-arms trade has been especially tough to stop. The end of the Cold War created a glut of rifles and other small arms that could cascade downward to all sorts of arms dealers and spread outward to many countries around the world (Klare 1999: 17). Not only do many countries make these weapons, creating a very difficult problem with tracing sales, but these small weapons are obviously much easier to smuggle than a battle tank. They can be shipped in boxes marked "farm implements" or easily off-loaded on almost any coastline, with small boats ferrying the arms from a cargo ship to shore.

Impressive efforts have been made at the global, regional, and national levels to carry out what former Secretary-General Boutros Boutros-Ghali has called "micro-disarmament." The UN organized the 2001 *Conference on the Illicit Trade in Small Arms and Light Weapons in All Its Aspects* and laid out a *Program for Action* to combat and eradicated this pernicious trade. The most immediate step was to add a firearms protocol to the 2000 *Convention against Transnational Organized Crime*.[32] The *Protocol against the Illicit Manufacturing of and Trafficking in Firearms, Their Parts and Components and Ammunition* calls for countries to make it a crime to illicitly manufacture and traffic in unlicensed firearms sales and to alter or falsify identification markings on firearms. It also requires documentation for all stages of trade.

At the regional level, Europe has taken some promising steps. The EU's Code of Conduct covers small arms as well as conventional arms in general. Additionally, the Organization for Security and Cooperation in Europe (OSCE) established strict standards for trade in firearms in 2003, especially paying attention to buyers in countries with poor human rights records (Stahl 2006: 7, 25).

A particularly impressive regional effort is that of the Latin American members of the OAS. These countries wrote the 1997 *Inter-American Convention against the Illicit Manufacturing of and Trafficking in Firearms, Ammunition, Explosives, and Other Related Materials*. This convention entered into force in 2002. To help carry out this treaty, the same countries created the 1997 *Model Regulations to Control the Movement of Firearms, Ammunition, and Firearms Parts and Components* (Model Regulations) that provides specific guidelines on imports and exports regarding paper work down to the registration number of each weapon. A paper trail is critical to know the origins, the final destination, and all points along the way of a weapon.[33] In 1998, the UN Economic and Social Council praised the OAS arms regulations and called for similar arms rules at the global level.

The Wassenaar Arrangement also helps guide states in their national policies on the export of small arms in addition to the larger conventional arms. To assist states, the Wassenaar Arrangement, as part of its 2002 "best practices" program, established the "Guidelines for Exports of Small Arms and Light Weapons" with a special focus on preventing firearms from reaching terrorists.

As in the area of landmines, and other weapons, NGOs have been important actors trying to stanch the trafficking in small arms. Amnesty International, the International Action Network on Small Arms (IANSA), and the Oxford Committee for Famine Relief (Oxfam), in particular, have banded together to promote the 2000 Arms Trade Treaty (ATA) to stop "gun-running." Having elicited support from dozens of countries, the NGOs promoted this treaty at the UN Review Conference on Small Arms in the summer of 2006.[34] The original conference was in 2001. The ATA grew out of a 1995 International Code of Conduct on Arms Transfers created by a list of Nobel Peace Laureates, now numbering 20 individuals and organizations that have won this prize. Another interesting NGO development is the *Small Arms Survey* begun in 1999 as an annual report. With help from the Swiss government at the start-up stage, the Graduate Institute of International Studies in Geneva researches and publishes each year its report on the small arms trade, and has developed a *Small Arms Trade Transparency Barometer* to gauge efforts aimed at stopping illicit trafficking (*Small Arms Survey* 2004: 134).

Chapter Summary

- States have long pursued the best arms to advantage themselves in conflicts or to increase their influence.
- Arms may not cause wars but they add to international tension through arms races.

- Most arms agreements to save money and lives have been of the arms control type rather than disarmament.
- The chief focus of the major states is on weapons of mass destruction – atomic, biological, and chemical weapons – and important agreements to stabilize the role of these weapons are in place.
- One of the greatest fears of international society is that "rogue" states, such as Iran or North Korea, might attach WMD warheads to a missile, greatly endangering other states.
- Despite the major concern with WMD, the most lethal weapons, currently in use, are small arms, such as assault rifles, in the hands of militias, terrorists, and gangsters.

Discussion Questions

1 What is the difference between disarmament and arms control? Which has the best prospects of being covered by arms treaties and why?
2 What is the START process and what makes it so significant?
3 What is the NPT and its role in arms limitations? How successful has it been?
4 Of the three categories of weapons falling under the rubric of WMD, which has the most effective control regime and why?
5 Small arms have killed more people than any other weapon in recent decades. Why is it so difficult to stop trade flows in this category of arms?

Useful Weblinks

http://www.armscontrol.org/
This is the website of the Arms Control Association offering treaties, country resources, reports, publications, and many other links. This site offers the most recent news on arms issues.

http://www.sipri.org/
This web site is the home page of the Stockholm International Peace Research Institute, one of the world's most respected research institutions on disarmament. Its databases are often the source on arms data found in many publications. It offers many publications and links.

http://www.hrw.org/en/category/topic/arms
Human Rights Watch is one of the best known human rights NGOs in the world. It has a focus on the role of arms and how they threaten the lives and well-being of people, especially women and children. This site offers recent news, publications, information on a country by country basis, and references to important films.

http://www.cns.miis.edu/
The Center for Nonproliferation Studies offers this website specializing in WMDs. The latest news in this field is readily available as are databases, monthly, and tri-monthly reports.

http://www.carnegieendowment.org/npp/
The Carnegie Endowment for International Peace, at this web page, provides links to films, news and analysis, and reports on WMDs. The commentary and publications of arms expert and in-house researcher Joseph Cirincione are important features of this website.

Further Reading

Cherif Bassiouni, M. (ed.) (2000) *A Manual on International Humanitarian Law and Arms Control Agreements.* Ardsley, NY: Transnational.

Craft, Cassady B. (1999) *Weapons for Peace, Weapons for War: the Effect of Arms Transfers on War Outbreak, Involvement and Outcomes.* New York: Routledge.

Dahinden, Erwin (ed.) (2002) *Small Arms and Light Weapons: Legal Aspects of National and International Regulations: Proceedings of the UN Conference on the Illicit Trade in Small Arms.* New York: United Nations Publications.

Falk, Richard A. (2008) *The Costs of War: International Law, the UN, and World Order after Iraq.* New York: Routledge.

Ferguson, Charles D. (Project Director) (2009) *U.S. Nuclear Weapons Policy.* Washington, DC: Brookings Institution Press.

ICON Group International (2009) *Arms Control and Disarmament: Webster's Timeline History, 1825–2007.* San Diego, CA: ICON Group International.

Larsen, Jeffrey A. (2005) *Historical Dictionary of Arms Control and Disarmament.* Lanham, MD: Scarecrow Press.

Schneider, Barry R. and Davis, Jim A. (eds.) (2006) *Combating Weapons of Mass Destruction: Avoiding the Abyss.* New York: Praeger Publishing.

Sinha, P. C. (ed.) (2005) *Encyclopedia of Arms Race, Arms Control and Disarmament.* New Delhi: Anmol Publications.

SIPRI Yearbook: Armaments, Disarmament, and International Security (annual) Stockholm: Stockholm International Peace Research Institute.

Notes

1   The paragraphs above draw on the useful history of earlier arms limitations arrangements by Bassiouni 2000: 1–95.
2   Available at http://www.sipri.org/contents/milap/milex/mex_trends.html.
3   Fidler 2003: 1–4; see esp. p. 1 at http://www.asil.org/ > Publications > Insights > ASIL Insights.
4   Levi and O'Hanlon 2005: 2. The NPT can be read at http://www.atomicarchive.com/ Treaties/Treaty6.shtml.
5   The CTBT is available at http://treaties.un.org/Pages/ParticipationStatus.aspx > Chapter XXVI.
6   This treaty is available at http://www.state.gov/www/global/arms/treaties/inf1.html.

7 For more information on the START process, see Larsen 2002: 389–91; Levi and O'Hanlon 2005: 145–7; and Waller 2002: 106–9.

8 SORT is at http://www.armscontrol.org/ > Treaties & Agreements > Strategic Offensive Reduction Treaty.

9 Go to http://www.armscontrol.org/ Enter Nuclear Weapons Free Zones in the website search engine.

10 A useful, brief summary of the nuclear legality case can be found in Meyer 2002: 227–34.

11 See the website of the ICJ at http://www.icj-cij.org/ > cases > Advisory proceedings 1993 > Request for Advisory Opinion by WHO.

12 The two previous paragraphs draw on Bello and Bekke 1997: 126–33; see also see Boisson de Chazournes and Sands 1999). In the latter source, see esp., Thirlway 1999: 390–1. Also, see the advisory opinions of the ICJ at http://www.icj-cij.org/ > cases > Advisory proceedings > 1993 "Legality of the Use by a State of Nuclear Weapons in Armed Conflict (1993–1996)."

13 The homepage of the Zangger Group is http://www.zanggercommittee.org/Zangger/default.html.

14 The homepage of the Nuclear Suppliers Group is http://www.nuclearsuppliers group.org.

15 Read about FMCT at http://www.fas.org/nuke/control/fmct. pp. 42–54.

16 Refer to http://www.un.org/disarmament/HomePage/treaty/Treaties.shtml.

17 Go to http://www.armscontrol.org > Treaties & Agreements > BWC.

18 The homepage of the Australia Group is http://www.australiagroup.net/

19 This list of suspect states is from Ainscough 2004: 175.

20 Go to http://treaties.un.org/Pages/ParticipationStatus.aspx > Chapter XXVI.

21 The OPCW's website is http://www.opcw.org/.

22 Cirincione 2002: 403–9; the homepage of the MTCR is http://www.mtcr.info/.

23 Institute for Defense and Disarmament Studies found at http://www.mtcr.info/english/objectives.html.

24 Husbands 2002: 168. For a general account on the transfer of conventional arms, see Klare and Lumpe 1999: 160–79.

25 This treaty is located at http://treaties.un.org/Pages/ParticipationStatus.aspx > Chapter XXVI.

26 Locate at http://treaties.un.org/Pages/ParticipationStatus.aspx.

27 The Cluster Munitions Treaty is at http://treaties.un.org/Pages/ParticipationStatus.aspx > Chapter XXVI.

28 Eamon Surry, "Transparency in the Arms Industry," SIPRI Policy Paper no. 12 (January 2006) found at http://www.sipri.org/ > "Transparency in the Arms Industry."

29 Cornish 1996: 65–7; Husbands 2002: 171; the UN's Register is at http://disarmament.un.org/cab/register.html.

30 The homepage for the Wassenaar Arrangement is http://www.wassenaar.org/.

31 Hill 2004: 6; Klare 1999: 1–2; and WHO has estimated 300,000 deaths each according to Lumpe 2003: 10–13; and the estimate is put at half a million deaths in the *Courier*, 44 (Summer 2004), 3–5.

32 This transnational crime treaty is at http://www.unodc.org/ > Treaties.

33 This treaty by the OAS is available at http://www.oas.org/ > Documents > Treaties & Agreements.

34 See the homepage of IANSA at http://www.iansa.org/ > "Small Arms at the UN." Also, at IANSA website enter "Arms Trade Treaty" in the internal search engine > "Control Arms Report."

No one can examine the grim history of the human race, repeatedly ravaged by the pain and horror of war, without feeling a great sadness at its ubiquity and perpetuity. (Donald Kagan)

Terrorism, like cavalry charges, is a tactic that has become largely obsolete. But it took cavalry officers decades to accept that, and terrorists will be with us for a while too. (Gwynne Dwyer, Journalist)

8

Law to Constrain Force

Contents

The more successful societies in history, whether tribes or modern states, have found ways to resolve disputes and accommodate change in a peaceful manner. Today's fledgling international society, however, continues to rely on frequent uses of military force. As actors, private militias, terrorists, and mercenaries are largely defined by their use of violent means. As for states, they remain the primary actors possessing the greatest force capabilities, although they perform other functions in addition to security. The history of states reflects the self-reliant methods of force including acts of military reprisals, intervention, and fighting wars when the stakes are high enough. The use of military force over many centuries has created its own momentum, making the effort to constrain force by law an ambitious task. Nonetheless, a progression of reforms through international law has tried to control violent conflict. Various actors of international society increasingly view warring violence as a great waste of human life, economic resources, and a despoiler of the natural environment.

This chapter begins with a historical overview of the effort to constrain force by law. Next, the twentieth-century evolution to the apex of efforts to limit force by UN rules is described. Then the major problems that threaten to undermine these rules are discussed in turn. There is disagreement over what constitutes aggression and under what circumstances self-defense can operate to blunt such an act. Another problem involves defense against terrorist attacks, a kind of violence unforeseen when the UN Charter was written in 1945. Intervention also is a problem that has plagued world peace, raising questions over its exact meaning and under what circumstances it can be used. A description of peacekeeping follows, a post-Charter innovation improvised to shore up peace. Finally, this chapter identifies some of today's most important issue areas that arise once a war has begun.

A Brief History of the Laws Governing Force

War and lesser levels of force have been so common and persistent in human affairs that ridding humankind of such violence might appear to be an errand of folly. Even the more modest ambition of reducing hardship and suffering in war, by creating so-called "humane warfare," has been called the ultimate oxymoron. Nevertheless, a rich history of rules regulating military violence has accumulated. The opposing groups in a war usually have been states, but recent history demonstrates that terrorists and private militias can also conduct significant military operations. For many international scholars, a conflict rises to the status of war when a thousand casualties occur over a period of several months.[1]

Until twentieth-century efforts to outlaw war altogether appeared, most rule-making energies were expended on how war was conducted. For centuries war was seen as natural and inevitable, and its causes obdurate. It is no wonder that many pragmatic policy-makers have concluded humankind has always suffered war and always will. One source claims 14,500 wars have taken place between 3500 BC and the late 20th century, costing 3.5 billion lives, leaving only 300 years of peace (Beer 1981: 20). Consequently, most efforts have been on constraining force by emphasizing laws during war, leaving the outlawry of war to the idealists.

Other observers are confident that war is not inevitable and thus indelibly stamped into human behavior. Some writers began to view war as a learned human invention, like slavery and dueling, and concluded that it can be unlearned. In a famous article published in 1940, shortly after the Second World War had begun, anthropologist Margaret Mead claimed that war would one day be replaced by something else, something better for resolving conflict, just as the car replaced the horse and buggy.[2]

In recent years, John Mueller has written about war's obsolescence and notes that most wars today are in the poor, underdeveloped region. He predicts that humankind, in time, will move away from military conflict (Mueller 1989; 2004). Keeping in mind the history of a conflict-prone world, efforts to reduce war's barbarity and to outlaw war altogether stand as a testament to human persistence that may yet outlast the human proclivity for turning to violence.

The effort to apply rules to war is ancient. By 700 BCE, the Greeks developed rules of war that included declaring war, respecting non-combatants, avoiding the burning of homes, and refusing to sell fellow Greeks into slavery, but imposed fewer restraints when fighting non-Greeks (Ober 1994: 12–26). The Romans too made declarations of war, scrupulously kept treaties, and fought in honorable ways as long as they were dealing with another city-state regarded as civilized; otherwise, it was all-out war using sword and torch, with little or no mercy shown to non-combatants. Long after the fall of the Roman Empire, a no-holds barred war has sometimes been referred to as a **bellum Romanum**, or Roman war (Stacey 1994: 27; Brand 1968).

After the recession of the Roman Empire from Europe, Europeans developed the Age of Chivalry (1100–1500) during the long medieval age, inspiring a warrior code of conduct. Armored knights on horseback were to apply Christian values of piety, charity, humility, courtesy to ladies, and mercy in battle (Stacey 1994: 27–39). The One Hundred Years War (1337–1453), primarily between France and England, saw a deterioration of the warrior code as the long-bow and cannon greatly diminished the status of the armored knight. In several battles, no quarter was given and prisoners were massacred (1994: 33). Despite some progress in rules for reducing the inhumanity of war, the Thirty Years War (1618–1648), largely contesting whether the Catholic or Protestant faith would prevail in Europe, was even more brutal than the One Hundred Years War had been (Neff 2005: 82). Customary law in Europe would evolve from the 1600s through the 1800s but, unfortunately, customary rules against looting, burning, and the mistreatment of prisoners were often ignored (Rothenberg 1994: 86–97).

A much more comprehensive war-control system than specific customary rules emerged during the early medieval period known as the **just war** tradition. It influenced the Age of Chivalry and later European efforts to wed ethics and war. Chivalrous knights were to defend the Roman Catholic Church and make war against infidels without cessation or mercy, as when conducting military crusades in the Holy Land. A just war involves a moral rationale for going to war and requires moral restraint when fighting a war. As a tradition, it has a long history reaching full-bloom by the time of St Thomas Aquinas (1225–1274). Five distinct principles came to make up the just war doctrine: (1) a war must be ordered by a proper authority, (2) fighting is restricted to combatants and the innocent are to be protected, (3) there must be a genuine grievance, such as lost territory, and the military response should be proportional to the injury suffered, (4) the injury should be repaired as an act of justice, and (5) those waging a just war should have a good motive, such as love of justice and a wish to defeat evil (Neff 2005: 50–1). Following a long decline in the emphasis on just war, by the nineteenth century, with legal positivism taking over, European leaders fought their wars purely for state interests without concern for moral questions (Franck 1995: 252).

From time to time, war aims are still stated in moral terms, such as the goal of protecting democracy in the First and Second World Wars or, more recently, at the outset of the brief Persian Gulf War of 1990–1991. Modern scholars continue to investigate the relationship of morality to war, with perhaps the best known example being Michael Walzer, author of *Just and Unjust War* (Walzer 1992; 2004).

Following centuries of customary development of the laws of war, a sharp turn toward their codification in written form began at least as early as Professor Francis Lieber's 1863 *Instructions for the Government of Armies of the United States in the Field* (also formally titled the *U.S. Army General Order No. 100*). The Lieber Code

---

Box 8.1 Just War Principles Applied to the Persian Gulf War, 1990–1991

- The cause must be just – frequently self-defense – the defense of Kuwait from aggression was based on a Western perception of threat.
- A lawful authority must decide to use force – the US Congress and the U N Security Council authorized the use of force, but only after some US forces were already on the scene.
- The use of force must be a final resort – the UN coalition applied economic sanctions first, but perhaps did not give them enough time to have a desired effect.
- The war must offer proportionality, meaning the good achieved must outweigh the damage done – the UN coalition freed Kuwait from Iraqi clutches, but with great ecological damage and the death of thousands of Iraqi soldiers, not to mention "friendly fire" killing some American and British troops.
- The war must carry at least a high probability of good success – the superior UN forces won a quick victory and with lighter casualties than expected.
- The methods of the war must minimize damage to noncombatants – the accurate bombing restricted collateral damage, but probably many civilians died in Iraq as a result of the war.

Source: These principles were offered by the George H. W. Bush administration and are followed by the author's opinion about their application.

---

was written in the middle of the American Civil War (1861–5) and used by both sides. Lieber had little in the way of written documents to draw on and, about his resources, he complained in a letter to US Army Chief of Staff H.W. Halleck that "nearly everything was floating."[3] In 157 articles, Lieber covered martial law, bombardment, POWs, spies, military necessity, civilians and partisans, retaliation, the protection of hospitals, occupation, giving quarter, flags of truce and deception, capitulation and armistice and assassination. He even defined *civil war* as a war distinct from international war.

Lieber's Code was a seminal work that inspired developments in Europe including the 1874 Brussels Declaration and the 1880 *Oxford Manual* drafted by the Institute of International Law, and finally the 1899 and 1907 *Hague Conventions on the Laws and Customs of War on Land* (Neff 2005: 186–7; Best 1994: 41). "Hague Law" is generally regarded as *jus ad bellum* because it concerns the rules on going to war, emphasizing justification for doing so, but also contains rules of engagement during fighting known as *jus in bello*. Many of the rules of these conventions still apply today. These rules aim at reducing the inhumanity of war.

Besides laws on land warfare, important developments have also taken place in the context of war at sea, or maritime war. In fact, "pride of place" belongs to the 1856 *Declaration of Paris* as the first multi-party treaty on war to appear in the nineteenth century. This treaty clarified the role of blockades, contraband, or cargo that might assist in a war effort, and privateering was abolished. This latter practice had allowed governments to authorize private merchant ships to arm and attack an enemy's shipping. More than four decades later, various specialized Hague Conventions would cover humanitarian law at sea for the sick and wounded, the status of enemy merchant ships, conversion of merchant ships into warships, tethering contact mines to the ocean floor, and rules to cover the bombardment of ports and towns. Between the Hague Conferences and the Second World War, several conferences held in Washington, DC, London, and Geneva tried to limit the number and size of capital warships, aircraft carriers and submarines, but a naval arms race still occurred among the major naval powers of the day before the Second World War began.

The advent of aerial warfare came much later of course than land and naval warfare. Consequently, international law for this type of war has remained comparatively underdeveloped. The 1923 *Hague Air Rules* (upgraded in 1938) never entered into force, but had they been, the extensive strategic bombing of cities during the Second World War, including the use of napalm and atomic bombs, should never have happened.

Fighting wars according to humanitarian principles is usually associated with the four 1949 Geneva Conventions, known as "Geneva Law." These conventions mostly concern *jus in bello*, the law during war. The term refers to right conduct while a war is ongoing requiring the maximum humanitarian practices that military necessity will permit. Even before 1949, there were important developments in humanitarian law. As primary examples, the 1863 Lieber Code involved rules of engagement but also military ethics that Professor Lieber felt were required of civilized existence (Wright 1971: 57). The 1899 and1907 Hague Conventions on land warfare also have a statement that addressed humane conduct, now known as the *Marten's Clause*. Russian diplomat Feodor Martens had inserted in the preamble of the Hague Conventions: "inhabitants and belligerents remain under the protection and the rule of the principles of the law of nations, as they result from the usages established among civilized peoples, from the laws of humanity, and the dictates of the public conscience."[4]

The first treaty dedicated to humanitarian concerns was the 1864 *Geneva Convention on the Amelioration of the Condition of the Wounded on the Field of Battle*, sometimes called the Red Cross treaty. A pioneering NGO, soon to be called the International Committee of the Red Cross (ICRC), lobbied European states to ratify this convention to protect the wounded, ambulances, and hospitals. Another important humanitarian development originally drafted by the ICRC was the 1929 *Convention Relative to the Treatment of Prisoners of War*, which was in place a decade before the Second World War.

With the unequalled destruction of the Second World War fresh in mind, states gave whole-hearted support to the four 1949 Geneva Conventions promoted by the ICRC: *Geneva Convention (I) for the Amelioration of the Condition of the Wounded and Sick in Armed Forces in the Field*, *Geneva Convention (II) for the Amelioration of the Condition of the Wounded, Sick and Shipwrecked Members of Armed Forces at Sea*, *Geneva Convention (III) Relative to the Treatment of Prisoners of War*, and *Geneva Convention (IV) Relative to the Protection of Civilian Persons in Time of War*. Amidst

---

Box 8.2 The International Committee of the Red Cross (ICRC)

After witnessing the carnage of the Battle of Solferino in Italy in 1859 between Austrian and French troops, Swiss Banker Henri Dunant (1828–1910) was shocked at the near-complete neglect of the wounded. He set in motion a train of events that would soon lead to the ICRC, which is headquartered in Geneva, Switzerland, but has national chapters in many countries. As their symbol of participation, Muslim countries use a Red Crescent on a white background instead of the Red Cross on white used in Christian countries. Dunant worked tirelessly for the cause of respecting humanitarian principles during times of war and persuading countries to sign appropriate treaties, beginning with the 1864 Geneva Convention on the Amelioration of the Condition of the Wounded on the Field of Battle. Toward the end of his life, existing in obscurity and poverty, he was sought out to receive the Nobel Peace Prize.

   The ICRC has become the sponsor and guardian of numerous humanitarian related treaties and texts. The 1949 Geneva Conventions are sprinkled with references to the ICRC's role in protecting POWs, civilians, and other victims of war. Its website contains 100 treaties and texts promoting in the humanitarian cause. These can be accessed and read along with the ratifications, reservations, declarations, objections, and the like.

Sources: The website of the ICRC is http://www.icrc.org/eng; also read David P. Forsythe, *Humanitarian Politics: The International Committee of the Red Cross* (Baltimore, MD: Johns Hopkins University Press, 1977); Martha Finnemore, *National Interests in International Society* (Ithaca, NY: Cornell University Press, 1996), pp. 69–88; Martha Finnemore, "Rules of War and Wars of Rules: The International Red Cross and the Restraint of State Violence," in John Boli, and George M. Thomas (eds.), *Constructing World Culture: International Nongovernmental Organizations Since 1875* (Stanford, CA: Stanford University Press, 1999), pp. 149–65; and David P. Forsythe, *The Humanitarians: The International Committee of the Red Cross* (New York: Cambridge University Press, 2005).

---

thousands of treaties on every imaginable subject, the four Geneva Conventions are among the most ratified.[5] The four Geneva Conventions were written primarily for international wars, but there is an obligation calling for humane conduct during internal conflict as well. It rests in Article 3 common to all four conventions.

   With time and experience behind them, the signatories of the Geneva Conventions added two protocols in 1977. *Protocol I Relating to the Protection of Victims of International Armed Conflicts* supplemented and clarified the four earlier conventions of 1949. The voice of the Third World is heard in the very first article, which calls for armed conflicts motivated by self-determination (against colonial, occupational, or racist regimes) to be treated as international conflicts. The much shorter *Protocol II Relating to the Protection of Victims of Non-International Armed Conflicts* explicitly imposes humanitarian responsibilities for parties engaged in conflicts

---

Box 8.3 Article 3 Common to all Four 1949 Geneva Conventions

Article 3

In case of armed conflict not of an international character occurring in the territory of one of the High Contracting Parties, each Party to the conflict shall be bound to apply, as a minimum, the following provisions:

(1)   Persons taking no active part in the hostilities, including members of armed forces who have laid down their arms and those placed *hors de combat* by sickness, wounds, detention, or any other cause, shall in all circumstances be treated humanely, without any adverse distinction founded on race, colour, religion or faith, sex, birth or wealth, or any similar criteria.

　　　To this end, the following acts are and shall remain prohibited at any time and in any place whatsoever with respect to the above-mentioned persons:
　　(a)   violence to life and person, in particular murder of all kinds, mutilation, cruel treatment and torture;
　　(b)   taking of hostages;
　　(c)   outrages upon personal dignity, in particular humiliating and degrading treatment;
　　(d)   the passing of sentences and the carrying out of executions without previous judgment pronounced by a regularly constituted court, affording all the judicial guarantees which are recognized as indispensable by civilized peoples.

(2)   The wounded and sick shall be collected and cared for.

An impartial humanitarian body, such as the International Committee of the Red Cross, may offer its services to the Parties to the conflict.

　　The Parties to the conflict should further endeavor to bring into force, by means of special agreements, all or part of the other provisions of the present Convention.

　　The application of the preceding provisions shall not affect the legal status of the Parties to the conflict.

Source: The Geneva Conventions are available at http://www.icrc.org.

---

internal to countries. Although the two Protocols are not as widely ratified as the four Geneva Conventions, they each have more than 160 ratifications. The U.S has signed the Protocols but has not gone on to complete the ratification process and yet claims to abide by them in general.[6] In 2005, a Protocol III was adopted to allow countries to use the emblem of a red crystal if their cultures were not receptive to either the red cross or red crescent symbols. Protocol III is not yet in force.

Evolution to UN Law

The rise in the use of arbitration and the growth of international organizations in the latter decades of the nineteenth century encouraged some leaders, especially President Woodrow Wilson, to believe that an IGO could take on the bold task of handling problems associated with war and peace, the core concern of states. The devastation of the First World War only reinforced the need for an innovative IGO. Instead of states depending on an unstable balance of power arrangement to deter an opponent from attacking, states were to advance to a new and more effective level of power management. The revolutionary step unfolded in three stages: first, the 1919 Covenant of the League of Nations; second, the 1928 Kellogg-Briand Pact; and finally, the Charter of the UN.

The Covenant of the League of Nations provided for **collective security**. This power management system calls for the combined power of many, even all, states to deter or punish an aggressor with diplomatic, economic, and voluntary military sanctions in the League era. Collective security assumes that the society of states will marshal a preponderance of power against a wrong-doer, a cause led by the League's Council. Collective security exists as a half-way house between international anarchy and world government (Claude 1971: 246). The Covenant expected states to settle disputes peacefully but in no case was a state allowed to resort to war until waiting for three months after peaceful settlement efforts had been concluded. If a member of the League did resort to war disregarding its League obligations, League members were to sever economic relations with the Covenant-breaking state and consider military sanctions. The League Council could only recommend military force.[7]

The League had some initial success dealing with the Greco-Bulgarian crisis of 1925 and the Chaco War between Bolivia and Paraguay, 1932–5, but a series of aggressive acts by major powers, beginning with Japan's incursion into Manchuria in 1931, led to the Second World War and the closing of the League's Geneva headquarters in 1939. The one enforcement case of note concerned Italy's aggression against Ethiopia. The League's economic sanctions nearly bankrupted the Italian economy but reflecting on the League's failed effort to stop Italy's assault on Ethiopia in 1935–6, Haiti's ambassador to the League remarked: "Great or small, strong or weak, near or far, white or colored, let us never forget that one day we may be somebody's Ethiopia" (Claude 1971: 251).

Because the League ultimately could only delay war, the 1928 *Kellogg-Briand Pact* tried to fill in this gap with a general prohibition on war.[8] Unfortunately, the decade of the 1930s was preoccupied with the aggressions of Germany, Japan, and the Soviet Union, rendering the Kellogg-Briand Pact more of a moral aspiration than a serious treaty to revolutionize international relations.

Near the end of the Second World War in 1945, international society demonstrated renewed determination to impose collective security by accepting the UN Charter. In the preamble to the Charter, the intent was expressed "to save succeeding generations from the scourge of war," but the founding states of the UN wanted broader coverage. The Charter's Article 2 (4) instructed states not to use or threaten to use *force*. This broad concept covers war, but also military measures short of war such as military reprisals, peaceful blockades, or temporary occupation of another state's territory. The only exceptions to Article 2 (4) are UN Security Council enforcement and a state acting in self-defense.

Chapter VII of the Charter provides the basis for collective security actions with respect to threats to the peace, breaches of the peace, or acts of aggression. A "threat to the peace" refers to gathering dangers that might rise to open fighting while a "breach of peace" is open fighting between two or more opponents. "Aggression" is much more complicated for political reasons but usually refers to one side attacking first without provocation. The Security Council can call for collective enforcement measures, including the interruption of economic and diplomatic relations, communications, and travel. If necessary, enforcement measures based on air, sea, and land military forces can be put into play. Unlike the League's requests for voluntary military action, the UN can order such enforcement action on the part of its members. The Charter provides for a Military Staff Committee, made up of the Chiefs of Staff of the five permanent members of the Security Council, to take charge of a multi-national force, but this Committee has never been operationalized.[9]

In its history, the UN has managed only two acts of collective security and these have been make-shift enforcement actions. When North Korea invaded South Korea in 1950, the Security Council authorized the United States to put together a coalition of 16 volunteer states to push the North Korean army back across the 38th parallel. These forces were placed under US "command and control" but were allowed to fly the UN flag over their positions. The Military Staff Committee called for in the Charter was not employed, and UN forces, led by the United States, certainly did not quickly overwhelm North Korean forces with a preponderance of power. The Korean War lasted three years and cost America alone 48,000 lives. The Cold War had created an early rift within the Security Council, and only the temporary absence of the veto-bearing Soviet Union from the Security Council's discussions provided a brief opportunity for authorizing the volunteer coalition led by the United States. The Soviet Union's departure was to protest the fact that mainland China was not given Nationalist China's seat on the Security Council, at least not at that time.

The UN would not exercise even a facsimile collective security operation for another four decades. In 1990, at the end of the Cold War, China and Russia withheld their vetoes allowing the Security Council to authorize, once again, the United States to organize a volunteer coalition of states to respond to Iraq's invasion of Kuwait. This time the coalition, organized by the administration of President George H.W. Bush, did achieve a preponderance of force over the invader in 1991, but UN authorization did not permit these forces to fly the UN flag over their headquarters. This great success buoyed confidence in what the UN might accomplish now that the Cold War was over and its divisive effects on the Security Council would be no more, or so it was hoped.

It can be argued that the US-led coalitions, in both the Korean and Iraqi cases, were acts of *collective self-defense*, not collective security. After all, the Security Council did not order enforcement in either of the two cases. These acts of enforcement can be placed under Article 51 of the Charter that allows states to help defend an attacked state on a voluntary basis, in addition to states defending themselves, at least until the Security Council can take charge. This distinction is important, no doubt, to the legally-minded, while to others, the UN simply improvised a bit to turn back aggression. It can be confidently observed that if the world's leading superpower had not wanted the two coalitions formed, they would never have materialized.

In 2003, President George W. Bush attempted to persuade the Security Council to approve another coalition to stop Iraq from developing suspected WMDs. Only the United Kingdom was supportive, while the other three permanent members holding veto power – China, France, and Russia – adamantly opposed military intervention in Iraq. Undaunted by a lack of UN approval, the U.S went its own course, as hegemons are prone to do. The United States sought legal justification through the "implied authorization" of previous Security Council resolutions; however, these clearly did not allow for military enforcement. Consequently, President Bush went around the UN and put together a "coalition of the willing," with most troops coming from the United Kingdom and the United States.

Ideally, states desirous of a peaceful world would treat the Charter prohibition against force as a *jus cogens* norm of inviolability, but the age-old tradition of self-help is dying a slow death. Some states are still prone to take matters into their own hands and use force, only now they are more likely to label their use of force as "self-defense," "humanitarian intervention," or camouflage their forceful acts with some other term their governments believe international society will accept.[10] So much of the application and enforcement of international law is about definitions: what do the terms of the Charter and other treaties and declarations mean? For instance, no consensus exists for delineating what constitutes aggression, an illegal act that would justify using collective security by the UN.

Aggression

Aggression is one of those terms that would appear easy to define. Our common sense assessments, however, will not always meet legal requirements that obligate the UN Security Council to condemn a country for an act of aggression. Is it not simply a conspicuous armed attack by one state against another? Unfortunately, complications immediately arise. Was the attacking state provoked in some way? Was the movement of troops across a border only a temporary occupation as an act of retaliation? Did both states commence hostilities about the same time? Was the attacking state reacting in a preemptive way to an attack known to be underway by an opponent?

Violating the sovereignty of another state is a serious category of misbehavior and, in the twentieth century, aggression was viewed as the worst instance of this category. Germany, Japan, and the Soviet Union brought down the League with flagrant acts of aggression in the 1930s. At the beginning of the Second World War, the Axis powers of Germany, Italy, and Japan were condemned by the Allies, led by the United Kingdom and the United States, and morally put on the defensive because of these acts of aggression. Aggression had become a very serious crime against peace for the Allies. With war's end, and Nazi leaders in the dock, the Nuremberg International Military Tribunal of 1945–6 stated:

> War is essentially an evil thing. Its consequences are not confined to the belligerent states alone, but affect the whole world. To initiate a war of aggression, therefore, is not only an international crime; it is the supreme international crime differing only from other war crimes in that it contains within itself the accumulated evil of the whole.[11]

The criminalization of aggression was upheld as well at the 1948 International Military Tribunal for the Far East (the Tokyo War Crimes Tribunal) (Dinstein 1994: 121).

The intent of the UN Charter was to give the prohibition against aggression a prominent place among the rules restructuring a post-war world. Article 1 of the Charter says a purpose of the UN is the suppression of aggression, and Article 39 assigns to the Security Council the role of determining if there is a threat to the peace, a breach of the peace, or an act of aggression. The often-cited 1970 *Declaration on Principles of International Law Concerning Friendly Relations and Cooperation Among States* is an important elaboration and reinforcement of Charter purposes. It states forthrightly that, "A war of aggression constitutes a crime against the peace, for which there is responsibility under international law."[12]

Lacking, unfortunately, was a policy tool for analyzing whether an act of force amounted to aggression. A 1974 UN General Assembly resolution, the "Definition of Aggression," attempted to fill this void. It defines aggression broadly as armed force by one state against another and offers seven specific acts that qualify as aggression.

General Assembly resolutions are of course non-binding, and the Security Council has been reluctant to refer to this "Definition on Aggression," despite its advance in specificity. Legal minds remain unsatisfied with this definition as well. Jurists working on the 1998 *Statute of the International Criminal Court* were unable to define "aggression" adequately so that charges of aggression could be filed in actual cases (Bloomhall 2003: 47). And shortly afterward, jurists developing *The Princeton Principles on Universal Jurisdiction* contended that "defining the crime of 'aggression' is in practice extremely difficult and divisive" (Macedo 2001: 47).

Besides legal issues, discord within the Security Council and the need for some degree of consensus make designating a country an aggressor politically difficult. Such a designation has been applied in at least three cases, however. Rhodesia's 1978 incursion into Zambia, Israel's 1985 attack on the Palestinian Liberation Organization in Tunisia, and South Africa's 1985 intervention in Angola resulted in these countries being branded as aggressors by the Security Council. In other seemingly unambiguous cases such as North Korea's 1950 invasion of South Korea, Iraq's 1980 invasion of Iran, Argentina's 1982 invasion of Britain's Falkland Islands, and Iraq's 1990 invasion of Kuwait, the Security Council preferred to use the safer label of *breach of peace* to cover these acts of misbehavior. Breach of peace simply means states are fighting and the emphasis is on restoring peace rather than accusing one of the states of criminal conduct, namely, aggression (Gareis & Varwick 2005: 70; Gray 2004: 85, 116, 146).

Box 8.4 Excerpts from the Definition of Aggression

General Assembly Resolution 3314 (XXIX) (1974)

Article 1

Aggression is the use of armed force by a State against the sovereignty, territorial integrity or political independence of another State, or in any other manner inconsistent with the Charter of the United Nations, as set out in this Definition.

Article 2

The First use of armed force by a State in contravention of the Charter shall constitute prima facie evidence of an act of aggression although the Security Council may, in conformity with the Charter, conclude that a determination that an act of aggression has been committed would not be justified in the light of other relevant circumstances, including the fact that the acts concerned or their consequences are not of sufficient gravity.

Article 3

Any of the following acts, regardless of a declaration of war, shall, subject to and in accordance with the provisions of article 2, qualify as an act of aggression:
(a) The invasion or attack by the armed forces of a State of the territory of another State, or any military occupation, however temporary, resulting from such invasion or attack, or annexation by the use of force of the territory of another State or part thereof;
(b) Bombardment by the armed forces of a State against the territory of another State or the use of any weapons by a State against the territory of another State;
(c) The blockade of the ports or coasts of a State by the armed forces of another State;
(d) An attack by the armed forces of a State on the land, sea or air forces, or marine and air fleets of another State;
(e) The use of armed forces of one State which are within the territory of another State with the agreement of the receiving State, in contravention of the conditions provided for in the agreement of or any extension of their presence in such territory beyond the termination of the agreement;
(f) The action of a State in allowing its territory, which it has placed at the disposal of another State, to be used by that other State for perpetrating an act of aggression against a third State;
(g) The sending by or on behalf of a State of armed bands, groups, irregulars or mercenaries, which carry out acts of armed force against another State of such gravity as to amount to the acts listed above, or its substantial involvement therein.

What sets the first three states apart for the more serious charge of aggression is not using force differently but, rather, the distinction is based on the nature of their governments. At the time of the alleged aggressions, these three were regarded as racist and very unpopular in world opinion (Gray 2004: 16). Obviously, aggression is not purely a legal term but entwines with politics.

Self-defense

Although the creation and use of collective security through the world bodies of the League and UN elevated the management of power to a whole new level, states were still allowed to defend themselves if attacked. In practice, the Security Council has often been immobilized by political division, leaving states to self-judge when to use force. States are prone to stretch the meaning of self-defense because it is the only legitimate exercise of force under the Charter, except for cooperating with Security Council enforcement. However, if every state were allowed to be its own final arbiter of the meaning of self-defense, the fundamental purpose of the UN would be severely undercut.

Even if all parties were doing their best to adhere to a proper meaning of self-defense under Article 51, practical issues inevitably arise. Conflicts may be so entangled that it is hard to identify which party is the victim and which the attacker. Both parties in a conflict are likely to invoke the right of self-defense. Israel's 2006 summer conflict with Hezbollah, the well-armed militia in southern Lebanon, is a case in point. The war was provoked by Hezbollah's kidnapping of two Israeli soldiers, placing the onus on this militia, but then Israel's heavy response of aerial bombing and artillery attacks seemed out of proportion to the original provocation, and thus much sympathy in the Middle East shifted to Hezbollah. Both sides claimed to be on the defensive, protecting their rights and peoples. Instead of figuring out which side to blame, the UN wisely concentrated on establishing a ceasefire.

There is also the unsettled issue about a state asserting a self-defense rationale when rescuing citizens endangered while on the territory of another state. This issue is colored by the fact that it is strong states that perform these acts of rescue when weak or failing states are unable, or unwilling, to protect foreigners. Rescue may seem humanitarian to some observers, but to others any military intervention appears to violate the UN Charter. Strong states argue customary law prior to the Charter permits rescues and that Article 51 on self-defense should carry forward the same understanding. Weak states usually prefer a strict interpretation of Article 2, which prohibits the threat or use of force by one state against another. A quick-in, quick-out rescue without any complicating goals other than saving citizens is more likely to be accepted by international society than a long-term involvement. US Marines have rescued American citizens many times with similar rapid operations but, in some cases, as in Grenada in 1983 and Panama in 1989, it was clear that the United States wanted not only to extricate its citizens from danger but also put the governments of its choice in power

The application of *collective self-defense*, as opposed to collective security, has been troublesome as well, at least when used without the UN stamp of approval. President

Ronald Reagan, in the last decade of the Cold War, decided to undermine Marxist governments in the client states of the Soviet Union under a policy that came to be known as the *Reagan Doctrine*. He sent weapons and other aid to revolutionaries fighting the leftist governments of Afghanistan, Angola, and Nicaragua. The foremost challenge to the Reagan Doctrine came when Nicaragua brought a case before the ICJ beginning in 1984 over the United States mining its harbors, attacking a Nicaraguan naval base, and arming Nicaraguan revolutionaries known as the *Contras*. The United States claimed that these acts fell under collective self-defense in order to protect El Salvador. However, the ICJ ruled that collective self-defense did not apply because El Salvador had not declared it was under attack nor had it invited the United States to help. Moreover, the alleged trickle of arms from Nicaragua to rebels in El Salvador did not constitute an armed attack, in the ICJ's opinion.[13] It is the Nicaraguan case that led President Reagan to withdraw the United States from the optional compulsory jurisdiction of the ICJ.

The United States had better success using collective self-defense following the 9/11 crisis of 2001 when terrorists flew airliners into the towers of the World Trade Center. The 1947 Rio Treaty of the OAS and the 1949 NATO alliance offered collective self-defense to each regional grouping of states. Both IGOs immediately proclaimed that al-Qaida's terrorist assault on the United States was an attack on the other members of the two regional organizations as well. The UN Security Council also gave firm support to the United States the very next day, condemning this terrorist act as an "armed attack," although al-Qaida is of course a private and not a state actor. The American-British military response against Afghanistan, which soon followed 9/11, has generally been accepted as a legitimate exercise of military force in self-defense.[14]

The final and most controversial issue associated with self-defense is the exercise of anticipatory or **preemptive defense,** which is a first strike to stop an attack thought to be impending and near in terms of time. Customary law on this issue was established with the *Caroline* incident of 1837. While the *Caroline*, a schooner, was on the United States side of the Niagara River, a Canadian force set fire to this schooner and sent it over the Niagara Falls because it had been used to ferry arms to Canadian insurrectionists. Following a heated exchange between US Secretary of State Daniel Webster and the British diplomatic representative to Washington, Lord Ashburton, both sides appeared to agree to Webster's understanding of preemptive defense. In a letter to Lord Ashburton, Webster said what must be shown is a "necessity of self-defense, instant, overwhelming, leaving no choice of means and no moment for deliberation." Webster went on to say the level of force "must be limited by that necessity and kept clearly within it."[15] From the *Caroline* incident was born the strong customary law principle that self-defense must be *necessary* and *proportionate* to the danger.

The *Caroline* precedent stood mostly unchallenged until the UN Charter set out to create a new legal order that intended to greatly limit a state's options regarding force. A strict interpretation of the Charter's Article 51 would call for initiating defense only after an armed attack has begun, but in recent years, with the rapidity and surprise element today's technology allows, anticipating a potential threat seems more important than ever. It is not surprising that jurists of the international legal community are not in full agreement on this issue, especially when specific cases of preemptive defense are discussed.

In the 1967 Six Day War, Israel trounced several Arab states and took substantial territories from them. The Egyptian government had put its forces on alert, placing thousands of troops in a state of readiness in the large Sinai Peninsula between Egypt and Israel, and ordered UN Peacekeepers to leave the Sinai. Despite all this activity, Egyptian forces did not initiate an attack on Israel. This case is widely cited as an instance of preemptive defense, but the Israeli government did not use the anticipatory rationale. Israel instead claimed that Egypt started the war by blockading the Straits of Tiran to Israeli shipping. This case remains controversial, drawing both supporters and critics. In another case, Israel had virtually no support in 1981 when it sent newly acquired American F-15s and F-16s to the Osirik nuclear reactor located near Baghdad, Iraq and destroyed it so Iraq could not develop an atomic bomb.[16] Echoing this 1981 attack, Israel, in 2007, snuffed out a start-up nuclear project in neighboring Syria with a bombing attack. Apparently, Israel will not tolerate a neighboring Islamic state with an atom bomb.

Self-defense in an Age of Terrorism

The practice of terrorism is ancient, but the world has experienced an especially strong pattern of terrorism for the last several decades. Although the number of terrorist attacks has declined recently, this good news is largely negated by the scale of spectacular terrorist episodes. While some terrorist organizations, like the Tamil Tigers in Sri Lanka, remain localized, others, particularly al-Qaida, take full advantage of a globalizing world. Not only can terrorists make good use of more open borders, rapid travel, and telecommunications to commit their nefarious deeds, but the same facilitating globalization pattern provides tempting targets ranging from commercial aircraft to computer networks. Terrorists hope, of course, through surprise attacks, often involving random victims, to cause enough mayhem that governments, numbed into submission, will do their will. However, the history of terrorism shows little political success of consequence despite the great attention that terrorist acts attract (Laqueur 2001; 2002: 1–13).

Since terrorist organizations cannot afford to openly square off against the police and military forces of states, they turn to asymmetrical warfare and use stealthy hit-and- run tactics similar to guerrilla soldiers. One exception might be Hezbollah, which some observers credit with forcing the Israeli army to withdraw from southern Lebanon in 2000 and fighting the Israeli army to a stand-still in the summer of 2006 (Byman 2005: 1–5; von Krieken 2002: 192, see also 53–78).

Numerous UN resolutions and global and regional conventions condemn all acts of terrorism, calling these threats to the peace, and urge states not to support terrorism in any manner or form. The 1970 Declaration Concerning Friendly Relations says, "Every state has the duty to refrain from organizing, instigating, assisting or participating in acts of civil strife or terrorist acts in another State."[17] Since 1972, the

UN General Assembly has passed over 40 resolutions relative to terrorism on such subjects as WMDs and financing, with these resolutions sometimes leading to anti-terrorist conventions.[18] Of special interest is the watershed 1985 resolution on "Measure to Prevent International Terrorism" that unequivocally condemned as criminal all acts of terrorism regardless of where, by whom, and for whatever reason.[19] This all-inclusive language has been echoed again and again at the international level, including the UN-sponsored 2005 World Summit Outcome conference. Despite such a sweeping coverage of terrorism, states have nevertheless failed to agree on a definition of "terrorism" that is universally accepted for enforcement purposes.

Beginning in 1989, the UN Security Council has approved more than 30 resolutions opposing terrorism. Particularly noteworthy are the resolutions that brought economic and diplomatic sanctions against Libya in 1992 over its agents bombing an American airliner in 1988.[20] Also of special interest is the resolution that came on September 12, 2001, the day after the 9/11 crisis, which unequivocally condemned the horrifying terrorist attacks in New York City and Washington, DC, and called on all states to redouble their efforts to prevent and suppress terrorist acts. The United States enjoyed widespread support from most states and IGOs when it attacked the al-Qaida bases in Afghanistan and toppled the Taliban government that had given this terrorist groups safe-haven. Then, on September 28, 2001, the Security Council passed very important resolutions asking states to fully implement all terrorist-related conventions, prevent the funding of terrorist cells and recruitment of their citizens, deny safe haven for terrorist organizations, and set up within the Security Council a Counter-Terrorism Committee for monitoring enforcement activities of all states.[21] When states attack terrorist nests in other countries, their governments do not always receive the support the United States drew after the 9/11 massive terrorist attack in New York City. In fact, they may be sharply criticized at the UN as in the cases of Israel's attack on Palestinian positions in Tunisia in 1985 and the US bombing of Libya in 1986.

The evidence and responsibility connecting states to terrorists is not always clear. When these states, such as Israel or the United States, counter-strike the bases and leaders of these terrorist groups, are they acting in self-defense or are such attacks the punitive measures of reprisal? The answer is important since military retaliation in peacetime is no longer legal under international law, although it once had more support under customary law. Most jurists today would agree that self-defense means to halt and repel an attack but not to act punitively. Countries contending with terrorist strikes say they are exercising self-defense because their purpose is to deter future attacks and not to seek revenge, but critics of Israel and the United States maintain these states have broadened the meaning of self-defense to give their vengeful military acts a veneer of legality. The support the United States had after 9/11 is a major exception.

The first effort at producing a terror convention was the League's 1937 *Convention for the Prevention and Punishment of Terrorism*, but it never entered into force. Since the early 1960s, at least 16 specialized conventions on terrorism dealing with such subjects as aircraft safety, protection of diplomats, hostage taking, maritime safety, plastic explosives and bombings, financing of terrorism, and, most recently in 2005, a convention on nuclear terrorism have been offered as rules to combat specific acts of terrorism. These

Box 8.5 The Status of Reprisal as a Self-help Measure

Traditionally, states have possessed an array of *measures short of war* to which they could easily turn. *Retorsion acts*, such as recalling diplomats from foreign countries, employing boycotts and embargo restrictions in trade, and freezing a country's bank assets, are legal but unfriendly measures to take. More serious acts are acts of *reprisal*, or retaliation. These are illegal acts but were once regarded as justified to punish a prior illegal act by another state. Reprisals have often contained a military element. The classic case of reprisal, or military retaliation, is the 1914 *Naulilaa* incident in Portuguese Angola, when German officers from Southwest Africa had a misunderstanding with Portuguese soldiers, leading to the deaths of several Germans. In 1928, an arbitration panel of three Swiss lawyers ruled against Germany because they had not tried peaceful settlement first. And the panel found the burning of several Portuguese posts in Angola as retaliation was out of proportion to the harm Germany suffered.

Military reprisals in peacetime are now widely recognized as illegal based on Article 2 (4) of the UN Charter, a position reaffirmed by the 1970 Declaration on Principles of Law Concerning Friendly Relations. When a country does use reprisal today, it almost certainly will claim that its action is a matter of self-defense.

Belligerent reprisals in wartime, however, are legal if they are proportionate to the harm suffered and do not affect POWs and civilians, as helpless victims of war. For example, although outlawed in 1925, if lethal gas had been used by Germany in the Second World War, then the allies would have been allowed to use deadly gas as well.

Source: The Naulilaa case can be read in Mary Ellen O'Connell, *International Law and the Use of Force* (New York, NY: Foundation Press, 2005), pp. 5–7.

conventions have generally been widely ratified except for the one on nuclear terrorism, which has 47 parties and entered into force in 2007. Typically these conventions contain a provision requiring that terrorist suspects be prosecuted or extradited to a country that will prosecute for the specific crime addressed in the convention.[22]

A convention under consideration for over a decade and, as yet unfinished, is the 1996 *UN Draft Comprehensive Convention* on terrorism.[23] This convention could prove invaluable if it finally eradicates the distinction between "terrorist" and "freedom fighter." In some places, particular terrorists have been given the latter name and treated as heroes. Additionally, several regional conventions are in operation, including the 1977 *European Convention on the Suppression of Terrorism* and the 2002 *Inter-American Convention against Terrorism*.[24]

A strong legal regime has been tightening around terrorism for decades but, even with international law on the books, commitment to the anti-terrorist rules remains critical. By now, most of the world and its various actors are probably prepared to place the terrorist in the status of *hostis humani generis* (the enemy of all humankind), along with pirates, slavers, and war criminals. Increasing numbers of people and governments have tired of the terrorist-created gray zone of neither peace nor war where agents of terrorism randomly strike civilians as they try to go about normal lives. The very nature of terrorist acts overrides the long-standing distinction between combatants and non-combatants during armed conflict.[25]

Despite progress, the legal regime on terrorism is not as strong as it could be. Just as the jurists writing *The Princeton Principles on Universal Jurisdiction* failed to place terrorism under universal jurisdiction because of a definitional problem, the writers of the 1998 *Statute of the International Criminal Court* did not locate terrorism within this court's jurisdiction. The failure, thus far, to complete a comprehensive terror convention also leaves an enforcement gap. The prosecution of terrorism remains mostly on the national level and must use charges for specific crimes, such as hijacking planes or carrying out bombing attacks.

Whatever the thoroughness of the legal regime, the process of enforcement must come next. The process of enforcement itself has raised an interesting legal issue between the policy-makers who advocate a Criminal Campaign against Terrorism (CCAT) and those favoring a War on Terrorism (WOT). These two approaches call for very different methods to get at the perpetrators of terrorist acts.

Some legal scholars prefer the British method, as used against the Irish Revolutionary Army, which involves pursuing terrorists as criminals through police and intelligence operations and then locking them up in a prison after trial and conviction (e.g. Rose 2002: vii–xiii; Howard 2002: 149–56). The screening of immigrants, customs control, cargo inspections, biometric passports, and shared data bases are the stuff of the criminal approach. The dichotomy between a CCAT and a WOT is not pure, however, since the British government has maintained a significant number of soldiers in Northern Ireland to help with security.

The thunderbolt of the 9/11 disaster led President George W. Bush to go for the other option, and he hurriedly announced a WOT. In a September 20, 2001, address before Congress, President Bush said, "Every nation, in every region, now has a decision to make. Either you are for us or you are for the terrorists. From this day forward, any nation that continues to harbor or support terrorism will be regarded by the United States as a hostile regime." The UN Security Council resolutions that came on the heels of the 9/11 disaster supported the US position on choosing a WOT, observing that the United States had been struck by an "armed attack," and that it could exercise its inherent right of self-defense under Article 51 of the UN Charter.

It was the magnitude of this shocking attack that made all the difference. More innocent civilians died in this attack than the military deaths suffered at Pearl Harbor from Japan's surprise attack in 1941. The laws of war do not take into account a non-state actor, such as a terrorist organization, being treated as an entity with legal personality, but these same laws do not prohibit military assaults on terrorists either, or prevent the attribution of blame to a state sponsoring terrorism, as Afghanistan did with al-Qaida in the 9/11 case (Vöneky 2004: 925–49, esp. 925–31). It can now be understood that a new rule is in place. States can exercise self-defense of a military nature against terrorists that constitute a large-scale threat to international peace and security (Franck 2001: 839–43).

Actually, a hard choice between a CCAT and a WOT does not have to be made because the two can be pursued as parallel policies (Neff 2005: 385–8). Criminal indictments have been filed against Osama bin Laden, head of al-Qaida, and he could conceivably be arrested, extradited to the United States, and put on trial. At the same time, he has been pursued by thousands of American soldiers and intelligence agencies since 2001, and bin Laden is still at risk to an unmanned drone equipped with a Hell-fire missile, even though he may now have left Afghanistan for Pakistan. Apparently the new Barack Obama presidency does not plan to use the term, "War on Terror."

Intervention

Intervention is a highly politically charged term that that often involves the use of force. In a broad sense, it refers to external actions that have effects in the domestic affairs of a sovereign state (Nye, Jr 1993: 132). The more traditional meaning of the term is based on *dictatorial interference*, which involves one or more states pressuring another to change its policies or even the character of its government. A newer sense of the term concerns *humanitarian intervention*, either by states or IGOs using force to cross the border of a state to stop gross violations of human rights.[26] Both types of intervention violate the cardinal principle of state sovereignty. The illegality of dictatorial interference is fairly clear, but the prominence that human rights has achieved in recent times as a *jus cogen* or inviolable norm now challenges the much older principle of sovereignty. Has the society of states created a new norm that allows intervention, for the sake of rights, to trump sovereignty? (Wheeler 2000: 2, 6; see also Franck 2003; Roberts 1993: 429–49).

The law against intervention seems clear and firm. In addition to several centuries of customary law protecting state sovereignty, there is written UN Charter law. Article 2 (4) explicitly instructs member-states to refrain from threatening or using force against the territory or political independence of another state, and Article 2 (7) prohibits the UN itself from intervening in matters within the domestic jurisdiction of a state. The 1965 UN *Declaration on the Inadmissibility of Intervention in the Domestic Affairs of States* affirms that direct or indirect intervention, for any reason whatever, is prohibited, and the 1970 UN *Declaration on Principles of International Law Concerning Friendly Relations and Cooperation Among States* repeats almost verbatim Article 2 (4) of the Charter.[27]

When violations of an interventionist kind do occur, they are often instances of the "rule of the strong" prevailing over the "rule of law." The violations may be as low level as radio propaganda and bribery of a state's officials or the mid-level use of money and arms to help a rebellion. A high-level intervention would be a military invasion, even if it is for temporary purposes. Since the latter part of the nineteenth century, strong states have often cast moral cloaks over their interventions. Since the Second World War, multiple cases of strong powers intervening in Third World states have occurred. Humanitarian concerns may well be genuine in some cases but still easily perceived by the Third World as freighted with great power interests.

Acts of forceful intervention are not restricted to Western states, however. In 1971, India claimed both humanitarian and national interests as it defeated Pakistan, helping this state's eastern section to become the independent country of Bangladesh. In 1978, the border incursions by Cambodia into Vietnam finally provoked Vietnam to invade and remove the Khmer Rouge government, which also had the result of ending one of the worst genocidal episodes since the Second World War. Tanzania fared better than India and Vietnam in terms of international acceptance following its intervention into Uganda in 1979. When the Tanzanian army, weary of border intrusions by Idi Amin's despotic government, drove him from Uganda and into exile, the world breathed a sigh of relief, for Idi Amin's horrific human rights record was widely known.

Interest in a purer form of humanitarian intervention, apart from states' national interests, developed in the latter half of the twentieth century, growing out of the modern human rights movement that was spawned with the creation of the UN. Perhaps infused with optimism following the end of the Cold War, UN Secretary-General Boutrous Boutrous-Ghali, in 1992, surprised sovereignty-oriented governments by suggesting that the consent by a host state may not always be required if help for its citizens needs to be sent. Then, in 1998, UN Secretary-General Kofi Annan claimed that humanitarian intervention was a lesser evil than letting massacres and extreme oppression continue. Moreover, he did recommend that intervention be *collective*, meaning that it would be carried out by a group of states authorized by the Security Council (Goulding 2003: 24). A few years later in a 2005 speech at the World Summit, Annan encouraged the UN to embrace the "responsibility to protect" in cases of genocide and ethnic cleansing.[28] This responsibility appears to be nothing less than a "duty to intervene," which has been spoken of since at the 1994 Rwanda genocide when few did little to help. Such a duty calls for nothing less than contravening the sovereignty of the state where terrible deeds are happening.

Enthusiasm for overriding sovereignty with human rights priorities has hardly been universal. Third World states, those usually at the receiving end of both dictatorial and humanitarian intervention, are less supportive because of long-held fears over neo-colonial behavior by powerful Western states. China and Russia, both with veto power in the Security Council, are also suspicious of humanitarian intervention since both states have serious patterns of human rights violations that are often brought to public attention by Western human rights NGOs.

The basis for selecting cases for humanitarian intervention is unclear and actual efforts of this kind are uneven in results. The UN's effort in Bosnia in the early 1990s to stop ethnic violence and bring food and medicine to the needy found itself caught in the cross-fire of numerous private militias. By 1995, NATO had to rescue the UN's humanitarian effort. The UN also tried to provide humanitarian help to Somalia from 1992 to 1994, but gave up and left because of the sharp conflict among clan-based militias. When Rwanda imploded into genocide in 1994, the UN was largely unresponsive, and its tiny force on the scene was unable to stop the slaughter of 800,000 people in a two-month period.

The Kosovo case of 1999 has been trumpeted by some observers as a much more positive example of humanitarian intervention, and its supporters believed it could provide a template for future cases. After Serbia rescinded the semi-autonomy for the province of Kosovo, containing mostly an ethnic community of Albanian people, tensions grew to the point that the Serbs began an ethnic cleansing policy of rape and murder, putting thousands of Kosovo refugees into flight for the nearest border. The Security Council declared this case a threat to international peace, but it was clear that China and Russia would veto a resolution calling for intervention. Completely without UN authorization, NATO intervened anyway by bombing Serb targets for two and a half months in 1999 until the Serbian government agreed to accept an international force in Kosovo. The "CNN effect" of thousands of Kosovo refugees broadcast around the world brought much sympathy for this intervention. When a Security Council resolution approved the settlement between NATO and Serbia over Kosovo, supporters argued tht the UN had ratified the NATO action after the fact.

Whether NATO's intervention in Kosovo can be repeated or will stand as an exceptional case remains to be seen. The limited number of humanitarian interventions and their mixed methods and outcomes, so far, do not add up to a new direction in international law that seriously loosens the strong moorings of state sovereignty. As Professor Mary O'Connell has observed, humanitarian intervention remains an inchoate principle, occasionally forgiven but not endorsed (O'Connell 2005: 318).

Peacekeeping

Following the demise of the League and the most destructive war in history, the Second World War, the UN Charter was a rebirth of hope that force could be controlled. Limited versions of collective security, however, proved possible only in the cases of Korea in 1950 and Iraq in 1990. The UN Security Council moving with dispatch against straightforward cases of aggression has not been the international reality. Internal civil wars, revolutions, guerrilla warfare, fights among multiple militias, and terrorism, with these conflicts often smoldering for years, have easily outnumbered the international wars the UN had expected to handle. The five permanent members with veto power, especially the Soviet Union and the United States, were sometimes the problem rather than the solution. Instead of the major powers contributing to UN efforts by policing aggression, much of the UN's energy during the Cold War had to be spent on keeping the two from taking sides and escalating local and regional conflicts.

To meet this unexpectedly complex environment regarding force, the UN, like many institutions confronting new conditions, improvised. Early in its history, the UN began an evolving process of **peacekeeping**. Without assigning blame, the UN calls for a ceasefire between disputing parties and then places a neutral force between them that can range in size from a few observers to a lightly armed multinational force of several thousand soldiers. Because of their distinctive blue head-gear, UN Peacekeepers are referred to as a thin blue line, a moral presence, creating a buffer-zone between parties in conflict until peaceful settlement efforts can resolve issues and bring lasting peace. Peacekeeping operations are usually authorized by the Security Council and operate under the direction of the Secretary-General, with the costs apportioned to states according to their ability to pay. Finally, peacekeepers can be deployed in a country only with the approval of its government.

This bold innovation, without a mention in the Charter, is said to fall somewhere between Chapter 6 on peaceful settlement and Chapter 7 on enforcement. Peacekeeping began with observer teams put in Palestine in 1948 and placed between India and Pakistan in 1949, but it reached full-form with the 1956 UN Emergency Force (UNEF) and the 1960–1964 UN Operations for the Congo (known by the French acronym ONUC) during Dag Hammarskjöld's tenure as Secretary-General. While these two operations were authorized by the General Assembly rather than the Security Council, they did separate combatants and bring a semblance of peace. With 6,000 peacekeepers from ten countries, UNEF supervised the departure of British, French, and Israeli troops after they had retaken the Suez Canal from Egyptian forces. ONUC had as many as 20,000 troops at one time coming from 34 countries and spent $400 million (well over $2 billion in today's money) This peacekeeping mission restored order in the new state of the Congo, recently freed from Belgium colonialism. ONUC quickly experienced "mission creep," becoming more than a moral presence. To establish peace, it first had to disarm army mutineers, arrest mercenaries, and defeat the forces of the secessionist province of Katanga.

Besides pulling apart warring parties and giving peace a chance, the UN Peacekeepers have disarmed militias, monitored borders, dug wells, taught in schools, delivered mail, removed landmines, and helped develop democracy by supervising elections and creating civil institutions for the administration of human services. The UN has had over 60 peacekeeping missions since 1948, costing a total of over $36 billion and the lives of almost 2000 peacekeepers. Often 15–20 operations are in place involving over 60,000 to 70,000 soldiers and police at a cost of about $5 billion.[29] In 1988, near the end of the Cold War and as the UN began to experience case overload, the UN Peacekeepers were awarded the Nobel Peace Prize. The current largest mission is again in the Congo, in the eastern part of the Democratic Republic of the Congo. Known by the French acronym MONUC, this mission has operated since 1999 with 20,000 soldiers from 18 countries and is spending $1.1 billion annually.

Peacekeeping, as an innovation going beyond the Charter, has evolved with experience. Over the years three additional concepts are now associated with peacekeeping. For several decades, the UN has tried *preventive diplomacy*, to defuse by diplomatic means a threatening crisis before it can erupt into serious fighting. Secretary-General Kofi Annan has pledged to move the UN from a "culture of reaction to a culture of prevention," calling for recognition of the danger signs of a conflict at an early stage.[30] More recently, UN diplomats speak of *peacebuilding*, which aims at marshalling resources to help with the root causes of conflict. In 2006, the UN inaugurated a Peacebuilding Commission that can go to work after peacekeeping stops the fighting to deal with poverty, ethnic conflict, and inadequacies in the areas of civil administration and rule of law.

Because in some cases UN Peacekeepers have been ignored as a weak, moral presence, there has been a need in some crises for more military clout. Consequently, the UN has turned to *peace enforcement* by enlisting large and medium powers to help. US Marines helped with Somalia in the early 1990s and Haiti in 1994. The French were authorized to provide a safe haven in Rwanda in 1995 for the Hutu fleeing Tutsi revenge following the Hutu acts of genocide. In 1999, the UN asked Australia to lead a force into East Timor to help this ex-colony of Portugal to set up an independent government free of Indonesian pressure and intrigue. Sub-contracting peace enforcement responsibilities by the UN to willing powers might well become a regular pattern.

Matters of peace and security are not intended to belong to UN alone, for Chapter 8 of the Charter allows regional IGOs to assist with peace as long as they keep their activities consistent with the Charter and seek prior approval of the Security Council before attempting enforcement action. The UN General Assembly has tried to reaffirm these rules with the 1994 *Declaration on the Enhancement of Cooperation between the United Nations and Regional Arrangements*.[31]

During the Cold War, misuse of regional organizations occurred with regularity. The United States used the OAS as a legitimizing cover for its interventions in Latin America to block leftist governments from coming to power, or to overthrow them if they did. The Soviet Union used the Warsaw Pact several times as a cover for policing wayward communist client-states in Eastern Europe. This practice can be found in Third World states as well. Syria led the League of Arab States into Lebanon in 1976 to quell a civil war there, but stayed to promote its own interests until 2005.

The role of the Economic Community of West African States (ECOWAS) comes closer to matching the role for regional IGOs provided in Chapter 8. Willing to embrace a security function as well as an economic one, ECOWOAS intervened in the Liberian and Sierra Leone civil wars, characterized by horrific atrocities that lasted for over a decade. With the consent of both governments, ECOWAS sent in peacekeepers to Liberia in 1990 and Sierra Leone in 1997, both times led by the Nigerian army. ECOWAS failed to acquire prior consent from the UN Security Council as required by the Charter, but in both cases ECOWAS was still commended retroactively by the Security Council for its good work in helping restore peace. In 2003, the Security Council also welcomed ECOWAS, along with French troops in 2002, to handle serious human rights violations that took place in the Ivory Coast.

The African Union (AU), replacing the Organization for African Unity in 2002, created bold power in Article 4 of its constitutive treaty to intervene in member-states to halt war and humanitarian crimes, if necessary, without the permission of the state in stress. This step is radical because it flies in the face of the foundational value of the sovereign independence of a state. The AU acted early in its history, sending in 7,000 peacekeepers to Texas-sized Darfur in western Sudan in 2003 but, in this case, with Khartoum's permission. Unfortunately, this small force has been unable to stop the deaths of 200,000 people or the homelessness of 2.5 million others.

Today's Salient Issues concerning the Laws of War

Declarations of war

War involves a strange paradox. Under the UN Charter, war is illegal except for self-defense but, if war breaks out, rules exist to guide its conduct, to limit the worst cruelty of a ferocious human enterprise. The *jus in bello* immediately apply. One interesting issue of war is whether a *declaration of war* is necessary to carry on a legal armed conflict. Many ancient peoples, including the Romans, issued declarations of war. The Romans did so by throwing a spear into the territory of an opponent to symbolize that war had begun. In medieval Europe, written declarations were fairly common. The 1907 *Hague Convention on the Opening of Hostilities* called for such declarations or the issuance of an ultimatum with a conditional declaration of war.[32] Even so, many wars, before and after the Hague Convention, were fought without formal declarations. As it happened, most states involved in the First and Second World Wars did issue declarations of war. By the time UN law was in place, states using military force shifted to the justification that they were acting under the legitimatizing concept of self-defense and dispensed with declarations (O'Connell 2005: 7).

According to Brien Hallett's *The Lost Art of Declaring War*, declarations of war are increasingly becoming obsolete. Hallett argues that declarations of war should be brought back into use because they are not merely statements to initiate war but public announcements of policy about war aims (Hallett 1998: 25–6). The US Congress did declare war for the War of 1812, the Mexican–American War of 1846–8, the Spanish-American War of 1898–1900, and the two world wars of the twentieth century. More recently, the United States has also fought several bloody wars without declarations, including the Korean War 1950–3, the Vietnam War 1963–75, the Persian Gulf War of 1990–1, and intervened militarily in Afghanistan in 2001 and Iraq in 2003 on a major scale. In these undeclared wars, presidents ask Congress for resolutions of support, which provide the executive branch with broad discretion in its use of constitutional war powers.

Whether wars begin with a declaration or not, the difference between a state of peace and a state of war involves grave consequences for states and their citizens. In times of war, diplomats are called home, enemy aliens can be interned and their property used in the war effort, treaties between belligerents are generally suspended for the duration of the war, neutral states and their citizens are often harmed in the midst of someone else's war, and, above all, the armed forces of a state at war will try to kill or incapacitate the forces of an opponent.

A return to the laws of peace comes with the cessation of hostilities. Surrenders, truces, ceasefires, armistices, or notifications by the side with the upper-hand in the fighting that its forces will cease hostilities on a certain day and time may all lead to peace. A peace treaty likely follows, but it is not a prerequisite to end a formal state of war. The war between the United States and Germany ended with the United States withdrawing its declaration of war in 1919, a necessary step because the United States would not sign the Versailles Treaty of 1919 with its entanglement of League membership.

Internal wars

Wars taking place inside countries have also been a special issue. There is no rule of international law that prohibits the use of force within countries as there is among states. Insurgents may carry out a limited revolt or cause a persistent and widespread rebellion. When the insurgency becomes a rebellion controlling a significant portion of the population and territory of the country, a **civil war** is at hand. The rebellion may attempt to either take control of the central government and all the population and territory, or secede taking a part of the territory and population to create a new state.[33]

There are several distinct features of internal wars which deserve special attention. In times past, while a rebellion was ongoing, other states have had the option to recognize the rebellion as a *belligerent*, allowing it to be viewed as possessing a limited legal personality. Great Britain recognized the Confederate government as a belligerent during the American Civil War of 1861–5. More recently, several states recognized one side or the other in the Spanish Civil War of 1936–9. Most states today, however, are reluctant to recognize a belligerent, fearing they will be accused of interfering in the domestic affairs of another state. Article Three of the 1977 Protocol II to the Geneva Conventions on Non-International Armed Conflicts appears to provide a clear rule against intervention for any reason, yet excuses are still sometimes found. The United States, for instance, has provided large amounts of military aid to the Colombian government for years as it struggles against three Marxist guerrilla armies, but the United States claims that this aid is intended only to fight the war on cocaine trafficking.

Another aspect of internal wars is the viciousness with which they are often fought. Although the history of international law has focused on international warfare, international rules are present calling for humane conduct during a conflict inside a country. The common Article 3 of all four 1949 Geneva Conventions certainly calls for humane treatment in "armed conflict not of an international character." Article 75 of the 1977 Protocol I of the Geneva Conventions on International Armed Conflicts requires humanitarian guarantees "at any time and in any place whatsoever, whether committed by civilian or by military agents." Also, Protocol II on Non-International Armed Conflicts has several lengthy articles addressing humane behavior.

Finally, the Third World, made up of a large number of states and the strong voice that goes with numbers, wanted to make sure that several problem area would not be regarded as in internal issues. These governments insisted that the 1977 Protocol I on International Armed Conflicts include the provision in Article 1 (4) that the exercise of self-determination "against colonial domination and alien occupation and against racist regimes." fall under humanitarian law governing international armed conflicts. In the past, the governments of colonial powers and white regimes in Africa might argued that self-determination struggles were internal matters and not the business of international society. Nowadays almost all colonial regimes and certainly countries with white-minority rule have passed into history, leaving only a few cases of alien occupation such as Israeli troops in Palestine.

Belligerent occupation

If states refrained from fighting wars, the question of *belligerent occupation* would not arise, but states occasionally do fight them, leading alien territory and people to sometimes fall into the victor's hands. Traditionally, occupation was expected to be a harsh experience. Article 52 of the Lieber Code regarded resistance to occupation as a violation of the laws of war, and Article 82 allowed partisans, soldiers not of a regular army, to be treated as robbers or pirates. The argument has even made that those occupied had a duty to obey the occupiers and not put up any resistance.[34] Resistance to the occupier could be met with harsh punishments, and modern history, from Napoleon's occupation of Spain to Hitler's of France, reflects a heavy-handed approach.

Calls for a more responsible form of occupation started well before Hitler's time with the 1899 and 1907 Hague Conventions on Laws and Customs of War on Land that devote over a dozen articles to what the occupier can and cannot do. Article 55 of both conventions, for example, requires the occupying state to treat public property of another as a trust and to it no harm. The 1949 Fourth Geneva Convention Relative to the Protection of Civilian Persons in Time of War leaps to a whole new level of humanitarian protection for civilians in occupied territory. It primarily prohibits annexation of the occupied territory, transfers and deportation of the population living in the territory, and the taking of hostages.

Occupation is assumed to be temporary. Yet, when it persists for a lengthy period, the lawful practice of occupation during hostilities can understandably cause those occupied to invoke the principle of self-determination and provoke resistance to alien rule. The prime example is the decades-long struggle of the state of Israel with the Palestinians living in the occupied territories, namely the Gaza Strip and the West Bank, or Trans-Jordan area. After several successful wars against Arab states, the Israelis have become bogged down in an asymmetrical war, mainly against Palestinian guerrillas and terrorists who engage in sporadic uprisings and, on occasion, the Hezbollah militia of southern Lebanon.

The Israelis have tried for years to win peace by trading land captured in the 1967 Six Day War to the Palestinians on which to form their own state. Israel has already given back the Sinai Peninsula to Egypt in 1979 and more recently, in 2005, turned over the very poor and crowded Gaza Strip to the Palestinian Authority, the government-in-waiting of the future Palestinian state. The Israelis briefly intervened in Gaza in January 2009 to stop rocket attacks from this territory. However, according to past-Israeli Prime Minister Ehud Olmert, as recently as June 2006, the Israelis expect permanently to retain Jerusalem, part of the Golan Heights, and major pieces of the West Bank, where substantial Jewish settlements have been located. In these occupied territories the Israelis have illegally placed a total of nearly 450,000 settlers, creating a *de facto* annexation (Segev 2006: 145). The Israelis are in clear violation of an international norm that began to crystallize at the end of the First World War. "To the victor belong the spoils" is no longer a valid option for a country coming out on top following a war. Apparently, the Israelis are not that impressed with this change in norms and, on a practical basis, may have reached the conclusion that captured territory cannot be traded for peace.

Besides possessing only a fraction of the UN Palestine Trust of 1947 that the Palestinian people once expected to receive, they have other problems with the ongoing Israeli occupation. These include an unfair distribution of water between Israelis and Palestinians, thousands of Palestinians held in detention, and cabinet officers of the Palestinian Authority arrested when their policies displease the Israelis. Furthermore, Israel has refused to accept the return of 800,000 Palestinian refugees to its territory and built a lengthy 25-foot-high security wall to keep Palestinian suicide-bombers from reaching its citizens. This wall separates 17 percent of the West Bank and 400,000 Palestinians from their fellow Palestinians. The Israeli Supreme Court ruled in 2004 that the wall is legal for security reasons but cannot be erected to demarcate final political borders. In the same year, the ICJ, in an advisory opinion, did not agree that the wall could be built under the doctrine of self-defense claimed by Israel, and certainly that it did not need to be erected mostly on occupied territory belonging to the Palestinians.[35] The other option would have been to construct the wall just inside the Israeli border.

Other occupations exist with their own troubles. The US invasion of Iraq in 2003 led to an interim government in 2004 endorsed by the UN Security Council, but many Iraqis have fought an insurgency against the "crusaders" on their soil instead of viewing US troops and other soldiers of the "Coalition of the Willing" as legitimate guests of the new Iraqi government (Diamond 2005). Although the Iraqi government has increasingly regained control, the US occupation will officially end on January 1, 2012. The United States has a similar situation in Afghanistan, except there its occupation started as a legitimate act of self-defense. Attacking al-Qaida and the Taliban in Afghanistan has morphed into a lengthy occupation of nation-building, including developing a democratic government. Then there is the case of Turkey occupying part of Cyprus in 1974 to protect the Turkish minority from the Greek majority. The Turkish section of Cyprus has become a *de facto* state, known as the Turkish Republic of Northern Cyprus. Finally, the division of Kashmir between the Indian and Pakistani armies has created two occupations since 1947, with each side continuing to claim the whole of Kashmir for itself.

Civilians in war

Protecting civilians in war is an old issue that has grown in importance with changes in weapons and modes of fighting. A century ago civilians accounted for only 15 percent of casualties but, in the wars since the Second World War, 90 percent of war victims are civilian (Cranston 2004: 30). From guerrilla warfare to strategic bombing of industries and cities, civilians are thoroughly in the mix of war. This tragedy has happened in spite of considerable efforts to provide international rules in war for the protection of civilians. For instance, the Lieber Code called for undefended cities not to be shelled. The Hague Conventions prohibited dropping bombs from balloons because of the likelihood of indiscriminate killing. However, efforts to restrict bombing between the two world wars, with the Hague Air Rules, gave way to all-out bombing strategies early in the Second World War. Relatively accurate laser and geo-positioning bombs of today are still no guarantee of striking military targets without harm to civilians. In the NATO attack on Serbia in 1999, 500 civilians died as a result of collateral damage, some of them Kosovo Albanians that NATO set out to protect (Wheeler 2003: 189–216, esp. 189, 198). Similar efforts to prevent unrestricted submarine warfare before the First and Second World Wars failed as all ships, including merchant and passenger ships, were sunk on sight.

Article 33 of the Fourth Geneva Convention and Article 51 of Protocol I also prohibit the use of terror against civilians in time of war. These restrictions on terror as a method of war could conceivably apply to the low-intensity warfare of either the Tamil Tigers in Sri Lanka or the several Palestinian groups and Hezbollah which strike at Israeli civilians with bombs and rockets.

Article 51 of Protocol I also forbids exposing civilians to indiscriminate attacks, using civilians as shields, or using reprisals against civilians. Article 54 disallows destruction of water, food resource, and other objects essential to human life. Article 4 of Protocol II focuses on many inhumane practices that have been occurring during internal wars and protects civilians against pillage, rape, slavery, hostage-taking, enforced prostitution, and the use of child soldiers. The factions fighting in several wars in African states in the 1990s gave little or no heed to the rules of Protocol II.

The status of civilians during conflict often brings up the customary law of *necessity* and *proportionality*, as the Israeli military actions in the summer of 2006 illustrate. When the Israelis were provoked by the killing and capture of several of their soldiers, first by a Palestinian raid from the Gaza Strip and then one by Hezbollah from Lebanon, were their retaliatory strikes in Gaza and southern Lebanon all out of proportion and excessively damaging to civilians relative to the harm Israel had suffered? Israel responded as if self-defense, an inherent right of a state, was necessary in this case. From the Palestinian point of view, destruction of the only electric power plant in Gaza Strip, needed for pumping water, was a disproportionate humanitarian hardship that should not have been imposed. The Israeli bombing of Beirut and many other towns in southern Lebanon, as well as bridges and highways, was also widely criticized as excessive. It would be difficult to predict what an international judicial body would say about the Israeli military attacks in Gaza and Lebanon because what is necessary and proportionate can be very subjective.[36]

Prisoners of war

The issue of POW status has been a legal thorn in the side of President George W. Bush's administration since he declared a WOT following the 9/11 attack. Accusations of abuse, even torture, and unjust trial formats for terrorist suspects have been laid at the feet of the Bush administration. This issue about status began with whether detainees, captured in Afghanistan in the fall of 2001, are POWs and, if not, what should their status be and what can be done with them legally. Despite a rich legal history of protecting detainees in wartime – starting with the Lieber Code and continuing through the Hague Conventions, the 1929 Geneva Convention on POWs, the third 1949 Geneva Convention, and the Protocols to the Geneva Conventions – the Bush administration moved about 800 prisoners from Afghanistan to a prison built for them at the US naval base at Guantánamo, Cuba. This move, so the Bush administration reasoned, would keep any treatment meted out to the detainees from the reach of the US federal courts. The US authorities have called the detainees "illegal combatants," a term not sanctioned by the Geneva Conventions. While holding these individuals for an indefinite period, military and intelligence personnel began sorting through them in search of those who could be tried for acts of terrorism or provide useful intelligence. The Bush administration planned to use military tribunals (sometimes called military commissions) with restricted trial rights to protect government secrets as opposed to military courts martial or civilian federal trials, either of which would provide a more extensive set of rights for defendants.

The Bush administration chose to ignore Article 5 of the 1949 Geneva Convention Relative to the Treatment of POWs, which states that if there is any doubt about the status of a captured person, his or her status "should be determined by a competent tribunal." Within months of US military activities in Afghanistan, calls from the EU Parliament, the OAS Inter-American Commission on Human Rights, the UN High Commissioner on Human Rights, and numerous human rights NGOs urged the government of the United States to organize such a tribunal.[37] Instead, the Bush administration argued that the Geneva Conventions were obsolete and inapplicable when it came to terrorism. The US Supreme Court, however, did not ignore the Geneva Conventions and ruled in the 2006 *Hamdan v. Rumsfeld* case[38] that Article 3, common to all four Geneva Conventions requiring humane treatment for all persons in a conflict, calls for a judgment through "a regularly constituted court affording all the judicial guarantees which are recognized as indispensable by civilized peoples." Individuals can be charged with terrorist acts as war crimes, but the accused must receive a fair trial and be granted the standard rights of a defendant. The Bush administration's plans for the "illegal combatants" finally collapsed, and the new president, Barack Obama, promised to close the prison at Guantánamo.

Mercenaries

The last issue concerns mercenaries and whether they can be distinguished from the personnel of the private military companies (PMCs), which have greatly increased in number since the end of the Cold War. Mercenaries, private individuals or groups who hire themselves out for military purposes, date back to antiquity; in medieval times, they were a significant element of most European armies. The French Foreign Legion and British regiments of Gurkhas from Nepal, both organized during French and British colonial periods, are a vestige of this European practice and continue to operate today (Botha 1999: 133–481). Increasingly, however, mercenaries have transformed into the modern business structures of PMCs.

By the late eighteenth century, however, mercenaries were beginning to be viewed more as a scourge, as the "dogs of war." With the influence of the French Revolution of 1789 and Napoleon's *mass levees* of troops, the expectation grew that armies should be made up of citizen-soldiers, loyal and patriotic to their government and country (Botha 1999: 136; Mandel 2002: 31–2).

Earlier examples can be found, but most PMCs began after the Cold War's end. The downsizing of military forces left many capable officers available, and often governments, MNCs, and humanitarian NGOs found it cost-effective to contract with PMCs instead of relying on their own security arrangements. Most PMCs are from the United Kingdom and the United States and also have the majority of their contracts with the governments of these two countries. PMCs form as corporations, often have web sites, can be listed on stock markets, and provide an array of services including training, logistics, consulting, communications and satellites services, intelligence analysis, and bodyguard protection for leaders, among other security functions. It is exceptional when PMCs take up combat roles. The dependence of

---

Box 8.6 Status and Definition of a Mercenary

Article 47

Mercenaries

(1)   A mercenary shall not have the right to be a combatant or a prisoner of war.
(2)   A mercenary is any person who:
    (a)   Is specially recruited locally or abroad in order to fight in an armed conflict;
    (b)   Does, in fact, take a direct part in the hostilities;
    (c)   Is motivated to take part in the hostilities essentially by the desire for private gain and, in fact, is promised, by or on behalf of a Party to the conflict, material compensation substantially in excess of that promised or paid to combatants of similar ranks and functions in the armed forces of that Party;
    (d)   Is neither a national or a Party to the conflict nor a resident of territory controlled by a Party to the conflict;
    (e)   Is not a member of the armed forces of a Party to the conflict; and
    (f)   Has not been sent by a State which is not a Party to the conflict on official duty as a member of its armed forces.

Sources: From the 1977 *Protocol I Relating to the Protection of Victims of International Armed Conflicts* to the 1949 *Geneva Conventions*. See the ICRC website.
for this protocol at http://www.icrc.org/. The 1989 convention opposing mercenaries is at http://www2.ohchr.org/english/law/mercenaries.htm.

---

governments on PMCs during the recent conflicts in the 1991 Persian Gulf War, the Bosnian and Kosovo conflicts in the 1990s, and the Iraqi occupation, among others, has steadily grown. Correspondingly, the revenue of PMCs has risen from $55.6 billion in 1990 to $100 billion in 2000 and may reach an income of $202 billion by 2010 (Leander 2005: 803–26; see also Singer 2005: 119–32).

International society has definitely spoken out against traditional mercenaries in UN General Assembly declarations as well as through various regional and global treaties. The clearest prohibition against mercenaries is Article 47 of Protocol I, which defines a "mercenary" as a person fighting in an armed conflict for pay but who is not a member of the armed forces or a citizen of either party to the conflict. This article disallows mercenaries a right to be a combatant or have POW status, but they still qualify for humane treatment. Given the clarity of this rule it may seem surprising that many states were reluctant to ratify the 1989 *International Convention against the Recruitment, Use, Financing and Training of Mercenaries*.[39] This convention barely had enough parties to enter into force in 2001, possibly reflecting the ambivalence many governments, as well as scholars, have toward PMCs. Are they or are they not mercenaries? There has been a trend to make a distinction between the two. Thousands of contracts between governments and PMCs, the support of the UN Rapporteur on Mercenaries, and at least the consideration by Kofi Annan, when he was Undersecretary-General for Peacekeeping, to use the South African PMC Executive Outcomes to protect refugees in Rwanda in 1994, suggest a growing legitimacy for PMCs. Although their legal status remains somewhat murky, PMCs may continue to gain acceptance if they focus on support roles and stay out of combat.

Without a doubt, the misbehavior of some will tarnish PMCs making the distinction from mercenaries a difficult one to maintain. Five employees of Blackwater USA went on trial in 2008 in US federal court accused of murdering 17 Iraqi civilians in an intersection of Baghdad in 2007.

Chapter Summary

- The most ambitious undertaking of international law has been to create rules to prevent war or to control its conduct for humanitarian reasons once it begins.
- After important historical precedents, such as the Lieber Codes, laws on force centered first on the Hague Conventions at the turn into the twentieth century and today on the four Geneva Conventions of 1949.
- A major effort for international society has been to identify aggressors and stop their use of force under the rubric of collective security, an ambition only sometimes successful.
- With collective security often unavailable, the UN improvised peacekeeping operations to halt conflicts so negotiations can settle the issues.
- Self-defense has often been claimed by states choosing to use force but becomes complicated when determining whether a state's justification for self-defense is acceptable at forums such as the UN.

Discussion Questions

1   Is war and violent conflict inevitable among humankind, or is it a learned practice that can change? What is your opinion of the prospects of outlawing war?
2   The Hague and Geneva rules call for humane conduct during war regarding civilians, POWs, and other concerns. Are such rules naive or are they likely to be more respected today since international tribunals and the ICC stand ready to back enforcement with judicially determined punishments?
3   What is the Lieber Code and what is its historical role?
4   What is the International Committee of the Red Cross and why does it have an almost unique status among NGOs?

5   What is collective security and why is the UN version improved over that of the League? What are peacekeeping operations and why has the UN had to rely mostly on these non-Charter missions?

Useful Weblinks

http://www.icrc.org/
This is the web site of the International Committee of the Red Cross. It contains copies of 100 treaties and other texts focused on humanitarian law, including the Geneva Conventions and their two 1977 Protocols. The treaties are conveniently listed by both topic and date.

http://www.crisisgroup.org/
A web site of a non-profit NGO aimed at identifying potential conflicts before they erupt. Specializing in field research, teams for Crisis Group provide careful analysis along with maps of troubled spots. This NGO also offers monthly the *CrisisWatch*, a 12-page bulletin providing a succinct regular update on the current crises around the world.

http://www.correlatesofwar.org/
The decades-old Correlates of War (COW) studies program has accumulated a large amount of data-sets related to war on such subjects as alliances, national capabilities, colonial/dependency, and militarized interstate disputes. The COW program transferred its central operations from the University of Michigan to Pennsylvania State University in 2001.

http://www.terrorism.com/
Founded in 1996, the Terrorism Research Center (TRC) is an independent institute dedicated to the research of terrorism, terrorism and war, and homeland security. It offers country profiles, advisories, and a variety of related web links. Among these is a long list of articles on terrorism as direct links.

http://www.un.org/en/peace/index.shtml
A major page of the web site of the UN, "Peace and Security" offers among other subjects Peacekeeping, the Peacebuilding Commission, Preventive Action, and specific issues such as the current situation of the Palestinians and conditions in Iraq.

Further Reading

Benvenisti, Eyal (2004) *The International Law of Occupation*. Princeton, NJ: Princeton University Press.

Bouchet-Saulnier, Francoise (2002) *The Practical Guide to Humanitarian Law*. Lanham, MD: Rowman & Littlefield.

Bowden, Brett, Charlesworth, Hilary, and Farrall, Jeremy (eds.) (2009) *The Role of International Law in Rebuilding Societies after Conflict: Great Expectations*. New York: Cambridge University Press.

Byers, Michael (2006) *War Law: Understanding International Law and Armed Conflicts*. New York: Grove Press.

Byron, Christine (2009) *War Crimes and Crimes against Humanity in the Rome Statue of the International Criminal Court*. New York: Palgrave Macmillan.

Cassese, Antonio (2003) *International Criminal Law*. New York: Oxford University Press.

Doyle, Michael and Sambanis, Nicholas (2006) *Making War and Building Peace: UN Peace Operations*. Princeton, NJ: Princeton University Press.

Engdahl, Ola and Wrange, Pål (2008) *Law at War: The Law as It Was and the Law as It Should Be*. Boston, MA: Martinus Nijhoff.

Gray, Christine (2004) *International Law and the Use of Force*, 2nd edn. New York: Oxford University Press.

Karoubi, Mohammad Taghi (2004) *Just or Unjust War? International Law and Unilateral Use of Force by States at the Turn of the 20th Century*. Burlington, VT: Ashgate.

May, Larry (2008) *Aggression and Crimes against Peace*. New York: Cambridge University Press.

Nasu, Hitoshi (2009) *International Law on Peacekeeping: A Study of Article 40 of the UN Charter*. Boston, MA: Martinus Nijhoff.

O'Keefe, Roger (2007) *The Protection of Cultural Property in Armed Conflict*. New York: Cambridge University Press.

UK Ministry of Defence (ed.) (2004) *The Manual of the Law of Armed Conflict*. New York: Oxford University Press.

Westra, Joel (2008) *International Law and the Use of Armed Force: The UN Charter and the Major Powers*. New York: Routledge.

Notes

1   This widely used definition is from Singer and Small 1972: 19–22. This work helped launch a program of studies still ongoing known as the Correlates of War Program, found at http://www.correlatesofwar.org.

2   Mead 1996: 222–6. Mead's article was originally published in 1940.

3   Wright 1971: 30–109, esp. 54–5. The Lieber Code can be read at http://www.icrc.org. eng > IHL Data Base > Treaties and Documents by Date > Instructions for Government of Armies (Lieber Code).

4   The Martens Clause is in the 1899 and 1907 Hague Conventions findable at http://www. icrc.org/.

5   Elsa 2002: 6. The Geneva Conventions and virtually all others relating to humanitarian matters in war can be read at the web site of the International Committee of the Red Cross, http://www.icrc.org/.

6   The conventions and protocols cited above can be found in Reisman and Antoniou 1994; and O'Connell 2005. They can also be found at http://www.icrc.org/.

7   See Articles 10, 11, 12, 13, 15 and 16 of the League of Nation's Covenant, which can be found in many sources, including O'Connell 205: 220–9.

8   Dinstein 1994: 83; The Kellogg-Briand Pact can be found in O'Connell 2005: 242–3.

9   The UN Charter is easily located, but certainly can be found in O'Connell 2005: 269–94; Henkin 1989; see also Glennon 2003: 6–35.

10   The self-labeling by states has been noted by Neff, *War and the Law of Nations*, p. 286.

11   Quoted from Bloomhall 2003: 47.

12   For instance, see the 1970 *Declaration on Principles of International Law Concerning Friendly Relations and Cooperation Among States in Accordance with the Charter of the United Nations*, found in O'Connell 2005: 568–75. Also it can be found at http://www.un.org/English > Main Bodies > General Assembly > Resolutions > Quick Links > UN GA A/RES/2625 (XXV); and the 1987 *Declaration on the Enhancement of the Effectiveness of the Principle of Refraining from the Threat or Use of Force in International Relations*. This declaration can be found at the same web site as the one just cited, but its number is UN GA A/RES/42/22.

13   The Nicaraguan case can be read at http://www.icj-cij.org/ > cases > Contentious Cases Listed in Alphabetical Order by Country > Nicaragua > Military and Paramilitary Activities in and against Nicaragua (*Nicaragua v. United States of America*) (1984–91); also excerpts of the case can be read in Reisman and Antoniou 1994: 12–23.

14   This resolution can be found at http://www.un.org/english/ > Main Bodies > Security Council > Resolutions > 2001 > Security Council Resolution 1368 (2001); also, for this resolution, see O'Connell, *International Law: Documentary Supplement*, pp. 745.

15   Quotes are from Arend 2003: 90–1.

16   An exception is D'Amato who has argued that the Israelis had a justifiable case of preemptive defense (1983: 584–8). On preemptive self-defense, see O'Connell, "The Myth of Preemptive Self-Defense," http://www.asil.org/ > Publications > Insight > ASIL Insight, August 2002, pp. 1–21.

17   See the 1970 Declaration Concerning Friendly Relations as cited in note 12.

18   See the UN web site at http://www.un.org/terrorism/resolutions.shtml.

19   Kolosov and Levitt 1995: 141–63, esp. 147. The resolution of concern is http://www.un.org/ > Main Bodies > General Assembly > Quick Links > UN GA A/RES/40/61 on "Measures to Prevent International Terrorism." (1985)

20   These resolutions can be found at http://www.un.org/ > Main Bodies > Security Council > Resolutions > 1992 > S/RES/731 and S/RES/748 dealing with Libya.

21   These resolutions can be found in O'Connell, *International Law: Documentary Supplement*, pp. 745–9; or accessed at http://www.un.org/ > Main Bodies > Security Council > Resolutions > 2001 > S/RES/1368 and S/RES/1373 dealing with acts of terrorism.

22   The UN list of terrorist conventions is at http://www.un.org/Docs/sc/ > Subsidiary Bodies > CTC > Laws.

23   This draft convention can be read in van Krieken 2002: 290–304.

24   These conventions can be found in van Krieken 2002; and Walter, Vöneky, Röben, and Schorkopf 2004.

25   Useful works on terrorism are by Richardson 2006b; 2006a; 2007.

26   This definition is similar to the one used by Keohane 2003: 1.

27   The 1965 Declaration can be found at http://www.un.org/ > Main Bodies > General Assembly > Quick Links > 1965 > UN GA A/RES/2131 (XX). And the 1970 Declaration Concerning Friendly Relations as has been cited in footnote 28.

28   Speech reported in *The New York Times* (March 28, 2005).

29   See the Department of Peacekeeping at http://www.un.org/Depts/dpko/dpko/index.asp.

30   Report of the Secretary-General of the 55th Session, "On the Work of the Organization," (June 7, 2001), pp. 1–37. Can be accessed at http://www.un.org/ > Main Bodies > General Assembly > Quick Links > UN GA A/55/985–5/574.

31   This Declaration was prepared in 1994 by the Sixth Committee of the UN General Assembly and presented February 17, 1995. It can be accessed at http://www.un.org/ > Main Bodies > General Assembly > Resolutions > Quick Links > UN GA A/RES/49/57.

32 This convention can be read in O'Connell 2005: 93–5.

33 These distinctions go back at least to the Leiber Code, see Articles 149–151. The Lieber Code is in O'Connell, *International Law: Documentary Supplement*, pp.17–36 and the aforementioned articles are on p. 35.

34 Roberts 1994: 133. Also, for a general work on occupation, see Benvenisti 2004.

35 O'Connell 2005: 261–4, 488–500. See also, case in 2004 http://www.icj-cij.org/ > cases > Advisory Proceedings > 2003–2004 "Legal Consequences of the Construction of a Wall in Occupied Palestinian Territory."

36 On this subject, see Frederic L. Kirgis, "Some Proportionality Issues Raised by Israeli's Use of Armed Forces in Lebanon," at http://www.asil.org/ > Publications > Insights > ASIL Insights, August 17, 2006, pp. 1–6.

37 Elsa 2003: 1–6.

38 *Hamdan v. Rumsfeld* found at http://www.supremecourtus.gov/ > Recent Decisions > Hamdan v. Rumsfeld (6/29/06).

39 This convention can be read at http://www2.ohchr.org/english/law/mercenaries.htm.

Referring to core international crimes, Justice Jackson said the Nuremberg IMT needed to address crimes "so calculated, so malignant, and so devastating, that civilization cannot tolerate their being ignored, because it cannot survive their being repeated." (Justice Robert H. Jackson, US Supreme Court, Temporarily serving as prosecutor at Nuremberg)

Rape has long been mischaracterized and dismissed by military and political leaders as a private crime, the ignoble act of the occasional soldier. (International Security Report 2005)

9

Core International Crimes
Atrocities That Shock the Conscience
of Humankind

Contents

For the sake of human well-being, international society has identified certain practices that are regarded as strikingly reprehensible. As in national legal systems, these practices have been made criminal. A wide array of customary and treaty law to suppress crimes ranging from piracy and slave-trafficking to kidnapping diplomats and nuclear terrorism are the creation of an international society determined to have a more livable international world order. For over a century, a specialized and interesting area of law has been evolving to protect humankind from atrocities in war and in peace.

These atrocities are so heinous that they are referred to as *core international crimes*. While these crimes reach across history, their apex of horror happened in the Second World War. Continuing to today's times, impunity for transgressions is clearly no longer assured. From privates to prime ministers, appearing before an international tribunal or national court for committing core crimes is a real possibility.

This chapter begins with a brief history of the development of international core crimes as a jurisdictional area of international law. A discussion of *crimes against peace* follows which will emphasize the crime of aggression. Next, *crimes against humanity* are covered. They deal with harms leveled against unarmed civilians on a widespread basis, in both peace and war. One specialized humanitarian atrocity has evolved into a core crime in its own right, the crime of *genocide*, when an attempt is made to kill a particular group in whole or in part. Some of the more prominent *war crimes* that states have committed against the military and civilians of other states are then identified and described. Finally, an evaluation of the status and effectiveness of tribunals trying these various crimes will be offered.

A Brief History of Core International Crimes

Historically, punishment for international crimes has been the exception, not the rule. Some empires and kingdoms established military codes of conduct but, for centuries, widespread looting, massacres, burning of cities, and enslavement of survivors made it difficult for an individual soldier or commander to stand out in such disrepute that a trial was warranted. One of the earliest exceptions was the trial of Peter von Hagenbach in 1474. Hagenbach was appointed as the governor of the City of Breisach on the upper Rhine River in Austria by Charles the Bold, the Duke of Burgundy. He was an overzealous governor who allowed his soldiers to attack citizens, commonly using rape and murder, and to prey on surrounding towns and merchants by extorting money. Once defeated and captured, he was tried by what can be called the first *ad hoc* international tribunal and promptly beheaded (Cryer 2005: 17–21). An *ad hoc* tribunal is limited in time and place regarding its jurisdiction and authority and is not set up to be a permanent court. Before the twentieth century, military tribunals usually involved an army trying one of its own or, rarely, a trial might be held for an individual enemy as happened in the infamous case of Henry Wirz at the end of the American Civil War.

During the latter nineteenth century, customary rules about conducting war and committing war crimes began to take written form, such as the Lieber Code and the *Oxford Manual*, and then the important Hague Conventions appeared at the turn of the twentieth century. These manuals and treaties set out in fairly clear terms what practices in war were impermissible. Although the Hague Conventions were based on obligations of states, atrocities committed by the Axis powers of Germany and Turkey in the First World War led to the revolutionary idea of bringing charges against individuals and placing them before war crimes tribunals for such crimes as sinking hospital ships and mistreating POWs.

The embryo of *crimes against humanity* began with what is now known as the Armenian genocide. The term "genocide" was not yet in use, but this crime was thought of by the Allies as a violation of the "laws of humanity," rather than as a war crime. Turkey massacred its own Armenian citizens, after all, not the citizens of an enemy state. Early in the war, Belgium, although a declared neutral, was quickly occupied and terrorized into submission by the German Army through the burning of houses, rape, forced labor, torture, and the murder of Belgium citizens.[1]

Box 9.1 Captain Henry Wirz: The Only Man Hanged for War Crimes in the American Civil War

Henry Wirz was born Heinrich Hartmann Wirz in Zurich, Switzerland, but left to escape debt and to pursue his medical ambitions. He wound up in Louisiana working as a "slave doctor" using a homeopathic approach for treating slaves. Embracing the Confederate cause, he joined the Confederate army but was badly wounded at the Battle of Seven Pines. Wirz was then assigned to guarding prisoners. At Camp Sumter, known in its infamy as "Andersonville" after a nearby village, he was given the impossible task of accommodating 30,000 to 45,000 Union prisoners in a space that would be crowded with the 10,000 prisoners for which the stockade was designed. In 1864, in a matter of months, 13,000 prisoners died due to poor rations and exposure, despite Wirz's numerous appeals to the Confederate government for help.

Captain Wirz was convicted by a US military commission in October 1865 of deliberately murdering prisoners in his care. His responsibility for prisoner deaths and the fairness of his conviction remain highly controversial. Demonized in the North and viewed as a martyr in the South, he was sentenced to hang. The execution took place in Old Capital Prison in Washington, DC, with spectators chanting "Remember Andersonville!" Always an unlucky man, the rope failed to break his neck and he slowly strangled to death.

Source: See James B. Daniels, "Personal History: Henry Wirz," *Military History*, November (2006), pp. 25–6; *Criminals, War Victims: Andersonville, Nuremberg, Hiroshima, My Lai*, prepared under the direction of Betty Reardon, (New York: Random House, 1974), pp. 5–12.

The 1919 Treaty of Versailles that ended the First World War forced Germany to accept responsibility for all the harms done to the Allies as a consequence of Germany's "aggression" and to cooperate with the Allies in providing evidence and handing over accused Germans to Allied tribunals. The most daring step the Allies took was to "publicly arraign William II of Hohenzollern, formerly German Emperor, for a supreme offense against international morality and the sanctity of treaties."[2] This wording was a roundabout way of charging the German Emperor with aggression (Bass 2001: 76). Not only was William II head of an important state but a monarch at a time when kings still had real power. William II wisely went into exile in neutral Holland and was granted asylum there in 1918. Since the Dutch, like other states at the time, did not consider aggression an established crime, they argued no legal basis existed for extradition. William II died in exile in 1941 just as the Netherlands was falling under Nazi Germany's occupation (Bassiouni 1997: 19; Bass 2000: 59, 76–8; Shabas 2004: 3). Aggression would be more clearly designated a crime at the end of the Second World War.

If efforts to prosecute the German Emperor fizzled out completely, attempts to bring German and Turkish military personnel to justice fared little better. Instead of Allied tribunals trying 2,000 to 3,000 accused, the number was gradually whittled down to around 900 and then reduced to about 45 cases due to German resistance, and these trials were in a German court.

Only a dozen minor cases went to trial and half of these ended in acquittal. Throughout the period of the trials, 1921–5, any German accused or tried was hailed as a war hero by German public opinion. In their frustration, the Belgium and French governments used military court martial proceedings to convict hundreds of Germans for war crimes *in absentia* (Horne & Kramer 2001: 340–55).

At first, the Turkish situation looked more promising. Great Britain at first received a favorable response from Turkey given the signing of the 1920 *Treaty of Sèvres*, which called for war crimes trials over Turkish mistreatment of British POWs and trials for massacring the Armenians. Punishing leaders for terrible mistreatment of their own subjects was a radical step at the time and, as it turned out, few Turkish leaders were actually tried and punished for these widespread killings. Once Britain began to draw down its occupation forces, Turkish nationalists became bold and resisted any further prosecution of the Ottoman Turks (Bass 2000: 112–19, 127, 139). The Treaty of Sèvres, never ratified, was replaced by the 1923 *Treaty of Lausanne*, which provided amnesty for all offenses committed between August 1914 and November 1922 (Shabas 2004: 4).

The principal allies of the Second World War – the Soviet Union, the United Kingdom, and the United States – were determined not to repeat the dismal prosecutorial failures that occurred at the end of the First World War, and made that clear to German and Japanese leaders. The Allies announced in the 1943 *Moscow Declaration* that they had received "from many quarters evidence of atrocities, massacres, and cold-blooded mass executions." The Allies further stated that German criminals "will be brought back to the scene of their crimes and judged on the spot by the peoples whom they have outraged." The Allies promised to "pursue them to the uttermost ends of the earth."[3]

Following a decisive victory by the Allies, the top Nazi leaders were tried at Nuremberg, Germany before a military tribunal provided for in the 1945 Nuremburg Charter.[4] The tribunal was known as the Nuremberg International Military Tribunal (Nuremberg IMT) and would have jurisdiction over three core international crimes: crimes against peace, crimes against humanity, and war crimes. Only war crimes were a category of jurisdiction well established in customary law and in the Hague Conventions. A similar Charter of the International Tribunal for the Far East (Tokyo Charter) was established at the Potsdam conference held in Germany in July 1945 to provide a Tokyo IMT for trying the top Japanese war criminals. A difference was that the Tokyo IMT had a larger panel of judges, representing 11 countries instead of 4.[5] When these tribunals were underway, the jurisdiction of core international crimes received further validation because the UN General Assembly passed a unanimous resolution in 1946 affirming that the Nuremberg Charter contained recognized principles of international law.[6]

After a long hiatus of nearly half a century, international society was forced again to confront shocking atrocities. The UN Security Council provided the International

Criminal Tribunal for the former Yugoslavia (ICTY) in 1993 located at The Hague, Netherlands, and the International Criminal Tribunal for Rwanda (ICTR) in 1994 at Arusha, Tanzania. These were to be *ad hoc* tribunals focusing on core international crimes in their locales for a limited period of time. These two *ad hoc* tribunals have heard numerous cases concerning core international crimes and are still in operation. Because these tribunals are limited in time and place, the permanent International Criminal Court (ICC) was created in 1998, also at The Hague, and authorized to hear cases about crimes committed after 2002.

The history of the twentieth century, the bloodiest and most violent of all time, reflects extensive efforts to use treaties to suppress a wide range of crimes – drug and arms trafficking, crimes against diplomats and UN personnel, hiring mercenaries, torture, and a panoply of terrorist associated crimes among others – but none surpasses in importance restraining core international crimes if humankind is to enjoy a safer world in which to live. Fortunately, the legal regime on core crimes has been evolving and strengthening.

Crimes Against Peace

The Nuremberg Charter specified **crimes against peace** as "planning, preparation, initiation or waging of a war of aggression, or a war in violation of international treaties, agreements or assurances, or participation in a common plan or conspiracy for the accomplishment of any of the foregoing."[7] "Aggression" was never specifically defined despite the fact that it was given more priority at the Nuremberg IMT than the Holocaust involving the systematic killing of millions of Jews and other peoples (Bass 2000: 148). No doubt with some bias at work, aggression at least meant the force used by the defeated Germany and Japan. Germany's unprovoked attack on Poland in 1939 and Japan's sudden attack on Pearl Harbor in 1941 ignited the European and Pacific theaters of the Second World War (Minear 1971: 56–8). The Tokyo IMT echoed the Nuremberg tribunal's emphasis on aggression.

Nonetheless, the Nuremberg IMT judges and the majority of the Tokyo IMT judges proceeded as if the crime of aggression was known to the rules of international law and was within the two tribunals' jurisdiction. Scholars still debate the legality of the aggression charge leveled against German and Japanese leaders at the end of the Second World War, a charge that resulted in men being hanged or sentenced to lengthy prison terms. Clarity as to what constitutes aggression remains elusive to this day. The attempt to punish the German Emperor for aggression at the end of the First World War had failed completely and obviously could not serve as a precedent. The Assembly of the League of Nations in 1927 passed a non-binding resolution stating that aggression was an international crime but without agreeing on a definition. It was to the 1928 Kellogg–Briand Pact that the Nuremberg IMT turned for authority to back the aggression charge (Cryer 2005: 242). However, the Kellogg–Briand Pact only called on states to outlaw war in general and did not specifically address aggression. Not even the UN General Assembly's 1974 Declaration on Aggression, with its fairly explicit language, has produced a meaningful consensus over the definition of aggression.

The most serious criticism of the aggression charge, as applied by the two IMTs, is that such a charge amounted to an ***ex post facto*** violation. Critics claimed the law was created after the fact, after the so-called crime was committed. The *ex post facto* legal principle is important in many national legal systems, including that of the United States where it was enshrined in the body of the US Constitution before the Bill of Rights was even conceived. If the Nuremberg and Tokyo tribunals violated this principle, another closely related and widely accepted legal principle was violated as well, ***nullem crime sine lege***. "No crime without law" means that law must pre-exist before criminal charges can be made. Understandably, for this reason, some critics view the tribunals with skepticism and derisively refer to them as producing a "victor's justice." Few would doubt the guilt of those sentenced for an assortment of crimes, but it is always appropriate to raise questions about the process of justice as well as its final outcome. Defenders of the charge of aggression have argued that customary law, morality, and the blatant fact of conspicuous first attacks make it clear that aggressions were committed in the opening period of the Second World War.

Aggression's best moment of legality quickly passed and went into retreat. Aggression was largely pulled back into the political arena despite worthy efforts to give it a legal footing. States, especially the more powerful ones, want flexibility in their options. "Aggression is what others do, not what we do." The 1974 UN General Assembly's Declaration on Aggression, although enumerated with specific acts that constitute aggression, has never been sufficiently agreed upon as a definition. The UN's International Law Commission's 1996 *Draft Code on Crimes against Peace and Security of Mankind*, including aggression as a crime, so far has been an unsuccessful effort to provide this area of jurisdiction with a supporting treaty.[8] Nor were the 1993 ICTY and the 1994 ICTR granted jurisdiction for aggression as these tribunals tried to provide justice for core crimes committed in the former Yugoslavia and Rwanda. The relatively new ICC possesses aggression as a potential jurisdiction if its statute is amended following the acceptance of a definition of aggression.

Crimes against Humanity

The 1945 Nuremberg Charter is the first effort to codify **crimes against humanity**, although there are the earlier references to "laws of humanity" in the Martens Clause of the 1899 and 1907 Hague Conventions and in the charges against Turkish leaders for the massacre of Armenians in 1915. The Nuremberg Charter includes in this category, "murder, extermination, enslavement, deportation, and other inhumane acts committed against any civilian population, before or during the war; or persecutions on political, racial or religious grounds in execution of or in connection with any crime within the jurisdiction of the tribunal, whether or not in violation of the domestic law of the country where perpetrated."[9] The Tokyo Charter covers the same acts but adds a sentence about conspirators being held equally accountable for any crimes they commit.[10] Crimes against humanity involve a widespread, systematic attack against any civilian population, including the citizens of the very government accused of these crimes. The charge of crimes against humanity allowed the

Nuremberg IMT to convict German leaders for horrid deeds against their own citizens, including Jews, Roma people (gypsies), and communists during the war, as well as millions of foreigners.

A specialized convention covering crimes against humanity has yet to develop, but planners of the Nuremberg and Tokyo Charters gave these crimes legal standing by linking them to war crimes, a well-established criminal jurisdiction (Bassiouni 1997: 26). The Nuremberg tribunal can be said to have created a precedent by convicting two defendants for crimes against humanity without associating this charge with war crimes (Cassese 2003: 70–1).

The numbers of those killed in the Second World War staggers the mind, although estimates of death vary. R. J. Rummel claims Nazi Germany killed almost 21 million unarmed, helpless people, both Germans and other European nationalities. He also estimates that militaristic Japan killed nearly 6 million people in the Second World.[11]

However, Iris Chang claims the Japanese killed 19 million people, mostly civilians in China alone (Chang 1998: 166–7, 215–17), while James Bradley puts the Japanese killings at 30 million deaths in China. Bradley even asserts that more people, mostly Chinese, were executed by Japanese samurai swords than were killed by the two US atomic bombs dropped on Japanese cities.[12] Starting well before the Second World War and continuing for years afterward, Joseph Stalin's communist Soviet Union killed far greater numbers than the German Nazis or Japanese militarists. According to one estimate, almost 62 million people died, the large majority being Soviet citizens. Mao Zedong's Communist China, from the 1930s until the 1970s, managed to take 35 million Chinese lives.[13]

The jurisdictional area of crimes against humanity has continued to grow in legitimacy despite the absence of a convention dedicated to this area of international law. Following on the heels of the Second World War, with its unrivaled horrors, the 1949 Four Geneva Conventions were a major upgrade in the laws of war aimed at providing humanitarian protection. Since the intent of the Geneva Conventions is to reduce suffering by providing a measure of humanitarianism during armed conflict, violators of Geneva Convention rules can be prosecuted as war criminals. Article 3, common to all four conventions, protects the sick and wounded, members of armed forces that have surrendered, and civilians. All these persons enjoy the status of *hors de combat*, meaning they are set aside from combat and should be protected from its dangers. Moreover, the 1977 Protocol I to the Geneva Conventions is an update in protections for victims in international armed conflicts, while the 1977 Protocol II to the same conventions provides protection for victims in non-international armed conflicts.[14]

More than four decades would pass before crimes against humanity would receive additional attention and reinforcement. The barbarity in Yugoslavia in the early 1990s as that country splintered apart amidst ethnic conflict and, shortly afterward, the African country of Rwanda imploded into widespread killings of genocidal proportions leading to the UN Security Council setting up a tribunal for each country. In Article 5 of its statute, the ICTY specifies a list of crimes against humanity similar to the list of the Nuremberg IMT, but the ICTY statute adds rape and torture to its punishable crimes. The jurisdiction of the ICTY for these crimes was tied to armed conflict; however, the 1995 *Prosecutor v. Tadić* case before the ICTY ruled that this connection was now obsolete.[15] The 1994 ICTR has the same list of crimes against humanity in its Article 3 and avoids any necessary tie to armed conflict.[16] Today's jurists consider crimes against humanity in peacetime just as relevant and prosecutable as those in wartime.

The ICC may offer the greatest hope for prosecuting and punishing crimes against humanity, along with other core crimes. In addition to being permanent and able to hear cases brought from anywhere in the world, Article 7 of the court's statute has a longer list of crimes against humanity than has appeared in any legal document before. There are eleven specific crimes. Several relatively new crimes are on its list, including forced prostitution and pregnancy associated with rape, disappearing persons, and the crime of *apartheid* (strict racial segregation).[17]

Genocide

Genocide is the mass killing of a people because of its ascribed group characteristics such as religion, language, race or skin color or some other ethnic trait. Genocide is a particular type of crime against humanity, but it became a crime in its own right soon after the Second World War. The 1948 *Convention on the Prevention and Punishment of the Crime of Genocide* (Genocide Convention)[18] emerged from a 1946 UN General Assembly resolution declaring that "genocide is a crime under international law."[19] This convention entered into force in 1951. The term "genocide" was coined by Professor of Law Raphael Lemkin in his *Axis Rule in Occupied Europe* (Lemkin 1944), published a year before the Second World War's end. Lemkin combined the Greek syllable *genos* for nation or tribe with *cide*, a Latin syllable referring to killing, hence, *genocide* (Weitz 2003: 8). This term was not used by judges at the Nuremberg IMT in 1945, but the prosecutors did make use of the word in their closing arguments. Prior to the coining of the term of "genocide," widespread murder committed against peoples like the Armenians in Turkey in 1915 were called "massacres" or "persecutions."

It is now recognized that genocide has taken place in all periods of history, as the Genocide Convention acknowledges in its preamble. There are biblical accounts of the deliberate exterminations of tribes. The European colonial onslaught toward indigenous peoples that lasted several centuries, employing bullets, liquor, and contagious diseases, managed to kill off entire tribes, and has been referred to by some as genocide. Perhaps the last colonial case was that of the Herrero tribal people slaughtered by German soldiers in Southwest Africa in 1904–5. At the same time, this case was the twentieth century's first genocide. The use of mustard gas on Ethiopians by Benito Mussolini in 1935–6, the attempted destruction of the Jewish and Roma peoples in Europe by the Nazis in the early 1940s, the killing of over two million Cambodians in a bizarre communist experiment in the 1970s, the gassing of thousands of Kurds in northern Iraq by Saddam Hussein's Iraqi government in 1987–8, and the killing of over eight hundred thousand Tutsis by the Hutu in Rwanda

---

Box 9.2 Selected Articles from the 1948 Genocide Convention

Article I

The Contracting Parties confirm that genocide, whether committed in time of peace or in time of war, is a crime under international law which they undertake to prevent and to punish.

Article II

In the present Convention, genocide means any of the following acts committed with intent to destroy, in whole or in part, a national, ethical, racial or religious group, as such:
(a)   Killing members of the group;
(b)   Causing serious bodily or mental harm to members of the group;
(c)   Deliberately inflicting on the group conditions of life calculated to bring about its physical destruction in whole or in part;
(d)   Imposing measures intended to prevent births within the group;
(e)   Forcibly transferring children of the group to another group.

Article III

The following acts shall be punishable:
(a)   Genocide;
(b)   Conspiracy to commit genocide;
(c)   Direct and public incitement to commit genocide;
(d)   Attempt to commit genocide;
(e)   Complicity in genocide

Source: This convention is available at http://treaties.un.org/Pages/ParticipationStatus. aspx > Chapter IV.

---

in 1994 in a little over two months are other cases of genocidal behavior. R. J. Rummel estimates that over thirty-eight and a half million people have died because of genocidal killing during the twentieth century alone (Rummel 1994: 4, Table 1.2). Eric Markusen and David Kopf have identified 44 genocidal episodes during the fifty years following the Second World War (Markusen & Kopf 1995: 28).

The grave nature of this heinous crime has made it the subject of an enormous amount of research and thought.[20] The most provocative question is why would a government choose to murder people *en masse*. Part of the answer may involve dictatorial leaders, with much power in their hands, becoming animated by a vision of a "pure" national society based on an ethnically homogeneous population

---

Box 9.3 Raphael Lemkin: A Life Devoted to Preventing Genocide

Raphael Lemkin (1900–1959), a Polish Jew and international lawyer, devoted most of his adult life to stopping the attacks and efforts to exterminate communities of people, for no more reason than simply being who they were. Years before the Second World War, he was hard at work; for instance, he made an appeal before an international law conference held in Madrid, Spain, in 1933 asking for a treaty to stop what he would later label "genocide" in his 1944 book, *Axis Rule in Occupied Europe*. He was one of the first to reveal the horrors that the Nazis were perpetuating against Jews and other ethnic groups in Europe. Almost all of Lemkin's family, including his parents, died in the Holocaust. At the Nuremberg IMT, the prosecution used his concept of "genocide" for the atrocities that Prime Minister Winston Churchill had previously called a "crime without a name."

   Working tirelessly, and with little regard for his health, Lemkin's poverty showed in his pale and shabby image that, nonetheless, became a lobbying power for international law to prevent genocide. Fortunately, his relatively short life did witness the emergence of the 1948 Genocide Convention and its wide acceptance based on numerous state ratifications.

Sources: Samantha Power, *A Problem from Hell: America and the Age of Genocide* (New York: Basic Books, 2002), pp. xix–xxi, 19–21, 26–9, 42–52; and Eric Markusen and David Kopf, *The Holocaust and Strategic Bombing: Genocide and Total War in the Twentieth Century* (Boulder, CO: Westview Press, 1995), pp. 39–41.

(Weitz 2003: 14).[21] If a state's leaders possess this purity ambition and, at the same time, are faced with the crisis of war, then the danger for minorities will greatly increase. The minorities might very well be seen as disloyal "fifth columns" or the "scapegoats" for whatever has gone wrong for the state.

Unlike the more general crimes against humanity, the legal regime on genocide has the clear advantage of being anchored in a specialized treaty, the 1948 Genocide Convention. Despite an affirming convention, the enforcement provisions could have been stronger. A serious failing is the absence of an *aut dedere aut judicare* clause, requiring states to either extradite or try a suspect in a genocide case. This type of compelling extradition can still apply when the crime is viewed as falling under universal jurisdiction. Seeing little chance for extraditing Adolf Eichmann, Israel kidnapped this chief Nazi architect of the Holocaust from Argentina in 1961 and then tried and hanged him. The Israeli courts claimed genocide was covered by customary law and universal jurisdiction, even if their agents had to violate Argentine sovereignty to "arrest" Eichmann.

Prosecuting the numerous episodes of genocide will likely remain problematical since leaders of states are often the chief perpetrators. Obviously, these leaders are unwilling to arrange their own extradition. The shadow of a lasting military victory over accused leaders may be necessary before justice can be done in genocidal cases. While trials of Turks halted as Great Britain's army began leaving Turkey after the First World War, the trials of Germans for atrocities after the Second World War resulted in hangings and prison sentences because of the entrenched Allied occupation. The Tutsis' victory over their Hutu oppressors in 1994 landed many Hutu in Rwandan jails and placed others before the ICTR in Arusha, Tanzania. The trials of Saddam Hussein by an Iraqi court were possible only because of the US invasion of Iraq in 2003, his over-throw, and an occupation that continued past his day of execution. He was on trial for genocide for gassing thousands of Kurdish people in northern Iraq in 1987–8 when he was hanged on the next to last day of 2006 for an earlier conviction of massacring Shi'as. Saddam had already been found guilty of crimes against humanity for having 148 people killed in the small city of Dujail in 1982 as an act of revenge because an assassination attempt on his life had occurred in this city. In the summer of 2007, three senior aides of Saddam were found guilty of genocide and other core crimes and were sentenced to death for the gas attack on the Kurds that took as many as 180,000 lives.

In most cases of genocidal threat, the best hope is that help will arrive from out-side the country where the threat exists. Is there an international duty to stop the destruction of an entire ethnic community? Will states and IGOs, such as the UN, respond? Outside actors were slow to halt the blood-letting in Bosnia in the early 1990s and acted in Rwanda only after two months of the uninterrupted genocidal murder of 800,000 people in 1994. NATO did act with some alacrity over Kosovo in 1999 to save the Albanian people from Serbian persecutions. Since 2002, however, the UN and concerned states have not yet found the means to put an end to the ter-rible attacks on people living in the Darfur region of western Sudan. These observa-tions are simply reminders of the question about the feasibility and legality of *humanitarian intervention* but, for cases of genocide, the pressure to act is profoundly felt. It has to be said that the record of international society is at best spotty when it comes to dealing with genocide.

While nearly half a century would pass after the 1948 Genocide Convention, the legal regime on genocide has been strengthened by placing it as a crime within the jurisdictions of the ICTY and the ICTR, and the ICC. Their statutes basically repli-cate the Genocide Convention as to what constitutes genocide.[22] The ICTY and ICTR have faithfully charged and convicted numerous persons for genocide as well as the broader crimes against humanity. In some cases, the genocide charges have been accompanied by indictments of rape and torture since these have helped carry out genocide.[23] The ICC case docket is at an early stage and has yet to try a genocide case. If the 2008 arrest warrant for President Omar Hassan al-Bashir of the Sudan can be served, and Hassan al-Bashir brought before the bar of the ICC, the charges will undoubtedly include genocide for his orchestration of a campaign that led to hundreds of thousands of deaths in the Darfur region.

The Most Notorious Episodes of Genocide

A brief review of the last century's worst genocides can be helpful. These reviews illustrate not only what dreadful, inhumane practice genocide is, but also some of the problems that hinder the suppression and punishment of this core crime. These episodes are presented in chronological order.

Armenian genocide

At the beginning of the First World War, the Ottoman Turkish Empire, feeling the encroachment of Christian countries on its periphery, decided to eliminate all two million Christian Armenians within their borders (Weitz 2003: 2–5). The Turks feared the Armenians might prove to be a "fifth column," disloyal and able to undermine the Turkish war effort. The genocide started with the goals of their forced assimilation by religious conversion and then the removal of the Armenians from Turkey. The rise in suspicion and hatred toward Armenians then quickly turned into widespread murder in 1915 (Bloxham 2005: esp. 96). Armenian men were shot outright or worked to death while the women and children commonly died on forced marches to the deserts of Iraq and Syria. Estimates vary, but Eric D. Weitz says one million died out of a total population of 2.1 million Armenians (Weitz 2003: 1–7, esp. 5).

At least two high-ranking Turkish officials, under the watchful eye of British occupation, were punished by a Turkish court for these massacres, one by hanging (Power 2002: 14–15). With the withdrawal of British forces and the rise of Turkish nationalism, further prosecution of the violation of the "laws of humanity" came to a halt. The term "genocide" was of course not yet available. The only means of justice left was vigilantism, with Armenian survivors hunting down and assassinating Turkish officials seeking refuge in Germany in 1921–2 (Bass 2000: 145). To this day, nationalistic Turks will not forthrightly acknowledge that genocide was committed against Armenians.

Nazi genocide

The Holocaust has been called the ultimate and archetypical genocide. Carefully laid plans, employing factory-like efficiency through the use of labor camps, gas chambers, and crematoriums, killed millions of innocent people. These plans, known as the "final solution," were devised by fifteen top Nazi leaders, including Adolf Eichmann, at the lakeside Wannsee villa near Berlin in January 1942. Driven by a strong sense of racial purity as policy, the Nazis moved quickly from socioeconomic discriminatory policies toward Jews of the pre-war 1930s, as well as persecuting other minorities, to the out-and-out killing of their numbers on a massive scale during the Second World War (Weitz 2003: 102–43).

The Nazis killed over 16 million people in a genocidal manner. Of these, they had a special enmity for Jews, homosexuals, and Roma people (gypsies). These three groups they wanted to extirpate, to rip up root and branch and totally destroy them. The Nazis killed well-over 5 million of the 14 million European Jews, 220,000 of the 1 million homosexuals thought to live in Germany, and 258,000 Roma people of the nearly 1 million found in Europe at the time. The Nazis probably killed more Slavic people than any other ethnic group, especially Poles and Russians, during the Second World War, but it is the factory-style extermination plan, directed at Jews, that is indelibly stamped into the memory of humankind (Rummel 1994: 112, Table 6.1, 111–22; 1991: 181–9, 29, 31–43). Without question, the tide of war turning against Germany is all that saved millions of people from the Nazis' genocidal ambitions.

Cambodian genocide

To achieve a pure form of rural communism, the Khmer Rouge leadership began a reign of terror in 1974 that murdered the entire educated class of Cambodia and drove all city-dwellers onto farm collectives. Only war and an invasion by Vietnam in 1979 brought this nightmare of repression to an end. Two million Cambodians died out of a total population of seven million, making this genocide, proportionately speaking, one of the worst in history (Rummel 1994: 159–207; Weitz 2003: 9). Since Cambodians mostly killed other Cambodians, is this case one of true genocide? The Genocide Convention clearly refers to the intent to destroy in whole or part a particular ethnic community, not one's own kind. The Cambodian episode has come to be known as a case of *autogenocide*. The Khmer Rouge killed their fellow Cambodians based on their social class status and for political ideological reasons, but hardly because of ethnic hatred.

Raphael Lemkin wanted class and political distinctions included in the definition of genocide. Such a definition was impossible, however, because the Soviet Union and its communist allies did not want their policies of eradicating peasants, the business class, old regime army officers, and political opponents in general associated with the odious practice of genocide (Weitz 2003: 9).

Genocide in Bosnia

As Yugoslavia broke up into half a dozen states following the general collapse of European communism, terrible events reminiscent of Nazi horrors of the previous generation, took place in the early 1990s. Three ethnic groups in particular, the Bosnian Muslims, the Serbs, and the Croatians, were in strong contention over part of the former Yugoslavia known as Bosnia-Herzegovina. All three groups suffered in the fighting that followed during the period 1992–5, with the Bosnian Serbs best able to press their territorial claims. They were backed by the nearby state of Serbia, clearly the strongest entity to emerge from the disintegration of Yugoslavia. After NATO imposed order in 1995, with the UN's blessing, individuals from all three ethnic communities were indicted for core international crimes before the ICTY, but the majority of atrocities were laid at the feet of the better armed Bosnian Serbs. The Serbs did not start with a blueprint for genocide as had the Nazis, but they did gradually develop a general notion about a "Greater Serbia," an exclusive homogeneous state for Serbs covering not only Serbia but as much of neighboring Bosnia as possible (2003: 198–201).

Military attacks, beatings, torture, the systematic use of rape, starvation, forced deportation, and murder were the main tools of terror used to drive non-Serbs from their homes and villages. Conservative estimates are that 200,000 people died, 12,000 women were raped, and about a million people left Bosnia as refugees and well over a million others were displaced as internal refugees. The large majority of victims were Bosnian Muslims.[24] Adding to the regions horrors was the Serbian Army's use of rape and murder in 1999 to force hundreds of thousands of ethnic Albanians to leave the Serbian province of Kosovo and flee to the nearest border for safety. Two and a half months of constant bombing of Serbian targets by NATO air forces finally halted this latest round of atrocities.

The growing numbers of indictments before the ICTY often have included charges for a mixture of genocide, crimes against humanity, and war crimes. One of the most interesting cases is that of General Radislav Krstić, a Bosnian Serb and Commander of the dreaded Drina Corps. He has the dubious distinction of being the first person in Europe convicted by an international tribunal for genocide, chiefly for aiding in the massacre of seven to eight thousand Muslim men and boys at Srebrenica in 1995. Srebrenica was supposed to be a safe-haven where Muslims could gather under UN protection. Krstić was found guilty in 2001 before the ICTY and given a 46-year sentence. His guilt was affirmed by the Appeals Chamber, but his sentence was reduced to 35 years.[25]

The most important trial from the former Yugoslavia could have been that of Slobodan Milošević, the ex-president of Serbia, but it will never be completed since he was found dead of natural causes in his cell in March 2006 at the headquarters of the ICTY at The Hague. Widely perceived as the principal force behind the bloody Balkan wars of the 1990s, Milošević was arrested in 2001 and his trial started in 2002. The prosecution had concluded its case in early 2004, and his defense began soon after with an end to the trial and a verdict expected at the end of 2006. Milošević had been indicted on 66 counts of crimes against humanity, genocide, and war crimes committed in Bosnia, Croatia, and Kosovo.[26]

Rwandan genocide

As the Hutus rose to power through democratic opportunities between 1992 and 1994, they began a campaign of discrimination and hateful anti-Tutsi rhetoric through the media. Finally, with the shooting down of the Hutu President Juvenal Habyarimana's plane under mysterious circumstances, tensions between the tribal groups exploded into a firestorm of genocidal carnage that swept across the country in a little over two months and killed an estimated 800,000 Rwandans, mostly Tutsis. Thousands of other Tutsis fled to neighboring countries. Without help from other countries or the UN, Tutsi militia managed to re-seize control in Rwanda, placed many Hutu suspects in Rwandan jails for their crimes, and surrendered other Hutu to the ICTR in nearby Arusha, Tanzania, many to face charges of genocide.

The trial of Jean-Paul Akayesu before the ICTR in 1998 was the first conviction worldwide for the crime of genocide by an international tribunal. His case preceded that of Bosnian Serb General Radislav Krstić by several years. Akayesu was also convicted of torture, rape, and murder, and received a life sentence. Noting the horror of genocide, one of his judges said that "genocide constitutes the crime of crimes."[27] In another important case, in 1998, the interim Prime Minister, Jean Kambanda, became the first head of government convicted of genocide and his life sentence was affirmed by the Appeals Chamber at The Hague in 2000. His trial judges held that his position as prime minister constituted an aggravating element of the crime. Kambanda used his power of office not to stop genocide but to encourage it.[28]

Special Dimensions of Genocide

Because of the atrocities in Bosnia and Rwanda, world opinion, led especially by human rights and humanitarian law specialists, began to give careful attention to *ethnic cleansing*, widespread *rape*, and *gendercide*. These important dimensions of genocide were mostly neglected until the 1990s.

Ethnic cleansing

The main question about ethnic cleansing is whether it is a category of harm distinguishable from genocide. If it is not genocide, it is surely its evil first cousin. Basically, **ethnic cleansing** is the use of force – murder, torture, rape, and the burning of homes – to terrorize a certain ethnic group so that its members will leave an area. Some are killed or treated in a barbaric way to frighten the others into a quick departure as refugees, leaving the victorious group in charge of the disputed territory. Raphael Lemkin wanted this kind of abuse included in the Genocide Convention just as he had wanted social class and political distinctions placed in the convention, but ethnic cleansing was not made part of genocide's treaty definition (Weitz 2003: 10).

This evil practice has gone on for centuries. According to the Old Testament, Jews drove Canaanites out of their "promised land" only to suffer at least two diasporas themselves. Indigenous peoples around the world regularly lost lives and land as European explorers and settlers showed up to claim their territories. Ethnic groups in Europe have pushed and shoved each other for centuries, especially in the Balkans. Adolf Hitler, early in the Second World War, expelled 100,000 French people from Alsace-Lorraine to Vichy France and a million Poles from western Poland to eastern Poland or to Germany as forced labor (Gutman 1999: 124). The largest and probably least studied case of ethnic cleansing is that of the expulsion of 15 million Germans from Germany's eastern provinces and from several East European countries between 1944 and 1950. Through murder, looting, and widespread rape, Russians and other Slavic peoples took their revenge for the German invasion of their lands in 1941. The taking of German territory after the war was approved as a joint decision by the Allies, and the perpetrators in this case of ethnic cleansing have enjoyed complete immunity (de Zayas 1994; Neary & Schneider-Ricks 2002).

The ethnic cleansing in Darfur in western Sudan has been widely attended to because of the modern, global communications system, the "CNN effect." With well-over 250,000 dead and more than two million people out of a total population of six million displaced, many have fled for their lives to neighboring Chad.[29] After debating the issue, the US Congress and President designated this tragedy as a case of genocide in 2004 (Straus 2005: 123–33). The policy implications are great. Genocide is at the pinnacle of core international crimes for many, and its occurrence constitutes a huge moral demand that international society do something about it.

Deciding to move a case of ethnic cleansing into the category of genocide may depend more on the intent of the perpetrators than the numbers of people killed. The perpetrators may wish for all of an ethnic group to die, as the Nazis did for the Jews, or they may be content only to destroy a people as a viable group, leaving them unable to assert its political and economic interests. After all, the Genocide Convention refers to "intent to destroy, in whole or in part," an ethnic group; it does not refer necessarily to total extinction. At the ICTY and ICTR prosecutors have successfully brought genocide charges for killing a few people or a few thousand based on the intent of the perpetrators. As the prosecutor said in the Radislav Krstic´ case, in which over 7,000 Muslim males were slaughtered, he did not have to demonstrate that Krstic´ intended to kill every last Muslim in Bosnia for it to be a case of genocide (Weitz 2003: 233–4). It must be said that ethnic cleansing edges very close to genocide.

The widespread use of rape

Susan Brownmiller's 1975 *Against Our Will: Men, Women and Rape* dispelled forever the myth that rape in armed conflict is no more than the private actions of a few misguided soldiers.[30] However, it took the systematic, widespread use of rape as a weapon of armed conflict in Bosnia, Rwanda, Sierra Leone and other places in the 1990s before Brownmiller's message began to resonate to the world. Except for some rape charges against Japanese officers at the Tokyo IMT, the common use of rape in wartime was not taken seriously until the tribunals for the former Yugoslavia and Rwanda began hearing cases. The statutes for the two tribunals and the ICC cover rape as a crime against humanity, but it was from news reports and hearing witness accounts before the tribunals that this despicable treatment of women became clear as an often-repeated pattern. The ICC Statute goes furthermost prohibiting not only rape, but sexual slavery, enforced prostitution, forced pregnancy, enforced sterilization, or any other form of sexual violence of comparable gravity. The ICC statute, coming several years after the Bosnian and Rwandan experiences, reflect what was learned about the large-scale use of rape as a tool of conflict and ethnic cleansing.

During the Paul Akayesu case before the ICTR, a coalition of NGOs persuaded the prosecutor to amend Akayesu's indictment to include sex crimes (Gardam & Jarvis 2001: 214). Not only was Akayesu the very first to be convicted for genocide by an international tribunal, but rape was determined to have been an integral part of his crime of genocide, a means to foment the destruction of an ethnic group. During the short-lived but still devastating genocide in Rwanda, between 250,000 and 500,000 women were raped and many of them killed.

The rape associated with Rwandan genocide continues to echo as late as the fall of 2007 in the eastern part of the Democratic Republic of the Congo where Hutu militias escaped and continue a rape epidemic concentrated in the South Kivu Province.

Gendercide

Scholars specializing in genocide have noticed that this heinous crime often involves a pattern based on gender, with men and women being treated differently. If one sex is killed and the other is not, or murdered in a very different way, it is **gendercide**. Armenian men were killed immediately while most women died on forced marches (Bloxham 2005: 86–7). Facing the gas chambers of the Nazis, pregnant Jewish women were among the first to be selected for death while young, healthy males were kept alive for a few months to perform labor (Gardam & Jarvis 2001: 21). During the expulsion of Germans at the end of the Second World War, the victims of rape, murder, and torture were predominantly women because the men were away as soldiers, had died in battle, or were POWs (Neary & Schneider-Ricks 2002: xxvii). In the ongoing Darfur genocide, men are routinely killed while women are raped. According to Adam Jones, the most consistently targeted group across history for murder and lesser abuses are men and boys of military age, ranging from 15 to 55 years of age.[31] The Srebrenica genocidal act in Bosnia is a case in point.

War Crimes

Among the core international crimes, war crimes are the oldest and most established as a specialized area of international law. They have long been recognized from customary law and the Lieber Code and Oxford Manual of the nineteenth century to the twentieth century's Hague and Geneva Conventions. The Nuremberg Charter defined **war crimes** simply as "violations of the laws or customs of war." It went on to offer a list of specific acts of war crimes, including murder, ill-treatment or deportation of civilians for slave labor, murder or ill-treatment of POWs, killing hostages, plunder of public or private property, and wanton destruction of cities not justified by military necessity.[32] Laws on war crimes have continued to be elaborated in the statutes of several tribunals.

The statute of the ICTY provides jurisdiction for grave breaches of the 1949 Geneva Conventions concerning protection of such persons as POWs and civilians and for violations of the customs and laws of war.[33] Much of the fighting in Yugoslavia began as an internal war before this country disintegrated into multiple states. In another important ruling from the 1995 Dusko Tadić case, the ICTY said that the laws of war applied, in any case, to internal wars as well as international armed conflict.[34] The jurisdiction of the ICTR was created specifically for an internal war based on Common Article 3 of the 1949 Geneva Conventions and Protocol II of these conventions, both of which cover the rules for internal armed conflict. Basically, the armed conflict of Rwanda was viewed as involving a civil war between two Rwandan ethnic groups.

The ICC draws appropriately on the two main sources of the rules of war, the Hague and Geneva Conventions, but at the 1998 Rome conference for creating its statute, controversy persisted over distinguishing war crimes in international wars from those occurring during internal wars. As a compromise, 26 war crimes are listed for international wars, and a list of 12 prohibited practices in internal wars is provided. The two lists overlap substantially on prohibitions against such practices as refusing quarter, killing or wounding treacherously, intentionally attacking civilians, recruiting children, pillaging a town, and committing rape and other sex crimes.[35]

The long list of possible war crimes and the many cases of violations would fill volumes. Only some of the more interesting and controversial cases can be described here.

Bombing

The puny bombs of the First World War gave rise to the expectation that war would be too frightful to contemplate. By the time of the Second World War, bomber aircraft would be capable of carrying ten-man crews, tons of high explosives and incendiary devices or "fire-bombs," and able to fly hundreds of miles to target. Within the first two years of the war, both sides allowed bombing policy to migrate from targeting specific military targets to the strategic bombing of entire cities, known as "carpet bombing." The rationale was that with the destruction of cities, not only would an enemy's wherewithal to fight be destroyed but so would the enemy's morale and willpower. Hundreds of thousands of civilians in multiple countries died in what would appear to be a clear contravention of the age-old distinction between attacking civilian and military objectives.

During the 1930s, the League of Nations and the governments of Great Britain and the United States condemned the German and Japanese bombing of cities as contrary to the laws of war and humanity (Markusen & Kopf 1995: 151–2); yet, once in the Second World War, these two states went all-out in attacking cities in Germany and Japan. In part, the bombing escalation was tit-for-tat, with one side escalating and the other retaliating. If one side attacked a capital city, the other side followed suit, and it was the same for incendiary bombs. Germany first bombed Britain's capital of London, claiming it was by mistake, and began the use of incendiary explosives against the same city in 1940, as it had done previously to Warsaw in 1939. If American and British air forces had greater success at gutting enemy cities than the Axis powers, it was simply because, as the war wore on, they had more bombers, bombs, and air crews (Grosscup 2006: 63–9).

The strong distinction between civilian and military targets reaches from customary law through the 1923 Hague Air Rules, which never entered into force, to post-Second World War laws of war such as the 1949 Geneva Conventions and the 1977 Protocol I to these conventions. Even the Nuremberg Charter for trying German war criminals listed the wanton destruction of cities as a war crime. The temptation to blow up and burn cities simply overrode any sensible interpretation of the laws of war. On the criminality of the bombing campaigns, General Curtis LeMay, the overseer of the US bombing campaign against Japan, said if America had lost the war, he would have been tried as a war criminal (Bass 2000: 8–9). German and Japanese air force generals and pilots were not charged with war crimes because American and British pilots had carried out the same policies, only had been much better at it (Markusen & Kopf 1995: 252).

The only punishment for bombing attacks came from the Japanese, surprised and embarrassed by the famous Doolittle air raid in April 1942. In a daring plan, sixteen medium Army Air Corps B-25 Mitchell bombers took off from the naval aircraft carrier *Hornet* and bombed Japanese targets in five cities. The material damage was not great, but the psychological impact on Japan was. After all, Japanese leaders had promised their people that American forces would never reach Japan. All the planes were lost in the effort to reach China, and eight US airmen were captured. They were charged with war crimes for bombing industrial targets in cities and strafing schools, fishermen, and farmers, according to their Japanese accusers. The eight were sentenced to die but only three were executed, the others having their sentences commuted to life by Emperor Hirohito (Bradley 2003: 107–11, 121).

The Second World War's bombing record only seemed to confirm for American generals the effectiveness of the wide use of bombing rather than appall them because of its massive destruction. During the Korean War (1950–3), almost all cities of North Korea were destroyed, and General Douglas MacArthur wanted to escalate to atomic bombs for use against Chinese targets. Later, more bombs were dropped on North Vietnam during the war in Vietnam (1963–75) than had fallen on Germany in the Second World War (Grosscup 2006: 78–87). Throughout the Cold War, the Soviet Union and the United States had each other's cities targeted for mass destruction with nuclear weapons carried first by long-range bombers and then ICBM missiles. High-value is still placed on aerial attacks as the 1991 Persian Gulf War, the 1999 NATO attack on Kosovo, and the 2003 attack on Iraq demonstrate. The bombs are much more accurate with GPS and laser guidance systems, but collateral damage to civilians, mostly women and children, remains common.

Submarine warfare

At first not much was expected of submarines in their early history. They were only given the task of guarding harbors and coasts until the diesel engines and underwater battery systems improved allowing submarines to become ocean-going, lethal vessels of the deep sea. In the First World War, despite their special facility for undersea operations, submarines did not have special rules of engagement but were expected to comply with the same Hague rules governing surface warships. Thus, submarines also had to allow for the safety of crews and passengers of any ships sunk, which almost certainly meant operating on the surface. These rules did not last after Germany blockaded the British Isles in the First World War and began to practice a war on commerce. Unrestricted submarine warfare allowed for the sinking of any ship bringing cargo to Great Britain, and with little heed given to crews and passengers. Germany's unrestrained submarine warfare caused moral outrage and helped bring the United States into the war in 1917 on the side of the Allies (Blair 1996: vol. I, 3–39).

During the interim between the world wars, efforts were made at the 1930 London Naval Conference to outlaw the submarine altogether. This effort failed, but some naval powers did agree to limit the size of submarines and to reinforce the rule that submarines had to surface and allow crews and passengers to reach safety before their ship was sunk (vol. I, 27–35).

Germany, early in the Second World War, under Admiral Karl Dönitz's leadership, returned to unrestricted submarine warfare by attacking Atlantic convoys with "wolf packs" of four or five submarines coordinating their attacks and striking without any warning (vol. I, 37–8). This strategy was fairly successful from 1939 to 1942. With better sonar and long-range planes equipped with depth-charges and the breaking of German naval ciphers by British intelligence officers, fewer and fewer German submarines returned to port after 1943 (Blair 1996: vol. II, 57–66).

Admiral Dönitz was tried at the Nuremberg IMT with the expectation that his unrestricted submarine warfare would bring a severe sentence, but that was not to be the case. His defense attorney argued that Admiral Chester Nimitz had followed similar policies in the Pacific against Japanese shipping and had refused to pick up Japanese survivors, a policy Nimitz affirmed for the Dönitz trial. It was essentially a *tu quoque* ("same as you") legal defense. It is awkward to try an enemy for something that has been done by the victors, a point that was clearly taken in the context of carpet bombing. Dönitz did receive a ten-year sentence for ordering the suspension of a rescue of British and Poles in lifeboats, following the 1942 sinking of the *Laconia*, a troop-ship, even though his several submarines were under a US air attack and needed to dive. Probably he should not have been tried at all, but Dönitz's strong support for Hitler made American prosecutors want to tag him with something (vol. II, 700–5).

The mistreatment of POWs

The history of POWs is mostly a litany of horrors despite considerable efforts at reformative international law. From bilateral agreements in the eighteenth century prohibiting the chaining of prisoners like convicts, to the 1863 Lieber Code, the Hague Conventions of 1899 and 1907, the 1929 Geneva Convention on POWs, and finally the 1949 Third Geneva Convention on POWs, strong legal efforts have been made to treat prisoners with decency and respect. The laws of war view a POW as a privileged person enjoying *hors de combat* status until he or she can be repatriated to home and family at war's end.

The gap between law and actual treatment of POWs often involves great tragedy, however. More Americans died in captivity in the American Revolution (12,000) than died from wounds (10,000) or battle deaths (6,000).[36] The poor hygiene, food shortages, and contagious diseases in Civil War POW camps turned places like Andersonville in Georgia and Elmira in New York into hellholes, unnecessarily costing the lives of many helpless men. Conditions improved remarkably in the First World War for prisoners, at least between Germany and Great Britain. An exception was the very poor treatment of British prisoners captured in Iraq by the Ottoman Turks, a case the British wanted prosecuted as a war crime, an effort that failed.

The Second World War witnessed egregious treatment of millions of POWs. Never in history have so many men and women been held in this form of captivity; consequently, this record deserves some examination. Intense racist and ethnic views of enemies, coupled with the fact that several of the major powers were led by totalitarian dictatorships with slight interest in law on POW treatment, allowed terrible depredations toward prisoners to occur.

None can surpass the Japanese for deliberate cruelty and mercilessly causing the deaths of POWs. The Japanese held 350,000 Allied POWs, 132,000 of them Westerners. Their death rate was 27 percent compared to 4 percent for German-held American and British POWs (Bradley 2003: 294–5, 319). According to Gavan Daws' *Prisoners of the Japanese*, "They beat them until they fell, then beat them for falling, beat them until they bled, then beat them for bleeding." He goes on to say, "If the war had lasted another year, there would not have been a POW left alive" (Daws 1994: 18). Linda Holmes interviewed 400 ex-POWs and noticed how similar the stories of abuse were among prisoners held across the far-flung region of Asia and the Pacific (Homes 2001: esp. xix–xx). American prisoners of the Japanese suffered much more than German-held Americans long after the war, experiencing higher rates of disease, nightmares, alcoholism, insomnia, divorce, and suicide (Daws 1994: 384–5).

Australian and British POWs were forced to build the Thai-Burma railway under extremely harsh conditions and suffered a high mortality rate (Breckman 1919: 253–5). Following the largest surrender in the US Army's history in the Philippines, 12,000 American and 66,000 Filipino soldiers were subjected to the Bataan Death March of 60 miles with little food or water and then put in tightly packed train cars for the rest of the journey to POW camps.[37] A little known story of brutality and death for POWs is the fate of 2,000 Australian and 500 British soldiers held at the Sandakan POW camp in North Borneo in present-day Indonesia. They were worked, starved, force-marched and finally, too sick to carry on, prisoners were shot or bayoneted. Of 2,500 prisoners, only 6 survived by escaping near the end of the war (Tanaka 1996: 8, 11–43, 45–78; see also Li 2003).

The Japanese also conducted chemical and biological warfare methods on unwilling subject, including POWs. The best known of 10 "death factories" in China and Manchuria was Unit 731 near Harbin, Manchuria directed by Lt General Ishii Shiro. The Japanese claimed the large well-equipped facility was a lumber mill and, in a nod to dehumanization, referred to their subjects as "maruta," or logs. Chinese and Soviet POWs, captured in the 1939–40 border war, were the "logs" along with Han Chinese, Koreans, and Mongolians. The purpose of these death factories was to discover the most lethal diseases and the best way to spread them as a tool of war. For example, three thousand Chinese POWs were given dumplings injected with typhoid and then released to spread the disease to their families. It is unclear whether American POWs were ever used as "logs." Instead of severe punishment, Lt General Ishii was given immunity in 1948 by the United States for sharing his germ warfare expertise with the US government (Harris 1994; see also Tanaka 1996: 135–55).

One of the most shocking reports to come out about Japanese mistreatment of POWs concerns the practice of cannibalism. The Japanese committed cannibalism on their own and Allied war dead to avoid starvation, mostly in New Guinea and the Philippines. Australia was the only country among the Allies publicly to investigate and punish this crime. The Australian courts managed only 2 convictions out of 15 Japanese prosecuted for this offense (Tanaka 1996: 111–34). The laws of war prohibit mutilation and desecration of bodies and improper burial, but cannibalism as a war crime was unforeseen. The Japanese also practiced a form of ceremonial cannibalism, eating the liver and other body parts of downed and beheaded flyers on

Chichi Jima. President George H. W. Bush narrowly escaped the same fate as a young pilot when he attacked this tiny island just north of Iowa Jima. This island was critical for its role as a communications relay station and heavily fortified. Fortunately, he was rescued by an American submarine after his navy plane was shot down and before Japanese boats could reach him. At least eight American aviators were bayoneted and beheaded and then their livers and gall bladders served at drunken Japanese officer parties, presumably to instill fighting spirit by killing and eating one's enemies. American war crimes trials were held over this form of cannibalism at Guam Island but kept secret for decades after the war. Five Japanese officers were hanged and others received sentences from five years to life.[38]

Among the highest-ranking Japanese war criminals, based on the extent of their crimes, eight were convicted by the Tokyo IMT for crimes against POWs and four of these sentenced to hang. Many other trials were held outside of Japan in or near the place where crimes took place. Two soldiers were sentenced to death for the Bataan Death March, including Lt General Masaharu Homma, who was executed in the Philippines in 1946. For the Thai–Burma railway cruelties, 32 death sentences were handed down from senior officers to guards. For all POW crimes by the Japanese, 3,000 were convicted out of 5,700 accused, and 920 were executed by the various countries bringing charges (Daws 1994: 369–70). Only the Soviet Union, however, prosecuted Japanese for the biological experiments of Unit 731, with 12 Japanese receiving prison sentences (p. 373).

Germany's record concerning POW treatment in the Second World War is a mixed one. The earlier favorable comparisons between Japanese and German treatment of POWs is based on the mostly reasonable treatment accorded to American and British POWs. The biggest problem for these POWs was probably food shortages in Germany in the latter part of the war. Germany's harsh handling of Soviet prisoners was a very different matter. The suggestion has been made that the more severe treatment meted out to Russians took place because their government had not signed and ratified the 1929 Geneva Convention on POWs (Markusen & Kopf 1995: 112). It is more likely that centuries of animosity between Teutonic and Slavic peoples finally spilled over into a merciless blood-letting by both sides. The first people put into the new German gas chambers in early 1942, to make sure they worked, were Russian POWs (Jones 2004: 26). The Germans captured huge numbers of Russian prisoners, especially early in the war. Through forced marches, hard labor, and little food, they killed 3 million of their 5.75 million Soviet POWs (Maogot 2004: 85; Rummel 1994: 40–2).

As for the Soviet Union, its army crushed the German Sixth Army at Stalingrad in 1942–1943 – perhaps the battle that turned the tide of the war against Germany – and captured approximately 100,000 surviving German soldiers and, by the end of the war, they had taken several million more Germans as POWs, many of whom never returned home. Some German soldiers were still coming home as late as 1955, only as indoctrinated communists. The Russian Army also captured at least 350,000 Japanese prisoners in Manchuria in 1945 and placed them in their slave-labor "gulag," with few of them ever to see Japan again.[39] However, what the Soviets are most infamous for is their capture and murder of Polish officers and civilian leaders.

The Soviets shot over 25,000 Polish leaders, many of them army officers, with over 4,000 murdered in the Katyn Forest near Smolensk in the Soviet Union. The Soviet government tried to blame this evil deed on the Germans, but after European communism collapsed in 1989, the new government of Russia admitted the perpetrators had been Soviet communists. The Poles wanted to call this mass murder genocide, but true to their earlier position on the definition of "genocide," the Russians said political or class identities were not relevant as elements in genocidal crime.

The United States and Great Britain have had very good records in handling POWs in wartime compared to most countries. However, in his 1989 *Other Losses*, James Bacque claims that General Dwight Eisenhower changed the status of German POWs to "disarmed enemy forces," ending their privileges and resulting in the death of 900,000 German prisoners due to cold and hunger. The number of deaths is probably a great exaggeration but some neglect and deaths of German prisoners may have happened (Bacque 1991). With massive US supplies on hand in 1945, it is unimaginable that it was necessary for a single POW of the US Army to suffer any deprivation as the war came to a halt in Europe.

Two special problems should be mentioned that often arise at the onset of POW status and at its termination. Soldiers of all armies have responsibility for taking prisoners and cannot refuse *to give quarter*, meaning they must accept the surrender of an enemy. This customary rule first appeared in written form in the Lieber Code and continues to be found in the most modern accounts of the rules of war. Troops that violate this rule are sought as war criminals, which happened when German SS troops machine-gunned American prisoners at the Battle of the Bulge in the winter of 1944.[40]

Also, at the end of a war, prisoners are to be *repatriated without delay* according to the 1929 Geneva Convention and the 1949 Third Geneva Convention on POWs. Violations, however, happen with some frequency. The Soviet Union did not go by such a rule at the end of the Second World War regarding its German and Japanese prisoners. The British and French also kept German POWs for a year or two after the war to use them in war reconstruction. A recent case involved hundreds of Moroccan prisoners held for many years by the Polisario Front following a ceasefire arranged in 1991 with Morocco. The Polisario Front had been fighting to gain the independence of Spanish Sahara as a new country while Morocco insisted on annexing it. These POWs were finally released in 2005. Apparently the poor, unfortunate prisoners were held back as bargaining chips despite the compelling law of war calling for their repatriation.[41]

Do Americans torture?

As long as there has been written law on prisoners, mistreatment and certainly torture have been banned. Yet, Americans have used torture against their enemies at times. Notorious cases of torture occurred during the Filipino Insurrection of 1900–2 by both the US Army and the Filipino insurgents. In the Second World War, forceful means were used on German POWs on American soil concerning the murder of one of their own believed to be a traitor. American interrogators applied steam heat to the sexual organs of one POW and placed an air-tight gas mask on his head until he passed out. Gaining his confession, the US Army then moved forward to try and finally hang seven German sailors for the murder (Whittingham 1977).

Since the 9/11 crisis of 2001, prisoners taken in the WOT by the United States have caused this country considerable consternation. Terrorist suspects by the thousands have landed in prisons in Afghanistan, Cuba, and Iraq. The United States applied aggressive interrogation techniques to many of them, while denying most of them POW status. The US handling of these prisoners has led to sharp criticism for a country accustomed to receiving plaudits for its historical promotion of human rights. Common Article 3 and other articles of the Third Geneva Convention on the Treatment of POWs require humane treatment for all persons in custody.[42] Also, the 1984 *Convention against Torture and Other Cruel, Inhumane, or Degrading Treatment or Punishment* (CAT) has broad application in peace or war. In its first article, this convention covers any severe pain or suffering either caused or ordered by a public official.[43] The United States signed the CAT in 1988 and completed the ratification process in 1994.

Following the 9/11 crisis, President George W. Bush could fairly conclude he was leading his country into an unconventional war with enemies who did not wear uniforms or necessarily obey the orders of a state prepared to comply with the laws of war. Although the United States faced an unusual and dangerous security climate, it could be argued that President Bush veered too far from a lawful path by trading the civil liberties of citizens and the privileges of prisoners for a modicum of national security. His administration, by early 2002, asserted that the Third Geneva Convention on POWs did not apply in the terrorist type of war at hand. This same office even claimed that the wartime powers of the President allowed the use of torture as long as mistreatment did not rise to the level of organ failure or death. The plan of the administration also included keeping prisoners off US soil so the executive branch would not have to face judicial and Congressional challenges to its treatment of prisoners. It is exactly for this reason that prison facilities were built at Guantánamo, Cuba.

The term "unlawful combatants," a term unrecognized in international law, has been applied to thousands captured in Afghanistan and Iraq. Interrogators suddenly found themselves on a slippery slope about what was allowed and what was not. Hooding, handcuffing, beatings, nudity, loud music, long hours in stress positions, threatening police dogs, slaps, kicks, gags, the questioning of Muslim men by scantily clad female soldiers, and, most notoriously, water boarding to simulate the feeling of drowning are among the forceful interrogation techniques used. Released prisoners have also complained about the common use of electric stun devices. Forced feedings of prisoners on hunger strikes took place at Guantánamo, and suicides have also occurred.[44]

Then, in Iraq, in early 2004, horrid pictures of sexual abuse of some detainees were reported to US Army investigators, and, two months later, these photographs migrated to the global communication grid, with their shocking effect instantaneously ricocheting around the world. Numerous investigations took place over prisoner abuse, resulting in mostly "misguided" enlisted personnel receiving punishment. The reputation of the United States was clearly at low tide.

Box 9.4 When Is Abuse Torture?

Torture, never a very reliable method of generating usable information, fell from grace as a legitimate police tool in eighteenth-century Europe. Few Americans realize that their Fifth Amendment right originated as a protection against torture. If one's own information cannot be used in prosecution, why bother to induce this information by inflicting pain? The dreadful practice of torture was returned to Europe before the Second World War by the Nazi and communist dictatorships. Since this greatest of all wars, the evolution of democracies in the Americas, Europe, and elsewhere has extolled the value of human rights and embedded them in numerous treaties, including the right to be free of torture. Nevertheless, democracies, faced first with colonial revolutions and then plagued by incidents of terrorism, have been tempted to take retrograde steps and use some types of torture.

Frantz Fanon's *The Wretched of the Earth* reveals the ugly use of electric shock, a severe torture, by France as it attempted to hold onto Algeria in the early 1950s. John McGuffin's *The Guineapigs* depicts the plight of unfortunate IRA suspects in 1971 in Northern Ireland at the hands of British police, who subjected the suspects to kicks and punches, stress positions, sleep deprivation, blindfolds, and sensory deprivation techniques such as "white noise" to cause paranoia and disorientation. These methods are very similar to the ones the United States is accused of using on terrorist suspects in its war on terrorism since the 9/11 attack. To claim these techniques fall below the torture threshold is disingenuous at best. It is highly doubtful that enough intelligence is gained to offset the blow to the US image and prestige as a democratic state promoting human rights.

Sources: Frantz Fanon, *The Wretched of the Earth* (New York: Grove Press, 1968; 1982 printing); John McGuffin, *The Guineapigs* (Baltimore, MD: Penguin, 1974).

The abuse, or torture, in the WOT has been compounded by the Bush administration's use of "extraordinary rendition." This policy remains murky as to its exact motive and extent, but critics in America and Europe claim that terrorist suspects, without any sort of judicial hearing, are flown to countries with unsavory human rights records and where torture commonly happens. Not only is the quality of intelligence gathered from the victims of extraordinary rendition in question, but this practice has been a body blow to US standing in international society (Grey 2006). This practice has put the United States in violation of Article 3 of the CAT prohibiting sending people to another country where torture can happen. Italian courts began an attempt in early 2007 to prosecute American CIA agents accused of kidnapping a Muslim cleric off the streets of Milan in 2003 and sending him to Egypt, where he claimed he was subjected to electrical torture. Germany is preparing similar indictments for abductions from its soil, and the EU's European Parliament has cited numerous European countries for allowing their airports and air spaces to aid in such abductions and transfers to states that torture. In the US, federal courts have declined rendition cases as recently as the fall of 2007 citing the "state secrets privilege," a doctrine asserting that national security secrets would be exposed.

Resistance to President Bush's unchecked power perhaps began with Congressional insistence that the 1996 *War Crimes Act* be obeyed. It prohibits US nationals or members of the armed forces from committing a breach of the 1949 Four Geneva Conventions, including cruel treatment or torture as referred to in Common Article 3. A major challenge came in the federal courts with none more important than *Hamdan v. Rumsfeld*, a Supreme Court case in the summer of 2006. Bush's plan to use a secret military tribunal with few rights for the detainees was denied by the court, which called for a fairer trial that would accord with Common Article 3 (d) of the Geneva Conventions. US Senator Lindsey Graham, a reserve colonel in the Air Force Judge Advocate Corps, and US Senator John McCain, a former POW in Vietnam and one tortured at that, encouraged President Bush to accept a compromise that became the *Military Commission Act of 2006*. Senator McCain had already led a successful fight to pass the *Detainee Treatment Act of 2005*, which forbade military personnel from using any form of cruel or inhumane acts on prisoners. The Military Commission Act provides trials closer to that of courts-martial, including defendants' rights to challenge the evidence of the prosecution. This act, however, still allows classified interrogation techniques, presumably by the CIA, and prevents detainees from bringing civil suits against CIA agents over mistreatment. It also excludes the normal use of *habeas corpus* to challenge in the federal courts why a person is incarcerated, incarcerations that appear to remain indefinite. The Supreme Court's 5–4 ruling in the *Boumediene v. Bush*, however, extended the *habeas corpus* writ to foreigners in US custody outside US territory.[45] The Bush plan of isolating prisoners and doing with them as this administration wished had been legally throttled.

Despite the UN Committee on Torture, in 2006, calling for the Guantánamo prison to be closed down, the US government announced in November 2006 that a $125 million courtroom facility would be ready in mid-2007. Fourteen high-value prisoners from CIA "black-sites" – secret prisons – were flown in September 2006 to Guantánamo for trial. The plan is to try them under the 2006 Military Commission Act. Apparently, only a small percentage of all the thousands of people caught in the US dragnet since 2001 were to face trial. At the outset of his presidency, President Barack Obama announced the closing of Guantánamo and promised accused terrorists a proper trial. The main problem remaining is to persuade countries to accept the 250 prisoners still at Guantánamo.

Assassination: an act of war or murder?

The traditional meaning of "assassination" is the killing of an individual for political purposes and usually within a national political context. Men of peace, with some frequency, suffer this fate. Mahatma Gandhi and Martin Luther King are well-known examples. Others are killed according to the ancient motto, *sic semper tyrannis* (ever thus to a tyrant), meaning his or her death is the only way to be rid of a terrible dictator. Assassination has been an issue at the international level as well.

In 1976, President Gerald Ford issued an Executive Order against assassination at the international level as illegal and unethical, at least outside of war. Would such a rule cover a "drug war," a counter-insurgency policy as in the Vietnam War, or the recent WOT? Of course Presidents can change Executive Orders as they see fit, and "targeted killings," the preferred term when national security is at stake, were used against the Viet Cong political cadre under the "Phoenix Program" in the Vietnam War, drug lords in Latin America, and known terrorists in a wide range of places. In 2002, the United States used a Predator drone to fire a Hellfire missile in a *non-combat zone* in the country of Yemen and killed a planner of the terrorist attack on the *USS Cole* harbored in Sanaa, Yemen.[46] Numerous attacks of this kind by the United States have occurred in Pakistan's frontier area bordering Afghanistan and at least once in Somalia in 2007.

Since the attack on their athletes at the Munich Olympics in 1972, the Israelis have led the way in carrying out "targeted killings," often receiving sharp criticism from the UN, European states, and the United States until recently. Since 2000, it is estimated Israel has killed 210 suspected enemy fighters with targeted killings, but in the process 129 innocent by-standers. Some of these attacks bring more scorn than others. In March 2004, Israel fired a missile from a helicopter at Sheikh Ahmed Yassin, founder of the Hamas group, who, at age 67, was a blind quadriplegic in a wheel chair leaving prayer service when killed.[47] The governments of Israel and now the United States believe they are fighting a kind of "twilight war," between clear-cut traditional war and peace. For them, special measures are needed if they cannot have terrorist suspects apprehended and extradited to their national courts for trial.

Does international law provide any guidance as to the acceptability or unacceptability of targeted killings? The Lieber Code of the American Civil War era forbade assassination outright, but of course Lieber was prescribing for two uniformed armies more or less respectful of the laws of war. The Hague Conventions prohibited killing "treacherously" and the more modern Protocol I of the Geneva Conventions forbids killing by "perfidy." Customary law also banned the killing of national leaders, especially monarchs. Unfortunately these rules do not provide unambiguous guidance for treating terrorists as combatants subject to being "taken out," like a soldier killed by a sniper on the battlefield.[48]

Only the Israel High Court of justice has tried to deal with the legality of targeted killings against terrorists and, unsurprisingly, provides basic acceptance of the practice. In December 2006, the High Court left targeted killings in place as a legal option but did set guidelines for the practice, such as using sound intelligence and avoiding collateral damage to innocents.[49]

Targeted killings are one of the most controversial issues in international law today. The law is not definitive and new rules of engagement may be developing in the face of terrorist threats. The temptation to turn to an unconventional method is strong because it might save lives and keep a terrorist organization off-balance as it keeps losing leadership. The downside is that dead leaders can become martyrs and, at the same time, more radical individuals might replace them. Or, one's own leaders might be similarly targeted in retaliation. The moral burden can be heavy too. Collateral damage to innocents is almost inevitable (Eichensehr 2006: 95–111).

In a carefully done study, Mohammed M. Hafez and Joseph M. Hatfield considered the impact of 151 Israeli targeted killings between 2000 and 2004 and found they had no significant effect on the rate of Palestinian terrorist attacks against Israelis. Improvements in security, they found, came from better defensive measures on the ground (Hafez & Hartfield 2006: 359–82).

In her article, "Mercy Killings: Why the United Nations Should Issue Death Warrants against Dangerous Dictators," Anne-Marie Slaughter finds a different use for targeted killings. Professor Slaughter argues that sanctions should be aimed at individual people instead of making whole countries suffer. For a terrible dictator, the UN Security Council, she suggests, should issue an arrest warrant but, if the dictator cannot be arrested, then a death warrant for that person could be issued instead of careening toward the massive destruction of an interventionist war (Slaughter 2003: 72–4). Slaughter's idea, if ever accepted by the UN, will make targeted killings even more controversial.

Rape as a war crime

An act of rape associated with an armed conflict is a war crime. Long before its role as a tool of genocide and ethnic cleansing was comprehended, rape was viewed as an unfortunate part of war. Rape and pillage were often part of the spoils of war for many an army. In time, rape would become a prosecutable crime but primarily as the wrongful act of individual soldiers.[50] Only in recent years have journalists, scholars, and international tribunals come to recognize that rapes on a massive scale help to conquer a people or defeat a country. The message of the conqueror is "we can do anything we like with you – resistance is futile." To send this message, tens of thousands of Chinese women were raped by Japanese soldiers in the 1930s and 1940s, German women by Russian soldiers in 1945, and Bengali women in Eastern Pakistan (now Bangladesh) by Pakistani soldiers in 1971, just to offer a few examples.[51] While all rapes are brutal attacks, the ICTY has heard some cases of rape so heinous as to amount to torture, creating an extra indictment as a war crime.[52]

Efforts to punish rape as a war crime date back at least to the Peter von Hagenbach case in the fourteenth century and prohibitions against this vile act appear in several military codes of kings. The Lieber Code considered rape to be a capital offense during the American Civil War. The 1907 Hague Convention covered rape with oblique, genteel language by stating that "Family honor and rights…must be respected." An article in the 1949 Fourth Geneva Convention on the Protection of Civilians is the first express mention of rape in an international treaty. The 1977 Protocols to the Geneva Conventions continue the explicit prohibition against rape as a war crime, as does the statute of the ICC.[53]

Despite the common practice of rape by the German army in Poland and the Soviet Union, the Nuremberg IMT did not prosecute for rape, but the Tokyo IMT did in several cases. A few Japanese generals were held accountable for what their troops did in the field under the rubric of "command responsibility." For a time after the capture of a Chinese city, Japanese troops were allowed to run amok, looting, burning and raping for several weeks. General Matsui Iwane was sentenced to death by the Tokyo IMT over the horrors that beset Nanking (Nanjing) in 1937–1938, where thousands of Chinese women were gang-raped and often murdered (Gardam & Jarvis 2001: 207).[121] General Tani Hisao was found guilty of personally raping 20 women in Nanking as well as inciting his troops to rape and massacre. He was found guilty after the war by a Chinese court and executed. These prosecutions were easily justified because rape, as a war crime, was well-established in customary law, even if rape on a massive scale, as the tool of the conqueror, was not fully appreciated at the time.

One of the very worst episodes of mistreatment of women to come out of the Second World War concerns the so-called "comfort women." In a different kind of mass rape, one to two hundred thousand women mostly from China, Korea, and the Philippines were forced to serve in military brothels across Asia in the 1930s and 1940s. This case can be called the most methodical and deadly mass rape of women in history since many did not survive their ordeal. Like the POWs forced into slave-labor, they were dehumanized and treated as "military supplies."[54] The Japanese government has done little by the women on the matter of compensation. Ex-comfort women have sued in Japanese courts, the UN has investigated and criticized Japan's inadequate response, and world opinion has excoriated the Japanese handling of the matter.

Child soldiers

Children have gone to war for centuries as drummers, messengers, and trainees to become officers, but warfare in Third World countries in recent decades reflects an alarming pattern to use children as young as ten as combatants. The estimates of child soldiers are as high as 300,000 youngsters taking part in some aspect of war, and they are found in multiple African countries and Burma (Myanmar), Colombia, Nepal, and Sri Lanka, among other places. Iran used thousands of children to clear minefields in the Iran-Iraqi war of the 1980s by having them simply walk across fields and set off the mines.[55]

Hardly any issue riles and motivates humanitarian NGOs as much as the issue of child soldiers. Save the Children and the Coalition to Stop the Use of Child Soldiers are among several NGOs that have pressured the UN and the involved states to try to bring this war crime to an end.[56] Their efforts have had some success because at least the law on this issue has been made firm and clear. From the 1977 Protocols of the 1949 Geneva Conventions to the 1998 statute of the ICC, countries must refrain from recruiting child soldiers age 15 or under, and certainly are not to engage people this young in combat. The widely ratified 1989 *Convention on the Rights of the Child* reaffirms this rule and offers an optional protocol restricting combat to persons 18 years of age or older. This protocol went into force in 2002.[57]

Of the numerous war crimes listed in the statute of the ICC, it is cases concerning the use of child soldiers that are heading its docket. This court's first warrants were issued for leaders of the Lord's Resistance Army, a militia group operating in northern

Uganda that has kidnapped thousands of children. The first war crimes trial, however, will probably focus on Thomas Lubanga Dyilo, a rebel leader in the Democratic Republic of the Congo who has forced children into military service. He was arrested in 2005 and transferred to ICC authorities in 2006. His trial process was tainted by "confidential evidence" supplied by sources in the UN providing grounds for a defense motion for dismissal. After a review of the situation, Dyilo's trial at the ICC got underway in January 2009.[58] Whether clear international law and court trials will stanch this terrible war crime remains in doubt. Children are seen as a cheap commodity in war, easily controlled with drugs and threats, and ready, with an undeveloped conscience, to pull the trigger of an AK-47 assault rifle.

The Contributions of International Tribunals

The Nuremberg and Tokyo tribunals are sometimes called first-generation tribunals, while the ICTY and ICTR, arriving about five decades later, are second generation. Several hybrid judiciaries, developed at the turn into the twenty-first century, are called third generation tribunals. Given that authority at the international level is still basically horizontal in nature, the creation of tribunals for coping with core international crimes is an impressive accomplishment.

The question of whether justice was properly served through the tribunals at the end of the Second World War turns not on guilt or innocence but on due process questions, that is, the rightful procedures of the two tribunals. Some critics call the Nuremberg and Tokyo IMTs "victor's justice" because the Allies tried their enemies, not unlike cattle ranchers trying rustlers, but what other means existed for trying German and Japanese war criminals? The evidence of their atrocities was massive, yet when doubt arose, several acquittals did result at the Nuremberg IMT (Smith 1977: 266–98). Besides the issue of victors trying the vanquished, there is the matter of applying new law. Since crimes against peace and crimes against humanity were not well-established law, were indictments in these two areas of law appropriate? Legal experts continue to debate this issue even today. At least the Nuremberg and Tokyo IMTs set a precedent for establishing these newer categories of core crimes as firm international law for the future. Crimes against peace and crimes against humanity now appear in the statutes of international tribunals alongside the much older category of war crimes.

The IMTs were innovative in holding individuals accountable instead of regarding war as an "act of state" with amnesty granted to individuals for any questionable acts they may have performed during a war, as had been the practice before the twentieth century. This time the Allies refused to allow the slipshod handling of individual accountability following the First World War to be repeated. Some individuals were even found guilty on the basis of "command responsibility" for what their troops did in the field and also for "conspiring" to commit core crimes, a charge pressed primarily by the American prosecution team. "Obeying orders" was reduced to a mitigating factor that could not constitute a defense absolving an individual of criminal acts. Finally, the IMTs handed down numerous death penalties that the second- and third-generation tribunals would not be empowered to use.

Whatever legal niceties are lacking in the first-generation tribunals, these judicial bodies, cobbled together as they may have been, had to be better than the speedy executions without trial that Prime Minister Winston Churchill of the United Kingdom and Premier Joseph Stalin of the Soviet Union wanted for their enemies.

At the Nuremberg IMT, the "Big Four" (France, the Soviet Union, the United Kingdom, and the United States) sat in judgment of the top Nazi leaders for 11 months beginning in the fall of 1945. Twenty-four persons were indicted with 22 of them actually tried and 3 acquitted. Twelve were sentenced to hang, 3 to life in prison, and the others to 10 to 20 years imprisonment. Four of the highest tier of Nazis escaped justice by suicide: Adolf Hitler, Joseph Goebbels, Heinrich Himmler, and, later during the Nuremberg proceedings, Hermann Göering. Those hanged were cremated and their ashes spread to the four winds to prevent pilgrimages and memorial services at grave sites by Nazis of the future. Thousands of lower ranking Nazis, both military and civilians, were also tried under the auspices of the 1945 Control Council Law No.10, which authorized the Allies to conduct trials in their respective zones of occupation of Germany.[59]

At the Tokyo IMT, 11 judges, representing France, India, the Netherlands, the Philippines, the United Kingdom, and the United States, among other countries harmed by Japan, tried 28 of the highest-ranking defendants between 1946 and 1948. Two defendants died during the trial and one became mentally ill. Seven were sentenced to hang, including Tojo Hidki, the Prime Minister of Japan. Sixteen defendants were given life imprisonment; one defendant got 20 years, and another received a 7-year sentence. Many other trials were also conducted in Australia, China, the Dutch East Indies (today's Indonesia), and the Philippines, among other countries, with well over 5,000 Japanese, plus some Formosan and Korean minions of the Japanese, put on trial. Out of all these trials, more than 900 executions took place and hundreds more of those convicted received long prison terms.

Unlike post-war Germany, which attempted to atone for the wrongs of the Second World War with apologies, reparations, and its own prosecutions of Nazis, Japan continues to celebrate the memories of some of its top war criminals at the famous *Yasukuni* Shrine built in 1869 to honor Japan's war dead. In 1978, the administrators of the shrine secretly memorialized 14 of their major war criminals, including those hanged and cremated such as Prime Minister Tojo. Despite an ignominious end for these leaders, their lives are still celebrated annually at this shrine by some of Japan's most prominent leaders. This annual pilgrimage causes diplomatic friction with Asian neighbors including especially China and Korea whose peoples remember well the heavy boot of Japanese conquest and occupation.

Also, the 1951 peace treaty with Japan permitted convicted Japanese, wherever they were serving their sentences, to be transferred back to Japan, allowing them to enjoy early releases. Emperor Hirohito escaped justice altogether. He may well have deserved to be put on trial for his knowledge and approval of what Japanese military forces had done across Asia and the Pacific, but he was needed as a symbolic leader to help stabilize Japan during the American occupation. The Tokyo IMT has often received the same criticism as the Nuremberg IMT for representing "victor's justice" and applying *ex post facto* law. There was more dissent among the larger number of

Box 9.5 General Tomoyuki Yamashita: Rush to Judgment?

General Tomoyuki Yamashita was known as the "Tiger of Malaya" for defeating a much larger British army and capturing Britain's Malayan colony for Japan in 1942. His last assignment was to take command of a doomed Japanese army and naval force in the Philippines in 1945, only to surrender after being in command for one month. Japanese naval forces refused Yamashita's orders to evacuate Manila and instead caused in that city a "bloodlust in defeat," including rape, torture, and the deaths of 100,000 Filipinos.

General Yamashita was promptly tried by an American military court in December 1945 at Manila, well before the Tokyo IMT got underway. He was charged with numerous atrocities in the Philippines, not for ordering them to take place but for failing to exercise proper "command responsibility" over all Japanese troops. The deep division between army and navy (including Japanese marines) commands that continuously plagued Japan's war effort, and General Douglas MacArthur's relentless attack on Yamashita's command and control facilities during the US retaking of the Philippines raise questions about Yamashita's practical and effective control of the offending troops.

He was sentenced to die and was hanged February 1946. His defense team's appeals to the Philippine high court, the US Supreme Court, and to President Harry Truman were to no avail. The claim could be made that his execution was poetic justice because, had he been tried by the British in Malaya, Yamashita could have been held directly accountable for the deaths of 100,000 Chinese.

Source: George F. Guy [a member of the defense team of Yamashita] "The Defense of General Yamashita," *Wyoming Law Journal*, Spring (1950), pp. 153–71.

Tokyo IMT judges, with Judge Radhabinodh of India, in particular, asserting that war crimes charges were a product of "victor's peace."[60]

The second-generation tribunals of the ICTY, ICTR, and the ICC, after a hiatus of decades, could draw on and make good use of the core international crimes the Second World War tribunals helped establish as firm international law. The ICTY and ICTR have helped to end a culture of impunity and create one of accountability, brought justice to thousands of victims, encouraged the international rule of law and further defined, through judicial interpretation, core international crimes. These *ad hoc* tribunals especially have done much to protect women by recognizing how the systematic crimes of rape, enslavement, and genocide fall heavily on them.

The ICTY has been able to apply justice in cases stemming from core crimes committed in the former Yugoslavia since 1991. It has handled 161 indicted cases with 117 concluded 44 cases still in process. The judges of the ICTY remain hopeful of concluding the tribunal's business by 2010. Its biggest failing, so far, is the inability to acquire custody of a major accused person, General Ratko Mladić of the Bosnian

Serbs. At least ex-President Radovan Karadžić of the Bosnian Serbs is in a jail cell at The Hague awaiting trial.[61]

The ICTR has tried crimes committed during the internal armed conflict of Rwanda. It has completed 29 cases and has 23 in progress. There are 7 appeals ongoing and 8 accused are awaiting trial. Over a dozen wanted persons are at large.[62] The same appellate panel at The Hague in the Netherlands is shared by both tribunals, a matter that has caused some difficulty especially for the ICTR since its headquarters in Arusha, Tanzania, is so far from Europe.

Unlike these tribunals, the ICC has the great advantage of being permanent and maintains jurisdiction over all international core crimes potentially on a worldwide basis, depending on the amount of cooperation of states. It can even hear cases on aggression if a legal definition of the crime is approved in the future. Cases can be brought to the ICC by states party to the ICC, the Security Council, and at the initiative of the Prosecutor of the ICC. Nearly a dozen individuals from four countries are in different stages of prosecution for humanitarian crimes, including recruiting child soldiers, rape, sexual slavery, murder, and pillage. Countries referring cases are the Central African Republic, the Democratic Republic of the Congo, and Uganda. The Sudan has two cases in a pre-trial chamber of the ICC but only because the UN Security Council has recommended these cases. So far, The Sudan government has all but ignored the ICC.[63]

The future usefulness of the ICC will depend heavily on whether countries wish to send defendants to this international court since governments have the option of trying individuals in their national courts instead. The ICC must also count on states to help apprehend suspects, locate witnesses, and provide jail space to enforce sentences. Like the *ad hoc* tribunals, the ICC does not have the option of a death penalty.

The third-generation tribunals are hybrid courts, or national courts that have been internationalized in some way through treaty arrangements with the UN. Typically, internationally appointed judges join national judges in a special panel that can apply both international law on core crimes and relevant national law. Taking part in the hybrid court system are Cambodia over the Khmer Rouge atrocities, East Timor following 25 years of invasion and abuse by the Indonesian army, Kosovo because of Serbian induced ethnic cleansing, and Sierra Leone after more than a decade of vicious fighting over the illicit diamond trade.[64] The major accomplishment so far is the arrest and trial of Charles Taylor, the ex-President of Sierra Leone before a special bench of the Sierra Leone hybrid court at The Hague.

Despite some impressive international efforts to prosecute core international crimes, if a full accounting in the name of justice is to be accomplished, national efforts will still have to handle most of the case load simply because so many violators exist. Using national courts, but sometimes asserting universal jurisdiction, states can and do make many cases. The Adolf Eichmann 1961 trial in Israel for genocide against the Jews, the military court martial of Lt. William Calley for the 1968 My Lai massacre in the Vietnam War, the Klaus Barbie trial in 1987 in France for crimes against humanity during the Second World War, and the Belgium trial in 2001 of two nuns for assisting the genocide against the Tutsi in Rwanda are just a few of the cases handled at the national level. In 2005, the US Judge Advocate Corps began court martial trials for several groups of American military personnel for mistreating prisoners and murdering innocent Iraqi citizens. In one notorious case, in early 2007, Sergeant Paul E. Cortez pleaded guilty to taking part in a gang-rape of a 14-year old Iraqi girl and then participating in killing her and her family. He received a 100-year sentence, which may be lessened if he testifies against others charged in the case.

Chapter Summary

- Core international crimes are crimes against peace, crimes against humanity, and war crimes.
- Crimes against peace have focused on aggression since the end of the Second World War, although aggression is difficult to define and as yet is not assigned to the jurisdiction of the International Criminal Court.
- The most severe crime against humanity is genocide, the deliberate attempt to destroy in whole or in part a group of people.
- Ethnic cleansing involves murder and rape to drive a people from their homes and territory; it grays toward genocide but whether it belongs under this rubric is in dispute among scholars.
- War crimes are common during conflict and include behaviors of looting, rape, attacking civilian targets, and mistreatment of POWs.
- A fascinating judicial legacy has evolved ranging from the Nuremberg and Tokyo tribunals to the ICC.

Discussion Questions

1 Why is the crime of aggression yet to be added to the jurisdiction of the ICC when this crime appears to be straight-forward and definable?
2 What is the most often voiced criticism of the Nuremberg and Tokyo war crimes tribunals? Do you think the legitimacy of these tribunals is in serious question?
3 Does ethnic cleansing spill over into genocide, or should the two be treated as separate phenomena and crimes?
4 Rape in war is no longer seen as simply a wrongful individual act but is now established as a tool of genocide and war practiced at a mass level. How did this important legal development come about?
5 Should strategic, or carpet bombing, of entire cities, as happened in the Second World War, be considered a war crime?

Useful Weblinks

http://www.crimesofwar.org/
The web site of the Crimes of War project maintains a current list of ongoing war crimes and offers numerous articles archived on war crimes. Other links on humanitarian law are available under "Resources."

http://www.dannen.com/decision/int-law.html
At this web site, offered by Gene Dannen, many treaties, UN resolutions, and other pertinent materials related to the bombing of citizens are offered.

http://www.ushmm.org/
This is the web site of the US Holocaust Memorial Museum. It offers a "Holocaust Encyclopedia" with 473 articles readily available, personal histories, views of exhibits, and commentary on present-day genocidal threats such as the one going on in Darfur.

http://www.globalpolicy.org/intljustice/index.htm
This web site of the Global Policy Forum, a think tank in New York City, does not specialize in international law, but it does have a useful sub-section on "International Justice," with useful information about international courts, including the hybrid courts.

http://avalon.law.yale.edu/default.asp
This Yale University web site is an excellent source for international law, history, and diplomacy. Using the internal search engine, a number of materials related to thez Nuremberg tribunal are available. As for the Tokyo tribunal, the offerings are limited. Many of the resources are offered on a century-by-century basis.

Further Reading

Bohlander, Michael (2007) *International Criminal Justice: A Critical Analysis of Institutions and Procedures*. London: Cameron May.

Broomhall, Bruce (2004) *International Justice and the International Criminal Court*. New York: Oxford University Press.

Cohen, Roger (2005) *Soldiers and Slaves: American POWs Trapped by the Nazi's Final Gamble*. New York: Knopf.

Cryer, Robert (2005) *Prosecuting International Crimes: Selectivity and the International Criminal Law Regime*. New York: Cambridge University Press.

Grünfeld, Fred and Huijboom, Anke (2007) *The Failure to Prevent Genocide in Rwanda: The Role of Bystanders*. Boston, MA: Martinus Nijhoff.

Lang, Anthony F. (2003) *Just Intervention*. Washington, DC: Georgetown University Press.

Lang, Anthony F. and Beattie, Amanda Russell (2008) *War, Torture and Terrorism*. New York: Routledge.

Lutz, Ellen L. and Reiger, Caitlin (eds.) (2009) *Prosecuting Heads of State*. New York: Cambridge University Press.

Osiel, Mark (2009) *The End of Reciprocity: Terror, Torture, and the Law of War*. New York: Cambridge University Press.

Quigley, John (2006) *The Genocide Convention: An International Law Analysis*. Burlington, VT: Ashgate.

Shaw, Martin (2007) *What Is Genocide?* Malden, MA: Polity Press.

Simpson, Gerry J. (2007) *Law, War & Crime: War Crimes, Trials and the Reinvention of International Law*. Malden, MA: Polity Press.

Stahn, Carsten and Sluiter, Göran (eds.) (2009) *The Emerging Practice of the International Criminal Court*. Boston, MA: Martinus Nijhoff.

Tams, Christian J. (2005) *Enforcing Obligations Erga Omnes in International Law*. New York: Cambridge University Press.

Winters, Francis X. (2009) *Remembering Hiroshima: Was It Just?* Burlington, VT: Ashgate.

Notes

1   General reading on Allied complaints against the Axis powers can be found in Bass 2001.
2   See Articles 227–31 of the Treaty of Versailles in O'Connell's 2005: 135–219. This treaty can also be accessed at http://avalon.law.yale.edu/subject_menus/versailles_menu.asp.
3   These quotes are from the "Statement on Atrocities" as part of the Moscow Declaration at http://avalon.law.yale.edu/subject_menus/wwi.asp.
4   The Nuremberg Charter can be found in O'Connell 2005: 309–16, or at http://avalon.law.yale.edu/imt/imtconst.asp.
5   The Tokyo Charter can be found in O'Connell 2005: 321–6, or at the website of Trial at http://www.trial-ch.org/en/international/the-international-military-tribunal-for-the-far-east.html.
6   This resolution can be found at http://www.un.org/english > General Assembly > Quick Links > Resolutions > Other > Earlier Regular Sessions > 1st - 1946 > 95 (1) 11 December 1946.
7   Article 6 (a) Nuremberg Charter, see note 4.
8   The Draft Code is at http://www.un.org/english/ > Main Bodies > General Assembly > Subsidiary Organs > International Law Commission > Activities > draft code of crimes against the peace and security of mankind.
9   Article 6 (c) Nuremberg Charter. See note 4.
10   Article 5 (a) Tokyo Charter. See note 5.
11   Rummel 1994: esp. 4, table 1.2; ch. 6 Germany, 111–22; and ch. 8 on Japan, 143–57.
12   Bradley 2003: 300. On the point about death by the samurai sword, see p. 297.
13   Rummel 1994; on the Soviet Union, see ch. 4, pp. 79–89; and on China, see ch. 5, pp. 91–109.
14   Find at http://www.icrc.org/eng > Treaty Database > 1949 Conventions and Additional Protocols & Commentaries. Or, see O'Connell 2005: 585–650.
15   The point about the Tadić case is found in Shabas 2004: 43. The Tadić case can be read at http://www.icty.org/ > ICTY Cases & Judgments > Tadić. The Statute of the ICTY can be found in O'Connell 2005: 691–701. Article 5 is on pp. 692–3. Or got to http://www.icty.org/ > Legal Library > Statute of the Tribunal.
16   The Statute of the ICTR can be found in O'Connell 2005: 702–12. Article 3 is on p.703. Or, go to http://www.ictr.org > Basic Legal Texts > Statute of the Tribunal.
17   The Statute of the ICC is in O'Connell 2005: 713–33. Article 7 is on pp. 715–17. The Statute is also available at http://www.icc-cpi.int/ > Legal Texts and Tools.
18   The Genocide Convention can be found in O'Connell 2005: 336–9; or see http://www.icrc.org/eng > Treaty Database > Treaties and Documents by Date > 1948 Convention on the Prevention and Punishment of the Crime of Genocide.
19   This resolution can be found at http://www.un.org/english > Main Bodies > Resolutions > Other > Earlier Regular sessions > 1st - 1946 96 (1) 11 December 1946.
20   See, for example, Horowitz 1997: ch. 15, "Researching Genocide," pp. 275–95, and the notes of the book, pp. 297–320; and the bibliography of Weitz 2003.
21   For the enforcement options in the 1948 Genocide Convention, see also Articles I and VII. See note 19.

22 Articles II and III of the Genocide Convention define genocide and list its punishable acts. See note 19. The content of these articles essentially reappears in Article 4 of the statute of the ICTY, Article 2 of the statute of the ICTR, and Article 6 of the ICC. These articles can be accessed, respectively, on p. 692, p. 702, and p. 715 of O'Connell 2005. See also Quigley 2006.

23 The growing list of cases, many of which involve genocide charges, can be accessed at http://www.icty.org/ >ICTY Cases & Judgments, and for the ICTR, see http://www.ictr.org/ > latest decision > status of decisions.

24 These figures are from Weitz 2003: 198–201; for a good discussion of Serbia and the Bosnian atrocities, see his ch. 5, pp. 190–235.

25 Read the Krstić case at http://www.icty.org/ > ICTY Cases & Judgments > Krstić.

26 Kelly Askin, "The Milosevic Trial – Part I" (March 13, 2002) at http://crimesofwar.org/ > use the internal search engine and enter "Kelly Askin." Also, see Anthony Dworkin, "Slobodan Milosevic Found Dead at the Hague" (March 11, 2006) at http://www.crimesofwar.org/ > use the internal search engine and enter "Anthony Dworkin.

27 Go to http://www.ictr.org/ > latest decisions > status of cases > Akayesu, Jean-Paul (ICTR-96–4) > 2 October 1998: SENTENCE.

28 See at http://www.ictr.org/ > latest decisions > status of cases > Kambanda, Jean (ICTR-97–23).

29 The Save Darfur NGO puts the deaths at 400,000, http://www.savedarfur.org/.

30 Brownmiller 1993. Originally published by Simon and Schuster, 1975. For developments in Bosnia and the role of the Yugoslavia tribunal, see Niarchos 1995: 649–90.

31 Jones 2004: 1–38. See, in particular, p. 10. The first book published on gendercide may be Warren 1985.

32 See Article 6 (b) of the Nuremberg Charter. Refer to note 4.

33 See Articles 2 and 3 of the statute of the ICTY in O'Connell 2005: 691–2.

34 For an excerpt on the Tadić case, see O'Connell 2005. The complete case can be accessed at the ICTY's website, see note 23.

35 See Article 8 of the statute of the ICC in O'Connell 2005: 717–21.

36 Based on an excerpt from history professor Edwin G. Burroughs forthcoming book, "The Prisoners of New York," reported in *The New York Times* (July 3, 2006).

37 Markusen and Kopk 1995: 100–102 for the Bataan Death March. A useful, albeit brief, description of major Japanese atrocities are on pp. 97–105.

38 Tanaka 1996: 8, also 11–43, 45–78; see also Li 2003.

39 Bradley 2003: 299. Estimates of Japanese POWs in Soviet hands at the end of the war has varied from 350,000 to 700,000.

40 John Burns, "Quarter, Giving No," in Gutman and Rieff 1999: 298–300; and Reoch 2006: 16–19. Of various laws of war treaties, this rule appears recently in Article 40 of the 1977 Protocol I of the 1949 Geneva Conventions.

41 Hubband 1999: 286–7. This rule of war is covered in Article 75 of the 1929 Geneva Convention on POWs and Article 118 of the 1949 Third Geneva Convention dealing with POWs.

42 See Common Article 3, and Articles 13 and 17 of the 1949 Third Geneva Convention on POWs in O'Connell 2005: 392–3. Or locate at http://www.icrc.org/.

43 The CAT can be read in O'Connell 2005: 651–6; or it can be accessed at http://www.ohchr.org > Human Rights Instruments > CAT.

44 Danner 2004. See the useful work on torture by Karen J. Greenberg and Joshua L. Dratel 2005).

45 For a critical view of the Military Commission Act, see Cerone 2006: 1–6. Article can be accessed at http://www.asil.org/ > Publications > Insights > ASIL Insights.

46   Anthony Dworkin, "The Strike Against Zarqawi: An Acceptable Case of Targeted Killing," (June 8, 2006), access at http://www.crimesofwar.org/onnews/news-zarqawi.html.

47   Anthony Dworkin, "The Killing of Sheikh Yassin: Murder or Lawful Act of War?" (March 30, 2004), access at http://www.crimesofwar.org/onnews/news-yassin.html.

48   See Article 148 of the 1863 Lieber Code, Article 23 (b) of the 1907 Hague Convention, and Article 37 of the 1977 Protocol I to the 1949 Geneva Conventions. These articles can be found in O'Connell 2005. On this issue, read Eichensehr 2003. This article is available at http://hir.harvard.edu/ > Archives > Volume 25, Issue 3 > "On the Offensive," pp. 1–5.

49   Anthony Dworkin, "Israel's High Court on Targeted Killings: A Model For the War on Terrror?" (December 15, 2006), access at http://www.crimesofwar.org/onnews/news-highcourt.html.

50   *Human Security Report 2005: War and Peace in the 21ˢᵗ Century* 2005: 107–9.

51   Brownmiller 1993. Also, see Henderson 2004: 1028–49, esp. 1029–30, 130 fn. 3. For the general problem of war's impact on women, see Charlotte Lindsey, *Women Facing War: ICRC Study on the Impact of Armed Conflict on Women* 2001.

52   See, for instance, the cases of Anto Fundžija and Hazim Delić at http://www.icty/ > ICTY Cases and Judgments.

53   See Article 44 of the 1863 Lieber Code, Article 46 of the 1907 Hague Conventions, and Article 27 (c) of the 1949 Fourth Geneva Convention on Civilians, and Articles 75 (2b) and 76 (1) of the 1977 Protocol I and Article 4 (e) of the 1977 Protocol II. Also, see Article 8(b) xxii of the Statute of the ICC. These documents are in O'Connell 2005. These documents can also be found at http://www.icrc.org/.

54   Tanaka 1996: 96–9: Also, see Dolgopol 1995: 127–54, and for personal accounts of comfort women, see Schellstede 2000.

55   *AI* (Winter 2006), p. 6; *Human Security Report 2005*, pp. 111–16.

56   Their web sites are http://www.savethechildren.org/ and http://www.child-soldiers.org.

57   The specific articles prohibiting child soldiers are Article 77(2) of Protocol I, Article 4 (3c) of Protocol II, associated with the 1949 Geneva Conventions, and Article 8 (2b) xxvi of the statute of the ICC. These are available in O'Connell 2005. This issue is also addressed in Article 38 of the 1989 Convention on the Rights of the Child, which is accessible, along with this convention's two protocols, at http://www.unicef.org/cfc/. Also, refer to Kuper 1997.

58   Lauren McCullough, "First International Criminal Court Case Going to Trial," (February 7, 2007) at http://www.crimesofwar.org/. Also, see the article on Dyilo at http://www.fidh.org/.

59   For general reading on the Nuremberg IMT, see Smith 1977; Taylor 1992); and Marrus 1997.

60   For general reading on the Tokyo IMT, see Brackman 1989; Minear 1971.

61   See the web site of the ICTY at http://www.icty.org.

62   See the web site of the ICTR at http://www.ictr.org.

63   The ICC website is http://www.icc-cpi.int/ > Situations and Cases.

64   Some reading on the hybrid courts can be done at http://www.pict- pcti.org/courts/hybrid.html; and see Romano, Nollkaemper, and Kleffner 2004.

Part III

Making the World Better

Human rights are a powerful and persuasive ideology because it represents a progressive program for the realization of universal human dignity. (Alison Brysk)

Human rights have gone global not because it serves the interests of the powerful but primarily because it has advanced the interests of the powerless. (Michael Ignatieff)

10

Human Rights
Freedom and Protection for Humankind

Contents

One of the most revolutionary developments in the several hundred years of sovereign state history has been the emergence of the global human rights movement. The international law of human rights runs counter to the notion of hard-shelled, independent states doing as they please at home. The human rights movement calls for states to treat their citizens not as they please but according to universal standards. Since the Second World War, human rights have held a prominent place on the agenda of global governance. The UN and other IGOs, a phalanx of benevolent states plus numerous human rights NGOs, such as Amnesty International and Human Rights Watch, have marshaled the political power to place human rights norms into declarations, treaties, national constitutions and laws.

This chapter begins with a brief history of the human rights movement to clarify why a world of states, accustomed to a jealous guarding of their sovereignty, would accept revolutionary changes concerning the treatment of their own peoples. This history is followed by description and analysis of the two broad traditional categories of human rights, civil and political rights as well as economic, social, and cultural rights. Attention will then be given to the enjoyment of group rights for special categories of people as opposed to viewing rights as belonging only to individuals. Examples are women, children, and indigenous peoples. Next, the human rights regimes based on institutions and their rules and norms will be covered, including the roles of the UN and various regional IGOs. Finally, the role of private actors will be noted, especially the positive role of NGOs, the mixed record of MNCs, and the negative impact of actors such as private militias.

A Brief History of the Human Rights Movement

The human rights movement calls for a radical realignment between government and the governed. For centuries rulers could view their subjects as mere resources to be used at will, as cannon fodder on battlefields, unpaid labor for public projects, and servants to provide food and other needs for the privileged upper class. In modern times, declarations, treaties, and international monitoring bodies have chipped away at states' sovereign prerogatives regarding their citizens. Unlike state-to-state obligations in the form of peace or trade treaties, human rights commitments are what states owe to their own populations. To many, Charter Article 2 (7) requiring the UN not "to intervene in matters which are essentially within the domestic jurisdiction of any state"[1] seems inconsistent with the UN's global effort to promote human rights.

Human rights are the freedoms people enjoy to make choices about their lives and the legitimate expectation that they will be treated in appropriate ways. The enjoyment of rights involves a moral entitlement and calls for a recognition of human dignity, meaning that every person has honor and worth. As part of the post-Second World War global movement, human rights are to belong to every person on the planet and are inalienable in the sense that they are an inherent part of each person. If a government or private party denies a right, it is a wrongful act.

The historical development of human rights has a connection to the natural law tradition, although today this tradition has partly fallen out of favor as a justification for the enjoyment of rights. Seventeenth-century philosopher John Locke is probably the best known for advocating that natural law conferred rights on human beings, at least white males. This view of innate, self-evident rights had a strong influence on the 1776 American Declaration of Independence and the French 1789 *Declaration of the Rights of Man and of the Citizen*, documents which justified revolutions against governments perceived as oppressive. Thomas Paine, best known to Americans for his 1776 political pamphlet "Commonsense," supporting the American Revolution, published his influential 1791 *Rights of Man* drawing heavily on the natural law tradition. Paine may well have been the first to have used the concept "human rights" as opposed to the common term of reference of the time, the "rights of man" (Lauren 1980: 18–20). The natural law tradition persisted for a long time and was reflected in the UN's 1948 *Universal Declaration of Rights* (UDHR).[2] Criticisms of the natural law tradition, as a rationale for rights, began early when the philosopher Jeremy Bentham, a contemporary of American and French revolutionaries, scoffed at natural rights as "nonsense on stilts" (O'Byrne 2003: 34).

Today's scholars are more apt to view human rights as *socially constructed*. From this perspective, rights are moral values that people choose to create and embrace instead of waiting for "laws of nature" to have a good effect. Through a widening social process, the acceptance of chosen moral values are promoted around the world.[3] People's shared sense of humanity and reflection on terrible episodes such as the Holocaust have propelled this social process (Blau & Mocado 2004: 24–6, 63).

Some notion of rights, as well as duties, is ancient, but the modern notion of rights is traceable in a direct way to European developments such as the English 1215 *Magna Charta* and the 1689 *Bill of Rights* plus the French 1789 Declaration of the Rights of Man and the Citizen. These developments began to check monarchical absolutism and laid the groundwork for democracy.

Special events propelled human rights forward as well. Stopping slave trafficking and then slavery itself has been called the first great human rights crusade. Millions of people from the sixteenth to the twentieth century were forcibly transferred from Africa to the Americas, Arabia, and the Persian Gulf kingdoms. The most effective action against slavery was by the British Navy. The unrivaled "Mistress of the Seas," which waged a mighty effort to stop the transportation of slaves on the Atlantic Ocean and the Red Sea, was encouraged by an early NGO called the Anti-Slavery Society (Miers 2003: 14–25; see also Fairbanks, Jr & Nathans 1982: 87–135).

IGOs have played a central role in this global cause. The 1919 League of Nations was the first prominent IGO to promote human rights even though its Covenant did not commit to this mission. The League is best known for arranging minority treaties with states carved out of defeated empires at the end of the First World War, including Czechoslovakia, Hungary, Lithuania, Poland, and Romania. The governments of these new states had to promise in treaties that ethnic minorities would have political, religious, and language rights respected. The League also developed a Temporary Slavery Commission and encouraged member-states to accept the 1926 *Convention on the Abolition of Slavery and the Slave Trade*, tried to halt trafficking in women and children, and set up the 1919 International Labor Organization (ILO) to improve workers' wages and safety (Lauren 1998: 115–18).

Because of the terrible war and humanitarian crimes that occurred during the Second World War, the League's replacement, the UN, became even more dedicated to the human rights cause. The Preamble of the UN Charter refers to "We the Peoples" suggesting a major concern will be the welfare of people despite the UN's creation by states. Unlike the League Covenant, the UN Charter mentions human rights in a half dozen places. Particularly important is Article 55 which recognizes a role for human rights in helping develop peaceful and friendly relations among states.[4] The UN was ready to back human rights worldwide, but exactly which rights were to receive attention?

The newly formed 1946 Commission on Human Rights was given the task of elaborating the rights referred to in the UN Charter. In the 1948 UDHR, a wide gamut of both civil and political rights and economic, social, and cultural rights were identified. As a declaration, it was a moral admonition, and while many states thought it might come to nothing, it became a fountainhead for numerous human rights treaties (Falk 2000a: 43). The acceptance of the UDHR on December 10 led to this date being celebrated each year as Human Rights Day by many around the world.

So successful has been the treaty-making process in the human rights field that questions have been raised about whether it would be a better strategy to focus on human rights conventions already on hand instead of creating more conventions. In *The Proliferation of Rights: Moral Progress or Empty Rhetoric?*, Carl Wellman worries that the "vast proliferation of rights" may devalue them as a category of international law (1999: esp. 2–3). The danger is that more conventions will merely have a "feel good" effect that something is being done without actually improving the rights and living conditions of people in their daily lives.

When the effort to convert the UDHR into an "International Bill of Rights" as a single treaty failed, the decision was made to divide the UDHR rights into two separate covenants so states might ratify at least one, if not both. The UN-sponsored 1966 *International Convention on Civil and Political Rights* (ICCPR) contained what came to be known as "first generation rights" that had enjoyed a long and hallowed history among Western democracies such as rights the rights to life, freedom from torture, and voting. First generation rights of the ICCPR are *negative rights* by their nature because they are enjoyed when governments, and even private actors, are restricted from interfering with them. At the time, the view that only civil and political rights were "real rights" held sway in the Western states (Cranston 1964).

The 1966 *International Covenant on Economic, Social and Cultural Rights* (ICESCR) enshrined "second-generation rights" to work, receive an education, enjoy health, and participate in cultural affairs, among others. Besides appearing later historically than civil and political rights, second-generation rights are *positive rights*, requiring an active role by governments to provide food, medicine, housing, and other basic needs. The communist and Third World states were ideologically much more comfortable with these rights as they did not provide a basis for challenging authoritarian governments unlike citizen challenges through the expression of civil and political rights. Both covenants, sometimes referred to as the "twin covenants," entered into force in 1976. In time, many states from all political camps ratified both, sometimes with sincerity but no doubt in some cases for propaganda purposes.

"Third-generation rights" refer to rights enjoyed by groups on a broad level as opposed to individual rights, possibly as an ethnic group, an entire country's population, or all of humanity. These rights are frequently called *collective rights* and can involve the right of self-determination, the enjoyment of natural resources, environmental security, the right to development, and the benefits of peace. Third-generation rights have their clearest expression in the 1981 *African Charter of Human and Peoples' Rights* (African Charter), which entered into force in 1986.[5] The right of self-determination, however, appears as the first article in both the ICCPR and the ICESCR, well before its appearance in the African Charter.

The proliferation of rights shows little sign of abating. Rights for victims of natural disasters, the mentally retarded, sexual minorities, and restrictions on human cloning, among other conceivable rights, have been recently articulated. Attempts to rein in this proliferation have argued for emphasis on basic subsistence rights like food and clean water (Shue 1980; Vincent 1986; Talbott 2005: 163), but the view adopted at the 1993 World Conference on Human Rights in Vienna will probably continue to prevail. There it was decided that all human rights are interdependent and reinforce one another, that a kind of synergy among the wide spectrum of rights enhances them all.

Another issue that has accompanied the history of the human rights movement, but has probably not received proper attention, is the role of duties. Henry J. Steiner and Philip Alston ask the intriguing question: "Why do we have a human rights rather than a human duties movement?" (Steiner & Alston 1996: 1661). The Western liberal tradition presupposes that citizenship involves a social contract between individuals and their governments based on both rights and correlative duties (O'Byrne 2003: 352). Yet, whether determined by human nature or culture, most citizens are much more interested in receiving their rights than meeting their duties such as jury duty, military service, and paying taxes. In some Western states, voting is regarded as both a right and a duty, as is the case in Australia.

Duty can also be exercised by leaders as well as citizens. In most non-Western societies, benevolent treatment for the general population came about through a sense of duty on the part of the leaders that they should provide for the welfare of their peoples (Donnelly 2003a: 71–88). In the time of strong European kings, such benevolence was known in the West as well. In the eighteenth century's Age of Enlightenment, philosopher Voltaire urged the monarchs of Europe to look to the well-being of their subjects as part of their monarchical obligations.

In more recent history, those promoting the enjoyment of rights have not ignored duties entirely, as is shown in some declarations and treaties backing human rights. The 1948 *American Declaration of the Rights and Duties of Man* has several specific articles on the duty to vote, obey the law, pay taxes, and, somewhat vaguely, to serve the community and nation.[6] In the same year, the UDHR's Article 29 stated that everyone has duties to his or her community.[7] The preambles to the 1966 twin Covenants, elaborating the UDHR, refer to the duties people have to other individuals and to their communities. As with group rights, the 1981 African Charter offers the most pronounced commitment to duties, with Chapter II of this treaty devoted to the subject.[8]

Finally, in the history of the human rights movement, the issue that has been most controversial concerns **cultural relativism**. Supporters of this view believe that global regions and countries have their own unique cultures and that a universal conception of human rights may not be a good fit for all ways of life. In fact, the most ardent critics assert that human rights are nothing more than another example of Western cultural imperialism forced on Third World states like capitalist trade rules that favor the wealthy West. Lee Kwan Yew of Singapore, prime minister of this country from 1959 to 1990, has claimed that "Asian values" place duties before rights. Many Islamic states see universal human rights as sharply conflicting with Muslim *sharia* laws that allow for the subordination of women and corporal punishment, among other practices (Lee Kuan Yew 2007: 2–7; Beotz 2001: 271–2; Marks & Clapham 2005: 37). It seems that it is mostly leaders who object to human rights, while general populations welcome rights when they have the opportunity to receive them (Ignatieff 2001: 70–2).

In the debate over cultural relativism, the supporters of universal human rights have managed to hold the moral high ground. At the 1993 World Conference on Human Rights, cultural relativist arguments were beaten back when the universal approach was accepted by consensus.[9] After all, without reforms of a human rights kind, human sacrifice, dueling, foot-binding of Chinese girls, slavery, and cannibalism might still be allowed.

Civil and Political Rights

The 1966 ICCPR was readily accepted by Western democracies and had the required 35 ratifications to go into force by 1976; it continues to enjoy growing support from additional states, with 164 ratifications by 2009. Its 53 articles identify almost two dozen specific rights, thus selective coverage is unavoidable.[10]

Self-Determination

The first article concerns self-determination, which is duplicated in the twin covenant on social and economic rights. Although the exact meaning of this collective right is not entirely clear, Antonio Cassese has argued that it entails at least an end to colonialism, military occupation, and *apartheid*, the racist rule once practiced in South Africa (1995). The placement of this article first in these core conventions reflects the growing influence of Third World states.

Slavery

The ICCPR also contains a clear prohibition against slavery, the slave trade, and compulsory labor in general, an issue that gave the global human rights movement its first impetus. This prohibition is a rule of international law in the early nineteenth century. By that time, strong moral questions had arisen over the practice of slavery that stretched back across the millennia. Slavery has persevered in several distinct forms. There is *chattel slavery*, with people owned like livestock. The Persian Gulf state of Oman was the last state to formally abolish this explicit form of slavery in 1970, but chattel slavery is still thought to exist in Mauritania in northwestern Africa despite being outlawed. Another form is *forced labor*, with persons held in debt bondage, a practice that remains fairly common in South Asia. Today a troubling pre-stage of slavery is *human trafficking*, usually involving women and children transported across borders to be used in the illegal sex trade industry. They find themselves entrapped in a nightmarish involuntary servitude. Although trafficking was an issue at the forum of the League of Nations, this odious practice always seems to have a new chapter. At the end of the Cold War, thousands of newly impoverished people in the ex-communist states were tricked into believing they were being transported to legitimate jobs in the West only to discover these jobs were as sex workers (*Amnesty International* 2005: 12–16; Kapstein 2006: 103–15).

Right to life

If any right can claim to be an inherent natural right, it might well be the right to life. The ICCPR and regional human rights conventions protect the right to life, at least to the extent of prohibiting the arbitrary taking of life by the state. Traditionally, the death penalty has been an exception. However, to many, the death penalty appears to be a direct violation of the right to life, and it has come under strong moral and legal attack in recent decades. One of the best known scholars on the subject, William A. Schabas, believes an inexorable progress toward the universal abolition of the death penalty is underway (Schabas 1996; 1997).

The trend toward ending the death penalty shows promise. The UN General Assembly adopted the Second Optional Protocol to the ICCPR in 1989 calling on states to abandon the death penalty, and 71 states had become signatories by 2009.[11] European states acted earlier in 1983 to add the Sixth Protocol to the 1950 *European Convention for the Protection of Human Rights and Fundamental Freedom* (more commonly called the European Human Rights Convention[ECHR]) to terminate the death penalty except in time of war, and, with the 2002 Thirteenth Protocol, these states removed the wartime exception.[12] The Council of Europe (COE) in 1994 and the EU in 1998 have made it a condition for countries joining these IGOs to end the death penalty. Of the major democracies, only Japan and the United States have retained the death penalty, but Japan's executions are fairly rare. Latin American states have also moved away from capital punishment, although a 1990 protocol to their 1969 *America Convention on Human Rights* (ACHR) permits an exception for war crimes. Interestingly, Article 4 (3) of this convention does not permit a state to return to capital punishment once abandoning it.[13] Communist Cuba however still makes use of the death penalty. African states are not prohibited from using capital punishment by their regional human rights conventions, but these states appear increasingly to be turning away from the death penalty. Asian and Islamic states still carry out executions with some frequency; in fact, China, with the world's largest population plus an authoritarian government, leads the world in the number of executions per year.

The right to life brings up other issues as well. Abortion has been controversial internationally and within many countries for years. China's "one child" policy, requiring forced abortions, even late-term ones, has been regularly criticized for violating a human rights principle that parents should be allowed to determine the number and spacing of their children. In the United States, the issue is often framed as pro-choice leaving it to a mother to choose to abort or not versus pro-life which allows very limited abortion options or no abortions. Relevant to the debate is the critical question of when human life begins. When does an embryo become a human being? Except for expressing a right to life, human rights conventions do not provide clear guidance for resolving this issue, with the exception of the ACHR. Probably due to the historical influence of the Roman Catholic Church in Latin America, its Article 4 (1) calls for the right to life to be protected "from the moment of conception."

Finally, the right to life has raised the question of a correlative right to die. When people are very ill and have lost all quality of life, should they be given the means to take their own lives or receive suicide assistance? Generally, states assert a strong interest in safeguarding all human life, and only a few jurisdictions have considered euthanasia. The Australian Northern Territory was the first to introduce euthanasia in 1996 before the federal parliament overruled this law. Euthanasia is more established in Belgium and the Netherlands. In a 2002 case before the European Court of Human Rights, Diane Pretty appealed from the United Kingdom asking that her

---

Box 10.1 A Summary of the Rights Contained in the ICCPR

Article 1	The Right of Self Determination
Article 6	The Right to Life
Article 7	Freedom from Torture, Cruel, and Inhumane or Degrading Treatment
Article 8	Freedom from Slavery and the Slave Trade
Article 9	The Rights to Liberty and Security
Article 10	The Right to Humane Treatment when Detained
Article 11	Freedom from Imprisonment for Indebtedness
Article 12	Freedom of Movement, Including the Right to Leave and Return to One's Country
Article 13	An Alien Lawfully within a Country Cannot be Arbitrarily Expelled
Article 14	Everyone Has the Right to a Fair Trial
Article 15	Criminal Law Cannot be Applied Retroactively after the Act
Article 16	Everyone Has the Right to Status as a Legal Person
Article 17	Everyone Has the Right to Privacy
Article 18	Freedom of Thought and Religion
Article 19	Everyone has the Right to Hold Opinions and Express Them
Article 20	Propaganda for War and for Racist or Religious Hatred is Illegal
Article 21	Everyone Shall Enjoy Peaceful Assembly
Article 22	Everyone Shall Enjoy Freedom of Association
Article 23	Men and Women Have the Right to Marry and Raise Children
Article 24	No Child Shall Experience Discrimination and must enjoy a Nationality
Article 25	Each Citizen Shall Have the Right to Vote and Hold Office
Article 26	Everyone is Equal before the Law
Article 27	Minorities Have the Right to Enjoy Their Own Culture

Source: This convention is available at http://treaties.un.org/Pages/ParticipationStatus.aspx > Chapter IV.

---

husband be allowed to assist her death without facing prosecution. She was paralyzed from the neck down and her quality of life was diminishing. The European Court of Human Rights, however, agreed with the United Kingdom's highest court that the right to life could not be interpreted to mean a right to die. Diane Pretty died a short time later in a hospice facility. Even in the few jurisdictions allowing euthanasia, most terminally ill patients are accepting hospice programs to ease their way to a natural death.[14] Taking individuals, without detectable brain activity, off feeding tubes is also quite controversial. In early 2009, 38-year-old Italian Eluana

Englaro died when her tube was removed. She had been on life-support for 17 years. Objecting to this, Prime Minister Silvio Berlusconi said, "Eluana did not die a natural death. She was killed!"

Religious freedom

For a person raised in a country with a strong tradition of separation of church and state, the placement of the freedom of religion under the heading of civil and political rights might at first seem an oddity, but it is not. Religious strife has often been intertwined with political conflict. Religious differences played a major role in the long wars of Europe that eventually led to the 1648 Peace of Westphalia, underpinning the sovereign state system that continues to structure the international politics of modern times. Much more recently, religious identities helped draw up the battle lines in Northern Ireland between Catholics and Protestants, in the Balkans among Croats, Muslims, and Serbs, and in the sectarian violence that currently plagues Iraq's Shi'a and Sunni populations. The fundamental idea behind the promotion of religious freedom, and with it religious tolerance, is to create more peaceful conditions, both within and among countries.

Modern international efforts began with the League Covenant's requirement that states ruling colonial or other dependent peoples respect their freedom of religion. At the end of the Second World War, the UN's Charter contained a requirement that respect for human rights show no distinctions such as religious differences. Numerous other human rights documents would also support religious freedom, including the UDHR and the ICCPR, but an entire convention devoted to this right has never materialized.[15] The UN General Assembly has at least produced the 1981 *Declaration on the Elimination of All Forms of Intolerance and of Discrimination Based on Religion or Belief*, and reaffirmed it in 1995, to be followed some years later by the 2003 *Elimination of All Forms of Religious Intolerance*, laying out the duties of states in this area.[16] Declarations are of course "soft law" setting firm norms but do not impose legal obligations on states.

Political repression

The issue of **political repression**, also known as state terror, affects a broad set of rights. Creating an atmosphere of fear through threats and actual harms, willful leaders use a well-known pattern of human rights violations to control their populations so they can stay in power and carry out the policies of their choosing. Violations typically involve "disappearing people," illegal detention, torture and political murder. These violations are prohibited in the ICCPR, major regional conventions, and specialized conventions as those on disappearance and torture. This pattern of human rights harms is recognized in the widely used annual *Country Reports* of the US State Department where they are referred to as violations of the rights involving "respect for the integrity of the person." These kinds of violations are also reported by Amnesty International each year on a country by country basis.[17]

A rich body of literature has been developed by scholars specializing in political repression.[18] If there is any bulwark that can stave off repression, it is the rise of a viable democracy preferably aided by a healthy national economy. Democracy requires a government to answer to its voters who will obviously not react well to repression, and a healthy economic growth rate raises hopes on the part of the general population that the standard of living will become better, thus reducing the chances of serious confrontations with the government.[19] The enjoyment of democracy is at least implicitly called for as a right in Article 21 of the UDHR and Article 25 of the ICCPR.

Refugees

The last civil and political rights issue considered here is the status of refugees. Once considered a temporary issue following in the wake of a war, millions of people fleeing across borders or to safe havens within their own countries have become a perennial problem for international society. National disasters, civil wars, the two world wars, and the chaos of failed states have driven masses of people to seek security elsewhere. On an individual basis, the fear of persecution based on political, religious, ethnic or other statuses forces these persons to seek a safer political environment.

The UN High Commissioner for Refugees was created in 1950, followed by the development of the 1951 UN *Convention Relating to the Status of Refugees*. A 1967 protocol extended the authority of the High Commissioner beyond the post-Second World War context.[20] The 1951 Convention defines a refugee as a person located outside his or her country who has a well-founded fear of persecution. The Convention enshrines the principle of **non-refoulement**, which calls on states not to return persons to a place where their lives or freedom would be threatened. Several regional treaties in Africa, the Americas, and Europe reinforce the global regime protecting refugees.[21] Despite years of considerable emphasis on refugee problems, there are currently over 20 million living outside their countries and nearly 24 million internally displaced persons occupying temporary camps within their own countries.[22]

Economic, Social, and Cultural Rights

A strong interest in socioeconomic rights has been around for a long time. The social welfare state was already in a formative stage in nineteenth century Europe, and the League of Nations committed member-states to press for better health conditions, protection of women and children, and the establishment of better working conditions, which led to the founding of the ILO. Among its half dozen references to human rights, the UN Charter's Article 55 mentions mostly socioeconomic rights as bettering prospects for peace and stability in the world. Shortly afterward, the UDHR devoted Articles 22 to 28 out of its 30 articles to social security, workers' rights, vacations, health improvement, and access to education and cultural experiences. Some regional efforts echo these kinds of rights, with the European Social Charter being particularly noteworthy.[23]

The 1966 ICESCR went into force in 1976, with at least 10 distinguishable rights contained within its 31 articles. The United States, however, dug in its heels despite the support of President Jimmy Carter, a strong supporter of human rights. By 2009, its support grew to 160 states based on ratifications.[24] The most likely explanation for America standing alone among Western democracies on this issue is that nineteenth-century classic liberalism still has a hold on the mindset of many of the country's leaders, especially among the ranks of the Republican Party. In the 1940s and 1950s, Senator John W. Bricker, a conservative Republican from Ohio, tried to throw roadblocks in front of any human rights commitments once calling the UDHR "socialism by treaty" (Greenberg 1982: 42–3). Although the United States has ratified several human rights treaties, such as the very important ICCPR, the "ghost of Brickerism" still lingers in the U. S. Senate.[25]

When countries do commit to the ICESCR, many Third World states lack the economic resources to fulfill adequately the obligations of good pay, health care, and educational opportunities, among other socioeconomic reforms (Felice 2003). Fortunately for these states, Article 2 (1) of the ICESCR provides poorer states with some leeway since a state is only responsible to realize socioeconomic rights "to the maximum of its available resources." Although benchmarks for the successful promotion of socioeconomic rights are undeniably vaguer than those associated with civil and political rights performances, major efforts by the UN system, especially the World Bank, continue to urge economic growth to benefit the citizens of the less developed countries. Attention can only be given to a selection of these rights.

Labor rights

Headquartered in Geneva, Switzerland, the ILO formed under the auspices of the League based on the realization that the great majority of people are destined to be workers and not employers; yet, they deserve protection from exploitation and mistreatment. When the UN replaced the League, the ILO in 1946 became the first specialized agency of what would become a complex UN System, and is the only "tripartite" UN agency. This status means that this IGO brings together workers, employers, and governments to cooperate in shaping mutually satisfactory labor policies. The ILO establishes and monitors labor standards mostly through more than 180 conventions it has sponsored; it disallows reservations by states to any of these treaties. In general, the ILO activities are very supportive of the rights contained in the ICESCR. It has promoted the right to unionize, equal pay on a gender basis, social security for retirement, safe and healthy work environments, and has given attention to the rights of groups as far-reaching as aboriginal, or tribal peoples, and maritime labor. This IGO can be regarded the oldest and possibly most successful of human rights IGOs.[26]

Health rights

Also headquartered in Geneva and created as a specialized UN agency in 1948 is the World Health Organization (WHO). WHO is the primary IGO that promotes the

---

Box 10.2 A Summary of the Rights Contained in the ICESCR

Article 1	The Right to Self-Determination
Article 6	The Right to Employment
Article 7	The Right to Good Working Conditions
Article 8	The Right to Form Unions and Strike
Article 9	The Right to have Social Security
Article 10	The Right of Protection for the Family, especially Mothers and Children
Article 12	The Right to Enjoy Physical and Mental Health
Article 13	The Right to an Education
Article 14	Primary Education is to be Free
Article 15	The Right to Enjoy Cultural and Scientific Benefits of Society

Source: This convention is available at http://treaties.un.org/Pages/ParticipationStatus. aspx > Chapter IV.

---

right to good health called for in Article 12 of the ICESCR. WHO tries to eradicate dozens of diseases, ranging from AIDS to Zoonoses, animal diseases that might spread to humans such as Ebola virus or avian flu. Some of its chief concerns have been substance abuse, domestic violence, leprosy, and obesity. Its greatest service in a world of about 200 state jurisdictions is the coordination of detection and containment of diseases that could become epidemics or even global pandemics like the influenza of 1919–20, that killed over 20 million people worldwide. Unlike the ILO, WHO does not have a lengthy record of conventions, but one important exception is the 2005 *Framework Convention on Tobacco Control* with 164 parties ratifying by 2009. WHO has taken this exceptional step because tobacco-related illnesses are a leading cause of death in the world.[27]

Education and cultural rights

Article 13 of the ICESCR calls for progress in education, but state efforts are reinforced by the UN Educational, Scientific and Cultural Organization (UNESCO) formed in 1945 and is headquartered in Paris. UNESCO operates on the assumption that education is a fundamental building block for all socioeconomic progress. It has been particularly attentive to gender equality in education, not just to be fair to girls and women but to advance the well-being of developing countries. Few developmental experts would disagree with using a strategy of educating women to improve the social and economic conditions of any country. Discrimination toward women is widespread, and especially so among countries practicing a fundamentalist Muslim faith. At least some Islamic states embrace educational progress for women as has happened already in Turkey and Tunisia and even more recently in Jordan, Morocco, and Qatar (Coleman 2004: 80–95; 2006: 14–38).

UNESCO also has endorsed Article 15 of the ICESCR, referring to the right of people to take part in cultural life and enjoy the benefits of scientific progress. The various arts and media were to be available to all and not just privileged elites. Important conventions developed through UNESCO are the 1954 *Convention for the Protection of Cultural Property in the Event of Armed Conflict* and the 1970 the *Convention on the Means of Prohibiting and Preventing the Illicit Import, Export and the Transfer of Ownership of Cultural Property*, which entered into force in 1972.[28] These conventions aim to halt the plundering of cultural artifacts as happened in Iraq. The US intervention in Iraq, in the spring of 2003, triggered wholesale looting in Baghdad, containing some of the finest cultural treasure troves in the world.

Box 10.3 The Demise of Property Rights

As Part of the natural rights tradition, 17th century philosopher John Locke spoke of "life, liberty, and property rights," but Thomas Jefferson, penning the 1776 Declaration of Independence, thought it would be a more ringing phrase to say "life, liberty, and the pursuit of happiness." James Madison's concern with the omission of property rights was repaired in the US Constitution when the Fifth Amendment stated that private property will not be taken without just compensation. Private property is taken in the United States under the eminent domain concept but with compensation to the owner. However, a set-back to the protection of property rights resulted from a bitter 2005 US Supreme Court 5–4 decision that allowed comfortable, well-kept neighborhoods to be taken from their owners and their land given to for-profit enterprises, such as shopping centers, that would generate more tax revenue for local governments responding to the interests of developers. Previously, the emphasis was on blighted, run-down areas that were taken for the general public good to build such things as roads and schools.

At the global level, the 1948 UDHR's Article 17 covered the protection of private property, but this article did not carry over to the two 1966 covenants that spring from it. Many socialist-oriented Third World states and certainly communist countries objected because they viewed private property as representing improper power and privilege. Their representatives raised the question of whether property rights should even be acknowledged as a right at all. Regional conventions refer to property rights but do not sanctify them. Latin America, in particular, has a strong tradition of expropriating privately-held industries.

Sources: Louis Henkin et al., *Human Rights* (New York: Foundation Press, 1999), pp. 111–49; Gregory Robertson, *Crimes against Humanity: The Struggle for Global Justice* (New York: The New Press, 2006), pp. 132–6.

Cultural rights have also been expressed as minority rights with ethnic groups often insisting on practicing their own way of life apart from a national culture. French speakers in Quebec, Canada and Russian minorities left behind in the Baltic states after the Soviet armies pulled out are good examples. Cultural diversity has long been a concern of UNESCO, and it proposed the 2001 *Universal Declaration on Cultural Diversity*, which was adopted in 2003. A convention on this matter followed in 2005 and entered into force in 2007.[29] These cultural rules call for ethnic groups to enjoy their own values and sense of identity as well as to be protected from forced assimilation into the mainstream national culture. Of course the declaration and convention are not intended to encourage secessionist movements and the likely violence associated with movements of this kind.

Group Rights

Although the League of Nations developed treaties for protecting minorities after the First World War, the emergent human rights movement had a definite slant favoring the individual over the group.[30] This movement largely began on the fallacious assumption that if all individuals received rights, groups would automatically be safeguarded at the same time. The claim has been made that groups are not real entities but mere aggregations of individuals. While the concept "group rights" still carries some controversy, in truth, much human suffering is experienced because of group identities. People often think and act in a certain way because they belong to certain groups and, more importantly, they are the recipients of different treatment from the general population, often negative and even violent, due to their group affiliation and not because of anything they have done as individuals (Felice 1996: esp. 1–3).

Protection of ethnic groups

The UN Charter, the UDHR, and the major human rights conventions that followed proscribed discrimination against people on account of such distinctions as their race, gender, religion, language, and political views.[31] Among the approximately 200 states, 5,000 ethnic groups occupy the territories of these countries, and some with real fears for their futures (Jackson-Preece 2003: 49–71). Ted R. Gurr, in his *Minorities at Risk*, identified over 230 groups facing potentially dangerous futures at the hands of majority populations (Gurr 1993; 2000). Some recent assurances for ethnic groups have come from the 1993 UN *Declaration on the Rights of Persons Belonging to National or Ethnic, Religious and Linguistic Minorities* and the 1994 COE's *Convention for the Protection of National Minorities*, which entered into force in 1998.[32]

Race, as an ethnic group characteristic, has been especially troublesome. It is a social concept rather than a scientific one, but people in many places still discriminate according to what is perceived as racial differences. These differences can involve the shape of eyes, noses, and ears but especially the color of a person's skin. Some national societies are structured hierarchically according to the lightness or darkness of skin, with lighter-skinned persons possessing more political power, wealth, and education (Felice 2003: 128–9). A human rights treaty aimed at alleviating racism appeared just before the twin covenants, the 1965 UN *Convention on the Elimination on All Forms of Racial Discrimination*, which entered into force in 1969. A particularly harsh form of racism is *apartheid* as once practiced in South Africa, where a small minority of whites ruled for decades over a much larger number of Indians and black South Africans. There were white regimes also in Portuguese Guinea (Guinea) and Rhodesia (Zimbabwe). In time, all three gave way to black majority rule but, before the collapse of all-white regimes, apartheid became an international crime based on the 1973 UN *Convention on the Suppression and Punishment of the Crime of Apartheid*. To call attention to the continuing problem of racism in the world, a 2001 *World Conference against Racism, Racial Discrimination, Xenophobia and Related Intolerance* was held in Durban, South Africa, where apartheid once prevailed.

Women's rights

Women are the largest single group in the world, and they have probably been discriminated against more than any other, often with callous treatment harmful to their well-being and very lives. Until modern times, women have largely been excluded as rights-bearers. When the "rights of man" came into vogue in the eighteenth century in America and France, it was a literal advocacy. A few voices, however, noted the serious omission of women from the human rights equation. For instance, impassioned by the American and French revolutions, Mary Wollstonecraft's 1792 *A Vindication of the Rights of Women* attacked the oppression of women and pushed for gender equality.[33]

Even today, women around the world receive less than men regarding education, food allotments within families, health care, inheritance rights, sports opportunities, income, job opportunities, and political power among other disparities between the sexes. What women do experience more of is violence, including "honor killings," female circumcision that eliminates sexual desire, dowry deaths, the abortions of female fetuses in China and India, and battery through domestic violence in almost every country.[34] Even when it comes to political repression, women are much more likely to face not only the familiar disappearance and torture pattern but to be held as hostages and subjected to sexual abuse (Henderson 2004: 1028–49). Despite improving respect for the human rights of women in Canada, Europe, and the United States, along with a few other countries, Clair Apodaca is correct to observe that all countries still treat women less well than men (Apodaca 1998: 139–72; esp. 146). The rights of women in Islamic states have been a special concern, although the conditions of women in more than 50 Islamic states vary considerably.[35]

The issue that brings more feminist condemnation than any other regarding women's rights is female circumcision, or female genital mutilation (FGM) as its many critics refer to it. Although unassociated with any particular religion, over a hundred million women and girls are affected by this tradition in 20 countries

---

Box 10.4 A Heinous Case of Injustice

Ordered gang-raped in 2002 by a local Pakistani village council, supposedly for something her brother did, Mukhtar Mai did not take the usual option of suicide but fought back. Her case reached international notoriety, forcing legal action against the rapists, although their convictions were overturned on appeal. After testifying in court, Mukhtar Mai received some financial compensation from the Pakistani government and donations from outside Pakistan. She began new schools in her village with the money. The government tried at first to keep her in detention as international attention grew but then relented and let her travel outside her country by 2005. During her travels she received honors and financial aid. Her life continues to be under threat in a remote area run by local Muslim warlords who practice a culture that chews up women and spits them out, according to a respected journalist for the *New York Times*, Nicholas D. Kristof.

Source: Mukhtar Mai's autobiography is *In the Name of Honor: A Memoir* (New York: Atria Books, 2006).

---

spread across Africa and the Middle East. WHO and the World Medical Association have condemned female circumcision. Moreover, the 1993 *Declaration on the Elimination of Violence against Women* states that violence against women includes FGM.[36] The UN's role has been central in coming to the aid of women's rights. The Charter of the UN, the UDHR, and the twin covenants all require an end to discrimination based on gender. The UN had barely got underway when in 1946 it created a Commission on the Status of Women that, along with other UN bodies, has created a constellation of legal protections for women. These include the 1952 *Convention on the Political Rights of Women*, the 1957 *Convention on the Nationality of Women*, and the 1962 *Convention on the Consent to Marriage, Minimum Age for Marriage and Registration of Marriages*. In 2000, the UN promoted a protocol to the *Convention against Transnational Crime* to stop trafficking in women and children. The UN also designated 1975 as International Women's Year and 1976–85 as the UN Decade for Women. Annually, March 8 is International Women's Day.

The centerpiece of UN efforts to promote women's rights began as a 1967 declaration and became the 1979 *Convention on the Elimination of All Forms of Discrimination against Women* (CEDAW) that entered into force in 1981. It is intended to be a comprehensive, universal framework of rules to prohibit all discrimination against women. As of 2009 a large majority of states had given 185 ratifications to this convention but, regrettably, more than 20 countries have attached over 80 substantive reservations regarding their obligations.[37] In general, treaty discussions, the CEDAW is often cited as a prime example of how reservations can undercut the good purposes of a treaty. Reinforcing the UN's global efforts to promote women's rights are useful steps taken at the regional level by the COE, OAS, and the African Union.[38]

Children's rights

Children's vulnerabilities and suffering frequently match that of women because the two groups are regularly together, including during wartime and civil unrest. Children are killed in wars, forced to watch their mothers raped, and, if they are lucky, find their way to refugee camps alongside their mothers to face uncertain futures. In one decade alone, 1990–2000, two million children were killed in the world's armed conflicts (Ishay 2004: 303). They are conscripted into armies and private militias, suffer from forced labor, denied education and health care, subjected to sexual abuses, including forced prostitution and pornography, and questionable adoption practices that amount to little more than the selling of children. Between 1990 and 2003, the fate of children in Iraq was probably even worse than that of women because of UN sanctions. The children were less able to survive malnutrition and contaminated water. What happens to children is clearly one of the largest of human rights concerns since persons under the age of 18 make up about one-third of the world's population.

Children, once the concern only of their parents and possibly the country of their nationality, eventually became a focus of international attention. In 1924, the League adopted the very brief *Declaration of the Rights of the Child*, and the UN followed up in 1959 with a more elaborate declaration. The major international accomplishment on behalf of children is the 1989 *Convention on the Rights of the Child* with extensive obligations for states.[39] It soon after entered into force with almost all states ratifying and many accepting its two protocols prohibiting the death penalty and military service for persons under 18 years of age.

Focused on children are UNESCO and the UN International Children's Fund (UNICEF has been retained as this IGO's well-known acronym, although "Emergency" was dropped from the name as its work became permanent), which have worked to improve children's health and education as global policies. Despite the hard work of these two IGOs, 40,000 children a day die from starvation and disease.[40] Millions of others live the misery of what Lawrence J. LeBlanc has called the "half-life of malnutrition" (Le Blanc 1995: xiii). Educational opportunities have eluded millions of children who have no access to schooling at all, a problem that falls especially heavily on girls (Drinan 2001: 47). Millions of children labor under conditions little better than slavery, baking bricks or weaving at looms for long hours per day. A major protection that needs fuller implementation is the ILO's 1999 *Convention on the Worst Forms of Child Labor*, which prohibits the trafficking of children, placing them in debt bondage and using children as soldiers, or for pornography or prostitution. The convention entered into force the next year and reinforces some of the provisions of the 1990 Convention of the Child.[41]

Some very specialized child protections are the 1980 *Hague Convention on the Civil Aspects of International Abduction* and the 1993 *Hague Convention on Inter-Country Adoption*.[42] The first is used primarily in cases where one parent, possibly not the custodial parent, takes a child or children across borders and denies access to the other parent. The convention on abduction requires that any children abducted be returned to the country of residence. The convention on adoption calls on states to distinguish carefully between legitimate adoptions and "baby selling," conducted through exorbitant fees that operate behind a thin veneer of legality.[43] Several significant conventions at the regional level also protect children, such as the 1990 *African Charter on the Rights and Welfare of the Child* and the 1996 *European Convention on the Exercise of Children's Rights*. The OAS has several conventions for the protection of children.[44]

The rights of indigenous peoples

If any special group needs to be first in line for human rights protection, it is **indigenous peoples**. Richard A. Falk has called these peoples the most vulnerable of all (Falk 2000a: xiii). People in this category are the descendents of the original inhabitants of a territory but who are now confronted with much larger, more powerful ethnic groups that came afterward as invaders and colonizers.[45] Amer-Indians in some Latin American countries, Inuit in Alaska and Canada, Maori in New Zealand, Aborigines in Australia, Ainu in Japan, Hmong in Laos, Montagnards in Vietnam, and Saami living in the several Nordic countries and Russia are examples of the original inhabitants, now far outnumbered by people of more sophisticated cultures with complex political institutions and numerous modern technologies. Estimates of the total number of indigenous peoples and the countries where they are located vary, but in a careful estimate, Franke Wilmer calculates these numbers as being about 300 million indigenous persons living in 47 countries (Wilmer 1993: 217–19).

From the sixteenth through the nineteenth centuries, European explorers found new lands they considered *terra nullius* (belonging to no one) and claimed these by "title of discovery," frequently pushing aside indigenous peoples and their interests. Following European conquest, enslavement, genocide, and forced migrations occurred, as when the Cherokee were forced onto the "Trail of Tears" in 1838, traveling from western North Carolina to Oklahoma with many dying along the way. As many as 100,000 Aboriginal children in Australia were taken from their families and placed with white foster families from 1910 to the 1970s. They are referred to as the "Stolen Generation." Some attacks on Amer-Indians in Brazil have taken place recently because gold miners and cattle ranchers have been eager to encroach on Amer-Indians' landed reserves. Currently, poverty, alcoholism, contagious diseases, and high rates of incarceration have been the worst common experiences for indigenous peoples around the world.[46]

In time, IGOs joined what became a significant global campaign on behalf of indigenous peoples. Taking the lead, the ILO began to investigate the labor conditions of indigenous groups as early as 1930 and has developed several important conventions for the protection of indigenous peoples (Wilmer 1993: 215; appendix B). The ILO's 1989 *Convention Concerning Indigenous and Tribal Peoples in Independent Countries* (No. 169) stands today as international law's most concrete response to indigenous peoples' needs. This convention resists assimilation into the majority population and encourages some measure of cultural autonomy (Anaya

1996: 47; Hannum 2003: 72–99). It came into force in 1991 but does not have a large number of ratifications.

Compared to the ILO, the UN was a Johnny-Come-Lately to the indigenous cause. Only in 1971 did the UN abandon the view that indigenous issues are domestic concerns. Between 1989 and 1993, the UN worked on a *Declaration on the Rights of the Indigenous Peoples*, which was only adopted in 2006 by the new Human Rights Council. Several countries, including Australia, New Zealand, and the United States, have opposed its acceptance by the UN General Assembly, presumably because these countries fear their indigenous peoples would be encouraged to pursue greater autonomy than they already enjoy.[47]

It is safe to say that of the regional IGOs, the OAS has distinguished itself the most in recognizing indigenous rights, partly because of numerous Amer-Indian tribes in multiple countries of the region, but also due to some compassion by the relevant governments. The Inter-American Human Rights Commission has addressed these rights on numerous occasions and, in 1997, approved the "American Declaration on the Rights of Indigenous Peoples." In what may be the best known international court case about indigenous peoples, the Inter-American Court on Human Rights ruled in 2001 that Nicaragua could not contract part of the land of the Awas Tingni tribe to a South Korean corporation because doing so would interfere with the tribe's collective property rights and close spiritual connection with its homeland (Hannum 2003: 86–7).

If one issue stands out about indigenous peoples as a special group, it is their determination to have a meaningful version of self-determination, perhaps short of an independent state but entailing greater autonomy than is generally experienced by other minorities. Importantly, the ILO and UN have both shifted from referring to "indigenous populations" to "indigenous peoples," an important symbol concerning autonomous claims. The use of indigenous populations would imply these special groups were merely another ethnic minority, but indigenous peoples entail a stronger claim for self-rule. As Franke Wilmer has observed, it is impossible to reform the indigenous problem without some kind of self-determination for these peoples (Wilmer 1993: 128).

A Human Rights Frontier?

Because human rights have never been a fixed, bounded list and tend to expand, one category of people who may be considered for group status is that of homosexuals. On the furthermost edge of human rights law is a struggling global effort to end all forms of discrimination regarding a person's sexual orientation. Whether various types of transgender persons will ever be able to embrace the status of group rights around the world is presently unknown. Very much at issue is whether a person's sexual status is to be considered a moral variable or a fundamental aspect of the person and an immutable part of his or her self-identity. Is transgender behavior natural for some people? Several major religions, including the Roman Catholic Church, Evangelical Christian churches, and Orthodox Judaism, would answer in the negative and regard this behavior as biblical sin. Most of the attention has focused on *homosexual persons* who make up as much as 10 percent of society and desire equal treatment with heterosexuals, including being able to live together as life partners. A growing number of national and international NGO gay, lesbian, bisexual, and transgender peoples' organizations (GLBTs) have been vigorously pursuing the goal of enjoying a full set of rights by ending discrimination in jobs, sports participation, child adoption, marriage, housing, conjugal visits in prison, service in the military and clergy as well as representation for GLBTs at international conferences and IGOs.[48]

The UDHR, the twin covenants, and major regional human rights conventions all prohibit discrimination on the basis of race, color, language, religion, politics, national origin, and sex, the latter presumably referring to the traditional gender categories of heterosexual men and women. Sexual minorities have generally not been protected from discrimination on such lists. The one exception is the EU's 1997 *Treaty of Amsterdam*, which entered into force in 1999. Its Article 6 (a) adds sexual orientation to the usual list of categories of persons at danger because of discrimination.[49]

Reforms to help GLBTs are underway but taking place in an uneven patchwork. Some positive steps have occurred within the UN System. In 2004, Secretary-General Kofi Annan decided to recognize spousal benefits for homosexual employees, but only if their home countries had similar policies. The UN High Commissioners for Human Rights have also been sympathetic to the enjoyment of rights by gays and lesbians. Several UN human rights monitoring committees have been concerned over issues of discrimination against homosexuals. Finally a handful of GLBTs groups have been given NGO consultative status with the UN.

The region of the world most supportive of sexual minorities is Europe. In addition to the explicit ban against discrimination in the Treaty of Amsterdam, the European Court of Human Rights, as a major institution of the COE, has protected sexual minorities by using rationales associated with the legal principles of privacy and equal treatment legal principles, but not consistently. Two of its most famous cases came from the United Kingdom, with the court ruling in 1999 that homosexuals could join the military and, in 2002, overturning one of its own earlier decisions by deciding that a male having undergone reassignment surgery could marry as a woman.[50]

On the downside, Islamic and African countries have strongly opposed rights for sexual minorities at home and at the fora of the UN. Under pressure from these states, the UN Development Program (UNDP) modified its "Human Freedom Index" to drop "freedom for homosexual activity" from its composite measure of freedom (De Laet 2006: 131). No less than 85 UN member-states criminalize same-gender sex.[51] In some Islamic states, homosexuals are imprisoned and even executed.

As for the United States, discrimination against homosexuals in jobs, housing, and adoptions are beginning to be quashed by state and federal courts using the equal protection legal principle of the Fourteenth Amendment. Same sex partnerships have been legalized as civil unions in several states and the District of Columbia, and four states of the US federal system allow same sex marriage. Anticipating this development, the US Congress passed the 1996 Defense of Marriage Act. Under this law, states do not have to recognize a same sex marriage sanctioned in another state.

Also, it remains unlawful for homosexuals to be in the US military; hence, the "don't ask, don't tell" policy, which allows this minority to participate in military service as long as their status remains unknown to authorities.

Human Rights Regimes

As in other areas of international law, the cumulative norms and treaties that states agree to and generally observe are often called *regimes*. At the global and regional levels, numerous institutions have been developed to promote human rights and even to monitor states' performances in this area of international law. These regimes are not governmental in the sense that they have enforcement powers but can only hope to induce sovereign states toward better records. In fact, many states often prove recalcitrant in the face of human rights reforms insisted on by others.

Global regime

The global regime is ensconced in the UN. The 1945 UN Charter made a clear commitment to the advancement of human rights. The Economic and Social Council (ECOSOC), one of the six primary bodies of the UN System, quickly implemented this commitment in 1946 by establishing the Commission on Human Rights, for a long time the hub of the UN rights regime. The Commission was made up of 53 states representing the various regions of the world. An increase in its authority came with a 1967 resolution allowing public examination of patterns of gross violations of human rights and another 1970 resolution that permitted confidential petitions from aggrieved individuals. The Commission soon created a 26 member Sub-commission on the Prevention of Discrimination and Protection of Minorities, which in 1999 was renamed the Sub-Commission on the Promotion and Protection of Human Rights to reflect the sub-commission's broadening range of concerns.

Both the Commission and Sub-commission study human rights problems in a specialized way, by creating numerous *working groups* and assigning individuals as *special rapporteurs* to research and report on such issues as women's rights, slavery, indigenous peoples, and torture. By the turn into the twenty-first century, dissatisfaction began to grow over the Commission. Many states began to view it as too political in nature because it focused on protecting its member-states' reputations regarding their own performance records instead of actually furthering the cause of human rights.

The ECOSOC also started a Commission on the Status of Women and a department known as the Advancement of Women Division attached to the Secretariat, the central administrative body of the UN. In 1950, a High Commissioner for Refugees was established and, in 1993, a long-awaited High Commissioner for Human Rights was set up to help interweave human rights throughout UN policies.[52]

Additionally, seven specialized committees created by human rights treaties and protocols, answering to the UN General Assembly, have been formed to monitor compliance with each treaty's specific requirements. These are the Human Rights

Committee on Civil and Political Rights and the Committee on Economic, Social and Cultural Rights. Other committees focus on race, women, children, migrant workers, and torture. Some committees can receive individual petitions, interstate complaints, and make on-site visits, while others are more limited in what they can do. It is to the credit of the UN regime that large numbers of countries accept the monitoring process; however, actual state cooperation in filing accurate, on-time, and useful reports is spotty.[53]

The effectiveness of the UN regime does not surpass "soft enforcement" based on monitoring states' practices and then encouraging improvements. Ultimately, in the worst cases of abuse, this type of enforcement can only exercise the "power to embarrass," which may or may not change a state's policies. A reform that may enhance the UN human rights regime is replacing the Commission on Human Rights with the Human Rights Council in 2006, a move receiving overwhelming support from the UN General Assembly. The Council is expected to have a much more proactive mandate. It has 47 state members (smaller than the 53 of the Commission), and the members will be chosen by an absolute majority of the General Assembly and not by the ECOSOC. The members will be elected for three-year terms and can be re-elected only once, and their records on human rights must undergo careful scrutiny. The new Secretary of State, Hilary Clinton, pursued membership for the United States in early 2009. Finally, the Human Rights Council will meet three times a year instead of once as was the case for the Commission.[54]

European regime

Through a fortuitous development of a culture favoring rights and the acceptance of supranational authority, Europeans have been able to converge around the standards of the most effective human rights regime in the world. Soon after the Second Word War, Western Europe at least had accepted the 1950 European Convention on Human Rights and then a European Commission on Human Rights, as well as a European Court on Human Rights, to make sure the lengthy list of civil and political rights would be grounded in the policies of member-states. The Commission would screen cases from applicants and send a few of them on to the court established in 1953 and headquartered in Strasbourg, France. In 1998, the Commission was eliminated and the court became full-time, screening its own cases. The Court now serves 47 states since Eastern Europe, including Russia, has joined the COE. Its chief problem is that it is swamped with applicants. It can be said the European Court of Human Rights has become the "constitutional court of Europe," with its decisions almost always complied with, thus creating common human rights standards for the whole region. In addition, the COE also created a Commissioner for Human Rights in 1999.[55]

Besides civil and political rights, COE states have also promoted socioeconomic rights through the 1961 *European Social Charter*, substantially revised in 1996. While the Social Charter is not backed up by robust court enforcement, its provisions are overseen by a European Commission of Social Rights. Also, the EU created the non-binding norms of the 2000 *Charter of Fundamental Rights* which, nonetheless, are often vigorously applied as firm norms by the powerful European Court of Justice (ECJ) of the EU. The ECJ was originally created to settle trade disputes but its decisions impact on human rights.[56]

American regime

The Inter-American human rights regime is nested in the OAS and was launched, as was the UN and European regimes, after the Second World War as part of the modern human rights movement. All 35 American states belong, but Cuba has been prevented from participating since 1962. At first glance, its institutional machinery resembles the European regime, but the Inter-American regime has never been able to structure human rights policies in its region as much as the European arrangement.[57] Perhaps its greatest accomplishment is that the Inter-American regime survived the sharp swerve toward dictatorships in the 1970s and early 1980s in Latin America and continues today to work on improving human rights conditions.

Certainly the Inter-American regime has built up an impressive set of declarations, conventions, and protocols to protect human rights, including the 1948 *American Declaration on the Rights and Duties of Man* and the 1969 *Inter-American Convention on Human Rights*, along with the latter's 1988 protocol to promote socioeconomic rights and its 1950 protocol to abolish the death penalty. Other OAS specialized conventions reject torture, violence toward women, and the practice of "disappearing" opponents of governments. The OAS has also produced the 1991 *Santiago Declaration* claiming democracy's survival in any state is an international concern and not strictly a domestic matter. This commitment to democracy is fairly strong in most of the American states and critical to sustain human rights. The chief exceptions are the cases of communist Cuba, led for nearly five decades by Fidel Castro and Hugo Chavez's worrisome tilt toward dictatorial powers in oil-rich Venezuela.

The *Inter-American Commission on Human Rights* began its work in 1959 and was incorporated into the OAS framework by 1979.[58] It is headquartered in Washington, DC. Unlike Europe's decision to drop its commission and rely only on its court, the Inter-American commission continues to be the workhorse of the Latin American regime. Its 11 members carry out fact-finding missions on-site, receive complaints from individuals and NGOs, lodge complaints with governments and, most importantly, bring cases before the *Inter-American Court on Human Rights* (IACHR). The IACHR can both hear contentions cases and offer advisory opinions. So far, 21 states have accepted the court's jurisdiction, but the Commission remains the chief instrument to place cases before the court. The states are reluctant to offend one another with legal challenges to each others' domestic practices. The IACHR is headquartered in San José, Costa Rica, holds two sessions a year, and is staffed by seven judges acting in their individual capacity. The court's case load is light compared to the European Court of Human Rights, but it has had a few interesting cases, including protecting the rights of Amer-Indians and overturning amnesty laws that once protected agents of repression after they left office.[59]

African regime

If Europe is a strong regime and the Inter-American regime a fairly viable one, then the African regime must be regarded as weak. Under the auspices of the 53-member OAU, the *African Charter on Human and Peoples' Rights* (African Charter) was approved in 1981 and went into force in 1986. On the positive side, the African Charter is best known for containing all "three generations of rights." The negative side is its "claw-back" articles that allow states to shelve their rights obligations in the face of problems such as security issues. Pleasing some and disappointing other observers is attention to duties as well as rights. The African regime in practice shows much deference to the sovereignty of states, mostly dictatorships.

The African regime has an *African Commission on Human and Peoples' Rights* (African Commission) located in Banjul, Gambia. It is derived from the African Charter and has 11 members, but they are appointed by African heads of state which may diminish them as an independent body. The Commission is to receive country reports every two years on a confidential basis but can only offer advice.[60]

The weakness of the African Commission led to proposals for an *African Court on Human and Peoples' Rights* (African Court of Justice). The court was established by a 1998 protocol to the African Charter that entered into force in 2004. The African Court judges were selected in 2006 and sit in Arusha, Tanzania, to take advantage of the court facilities placed there to try Rwandan genocide and war criminals in an international tribunal. During the court's development, the OAU reconstituted itself as the African Union in 2002. The 11 judges of the court can hear contentious cases and requests for advisory opinion. Just what the Commission's relationship to the court will be is unclear. It is too early to tell if the African Court can pull itself free from the strong African proclivity to defer to states. One rather interesting feature of this court is that any human rights treaty ratified by a state accepting the court's jurisdiction (now at 20) can be taken into consideration by the judges.[61]

Other regimes

Islamic and Asian states have not done much in the way of developing human rights regimes. The Organization of Islamic Conference in 1990 produced the *Cairo Declaration of Human Rights* as an alternative to Western originated conceptions of rights (Mayer 2005: 209–11). With a similar motive, a sub-set of Islamic states, the League of Arab States, came up with the 1971 *Arab Charter of Human Rights* that was not approved by the League until 1994. This League also established the 1968 *Arab Commission on Human Rights*, but its limited activities have centered on Israel's treatment of Palestinians.[62] Except for a few bright spots such as Tunisia and an improving Turkey, the human rights record of the Islamic states is generally poor. The Islamic states are mostly controlled by authoritarian governments and are sometimes under pressure by fundamentalists to put sharia rules ahead of human rights.

Asian states have been particularly reluctant to develop institutional arrangements on behalf of human rights, although at least three large democracies – India,

Japan, and the Philippines – are in the region. Nonetheless, the 1993 *Bangkok Declaration on Human Rights* was created, followed by the 1997 *Asian Human Rights Charter*, but these are of dubious utility. Leaders in Asia, more so than other regions, have championed the "cultural relativism" doctrine and prefer to emphasize economic advances over civil and political rights (Castellino 2005: 16–18).

The Role of Non-state Actors

Human rights conditions are not shaped only by states and the IGOs that states create. Private actors both help and harm the enjoyment of rights (Brysk 2005; Clapham 2006). Several hundred human rights NGOs around the world monitor and report on human rights practices, often working in collusion as advocacy networks lobbying states and IGOs for reforms. One of their best services is to provide "shadow reports" on governments that do not respond to the seven monitoring committees or provide inadequate reports. Undoubtedly the best known is Amnesty International, with a membership of two million people spread across 150 countries. Other well-known human rights NGOs are Human Rights Watch, Doctors Without Borders, Physicians for Human Rights, Freedom Writers Network, and the Arab Lawyers Union, to name but a few.[63] Human rights activists often expose themselves to great dangers and sometimes become the victims of political repression. Their fate may start with threatening phone calls and escalate to torture and even murder. A few NGOs, such as Peace Brigades International, have specialized in serving as unarmed bodyguards for other activists (Mahoney & Eguren 1997). Without human rights activists, states would get away with far more human rights abuses than already occur.

Box 10.5 Peter Benenson, 1921–2005: Human Rights Hero

As one individual, Peter Benenson, an English human rights lawyer, launched a revolution in human rights advocacy in 1961 by founding Amnesty International, today's largest and most influential human rights NGO. His basic concept, still used today, was based on a letter writing campaign to free political prisoners. His first case involved two Portuguese students arrested for toasting freedom in then dictatorial Portugal. Amnesty International, since then, has fought for the freedom of thousands of prisoners of conscience, promoted the Convention against Torture, pressed for the end of the death penalty around the world, supported the creation of the International Criminal Court, and won the Nobel Peace Prize, all from the germ of an idea of an outraged lawyer.

Source: *Amnesty International*, Spring (2005), p. 3; and "Peter Benenson (1921–2005)" in Zehra F. Kabasakal Arat, *Human Rights Worldwide* (Santa Barbara, CA: ABC/CLIO, 2006), pp. 150–1.

Private celebrities have also stepped forward in a promotional manner to advocate for improvements in the human rights field. Movie star and academy award winner Audrey Hepburn made appearances as a goodwill ambassador for UNICEF from 1988 until her death in 1993. Actress Agelina Jolie has been serving as a goodwill ambassador for the UN High Commissioner for Refugees since 2001. In the summer of 2007 she visited displaced Iraqis in both Iraq and Syria to draw attention to their plight. Other examples are the English rock star Sting, who has organized benefit concerts for human rights, and Bono, lead singer for the U-2 band from Ireland, who has raised funds and lobbied governments to reduce human suffering in African countries. Bono was once nominated for the Nobel Peace Prize. In 2007, comedian and actor Jim Carrey made a *YouTube* video on behalf of the Human Rights Center calling for Nobel Laureate Aung San Suu Kyi to be freed from years of house arrest by the Myanmar military dictatorship. Recognizing the role that private groups and persons can play in the human rights movement and wishing to encourage it, the UN General Assembly has approved the 1999 *Declaration on the Rights and Responsibility of Individuals, Groups and Organs of Society to Promote and Protect Universally Recognized Rights and Fundamental Freedoms.*[64]

Some actors have a mixed record, an observation that can even apply to churches. For example, although the Roman Catholic Church has done charitable work in many countries for centuries, deplorable reports of pedophilia by priests in Europe and the Americas have come to light in recent years (Brysk 2005: 9). In 2007, this church agreed to pay out $2 billion to settle civil suits in the United States alone.

Another actor with a mixed record and great potential for harms is the multinational corporation, or MNC. Although providing jobs, raising standards of living, and sharing needed technology with underdeveloped countries, some MNCs have also operated "sweatshop" industries, damaged physical environments, sold torture devices and firearms to dictators, bribed officials to look the other way when laws are broken, cheated local governments out of tax revenues with "double accounting" practices, and supported repressive governments that control local labor for the benefit of the MNCs.[65]

Typical actors that categorically have bad effects on human rights are transnational criminal organizations and private militias. Completely outside the pale of law, criminal organizations smuggle guns, distribute illicit drugs, and are behind human trafficking. These organizations undercut the health and welfare of millions of people and take the lives of uncounted innocents. Militias ignore both humanitarian law and a broad range of human rights in general as they perform their nefarious acts of murder and torture in many places, such as several African states and the Balkans in the 1990s. The worst current example might be found in Colombia, suffering from a decades-long long revolutionary war. An alliance of military, business, and political leaders have kept militias in the field to help counter three leftist guerrilla armies. These operate apart from the Colombian Army and cause some of the worst human rights depredations along with the guerrilla armies. Only in the last several years has Colombia's government sought to demobilize its paramilitaries (Ambrus 2007: 16–20).

Chapter Summary

- The development of human rights for individuals and groups has been a radical departure from a state-system that originally allowed sovereign states to do as they wished at home including treating their citizens as governments pleased.
- Human rights have expanded across "three generations" from a concern with civil and political rights to social and economic rights, and now also include broad based peoples' rights such as enjoying peace and environmental security.
- The accumulated norms and rules regarding human rights are known, institutionally speaking, as a human rights regime; there is a global regime sponsored by the UN and several regional regimes promoted by such IGOs as the COE, OAS, and AU.
- NGOs, such as Amnesty International and Human Rights Watch, have proven to be critically important to the worldwide human rights movement by sponsoring human rights conventions and reporting violations of these conventions

Discussion Questions

1   Human rights may have both natural rights and a constructivist heritage. Make clear these two distinct sources of human rights. Which is the more likely explanation for the development of human rights?
2   A long-standing distinction exists between civil and political rights and social and economic rights. Is it plausible that one set is more important and should receive priority over the other, or are types of rights interdependent in the sense that they reinforce one another?
3   How much credence should be given to the concept of cultural relativism? Since women are treated as second-class citizens in many countries, should other governments, as well as human rights NGOs, respect these countries' sovereignty and leave them to their own way of life?
4   What is political repression and what are the rights it typically denies?
5   How do human rights NGOs help protect and promote human rights?

Useful Weblinks

http://www.un.org/rights/index.shtml
This website is the main UN portal to human rights activities by the IGO. It provides direct access to the UN activities in the human rights field, including treaties the new Human Rights Council, and a useful research guide.

http://www.ohchr.org/english
The Office of the High Commissioner on Human Rights can be accessed from the main UN portal but deserves a place in the list of Top Picks in its own right. By using the "International Law" tab numerous human rights treaties are available with full text and arranged by appropriate categories.

http://www.amnesty.org/
Undoubtedly the larges and best known human rights NGO, the website of Amnesty International features special campaigns such as political prisoners, protection of women, stopping torture, control of arms, urging action over Darfur, all of which are easily accessible. It also leads to other human rights links and the national chapters of Amnesty International in other countries.

http://www.freedomhouse.org/
Freedom House is one of the older human rights NGOs and specializes in democracy and civil and political rights. It provides annual assessments of freedoms such as the enjoyment of democracy and especially the status of the freedom of press in countries.

http://www1.umn.edu/humanrts/treaties.htm
This website is particularly user friendly and offers lists of treaties on human rights by subject-matter plus information about the ratification of treaties by country. These treaties can be researched by entering a "key word" in a search engine.

Further Reading

Arnold, Roberta and Quénivet, Noëlle (eds.) (2008) *International Humanitarian Law and Human Rights Law*. Boston, MA: Martinus Nijhoff.

Carey, Sabine C. and Poe, Steven C. (eds.) (2004) *Understanding Human Rights Violations*. Burlington, VT: Ashgate.

Champagne, Duane, Torjesen, Karen Jo, and Steiner, Susan (eds.) (2005) *Indigenous Peoples and the Modern State*. Lanham, MD: Rowman & Littlefield.

Cottier, Thomas, Pauwelyn, Joost, and Bürgi, Elizabeth (eds.) (2005) *Human Rights and International Trade*. Oxford: Oxford University Press.

Francioni, Francesco and Scheinin, Martin (eds.) (2008) *Cultural Human Rights*. Boston, MA: Martinus Nijhoff Publishers.

Gibney, Mark (2008) *International Human Rights Law: Returning to Universal Principles*. Lanham, MD: Rowman & Littlefield.

Hood, Roger and Hoyle, Carolyn (2008) *The Death Penalty: A Worldwide Perspective*, 4th edn. New York: Oxford University Press.

Kneebone, Susan (ed.) (2009) *Refugees, Asylum Seekers and the Rule of Law*. New York: Cambridge University Press.

Krivenko, Ekaterina Yahyaoui (2009) *Women, Islam and International Law*. Boston, MA: Martinus Nijhoff Publishers.

Ranstorp, Magnus and Wilkinson, Paul (2007). *Terrorism and Human Rights*. New York: Routledge.

Richardson, Diane and Seidman, Steven (2002) *Handbook of Lesbian and Gay Studies*. Thousand Oaks, CA: Sage.

Weston, Burns H. (ed.) (2005) *Child Labor and Human Rights: Making Children Matter*. Boulder, CO: Lynne Rienner.

White, Richard Alan (2004) *Breaking Silence: The Case that Changed the Face of Human Rights*. Washington, DC: Georgetown University Press.

Notes

1   This point is made by Charlesworth and Chinkin 2000: 201–3. Article 2 (7) of the UN Charter can be read at http://www.un.org/aboutun/charter.

2   Brems 2003: 101–3; The UDHR can be read at http://www.un.org/cyberschoolbus/humanrights/resources/universal.asp.

3   As an example of this perspective, see Howard 1995: 12–15.

4   Human Rights are mentioned in the UN Charter in the Preamble, Article 1 (3), Article 13 (1) b, Article 55, implicitly in Article 56, and Article 62. For a convenient access to the Charter, see endnote 1.

5   First and second generation rights can be read of the International Covenant on Civil and Political Rights 1966 and the International Covenant on Economic, Social and Cultural Rights can be read at http://treaties.un.org/Pages/ParticipationStatus.aspx > Chapter IV. The African Charter can be located at www.africa-union.org/ > Documents > Treaties, Conventions & Protocols > scroll down to the African Charter on Human and Peoples' Rights. See especially Articles 19–24 of the African Charter. Also, all three are conveniently located in the Annex on Documents in Steiner and Alston 1996.

6   Go to http://www.hrcr.org/docs/OAS_Declaration/oasrights.htlm.

7   See note 2 for a website for the UDHR.

8   See note 5 for a website on the African Charter.

9   For analysis in depth, see Donnelly 2003: 20–45; An-na'im 1992; Booth 1995: 119–20; Pollis and Schwab 2000: 1–8; Ignatieff 2001: 62–77.

10   See, http://treaties.un.org/Pages/ParticipationStatus.aspx > Chapter IV.

11   The Second Optional Protocol to the ICCPR can be read at Scott 2006: 392–5; or accessed at http://treaties.un.org/Pages/ParticipationStatus.aspx > Chapter IV > Scroll down to item 12.

12   See the website of the Council of Europe at http://www.coe.int/ > Human Rights > The Convention > Protocol No. 6 and Protocol No. 13.

13   The Protocol forbidding the death penalty but with a wartime exception can be read at the OAS website of http://www.oas.org/main/english > Treaties and Agreements > By Subject > Death Penalty – see Human Rights in general > Human Rights to Abolish the Death Penalty, Protocol to the American Convention (A-53); to read the American Convention on Human Rights, including its Article 4 (3), see the same site. After "By Subject" > Human Rights "Pact of San Jose, Costa Rica," American Convention (B-12). The ACHR can also be read at Steiner and Alston 1996.

14   Good coverage of this case is the website of ASIL found at http://www.asil.org > enter "Pretty" in the search engine and > International Law in Brief-May 22, 2002.

15   Some primary references to the freedom of religion are the UN Charter's Article 55, the UDHR and ICCPR's Article 18, ICESCR's Article 13 (1), the ECHR's Article 9, ACHR's Article 12, and the African Charter's Article 8. These conventions can be found in Steiner and Alston 1996, and in previously cited websites. Or, see note 5.

16   For the 1981 declaration on religion, refer to http://www.ohchr.org/english/law/religion.htm.

17   State Department *Country Reports* can be found at http://www.state.gov/g/drl/rls/hrrpt/; Amnesty International reports are at http://www.amnesty.org. Enter "Annual Reports" into AI's search engine.

18 Much of this impressive literature on political repression is cited in Davenport 2000 and in Carey and Poe 2004.

19 An article providing evidence that supports the importance of democracy and economic improvements to dissuade repression is Henderson 1991: 120–42.

20 http://www.unhcr.org/ > quick find topics > 1951 Refugee Convention. And see http://www.ohchr.org/english/ > International Law > Nationality, Statelessness, Asylum and Refugees.

21 For regional efforts on behalf of refugees, see http://www.unhcr.org/basics.html > OAU Convention Governing the Specific Aspects of Refugee Problems in Africa; and > Cartagena Declaration on Refugees (in the Americas). For Europe, see http://conventions.coe.int > full list > 031 Abolition of Visas for Refugees, 061-A Protocol to the European Convention on Consular Functions Concerning the Protection of Refugees, and 107 European Agreement on Transfer of Responsibility for Refugees.

22 These figures are from http://www.unhcr.org/basics.html > "Refugees by Numbers, 2006 Edition" and "Internally Displaced People 2006 Edition." Also, read Kane 2003: 301–22.

23 For the European Social Charter, see http://www.coe.int/T/E/Human_Rights/Esc/.

24 Findable at http://treaties.un.org/Pages/ParticipationStatus.aspx > Chapter Four.

25 Numerous references are made about Senator Bricker and "Brickerism" in Van Dyke 1970: 55, 74, 120, 127, 130–141, 149, 164, 182, 236, and 246.

26 The ILO's homepage is at http://www.ilo.org/global/lang-en/index.htm; also see Alston 2005.

27 See http://www.who.int/ > Programs > Projects > Scroll to Tobacco Free Initiative; also see Fidler 1999; Bruntland 2003: 7–12; Farmer 2003; and Garrett 2007: 14–38.

28 For the cultural conventions see, http://www.unesco.org/.

29 The declaration and convention are at http://www.unesco.org/.

30 See the preface and the first article by Lyons and Mayall 2003: vii–viii, 3–19.

31 As examples, see Article 55 of the UN Charter, Article 2 of the UDHR, and Article 2 of both the ICCPR and the ICESCR.

32 To read the 1993 UN Declaration, see http://www.un.org/documents/ga/res/48/a48r138.htm, and the 1994 COE Convention can be read at http://www.coe.int/T/E/Human_Rights/Minorities/ > Text of the Framework Convention.

33 Republished as Wollstonecraft, *A Vindication of the Rights of Women*, 1988.

34 Excellent general sources on women's rights are the UN Development Program's *Human Development Report 1995*; Steiner and Alston 1996: 887–967; Askin and Koenig 1999); Ashworth 1999: 259–76; and Lockwood 2006.

35 On Muslim women see Coleman's articles; also see Arat 2000: 69–93.

36 Steiner and Alston 1996: 242–3. Also, see Walker 1993; Robert F. Drinan 2001: 42–3. And see Article 2 (a) of the 1993 Declaration at http://www.ohchr.org/english/law/index.htm > Rights of Women > Declaration on the Elimination of Violence against Women.

37 Refer to http://treaties.un.org/Pages/PartictpationStatus.aspx > Chapter IV.

38 For a good general review of conventions on the rights of women, see Cook 1997: 181–207; also some of the international legal documents on women's rights can be read at http://www.ohchr.org/english/law/index.htm > Rights of Women.

39 For the development of the convention, see LeBlanc 1995. The two declarations and the convention can be read in the appendices, pp. 289–316.

40 Rehman 2003: 377; see also http://www.unesco.org/education; and http://www.unicef.org/.

41 For the convention dealing with the worst forms of child labor, see http://ilo.org/global/lang–en/index.htm. Enter "child labor 182" in the site's search engine.

42 For the 1980 child abduction convention, see http://www.hcch.net/ > Child Abduction Section; and for the adoption convention, > Intercountry Adoption Section.

43   AP news story by Juan Carlos Lorca, May 22, 2007.

44   For the 1990 African Charter on Children, see http://www.africa-union.org/ > Documents > Treaties, Conventions & Protocols > scroll down by date to the charter on children; also for OAS protection of children, see http://www.oas.org/main/english > Documents > Treaties and Agreements > Multilateral Treaties > By Subject > Children (click on human rights, minors). And for the 1996 European children's treaty, refer to http://conventions.coe.int/Treaty/en/Treaties/Html/160.html.

45   This definition is compatible with the "UN Working Definition of Indigenous Peoples," UN Document E/CN.4/Sub. 2/ L 566, Chapt. II; or see the UN working definition in Wilmer 1993: 216.

46   For good general descriptions of the plight of indigenous peoples, see Wilmer, 1993: pp. 58–126; Anaya 1996: 95–126.

47   *Amnesty International: Maze of Injustice: The Failure to Protect Indigenous Women from Sexual Violence in the USA*, pp. 21–22, go to http://www.amnestyusa.org/women.

48   Useful background reading can be found at Douglas Sanders, "Sexual Orientation in International law," at http://www.ilga.org, pp. 1–23; and see Sander 1996: 67–106.

49   The article in the Treaty of Amsterdam can be read at http://europa.eu.int/eur-lex/en/treaties/dat/amsterdamn.htl > scroll down to Article 6 (a).

50   The status of homosexuality in Europe can be read in Sander's "Sexual Orientation in International Law."

51   "State of Homophobia: World Map on LGBT," at http://www.ilga.org/.

52   A good starting point for examining the UN's role on human rights is http://www.un.org/rights/. For a critical appraisal of this role, see Alston 1995; Mertus 2005; and see the Canadian NGO Human Rights Internet for additional evaluation at http://www.hri.ca/index.aspx > UN Information.

53   Further reading on these monitoring committees can be found at Gomez, 2005: 262–6; see also Donnelly 2003: 84–9.

54   Refer to http://www.un.org/english/ > Human Rights > Human Rights Council.

55   Go to http://www.coe.int > Commissioner for Human Rights; > European Court of Human Rights; and > Human Rights.

56   http://www.coe.int > Human Rights > European Social Charter; and see the EU's Charter of Fundamental Rights of the European Union at http://europa.eu/index_en.htm > Human Rights > Charter of Fundamental Rights.

57   Find at http://www.oas.org/main/english/ > OAS Sectors and Topics. Listed are human rights and specialized subjects on children, indigenous rights, and more.

58   Read about at http://www.oas.org/main/english > Inter-American System > Inter-American Commission.

59   See http://www.oas.org/main/english > Inter-American System > Inter-American Court of Human Rights.

60   Find at http://www.africa-union.org/root/au/organs/The_Commission_en.htm.

61   See, http://www.africa-union.org/root/au/index/index.htm > AU Organs > The Court of Justice.

62   Go to http://www.al-bab.com/arab/docs/league.htm > special topics > human rights.

63   For directories on the many human rights NGOs, go to http://www.idealist.org; or to the website of Human Rights Internet at http://www.hri.ca/.

64   Refer to http://www.ohchr.org/english/ > International Law > scroll down to Promotion and Protection of Human Rights.

65   Zerk 2006: esp. 7–59. The point about human rights policy reports is on p. 42; Love and Love 2003: 98–9.

There must be a fundamental change of politics and economics if the planet is to stay alive ... Eco-justice is nothing less than taking seriously the destiny of humanity and the planet on which we live. If there is a future, it will be green. (Petra Kelly)

Regarding natural catastrophe: "We don't have generations now, it's years, at best. Climatic natural thresholds – we don't know where they are. Nature is the timekeeper, and we can't see the clock. (Lester Brown)

11

The Global Environment
in Jeopardy

Contents

Threats to the world's **environment**, the physical features of the planet and their interaction, have helped crystallize the commonly held view that humankind faces an imperiled future. Humankind has occupied Earth for thousands of years but, by the early twenty-first century, the human "footprint" on this shared world has created unprecedented danger for well over six billion people who wish not only to survive but to live well materially. Confronting humankind today are, among other harms, fouled air, global warming and melting polar ice caps, polluted oceans, shortages of fresh water needed for drinking and irrigation, depleted soil quality, shrinking forests, and the rapid loss of many animals and plants to extinction.

A jeopardized world environment does not easily rise to the top of everyone's priority list in the way that a war or economic depression does. Nonetheless, environmental problems are a set of slow-motion crises that grind away with relentless effect. Facing these problems are about two hundred governments controlling varying amounts of the Earth's territories and representing a wide range of interest in the environment as well as differing capability to do something about environmental problems. Then there are the gigantic international spaces of the open seas, outer space, and Antarctica, known as the global commons, also requiring protection. A politically fractured world makes it especially hard to deal with environmental issues that stretch across regions and even the globe. Fortunately, foot-dragging states are pushed to take some positive steps by an active global civil society made up of IGOs and many NGOs specializing in the environment. The various actors of this global society regrettably have been far more successful at generating hundreds of environmental treaties than achieving treaty enforcement and environmental reform.

This chapter begins with a brief history of the international environmental movement, a relatively recent phenomenon compared to traditional topics of international law such as diplomacy and warfare. The global environment is then divided into its various natural dimensions, each being given a chapter section. Regimes of rules and norms have built up around each of these with varying degrees of success. They are the Earth's atmosphere, the oceans and rivers, soil and desertification, forests, and wildlife. A chapter section will also be devoted to the special issues of environmental impact on the human rights of women and indigenous peoples and the role that environmental scarcity plays in conflicts and warfare. Finally, the critical part played by a very active global civil society to encourage all actors to focus on a progressive environmental agenda will be described.

A Brief History of Environmental Developments

The 1972 UN Conference on the Human Environment (the Stockholm Conference) is usually referred to as the beginning of the new sub-field of international environmental law (Magraw & Vinogradove 1995: see also French 2000: 144). Actually there were earlier treaties, aimed at conservation, such as the 1900 *Convention for the Preservation of Wild Animals, Birds and Fish in Africa* and the 1911 *Treaty for the Preservation and Protection of Fur Seals*. These kinds of conventions, however, were for the "preservation" of a particular animal species for future "harvesting" and not the "protection" of the species as a valued participant in the animal kingdom. Since 1972, 900 to 1,000 environmental agreements have been created bilaterally, regionally, and at the global level (Vig 1999: 2; Bell 2006: 107). In general, these treaties represent a move away from an *anthropocentric* function centered on human needs and wants and one toward a *biocentrism* calling for the protection of animals and plant life and the natural features of the planet such as air and water quality for their own sake.

Only a generation old, the rapidly developing field of international environmental law has produced impressive conventions, treaties, principles, and reports. The Stockholm Conference was attended by 113 states and several hundred governmental agencies and NGOs.[1] In less than two weeks this conference accomplished a lot. While no treaties were produced, the *Stockholm Declaration on the Human Environment*, with 26 principles, was accepted. Probably the most cited is Principle 21, which recognizes a state's sovereign rights over its own resources as well as state responsibility for environmental damages caused to another's territory. At this conference, an *Action Plan* with 109 recommendations was also produced. The most concrete contribution was the creation of the UN Environment Program (UNEP) headquartered in Nairobi, Kenya, which coordinates research and policy at the global level. Many countries followed up by creating their own national departments or ministries for dealing with environmental concerns. Perhaps the single most important, lasting accomplishment was to attune governments and public opinion to the notion that worldwide cooperation is needed to cope with global environmental problems.

The World Charter for Nature was accepted at a Nairobi conference in 1982 with 111 states voting for it and only the United States voting against.[2] The relatively new government of President Ronald Reagan was not convinced that the environment needed protection from business practices. This Charter is a brief document best known for its five General Principles, which draw attention to the protection of all life forms for their own sake instead of a focus only on a salubrious setting for human living as was the emphasis at Stockholm a decade earlier.

One of the best known contributions to environmental principles is the report of the 1987 *World Commission on Environment and Development*, commissioned by the UN General Assembly, but better known as the Bruntland Commission, named after its distinguished chair. Chair Gro Harlem Bruntland, a former prime minister of Norway, led 23 commissioners for 4 years in visits to many countries, addressing a growing concern over the deterioration of the human environment and natural resources and the implications for economic and social development. The 1987 report of the commission, titled *Our Common Future,* (UN 1987) emphasized the most appropriate ways to practice **sustainable development**. This concept refers to economic development that provides for the needs of the present generation without compromising future generations' needs by overusing and harming the environment. A few years later in 1992, another environmental conference would create the Commission on Sustainable Development (CSD). It would answer to one of the six principal bodies of the UN, the Economic and Social Council.

During this period, some countries began to "green" their international trade relations by placing environmental rules on imports and exports, often causing court cases and arbitration procedures to arise. The famous 1988 *Danish Bottle* case is now an important development in environmental history. This case began in 1977 when Denmark required returnable bottles for imported beer and soft drinks instead of cans. Basically, the European Court of Justice, now of the EU, supported this environmental requirement and, in time, the EU harmonized "green rules" for trade among its now 27-state membership. The best known environmental conference is the 1992 *UN Conference on Environment and Development*, commonly called the Earth Summit. It was held in Rio de Janeiro, Brazil and is one of the largest conferences ever held regardless of the subject. In attendance were 178 national delegations with over 100 presidents and prime ministers making appearances for at least part of the 11-day program. Also in attendance were over 1,400 environmental NGOs working out of the parallel NGO Forum and an estimated 8,000 journalists. The size was much larger than the Stockholm Conference not only because environmental issues had moved further up the global agenda in importance during the intervening 20 years, but also because the Cold War's end left the world in high spirits over all the positive good that might be achieved.

The immediate accomplishments were the Rio Declaration, or Earth Charter, calling on both developed and developing states to confront the challenges of sustainable development, *Agenda 21*, with 800 pages outlining the implementation of sustainable development, and the *Forest Principles*, calling for the conservation and sustainable development of all types of forests.

While these three sets of principles are significant accomplishments, the Earth Summit is especially distinguished through its creation of two treaties opened for ratification by states. Principles are soft law and represent strong norms for states to comply with, but treaties are hard law and operate at the pinnacle of expectations about state compliance. The two treaties are the *Framework Convention on Climate Change*, dealing with greenhouse gases, and the *Convention on Biological Diversity*, recognizing the importance of scientific developments for the good of all humankind but also acknowledging the property rights of countries possessing shares of such diversity.[3] Following a decade of sober reflection over the Cold War's end, less enthusiasm characterized the Johannesburg *World Summit on Sustainable Development*, sometimes called Earth Summit Two. Despite the appearance of a growing number of environmental treaties, environmental conditions had further deteriorated, optimism about the future was at low ebb, and the prospects for cooperation between the richer and poorer states were

---

Box 11.1 The Earth Charter

The Earth Charter is a stronger set of norms and goals than a majority of states have been willing to support, at least so far. It involves a firm moral commitment by states to build democracies and practice peace on the way to a healthy global ecosystem that can provide for humankind's social and economic needs in a sustainable manner. An early draft of the Earth Charter was presented at the 1992 Earth Summit but turned down in favor of the milder Rio Declaration. In 1994, the draft version attracted the support of Maurice Strong (the former Secretary-General of the Earth Summit) of the NGO Earth Council and Mikhail Gorbachev (the last chief executive of the Soviet Union), now heads Green Cross International, an environmental NGO. These two formed an Earth Charter Commission in 1997 and completed the Earth Charter in 2000.

The completed Earth Charter was submitted to the 2002 the World Summit on Sustainable Development in Johannesburg, South Africa, with much state support but again was not accepted by a global environmental conference. Although the Earth Charter may not represent an achievable consensus among a majority of states, this charter has the support of many actors of international society, including many state leaders, 2,500 environmental NGOs, and IGOs such as UNESCO.

Source: The Earth Charter and its history can be found at http://earthcharterinaction. org/.

weaker (Van de Veer 2003: 55–60). The Johannesburg Declaration on Sustainable Development was adopted, but no treaties were promulgated. The Johannesburg Declaration did at least call attention to the litany of problems that make it diffi-cult for poor, developing states to protect their share of the global environment. These problems include hunger, disease, armed conflict, corruption, terrorism, and ethnic violence, among others.[4]

A gloomy outlook on the environment is not inappropriate, at least according to the Millennium Ecosystem Assessment commissioned by Secretary-General Kofi Annan in 2000 and reported in 2005, with 1,360 environmental experts taking part worldwide. An **ecosystem** involves a special perspective on the environment. A healthy ecosystem is one in which animals, plants, and humans are able to interact with their physical environment in a way that meets their needs and allows them to function successfully. The assessment study found that many of the resources needed for sustaining life are being degraded.[5]

Actually a consensus among environmentalists is lacking over how bad environ-mental problems are and just what needs to be done. Varying opinions on these problems are reflected as well among and within governments, IGOs, and NGOs, thus hampering concerted policy remedies. Unfortunately, a litmus test that can either prove or disprove **ecocide** – the destruction of the natural environment as a result of human activity – is unavailable and so debates over the environment con-tinue. The alarmists believe time is running out and environmental collapse is a rising crisis. In the early 1970s, Donnella Meadows and associates, using a computer model, predicted that a world of finite resources would soon face serious limits to growth.[6] Since the 1960s, Paul and Anne Erhlich have written pessimistic accounts of rapid population growth and its impact on scarce resources.[7] Recently ex-Vice President Al Gore's documentary, *An Inconvenient Truth*, resonated with millions of viewers over his deep concern for global warming and the resulting melting polar ice caps and rising seas that could turn millions of people into refugees. Gore's documentary won a 2007 Oscar, and he shared the 2007 Nobel Peace Prize with the UN Intergovernmental Panel on Climate Change (IPCC)), led chiefly by Susan Solomon.

Other writings have pointed to serious problems but offer a solution claiming that time is available to carry out reforms, if only proper action is taken. Rachael Carson's classic 1962 book, *Silent Spring*, convinced many governments to stop using the pesticide DDT to save birdlife (Carson 1962). To encourage the Stockholm Conference to move toward environmental reform in time, Barbara Ward and René Dubos wrote the 1972 book, *Only One Earth: The Care and Maintenance of a Small Planet* (1972). Finally, a list of important writers on the environment would not be complete without referring to an eco-optimist. In an impressive *tour de force*, Danish political scientist Bjørn Lomborg, in *The Skeptical Environmentalist*, covered almost every imaginable environmental issue while arguing that the world still basically possesses a healthy environment (2001). These authors are but a few of those who have contributed to a large and rich body of environmental literature.

The problems facing environmentalists, whether they are located in the scholarly community, employed by IGOs such as the UNEP, or engaged with NGOs like the well-known Greenpeace, are truly obdurate and resist the reforms intended by environmental law. The three core variables of population size, economic growth, and technological developments combine to make systematic environmental reform for the planet problematical at best.

Obviously more people inhabiting Earth means more resources will be consumed and pollution will increase. Today's 6.6 billion people already place a great weight on the **carrying capacity** of the planet, the ability of an ecosystem to remain healthy and able to meet the needs of the species that inhabit it. In this case, the ecosystem is global. By the middle of the twenty-first century, the human population could reach 9.3 billion, although estimates of future population growth vary. Ninety percent of population growth is occurring in Third World countries where it is a sensitive cultural issue involving women's role in society. Women are expected to have multiple children, and a woman's status may depend on the number of sons she bears. The best hope for bringing population size under control is for women to be allowed the choice of wanting *more for their children* and not *more children*. Anne and Paul Ehrlich, as well as the NGO Population Connection, have long advocated a policy of **zero population growth** (ZPG), which calls for a couple to have only two children to replace themselves.[8] If this policy were followed, a **steady state** might occur with the human population using natural resources no faster than they can be replenished.

Today's human population is probably already living beyond Earth's means, consuming more forests, soil, fresh water, and other resources than the planet can afford (Flavin & Gardner 2005: 15–16). Environmentalists' strategic goal of sustainable development may be rendered impossible to achieve (Brown 2008: 7; Salzman & Thompson 2003: 25–6). The market forces prevalent in the world are programmed to respond to the needs and wants of growing numbers of people, not the creation of a steady-state planet. The pressure for more economic growth, and the extraction of natural resources that goes with it, is enormous especially among Third World populations increasingly aware of the gap between their lives and the affluence of the Western lifestyle.

Perhaps the best hope rests with technological improvements. Technology has allowed humankind to extract, transform, consume and discard the substances of nature as people have seen fit, sometimes recklessly, yet it has another side. Technology also allows for the more efficient use of resources, such as drip irrigation, hybrid cars, wind turbines, and solar panels, among many other helpful devices. Ultimately, the wise use of technology can only buy time as population growth and consumption rates must be brought into balance with what Earth can provide.

Atmosphere

The most far-reaching theoretical understanding of the planet's environment is the **Gaia Hypothesis**, first suggested by novelist William Golding, but brought into scientific circles by atmospheric chemist James Lovelock. He named his hypothesis after the ancient Greek goddess whose task was to nurture and care for Earth.

Lovelock took the view that the **biosphere** of the planet – the layers of soil, ocean, climate, and air that envelop Earth and sustain all animal and plant life – is a living super organism. Lovelock's approach is *holistic* in the sense that the Earth amounts to an organic whole greater than its elements. For him, the elements are interdependent and so damage to one part of the biosphere can easily spread to other parts (Myers 1993; Lovelock 2003).

Harmful interference has occurred all across the biosphere because of the human tendency to approach the environment with an anthropocentric outlook that places people at the center of existence, with environmental resources completely at their disposal for exploitation. No dimension of the biosphere has been abused more than the **atmosphere**, the envelope of gases, or air, surrounding the planet. Human interference with the atmosphere can range from cigarette smoke to clouds of nuclear radiation resulting from testing nuclear bombs, an activity that may have passed into history. The most persistent threat to the atmosphere comes as a by-product of decades of industrialization and modern living, including the use of multiple millions of automobiles and trucks around the world and the widespread use of refrigeration and air conditioning. The energy sources supporting our advanced industrial system are still heavily dependent on coal-burning furnaces and fossil fuels for internal combustion motors. The waste products from the uses of these energy sources are carbon monoxide and dioxide, sulfur dioxide, and nitrogen oxide. Escaping gases still used in the cooling systems of many countries can cause or worsen a litany of health issues, such as asthma, bronchitis, cancer and heart conditions, to name but a few.

Although air pollution remains a serious health threat in most countries, many countries in the West have had considerable success at improving their air quality, and more newly industrialized ones are trying to do the same. What has increasingly come to be recognized is that these problems are not operating just at the national level but are transnational and spill over into regional and global arenas, thus making air pollution an appropriate subject of international law. For instance, China's remarkable economic success has come at a price, one of the worst cases of air pollution in the world. China's pollution is easily measured on the Pacific coast of the United States, a country that has long shared its own air pollution with other states, especially Canada.

International environmental law is often thought to have begun with the *Trail Smelter* arbitration case between Canada and the United States. A Canadian smelter company located in British Columbia, just 12 miles north of the state of Washington, emitted a large amount of sulfur dioxide as a form of air pollution between 1926 and 1937, causing much damage to privately owned agricultural land and forests. Decisions by a joint commission and then an arbitration panel decided on financial compensation for American farmers and called for remedial measures to avoid a reoccurrence of this misfortune. With no environmental treaty to draw on, the commissioners and arbiters used a precedent from the US federal system, in which one federal state is responsible for harm it does to another. As a source of international law, relevant principles have often been drawn from domestic experiences. It was an easy step in the Trail Smelter case to apply the international legal principle of *state responsibility*, meaning that sovereign states cannot allow their territories to be used in a way that causes harm to another country.[9] Today, the mention of the *Trail Smelter* case will readily be identified with the beginnings of international environmental law but, at the time, the case was more likely viewed as an issue of state responsibility. The role of this case in helping launch the new field of environmental international law was probably unforeseen.

One of the most dangerous kinds of air pollution is nuclear radiation released by the atmospheric testing of atomic and hydrogen bombs during the Cold War, even if the explosions were on a remote Pacific island. Air currents can carry radiation great distances. In 1954, the United States made a financial settlement for exposing the crew of a Japanese fishing boat named the *Fukuryu Maru* to nuclear radiation from the testing of nuclear bombs near the Marshall Islands and later made a financial arrangement for the people of Bikini Island who had to abandon their homes permanently. In 1973–4, Australia and New Zealand brought separate but similar cases before the International Court of Justice (ICJ) calling for a halt to French atmospheric tests, claiming that radiation would damage their peoples and territories. The court ordered France to cease the tests while the cases were under consideration, an order the French did not respect at first. Shortly afterward, however, the French government changed policy and decided to halt atmospheric testing, thus ending legal action before the ICJ.[10] It is hard to imagine that the ICJ would not have ruled against France had the cases gone forward. France and other technologically advanced nuclear powers gradually moved tests underground and finally halted even these tests after accepting the 1996 Comprehensive Test Ban Treaty. The most modern nuclear-armed states have been able to convert to computer models that permit testing by simulation.

A major step forward in the legal protection of the atmosphere was the first convention binding states to rules governing a broad region, the 1979 *Geneva Convention on Long-Range Transboundary Air Pollution* (LRTAP). This convention was sponsored by the UN Economic Commission for Europe, but it might not have come about without the support and expertise of a community of scientists working together across national boundary lines. The worst pattern the scientists noted involved the tall smoke stacks of Great Britain and Germany, pushing polluted smoke into air streams high enough to carry sulfur dioxide and other pollutants to Scandinavian forests. These researchers had studied and reported on the acidification effects from sulfur for two decades before European states plus Canada and the United States ratified the LRTAP. This treaty entered into force in 1983 and now has over 50 state parties. The LRTAP is designed as a framework treaty, meaning that it is open for the addition of protocols that can deal with specific problems as they arise and are recognized. There are presently eight protocols, such as the 1988 *Protocol on Control of Nitrogen Oxide* and the 1998 *Protocol on Persistent Organic Pollutants*, or POPs.[11]

Among the many environmental worries that confront the planet, none exceeds *global warming* for the attention that it has received. The atmospheric belt around Earth traps much of the sun's warmth and contains it in a way known as the "greenhouse effect." Actually this is a natural occurrence that allowed animal and plant life to develop. Were it not for the greenhouse effect, the Earth would be cold and lifeless. The

problem arises when human activities, such as burning coal and wood and using petroleum products to fuel millions of cars and other vehicles, add an unnaturally large
volume of gases to the atmosphere that cause temperatures to rise and stay at injurious
levels. Since 1991, the NGO World Resources Institute has ranked countries with a
Greenhouse Index,[12] and many states have tried to improve their records. China and
the United States are the worst offenders releasing harmful emissions such as carbon
dioxide, with China's surging industries taking this country into the lead. The pollution in Beijing was so bad during the 2008 Summer Olympics that some athletes
trained in neighboring countries and arrived in China just in time for their sports
event. Partially masking the warming effect on China and other parts of Asia is a phenomenon known as the "Asian brown cloud," which is made up of relatively dense
carbon and other pollutants. While reducing temperatures slightly, this cloud also
reduces rainfall and denies crops some of the sun's radiation needed for growing.

Concern over global warming continues to be on the rise, and the priority this
issue has received is reflected in the awarding of the 2007 Nobel Peace Prize for work
in this area. The 2007/8 UN Development Program issue of the *Human Development
Report: Fighting Climate Change* gave much of its space to the problem. The appre-
hension over global warming has percolated down from IGOs, governments' environmental departments and university scientists to the general public. People are
voluntarily identifying ways to lighten their impact on global warming. College dor-
mitories are trying to reduce electrical usage, families are buying energy-efficient
appliances, and some buyers of cars want fuel-efficient hybrids. The impact individuals or families can have on climate change through carbon emissions has come
to be known as their "carbon footprint." The NGO, the Nature Conservancy, offers
on its website a "carbon footprint calculator" to measure an individual's or group's
production of carbon dioxide and other greenhouse gases.[13] The UN's World
Environmental Day, June 5, had the theme in 2008 of "Kick the Carbon Habit."

Global warming has come to the forefront among environmental dangers because
of the range of damage it can cause. The IPCC has estimated that sea levels will rise
from only a few degrees increase in temperature, a serious threat for countries with
low-lying coastal plains and numerous island states spread about the world, a problem that could create millions of desperate refugees who will have to find a place to
flee to higher ground. The rise in sea level will come from melting glaciers, the ice
caps at the North and South Poles, as well as the ice sheet covering much of Greenland.
The areas at the poles appear to be melting twice as fast as other ice fields. Loss of ice
and snow at the poles is especially devastating because of the desirability of the
albedo effect. This effect results from the white surfaces at the poles reflecting sun-
light off the Earth's surface, which helps cool the planet. The danger of the frozen
Arctic Sea completely melting in summer is very real. If global warming continues,
devastating effects will happen not only for the 155,000 Inuit people living in the
circumpolar region, but also for polar bears, seals, and bird life. In the temperate
zone, food chains will be affected through crop failures, with famine to follow, and
even the spread of tropical diseases.[14]

As offered by Bjørn Lomborg in his *Cool It: The Skeptical Environmentalist's Guide
to Global Warming*, a cautionary note about global warming is worth keeping in

---

Box 11.2 Alliance of Small Island States

Consisting of 43 members, the Alliance of Small Island States (AOSIS) is based on both small states with low-lying coasts and many island states. These states are in every region of the world and include, for example, Aruba, Belize, the Maldives, Nauru, Puerto Rico, the Seychelles, and Tonga. The AOSIS represents 5 percent of the world's population.

These states have much to worry about regarding global warming and the resulting melting of glaciers and polar ice caps. It has been speculated that if all the ice of Greenland melted, the world's oceans would rise 20 feet, inundating most of the AOSIS states. The reality is that global ice-melting is a matter of degree, but this problem is a legitimate concern and potentially could turn toward disaster. If the oceans rose significantly, tens of millions of disaster-refugees would join the approximately 35 million mostly conflict refugees that the International Refugee Organization struggles to help.

Source: See http://www.sidsnet.org/aosis/.

---

mind. While not denying that global warming is a serious problem, he sees it as less apocalyptic as a crisis than other environmentalists see it and instead urges the public, governments, and scientists to avoid excitable overreactions. Lomborg fears overreaction will launch terribly expensive programs that may not work. Lomborg prefers a slow, calm approach focusing on the careful development of technology that could take a century to bring global warming under control. It is always healthy intellectually, and for policy reasons, to consider challenging points of view, but Lomborg's *Cool It* is up against some very weighty evidence marshaled by Lester Brown's Earth Policy Institute and the several thousand scientists affiliated with the IPCC, environmentalists who would argue that the danger is closer and more serious than Lomborg allows.[15]

The voluntary work of citizens around the world and environmental NGOs are helpful, but the role of IGOs and states at putting environmental treaties in place is critical since these are better able to bring about reform through the creation of norms and rules. One of the major accomplishments of the 1992 Earth Summit was the development of the *UN Framework Convention on Climate Change* (UNFCCC), which entered into force in 1994 after the 50th ratification was deposited in 1993, and now has the support of 192 states. As a framework convention, it offered a future method for states to accept protocols for stabilizing levels of greenhouse gases and even reducing them.[16]

Lengthy negotiations finally produced the *Kyoto Protocol* of the UNFCCC, which was signed in Kyoto, Japan in 1997, but it did not enter into force until 2005.[17] A sufficient number of states had to ratify so as to account for at least 55 percent of the total carbon dioxide emissions released in 1990, with this year having been chosen as a baseline. Under the protocol, the signatories are expected to reduce their greenhouse gases to 1990 levels, or below, during the 2008–12 period. Unlike many environmental treaties, the Kyoto arrangement has an enforcement mechanism with signatories required to monitor and keep precise records of their emissions. The parties backing the Kyoto Protocol are 183 in number. By 2012, a new protocol is to be negotiated and ready to replace the present one.

The Kyoto Protocol has been able to enjoy a measure of success without the endorsement of the reigning hegemon, in this case one that has played an obstructionist role in environmental matters. The United States readily signed and ratified the UNFCCC, but only signed the Kyoto Protocol in 1998 without a follow-up ratification. After 2000, the new presidency of George W. Bush proved resistant to reducing greenhouse gases because of the costs US energy and manufacturing interests would have to bear. These interests were concerned that developing the technology needed to protect the atmosphere would eat into profits (Eckersley 2004: 104–5). President Bush especially disliked the provision in the Kyoto Protocol that places a heavier burden of commitment on the economically developed Western states, under the principle of "common but differentiated responsibilities," than was the case for Third World countries. Some of the Third World states, especially China and India, have become economic dynamos able to compete forcefully with Western industries while enjoying less stringent environmental rules.

While meeting in Bali, Indonesia, in December 2007, the Conference of Parties (COP), or parties to the Kyoto Protocol, brought to a head US resistance to reducing greenhouse gases. This country faced strong pressure from most of the other states in attendance. Yet, of the industrialized European states, less than half are on track to meet Kyoto expectations concerning air quality, a fact revealed just before the December 2008 climate conference held in Poznan, Poland. The best hope for a replacement agreement to the Kyoto Protocol will be at the UN climate conference in Copenhagen, Denmark in 2009. The United States, having elected Democrat Barack Obama President in November 2008, may shift to a priority of carbon emissions limits and play a more constructive role at climate conferences.

Another major atmospheric concern has been *ozone depletion*. This issue is not discussed as much as global warming because the ozone protection regime has been relatively successful. Cooperation among states came quickly as a result of convincing scientific evidence (Chasek 2003: 193, 224; Salzman & Thompson 2003: 11). Ozone is a simple molecule of three oxygen atoms and concentrated as a thin layer in the middle of the stratosphere. It plays a crucial role in breaking up the sun's ultra-violent rays that otherwise can cause skin cancer, harm the photosynthesis process of some crops, cause cataracts on human eyes, and kill plankton, a microscopic floating plant critical to the marine food chain. The chief culprit for depleting the ozone layer is chlorofluorocarbons (CFCs), which leaked into the atmosphere from refrigeration and air conditioning devices. CFCs release chlorine that destroys ozone molecules. Ironically, the variant CFC-12, once used widely in air conditioning, was regarded in the 1920s as a safe substitute for the dangerous ammonia and sulfur dioxide refrigerants then in use in refrigerators (Salzman & Thompson 2003: 11).

In 1979, after a team of British scientists found a huge hole in the ozone layer over the Antarctic, states which are usually slow to reform moved with alacrity to do something about the problem. The UNEP sponsored a conference that led to the creation and ratification of the 1985 *Vienna Convention for the Protection of the Ozone Layer* that entered into force in 1988 and now has 193 parties. It called for cooperation in research among countries and IGOs and listed harmful chemicals, in addition to CFCs, to be better controlled or eliminated. Perhaps its most important provision was to call for COP meetings which could devise protocols with tougher rules. The December 1–12, 2008, climate conference in Poznan had as a top priority the goal of recharging the Kyoto process. A conference called the World Climate Conference–3 is to take place in September 2009.

Very quickly the COP came up with the 1987 *Montreal Protocol on Substances That Deplete the Ozone Layer*, which entered into force in 1989. A primary aim of this convention was to protect human health since the sun's rays, without the filter of the ozone layer, has been connected to skin cancer. Parties to the convention would be obliged to control releases of chlorofluorocarbons that destroy ozone. Follow-up meetings of the COP during the 1990s served to tighten standards and compliance, although some leeway was granted to developing states. The Montreal Protocol also has over 190 states supporting it. It was one of the first environmental reforms to confront a global problem and was precautionary in nature since it aimed to stop a growing crisis before it could mature into a reality (Salzman & Thompson 2003: 11). Scott Barrett finds that of several hundred environmental treaties he studied, few alter state behavior appreciably, but the big exception is the Montreal Protocol (Barrett 2005: xi). It is not uncommon for specialists in international environmental law to cite this protocol as the most successful among the hundreds of environmental agreements.

Until the world's energy needs can be met in a more environmentally friendly way, as with new technology, it may be impossible to clean up the world's atmosphere through reforms brought by international environmental law. Save for developing safe and practical hydrogen energy mechanisms that can be threaded through a country's energy grid, prospects for freeing the planet from oil and coal dependence are limited. A few new technologies are in place but provide only a small amount of the energy needed to run the world. Some 60 million Europeans get their residential electricity from wind farms, 40 million Chinese have hot water from solar water heaters, and Iceland heats 90 percent of its homes with underground thermal energy (Brown 2008: 21). Other examples exist but, for the foreseeable future, the vast majority of the world's population are likely to rely on fossil fuels and coal-fired furnaces that will pollute on a massive scale.

Renewed interest in nuclear power has returned to Europe and some other places despite the 1986 Chernobyl meltdown that spread dangerous radioactivity across northern Europe. Nuclear energy is the cleanest most efficient energy source, but its use has the drawback of requiring the permanent storage of spent radioactive fuel. Nevertheless, new nuclear plants are currently being built, adding to the 450 plants already in existence in 30 countries (Birnie & Boyle 2004: 454). The rise in the number of nuclear plants is found most recently in Europe and the United States, but with some increase in Third World continues. France's array of nuclear plants makes it energy-independent for electricity and even able to deliver it to other countries. Despite concerns over nuclear energy sources, even NGO Greenpeace has admitted that nuclear energy is the only clean energy source that currently can replace fossil fuels on a massive scale. Although nuclear plants are much safer today, one problem remains as serious. All countries with nuclear reactors have to find a way to store spent radioactive fuel. The spent fuel must be stored in a manner so that it cannot leak endangering public health, and it has to be safeguarded from terrorists and states ambitious to have nuclear weapons. The United States continues to struggle with nuclear waste storage sites scattered around the country rather than place its spent fuel in the well-prepared facilities under the Yucca Mountain in Nevada. Domestic politics continue to block the move of the spent fuel to the Nevada location. While these facilities are the best prepared, many Americans take a "not in my backyard" stance and insist each of the 50 states of the federal system must store its own spent fuel.

Much attention has been given recently to bio-fuels, but its use cuts into food supplies of corn, soybeans, and sugar (Hunt & Sawin 2006: 66–7). Thousands of hydroelectric dams have been built and currently supply 19 percent of the world's electrical needs. Viable places for their construction are available in the Third World, but unfortunately these dams, and the lakes behind them, displace millions of people and damage a river's varied life forms, including fish stocks and numerous plants (Postel 2006: 42–5). China is nearly finished with its gigantic Three Gorges Dam on the Yangtze River, with only the locks for moving boats around the dam to be completed. This project has mortified many environmentalists. So far, the various alternatives to coal and oil have not proven to be the holy grail for solving the energy conundrum. Protecting the Earth's atmosphere has eluded the grasp of humankind. The one piece of good news for the atmosphere remains the Montreal Protocol's protection of the ozone layer.

Water

For many people, the oceans and the powerful rivers that flow into them appear so vast that they should be able to supply an unlimited amount of water and food resources and provide a bottomless "sink" for disposing of wastes. Oceans and rivers are not limitless, however. Fearing that pollution of the world's waters and excessive uses of resources have created a huge threat to the viability of these waters, marine biologists and environmentalists consider restorative and protective actions to be long overdue.

Fresh water is a resource that people easily take for granted. Three-fourths of the planet is covered by water but 97 percent of it is salt water. For several generations, humankind has been fouling and exhausting a precious resource necessary for all life on the planet. Human need for fresh water will only increase with the growth of the world's population, with the use of water continuing to double in shorter spans of time (Postel 2006; Brown 2008: 68–84). More than one billion people around the world presently lack safe drinking water. Millions of women and children spend hours every day trekking miles to fetch water to their homes for drinking and cooking (Postel 1994: 6). Water shortages force people to drink water tainted by industrial chemicals and limit the amount of crops farmers can grow. A scarcity of good water is not only a problem in the Third World but is almost a universal concern. Iceland is one of the few countries that has an abundance of water. Farmers, cities, and resort communities compete for water in the richest countries. Perhaps the clearest measure of water's threatened status is that underground aquifers around the world are losing water faster than it is being replenished. Glaciers and snow packs around the world, that supply the head waters of many rivers, are disappearing at an alarming rate.[18] And the same can be said of large lakes, such as Lake Chad in Africa and Lake Aral in southwestern Asia, drained down to a small portion of their former size to irrigate crops. One of the largest freshwater lakes in the world is Lake Baikal in Russia's Siberia, a lake long despoiled by a paper mill plant. Since the collapse of the Soviet Union, activists have made some progress at protecting the lake, but still face some harassment from authorities.

In 1992, the International Conference on Water and the Environment met in Dublin, Ireland and produced four key principles to guide the world's water policy; these principles are known as the *Dublin Principles*. Briefly, they are: (1) water is a finite and vulnerable resource; (2) all users of water should participate in planning water usage; (3) women play a central role regarding water; and (4) water is an economic good and should be treated as such.

Serious concern over sharing fresh water at the international level began at least as early as 1911 at a meeting of publicists, or international law scholars, in Madrid, Spain. This meeting contributed ideas to the much better known 1966 *Helsinki Rules on the Uses of Waters of International Rivers*, which were written by publicists of the International Law Association.[19] The Helsinki Rules contain some articles on pollution and settling disputes, but "equitable utilization" of rivers shared by two or more states was the core concern. States sharing a so-called international river are known as **riparian states**. Fortunately for the sake of avoiding future conflicts, the United States's *Harmon Doctrine* of 1895 never gained traction at any later publicist meeting. US Attorney-General Judson Harmon had insisted that international law imposed no restraints on the United States's diversion of the Rio Grande River, and so the United States did not need to concern itself with whether a fair share of water was left for Mexico.

In 1970, the UN General Assembly decided to prepare something like the Helsinki Rules in treaty form, but what became the *UN Convention on the Law of Non-Navigational Uses of International Water Courses* was not ready for ratification until 1997. While today this convention has received less than half the necessary 35 ratifications to enter into force, it is recognized by jurists of the ICJ as an authoritative collection of customary law regarding international rivers. Hesitancy over ratification of this convention is probably due to the perception that it has not merely codified customary rules but has progressively developed the rules making for bolder international law. States, after all, are conservative about accepting new rules.

In a 2004 Berlin meeting, the International Law Association set out the *Berlin Rules on Water Resources* to update customary law developments since the 1966 Helsinki Rules. Compared to the older rules, the Berlin Rules are more advanced since they incorporate all customary law on national and international waters, environmental law, and even some human rights. For instance, Article 20 of the Berlin Rules calls for a special effort to protect indigenous peoples, and Article 21 requires compensation for any local community displaced when dams are built. It is too early to tell if the Berlin Rules will be as well accepted as the Helsinki Rules, with their simpler emphasis on the equitable sharing of rivers' waters.[20]

Numerous river basins are shared by two or more countries in many places around the world. It is not unusual for four to six riparian states to count on the water of the same river. The Danube River holds pride of place by originating in Germany and passing through or along the borders of nine other states. The surprise is that more conflict has not arisen over sharing rivers. In fact, some of the earliest cooperation in international relations started with the river commissions of Europe. Thomas Bernauer observes that the Central Commission for the Navigation of the Rhine River, founded in 1815, was the first IGO in history (1997: 170). Thomas F. Homer-Dixon, a specialist in environmental scarcity and conflict, regards conflict over rivers as potentially serious problems, but still notes that most conflict over river water is among competing groups within the same country (1999: 180).

Sharing the waters of rivers can still be a sharp international irritant in some cases, however. Iraq has long complained that Turkey's extensive dam system on the Euphrates River cuts down on its share of the Euphrates' water by half, and the Israeli occupation of the Palestinian territories has resulted in a stingy portion of water from the Jordan River and underground aquifers for Palestinians. The United States uses so much of the Colorado River that it is a trickle if it even makes it to Mexico; the United States tries to compensate its southern neighbor with free electricity generated from American dams on the same river. One of the most interesting river cases is the ICJ case known as the *Gabcikovo–Nagymaros Project* on the Danube River, which began to make its way through this global court in 1993, with a judgment in1997. The case evolved from a 1977 agreement between Czechoslovakia and Hungary during the communist era. They agreed to build together a set of locks for moving barges on the Danube. However, in 1989 Hungary reneged on the partnership, claiming the locks would cause environmental damages. Slovakia, continuing with the case after Czechoslovakia divided into the Czech and Slovakian Republics after the end of the Cold War, built its own locks but, in the process, limited Hungary's access to the Danube. The ICJ actually ruled against both parties, Hungary for breaching the treaty and Slovakia for restricting Hungary's use of the Danube with its unilaterally built locks. The court ordered the two states to negotiate the problem in good faith.[21]

While rivers and lakes fall within the sovereign control of the various states, the oceans and seas amount to a vast global commons shared by all and belong to no one. An unprecedented level of cooperation among states is necessary if the quality of ocean water and forms of marine life are to be protected. By the 1960s, trash from ships and boats floating in the oceans, oil slicks from ships ejecting spent fuel, and contaminated fish caught for food led to a general awareness that many countries were using the oceans as "sinks" for every kind waste, including household trash, hospital hazardous waste, raw sewage, fertilizer run-off, and even discarded radio-active devices. This awareness helped produce the important 1972 *Convention on the Prevention of Marine Pollution by Dumping of Wastes and Other Matter*. This is better known as the London Convention, which entered into force in 1975 and has 85 parties. A 1996 protocol strengthened the London Convention, which substantially reduced marine pollution.[22]

Close on the heels of the London Convention was the 1973 *International Convention for the Prevention of Pollution from Ships*, better known as the Marine Pollution Convention, or MARPOL. While the London Convention broadly covered ships, planes, and oil platforms, MARPOL focuses on all manner of harmful material that can be emitted from a ship such as sewage, burned fuel oil, garbage, and, above all, accidental oil spills from shipwrecks. Today 146 countries are parties and together account for virtually all of the world's ships. MARPOL was also strengthened by a protocol in 1978.[23] Today, this convention stands as the most important agreement for protecting the oceans and seas of the world.

One of the most impressive accomplishments in the history of multilateral diplomacy and international law is the development of the 1982 UN *Law of the Seas Convention* (UNLOS), one of the longest treaties to date and written by one of the largest international conferences ever held. Of its 17 parts and 9 Annexes, Part 12 is devoted entirely to "Protection of the Marine Environment." The UNLOS reinforces rules against dumping in the oceans or any other form of pollution caused by ships. One special contribution is its prohibition against "Land Based Marine Pollution" (LBMP).[24] Widely accepted among environmentalists is the realization that 70 percent or more of the pollution in the oceans originates from land-based sources.[25]

Complementing the global approach of the UNLOS is the UNEP's *Regional Seas Program*, which was launched just two years after the UNEP was set up and has become one of its most successful endeavors in its more than 30 years of operation. One hundred and forty countries take part in 13 regional efforts. Six of the 13 are directly administered by the UNEP while the rest are affiliated in "partner programs." They involve the Antarctica, the Arctic, the Black Sea, the Caspian Sea, the Mediterranean Sea, and the Red Sea and Gulf of Aden, among others.[26] The impressive success of the Regional Seas Program may have to do with countries willing to respond collectively as good neighbors to handle common problems close at hand that affect their economies and quality of life. When the 1982 UNLOS appeared, it encouraged regional seas cooperation in its Article 197 as well.

Two of the regional sea programs deserve special attention. The 1972 *Oslo Convention* encouraged 13 northeastern Atlantic states, from Portugal to Norway, to halt dumping in the ocean, and then "married" this convention with one to halt LBMP to form the 1992 *Convention for the Protection of the Marine Environment in the Northeastern Atlantic*, thus covering the effusion of pollution from both coastal areas and ships (Hunter, Salzman, & Zaelke 2002: 739–40). The other involves the Mediterranean Sea, covered under the 1976 *Convention for the Protection of the Mediterranean Sea against Pollution*. In the early 1970s, a more diverse set of governments – monarchies, communist regimes, democracies – and cultures surrounding the Mediterranean could hardly be imagined. Yet, the scientists of each country persuaded their respective governments to cooperate in order to save the quality of the deteriorating Mediterranean for commercial and sport fishing and tourism, an industry that would naturally appreciate the aesthetics of a clean and beautiful azure sea (Wagner 2003: 115–42).

Despite improvements in cooperation over reducing ocean pollution, one oceanic problem is growing worse and that is the seas' capacity for supplying food. Fishing technology in the form of factory ships, sonar, and sea-bed trawling with nets, among others, has allowed the world's fish catch to climb from 19 million tons in 1950 to 100 million tons today. The harvesting pressure on many species of fish has caused their serious decline. For instance, the highly prized blue fin tuna, wanted by the Japanese for their sushi bars, has been depleted by 94 percent (Brown 2008: 97–101). The UN FAO has reported that of the 17 major fisheries of the world's oceans, most have reached or exceeded their natural limits, with nine of them facing an especially dire future.[27] The collapse of the codfish stocks off Newfoundland ruined this fishery and harmed the economy of this province of Canada as well. Pollution of coastal wetlands, the nurseries of many fish species, is another major reason for the decline of fish stocks. Coral reefs likewise serve as a breeding area for many fish species as well as a rich plant life, are mostly close to shorelines, and are very fragile in the face of human intrusions. Dragging anchors, fishermen's nets, recreational divers, poison to stun and capture exotic fish for tanks, and most certainly the bleaching of reefs from global warming take their toll. Some coral reefs received relief from an unexpected source. Running counter to his usual policies on the environment, President George W. Bush created a huge marine national park in 2006, the Northwestern Hawaiian Islands National Monument, to protect marine life and a number of coral reefs.

Another problem for fishing is the creation of "dead zones" that sometimes cover thousands of square miles of ocean. Some scientists identify as many as 400 of these zones around the world. Dead zones are caused by a hypoxic state of low oxygen due to fertilizer run-off from farming in coastal areas. Occurring more frequently, these Dead Zones simply cannot support marine life (Postel 2006): 46). They destroy plankton, not only a fundamental element in the marine food chain, but an efficient plant for absorbing carbon. Some relatively well-managed fisheries, such as those in the waters around Alaska, New Zealand, and Iceland, are commendable examples of fishery management, but they will not nearly keep up with the growing numbers of people expecting to share in the world fish catch as an important food source. Unfortunately, humankind's capacity for cooperation has not begun to adequately regulate the fishing industry, which looks like an "every man for himself" operation and not a cooperative venture for the common good.

Soil

Just as fresh water can be replaced under favorable conditions, soil rich enough to grow crops can be renewed if weather conditions and human activities allow this process to happen. Unfortunately, soil erosion in many places is a strong pattern overpowering the replenishment topsoil. Arable land that can produce food for humans, livestock, and wildlife is definitely in decline (Postel 1994). As early as 1984, the UNEP reported that 35 percent of the Earth was in danger of experiencing **desertification,** the process of degrading arid and semi-arid areas into useless deserts (Kelleher & Klein 2006: 116–18). Wind, drought, overgrazing, poor farming practices, and cutting down forests are among the chief causes of soil degradation.

The UNEP report helped lead to the 1994 *UN Convention to Combat Desertification in Countries Experiencing Serious Drought and/or Desertification, Particularly in Africa* (UNCCD), with 193 states backing it.[28]

The UNCCD went into force in 1996 and contains detailed provisions for steps to take to combat the current assault on healthy land. In the preamble, the treaty recognizes the impact of desertification on food security, refugees, and the hardships women experience, at least in the Third World where their lives are closely tied to agriculture. The UNCCD calls for the eradication of poverty, because the poor often in desperation abuse the land by acts such as cutting down woodlands for firewood. The convention calls for help through research, financial aid, the transfer of technology, and education specific to the problem, all aiming to break up the pattern of poverty that contributes to desertification. The UNCCD ends with four annexes addressing particular conditions of troubled regions, with Africa heading the list. Especially of concern is the Sahara Desert that stretches across northern Africa and threatens to expand into the Sahel, the arid belt on the southern flank of the Sahara.

Although some of the numerous wars in Africa have been over the riches of diamonds, gold, and exotic lumber, it is environmental stress in the Sudan's arid Darfur region that contributes greatly to the conflict there among desperate peoples competing for the declining land needed to graze herds and grow food. The struggle to check desertification has not been particularly successful around the world overall. In some cases, such as Haiti, with its nearly treeless, gully-washed hills, this plight may be irreversible, condemning this country to the status of the poorest country in the western hemisphere. Every tropical storm that strikes this pitiful country washes away more of what is left of precious top soil.

One bright spot in the world is the nearly pristine continent of Antarctica. With a treaty regime dating back to 1959, the relevant countries have been willing to table territorial claims and agreed to keep this continent not only weapons-free but have produced an important environmental agreement, the 1991 *Protocol on Environmental Protection to the Antarctica Treaty* that entered into force in 1994.[29] It calls for extensive environmental protection of every kind, down to proper waste disposal on the part of scientific stations allowed to do research on the continent. The major threat to the Antarctica continent is global warming, with the most immediate threat being the loss of some of the massive ice field that covers the land mass.

Protecting the world's soil is critical if a world population rising to at least 9.5 billion in this century is to have enough to eat. Between the 1960s and 1980s, the "Green Revolution" – based on hybrid seeds producing bountiful crops, the widespread use of fertilizer and pesticides, and improved farm machinery – seemed to promise enough food for the world's population. This development appeared to cheat Thomas Malthus (1766–1834) out of any theoretical credibility (Malthus 1992). The Malthusian theory claimed population was growing at an exponential pace while food production advanced at only an arithmetical rate. Malthus expected great food shortages and mass starvation. A Malthusian crisis is probably not at hand, but food security has recently been shaken by several factors. The disruption of supplies by numerous wars, rising fuel costs, weather conditions, the growing purchasing power of the two most populous countries of China and India for grains, the conversion of corn for bio-fuel, and the expansion of cities and suburbs that gobble up farm land are making it difficult to supply enough food for everyone. Those hardest hit are the world's poor, who cannot afford to pay the recent spikes in food costs, with the sharpest edge of the problem occurring in Africa. Presently, it is safe to say that efforts to increase food supply are not keeping up with the hunger of millions of people. Finally, the Global Food Vault built by Norway in 2007 on Spitsbergen Island in the Norwegian Arctic, holding in safety seeds from all over the world, is an admirable contribution to humanity, but seeds frozen as a protection against plant diseases will always need healthy soil in which to grow.

Closely related to protecting soil is the issue of waste materials, which, except for space junk, finds its way into the Earth's land crust in some way unless it can be recycled for further use. Humans are messy animals, especially since the industrial age has allowed enormous amounts of natural resources to be converted into something people want. Then once done with their "wants," people discard and litter everywhere they go. China recently launched a program of cleaning up its face of Mt Everest that includes removing everything from backpacks and tents to the bodies of failed climbers.

Much more serious than litter are the hazardous and often radioactive wastes involving hundreds of chemicals and materials and how to properly dispose of these. Most modern industrial countries have become fairly adept at controlling and disposing of hazardous wastes, but the temptation to dispose of these in an inappropriate way to save money has occurred in all countries. On occasion, some modern countries have shipped wastes to poor Third World countries desperate for cash, a practice derisively called "environmental imperialism." A maturing international norm that wastes should be handled within the country that created them has tightened the grip on this kind of international trade, especially when the waste is of a hazardous nature. Non-hazardous waste, if it can be recycled, has led to a robust trade between some countries. One of the largest exports from the United States to resource-hungry China is waste paper, plastic bottles, and aluminum cans, already separated and packed into shipping containers. Trade in recyclables, however, has slowed to a crawl with the 2008–9 world recession.

When outrageous incidents of reckless dumping of hazardous waste in Third World countries came to light, treaties on this subject were not far behind. In one infamous case, the City of Philadelphia in 1986 attempted to ship 15,000 tons of hazardous burned ash on the freighter *Kia Sea* to the Bahamas but, after being turned away, this ship wandered the high seas for 18 months. Even after changing its name, the ship could not find a country that would allow the ash to be dumped, and it is suspected that the crew surreptitiously pushed the ash overboard in the Indian Ocean (French 2000: 72–3; Salzman & Thompson 2003). The major corrective treaty for this abuse by rich countries of poor ones is the 1989 *Basel Convention on the Control of Transboundary Movements of Hazardous Wastes and Their Disposal*.[30] This treaty entered into force in 1992 and now has over 170 supporting states. The Basel Convention is a global notification system that monitors shipments and creates a paper record, including the written consent of the receiving country. It covers all types of hazardous wastes except radioactive materials, which are left to the IAEA to handle.

Unsatisfied with anything less than a complete ban on shipping all wastes to Third World countries, African states, supported by the NGOs known as the Basel Action Network,[31] have moved from trying to amend the Basel Convention to adopting a new treaty appropriate for their continent. These countries embraced the 1991 *Bamako Convention on the Ban of the Import Into Africa and the Control of Transboundary Movement and Management of Hazardous Waste Within Africa.*[32] Entering into force in 1996, but with only 20 parties of the more than 50 African states, the Bamako Convention calls for a complete ban and makes no exception for radioactive materials. Unfortunately, plenty of countries are left that will be tempted by the easy money to be made, and of course illegal dumping at sea remains a potential problem. Another major step taken by a set of Third World countries was the 1990 *Lomé IV Convention* arranged among the small Asian, Pacific, and Caribbean countries (APC states), numbering 71, and the EU. Lomé IV primarily provided the APC states with preferential trade privileges to boost their economies, but it also prohibited the importation of radioactive wastes.[33]

Forests

The destruction of forests has become an urgent worldwide issue. Today forests cover about one-fourth less of the Earth's land surface than in 1700, and the present disappearance rate is 1.5 acres per second (Postel 1994; Gore 1992). Rainforests which gird the Earth at the equator receive the most attention. These once covered 16 percent of the Earth's surface but now cover just 7 percent, a loss involving millions of acres per year.[34] Although with some exaggeration, the rainforests have been called the "lungs of the Earth" for their capacity to convert carbon dioxide into oxygen. The *State of the World's Forests 2007*, a report prepared biennially by the UN Food and Agricultural Organization (FAO), reports an uneven record on a region-by-region basis, but overall the world has 4 billion hectares [1 hectare equals 100 acres] of forest covering about 30 percent of the world's land area, with a total world loss of 3 percent since the early 1990s. While developing countries continue to experience high rates of deforestation, there is some good news about other regions. Most countries in Europe and North America have reversed centuries of deforestation and now show small net gains in forest coverage.[35]

Environmentalists who have urged the preservation of the rainforests have run head-on into the North–South economic controversy. Leaders and many environmentalists of the North maintain cutting tropical forests is an environmental disaster. From their perspective, forests should be left standing and allow forest products to be harvested on a gradual, sustainable basis. The noted environmentalist Lester Brown fears that if as much as half the Amazon basin is cleared, the sensitive ecosystem of the rainforest will reach its tipping point and will be irredeemable (Brown 2008: 13). Yielding somewhat to the North's pressures, Brazil promised to slow down the rate of razing its rainforest during the 2008 climate conference held in Poznan, Poland. However, tropical states basically remain committed to economic development trumping rainforests. The South's point of view is that cutting and burning its rainforests is not a bad choice because timber can be sold and farms and cattle ranches will replace trees. In Brazil, Indonesia, and the Congo, and other tropical states, future economic dividends will come from roads, hydroelectric plants, power lines, mining operations, and the resettlement of burgeoning populations in previously forested areas. At some point, however, the damage could become irreversible.

Perhaps the worst episode of forest destruction in history is the case of Easter Island, a possession of Chile over 2,000 miles away in the Pacific Ocean. Settlers arrived from the Marquesas Islands to the north between 400 and 600 AD and, by the late seventeenth century, rapid population growth caused the complete deforestation of Easter Island. Tribal war erupted, and the desperate islanders even turned to cannibalism to survive. Today, Easter Island is famous for the giant carved stone heads known as *Moais*, which have led to a booming tourist industry creating yet another threat to the delicate island.

There are perfectly good reasons for not cutting down forests. Forests hold soil in place, prevent erosion, and also "scrub" the air by absorbing carbon dioxide and releasing oxygen. Rainforests, in particular, are home to many indigenous peoples, such as the Yanomamo Indians of Brazil and the Penan people of Malaysian Borneo. Rainforests are also rich in **biodiversity**, suffused as they are with a wide variety of plants and animals. Biodiversity is the genetic variability of all living organisms, including both animal and plant species. Numerous medicines depend on this tropical biodiversity. For instance, drugs for childhood leukemia and Hodgkin's disease derive from the periwinkle plant; the drug that stabilized President Ronald Reagan, after he was wounded by the bullet of a would-be assassin, came from the venom of an Amazon bush viper. Then there is income available from gathering food, such as nuts and fruits, the planting of flowers and bananas for sale in Europe and North America, and tapping trees for rubber products. The Brazilian government is fighting HIV/AIDS with a government-run free condom distribution program using latex harvested from rubber trees in its rainforest. Finally, forests provide opportunities for income from ecotourism, with resort communities built into natural settings, allowing many urbanites to commune with nature. These economic opportunities that would protect forests as income earners may seem inadequate to leaders under pressure to raise wealth in the immediate future.

The governments of countries are very prone to stand behind the shield of sovereignty taking the view that their own resources involve their policy choices alone. An effort to soften this outlook, however, led to one of the five major documents that emerged from the 1992 Earth Summit, the *Forest Principles*, more formally known as the "Statement of Principles for a Global Consensus on the Management, Conservation and Sustainable Development of all Types of Forests." The Forest Principles offer 15 non-binding principles for guiding national policy-making. While a policy guideline, rather than a treaty, these principles represent the first effort to put together some form of global consensus on managing forests for the sake of a healthy planet biosphere while at the same time meeting national needs.[36]

Although the world is losing slightly more trees than it is gaining, many interesting efforts to plant trees and preserve forests are, nevertheless, underway albeit uneven in success. National Arbor Day, usually celebrated on the last Friday of April, began in Nebraska 120 years ago and the organization behind this project plants millions of trees every year, and has a special program to save rainforests. Wangari Maathai of Kenya won the Nobel Peace Prize in 2004 for organizing the Green Belt Movement to plant trees in many African countries. Her award recognized the connection between the environment, democracy, and peace. Similar replanting organizations have sprung up in many developing countries.

The IPCC has estimated that deforestation leads to 15–20 percent of global greenhouse gas. This panel of scientists has urged the Kyoto meeting for 2012 to include a forest element in its agenda. Such a step might move forest protection from well-meaning principles to lawful requirements. In 2007, the World Bank launched the Forest Carbon Partnership Facility as a pilot program to compensate countries for preserving their forests.[37] Many states help by organizing national parks and forests that provide recreation but also preserve the world's biodiversity. The US Wilderness Act sets aside thousands of acres as off-limits to mining or logging. The EU states will not import bio-fuel from land that was previously rainforest. Costa Rica pays landowners for leaving their forests standing. All of these activities are encouraging, but the future of forestry cover on Earth remains in doubt, especially in the tropical areas.

Wildlife

Historically humans have interacted with animals in a variety of ways but, as the most intelligent animals, they have easily used other animals in a clearly anthropocentric manner: butchering animals for food, using their hides for homes and clothes, harnessing them for energy, and employing them in sport competition and in war. More recently, animals have been used in laboratories, testing medicines and cosmetics on them. In Africa, with its warfare and poverty, many animal species are endangered. For example, hippopotamuses, gorillas, elephants, and other animals are shot for their meat, ivory tusks, and various body parts for trophies. These wanton killings give little heed to the damage done to the survival prospects of many species or even to the harm to the ecotourism industry and the income it can produce.

In the latter twentieth century and continuing today, many governments and environmental NGOs have called for a reformative way of dealing with animals, ranging from protecting bees that pollinate crops and produce honey to saving African and Asian elephants now recognized for their intelligence and family-like behaviors. The wolves of North America, the polar bears around the Arctic Circle, the much adored panda bears of China, marine species such as dolphins, sea turtles, seals, and even the fierce salt water crocodiles of northern Australia, among many other animals, all have their supporters and preservationists, both in governments and NGOs. Many species desperately need human help, not human abuse. Sometimes that help is exemplary. In the fall of 2008, when hundreds of Magellan penguins washed up on Brazil's northern shores, the authorities restored hundreds of them to good health and flew them on airforce cargo planes to southern beaches of Brazil, a location closer to the penguin's natural range. Food shortages due to a scarcity of fish had likely driven the penguins northward.

Perhaps no animal has attracted more concern for protection than whales. The 1946 *International Convention for the Regulation of Whaling* was designed to continue agreements arrived at in the 1930s based on conservation and harvesting needs. The whaling convention was signed by 42 states in Washington, DC, and entered into force in 1948. Today, approximately 80 states are members. A protocol to the convention was accepted in 1956, which, among other terms, covered the use of helicopters for hunting whales.[38] Modern techniques, including fast ships and electric and explosive harpoons, had begun to deplete some of the 37 whale species to the point that the extinction of some species was a serious danger. Seven of the whale species are already considered seriously endangered. The whaling convention allowed for seasonal hunting, the protection of the more depleted species, and the provision for whale sanctuaries if countries chose to designate them in their respective regions. So far, the International Whaling Commission (IWC) has approved the Southern Ocean Whale Sanctuary around Antarctica and the Indian Ocean Whale Sanctuary, with both banning all types of commercial whaling.

To make adjustments according to needs, the whaling convention created the IWC with 17 commissioners serving, and the IWC has a permanent secretariat headquartered in Cambridge, England. A policy-making body, it underwent a major shift in its policies during the 1985/6 period, changing priorities from *conservation* to *preservation* of whales, with a moratorium on whale hunts following. The IWC continues to struggle over conservation/preservation approaches, with neither side able to mount a three-fourths majority needed to set policy in a firm way. Long past is the need for whale oil for lamps or their bones for hoopskirts. The principal reason whales continue to be hunted is that several countries – Iceland, Japan, and Norway – have cultures with preferences for whale meat. Japan and Norway especially have resisted this bold change of policy and continue to hunt the relatively numerous minke whales by exploiting a research exception of the whaling convention. The hundreds of whales these countries harvest annually actually wind up being sold for food (Friedham 2001: 3–48, esp. 11). The concern is that whale hunters will gravitate toward the larger species such as the right, gray, blue, and humpback whales, which are few in number. The small, white beluga whale in the Arctic waters of Alaska's Cook Inlet was added to the wildlife endangered list in the fall of 2008 by the United States. The IWC does permit whale hunting by indigenous peoples in Alaska and some other places as long as they use traditional methods (Gillespie 205: 194–246).

The major shift in policy away from hunting whales probably resulted mainly from the scientific recognition that whales live in social structures called pods and even develop their own languages, a phenomenon portrayed in movies and television programs leading to public outcries against hunting them (Frieheim 2001: 4–5). Besides some whale hunting, whales still face food shortages, abandoned fishing nets that entangle them, pollution, and powerful sonar beams of ships that can confuse their navigation and migration patterns by causing hemorrhaging around the brain and ears. In late 2008, the US Supreme Court nonetheless ruled against restricting the Navy's use of sonar during training maneuvers against potential enemy submarines, arguing that national security trumps the welfare of whales. Environmentalists fought this cause for a decade but lost.

Whales are faring reasonably well, at least compared to many land-based animals that are in shocking decline. Pollution, habitat destruction, and poaching of animals for Asian medicines, food, and capture for zoos or pets have caused many species to decline precipitously, including rhinoceros, tigers, monkeys, snakes, and fish. Many species are endangered and some may face extinction. One fortunate development in the summer of 2008 was the discovery of 125,000 previously unknown western lowland gorillas deep in the forests of the Republic of the Congo. This find more than doubles the estimates of these endangered primates. Unfortunately, many of the other more than 600 types of primates in the world may be on the path to extinction.

A major strategy of protection has been to prevent animals and plants from being removed illegally from the natural habitats of their countries and continents. This strategy is legally reflected in the *Convention to Regulate International Trade in Endangered Species of Flora and Fauna* (CITES). CITES was first proposed in 1963 by the NGO World Conservation Union, but a decade passed before a convention text was found agreeable to a large number of states. Eighty states accepted this convention in Washington, DC, and it entered into force in 1975 with 173 countries now supporting it. Switzerland serves as the depository government, meaning that countries wishing to be bound by CITES notify the Swiss government. Its purpose is to use an export–import licensing system to make sure all flora and fauna are approved for transnational shipment. The convention is up against a lucrative illegal trade in wildlife worth billions of dollars and so smuggling is rampant.[39]

Unfortunately, CITES is spotty in its record of effectiveness. Ideally all signatories would incorporate CITES into their national law and assign an agency dedicated to strict enforcement, as the United States and some other states have done. In many of the poorer Third World countries however, enforcement of CITES is undermined by corruption. Poorly paid officials are inclined to take bribes and look the other way. Moreover, countries simply do not have the resources to monitor what is happening to their animals and plants, unable to pay for a large, well-armed force of game wardens. Elephant ivory is especially a robust black market economy, although this trade was banned globally in 1989. Ivory carving in Asia is an ancient art and brings a fortune to poachers, sellers, and carvers. China in particular has kept slap-dash records on ivory inventories despite a requirement in CITES to monitor properly the licensing of sales. Countries can also apply for exceptions and buy ivory from several southern-most African states where elephants are not endangered. African states have tried to reinforce CITES in their region with the 1994 Lusaka Agreement to stop illegal trade in animals and plants but, so far, this agreement has only seven parties.

States sometimes try to protect wildlife through economic sanctions leveled at other states. The United States, for instance, tried to embargo Mexican tuna until Mexico changed from the use of enormous purse-seine nets to a net that would allow dolphins to escape instead of drowning. A 1991 ruling of the General Agreement on Tariffs and Trade (GATT) process found that the US action against Mexico violated free-trade principles. Following years of negotiation, the United States, Mexico, and several other states reached a compromise that would substantially reduce dolphin deaths by changing the design of the nets employed. Soon afterward, the successor organization to the GATT, the World Trade Organization (WTO), ruled against the United States in 1998 again for violating free trade principles. In this case, the United States would not accept shrimp imports if foreign fishermen did not use turtle exit devices (TEDs) in their nets to save sea turtles. The United States changed its enforcement to focus on individual shipments instead of excluding an entire country's trade in shrimp. WTO then accepted the US TEDs policy in a 2000 ruling (French 2000: 116–23; Vogel 2006: 354–72).

A particularly impressive development related to all manner of animals and plant life is one of the two conventions to emerge from the 1992 Earth Summit, the *Convention on Biological Diversity* (CBD), which entered into force in late 1993 and is well-supported with 191 parties. While the convention acknowledges state sovereignty over their own national resources, it also recognizes that biological diversity is a common concern of humankind and that everyone will be affected by the rapid loss of this diversity as habitats fall to so-called modern development. The CBD's intent is to conserve and sustain this diversity for the future, and it calls for fair and equitable benefits from all genetic resources.[40] The protocol to the 1991 Antarctica treaty also designates the Antarctic as a natural reserve and requires that its biodiversity be protected.

Extinction is a serious problem for the success of the CBD. While it is true that extinction of animal and plant species has been basic to natural history, human actions in modern times have greatly accelerated a massive loss of animal and plant life. The NGO Birdlife International points out that there have been 21 extinctions since the 1970s, and 139 other bird species are on the brink of extinction.[41] Of 9,817 known species of birds, 70 percent are in decline and may go the way of the Dodo bird or the Carrier pigeon (Brown 2008: 102–3). Along with amphibians, especially frogs, birds are usually the first harbingers of an unhealthy environment. A final example concerns human's closest animal, at least based on overlapping DNA evidence. The NGO World Conservation Union reports that of 394 primates, 114 are classified as an extinction threat.[42] The list of losses of animals and plant life is a long and sad one. Human economic development is destroying some species before they can even be identified. Environmentalists are not just concerned about the Amazon basin for its trees, but also because it is one of the richest treasure-troves of biodiversity in the world. How many medical benefits are lost before indigenous medicine men can reveal their knowledge is an unknown.

Finally worthy of mention are the Ramsar and Bonn Conventions. The formal name of the Ramsar treaty is *The Convention on Wetlands of International Importance, Especially as Waterfowl Habitat*, which was signed in Ramsar, Iran, in 1971. It entered into force in 1975. Today there are 158 parties, each of which must maintain at least one or more wetland sites for flora and fauna, particularly for water fowl which migrate across borders. More than 1,755 "Ramsar sites" exist among the supporting parties of the Ramsar treaty.[43] The Bonn Convention of 1979 is formally known as the *Convention on the Conservation of Migratory Species of Wild Animals*. The aim is to conserve land-based and marine bird life crossing borders, especially those threatened with extinction. The states accepting the Bonn Convention number over 110 and are located on several continents.[44]

The Environment and Human Rights

While no acknowledged individual right to a healthy environment, in the manner of free speech or freedom from torture, has yet found its way into treaty form, support does exist for a moral and legal collective, or societal, right to enjoy an environment in a way essential to humankind's well-being. Obviously, the more a right to a proper environment emerges the greater will be the duty of states to provide a wholesome setting for their citizenry. A broad connection between human rights and the environment was first expressed in Principle 1 of the 1972 Stockholm Declaration. Article 12 of the 1966 UN *Covenant on Economic, Social, and Cultural Rights* refers to improved environments and industrial hygiene.

Perhaps the most explicit reference to the interconnection between rights and the environment is by the 1981 *African Charter of Human and Peoples' Rights* in its Article 24, where the right to the enjoyment of natural resources and environmental security are placed alongside the right to development and self-determination. Then in 1994, a "Declaration of Principles on Human Rights and the Environment" of the UN Sub-Committee echoed the Stockholm Declaration's Principle One (Birnie & Boyle 2008: 252–4). Much more recently, the UN Human Rights Council adopted a position by consensus that climate change impacted on human rights and in 2008 called on the UN High Commissioner for Human Rights to do a detailed study of the problem.[45]

Environmental conditions affect everyone on the planet, but particularly the poor, women, indigenous peoples, and future generations (Sachs 1995; UNHDP 1998: 66–85). The negative side effects of mining, manufacturing, cutting down forests, building roads and dams, air pollution, and much else fall hard on the powerless, especially in Third World countries where protesting deleterious environmental conditions can be dangerous. The 1988 murder of Chico Mendes in Brazil is a famous case in point, as he tried to prevent ranchers from cutting down the rainforests.

The global environmental movement has been slow to recognize the critical role of women and how the environment impacts their lives. Working the land for food, trudging long distances for potable water and firewood, caring for sick children and the elderly, and living inside smoke-filled homes, caused by wood fires used for cooking and heating, are just some of the ways many women in the Third World lack a healthy environment. Yet, not until the 1992 Earth Summit did women begin to be recognized for their important and central role. From this conference came Principle 20 of the Rio Declaration referring to their "vital role," the Forest Principle 4 (b) stating that women's full participation is needed to sustain the world's forests, the preamble to the CBD calling for women to be recognized for their role in conserving this diversity, and finally the lengthy Agenda 21, a world blueprint for environmental protection. It devotes the entirety of Chapter 24 to women's role. In addition to the Greenbelt Movement in Africa and the Chipko Movement in India, in which women lead the cause of planting trees, numerous women's NGOs reinforce the efforts of IGOs and governments willing to promote the environment. The Women's Environmental and Development Organization (WEDO) is a notable example.[46]

Indigenous peoples are in the front lines of environmental threats because their lives are intimately connected to forests, the frozen tundra of the arctic circle, the seas and rivers, and other geographical settings. They draw their living directly from the land and water. Unfortunately, millions of these vulnerable people are facing the rapid destruction of their very homelands and food resources. The problem always seems to start with the building of a new road. Then the miners arrive to pollute streams, wielders of chainsaws to acquire lumber, ranchers to burn down forests for grazing land, and dam builders to create lakes on top of indigenous homelands to generate electricity for far away cities. Some governments make concessions and offer protection, but these efforts are not keeping up with the destruction of indigenous peoples' homelands and ways of life.

In addition to some earlier efforts of protection by the International Labor Organization, more broadly-based recognition of the need to protect indigenous peoples' environments began with the Earth Summit's agreements, principles, and articles. The CBD deserves to be singled out because it recognizes in its preamble not only the closeness of indigenous peoples to biological resources but that they should share equitably in the benefits arising from their traditional knowledge. The medicines provided with the help of Amer-Indians in the Amazonian rainforests are a prime example.[47]

Another important environmental right receiving growing recognition concerns intergenerational equity, a moral claim that those persons not yet born have a right to enjoy environmental conditions at least as favorable as those of the present generation. People now living on Earth hold in trust the environment for those yet to come (Weiss 1999: 106). Petra Kelly, a pioneering environmentalist in the German Green Party once said, "We must learn that as the motto of the German Green Party says we have only borrowed the Earth from our children" (Kelly 2004: 284). The intergenerational equity question had an early beginning as declarations and treaties began to appear in the relatively new area of environmental international law. The 1972 Stockholm Declaration referred to improving the environment for present and future generations as an imperative for humankind, and this right was the focus of its first two principles.[48] The concern for future generations is implicit in the concept of sustainable development that received much attention in the 1987 Bruntland Report, which calls for replenishing natural resources at a rate at least equal to the present rate of use.

The last example concerns scarcity and conflict among actors over scant resources, whether the actors are states engaged in international warfare or ethnic communities within the same country. The desertification in Darfur of Western Sudan that has pitched the African and Arab peoples there into a cruel no-holds-barred war and Japan's decision early in the Second World War to seize resources from its Asian neighbors, especially oil from today's Indonesia, are clear examples. It is widely understood that a healthy environment, able to provide for the wants and needs of people, will contribute to peace. The Nobel Peace Prize has been given on several occasions to environmentalists with this point in mind.

The connection between conflict and the environment is reflected in several places in the sources of international law. The 1972 Stockholm Declaration asserts in its Principle 26 that humankind is to be spared the effects of nuclear weapons and all manner of weapons of destruction. The most feared of all conflicts was the potential all-out nuclear war between the Soviet Union and the United States during the Cold War, a conflict that might have eliminated all life on the planet. Principle 5 of the UN's *World Charter for Nature* calls for nature to be free from any degradation caused by war and other hostile acts. In 1977 the *Environmental Modification Convention* was designed to prevent changing the environment for hostile purposes. In the same year, Protocol I to the 1949 Geneva Conventions prevented international warfare that could cause lasting harm to the environment, and Protocol II carries the same rule for internal war. These international rules appeared soon after the Vietnam War in which the United States used Agent Orange as a defoliant that probably caused birth defects and cancer for both the Vietnamese people and American service personnel. The 1992 Rio Declaration devoted 3 of its 27 principles (Principles 24–6) to draw attention to the nexus among armed conflict, the environment, and peace.[49]

In a rush to achieve advantage, warring parties unfortunately may not hesitate to use cancer-inducing defoliants, sow farmland and roads with landmines, burn oil wells creating nightmarish air pollution, and fire uranium-depleted shells that might cause radiation sickness. Wars that last for months or a few years may leave behind ill-effects for the environment that can trouble humankind for decades.

Environmental Governance

In addition to states' efforts to protect their environments at home through environmental agencies, laws bolstered by domestic environmental NGOs, and even green political parties in some countries, the environmental cause has been energized with global and regional efforts as well. IGOs, international NGOs, and scientific communities are important actors in international society working for the environmental cause. The interaction of these various actors in common cause generates a steady flow of rules and norms providing some governance, however inadequate it might seem at times. In our relatively new age of environmental awareness, this governance offers some order to environmental protection efforts in the absence of central world authority.

The UN has emerged as an impressive global environmental regime by promoting policy reform through specialized agencies, holding international conferences, and encouraging the creation of environmental international law. Following the suggestion of the Stockholm Conference, the UN created the UNEP headquartered in Nairobi, Kenya. This organization has a wide range of interests and activities. In 1975, it launched the Global Environmental Monitoring System (GEMS) that serves as a repository of environmental data collected from around the world that governments and scientists can use. The UNEP also provides expertise for the Global Environmental Facility (GEF) created in 1991 to provide funds for environmental projects, especially those in developing countries. The World Bank proposed GEF, at the suggestion of France, and manages its funds. As well, the UNEP publishes an annual yearbook on global environmental conditions.

Another important UN organ is the Commission on Sustainable Development (CSD), a specialized sub-commission of the UN Economic and Social Council, cre-

---

Box 11.3 Special Environmental Observances of the UN

March 22	World Water Day
April 22	Earth Day
May 10–11	World Migratory Bird Day
May 22	International Day for Biological Diversity
June 5	World Environment Day
June 17	World Day to Combat Desertification and Drought
Sept. 17	International Day for the Preservation of the Ozone Layer
Sept. 27	World Maritime Day
Oct. 16	World Food Day
Nov. 6	International Day for Preventing the Exploitation of the Environment in War and Armed Conflict
2008	International Year of Sanitation
2008	International Year of Planet Earth
2005–15	International Decade for Action: Water for Life

Source: See http://www.un.org/events/ and http://www.unep.org/Documents.

---

ated in 1992 as a follow-up to the 1992 Earth Summit. Its main function is to monitor and report on the implementation of the Earth Summit's global environmental blueprint known as Agenda 21. There is no exaggeration in saying that environmental concerns thread through much of the UN System, including, for instance, the World Health Organization, The Food and Agricultural Organization, the International Atomic Energy Agency, and the International Maritime Organization.[50]

To assist in encouraging the cooperation needed to support the soft authority of global governance, the UN has sponsored numerous conferences. Besides the well-known Stockholm Conference and Earth Summit, a few other examples of these global town meetings are the 1994 International Conference on Population and Development, the 1995 Conference on Straddling and Highly Migratory Fish Stocks, the 1997 Earth Summit + 5, the 2002 World Summit on Sustainable Development, the 2005 World Conference Disaster Reduction, the 2006 Fourth World Water Forum, and the 2007 UN Climate Change Conference held in Bali, Indonesia.[51] The most recent climate change conference is of course the one held at Poznan, which was attended by 190 states.

From the fora of UN conferences, some important environmental law has emerged. A few of these are the 1982 *Convention on the Law of the Seas* with some of its articles covering living resources of the oceans and pollution, the 1992 *Framework Convention on Climate Change*, the 1992 *Convention on Biological Diversity*, and the 1996 *Comprehensive Nuclear-Test Ban Treaty*.[52] Finally, the important 2000 Millennium Development Goals contain the objective of ensuring environmental sustainability.

Regional efforts at promoting environmental priorities have been useful also. The EU has raised standards in ex-communist and poorer member-states, offers businesses awards for environmental improvements, and celebrates "Green Week" each June. The EU eco-label can be found on a wide range of goods and services so consumers can direct their purchases in environmentally friendly ways. The EU Commission, Parliament, and the European Court of Justice have built up an impressive body of rules and laws calling for environmental protection. The EU in 1990 set up the European Environment Agency (EEA) to provide sound, independent information on the environment for its 27 members and 5 other European non-members. For its own membership, the EU has agreed to all manner of treaties covering, for instance, transnational air pollution, protecting the Baltic and Mediterranean Seas from pollution, safeguarding the transportation of animals, and even the conservation of bats. Outside Europe, the EU is best known for spearheading world efforts to implement the Kyoto Protocol and helping reduce the greenhouse effect of global warming.[53] In late 2008, at Brussels, Belgium, the EU committed itself to the "20–20–20" targets of reducing greenhouse emissions by 20 percent and ensuring that 20 percent of energy comes from renewable sources such as the wind and sun, all by the year 2020.

Latin American states, working through the Organization of American States (OAS), have also made some significant strides at environmental protection. As early as the 1950s, the OAS formed the Department of Sustainable Development (DSD), which has helped member-states with greening trade agreements, natural resource management, risk reduction during natural disasters, and poverty alleviation. A recent priority has been helping the small, poor Caribbean members. Among other conventions, a particularly important one is the 1978 *Treaty for Amazonian Cooperation* formed among the eight OAS members with territories overlapping part of the Amazon basin. This area contains probably the world's richest biodiversity area. The OAS celebrated its first "Green Week" in September 2008.[54]

The African Union (AU) has some impressive accomplishments worthy of mention too. The centerpiece of its success is the 2003 revision of the 1968 *African Convention on the Conservation of Nature and Natural Resources*, first created when the African states were organized as the Organization of African States. The revised convention will come into force when 15 of the members ratify it. Other worthwhile developments are the 2005 *Kinshasa Agreement* and the 2006 *Maputo Declaration*. The first was signed in Kinshasa in the Democratic Republic of the Congo and called for protection of threatened ape species, such as gorillas and chimpanzees, with donor states from Europe helping finance this protection. The second was signed in Maputo, Mozambique, and commits African states to take part in a multi-regional satellite program to monitor climate change and environmental risks. The AU holds annual conferences on the environment at the ministerial level and, for several years, has celebrated the third day of March as "Africa Environment Day."[55]

The environmental efforts of the UN and regional IGOs are thought of as regimes of rules and norms embedded within permanent institutions. Other regimes lack significant institutional frameworks and vary in their success. A few examples will make this point clear. The *whaling regime* is situated in the International Whaling Commission, which has managed to protect most whales from hunting except for the numerous, small minke whale. The *atmosphere regime* rests on several agreements, including the 1987 Montreal Protocol, the 1992 Convention on Climate

Change and the 1997 Kyoto protocol. These are noteworthy accomplishments, yet this regime has failed to win the cooperation of the United States and some newly emerging economic powers, most importantly China, which operates huge coal-burning industries. The *forest regime* is a particularly weak regime, with only the non-binding forest principles from the Earth Summit to its credit. The cutting of tropical forests has not slowed by much.

Forming a critical element of the global civil society are the international environmental NGOs, which are countable by the hundreds.[56] NGOs attempt to speak for and activate world opinion as they spend millions of dollars in private funds for their causes. Some are broad-based, working on many issues like Greenpeace and Green Cross International, but others are specialized like the World Wildlife Fund, Sea Shepherd, Rising Tide, and the Rainforest Action Network. Equipped with their expertise and money, NGOs can attend IGOs fora and international conferences, and often recommend what the rules and norms should be for governing the world environment. For many participants in NGOs, improving the world's environment is a moral issue as well as a practical necessity.

Finally, the scientific communities of many countries collaborate across borders in common causes, such as persuading diverse types of countries, on the coast of the Mediterranean Sea, to cooperate in protecting the ecosystem of this beautiful body of water. From 2001 to 2005, over 1,300 scientists from countries around the world worked on the UN Millennium Ecosystem Assessment report. Scientists with similar academic backgrounds are often referred to as *epistemic communities*.

Chapter Summary

- International environmental law is a relatively new field in international law but reflects a rapid build-up of treaties and global and regional conferences to deal with this important subject; unfortunately, policy results in this area of law have been somewhat disappointing.
- The global biosphere can be thought of as having the interdependent dimensions of air, water, soil, forests, and wildlife, each with its own treaty regime.
- Conventions to protect the oceans have had measurable success but climate/air pollution problems noticeably lag behind some other environmental improvements.
- Economic needs and wants, worsened by a rising world population, make it difficult to achieve environmental progress.
- Everyone shares environmental problems in common but women in Third World countries and indigenous peoples, both with lives intimately bound up with the land, probably suffer more than other identifiable groups.
- Global governance, made up of states, IGOs and NGOs working together, represents an impressive effort to develop cooperation and rules for a healthy environment.

Discussion Questions

1   What is the Earth Summit and what are its major contributions in terms of trea-
    ties and principles?
2   What is sustainable development and has the term found its way into any envi-
    ronmental agreements? What are the implications of population growth for sus-
    tainable development?
3   What is the impact of global warming on the Arctic and Antarctic regions? What
    treaties address this issue?
4   What problem does the Kyoto Protocol address and is this agreement doing enough?
5   What is the most successful environmental treaty or agreement, and why?

Useful Weblinks

http://www.un.org/climatechange/
This website is the gateway to the UN's environmental interests in climate change. It
is very broad in coverage and deals with climate conferences, a carbon "footprint"
indicator including a carbon footprint calculator. This site offers the *Human
Development Report: Fighting Climate Change 2007–2008*, the UNFCCC treaty, and
numerous other accessible sites in the left column of the front page concerning multiple UN agencies and how they relate to environmental problems.

http://treaties.un.org/Pages/ParticipationStatus.aspx
A very useful source is provided for the UN's Treaty System broken down by subject.
Scroll down to Chapter 27 for a specific list of environmental conventions. The sta-
tus of acceptance on a country-by-country is provided.

http://sedac.ciesin.columbia.edu/entri/
ENTRI stands for "Environmental Treaties and Resource Indicators." This website
offers environmental treaties, country profiles, the capacity for making tables with
data provided, and an internal search engine.

http://www.cnn.com/SPECIALS/2009/planet.in.peril/
This site is an informative and even entertaining website produced by CNN, covering numerous environmental issues through investigative reporting. This site has
blogs, video clips, an interactive map on conflict, and a gallery of photographs.

http://css.snre.umich.edu/
This website is maintained by the Center for Sustainable Development of the
University of Michigan's School of Natural Resources & Environment. It should be
of great interest to those planning for an education and career in the environmental
area. A useful site map and contact information are provided.

http://www.unep.org/
The website of the UN Environment Program, which covers global governance, climate change, natural disasters, resource efficiency, and other topics.

Further Reading

Al-Duaij, Nada (2004) *Environmental Law of Armed Conflict*. Ardsley, NY: Transnational.

Biermann, Frank, Siebenhüner, Bernd, and Schreyögg, Anna (eds.) (2009) *International Organizations in Global Environmental Governance*. New York: Routledge.

Birnie, Patricia W. and Boyle, A. E. (2002) *International Law and the Environment*. New York: Oxford University Press.

Bodansky, Daniel, Brunnee, Jutta, and Hey, Ellen (eds.) (2008) *The Oxford Handbook of International Environmental Law*. New York: Oxford University Press.

Chasek, Pamela, Downie, David L., and Brown, Janet Welsh (2005) *Global Environmental Politics*, 4th edn. Boulder, CO: Westview Press.

Louka, Elli (2006) *International Environmental Law: Fairness, Effectiveness, and World Order*. New York: Cambridge University Press.

Romano, Cesare (2000) *The Peaceful Settlement of International Environmental Disputes: A Pragmatic Approach*. Boston, MA: Kluwer Law International.

Sands, Philippe (2000) *Principles of International Environmental Law*. New York: Cambridge University Press.

Tremmel, Joerg Chet (ed.) (2006) *Handbook of Intergenerational Justice*. North Hampton, MA: Edward Elgar.

Nanda, Ved P. and Pring, George (2003) *International Environmental Law and Policy for the 21st Century*. Ardsley, NY: Transnational.

Watters, Lawrence (2004) *Indigenous Peoples, the Environment and Law*. Durham, NC: Carolina Academic Press.

Westra, Laura (2007) *Environmental Justice and the Rights of Indigenous Peoples: International and Domestic Legal Perspectives*. Sterling, VA: Stylus Publishing.

Notes

1 http://www.unep.org/ Enter "UN Conference on the Human Environment 1972" in the website search engine.

2 *The World Charter for Nature* was devised in Nairobi, Kenya at the UNEP headquarters, at a plenary meeting, October 28, 1982. It is recorded as UN GA/RES/37/7. Or, go to http://sedac.ciesin.columbia.edu/entri/texts/world.charter.for.nature.

3 Go to http://www.UNEP.org/Documents Enter "Commission on Sustainable Development" in website search engine.

4 *Report of the World Summit on Sustainable Development* (New York: United Nations, 2002); for a pdf file copy, see http://daccess-ods.un.or/access.nsf/Get?Open&DS=A/57/460&Lang=E.

5 For a summary, see http://ww.millenniumassessment.org/en/About.aspx, pp.1–7. Note: the entire report fills five volumes.

6 Donnella Meadows 1972); An updated edition (2004), is a little less pessimistic in its predictions.

7 See, as a few examples, Ehrlich 1971; Ehrlich and Ehrlich 1987; 2008. A strong critic of their work has been Simon: e.g. 1981; 1990; 1992.

8 An excellent source of human population numbers and estimates is http://www.prb.org.

9 For the Trail Smelter case, see Romano 2000: 261–78.

10   Found at http://www.icj-cij.org > cases > 1973 Nuclear Tests (New Zealand v. France) and (Australia v. France).

11   Available at http://www.unece.org/env/lrtap/lrtap_h1.html. See the second page. Also, refer to the convention found in Hunter 2002: 43–59.

12   See, http://ww.wri.org/ > Climate + Energy + Transport > Climate Analysis Indicator Tool (CAIT).

13   The human development report on climate change can be located as *Human Development Report: Fighting Climate Change 2007/2008* (2007); the carbon footprint calculator of the Nature Conservancy is at http://www.nature.org/initiatives/climatechange/calculator.

14   The array of problems can be effectively read about in a brief form in Brown 2008: 48–67.

15   Lomborg 2007). The Earth Policy Institute can be found at http://www.earth-policy.org/. The Intergovernmental Panel on Climate Change website is at http://www.ipcc.ch/.

16   The UNFCCC can be read in Hunter, Salzman, and Zaelke 2002: 119–33. Or, it may also be accessed at http://www.un.org/climatechange/.

17   The Kyoto Protocol can be read in Hunter, Salzman, and Zaelke 2002: 134–48; or, examined at http://unfccc.int/Kyoto_protocol/.

18   For a good description of fresh water threats, see Postel 1994: 57–60. Brown 2008: 68–9.

19   A good general discussion of regulating rivers is Thomas Bernauer 1997: 155–6.

20   Joseph W. Dellapenna, "The Berlin Rules on Water Resources: The New Paradigm for International Water Law." See this conference paper at http://cedb.asce.org/cgi/WWWdisplay. cgi?0603955 > Download full text. Or, contact the author at the Villanova Law School.

21   Several examples of water stresses are in Brown 2008: 82–84; the Hungary-Slovakia case can be read at http://www.icj-cij.org/ > cases > contentious cases > Gabcikovo-Nagymaros Project > 25/9/1997 Judgment.

22   Hunter, Salzman, and Zaelke 2002: 731–9. Also, accessible at http://www.imo.org/.

23   Hunter, Salzman, and Zaelke 2002: 707–31. The MARPOL Convention and its 1978 protocol can be found in Hunter, Salzman, and Zaelke 2002: 220–45. Or, found at http://www.imo.org.

24   Major excerpts of the UNLOS, including articles relevant to pollution, are in Hunter, Salzman, and Zaelke 2002: 149–96; Articles specific to pollution and enforcement are pp. 177–186. The UNLOS is available at http://un.org/Depts/los/convention_agreements/convention_overview_convention.htm.

25   See the interesting discussion in Hunter, Salzman, and Zaelke 2002: 747–54. See especially Articles 207 and 213 of the UNLOS on p. 752. The UNLOS can be located as well at the same website given in note 24.

26   http://wwww.unep.org/regionalseas/ > About Regional Seas.

27   Postel 1994: 11. An interesting article on fisheries written for the general public is, "Still Waters: The Global Fish Crisis" (*National Geographic*, April 2007: 33–98).

28   The UNCCD can be read in Hunter, Salzman, and Zaelke 2002: 400–24. As well, available at http://www.unccd.int/ > About UNCCD > Text of the Convention.

29   This protocol can be read in Hunter, Salzman, and Zaelke 2002: 384–95. Also, access is available at http://www.antarctica.ac.uk//about_antarctica/geopolitical/treaty/.

30   The Basel Convention can be read in Hunter, Salzman, and Zaelke 2002: 253–72; Or, use http://www.basel.org/ > About the Basel Convention>Basel Convention.

31   More can be learned about the Basel Action Network (BAN) at http://www.ban.org.

32   Blakesley, Firmage, Scott, and Williams 2001: 365–78. The convention is also available at http://www.ban.org/library/bamako_treaty.html.

33 A brief discussion of this agreement can be found in Hunter, Salzman, and Zaelke 2002: 853–4; To read Lomé IV, go to the Basel Action Network at http://www.ban.org/history/lome4_article39.html.

34 Wapner 1995: 311–13; *Our Global Neighborhood: The Report of the Commission on Global Governance* (1995: 66). Rainforest Action Network is at http://ran.org.

35 *State of the World's Forests 2007* at http://www.fao.org > Topics > Forestry.

36 These principles can be found in Hunter, Salzman, and Zaelke 2002: 396–9. Or, use http://www.ti.org/forestprin.html

37 See, http://worldbank.org/. Enter "Forest Carbon Partnership Facility" in the site's website.

38 For the whaling convention, see Hunter, Salzman, and Zaelke 2002: 340–4; Also, go to http://iwcoffice.org/ > Convention.

39 CITES can be read in Hunter, Salzman, and Zaelke 2002: 329–39. Also, see http://cites.org.

40 The CBD can be read at Hunter *et al*, *International Environmental Law and Policy: Treaty Supplement*, pp. 345–362; or, go to http://www.cbd.int/.

41 For Birdlife International, see http://www.birdlife.org.

42 Find the World Conservation Union at http://encyclopedia2.thefreedictionary.com+World+Conservation+U.

43 The Ramsar Convention can be read in Hunter, Salzman, and Zaelke 2002: 380–3; or go to http://ramsar.org.

44 The Bonn Convention can be read in Hunter, Salzman, and Zaelke 2002: 320–8. It can also be read at http://www.cms.int/documents/index.html.

45 http://www.ciel.org/Hre/UN_Resolution_26Mar08.html.

46 For WEDO, see, http://www.wedo.org/index.aspx.

47 For a general reading on this subject, see Westra 2008.

48 For general reading on this right, see Westra 2006.

49 For some of the best literature on the environment-conflict issue, see Homer-Dixon 1991: 76–116; 1994: 5–40. More of his work is identified in http://www.homedixon.com/academicwriting.html.

50 A useful gateway for UN environmental activities is at http://www.unep.org/; and see http://www.un.org/climatechange.

51 To see UN sponsored conferences, go to http://www.un.organ/events/conferences.htm.

52 These conventions, among others, can be accessed at http://www.unep.org/law/ > "Environmental Law Instruments" > "Global Environmental Agreements."

53 A useful gateway to EU activities is http://europa.eu/pol/env/index_en.htm.

54 A useful site for OAS environmental activities is http://www.oas.org/dsd/EnvironmentalLaw/EnvlawDB/Default.htm.

55 See http://africa-union.org/. Enter "Environment" into this website's search engine. For a list of many regional environmental conventions go to http://www.unep.org/Law_instruments/index.asp > "Environmental Law Instruments" > "Regional Environmental Agreements."

56 For a good description of environmental NGO activities, see McCormick 1999: 52–71. A useful article is Raustiala 1997: 719–40. Unfortunately, the website for the World Directory of Environmental Organizations ended in February 2008, but another helpful site is http://www.interenvironment.org/wd1intro/aboutorgs.htm. Scroll down to the bottom of the page for SEARCHInterEnvironment.org at the bottom of the page.

Interdependence is not simply a word created by idealistic world-order reformers, but a very real condition of life bonding the fate of the rich to the fate of the poor. (Seyom Brown)

The world is divided into three kinds of nations: Those that spend lots of money to keep their weight down; those whose people eat to live; and those whose people don't know where the next meal will come from. (David S. Landes)

12

Rules for Sharing the World's Wealth

Contents

Economic life is a fundamental dimension of humankind. Humans have always had to meet their *needs* of clothing, shelter, and food in some manner, whether with their own hands or through bartering and trading with others. At the first opportunity, people have also pursued *wants* such as silk, gold jewelry, and spices for their food. Across history, this pursuit of needs and wants first created a local, then national, and finally a global economic system of producing, distributing, and using wealth. Governance of global economic interchange emerged slowly, but then accelerated after the Second World War with a "thick" set of rules and IGOs. Differing views on organizing and managing the economic system have been contentious at times with the free market economists opposing Marxist views of the communist states as well as the socialist outlook of the Third World. The free market model, backed by the hegemony of the United States, has mostly prevailed. International law has played a key role in securing an economic world order based on free market principles. International law's contribution is borne out by the large number of agreements regulating bilateral and multilateral trade, the treaties creating regional and global IGOs for economic governance, and even the soft law involving codes of conduct for guiding the behavior of MNCs.

This chapter begins with a brief history of contesting economic philosophies and the free trade model's strong ascent in the face of its challenges. Governance under free trade rules, the preferred rules of the richer, more developed states, is covered in the next section. Sections on standardization, intellectual property rights, and arbitration follow as specialized aspects of global governance. A section then appears on the issue of whether a global or regional approach to governance is more effective. The subsequent section concerns the effort to rewrite the rules of the prevailing economic order on the part of the poorer developing states. After this, a section on four economic flows–trade, aid, investment, and loans–elaborates the relationship between the rich and the poor states. The last section deals with the economically counterproductive issues of crime, corruption, and the pursuit of non-economic goals.

A Brief History of Economic Relations

Trade undoubtedly predates the historical record since goods that are needed and wanted have always been geographically distributed in a haphazard manner. Known history is replete with trade patterns. Roman roads were not only for the movement of soldiers and tax collectors but for trade as well. The famous Silk Road stretching from northern China across Eurasia, the Vikings' trade across Europe as well as their conquests, and the movement of spices and perfumes from the Middle East to northern Europe are other examples. Early trade was governed mostly by the simple rule, *caveat emptor*, or let the buyer beware to avoid being cheated. Some of the earliest governmental rules were the Roman *jus gentium*, which covered trade with peoples on the periphery of the Roman Empire along with other kinds of interactions. The Romans also recognized *lex maritima* begun by the Greeks to govern trade on the Mediterranean Sea. These trade rules were used by Europeans well into medieval times. In the medieval period, private trade rules, known as the *lex mercatoria* or merchant law, evolved in Europe and gradually took on a public character as kings and courts applied merchant law.

As the kingdoms of Europe crystallized into territorial states, monarchs began to practice an economic philosophy known as **mercantilism**, or economic nationalism, which held sway from the sixteenth through the eighteenth centuries. The focus of these monarchs was on maximizing exports and minimizing imports so as to turn a national profit. The acquired wealth could then be used to enhance a country's military strength and security. European kings were practicing a strong form of **protectionism**, discouraging the purchase of foreign goods and encouraging the rise of domestic industries.

Mercantilism, with its protectionist character, faced a major challenge when the advocacy of a new order based on international **free trade** appeared in the eighteenth century. This order calls for the removal of border restrictions on trade. The major advocate for competitive free trade to benefit all states and their peoples was Adam Smith (1723–1790). He argued in his 1776 *Wealth of Nations* that if each country would sell what it makes best and cheapest, everyone across Europe would enjoy greater prosperity. David Ricardo (1772–1823) refined Adam Smith's thinking by adding the notion of "comparative advantage." Ricardo realized several countries could produce wool or wine, among other products, but the country able to provide a product with the most efficiency should be the one to sell it internationally.

International free trade seemed like the logical next step to the domestic practice of **capitalism**. This economic approach is based on private ownership of property and calls for commerce to be regulated by market forces of supply and demand, not government regulation. The role of government is only to provide a law and order environment and to protect property. This hands-off role by government is often referred to as *laissez-faire*, roughly translated as, "let it operate freely." Capitalism grew in importance during Europe's nineteenth-century industrial expansion.

Capitalist rules, with its global extension as a free market order, would mostly prevail, but it would confront the challenge of communism for a time. European communism claimed to have its roots in **Marxism**. Karl Marx (1818–1883) believed capitalism exploited workers for the benefit of rich factory owners. Relief for workers would happen only when revolution destroyed the capitalist class and the government apparatus that protected it, according to Marx. The revolution never came about, a failure that a disciple of Marx by the name of Vladimir Lenin (1870–1924) attempted to explain in his 1918 work, *Imperialism*. Lenin argued the workers' revolution was delayed because European capitalists shifted the exploitation of their workers to the oppressed peoples of European colonies spread across several continents (Gilpin 1987: ch. 2). Lenin would finally force revolution on Czarist Russia in 1917, leading to the creation of the communist Soviet Union. This revolution did not ignite spontaneously in other European states as Marx once predicted and as Lenin had hoped. Communism would reach other European states only through occupation by Soviet armed forces at the end of the Second World War. European communism was never very successful economically, and this fact contributed heavily to the downfall of communism in 1989–91. With the communist yoke lifted, ex-communist states scurried to embrace capitalism and free trade as the appropriate path for improving the material well-being of their citizens.

By the nineteenth century, a flourishing trade was taking place among European states, but not as a pure form of free trade. A generous use of protectionism, involving tariffs (fees on imports) and quotas (limits on the number of imports), was still in place. During the first half of the twentieth century, international trade received a series of hammer blows, namely the First World War (1914–18), fought among the major trade states of Europe, the Great Depression of the 1930s, with its shortsighted protectionism that worsened the economic downturn, and the wreck and ruin of the Second World War (1939–45). Only after this largest war in history did the free trade agenda have a realistic chance to be put into operation. The United States emerged from the war as a military and economic hegemon determined to rectify decades of mistakes by leading the world toward the free trade model.

US economic leadership actually started before the end of the war. In 1944, at Bretton Woods in New Hampshire, led by the United States, 44 states gathered for the UN Monetary and Financial Conference. The product of the conference would become known as the Bretton Woods system, featuring the institutions of the World Bank and the International Monetary Fund (IMF). The World Bank would make loans to war-torn European countries to rebuild infrastructures of roads, bridges, ports, and the like, and would later make loans to new countries freed from colonial empires. The IMF had the function of loaning money to shore up national currencies. The Bretton Woods banking system has its headquarters in Washington, DC.

In 1947, the United States wanted to strengthen economic governance further with the International Trade Organization. Its function would be to oversee an Adam Smith-like free trade system without tariffs or quotas. When the US Congress would not approve the International Trade Organization, the US executive branch retained the General Agreement on Tariffs and Trade (GATT) and helped keep it operating for five decades. The GATT was to be temporary but instead served effectively as a series of negotiating rounds to reduce tariffs and move free trade principles into more and more sectors of goods and services. In 1995, the creation of the World Trade Organization, with its enforceable trade dispute mechanism, would replace the GATT process and join the UN system as an independent agency.

Also in 1947, the United States, in an act generally regarded as enlightened, offered the Marshall Plan to Europe. This was a major package of loans and aid to rebuild Europe following the unparalleled destruction of the Second World War. Democratic Western Europe gladly accepted nearly $14 billion from the United States and put it to good use. In contrast, Eastern Europe and the Soviet Union, held in the grip of Joseph Stalin and communism, chose not to take US money. This separation into two economic and political camps, known as the East–West division, became bedrock to the Cold War.

If the Cold War division between the East and West has subsided with the collapse of European communist governments, the wide divide between the well-off states and the poorer states of the Third World has proven obdurate. This divide is frequently depicted as the world's North–South division, with the developed states generally north of the equator and the developing Third World states of Africa, Asia, and Latin America mostly south of the equator. As these states left colonialism in the decades between the 1940s and the 1980s, their numbers grew, as did their sense of identity as a special group of states. Starting with their 1955 conference in Bandung, Indonesia, and continuing with meetings held at the UN, these states have joined together to bargain economically with the developed countries of the North. In the 1970s, their approach finally coalesced into a challenge to the free market world economy controlled by the North. Essentially, the South wanted a redistribution of existing wealth to enable them to develop their countries. The capitalist West saw this goal on the part of the South as global socialism.

Meeting the resistance of the North, the South accused the richer states of practicing *neocolonialism*, a continuation of economic exploitation of ex-colonies through unfair trade practices. In its strongest form, this accusation is known as the **dependency theory**. Its origin is usually attributed to Argentine economist Raul

Prebisch. This theory was widely accepted in the 1970s as an explanation for the enormous gap in wealth between North and South. According to the theory, as in colonial times, the North draws on cheap raw materials and labor but sells expensive finished products back to the South. The South receives a meager share of the profits and cannot break the pattern of exploitation but has to participate in this unfair arrangement in order to subsist (Walters & Blake 1992: 45–55). It is safe to say the free market approach of the richer states has persevered so far as global economic rules are concerned.

Any historical account of the world economy would be incomplete without recognizing the current era of globalization, the sensitive interconnectedness of the world. An effect in one place can have major impact on the other side of the world. Although some scholars point to earlier epochs of globalization, the present era is unrivaled in the speed and sensitive interrelationships of the various elements of the global economy (Ohmae 1999; see also Moore 2003). The click of a computer mouse can relocate a fortune in investment monies from one national market to another. The currency default of a medium-sized country can send economic shock waves through the world's financial houses, including the Bretton Woods IGOs.[1] Many scholars, NGOs, and certainly anti-globalization protestors have raised strong objections to the globalization process because of its impact politically, socially, culturally, and certainly economically, but globalization is unlikely to go into reverse barring a major depression equal to that of the 1930s.[2]

The role of international law has been and will be critical in the governance of a complex world economy as states, IGOs, NGOs, and MNCs contest over the many rules and regulations needed for the mammoth global economy to function. If the elusive but desired consensus ever does materialize over the management of the world's wealth, it will be built on the framework of international law.[3]

Governance from the North

Global governance of the international economy is based on the rules and norms generated by states, IGOs, and NGOs, and especially the well-developed states of the North. The claim by some scholars that the world has become "borderless" and that the state has shrunk in importance, giving ground to the MNC, is probably misconstrued.[4] Only in some Third World states is government weak, and there it is due to internal causes (Rapley 2006: 95–103). It is true that influence has become more dispersed among the states of the North. The United States has experienced a relative decline since it was the economic hegemon that led in the development of the Bretton Woods system and the GATT process. Today, the United States is at best a *primus inter pares*, or first among equals. Still in possession of the world's largest gross domestic product (GDP), the United States increasingly has found it necessary to consult and bargain over rules with other significant economic powers. The GDP is a macro-measure at the national level based on the total worth of goods and services for one year. In early 2009, the United States had a GDP of $11.75 trillion, but it had a national debt of $10.8 trillion and was running huge annual budget deficits.

This country is paying for the long-running wars in Afghanistan and Iraq and providing over $1.5 trillion in bailouts for troubled banks and infrastructure funds to energize an economy in deep recession.

Consulting bodies among the major economic powers often infuse IGOs with policy ideas that the latter later apply as rules and norms in economic relations. Policy ideas often started with the meetings of the Group of Eight (G-8). This consulting body started in 1975 as the G-7, and included Canada, France, Germany, Great Britain, Italy, Japan, and the United States. With the Cold War's end, Russia was brought on board, as much for an opportunity to socialize this ex-communist state in the ways of Western democratic-capitalism as for this country's economic potential. Other national economies are larger and more robust than Russia's, and these countries can assert a claim that their representatives be included. Certainly Brazil, China, India, Mexico, and South Korea have worthwhile claims. Recognizing the oddity over their absence in 2005, Britain's Prime Minister, Tony Blair, invited additional states with economic prowess to join in talks when he hosted the G-8 summit. Gradually summit meetings began to be called G-20 conferences as more countries joined in to help find ways to jump-start the sagging world economy in 2008–9. These industrialized states want to lift their economies and have to be concerned with the developing countries of the Third World pulling them down further. The economies of these poorer states were worsening as international banks and investors cut credit lines to stanch their financial hemorrhaging. In April 2009, British Prime Minister Gordon Brown hosted another G-20 meeting of the top economic states, aimed at solving the finance problems of the sagging world economy and avoiding the pitfall of turning back to protectionism.

An interesting opportunity for consulting and suggesting management ideas for the world economy is the World Economic Forum (WEF) since it brings a variety of actors to one place and has done so annually since 1971. The WEF is a non-profit NGO registered with the Swiss government and has observer status at the UN Economic and Social Council. The WEF draws as many as 40 top heads of state, over 1,000 MNC executives, several hundred NGO representatives, journalists, and professors of business law for a total of 2,500 persons to the Davos resort near Geneva, Switzerland. The WEF's best known publication is its annual *Global Competitiveness Report*, which ranks countries according to how well they embrace free trade policies and operate their corporations efficiently. The United States has often been number one in this report and was again in 2008–9. The rest of the top ten in the same year are from Western Europe except for Japan and Singapore. The WEF is corporation-oriented in the sense that business profits are sought, but it also pays attention to uplifting socioeconomic conditions for society in general. It places this policy under the rubric of Corporate Global Citizenship.[5]

Some of the most important IGOs applying rules and norms are the World Bank, International Monetary Fund, Organization for Economic Cooperation and Development, and the World Trade Organization. Created with the 1944 *Articles of Agreement* at Bretton Woods, the World Bank is actually a group of banks.[6] There is the International Bank for Reconstruction and Development (IBRD), with 185 state members, that focuses on helping middle-income and credit-worthy countries. This affiliate of the World Bank had cumulated loans of $446 billion in 2008. The International Development Association (IDA), with 168 members, serves the poorest states by providing long-term, low-interest loans. Its commitments were at the $193 billion mark in 2008. The World Bank group also contains the International Finance Corporation (IFC) for private sector loans, the Multilateral Investment Guarantee Agency (MIGA) for insuring large foreign investments, and the International Center for Settlement of Investment Disputes (ICSID) to assist with arbitration procedures. The member-states provide the loan monies and have commensurate voting power with what they invest. The World Bank has 10,000 employees working in 100 countries. It shifted focus from war-torn Europe to infrastructure projects in the Third World such as highways, airports, and hydroelectric plants, and finally sought to achieve socioeconomic progress for the general populations of the less developed states. Under fire from critics, the World Bank has tried make gender equality and environmental issues priorities while advancing economic growth.[7]

The International Monetary Fund (IMF) was created in the same Articles of Agreement as the World Bank. If the World Bank is the first pillar of the Bretton Woods system, the IMF is the second. The membership of the IMF is the same 185 states that support the World Bank. Coordination between the two takes place through the World Bank/IMF Development Committee. The IMF is served by 2,500 personnel and had lendable assets of $250 billion in 2009. A recent investment by Japan of an additional $100 billion bodes well for reaching this goal of $500 billion in lendable assets. The purpose of the IMF is to stabilize the international monetary and financial systems for the greater good of encouraging international trade. Without confidence in currencies and national banking systems, economic exchanges would be quickly reduced to bartering for goods.[8] The task of the IMF was simple enough as long as the various national currencies could be pegged against the gold-based American dollar, but in 1971, President Richard Nixon took the United States off the gold standard, requiring the IMF to use a "float system" based on an average of several major currencies.

The IMF has become the "lender-of-last-resort" to help the poorest developing countries when these cannot secure loans elsewhere. Countries able to establish good credit with the IMF and the World Bank are said to have "seals-of-approval" that enable them to borrow from regional development banks and private banks. Both the World Bank and the IMF have been criticized as vehicles of Western capitalism that allow the rich states to impose control over the poor. Critics have called the IMF the "debt police" because it requires client countries to reform their economies by lowering the value of their currencies, reducing the national debt, or making loans harder to acquire. These belt-tightening measures might suit a capitalist banker but are very unpopular in poorer countries when, as a result of these measures, the standard of living drops even lower. The loss of food subsidies is especially dire and causes so-called "IMF riots."

The Organization for Economic Cooperation and Development (OECD) began in 1947 but reorganized under the 1960 *Convention on the Organization for Economic Cooperation and Development*.[9] Headquartered in Paris, France, the OECD is made up of 30 industrialized democracies committed to free trade as a way of boosting world economic growth. Besides South Korea and the United States, the OECD is made up of European states. In 2007, Russia was invited to consider joining, and Brazil, China, and India may soon be asked as well. This IGO has decades of experience and research accumulated in areas such as trade, agriculture, technology, and taxation. The meetings of the OECD allow governments to compare policy experiences and pursue answers to common problems. This organization shares its expertise with 70 other non-member countries, and its extensive publications in economics and public policy are useful tools for disseminating its philosophy and knowledge.[10]

The premier IGO for liberalizing and managing international trade is unquestionably the World Trade Organization (WTO), which succeed the GATT process in 1995. In addition to encouraging the removal of trade barriers, the WTO has a Dispute Settlement Body (DSB) that can allow an aggrieved state to level punitive tariffs against another state for violating fair trade practices. An appeal by either or both parties is possible. As of early 2009, the WTO has helped settle over one-third of more than 300 disputes, with others settled outside of WTO procedures or still in process. Not surprisingly, the United States, as the largest trade state, has led all others in the number of disputes. The United States has been involved in 92 cases as the complainant and 105 cases as the respondent. The EU, as a single trade entity made

---

Box 12.1 The Banana Wars

A dispute over trade in bananas developed between the United States and the EU during the 1990s before the WTO took over from the GATT process in 1995. Ironically, neither party grew bananas, but the United States had companies, such as Chiquita Brands, raising bananas in Central and South America. These American companies were accustomed to shipping their fruit to Europe. Although the American brand was cheaper than bananas imported from ex-colonies in Africa, the EU still decided to give preferential treatment to the ex-colonies' bananas as a way of boosting African economies.

The United States began charging EU countries punitive damages under its own laws. After this case went before the WTO Dispute Settlement Body, the United States won an award in tariff sanctions of nearly $200 million. The United States had asked for a $500 million settlement. What became known as the "banana wars" involved a puny amount compared to most trade sectors, but the danger is great that the situation could escalate into a full-blown trade war if these issues were not put to rest. In 2001, the United States and the EU, negotiating outside the WTO framework, agreed the United States would drop the sanctions if the EU would be more generous in licensing imports of Chiquita bananas.

Sources: From http://www.wto.int/ > Trade Topics > Dispute Settlement > By Subject > Bananas; http://www.asil.org/ > Publications > insights > ASIL Insights > Insights Archive 2001 > US-EU Agreement to Resolve the Banana Dispute.

up of 27 states, has also taken part in many disputes. Despite its rapid growth into a major trading power, China has had only a few cases before the DSB.[11]

The WTO has 153 members, including China, which joined in 2001, and 30 observer states with Russia in this group. This body is headquartered in Geneva, Switzerland and has a staff of 625 persons and a budget of $163 million. The WTO monitors compliance with a daunting list of 60 agreements, annexes, decisions, and understandings inherited from the Uruguay Round that cover tariffs, services, inventions, technical standards, safety, and much else.[12] The Uruguay Round was a lengthy trade negotiation and the last such round of the GATT process.

Standardizing the Global Economy

Trade agreements frequently have been fairly detailed, specifying exactly the goods covered and the quotas on how many can be imported. Setting technical standards for trade is even more detailed but is very important. For trade to go forward smoothly and with mutual confidence between suppliers and users, transparency regarding amounts, quality, and safety of goods must be present. Standardization refers to conforming to the same technical criteria as a common denominator. Failing that, reliable conversion tables should be available to interpret from one type of measure to another.

After decades of effort, standardization is far from complete in world commerce. Several types of electrical plugs, both 110 and 220 voltages, and direct as well as alternating currency flows are in use in various places around the world. There are both fahrenheit and celsius thermometers. Multiple ways of measuring shoe sizes still exist, and shoes are one of the most common export-import items in world trade. Mechanics have to keep both metric and American/English tool sets to work on cars, at least in the United States. There are still about 20 countries where cars require the steering wheel on the right side in contrast with most of the world placing steering wheels on the left side. Yet standardization has occurred in many areas and doubtlessly will continue to advance in more trade sectors as the world further integrates economically. Credit cards are the same size all over the world and usually work flawlessly through the fiber optic lines tying the world's telephone systems together. Picture symbols on the instrument panels of cars are alike, thus, minimizing the problem caused by drivers using different languages. Signage in airports, hotels, and on restroom (water closet) doors is often in the same easily understood picture symbols. Energy use is frequently calculated in British thermal units (BTUs).

Pressing for greater harmonization among products is the International Organization for Standardization, usually written as the International Standardization Organization (ISO).[13] This organization adds dozens of new standards each year to the 20,000 already in existence, which cover everything from quality control of underwater oil pipelines to the sweat resistance of a shirt. The ISO began its operations in 1947 and is headquartered in Paris, France. The ISO is an NGO, but it occupies a special position as a bridge between public and private sectors. It began with the support of 25 countries, and today over 150 countries' national standards institutes attend ISO meetings and contribute ideas, along with business and industrial organizations, IGOs, and consumer groups. Through its "World Standards Day," celebrated every October 14, the ISO tries to raise public awareness about the importance of common standards. The staff of the ISO contributes to global management of the world economy by helping monitor the application of WTO treaties. Probably most important to the ISO are the *Agreement on Technical Barriers to Trade* (TBT) and the *General Agreement on Trade in Services* (GATS), the latter dealing with standards in banking, telecommunications, and insurance, among other services. For the more advanced national economies, services are a growing sector of foreign income relative to trade in goods.[14]

Most trade partners welcome some sort of standardization or at least conversion tables to facilitate commercial interchange. An area particularly controversial, however, is the Internet and who controls it. The Internet has exploded into an unforeseen size and importance since its beginning as a communications network among elements of the US military. Private emails, access to massive data sets by banks, linkage among octopus-like MNCs operating in multiple countries, research of every imaginable subject, and the buying and selling of everything from automobiles to clothes can take place because of the Internet. It is an indispensable tool of modern international business.

The Internet, not unlike roadmaps, has to indicate routes and destinations to permit travel, in this case the travel of electronic communications. Some sort of management must exist over the choice of domain names, Internet protocol numbers, who possesses the powerful computers used for root servers, and standards that allow computers to interface. For about thirty years a California professor managed this complexity but, in 1998, the United States encouraged a non-profit private organization to take over. As a result, the Internet Corporation for Assigned Names and Numbers (ICANN) was established and registered in California.[15] Many other countries view this move with suspicion and want an international organization like the ITU to take over Internet responsibilities. Critics argue that the United States could, in an act of retaliation or war, remove a country's initials, for example ".ir" for Iran, from its domain name and shut down its Internet service. In the years 2003–5, the United States did contemplate allowing an IGO to take over in 2006, but backed away from this decision.[16] Essentially, the United States trusted ICANN operating from its soil more than an IGO where various political perspectives could lead to unwanted mischief.

Intellectual Property Rights

As national economies modernize, the wealth of a country depends more and more on **intellectual property** as opposed to manufactured goods or commodities that many countries have to sell. Intellectual property refers to creations of the mind such as artistic works, computer software, or inventions.[17] The creation might be essentially a mental construct, as with a pharmaceutical formula, or a hybrid development based on a researcher's ideas plus the extraction of a tropical plant. Intellectual property is a broad term covering patents for inventions, trademarks such as logos, copyrights on books, movies, and music, and trade secrets concerned with the preparation of food or beverages. The protection of intellectual property dates back in English history to the 1623 Statute of Monopolies on patents and the 1710 Statute of Anne on copyrights.[18]

Until recent times, the protection of intellectual property was a mishmash of national laws plus some bilateral and regional treaties. Margaret Mitchell and her husband spent much of their time and energy trying to sue over illegal translations and publications of her famous 1936 novel, *Gone with the Wind*. They had to secure legal aid in each country and go through that country's national courts. Protection at the international level received a major boost with the World Intellectual Property Organization (WIPO) established by the 1967 *WIPO Convention*, which entered into force in 1970.[19] The WIPO is headquartered in Geneva, Switzerland, and administers 24 Intellectual Property Rights (IPR) related treaties, including the well-known 1886 *Berne Convention for the Protection of Literary and Artistic Works* and the 1883 *Paris Convention for the Protection of Industrial Property*. Since 1995, the WIPO has reinforced the WTO's *Agreement on Trade Related Aspects of Intellectual Property Rights* (TRIPS).[20]

Intellectual property amounts to a significant portion of many states' wealth, with struggles taking place over some protecting this property and others trying to take it away. Improper use of another's ideas can involve counterfeiting of a drug, theft of an engineering design, or arguments over whether an idea is appreciably different or merely a copy of another's creation. Struggles over intellectual property are only partly contained by the WIPO and the two dozen treaties housed by this UN agency. The industrial democracies of the OECD are most likely to respect the IPRs of others because each wants its own respected (Marlin-Bennett 2004: 47). Much of the intellectual piracy seems to occur when a state is undergoing development as one of the newly industrializing countries (NICs) since these states are especially ambitious for further economic expansion. In the nineteenth century, the United States, a NIC in this era, not only printed copies of Charles Dickens' novels at will but copied English textile machinery whenever possible. Today's NICs, including Brazil, China, and Mexico, have industries that are following a similar pattern of using the ideas and creations patented or copyrighted in other countries without paying licensing fees for their use.[21] However, today's NICs also have MNCs with research and development facilities and original creations of their own, and the more they develop in this direction, the more these countries are likely to respect the IPRs of others.

International law on intellectual property is designed to protect owners' rights and indirectly encourage international business exchanges, but the temptation for an easy profit wins out in many instances. Through reverse-engineering, everything from bulldozers to air conditioning test gauges can be reproduced in nearly identical versions. Gucci purses, Rolex watches, movie and music CDs, the Harry Potter books, ex-President Bill Clinton's autobiography, *My Life*, and hundreds of other merchandise have illicit copies on the international market amounting to billions of dollars in wrongful trade. The profits of this illegal enterprise also attract organized crime and terrorists seeking funding for their operations (Naím 2005).

Contention often arises as the governments of states strive to protect individual and company intellectual property and, in turn, enhance national wealth. The sharpest conflict has been over medicines and their high costs. With killer diseases like cholera, tuberculosis, malaria, and especially the HIV/AIDS virus raging through many African

---

Box 12.2 *Microsoft v. Commission of the European Union*

In addition to protecting intellectual property rights, there are questions of unfair practices of excluding a competitor's creations, cases known as anti-trust activities or monopolization. Bill Gates' company, Microsoft, has struggled with the EU since at least 1993 when complaints began to surface about monopolization over Windows Media Player. Bundled with Windows, Media Player made it difficult for competitors to use their media players with the Windows framework.

The EU Commission ordered Microsoft in 2004 to sell a Windows version without Media Player and to pay nearly $800 million in fines. This case was before the Court of First Instance from 2004–7, but Microsoft lost and abandoned the issue. When the EU Commission fined Microsoft $1.44 billion for failure to adequately comply with the earlier 2004 decision, Microsoft appealed the astronomical fine in 2008 with the Court of First Instance. In the latest development, a Norwegian company, with a web browser called "Opera," filed another anti-trust action claiming Microsoft's use of Internet Explorer with Windows makes it difficult for other web browsers to work with Windows.

Source: The case filed with the EU's Court of First Instance in 2004 can be read at http://eur-lex.europa.eu > Access to European Union Law > Simple Search > European Court Reports > Enter "2004" and scroll down to the Microsoft case.

---

countries, as well as other places, hundreds of thousands of lives are at stake. Medications from the developed countries are so costly that most sick people in the Third World may as well entertain the desire to buy a luxury automobile. A market demand for cheap, generic versions of necessary drugs, such as the anti-viral cocktail of medicines to treat AIDS, has sprung up in many countries but, unfortunately, their manufacture commonly violates the patent laws of the rich, industrialized states. Brazil, India, and Thailand have thriving illicit national and international businesses in the generic manufacture of medicines. An AIDS generic imported from Thailand can be a small fraction of the cost of the original medicine in the United States or Europe. Third World countries implored the WTO to change the rules over copying medicines in generic form to save untold numbers of AIDS victims, but these states were turned down until 2003 when the WTO finally relented for humanitarian reasons and gave permission for the importation of life-saving generic drugs at substantially lowered costs.

Commercial Arbitration

The closest of allies and trading partners can have disputes over a trade agreement, but most states and corporations want these settled as quickly and inexpensively as possible so they can move on to future trade opportunities. In preference to the lengthy procedures of foreign ministries and court proceedings, arbitration is often preferred. Arbitration is a binding settlement by impartial arbiters relying on facts and law to determine an outcome. While arbitration historically is *ad hoc* and can involve a one-time use, arbitration bodies are available upon request. Lists of arbiters are retained and called upon when needed. Decisions by arbiters are regarded as final and compliance by the disputing parties is expected.

The Permanent Court of Arbitration, established at the turn into the twentieth century has not had a heavy case load but did show a rise in cases in the 1990s dealing with borders, the environment, and trade. The private organization of the International Chamber of Commerce has offered business interests the International Court of Arbitration since 1923 that has heard thousands of cases. This arbitration panel relies on the 1958 *New York Arbitration Convention*, with over 130 parties, for enforcement of its decisions. In 2005, the Hague Conference on Private International Law offered the *Convention on Choice of Court Agreements*. This convention reinforces the New York convention by governing the choice of forum as well as enforcement of decisions. Also useful to an arbitration forum is the 1985 *Model Law on International Commercial Arbitration*. Amended in 2006, this model of arbitration was developed by the UN Commission on International Trade Law (UNCITRAL) as a guideline for business arbitration.[22]

Another arbitration option of growing importance is the International Center for the Settlement of Investment Disputes (ICSID). Investment across national boundaries has come to rival trade in importance. The ICSID is provided in a convention sponsored by the World Bank, the 1966 *Convention for the Settlement of Investment Disputes* with the support of over 140 parties. Hundreds of bilateral investment treaties (BITs) in existence frequently call for using the ICSID. Over sixty cases have come before this forum so far, and these usually involve an MNC from the North as plaintiff and a Third World government as a respondent, or defendant. The investments of MNCs often entail permanent fixtures–such as factories, fleets of trucks, communications systems, and major agribusiness operations–worth millions of dollars. The complaining company naturally objects to any form of expropriation, either in whole or degree, or damage done to its properties during internal strife, experiences that are not uncommon in many Third World countries.[23]

Finally, arbitration has been used in numerous cases concerning a practice known as "cybersquatting." Individuals or companies register domain names involving celebrities' names hoping to cash in by selling this domain to the celebrity for a tidy sum. While it is easy and inexpensive to register a domain name with ICANN, WIPO has offered arbitration since 1999 to settle disputes over conflicting claims. Parties in dispute often accept a WIPO-appointed arbiter, or panel of arbiters, to save the high costs of a regular court. Many celebrities, including Pierce Brosnan, Richard Crichton, Celine Dion, and Kevin Spacey, have reclaimed their names from cybersquatters with the help of WIPO arbiters. WIPO's arbitration process allows for an appeal to be filed in a national court system within ten days after an arbitration ruling, if one or both parties are dissatisfied.[24] Allowing an appeal before a public court provides a generous option because, as a principle of international law, arbitration decisions are normally final.

Globalism versus Regionalism

Is governance of economic interchange better served from the global or the regional level? With the proliferation IGOs since the Second World War, scholars have often engaged in rounds of debate over this theoretical question. *Globalism* is the belief that resources, markets, and transportation and communication are worldwide and so governance through rules and norms should operate from this level. *Regionalism* involves the belief that regional management is more efficient because fewer states are at stake, they are in geographical proximity, and they often share a similar culture and problems. In practice, both levels can encourage development and prosperity without significant incompatibility between the two (Lawrence 1995: 411–12; Coleman & Underhill 1998; Cohen 2003).

The UN has long been operating on the assumption that economic expansion will depend on both levels of governance. The Bretton Woods institutions of the World Bank and the IMF plus the WTO are global and are independent agencies operating under the auspices of the UN Economic and Social Council. This same council also oversees five UN regional economic commissions for Africa, Asia and the Pacific, Europe, Latin America, and Western Asia.[25] The WTO readily accepts the formation of regional trade agreements (RTAs), only it expects to be notified of their formation, and states belonging to RTAs must still meet their WTO obligations.[26]

The ultimate question is whether regional economic organizations can undermine the global legal regime and its economic promotional role. The answer is that RTAs are very unlikely to do so. Strong forces are at work underpinning the global level. First, the Bretton Woods institutions and the WTO are firmly established, with non-members such as Russia anxious to join. Second, free-trade values were firmly established at the global level when the United States was clearly an economic hegemon pushing free trade ideas. The US effort seemed validated when the communist regimes of Europe collapsed and turned to democracy and capitalism. Despite some backward steps, especially by the Russian government, these values are holding fast. Third, the major trade states are scattered about the world and on different continents, thereby buttressing a global pattern. Fourth, MNCs, the major vehicles of world trade and investment, tend to spread out globally to achieve maximum efficiency and profits. In a final analysis, regional trade arrangements appear to make national economies stronger and better able to compete on a global scale. In fact, members of RTAs usually trade more outside than inside their respective regions. A major exception is the EU, where *intra*-regional economic activities surpass those that are *inter*-regional.

The regional arrangements are numerous and vary regarding the extent of **economic integration**, which is the merger of two or more national economies in some degree.[27] Most RTAs are free trade arrangements reducing tariffs in agreed-upon sectors of trade. The EU, as a union, is exceptional with substantially more integration. A union can have common tariff policies toward non-members, suspension of customs inspections among members, the free movement of labor and capital on an intra-regional basis, a central banking system, and even a common currency. The institutional basis of RTAs is established in the treaties of their creation, but decisions to go deeper into integration depend largely on the expected economic benefits. Obviously a major global recession such as the one in 2008–9 does not bode well for deeper integration among RTAs; however, this recession could easily prove to be a temporary setback. Several major examples can be offered to show the diversity among regional economic arrangements.

The EU has evolved over several decades into a well-integrated union of 27 states. Multiple treaties help account for today's EU, most importantly the 1986 *Single Europe Act* and the 1992 *Treaty of Maastricht*. The first calls for a borderless Europe with goods, persons, capital, and services able to move about without hindrance, and the second provides for a central bank and the opportunity to use a common currency, with 16 EU states so far joining the Euro Group. While Europeans backed away from agreeing to a European Constitution in 2004, the 2007 *Treaty of Lisbon*, providing for more transparency and democracy on the part of EU institutions, may be ratified in 2009.[28] The European Commission, European Parliament, and European Court of Justice possess a measure of *supranational authority* over the 27 countries to guarantee smooth operations as a single economic entity. Largely because of the EU, Europeans enjoy the highest standard of living in the world. In 2008, the EU states contained 456 million people or consumers and a total GDP of $18 trillion measured in US currency.

The North America Free Trade Association (NAFTA) was proposed in 1992 and its treaty of creation, the *North American Free Trade Agreement*, ratified in 1994. Additional agreements on labor rights and protection of the environment had to be reached before the United States would ratify. This agreement covers trade goods, services such as banking and insurance, and IPRs among Canada, Mexico, and the United States.[29] Trade has more than doubled among these countries since the creation of NAFTA, but questions still linger over the matter of MNCs benefitting at the expense of American labor and Mexican farmers. The three NAFTA countries have more than 440 million people living within them and a total GDP of over $16 trillion. The United States provides, by far, the largest portion of people and GDP. One outstanding issue is continue refusal by the US government to allow Mexican cargo trucks to travel freely within the United States Mexico retaliated in the spring of 2009 with higher tariffs on American imports.

Proposals have been made to extend NAFTA to all of North and South America, perhaps under the name of the Free Trade Association of the Americas. Thus far, this proposal has not been realized, perhaps due to sub-regional groups being unsure just what a hemispheric arrangement would mean for them. Already in place are the Andean Community, Mercorsur, and the more recent 2004 *Central American Free Trade Agreement* (CAFETA), with the United States and Central American countries as members.

Another well-known regional organization is the Association of Southeastern Asian Nations (ASEAN). This organization began as a political consultation group in 1967 and reorganized as a free trade association in 1992, a plan announced in the Singapore Declaration. In 2007, the 10 member-states signed the ASEAN Charter expressing ambition for a more economically integrated economic community by 2015.[30]

These states have a total of 560 million people and a combined GDP of $1.1 trillion. A much broader arrangement, but encompassing ASEAN, is the Asia Pacific

Economic Cooperation (APEC) arrangement, which has remained as a loose consulting body for 21 states located around the Pacific Rim. The membership includes the powerful trade states of China and the United States APEC has held summit meetings for heads of states annually beginning in 1993. Without much in the way of organizational structure or treaties, the purpose of APEC is to persuade members to reduce tariff barriers in more sectors of goods.[31]

The large African Union (AU), with 53 members, has not unified Africa as a single economic entity as the EU has done for Europe. The AU has focused on ambitions reorganizing its institutions and adding others. At the 2007 summit meeting in Accra, Ghana, leaders discussed the possibility of a "United States of Africa." Toying with the superstructure of the AU may seem grandiose in light of the many fundamental problems the African people are experiencing, such as poverty, AIDS, weak educational systems, bloody civil strife in several countries, and corrupt dictators, to name but a few. Economic cooperation on the African continent is divided among eight trade associations with overlapping memberships, for example, the East African Community and the Common Market of Eastern and Southern Africa.[32] Little is being done to draw these eight "islands" into a continental economic arrangement. The African states hold 850 million people having to share a total GDP of about $900 billion of which the Republic of South Africa alone accounts for almost one-third.

Governance of the South

The states of the South, or Third World, have long expressed grievances. In the second half of the nineteenth century, the states that evaded colonial bondage, such as China, Persia, and Japan, desired to be treated as sovereign equals to European states. Those states held in colonial empires sought their independence as well as wished to be accorded racial equality and enjoy respect for their cultures. Today, the injustice that remains falls in the economic domain.

As the Third World coalition of developing states grew in number with the shrinking of colonial empires, these states waited patiently, but in vain, for their old colonial masters to fulfill their moral obligation of making sure that the new states enjoyed prosperity. Husbanding their wealth and dealing with their own problems, the developed states of the North beckoned to the South, by the 1960s, to join in the free trade system pressed on the world by the United States. Instead, the South insisted on new rules, almost a revolution. The South was emboldened by an unexpected development, the early success of the Organization of Petroleum Exporting Countries (OPEC) as a commodity cartel. In 1973, OPEC sent the industrial states reeling backward for a time as it tightened the taps on the flow of oil and charged high prices. Taking a cue from OPEC for confronting the North, the South used its majority in the UN General Assembly to pass the 1973 *Declaration on Permanent Sovereignty over Natural Resources* and a 1974 *Charter on Economic Rights and Duties of States*. Later, these states also came up with the 1986 *Declaration on the Right to Development*. The centerpiece to the South's revisionist approach, however, was the 1974 *New International Economic Order* (NIEO). Basically, this vision of a new order included a free hand to regulate MNCs on their soil, enjoyment of a generous transfer of technology, power to expropriate foreign property on the South's terms, acceptance by the North of additional commodity cartels similar to OPEC, and preferential tariff treatment for the South.[33]

The reaction of the North was hard nosed. Rejected was the South's general appeal for economic justice as a redistribution of wealth. Self-development and finding something to sell to the world under the Bretton Woods model appeared to be the only path left for the Third World. The North's vast resources of investment capital, foreign aid, technology, desirable exports including arms and luxuries, plus the historical fact that the industrialized states had put the free trade system in place before the large majority of Third World states slipped the hobbles of colonialism, gave the developed states the upper-hand. Failed attempts at rational argument and moral suasion were compounded by the rise of the "Asian Tigers" in the early 1980s. Singapore, South Korea, and Taiwan (Nationalist China), and later the economic dynamo of China demonstrated that impressive economic growth was possible by following a free-market model. In all fairness to the South, this "free market" seemed to be *neo-mercantilist*, with emphasis on export-driven growth and strong resistance to imports.

If the South failed to achieve a redistribution of wealth from the North, these states at least built a solid platform within the UN for further advocacy. Many agencies of the UN contribute to socioeconomic development, but several are primary. The Group of 77 (G-77) formed in 1964 at the UN was based on the number of available developing states at the time. This coalition retains the same name although it now numbers over 140 states. With its large majority, the G-77 can often control the resolutions and declarations of the UN General Assembly and influence UN's many specialized agencies, such as the Food and Agricultural Organization, that relate to economic development.[34] In 1988, the G-77 proposed a trade arrangement among developing states that became the *Agreement on the Global System of Trade Preferences among Developing Countries* (GSTP), which still has only 43 parties. The aim of the agreement was to promote trade ties across Africa, Asia, and Latin America to raise the prosperity of the South in a self-help manner.[35] The relatively small number of ratifying states, out of a potential of at least 140 states, indicates that states of the South are well aware that what they need requires strong, beneficial economic ties with the North.

In the same year as the G-77 organized and with its support, the UN Conference on Trade and Development (UNCTAD) formed and became a strong champion of the Third World point of view. UNCTAD was informally known as the "poor man's lobby."

UNCTAD serves as a forum, research center, and a source of technical assistance to help developing states integrate into the world economy. For instance, it provides technical and administrative assistance for the GSTP.[36]

The most important body of the UN for assisting Third World states is the UN Development Program (UNDP). Its 2007 budget was $1.2 billion, a phenomenal sum for an IGO. This body coordinates the Millennium Development Goals (MDG), which is a broad partnership of many organizations and countries. The MDG started in 2000 and has the overarching aim of cutting world poverty in half by 2015. There are eight specific goals with a set of special targets associated with each goal.[37] Ideally, the MDG would be so successful that the yawning gap between North and South would close once and for all. The generosity of the North toward the MDG is undoubtedly weakened by the worsening recession of 2008–9.

Box 12.3 The Human Development Index

(Selected countries)

High human development

1	Iceland	0.968
3	Australia	0.962
4	Canada	0.961
8	Japan	0.953
12	USA	0.951
16	UK	0.946
22	Germany	0.935
25	Singapore	0.922

Medium human development

43	Lithuania	0.862
48	Costa Rica	0.846
51	Cuba	0.838
61	Saudia Arabia	0.812
67	Russia	0.802
74	Venezuela	0.792
81	China	0.777
121	S. Africa	0.674
128	India	0.619

Low human development

177	Senegal	0.499
158	Nigeria	0.470
168	DR of Congo	0.411
156	Sierra Leone	0.336

Source: From the *Human Development Report 2007/2008* (New York: Oxford University Press, 2007), Table 1, p. 229. The HDI is a composite measure based on (1) Purchasing Power Parity (PPP), which is GDP per capita converted to eliminate differences in spending power of national currencies, (2) longevity of life, and (3) education levels.

Another important role of the UNDP is to provide the annual *Human Development Report*, which contains the Human Development Index (HDI).[38] This index is a salient and meaningful measure of economic development, one that is focused on the welfare of people. Knowing only that the GDP of a country increased might simply reveal that the rich were getting richer. Instead of focusing on the GDP, as a national or macro-measure, the HDI measures how effectively the wealth of a country reaches individual persons. The HDI is a composite measure of income, longevity of life, and education. Countries are ranked according to the score achieved. A human rights view of development requires that improvements occur in the quality of life for the general population. When a country of modest means improves its HDI score, it is an invitation for other countries to study what the improving state is doing right in its policies.

Despite the North's efforts to draw the South into its circle of prosperity by following the free trade model and UN agencies pushing these same states to achieve developmental goals, the huge North–South economic chasm holds on. Barbara Ward's 1962 *The Rich Nations and the Poor Nations* called this "tragic division" the most urgent problem of that time, and it still is today.[39] At the turn into the twenty-first century, the world economy was enjoying vigorous growth and, as Martin Wolf observed in his *Why Globalization Works*, the integrating free trade system seemed set to close the North–South divide (Wolf 2004; see also Dollar & Kraay 2002: 120–33). Others have been less sanguine about reducing this inequality. Jeffrey D. Sachs believes the gap is actually widening if only because the North is getting rich faster than the South can improve.[40] Even in prosperous times, the extreme poverty of a "bottom billion" people of the Third World, living on hardly more than a dollar a day, can seem unyielding.[41]

Can blame be assigned for the North–South gap and the failure to develop the Third World more effectively? The North's indictment is well-known. The Third World countries need more democracy because of the special synergy between this type of government and economic prosperity. Widespread corruption by predatory elites who loot their own national treasuries undermine any hope of progress. Civil wars and revolutions have mostly occurred in developing states in recent decades, disrupting economic potential. The weak infrastructure of many underdeveloped areas discourages MNCs from wanting to locate and invest. Third World states are satisfied to depend mainly on a single commodity or industry and seem unable diversify. Social policies are inadequate for redistributing a country's wealth, polarizing national societies into the few rich versus the many poor.

If one criticism stands out among developmental experts and within agencies of the UN, it is that the traditional role of women must be reformed. Instead of staying home and raising a large family, women should receive equal education as men and enter the work force in an economically productive way. The Report of the South Commission, *The Challenge to the South*, has stressed that a gender-sensitive approach to development is a basic condition for economic and social progress.[42]

Spokespersons for the South can level charges as well. The research and development by the North's MNCs will always keep the North ahead unless the best technology is shared with the South. The debt load placed on the Third World in the 1970s and 1980s drains money from socioeconomic development to service loans. More rescheduling terms, if not complete forgiveness of the debt, is required. The North preaches free trade but indirectly restricts the South's agricultural products. The North's farm subsidies keep prices of crops at home so low that imports from the South cannot compete. The North resists the South trying to control its MNCs in effective ways, even when many of these companies already have far more money and personnel than the governments of most Third World states. Finally, the North never delivers all the aid it promises, making it difficult to plan development projects over the long term. Perhaps the best general assessment is that both sides have creditable positions and that there is enough blame to go around.

If a consensus did exist over a program for economic development, would there be enough "natural capital" or resources to allow such an expansion in wealth?[43] All the careful planning that can be marshaled cannot make something out of nothing. As the population of the world surpasses nine billion at mid-century, will there be enough wood, oil, natural gas, water, soil for crops, and other necessities to allow everyone on the planet to live as well as, say, a typical European? The world need not plunge into a Malthusian nightmare before realizing that sufficient natural resources may not be available to overhaul the standard of living for billions of people. Overstrained resources to produce a prosperous economy for all could even result in conflict and war, according to Michael T. Klare's *Resource Wars* (Klare 2002). Modern global communications makes the world's poor aware of how their elites at home and the populations of the North live. Increasing numbers of people experiencing "rising expectations" is the understandable result.[44] Hope rests on the human population leveling off at 9.5 billion people during the twenty-first century, according to UN demographers, and on improved technology stretching both old and newly discovered resources to better accommodate developmental demands.

Four Economic Flows in the North–South Relationship

The North–South economic relationship revolves around four flows: trade, aid, investment, and loans. Both above and below the equator, the four are regarded as mutually useful, but different perspectives are at work. The North's approach is of course the free market model with emphasis on trade and investment, and it has never been willing to give much ground on this model's rules. The South's approach calls for a partnership with the North to build up the South for the common good (South Commission 1990: 211). If the South cannot force a new economic order into place, some small accommodation over the four flows is at least expected by the South.

The trade flow

In the North–South relationship most income for the South depends on selling commodities such as coffee, bananas, and various metal ores, as well as finished products, especially wearing apparel. The standard complaint is still heard that this trade is neocolonial, with the South selling for what the North will pay, and the

North charging the South high prices for technology-based exports such as medical equipment or computers. One exception to this trade pattern has been OPEC, which had a dramatic early success in 1973 but less influence on world markets in recent times. The 40 percent of the petroleum market controlled today by OPEC allows this cartel to put its thumb on the scale but that is about it.

Ideally, the South would like to have concessionary trade, meaning low tariffs applied on its products by the North while charging higher tariffs on products imported from the North. The North has traditionally had a firm rule about trade being *reciprocal*, meaning trade partners grant the same and equal privileges to each other. The North also has long used the *most favored nation* (MFN) rule, with the trade terms given to a trade partner guaranteed to be as good as the terms allowed any other trading partner. States of the North generally assume trade partners can be on an equal footing, practicing symmetry in the relationship. Without concessionary trade terms, however, the developing states fear they cannot make economic progress and certainly cannot catch up with the developed states of the North. The South insists on some asymmetry in trade relations. Noted economist Ethan B. Kapstein believes that free trade will ultimately close the North–South gap but, since the North has tilted the playing field against the South in the first place with "rigged trade regimes," the North should, for a time, practice "relaxed reciprocity" (2006b).

Some concessionary trade has been won from the North. UNCTAD successfully lobbied the GATT process for the 1971 Generalized System of Preferences (GSP), which calls for waivers in symmetrical trade. The GSP, however, is a program and not an obligatory treaty. States of the North are free to handle the GSP as they see fit. Some developed states have reduced their tariffs without expecting the same reduction from an economically weaker state. As the GATT rounds lowered tariffs for all, the privileges of the GSP grew less important. Some states have special programs of the GSP type. One of these is the *Caribbean Basin Initiative* established by the United States in 1983, which continues today for 24 Caribbean and Central American countries. The EU used the four *Lomé Conventions* since 1975, and now the 2000 *Cotonou Agreement* signed in Cotonou, Benin, to extend lower tariffs to 71 poorer African, Caribbean, and Pacific countries, a privilege that will last until 2020.

The major trade issue that currently overshadows all others in the early twenty-first century is the question of agricultural subsidies. For decades, the industrialized democracies of the North have paid out subsidies, or price supports, to guarantee a level of income for their farmers allowing them to keep their farms going. The United States has a large agricultural subsidy program, but subsidies in Europe and Japan sometimes amount to triple those in the United States. Unfortunately, farm subsidies make cotton, peanuts, wheat, corn, and many other commodities so cheap that farmers in Third World countries cannot compete in domestic markets of the industrial democracies or even internationally. Agricultural products, after all, are the sector of trade that gives most states of the South their best chance for an export that will produce a national income. When subsidies create an artificially low international price, it is called *dumping*, that is, placing a product or commodity on the market at a price below the actual cost of production. Dumping is incompatible with free trade principles, along with tariffs and quotas. The North's subsidies clearly violate the spirit of the free market model.

The use of farm subsidies by states championing free trade is ironic at best. What can explain this contradiction to free market principles? The farmers of the industrialized states make up only a tiny percentage of the overall populations of the EU countries, Japan, and the United States, but these are democracies with farmers spread across most electoral districts. All kinds of farmers – tillers of the soil, herdsmen of cattle and sheep, and harvesters of fruit, among others – in a country join hands to form a powerful phalanx calling for protectionist policies for agriculture. In many cases, farmers are really corporations known as *agribusinesses* and able to lobby effectively for subsidies, or what critics call "corporate welfare."

At the 2001 Doha, Qatar, round of the WTO, the major offenders promised to cut farm subsidies, but at the 2003 summit in Cancún, Mexico, these same states reneged on their Doha promises. Countries have often preached free trade principles only to pull up short at international conferences to mollify domestic interests. In 2004, Brazil, weary of unfulfilled promises, took the United States before the WTO's dispute settlement process and won over the issue of US cotton subsidies.

Box 12.4 Brazil versus the United States on Cotton Subsidies

The United States has often found its trade practices challenged before the WTO. The United States did win a case against the EU over bananas in 1999, and had a partial success against Canada over the importation of Canadian softwood lumber in 2004. In other cases, however, especially while George W. Bush was president with his protectionist bent of mind, the United States has not fared so well. Brazil complained for years that US cotton subsidies created an artificially low international price for this commodity, in effect "dumping" American cotton on the world market. Brazil won the original case before the WTO's Dispute Settlement Body in 2004 and continued to consult with the foot-dragging United States on this issue. Both states appealed the decision in 2008 before the Appellate Body of the WTO, and this appeal confirmed the earlier decision in Brazil's favor.

Brazil, in early 2009, is attempting to be allowed to use WTO countermeasures of a punitive kind against the United States, and Brazil is seeking as much as $4 billion in compensation. If permitted, Brazil may use "cross-retaliation," meaning it will seek sanctions in the intellectual property rights sector instead of charging extra tariffs on some American imports. Brazil could possibly copy something the United States makes without paying a licensing fee.

Sources: http://www.wto.int/ > Dispute Settlement > Disputes by Subject > Cotton; http://www.asil.org/ > Publications > insights > ASIL Insights > Insights Archive 2005 > The WTO Decision on Cotton Subsidies.

The foreign aid flow

Billions of dollars gifted to Third World states over several decades have not made major differences in the living conditions of the peoples in these countries. There are several reasons for this disappointing outcome. Aid money turned over to corrupt dictators has simply vanished. When given as a tool for winning friends during Cold War competition, the aid furnished came with few guidelines for its use and was often squandered. Foreign aid has frequently been spread so thin over too many projects that a positive and telling effect has not been measurable. And finally, the aid promised by the states of the North, since the 1995 UN World Summit for Social Development (better known as the poverty summit) in Copenhagen, Denmark, has never been forthcoming. The rich states rather stingily offered a mere 0.7 percent of their national economy's worth, but only Denmark, the Netherlands, Norway, and Sweden have met this goal. Except for the pledges to donate aid money at conferences, foreign aid has been a matter of political policy by individual state donors and not agreements stemming from global governance. There are some exceptions, as when the EU offers aid as an organization. With the Cold War competition now past and with poor results from previous gifts of foreign aid, the donor states have begun to experience "compassion fatigue."[45]

As a policy strategy, private aid through NGOs, targeted at specific problems, may do more good than foreign aid by states. Ex-President Jimmy Carter's Carter Center and the Bill Gates Foundation have had some success with controlling diseases in Africa. CARE and Oxfam International have for decades taught the poor how to feed themselves and branched out into the empowerment of women and aid during natural disasters and conflicts.[46] One of the most interesting private aid projects is by the NGO One Laptop Per Child. Tens of thousands of low-cost, low-powered computers provide self-education opportunities for the children of Third World countries. Far more laptops are needed. It is too early to know how this project will impact on economic development and the quality of life if millions of poor children are connected to the Internet.[47]

The investment flow

Investment has been gaining on trade in recent years as an important economic flow. The major type of investment is *foreign direct investment* (FDI), involving the movement of a large amount of capital across borders on a long-term basis to develop a profit-making enterprise. FDI is distinguishable from an individual's stock portfolio in a foreign country. A US car manufacturer building an automobile plant in China, a French telephone company setting up and operating cell towers and line phones in an African country, or a Japanese company making fork-lifts in the United States are examples of FDIs. MNCs are normally involved in FDI and, for efficiency's sake, have operations in several or many countries. For example, Trelleborg, a Swedish-registered company, is a fairly average-sized company with 24,000 employees at 100 manufacturing sites in 40 countries. This MNC made the fabric for the escape slides of airliners in Spartanburg, SC, within the United States. These emergency devices permitted the crew and 150 passengers to escape from a plane forced to land in the Hudson River in New York City on January 15, 2009. This incident has come to be known as the "Miracle on the Hudson."

Many MNCs have not enjoyed a favorable public image within the context of economic development in the South. The view of the North is that MNCs are helping build an economy advantageous to all states and peoples. The other interpretation, one that many academic critics and Third World leaders espouse, is that MNCs are exploiting poorer countries, ignoring human rights, and harming the environment (Schwartz & Gibb 1999). It seems that with every possible advantage MNCs produce, a corresponding disadvantage occurs. There have been some particularly egregious episodes that have stained the reputation of MNCs. In 1973, International Telephone and Telegraph, apparently with the CIA's help, reputedly helped bring down the democratically elected government of Salvador Allende in Chile and, in 1984, Union Carbide accidentally leaked a poisonous pesticide killing over 3,000 people in Bhopal, India, to name but two. Starting with the WTO conference in Seattle, Washington in 1999, anti-globalization protestors began showing up at economic summits to object to the abuse of the poor and the environment due to international business practices (Broad 2002).

Many developmental NGOs and Third World governments would like to see international rules guaranteeing more social responsibility on the part of MNCs. Critics have become concerned that the most powerful MNCs are even beyond the control of the industrialized democracies where most are registered as corporate entities (Hertz 2001). Regulatory international law is not in place, and so *codes of conduct* are the make-do regulation available. These are moral norms calling for MNCs to do right instead of wrong as they pursue profit. These codes are numerous but only a few will be mentioned. The UN struggled for years for such a code, and finally Secretary-General Kofi Annan presented the 10 principles of a *Global Compact*. The ILO offered the *Tripartite Declaration of Principles Concerning Multinational Enterprises and Social Policy*. The OECD contributed the *Guideline for Multinational Enterprises*.[48] Numerous NGOs monitor MNCs and suggest their own codes, frequently within specific industries. The Clean Clothes Campaign (CCC),

---

Box 12.5 Good and Bad Effects of MNCs

Introduce technology	Offer ill-suited technology
Encourage economic growth	Retard economic growth
Encourage interdependency	Cause dependency
Elites learn to regulate MNCs	MNCs bribe elites
Promote human rights	Disrespect human rights
Protect the environment	Harm the environment
Economic actors in essence	Influential political actors
Promote a globalized world	Damage national cultures

with its interest in the notorious working conditions of women and children in the garment industries of the Third World, is one that is well-known.[49]

The loans flow

Loans for development were actually encouraged by the North in the 1950s and 1960s but, in time, loans ballooned in size. A particularly sensitive interdependence arose in North–South relations in the 1980s and continues today. Vast sums of money, known as petro-dollars, flowed to the OPEC states following the oil crisis of 1973 and the sharp rise in oil prices. Awash in unprecedented amounts of cash, Saudi Arabia and other OPEC members placed their money in Western banks. As good bankers, the executives of these banks put the money to work and loaned out huge amounts of monies to any state, including the poor Third World countries. At one point, the total owed across the South was $1.3 trillion in 1980s money, and the interest to service this staggering sum would amount to 30 percent of their total wealth for a year. These states had planned to invest the borrowed money wisely and so be able to service the massive debt. Such an outcome proved to be exceptional. By the early 1980s, the indebtedness of the developing states had come to be known as the "debt bomb" because default by a major borrower might trigger a chain reaction through a pyramid structure of interconnected banks, causing financial collapse on a major scale (Ferraro & Rosser 1994: 321–55; George 1992).

When bad planning, corruption, rampant consumerism, and recessionary trends in the 1980s caught up with the large indebted class of Third World states, it became apparent that servicing debts was seriously undermining states' budgets, meaning that national services in health care, education, and food supplies were strained. Environmental harms increased as states exploited their natural resources to pay off debts (Hertz 2004: 184). A debt strategy based on the North's rules – loan for profit and somehow exact repayment – obviously was not working. In particular, the World Bank's early role of focusing on infrastructure projects such as roads, ports, and dams was not doing well. One study reported less than half the developing states borrowing from the World Bank benefitted from its loans, and a goodly number were worse off than before (Moore 2003: 230).

A new policy of dealing with Third World debt was needed. The policy would involve rescheduling debt by lowering the interest rate and extending the repayment period, the policy already being followed by regional development banks, such as the Asian Development Bank.[50] Other approaches include simply retiring the debt with donations from others or forgiving the debt altogether. For the 40 poorest countries, mostly in sub-Sahara Africa, the IMF, the World Bank, and the Asian Development Fund began retiring debts of the heavily indebted poor countries (HIPC) in 1996, using funds provided by G-8 countries. The Inter-American Development Bank joined in with help in 2007.[51] Some environmental NGOs are willing to retire small amounts of debt when states agree to preserve some aspect of their environmental base.

From the private sector, hundreds of thousands of people have signed petitions calling for debt forgiveness, because payments on loans subtract from what developing states have to provide for human services. Perhaps an odd pairing, but noted development economist Jeffrey D. Sachs and U-2's lead singer Bono (Paul Hewson) have famously teamed up to be spokespersons for this option (Hertz 2004: 4, 10; see also Sachs 2005b: 355–76). The NGO Jubilee 2000 (now Jubilee Research) has also called for debt cancellation.

One of the most useful ways to help people with loans in the Third World is found outside the purview of states and the treaties they can create. This strategy involves micro-loans of $50 to $250 dollars. From these tiny loans, purchases of bamboo to make furniture, cows to provide milk for sale, and yarn for weaving stoles, for example, result in viable business ventures for great numbers of people. Bangladeshi economist Muhammad Yunus began this idea in the 1980s and, for his efforts, was awarded the 2006 Nobel Peace Prize. His loans grew into the Grameen Bank, and this simple concept has been duplicated in other regions outside of Asia.[52] An affiliate is *Pro Mujer* ("for the woman") operating in several Latin American countries.[53] Most of the recipients of micro-loans are women who have used the money to go into business and better their lives and that of their families (Sen 1999: ch. 8).

Counter-productive Issues for the Global Economy: Organized Crime, Corruption, and the Pursuit of Non-economic Goals

Organized crime has operated across borders for decades, if not centuries, and draws a significant portion of the world's wealth into a non-taxable underworld and away from useful investment and development. Close behind crime ventures is the practice of corruption. Crime and corruption are "cancers" on the world economy reducing its health and vitality. The pursuit of non-economic goals by economic means also undermine commerce and development, even though the goals sought may be legitimate

Crime

Transnational organized crime (TOC) is a growth industry enjoying prodigious profits roughly estimated to be from one-half to $1 trillion a year, generated through the loss and suffering of innocent people. Rampant crime is the dark underbelly of a surging interdependent world economy. TOC has ridden on the back of globalization, taking advantage of rapid travel and communication, including the use of privately owned jet aircraft, the ease of transferring and hiding bank funds, communications by cell phones, and encrypted messaging via the Internet. Illicit goods and trafficked persons can be moved with unprecedented speed and efficiency. Now, as Moisés Naím has said, "All borders leak, all the time."[54]

The pernicious effects of TOC involve bribery of officials, the murder of thousands of lives, courts tied up with numerous cases, billions of dollars spent on law enforcement and the operation of prisons, and even the spread of diseases such as

AIDS as a result of the illegal drug trade and prostitution. Criminally gained wealth may lay dormant as cash in bank lock-boxes or in numbered bank accounts, or spent frivolously on perishable luxuries. Wasted, this money will not build schools or hospitals, buy textbooks or medicines, construct roads or dig wells.

Criminal organizations typically start in one country but extend tentacles into others, both to increase profits and to thwart law enforcement by operating in multiple jurisdictions. Well-known criminal organizations are the Sicilian mafia, Russian mobs known as the *mafiya*, Japanese yakuza, Chinese triads operating from Hong Kong, the cocaine cartels of Colombia, and Mexican drug smugglers operating along the Mexican–US border. These gangs vary in the amount of international activity, but some are ascending above national and regional levels to form global connections. For instance, Colombian cartels have been known to sell heroin for the Sicilian mafia in the Americas if the mafia sells cocaine for them in Europe and Asia. And the yakuza have helped trans-ship Colombian cocaine from Lebanon to Japan. Trans-regional activities in the trafficking of persons, arms, counterfeit merchandise, and everything else sellable also take place. So far the global pattern has been restricted to cases of mutual assistance on a trans-regional basis, but international enforcement will need to gain traction before crime operations become more globally centralized.

While some treaties to halt trafficking in persons and drugs date back to the League of Nations era, the UN has energetically pursued crime and corruption as a priority. Today's most important global crime-fighting regime centers on the UN Office on Drugs and Crime, the widely supported UN *Convention against Transnational Organized Crime* (CTOC) and its three protocols dealing with trafficking in persons, the smuggling of migrants, and illicit manufacturing and shipment of firearms. The CTOC went into force in 2003 and its protocols shortly afterward. These four together create a strong, comprehensive regulatory framework.

Parties to the CTOC are obliged to create national laws against money laundering, joining a crime organization, and obstructing justice. They are also to confiscate illegal gains, use agreed upon sentences, and coordinate with police agencies of other states. The provision on extradition is particularly noteworthy, for it is similar to extradition in the humanitarian and war crimes context. Governments capturing suspects are to try them or send them to a state that will.[55]

The UN has long helped countries deal with drug abuse and the improper trade in a wide range of drugs. Barely having been created, the UN started the Commission on Narcotic Drugs in 1946 as its central policy-making body on drugs. One of its primary tasks is to monitor three UN treaties, and which are widely supported by states based on the number of ratifications of over 180 for each. The 1961 *Single Convention on Narcotic Drugs* covers a broad range of drugs and tries to limit their possession and movement to stop trafficking. The 1971 *Convention on Psychotropic Substances* covers illegal trade in synthetic drugs. And the 1988 *Convention against the Illicit Traffic in Narcotic Drugs and Psychotropic Substances* focuses on money laundering related to drug profits, the diversion of necessary chemicals in the manufacture of drugs, and extradition of drug traffickers.[56]

In a 1998 UN General Assembly special session, the year 2008 was set as a target-date for significantly reducing or eliminating the world's drug demand and illegal trade, but gains have been modest, if any. Drug addiction remains common and trafficking is both cleverly secretive and bloody. Several submarine-type vessels, carrying cocaine or marijuana, have been intercepted recently in the Gulf of Mexico and the Caribbean Sea. Long tunnels are dug under the Mexican–US border and replaced when authorities collapse them. Drugs flow to the United States and arms are smuggled from the United States to Mexico. Several small towns along this border have witnessed turf wars among drug gangs, with murder by decapitation not unknown. As opposed to lighter armed police officers, only the Mexican Army can enter parts of these towns. Shrewd smuggling methods and murderous behavior are replayed all too often in many areas of the world. Besides the usual greedy motive of huge profits, there are also the needs of terrorists and insurgents to acquire funds for their violent strikes and warfare. The Taliban in Afghanistan, for example, now encourage crops of heroin poppies to raise funds but, when in power, this religious group outlawed such crops. Apparently religious zealots can be practical when they need to be.

Regional efforts are in place too. The Council of Europe (COE), made up of 47 states, adopted the world's first *Convention on Cybercrime* that went into force in 2004. Crimes over the Internet have exploded in number, ranging from robbing bank accounts to exchanging pictures among rings of child pornographers. Europe has created the European Police Office (Europol), proposed in 1992 and operational in 1998. This office can help with intelligence-sharing and the coordination of national police forces during an investigation. The EU implemented the Shengen Agreement in 1995 to maintain strict border controls over non-EU citizens to prevent crime and terrorism. The OAS has useful regional treaties relating to crime but, in 2006, OAS members adopted the Hemispheric Plan of Action against Transnational Organized Crime, calling on OAS members to apply the UN's CTOC and its three protocols.

Corruption

Corruption and crime go hand in hand. Bribery induces the police and military to look the other way while criminal gangs ply their unlawful trade. The corruption of officials is the key determinant of whether organized crime thrives or withers (Thachuk 2007: 11). Corruption tends to worsen over time as individuals taking bribes become greedier and their associates decide they want in on the easy money too. The collapse of Chinese dynasties over the centuries was usually preceded by deep patterns of corruption that weakened tax collection. In turn, less tax revenue meant a decline in the ability to pay for a military able to provide centralized control. Eradicating corruption is critical if a country is to attract major investments, increase tax revenue, and deliver human services such as health and education (Mauro 1997: Hodder 2007).

Probably no country is entirely free of corruption, but some countries of the South have been hurt by especially strong patterns of this problem. Poor countries usually pay their civil service and police poorly, hence the temptation to take bribes. For those states with large revenues from oil, gold, diamonds, and exotic timber, pernicious corruption can also be the order of the day. Instead of these revenues going to the good of the general population, much of this commodity wealth is siphoned off into officials' foreign bank accounts and used to pay-off leaders' patronage groups. Shocking examples of embezzlement are well-known. Suharto of Indonesia took $15 to $35 billion, Mobutu Sese Seko of Zaire (now the Democratic Republic of the Congo stole $5 billion, and Sani Abacha of Nigeria awarded himself $2 to $5 billion.[57]

In 2007, the World Bank set up a program to help developing countries recover stolen assets. World Bank President Robert B. Zoellick has estimated that $1.0 to $1.6 trillion a year is stolen from the world's total wealth due to crime, corruption, and tax evasion. The problem is most acute in Africa, where 25 percent of national economies are lost to corruption. The World Bank recovery program operates in conjunction with the UN Office on Drugs and Crime. For the countries ratifying the *Convention against Corruption*, which went into force in 2005, their goverments are obliged to repatriate any stolen funds placed in their banks.[58] Regrettably, numerous states have failed so far to ratify, including Switzerland, which helped pioneer the numbered bank account concept absent a person's name. Switzerland at least signed this convention in December 2003.

Corruption is not restricted to states. The UN itself became caught up in a major corruption scandal concerning the $64 billion Iraqi oil-for-food program. Following the defeat of Iraq in 1991 by a UN multinational force, led by the United States, awareness of the deprivation of the Iraqi people in the post-war aftermath led to this humanitarian program. Iraq was allowed to sell oil to raise revenue for food and medicine. Kickbacks quickly followed. Companies wanting to do business with Iraq overpaid for oil creating a pool of money for Saddam Hussein's lavish spending and to pay off UN officials for ignoring the kickbacks. An investigation panel, headed by former Chair of the US Federal Reserve Paul A.Volcher, found substantial evidence against multiple individuals, including the ex-director of the oil-for-food-program, Benon Savan. Secretary-General Kofi Annan was at least sharply criticized for not monitoring UN personnel more effectively and apparently had a son involved in the corruption. The oil-for-food program lasted from 1996 to 2003; interestingly, the latter year was when the UN Convention against Corruption was proposed.

The legal structure aimed at corruption is impressive, but this problem is tough to eradicate. The UN convention has regional reinforcement. One is the 1996 *Inter-American Convention against Corruption*. In 1997, another was added as the OECD brought about the *Convention on Combating Bribery of Foreign Public Officials in International Business Transactions*. This convention, of which the United States is a party, helped the United States in business competition. When the US *Foreign Corrupt Practices Act* of 1977 went into effect, MNCs registered in the United States were forbidden to sweeten business deals with bribes, whereas companies from other industrialized states might not be constrained in this manner. The OECD convention helped level the playing field among the largest industrial and trade states. The COE's 2003 *Criminal Law Convention on Corruption* allowed charges to be brought against individuals in their own right and as agents of MNCs. Also in 2003, the AU devised a *Convention on Preventing and Combating Corruption*. It is the UN Convention against Corruption, however, that has the best chance for effectiveness because it can apply to the entire world, and has the critically important provision for repatriating stolen funds.[59]

National and international law are very important to control corruption, but the roots of this problem drive deep into many national cultures. Sadly, many of the countries most in need of economic development are also those prone to corruption (Lipset & Lenz 2000: 112–24). Transparency at least can help off-set proclivities toward corrupt practices. Transparency is openness and accountability, and usually practiced more thoroughly in mature democracies. Committees of legislatures scrutinize executive conduct, courts apply the rule of law to wayward individuals, attorneys-general investigate judges suspected of taking bribes, and the populace turns out officials suspected of wrong-doing via elections. Democracy is not an absolute guarantee against corruption, however. The Governor of Illinois, Rob Blogojevich, was charged by federal authorities in late 2008 for trying to "sell" President Barack Obama's US Senate seat, and the Illinois legislature impeached and convicted him in a 59–0 vote for the same offense in early 2009. In the private sector, until arrested in late 2008, financier Bernard Madoff once ran the world's record Ponzi scheme of $50 billion from New York City.

Since crime and corruption have become such transnational phenomena, the role of the International Criminal Police Organization, better known by its old telegraph address of Interpol, has become most important. Interpol, formed in 1923, coordinates investigations and pursuits of fugitives across national boundaries in the areas of organized crime, trafficking persons, drug smuggling, corruption, as well as terrorism and even art theft. Interpol maintains a Command and Coordination Center around the clock for the use of its 187 participating state-members. Interpol is headquartered in Lyons, France and was recognized by the UN in 1971 as an IGO, after first receiving consultative status as an NGO at the UN in 1949.[60]

NGOs have proven invaluable for imposing transparency on governments and IGOs. One of the best known in this field is Transparency International (TI), with its annual and carefully watched Corruption Perceptions Index. This NGO ranks countries according to the extent of their corruption. One World Trust works to ensure accountability in global governance, including the role of IGOs. NGOs even scrutinize each other for honesty and effectiveness, a service provided by NGO Watch and Charity Navigator.[61]

Non-economic goals

The pursuit of non-economic goals often diverts economic energies away from development's contribution to human prosperity, whether on the part of rich or poor states. Sanctions have often been leveled by well-meaning countries to protect human rights, consumer safety, and the environment. One of the more criticized sanctions policy still in effect, however, is the one leveled against communist Cuba by the United States. The standard of living for Cubans is undoubtedly hurt by US sanctions since Cuba, before its communist era, had traded heavily with the United States. This policy is a remnant of the Cold War but is still useful to American political leaders as a way to attract Cuban–American voters in Florida. The 1992 *Cuban Democracy Act* forbids trade with Cuba, even by foreign-located subsidiaries of MNCs registered in the United States. The 1996 *Helms–Burton Act* continues the trade embargo and allows Americans, who lost property due to Cuba's expropriation of American companies in the 1990s, to sue in US courts. The law suit can be directed at the company of a third country that does business with Cuba when the business arrangement involves seized American property. European trade partners and allies of the United States are especially upset over this sanctions policy. President Barack Obama was moving in early 2009 to keep a campaign promise to allow Cuban–Americans to visit Cuba, but not to end the trade boycott.

Multilateral economic sanctions have often been used by IGOs, such as the UN, to either stop or encourage particular behavior by other actors. The League of Nations sought to halt Italy's invasion of Ethiopia in 1936 with economic sanctions, and the UN wanted to bring down the white-ruled regime of Rhodesia (today's Zimbabwe) in 1965 with sanctions. Much more is known today about the side-effects of sanctions, as in the case of UN-sponsored sanctions against Iraq in the early 1990s. These were aimed at preventing Saddam Hussein from developing weapons of mass destruction. The side-effects included widespread illness, hunger, and loss of Iraqi lives, especially among children, and certainly raise serious questions about the way sanctions are applied and their general usefulness.[62] It can also be argued sanctions against Iraq were not necessary in the 1990s as Iraq was exhausted first by the war of the 1980s with Iran and then by fighting the US-led coalition over Kuwait in 1990–1.

Are the socioeconomic problems experienced by general populations from sanctions justified by the goals sought? The history of sanctions shows that they often do not work and may have undesired consequences. A great deal of careful thought has been given to sanctions in recent years resulting in a focus on "smart sanctions." Such sanctions target elite decision-makers, including freezing their bank accounts in foreign countries or prohibiting their travel by air, thus minimizing negative effeczts on general populations (Cartwright & Lopez 2002: O'Sullivan 2003). Smart sanctions are not a panacea, but they help protect the welfare of most citizens of a country.

Chapter Summary

- Once countries realized they needed or wanted the products of others, trade treaties developed first as bilateral arrangements and finally as regional and global agreements that included IGOs to supervise.
- Although different philosophies and policies have always characterized international commerce, a major effort by the United States after the Second World War to lead the world toward a consensus within a free trade system.
- A major problem for consensus over world trade is the huge gap between the industrialized states of the North and the poorer countries of the South, with the latter seeking different rules that will allow them to narrow the economic gap.
- Corruption, crime, and the use of economic potential for political leverage are "leaks" on the world's wealth that ultimately harm the well-being of many people.

Discussion Questions

1   How does the hegemon theory (regarding the development of international law) help explain the rapid build-up of treaties and IGOs backing the world economy that emerged after the Second World War?
2   Do treaties on economic relations operate better from the global or regional levels, or is such a distinction even important?
3   What are GSTPs and why do Third World states desire them in trade treaties?
4   How does the lack of ratification by Switzerland of the Convention against Corruption help sustain corrupt practices?
5   What is Interpol and what is its status regarding the UN?

Useful Weblinks

http://www.globalpolicy.org/reform/indxbiz.htm
This website began during Secretary-General Kofi Annan's tenure at the UN. He set up the Global Policy Forum to develop a close partnership between the UN and the international business community. This site offers pertinent publications and papers on the role of business in economic development, reports on relevant conferences, an available electronic newsletter, numerous reports by development-oriented NGOs, and useful additional links including the UN Global Compact site for guiding MNC conduct.

http://www.worldtradelaw.net/
For a legal approach to the international economy, this website is invaluable. Much of the focus is on the GATT/WTO process and dispute settlement. Also offered are quick links to Trade Law Articles, Trade News, a blog on international economic law, legal texts, IGOs, court/tribunal decisions, university programs, and even jobs.

http://www.icrw.org/
This website by the International Center for Research on Women (ICRW) is a leading NGO in the field of development as it relates to women. This NGO operates from the assumption that poverty, hunger, and disease can be better dealt with by focusing on the role of women in development. As a think-tank, the ICRW provides research to government policy-makers so they can weave research ideas into practical policy. This website offers its annual report in electronic format. ICRW receives a four-star rating by Charity Navigator for its efficiency and good management of finances.

http://www.asil.org/trade-investment.cfm
This website by the American Society of International Law offers legal and institutional developments in the areas of trade, foreign direct investment, intellectual property, and the transnational movement and regulation of goods, services, labor and capital.

http://www.jus.uio.no/lm/international.economic.law/toc.html
This site is hosted by the Law Faculty of the University of Oslo. It lists directly accessible links for consulting groups and IGOs, international economics, international trade law, international investment, and corruption. This website has a built-in

search engine and an "A–Z" index for the site. One of the accessible links is "Lex Mercatoria," covering electronic encryption, corruption, and cross-border crime, among many other topics.

Further Reading

Ala'i, Padideh, Broude, Tomer, and Picker, Colin (eds.) (2006) *Trade as Guarantor of Peace, Liberty and Security?* Washington, DC: American Society of International Law.

Andersen, Birgitte (ed.) (2006) *Intellectual Property Rights: Innovation, Governance and the Institutional Environment.* Northampton, MA: Edward Elgar.

Baldwin, Richard and Low, Patrick (eds.) (2009) *Multilateralizing Regionalism: Challenges for the Global Trading System.* New York: Cambridge University Press.

Datta, Rekha and Kornberg, Judith F. (2002) *Women in Developing Countries: Assessing Strategies for Empowerment.* Boulder, CO: Lynne Rienner.

Dewey, Susan (2008) *Hollow Bodies: Institutional Response to Sex Trafficking in Armenia, Bosnia and India.* Herndon, VA: Kumarian Press.

Dignam, Alan and Galanis, Michael (2009) *The Globalization of Corporate Governance.* Burlington, VT: Ashgate.

Guzman, Andrew T. and Sykes, Alan O. (eds.) (2007) *Research Handbook in International Economic Law.* Northampton, MA: Edward Elgar.

Kariyawasam, Rohan (2007) *International Economic Law and the Digital Divide: A New Silk Road?* Northampton, MA: Edward Elgar Publishing.

Kouladis, Nicholas (2006) *Principles of Law Relating to International Trade.* London: Springer.

Lambert, June (2009) *Enforcing Intellectual Property Rights: A Concise Guide for Businesses, Innovative and Creative Individuals.* Burlington, VT: Ashgate.

Lawrence, Robert Z. (2003) *Crimes & Punishment? Retaliation Under the WTO.* Washington, DC: Institute for International Economics.

Lea, David (2008) *Property Rights, Indigenous People and the Developing World.* Boston, MA: Martinus Nijhoff.

Smith, Fiona (2009) *Agriculture and the WTO: Towards a New Theory of International Agricultural Trade Regulation.* Northampton, MA: Edward Elgar.

Waelde, Charlotte and MacQueen, Hector (eds.) (2007) *Intellectual Property: The Many Faces of the Public Domain.* Northampton, MA: Edward Elgar.

Wolf, Ronald Charles (2004) *Trade, Aid, and Arbitrate: The Globalization of Western Law.* Burlington, VT: Ashgate.

Wouters, Jan, Noellkaemper, André, and de Wet, Erika (eds.) (2008) *The Europeanization of International Law: The Status of International Law in the EU and its Member States.* New York: Cambridge University Press.

Notes

1   The multifaceted nature and speed of globalization are made poignantly clear in the popular books by Friedman 1999; 2007.

2   Falk 1999); and see Broad 2002). For a favorable view of globalization, read Bhagwati 2007.

3   Bederman believes international law has a special, even if limited, role to play in many of the policy debates concerning today's globalization. See his 2008.

4   Korten 1995); and Strange 1996. For a view on state resilience, see Slaughter 2001: 177–205. Also, along this theme is Cohen 2006.

5   See the website of the World Economic Forum at http://www.weforum.org/.

6   The Bretton Woods Articles of Agreement can be accessed at http://www.worldbank. org/. Scroll down to "Index" > Articles of Agreement.

7   Go to http://www.worldbank.org/.

8   Refer to http://www.imf.org/.

9   The OECD Convention is at http://www.oecd.org/ > About oecd > History.

10   An extensive amount of information on this organization is at the website cited in end-note 13.

11   Visit http://www.wto.int/ > WTO Structure > Settling Disputes. And read Lanoszka 2009.

12   To investigate these, go to http://www.wto.int/ > introduction > understanding the WTO > the Agreements > Overview.

13   The website for the ISO is at http://www.iso.org/. Standardization can also be read about in Loya and Boli 1999: 169–97. Also, a recent, useful work is Murphy 2008.

14   See the "Information Center" of ISO at http://www.standardsinfo.net/.

15   This service is at http://www.icann.org/.

16   Much of this information on the ICANN issue is drawn from 2005: 7–13. Also, see Paré 2003.

17   This definition depends on the one given at the website of the World Intellectual Property Organization, http://www.wipo.int/about-ip/en/.

18   Neipert 2002: 145–7. For parallel developments in the United States, see Matsuura 2008.

19   For the WIPO Convention and the 24 conventions this IGO monitors, see http://www. wipo.int/treaties/en/convention/.

20   On TRIPS, read May and Sell 2006: 161–201. TRIPS can be read at http://www.wto.org/ > Legal texts > Annex 1C Trade Related Aspects of Intellectual Property Rights (TRIPS).

21   Written with sympathy for Third World states regarding IPRS is the edited volume of Drahos and Mayne 2002.

22   UNCITRAL's website is http://www.uncitral.org.

23   Information on the ICSID and the Convention for the Settlement of Investment Disputes is at http://www.icsid.worldbank.org/ICSID/.

24   The website of WIPO's Arbitration and Mediation Center is at http://www.wipo.int/ amc/en/index.html.

25   The regional economic commissions can be found at http://www.un.org/aboutun/ mainbodies.html.

26   WTO's stance on RTAs can be found at http://www.wto.int/ > Trade Topics > Regional Trade Agreements.

27   See note 26 and > RTA Database.

28   The treaties behind the EU can be accessed at http://europa.eu/abc/treaties/index_ en.html.

29   As a treaty, NAFTA can be read at http://www.export.gov/fta/nafta/doc_fta_nafta.asp and see http://www.naftanow.org/.

30   ASEAN's home web page is http://www.asean.org/.

31   More on APEC is at http://www.apc.org/.

32   These eight economic organizations can be located at http://www.african-union.org/ >
      RECs.

33   Hedley Bull, "Justice in International Relations," 1983–1984 Hagey Lectures (Waterloo
      Ontario: University of Waterloo). Given October 12–13, 1983, pp. 1–36. See, especially,
      pp. 2–5. The best single article on Third World expectations may still be Murphy 1997:
      201–15.

34   The Group of 77 has a website at http://www.g77.org/.

35   Refer to http://www.unctadxi.org.

36   UNCTAD's web page is http://www.unctad.org/.

37   The Millennium Development Goals can be viewed at http://www.undp.org/mdg/
      basics_ontrack.shtml.

38   This report is available at http://www.undp.org/ > Human Development Report.

39   Ward 1962: 36. Along the same theme, see Landes 1998.

40   Sachs 2008: 18; see also 2005b); and refer as well to Greig, Hulme, and Turner 2007.

41   Collier 2007; and see Isbister 2006). A recent World Bank re-evaluation of purchasing
      power and poverty places 1.4 billion persons at the bottom.

42   South Commission 1990: 128–31. Also, see UN 1999: ST/ESA/269. In addition, read
      Handelman 2000: 78–102.

43   An introductory work on this question is *Global Resources: Opposing Viewpoints* 2008.

44   For background reading on population and the environment, see Ehrlich and Erhlich
      2008.

45   See the articles on foreign aid in Oatley 2005: 377–94.

46   An interesting article on development NGOs is Veltmeyer 2005: 89–109.

47   This NGO's website is http://www.laptop.org/. A useful critique of the Internet's worth
      to economic development is Kenny 2006.

48   Annan's "Global Compact" is at http://www.globalpolicy.org/reform/indxbiz.htm > UN
      Documents > The Ten Principles of the Global Compact. The ILO Tripartite Declaration
      is at http://www.ilo.org/global/lang–en/index.htm. Enter "Tripartite Declaration" in the
      search engine. For the OECD Guideline visit http://www.oecd.org/. Enter "Guideline for
      Multinational Enterprises" in the search engine.

49   Many such NGOs and their websites are found in Broad 2002: 309–24. Also, the websites
      of numerous codes of conduct can be accessed at http://www.goodmoney.com/direc-
      tory_codes.htm. As well, see the website of the Center for Research on Multinational
      Corporations at http://somo.nl/. The Clean Clothes website is http://www.cleanclothes.
      org/ > Codes of Conduct.

50   Four regional development banks can be accessed at http://www.dfid.gov.uk/ > devel-
      opment banks.

51   The program for this category of indebted states is at http://www.imf.org/ > hipc.

52   Dowla and Barua 2006; and visit http://www.grameenfoundation.org/

53   The site of this bank is http://www.promujer.org/.

54   Naim 2005: 273. For general reading, see Aas 2007.

55   This convention and the three protocols, plus their ratification status, are available at
      http://www.unodc.org/unodc/en/treaties/ctoc/index.html.

56   A wide range of UN activities in this area are at http://www.unodc.org/unodc/en/illicit-
      drugs/index.html. For treaties at this site > Treaties > Drug-related Treaties.

57   Newspaper article on July 10, 2007 cites the NGO Transparency International at http://
      www.transparency.org/.

58   From Warren Hoge, "World Bank and UN to Help Poor Nations Recover Stolen Assets,"
     New York Times (September 18, 2007). Chapter 5 of the UN Corruption Convention is
     about Asset Recovery. This UN convention can be read at http://www.unodc.org/unodc/
     en/treaties/CAC/index.html.
59   There are 131 states that have ratified the UN Corruption Convention cited in note 58.
60   This international police agency can be found at http://www.interpol.int/.
61   Transparency International is located at http://www.transparency.org/; One World Trust
     is found at http://www.oneworldtrust.org/; Charity Navigator is at http://www.charity-
     navigator.org/; and NGO Watch is found at http://www.ngowatch.org/.
62   At least one study takes the position that the UN sanctions were successful in blocking
     Saddam Hussein's ambitions. See Lopez and Cortwright 2004: 90–103.

Part IV
Making the Future

13

The Problems and Prospects
of International Law

Making the world more lawful has a distinguished history. The success of international law as a set of rules most actors obey most of the time seems assured for the future. While it is relatively recent that political scientists have begun to study this subject, once left to law professors, they have come to appreciate how much international law helps shape international relations. The theoretical dominance of realists in the international relations field obscured international law's contribution for decades. It was inconceivable to realists that law could operate effectively without a central authority equipped with strong coercive tools for enforcement. As a horizontal system of mostly voluntary compliance, international law was first accepted by states, then by other actors, because they needed this law to fulfill a functional need. The preference on the part of most humans seems to call for avoiding wasteful conflict and settling differences in other ways. Creating rules, whether in war, trade, or in any area, tell actors what to expect and what to do, thus heading off many problems before they can materialize into major issues.

Besides the usefulness of international law, a growing population of states, IGOs, and NGOs embrace this law because they are socialized within the international society to do so. Beginning in Europe, modern international law has become a global structure helping bind the world together. The majority of states want acceptance within international society to better promote and protect their interests. States realize violations of international law damage their reputations and hurt their chances for achieving their goals. Non-colonized countries, such as Japan, the Ottoman Turkish Empire, Persia, and Siam were willing to embrace a Euro-system of rules to better cope with European states enjoying impressive military and economic power. Later, ex-colonies in Africa and Asia wanted the same acceptance, and their elites had the advantage of European educations and employment in European bureaucracies.

Within the state system, whether in Europe or worldwide, it might be useful to the development and future of international law for a benevolent hegemon to strongly back this law, as the United States did in the post-Second World War period to restart and improve a global economy. Hegemonic support may not be an absolute necessity, however, when one considers the continued expansion of treaties without US support. From the LOS convention to the Kyoto Protocol, rules in many areas have evolved without ratifications by the United States. This observation holds up even in the anti-treaty presidency of George W. Bush from 2001 to 2009. If the world were based on a small number of states, as was the case up through the Second World War, the power structure among states might be more determining. Now, with an international society of 200 states and hundreds of IGOs, plus thousands of NGOs characterized by varying degrees of legal personality, this society apparently can flourish even with an uncooperative hegemon present.

International law has also proven to be amazingly effective without the usual strong government institutions carrying out the three traditional functions of rule-making, rule-enforcement, and rule-adjudication. In facsimile fashion, make-do institutions manage to perform these functions, as when the UN begins the legislative process. The ILC of the UN has on several occasions proposed a treaty to states. If a sufficient number ratify, the international legislative process is completed. The sources of international law began as customs and principles, but treaties today are probably more important. Because of modern travel and communications, states and other actors can easily meet in large conferences to produce the LOS convention or the various documents of the Earth Summit. Judicial decisions and the research of scholars known as jurists also contribute to the content of international law. The efficacy of international law shows in another way as well. International law does not rest only on the international level, but frequently has to be incorporated into the domestic practices of states involving matters ranging from migratory birds to human rights.

The scope of international law has grown immensely from the traditional subjects of diplomacy and war to more recent interest in human rights and the environment. The fundamental distinction between private and public international law seems to be fading as governments regulate such transnational matters as business interactions and child adoptions. Inventions and change in human activities create new jurisdictions as well. The invention of aircraft and development of the Internet are but two examples. Not only are all spaces now governed, including outer space, but governance of persons has evolved. Citizenship is often no longer based on a single nationality since a growing number of states recognize dual nationality, however reluctantly. More states also apply extraterritorial jurisdiction because their governments are trying to protect their citizens living or traveling abroad from terrorists and pirates and communicable diseases.

International law has made the world not only more lawful but safer. The rules of diplomacy provide for the peaceful settlement of disputes according to well-known practices such as conciliation and arbitration. One of the most visited areas of negotiation concerns arms agreements resulting in numerous limitations on arms to protect lives and to save money. Terrible wars still occur but they are mostly internal and use conventional weapons. The UN regularly sends in negotiators and peacekeepers to end, or at least dampen conflicts. These conflicts have notoriously ignored humane rules involving civilians and POWs. Peacekeeping operations to separate warring parties have been improvised over the decades by the UN, and far outnumber the

Charter-provided collective security operations. Occasions to identify and stop an aggressor with an UN-sanctioned posse of states have been few. One of the greatest accomplishments of the UN has been the sponsorship of the criminal tribunals for the former Yugoslavia and Rwanda to punish individuals for committing humanitarian and war crimes. A permanent International Criminal Court was encouraged by the success of these tribunals.

Making the world better by means of international law is a fairly recent development, occurring mostly in the last several decades. The view by some leaders that they are in charge of a hard-shelled sovereign state has not entirely disappeared. Dictatorships in Africa, and several other places, treat their own citizens in shameful, inhumane ways and defy objections arising from the outside world. The notion of universal human rights necessarily must crack sovereignty's hard shell if people need protection from their own governments. Many governments have improved human rights because these rights are treated as having *jus cogens* standing, and international society, including thousands of human rights NGOs, will not view a government as fully legitimate without a proper human rights performance. The communist state of China, for instance, has become sensitive to outside criticism of its human rights policies and strives to persuade the world to focus on socioeconomic rights improvements and give less attention to the many executions, throttled free speech, and the oppression of ethnic minorities. Today, equality for women, an end to all forms of torture, and rights for same-sex relationships are among the many human rights around the world awaiting improvement.

The physical health of the world is another recent issue-area in need of being made better through international law. Probably no other area within the scope of international law has had as many treaties, statement of principles, and declarations as has the environment. These rules are much more impressive than the effect of the rules, however. Examples of progress can be found, but improvements have not yet caught up with the environmental damage caused by profligate human behavior. Major changes in lifestyle and technological breakthroughs will be necessary to better the environment. Rising population numbers with rising expectations about needs and wants continue to place the environmental cause in doubt.

Economic exchanges, enabled by trade treaties and other rules, have definitely made the material lives of billions of people better than they were several decades ago. Unfortunately, global inequality is still strongly present, with Western, industrialized states of the North living at a much higher economic level than states of the South. This observation is especially true for the "bottom billion" of the South who eek out a meager existence on a daily basis. Led by the UN system, including the UNDP and the WB, corrective measures have been pursued, but closing the huge inequality gap is a Herculean task. Not only has the North insisted on free market rules that benefit the industrialized economies, but these richer states refuse to apply these same rules to their agricultural sector, a step that would greatly help Third World states.

Finally, a *society of states* that emerged in Europe in the era of the Peace of Westphalia ultimately spread around the world, and would evolve into an *international society* as other kinds of actors began to participate, including especially IGOs and NGOs. These latter actors have helped form a global civil society, as a special dimension of international society, which would advocate for worthy causes and press states to accept international rule-making for a more lawful, safer, and better world. Globalization forces, and the resulting interdependence, will only call for more effective international law to help share benefits and manage problems that accompany multiple actors' deeper involvement in international society. International law is almost certain to become a thicker web of rules. This law sets agreement in place and extends patterns of cooperation into the future. International law institutionalizes international society.

Glossary of Terms

accession: the acceptance of a treaty by one or more states after it has entered into force.

acta gestionis: state involvement in commerce thus calling for restrictive immunity, which allows state commerce to be a party in the court cases of another state.

acta imperii: traditional acts of state concerning security and diplomacy, matters very unlikely to be involved in the court cases of another state.

Act of State doctrine: respecting state immunity for the acts of a government performed on its own territory, even when another state's citizens are involved.

actors: individuals and various groups of individuals, including entire states, which can make behavioral choices to obey or disobey international law.

adjudication: third party judicial settlement of disputes that are legally binding.

advisory opinion: a decision, as by the ICJ, stating a legal opinion on an issue but without litigants actually bringing a contentious case before the court. It is theoretically a moot action by a court but may, nonetheless, set norms.

agrément: a formal agreement by a host state to accredit a new ambassador.

alien: a non-citizen located on the territory of a state.

ambassador: the highest rank of diplomatic agent.

amendment: a formal change in an article or two of a treaty or it could refer to a general revision of the treaty.

anarchy: the absence of government in a particular social system.

arbitration: a binding third party adjudication that is *ad hoc* or for a one-time use.

archipelago states: states made up of several or more islands recognized as a geographical entity.

arms control: limitations or caps on the numbers of one or more kinds of weapons.

aut judicare aut dedere: either try or extradite to a country that will try an individual wanted for a crime involving universal jurisdiction.

baseline: the land–water demarcation, determined at low tide, serving as the starting point for several seaward jurisdictions of coastal states.

belligerent recognition: a provisional recognition by other states of an insurgent group with some prospects for success in their revolutionary war.

bellum Romanum: all-out war without restraint as Romans practiced against groups they considered to be barbarians.

biodiversity: the genetic variability of all living organisms, including both plant and animal life.

biosphere: the interdependent layers of soil, ocean, climate, and air that envelope earth and sustain life.

Calvo Clause: aliens are expected to rely on local remedies over a grievance and not turn to the diplomatic services of their home country.

Calvo Doctrine: the effects of a revolution may be beyond a state's control, and so the response under state responsibility should not have to be greater for aliens than it is toward a state's own citizens

capitalism: an economic system of private ownership of property and commerce regulated by market forces of supply and demand.

carrying capacity: the ability of an ecosystem to support the needs of the species inhabiting it and to remain healthy.

chargé d'affaires: a diplomat that runs the day to day affairs of an embassy and can stand-in for an ambassador at state functions.

civil war: a conflict involving a rebellious force in charge of a significant portion of a state's territory and people.

codification process: converting customary law into treaty law but, broadly speaking, can also be a study, as by the ILC, to determine what the law is in a given area.

coercive diplomacy: a skilled mix of diplomacy and force aimed persuading a state to halt further action, such as aggression.

collective recognition: a group of states, as in an IGO, extending diplomatic recognition to one or more states.

collective security: a power management system calling for preponderant force by a gathering of states to stop an aggressor, as provided for in the UN Charter.

comity: mainly courtesies exercised among states and their diplomats to facilitate the handling of serious issues.

commission: the credentials of a consul issued by his or her government.

conciliation: a third party negotiating technique involving an ascertainment of the facts to help parties in dispute, but usually done by a commission or group of experts.

consul: a diplomatic agent with lower immunity than an ambassador who works with fellow citizens' problems and commercial matters.

consulate: the offices of a consul which enjoy lesser immunities than that of an embassy.

contiguous zone: this strip of coastal waters extends 24 miles from the baseline and overlaps the territorial band of water. Its purpose is to allow law enforcement against smuggling and other violations against a state.

continental shelf: a geographical prolongation from a state's territory across the seabed providing the state with a 200-mile jurisdiction under the sea and in some special geographical cases 350 miles. Highly valued for natural resources such as oil and natural gas.

crimes against humanity: widespread, inhumane acts against civilian populations in peace or war.

crimes against peace: an international crime involving planning and waging war of aggression or in violation of treaties.

cultural relativism: the view that regions and countries have their own unique cultures and that a universal conception of human rights may not be a good fit for all societies.

customary law: rules that emerge from the experience of states over time, and a primary source of international law along with treaties.

dean: the ambassador with the longest tenure in a capital and who traditionally handles disputes between ambassadors or embassies.

delict: a wrong or harm done to aliens by a host state's agents or its citizens.

demonstration: a display of military force to indicate that a state is serious about its rights being respected.

dependency theory: a view that the South is bound to the North in a neocolonial relationship of exploitation.

deportation: a legal process for forcing an alien, even if naturalized as a citizen, usually for covering up an illegal past. Rule of law countries usually provide a hearing before a judge.

desertification: the process of degrading arid and semi-arid areas into useless deserts.

diplomacy: a process of communication and negotiation among states and IGOs to maximize cooperation and minimize conflict.

diplomatic bag: (or pouch) a device for carrying documents or equipment and given immunity.

diplomatic corps: the ambassadors of various countries located in a capital city and sharing a sense of community within their group.

diplomatic courier: a diplomatic agent that carries important documents from a home state to an embassy or consulate and may return with other documents.

disarmament: the complete or partial elimination of weapons.

dualism: the view that international law and municipal law are two separate legal domains which can operate independently of each other.

dual nationality: a person with two citizenships, a status more states are reluctantly accepting.

due diligence: a state responsibility to take care and avoid wronging another state or its citizens.

ecocide: the destruction of the natural environment as a result of human activity.

economic integration: the merger of two or more national economies in some form and degree.

ecosystem: the interaction of a species, animal or plant, with its environment, but with the question of whether it is a healthy, sustainable relationship.

embassy: the facilities of a permanent diplomatic mission enjoying substantial immunity.

entry into force: a prescribed number of ratifications, usually mentioned in a treaty, to activate the treaty as law.

environment: the physical features of the planet Earth and their interaction.

espousal doctrine: a requirement that states speak for individuals and corporations in international matters but is no longer strictly followed.

ethnic group: a collective of people sharing an enduring and special sense of identity, which can include language, religion, and racial characteristics, among others.

exclusive economic zone: a jurisdiction extending to 200 miles of sea from the baseline of a state for controlling natural resources such as fisheries.

exequatur: the certificate of acceptance by a host state extended to another state's consul.

ex post facto: after the fact, a charge created and leveled against a party after the so-called crime has been committed, thus violating a widely recognized principle of justice.

expropriation: the seizure of foreign-held property and its transfer to control of the seizing state. Proper compensation is at issue.

expulsion: immediate removal of an alien or a group of aliens for security or health reasons, a practice sometimes abused and turned into a human rights issue.

extradition: a treaty-provided process of requesting a wanted person by one state when that person is located in another state.

extraterritorial jurisdiction: exerting jurisdiction by a state beyond its borders.

flags of convenience: ships fly the flag of the state where they are registered. Some states provide their flags for a fee but provide little actual regulation allowing greater profits for ship-owners.

framework treaty: a basic treaty for which add-ons known as optional protocols can be used to elaborate and extend the terms of a treaty at a later time.

free trade: the removal of border restrictions on goods and services such as tariffs and quotas.

forum non conveniens: refers to the inappropriateness of a court for a case at hand, usually as a jurisdictional issue.

functional immunity: usually associated with IGOs, it provides sufficient immunity for an organization to perform its tasks but no more.

Gaia Hypothesis: Earth is viewed as a single biosphere, a living super organism.

genocide: the mass killing of people because of their group characteristics such as race or religion.

geostationary satellites: satellites placed about 22,000 miles above Earth in an orbit that allows the satellite to travel in a synchronized way with the planet.

global civil society: private persons and organizations which link up across borders, usually through non-government organizations, to pursue worthy causes in cooperation with IGOs and states.

global governance: a loose array of states, IGOs, and NGOs, exercising a weak supranational authority to influence global policy and law.

globalization: a combination of several forces, especially economic, drawing the world together into a pattern of interdependence.

good offices: a minimal third party role to help disputing parties by passing information between them.

hegemon: the world's most powerful state.

high seas: open waters of the oceans and seas of the world available to all for navigation, over flight, and fishing.

hors de combat: set aside from combat such as civilians and POWs and should be protected from the harms of war.

human rights: the freedoms and protections people should enjoy as individuals and groups simply because they are human.

humani generi hostis: the enemy of all humankind and involves universal jurisdiction as in the case of pirates and war criminals.

imputable: the harm done to an alien may be attributable to the host state.

incorporation: the process of applying the rules of international law within national jurisdictions, or municipal systems.

indigenous peoples: descendents of the original inhabitants of a country or region, such as Native Americans in the United States or Aborigines in Australia.

innocent passage: the continuous and expeditious voyage of a foreign ship through the territorial waters of another state on the condition that there are no harmful effects to that state.

inquiry: a third party communication link in a dispute that involves ascertaining the facts to help clarify the dispute. The term can also be spelled "enquiry."

insurgents: groups of citizens waging war against their central government and exercising control over part of a state's territory and population.

intellectual property: the creations of the mind such as artistic endeavors or inventions which can generate wealth.

internal waters: states have complete sovereignty over waters on the landward side of their baseline including lakes, rivers, ports, bays, and the like.

international law: a collection of rules and norms, covering a wide scope of activities and interests, that states and other actors are obliged to obey and commonly do so.

internment: the temporary detention of aliens living on a state's territory who are citizens of an enemy state.

intervention: the dictatorial interference by one state in another state's affairs ranging from its leadership choices to landing troops on its territory.

invalidity: conditions under which a treaty no longer applies for one or more states.

jurisdiction: a domain for making rules and enforcing them for either places or the activities of persons.

jus cogens: firm law that is based on a peremptory norm that all states are expected to obey.

jus gentium: law of the nations, first used by the Romans to deal with peoples on the periphery of their empire and then the term was used by the early state system of Europe.

jus sanguinis: law of the blood, used as a citizenship principle meaning that a person takes the citizenship of a parent regardless of where that person was born.

jus soli: law of the soil, used as a citizenship principle by some states meaning that anyone born on the territory of such a state can take that citizenship.

just war: a war fought for a strong moral cause and thus justified to be waged.

legal personality: the degree of rights and duties assigned to an actor whether a state, IGO, or an individual.

letter of credence: an ambassador's credentials presented to the head of state of the host country.

letters rogatory: sworn statements that are made before judicial authorities in one country to be used as evidence in the courts of another state.

lex ferenda: law in the process of being developed or the law that should exist.

lex lata: law as it presently exists.

liberals: leaders and scholars who believe international law helps structure international life in useful ways, including progressive results for humankind.

male captus bene detentus: bad capture is good detention. the courts of some countries will gladly try a person even if that person has been abducted from another state.

mare clausum: a closed sea, a jurisdictional claim involving the control of a great portion of the high seas by one state. Never valid after the seventeenth century, if it ever was.

mare liberum: a free or open sea as opposed to a closed sea controlled by one state.

Marxism: Karl Marx called for the revolutionary destruction of the capitalist system because it exploited workers to provide wealth for a few factory owners.

material breach: the clear violation of part of a treaty by a party or the unilateral rejection of the entire treaty.

meditation: a third party negotiating technique in which terms of settlement are suggested to the disputants.

mercantilism: an economic philosophy of the sixteenth through the eighteenth centuries that called for maximizing exports and minimizing imports, thus creating a national profit that kings could spend on military prowess.

mercenary: an economically motivated volunteer fighting for a government. The legality of this combatant is very much in question.

minister: the rank of diplomatic agent below an ambassador and almost entirely in disuse.

monism: the view that international and national legal systems share the same legal order in a reasonably compatible arrangement.

moot issues: involves theoretical points of law without a contentious case at hand.

multinational corporations: a special case of the NGO actor, it is a business enterprise operating in several or more countries. Sometimes written as transnational corporations.

municipal law: in international relations, this term refers to law within the domestic context of states.

National Liberation Movement: a special case of insurgency expressing self-determination, or self-rule, involving freedom from colonial rule, a racist regime, or foreign occupation.

nationality: the legal identification of an individual person with a particular state, which provides the legal protection of that state and accords certain rights and duties.

naturalization: the legal process of changing one nationality for another.

natural law: originating in ancient greece and based on the notation that laws of divine origin govern human affairs similar to laws of nature in the physical world.

negotiation: a bargaining process over issues between agents of states, often resulting in a compromise, as when treaties are written broadly to cover the positions of several states.

***non-refoulement*:** not to be returned, a principle calling on governments to avoid returning refugees to a place where their lives or freedoms would be threatened.

norms: informal, customary expectations about appropriate behavior by actors.

***nullen crime sine lege*:** no crime without law; as a principle, a law violated must be known and in place before a party is charged with this crime.

objects: an actor receiving the effects of international law but not necessarily enjoying a degree of legal personality.

***opinio juris sive necessitates*:** a known customary law for which compliance is expected. Often shortened to *opinio juris*.

order: an enduring pattern of values and behaviors which structure the relationships of actors over time, for decades and even centuries.

***pacta sunt servanda*:** one of the most fundamental principles of international law meaning that treaties must be obeyed.

passports: an internationally recognized travel document that verifies the identity and nationality of the bearer.

peacekeeping: a neutral military force placed between belligerent parties following a ceasefire, as practiced by the UN.

***persona non grata*:** a person from another country who is declared "unwanted" by a host state, usually occurring in the context of diplomats.

plenipotentiary powers: wide latitude in the freedom of decision and action allowed a diplomat, especially earlier in history with poor communications and travel.

political offense: a politically motivated act that governments object to, such as rebellion, but, in modern times, are unlikely to appear in a list of common crimes usually found in treaties of extradition.

political repression: state-sponsored terror to threaten and control its population.

positivism: a philosophy of international law that claims this law is no more than the rules to which states agree to be bound.

preemptive defense: a first strike to prevent an attack thought to be impending and fairly certain to occur.

premises: the grounds and facilities of an embassy.

preventive diplomacy: based on UN experience, it is early diplomatic intervention to avoid an escalating crisis.

principle: a firm guideline of law that falls below treaties and customs in a hierarchy of importance regarding sources of international law.

private international law: focuses on the activities of individuals and groups, as opposed to states, when family and business activities cross national boundary lines producing effects on two or more countries. The distinction between private and public international law is blurring.

private military companies: registered corporations that provide auxiliary military services ranging from security as bodyguards to monitoring satellite cameras. Often distinguished from mercenaries, especially if they remain outside direct combat roles.

protocol: established practices and courtesies that allow diplomats to focus on the substance of negotiation.

privileges and immunities: the protections and freedoms of action allowed to diplomats and their embassies to do perform their functions.

protectionism: discouraging the purchase of foreign goods and encouraging the rise of domestic industries.

protocol: established practices and courtesies that allow diplomats to focus on the substance of negotiation.

public international law: primarily deals with the rights and duties of states and IGOs.

publicists: legal scholars who contribute clarification of international law and sometimes contribute to its rules.

ratification: the stage at which a state agrees to be bound by a treaty as a lawful obligation. The state becomes a party to the treaty.

realists: leaders and scholars who focus on power relations and tend to hold disdain for international law.

rebus sic standibus: as long as conditions remain the same; a state might claim a condition undergirding a treaty has so altered that a treaty is invalid.

reciprocity: the mostly horizontal international legal system depends on states returning in like kind compliance with obligations.

recognition: one state acknowledging the rightful existence of another through an exchange of ambassadors.

regimes: rules and norms formed over an issue of common concern that states usually obey.

regionalism: an identity by a sub-set of states based on cultural and geographical connections; the claim has been made that many policy matters are better handled at this level rather than globally.

registration: the UN's Charter Article 102 requires that copies of all treaties be located with the UN and made public.

reprisal: a punitive act that is normally illegal but considered justified because of another state's prior offense; such an act had more support in customary law of an earlier time than today.

res communis: a commons available for the use of all states such as the oceans or outer space.

reservation: at time of signature or ratification a state may set aside one or more articles of a treaty so as not to be bound by them.

restrictive immunity: qualifies a state's immunity so that commercial transactions by a state could be involved in a court case in another state.

retorsion: a legal but unfriendly act, such as withdrawing an ambassador, to protest a wrongful act by another state.

rules: formal, usually written as in the case of treaties, expectations for the behavior of actors.

scope: the range of subjects regulated by international rules.

self-determination: a prominent group right to self-rule that was claimed especially by peoples of the Third World during the colonial era.

self-executing: a treaty that does not require enabling legislation for it to be implemented. National policy varies on the recognition and use of this concept.

self-help: a state acting on its own initiative to enforce international law or defend itself.

shuttle diplomacy: diplomacy involving back and forth travel by an envoy to help two disputants resolve their differences and made possible by modern jet aircraft.

signature: a stage of treaty development that provides provisional consent by diplomat, but formal approval by a state must occur to complete ratification.

sovereign: in adjective form (sovereign state), denotes that a state is a legal equal to other states and is unbound by higher authority without its consent.

sovereign immunity: an act of comity, or courtesy, to exempt a state's public acts and property from the court cases of another state.

sovereignty: the legal equality of a state with other states and the freedom from higher authority.

stare decisis: to stand by a previous decision by a court as a precedent while deciding a current case.

state: a sovereign actor with a central government that rules over a territory and population and represents that population in international relations.

state immunity: the same as sovereign immunity.

state responsibility: the circumstances under which a state is held accountable for a breach of an international obligation. Historically, the focus has been on the treatment of aliens on a state's territory.

state succession: the passing of treaty obligations, archives, treasury, debts, and other matters of the state to one or several other states when a state breaks up into new states or becomes extinct.

stateless persons: an unusual situation, individuals without documentation for international travel and who do not enjoy the diplomatic protection of a state.

steady state: the human population using natural resources at a rate no faster than they can be replenished.

strait: a narrow passage between two bodies of open sea within the jurisdiction of one or more states. Straits are often between an island and the coast of a particular state or lay between two separate countries.

subjects: an actor with the rights and duties of legal personality in some degree.

summit diplomacy: a personal meeting of leaders for direct negotiations, especially used in the age of jet aircraft.

supervening impossibility of performance: substantial change that makes a treaty, or some its articles, irrelevant, such as a river drying up that was once designated as a boundary.

supranational: authority exercised above the heads of sovereign states although they are sovereign entities. The best example is the EU.

sustainable development: economic development that meets the needs of the present generation without compromising the needs of future generations.

territorial sea: the band of water along a state's coast under a state's exclusive jurisdiction. Traditionally, 3 miles in width but 12 miles since the 1982 LOS convention.

terrorists: private actors that use or threaten sudden and surprising violence to intimidate a government and citizenry as a means to achieve a political goal.

track-two diplomacy: first track diplomacy is by diplomatic agents of states, and the second is by private parties of two or more states who volunteer to help resolve state differences.

transit passage: innocent passage through a strait.

treaty: an international agreement concluded between two or more states but can also be between IGOs or an IGO and a state.

visa: a stamp on a passport that is prearranged permission for a foreigner to enter a country.

war: a belligerent struggle either inside a country or between states lasting several months and causing a thousand battle deaths or more.

war crimes: the violation of the laws and customs of war including murder, ill-treatment of pows, plunder, and rape, among other crimes. country.

zero population growth: a stable population size achieved by each couple having two children to replace themselves.

Bibliography

Aas, Katja Franko (2007) *Globalization and Crime*. Los Angeles, CA: Sage.

Abi-Saab, Georges (1987) "The International Law of Multinational Corporations: A Critique of American Legal Doctrine," in Frederick Snyder and Sathirathai Surakiart (eds.), *Third World Attitudes Toward International Law: An Introduction*. New York: Kluwer.

Abi-Saab, Georges (1996) "The International Court as a World Court," in Vaughn Lowe (ed.), *Fifty Years of the International Court of Justice*. New York: Cambridge University Press.

Agha, Hussein, Feldman, Shai, Khadlidi, Ahmad, and Schiff, Zeev (2003) *Track II Diplomacy: Lessons From the Middle East*. Cambridge, MA: MIT.

Ala'i, Padideh, Broude, Tomer, and Picker, Colin (eds.) (2006) *Trade as Guarantor of Peace, Liberty and Security?* Washington, DC: American Society of International Law.

Albert, Mathias, Brock, Lothar, and Wolf, Klaus Dieter (eds.) (2000) *Civilizing World Politics: Society and Community Beyond the State*. Lanham, MD: Rowman & Littlefield.

Al-Duaij, Nada (2004) *Environmental Law of Armed Conflict*. Ardsley, NY: Transnational.

Aleinikoff, T. Alexander and Klusmeyer, Douglas (2002) *Citizenship Policies for an Age of Migration*. Washington, DC: Carnegie Endowment for International Peace.

Allman, T. D. (2004) *Rogue State: America at War with the World*. New York: Nation Books.

Allott, Philip (2000) "The Concept of International Law," in M. Byers (ed.), *The Role of Law in International Politics*. New York: Oxford University Press.

Alston, Philip (1995) *The United Nations and Human Rights: A Critical Appraisal*. Oxford: Clarendon Press.

Alston, Philip (ed.) (2005) *Labour Rights as Human Rights*. New York: Oxford University Press.

Alter, Karen J. (2001) *Establishing The Supremacy of European Law: The Making of an International Rule of Law for Europe*. New York: Oxford University Press.

Alterman, Jon B. (2003) "Coercive Diplomacy Against Iraq, 1990–98," in Robert J. Art and Patrick M. Cronin (eds.), *The United States and Coercive Diplomacy*. Washington, DC: United States Institute of Peace.

Alvarez, José E. (2005) *International Organizations as Law-Makers*. New York: Oxford University Press.

Ambrus, Steven (2007) "Dominion of Evil," *Amnesty International*, Spring.

Anaya, S. James (1996) *Indigenous Peoples in International Law*. New York: Oxford University Press.

Andersen, Birgitte (ed.) (2006) *Intellectual Property Rights: Innovation, Governance and the Institutional Environment*. Northampton, MA: Edward Elgar.

Anghie, Antony (2000) *Imperialism, Sovereignty and the Making of International Law*. New York: Cambridge University Press.

An-na'im, Abdullahi Ahmed (ed.) (1992) *Human Rights in Cross-Cultural Perspectives: A Quest for Consensus*. Philadelphia, PA: University of Pennsylvania Press.

Antoniou, Chris T. (1994) *The Laws of War*. New York: Vintage Books.

Apodaca, Clair (1998) "Measuring Women's Economic and Social Rights Achievements," *Human Rights Quarterly*, 20 (1).

Arat, Zehra F. (2000) "Women's Rights in Islam: Revisiting Quranic Rights," in Adamantia Pollis and Peter Schwab (eds.), *Human Rights: New Perspectives, New Realities*. Boulder, CO: Lynne Rienner.

Arend, Anthony Clark Arend (1999) *Legal Rules and International Society*. New York: Oxford University Press.

Arend, Anthony Clark (2003) "International Law and the Preemptive Use of Military Force," *Washington Quarterly*, Spring.

Arnold, Roberta and Quénivet, Noëlle (eds.) (2008) *International Humanitarian Law and Human Rights Law*. Boston, MA: Martinus Nijhoff.

Artz, Donna E. and Lukashuk, Igor I. (1995) "Participants in International Legal Relations," in Lori Fisher Damrosch, Gennady M. Danilenko, and Rein Müllerson (eds.), *Beyond Confrontation: International Law for the Post-Cold War Era*. Boulder, CO: Westview Press.

Ashworth (1999) "The Silencing of Women," in Tim Dunne and Nicholas J. Wheeler (eds.), *Human Rights in Global Politics*. New York: Cambridge University Press.

Askin, Kelly D. and Koenig, Dorean M. (eds.) (1999) *Women and International Human Rights Law*, 3 vols. Ardsley, NY: Transnational Publishers.

Aust, Anthony (2007) *Modern Treaty Law and Practice*. New York: Cambridge University Press.

Aviel, JoAnn Fagot (1999) "The Evolution of Multilateral Diplomacy," in James P. Muldroon, Jr, et al., *Multilateral Diplomacy and the Untied Nations*. Boulder, CO: Westview Press.

Bacque, James (1991) *Other Losses: The Shocking Truth Behind the Mass Deaths of Disarmed German Soldiers and Civilians under General Eisenhower's Command*. Rocklin, CA: Prima.

Baldwin, David (1993) *Neorealism and Neoliberalism: The Contemporary Debate*. New York: Columbia Univeristy Press.

Baldwin, Richard and Low, Patrick (eds.) (2009) *Multilateralizing Regionalism: Challenges for the Global Trading System*. New York: Cambridge University Press.

Ball, Nicole (1994) "Demilitarizing the Third World," in Michael T. Klare and Daniel C. Thomas (eds.), *World Security: Challenges for a New Century*, 2nd edn. New York, NY: St Martin's Press.

Banisar, David (2003) "Cyber-Policing Dissent: The Great Firewall of China," *Amnesty Now*, Spring.

Barker, J. Craig (2006) *The Protection of Diplomatic Personnel*. Burlington, VT: Ashgate.

Barrett, Scott (2005) *Environmental Statecraft: The Strategy of Environmental Treaty-Making*. New York: Oxford University Press.

Barston, R. P. (2006) *Modern Diplomacy*. New York: Pearson Longman.

Bass, Gary Jonathan (2000) *Stay the Hand of Vengeance: The Politics of War Crimes Tribunals*. Princeton, NJ: Princeton University Press.

Bassiouni, M. Cherif (1997) "From Versailles to Rwanda in 75 Years: The Need to Establish a Permanent International Court," *Harvard Human Rights Journal*, 10 (Spring).

Bassiouni, M. Cherif (ed.) (2000) *A Manual on International Humanitarian Law and Arms Control Agreements*. Ardsley, NY: Transnational.

Bassiouni, M. Cherif (2004) "The History of Universal Jurisdiction and Its Place in International Law," in Stephen Macedo (ed.), *Universal Jurisdiction: National Courts and the Prosecution of Serious Crimes under International Law*. Philadelphia, PA: University of Pennsylvania Press.

Beck, Robert J. and Ambrosio, Thomas (eds.) (2002) *International Law and the Rise of Nations: The State System and the Challenge of Ethnic Groups*. Washington, DC: Congressional Quarterly Press.

Bederman, David J. (2001a) *International Law in Antiquity*. New York: Cambridge University Press.

Bederman, David J. (2001b) *International Law Frameworks*. New York: Foundation Press.

Bederman, David J. (2008) *Globalization and International Law*. New York: Palgrave Macmillan.

Beer, Francis A. (1981) *Peace Against War*. San Francisco: W. H. Freeman.

Beitz, Charles R. (2001) "Human Rights as a Common Concern," *American Political Science Review*, 95 (1).

Bekou, Olympia and Cryer, Robert (eds.) (2004) *The International Criminal Court*. Burlington, VT: Ashgate/Dartmouth.

Bell, Ruth Greenspan (2006) "What to Do about Climate Change," *Foreign Affairs*, 85 (3).

Bello, Judith Hipler and Bekker, Peter H. F. (1997) "Legality of the Threat or Use of Nuclear Weapons," *American Journal of International Law*, 91 (1).

Benvenisti, Eyal (2004) *The International Law of Occupation*. Princeton, NJ: Princeton University Press.

Benvenisti, Eyal and Hirsch, Moshe (eds.) (2004) *The Impact of International Law on International Cooperation*. New York: Cambridge University Press.

Bernauer, Thomas (1997) "Managing International Rivers," in Oran R. Young, *Global Governance: Drawing Insights from the Environmental Experience*. Cambridge, MA: MIT Press.

Bernhardt, Rudolf (2001) "The International Protection of Human Rights: Experiences with the European Court of Human Rights," in Sienho Yee and Wang Tieya (eds.), *International Law in the Post-Cold War World: Essays in Memory of Li Haopei*. New York: Routledge.

Berridge, G. R. (1985) "Old Diplomacy in New York," in G.R. Berridge and A. Jennings (eds.), *Diplomacy at the UN*. New York: Macmillan.

Berridge, G. R. (2005) *Diplomacy, Theory and Practice*, 2nd edn. New York: Palgrave Macmillan.

Best, Geoffrey (1994) *War and Law Since 1945*. Oxford: Clarendon Press.

Bhagwati, Jagdish N. (2007) *In Defense of Globalization*. New York: Oxford University Press.

Bianchi, Andrea (2009) *Non-State Actors and International Law*. Burlington, VT: Ashgate.

Biermann, Frank, Siebenhüner, Bernd, and Schreyögg, Anna (eds.) (2009) *International Organizations in Global Environmental Governance*. New York: Routledge.

Biersteker, Thomas, J. (2007) *International Law and International Relations: Bridging Theory and Practice*. New York: Routledge.

Bilder, Richard B. (1998) "International Dispute Settlement and the Role of International Adjudication," in Charlotte Ku and Paul F. Diehl (eds.), *International Law: Classic and Contemporary Readings* (Boulder, CO: Lynne Rienner.

Binnendijk, Hans (ed.) (1987) *National Negotiating Styles*. Washington, DC: Foreign Service Institute.

Bing Bing Jia (1998) *The Regime of the Straits in International Law*. Oxford: Clarendon.

Bing Bing Jia (2001) "Judicial Decisions as a Source of International Law and the Defense of Duress in Murder or Other Cases Arising From Armed Conflict," in Sienho Yee and Wang Tieya (eds.), *International Law in the Post-Cold War World: Essays In Memory of Li Haopei*. New York: Routledge.

Birdsall, Andrea (2008) *The International Politics of Judicial Intervention*. New York: Routledge.

Birnie, Patricia W. and Boyle, A. E. (2002) *International Law and the Environment*. New York: Oxford University Press; 2nd edn. 2008.

Bishop, William H., Jr (1989) "The Authoritative Sources of Customary Law in the United States," *Michigan Law Review*, 10 (2).

Blair, Clay (1996) *Hitler's U-Boat War*. New York: Random House.

Blakesley, Christopher L., Firmage, Edwin B., Scott, Richard F., and Williams, Sharon A. (2001) *The International Legal System*, 5th edn. New York: Foundation Press.

Blau, Judith and Moncado, Alberto (2005) *Human Rights: Beyond the Liberal Vision*. Lanham, MD: Rowman & Littlefield.

Bledsoe, Robert L. and Boczek, Boleslaw A. (1987) *The International Law Dictionary*. Santa Barbara, CA: ABC-CLIO.

Bloxham, David (2005) *The Great Game of Genocide: Imperialism, Nationalism, and the Destruction of the Ottoman Armenians*. New York: Oxford University Press.

Bodansky, Daniel, Brunnee, Jutta, and Hey, Ellen (eds.) (2008) *The Oxford Handbook of International Environmental Law*. New York: Oxford University Press.

Bohlander, Michael (2007) *International Criminal Justice: A Critical Analysis of Institutions and Procedures*. London: Cameron May.

Boisson de Chazournes, Laurence and Sands, Philippe (eds.) (1999) *International Law, the International Court of Justice and Nuclear Weapons*. New York: Cambridge University Press.

Bolewski, Wilfried (2007) *Diplomacy and International Law in Globalized Relations*. New York: Springer.

Booth, Ken (1995) "Global Ethics: Human Wrongs and International Relations, *International Affairs*, 71 (1).

Botha, Christo Botha (1999) "From Mercenaries to 'Private Military Companies': The Collapse of the African State and the Outsourcing of State Security," *South African Yearbook of International Law*, 24.

Bouchet-Saulnier, Francoise (2002) *The Practical Guide to Humanitarian Law*. Lanham, MD: Rowman & Littlefield.

Boutros-Ghali, Boutros (1995) *An Agenda for Peace*. New York: United Nations Publications.

Boutwell, Jeffrey and Klare, Michael T. (eds.) (1999) *Light Weapons and Civil Conflict: Controlling the Tools of Violence*. Lanham, MD: Rowman & Littlefield.

Bowden, Brett, Charlesworth, Hilary, and Farrall, Jeremy (eds.) (2009) *The Role of International Law in Rebuilding Societies after Conflict: Great Expectations*. New York: Cambridge University Press.

Bozeman, Adda (1971) *The Future of Law in a Multicultural World*. Princeton, NJ: Princeton University Press.

Bozeman, Adda (1994) *Politics and Culture in International History*. New Brunswick, NJ: Transaction.

Bradley, James (2003) *Flyboys: A True Story of Courage*. New York: Little, Brown and Co.

Brand, Clarence Eugene Brand (1968) *Roman Military Law*. Austin, TX: University of Texas.

Brems, Eva (2003) "Protecting the Human Rights of Women," in Gene M. Lyons and James Mayall (eds.), *International Human Rights in the 21st Century: Protecting the Rights of Groups*. Lanham, MD: Rowman & Littlefield.

Brierly, J. L. (1990) The Law of Nations: An Introduction to the International Law of *Peace*, 6th edn. New York: Oxford University Press.

Broad, Robin (ed.) (2002) *Global Backlash: Citizen Initiative for a Just World Economy*. Lanham, MD: Rowman & Littlefield.

Brown, Lester R. Brown (2008) *Plan B 3.0: Mobilizing to Save Civilizing*. New York: W.W. Norton/ Earth Policy Institute.

Brownmiller, Susan (1993) [1975] *Against Our Will: Men, Women and Rape*. New York: Fawcett Columbine.

Bruntland, Gro Harlem (2003) "The Globalization of Health," *Seton Hall Journal of Diplomacy and International Relations*, 4 (2).

Broomhall, Bruce (2003). *International Justice and the International Criminal Court: Between Sovereignty and the Rule of Law*. New York: Oxford University Press.

Brown, L. David, Khagram, Sanjeev, Moore, Mark H., and Frumkin, Peter (2003) "Globalization, NGOS, and Multi-Sectoral Relations," in Joseph S. Nye, Jr and John D. Donahue (eds.), *Governing in a Globalizing World*. Washington, DC: Brookings Institution Press and Visions of Governance in the 21st Century.

Brownlie, Ian (1983) *State Responsibility*. Oxford: Clarendon.

Brownlie, Ian (ed.) (1995) *Basic Documents in International Law*, 4th edn. Oxford: Clarendon.

Brownlie, Ian and Brookfield, F. M. (1992) *Treaties and Indigenous Peoples*. New York: Oxford University Press.

Brysk, Alison (2005) *Human Rights and Private Wrongs: Constructing Global Civil Society*. New York: Routledge.

Bull, Hedley (1983) "Justice in International Relations," 1983–4 Hagey Lectures. Waterloo Ontario: University of Waterloo.

Bull, Hedley (1984) "The Emergence of a Universal International Society," in Hedley Bull and Adam Watson (eds.), *The Expansion of International Society*. Oxford: Clarendon.

Bull, Hedley (1995) *The Anarchical Society: A Study of Order in World Politics*, 2nd edn. New York: Columbia University Press.

Bull, Hedley and Watson, Adam (eds.) (1984), *The Expansion of International Society*. New York: Oxford University Press.

Burns, John (1999) "Quarter, Giving No," in Roy Gutman and David Rieff (eds.), *Crimes of War*. New York: W.W. Norton.

Burroughs, Edwin G. (2008) *Forgotten Patriots: The Untold Story of American Prisoners in the Revolutionary War*. New York: Basic Books.

Burroughs, Gideon (2002) *The No-Nonsense Guide to the Arms Trade*. London: Verso.

Buzan, Barry (1991) *People, States and Fear*, 2nd edn. Boulder, CO: Lynne Rienner.

Buzan, Barry (2004) *From International to World Society? English School Theory and the Social Structure of Globalization*. New York: Cambridge University Press.

Byers, Michael (1999) *Custom, Power, and the Power of Rules: International Relations and Customary Law*. New York: Cambridge University Press.

Byers, Michael (2000) "Introduction," in Michael Byers (ed.), *The Role of Law in International Politics: Essays in International Relations and International Law*. New York: Oxford University Press.

Byers, Michael (2006) *War Law: Understanding International Law and Armed Conflicts*. New York: Grove Press.

Byers, Michael and Nolte, Georg (2003) *United States Hegemony and the Foundations of International Law*. New York: Cambridge University Press.

Byman, David (2005) *Deadly Connections: States That Sponsor Terrorism*. New York: Cambridge University Press.

Byman, Daniel (2006) "Do Targeted Killings Work?" *Foreign Affairs*, 85 (2).

Byron, Christine (2009) *War Crimes and Crimes against Humanity in the Rome Statue of the International Criminal Court*. New York: Palgrave Macmillan.

Caminos, Hugo (ed.) (2001) *Law of the Sea*. Burlington, VT: Ashgate.

Campbell, Kurt M. and Einhorn, Robert J. (2004) "Avoiding the Tipping Point: Concluding Observations," in Kurt M. Campbell, Robert J. Einhorn, and Mitchell B. Reiss (eds.), *The Nuclear Tipping Point: Why States Reconsider Their Nuclear Choices*. Washington, DC: Brookings Institution Press.

Carey, Sabine C. and Poe, Steven C. (eds.) (2004) *Understanding Human Rights Violations*. Burlington, VT: Ashgate.

Caron, Daniel D. (2002) "The ILC Articles on State Responsibility: The Paradoxical Relationship Between Form and Authority," *American Journal of International Law*, 96.

Caron, David D. and Shinkaretskaya, Galina (1995) "Peaceful Settlement of Disputes Through the Rule of Law," in Lori Fisler Damrosch, Gennady M. Danilenko, and Rein Müllerson (eds.), *Beyond Confrontation: International Law For the Post-Cold War Era*. Boulder, CO: Westview Press.

Carr, E. H. [1946; 1966] (1997) *The Twenty Years' Crisis 1919–1939*, 2nd edn. New York: St Martin's Press.

Carson, Rachel Louise (1962) *Silent Spring*. Boston: Houghton Mifflin.

Carter, Jimmy (2009) *We Can Have Peace in the Holy Land: A Plan That Will Work*. New York: Simon & Schuster.

Cassese, Antonio (1995) *Self-Determination of Peoples: A Legal Reappraisal*. New York: Cambridge University Press.

Cassese, Antonio (2001a) "The Contribution of the International Criminal Tribunal for the Former Yugoslavia to the Ascertainment of General Principles of Law Recognized by the Community of Nations," in Sienho Yee and Wang Tieya (eds.), *International Law in the Post-Cold War World: Essays in Memory of Li Haopei*. New York: Routledge.

Cassese, Antonio (2001b) *International Law*. New York: Oxford University Press.

Cassese, Antonio (2003) *International Criminal Law*. New York: Oxford University Press.

Castellino, Joshua (2005) "The Asian Regional Human Rights System," in Rhona K. M. Smith and Christian van den Anker (eds.), *The Essentials of Human Rights*. New York: Oxford University Press.

Castles, Stephen and Davidson, Alastair (2000) *Citizenship and Migration: Globalization and the Politics of Belonging*. New York: Routledge.

Century of International Law: American Journal of International Law Centennial Essays, 1906–2006 (2007) Washington, DC: American Society of International Law.

Cerone, John (2006) "The Military Commission Act of 2006," *ASIL Insights*, 10 (30).

Champagne, Duane, Torjesen, Karen Jo, and Steiner, Susan (eds.) (2005) *Indigenous Peoples and the Modern State*. Lanham, MD: Rowman & Littlefield.

Chang, Iris (1998) *The Rape of Nanking: The Forgotten Holocaust of World War II*. New York: Penguin.

Charlesworth, Hilary and Chinkin, Christine Chinkin (2000) *The Boundaries of International Law: A Feminine Analysis*. Manchester: Manchester University Press.

Charlesworth, Hilary and Coicaud, Jean-Marc (eds.) (2009) *Fault Lines of Inernational Legitimacy*. New York: Cambridge University Press.

Chasek, Pamela (2003) "The Ozone Depletion Regime," in Bertram I. Spector and I. William Zartman (eds.), *Getting It Done: Postagreement Negotiation and International Regimes*. Washington, DC: United States Institute of Peace Press.

Chasek, Pamela, Downie, David L., and Brown, Janet Welsh (2005) *Global Environmental Politics*, 4th edn. Boulder, CO: Westview Press.

Chatterjee, Charles (2007) *International Law and Diplomacy*. New York: Routledge.

Chieh Hsiung, James (1997) *Anarchy and Order: The Interplay of Politics and Law in International Relations*. Boulder, CO: Lynne Rienner.

Chinkin, C. (1989) "The Challenge of Soft Law: Development and Change in International Law," *International and Comparative Law Quarterly*, 38.

Chinkin, C. (2000) "Human Rights and the Politics of Representation: Is there a Role for International Law," in Michael Byers (ed.), *The Role of Law in International Relations*. New York: Cambridge University Press.

Cirincione, Joseph (2002) *Deadly Arsenals: Tracking the Weapons of Mass Destruction*. Washington, DC: Carnegie Endowment for International Peace.

Clapham, Andrew (2006) *The Human Rights Obligations of Non-State Actors*. New York: Oxford University Press.

Clark, Grenville and Sohn, Louis B. (1985) "Introduction to World Peace Through World Law," in Richard Falk, Friedrich Kratochwil, and Saul H. Mendlovitz (eds.), *International Law: A Contemporary Perspective*. Boulder, CO: Westview.

Clark, Ian (2005) *Legitimacy in International Society*. New York: Oxford University Press.

Claude, Inis L., Jr (1971) *Swords Into Plowshares: The Problems and Prospects of International Organization*, 4th edn. New York: Random House.

Cohen, Raymond (1997) *Negotiating Across Cultures: International Communication in an Interdependent World*, revised edn. Washington, DC: United States Institute of Peace Press.

Cohen, Roger (2005) *Soldiers and Slaves: American POWS Trapped by the Nazis' Final Gamble*. New York: Knopf.

Cohen, Samy (2006) *The Resilience of the State: Democracy and the Challenge of Globalization*. Boulder, CO: Lynne Rienner.

Cohen, Theodore H. Cohen (2003) *Global Political Economy: Theory and Practice*. New York: Longman.

Coicaud, Jean-Marie and Heiskanen, Veijo (eds.) (2001) *The Legitimacy of International Organizations*. New York: United Nations University Press.

Coleman, Isobel (2004a) "The Payoff from Women's Rights," *Foreign Affairs*, 83.

Coleman Isobel (2004b) "Women, Islam, and the New Iraq," *Foreign Affairs*, 83.

Coleman, William D. and Underhill, Geoffrey R. D. (eds.) (1998) *Regionalism and Global Economic Integration: Europe, Asia and the Americas*. New York: Routledge.

Collier, J. G. (1996) "The International Court of Justice and the Peaceful Settlement of Disputes," in Vaughan Lowe and Malgosia Fitzmaurice (eds.), *Fifty Years of the International Court of Justice*. New York: Cambridge University Press.

Collier, Paul (2007) *The Bottom Billion: Why the Poorest Countries Are Failing and What Can Be Done about It*. New York: Oxford University Press.

Cook, Rebecca J. (1997) "Women," in Christopher Joyner (ed.), *The United Nations and International Law*. New York: Cambridge University Press.

Corbett, P. E. (1951) *Law and Society in the Relations of States*. New York: Harcourt, Brace and Company.

Cornish, Paul (1996) *Controlling the Arms Trade: The West Versus the Rest*. London: Bowerdean.

Cortwright, David and Lopez, George A. (2002) *Smart Sanctions: Targeting Economic Statecraft*. Lanham, MD: Roman & Littlefield.

Cottier, Thomas, Pauwelyn, Joost, and Bürgi, Elizabeth (eds.) (2005) *Human Rights and International Trade*. Oxford: Oxford University Press.

Couch, Dick (2003) *United States Armed Forces Nuclear, Biological, and Chemical Survival Manual*. New York: Basic Books.

Covell, Charles (2004) *Hobbes, Realism and the Tradition of International Law*. New York: Palgrave Macmillan.

Craft, Cassady B. (1999) *Weapons for Peace, Weapons for War: the Effect of Arms Transfers on War Outbreak, Involvement and Outcomes*. New York: Routledge.

Cranston, Alan (2004) *The Sovereignty Revolution*, edited by Kim Cranston. Stanford, CA: Stanford University Press.

Cranston, Maurice (1964) *What Are Human Rights?* New York: Basic Books.

Craven, Matthew C. R., Fitzmaurice, M., and Vogiatzi, Maria (2007) *Time, History and International Law*. Boston, MA: Martinus Nijhoff Publishers.

Cryer, Robert (2005) *Prosecuting International Crimes: Selectivity and the International Criminal Law Regime*. New York: Cambridge University Press.

Cukier, Kenneth Neil (2005) "Who Will Control the Internet?" *Foreign Affairs*, 8 (6).

Dahinden, Erwin (ed.) (2002) *Small Arms and Light Weapons: Legal Aspects of National and International Regulations: Proceedings of the UN Conference on the Illicit Trade in Small Arms*. New York: United Nations Publications.

D'Amato, Anthony (1970) "Manifest Intent and the Generation by Treaty of Customary Rules of International law," *American Journal of International Law*, 64 (4).

D'Amato, Anthony (1983) "Israeli's Air Strike Upon the Iraqi Nuclear Reactor," *American Journal of International Law*, 77 (3).

D'Amato, Anthony (1987) "Trashing Customary Law," *American Journal of International Law*, 8 (1).

D'Amato, Anthony (1995) *International Law: Process and Prospects*. Irving, NY: Transnational.

Danner, Mark (2004) *Torture and Truth: America, Abu Ghraib and the War on Terror*. New York: New York Review Books.

Danspeckgruber, Wolfgang (ed.) (2002) *Self-Determination of Peoples: Community, Nation, and State in an Interdependent World*. Boulder, CO: Lynne Rienner.

Datta, Rekha and Kornberg, Judith F. (2002) *Women in Developing Countries: Assessing Strategies for Empowerment*. Boulder, CO: Lynne Rienner.

Davenport, Christian (ed.) (2000) *Paths to State Repression*. Lanham, MD: Rowman & Littlefield.

Davidson, Scott (ed.), *The Law of Treaties*. Burlington, VT: Ashgate.

Davis, Jim A. and Schneider, Barry R. (eds.) (2004) *The Gathering Biological Warfare Storm*. (Westport, CT: Praeger Publishers.

Davis, Zackary S. (1998) "Nuclear Proliferation and Nonproliferation Policy in the 1990s," in Michael T. Klare and Yodesh Chandrani (eds.), *World Security: Challenges for a New Century*, 3rd edn. New York: St Martin's Press.

Daws, Gavan (1994) *Prisoners of the Japanese: POWS of World War II in the Pacific*. New York: William Morrow and Co.

Dekker, Ige F. and Post, Harry H. G. (ed.) (2003) *On the Foundations and Sources of International Law*. New York: Cambridge University Press.

DeLaet, Debra L. (2006) *The Global Struggle for Human Rights: Universal Principles in World Politics*. Belmont, CA: Thomson/ Wadsworth.

Deller, Nicole, Makhijani, Arjun, and Burroughs, John (2003) *Rule of Power or Rule of Law?* New York: Apex Press.

Delsol, Chantal (2008) *Unjust Justice: Against the Tyranny of International Law*. Wilmington, DE: ISI Books.

Denza, Eileen (1976) *Diplomatic Law: Commentary on the Vienna Convention on Diplomatic Relations*. Dobbs Ferry, NY: Oceana Publications.

Dewey, Susan (2008) *Hollow Bodies: Institutional Response to Sex Trafficking in Armenia, Bosnia and India*. Herndon, VA: Kumarian Press.

de Zayas, Alfred-Maurice (1994) *Terrible Revenge: The Ethnic Cleansing of the East European Germans, 1944–1950*. New York: St Martin's Press.

Diamond, Larry (2005) *Squandered Victory: The American Occupation and the Bungled Effort to Bring Democracy to Iraq*. New York: Times Books/Henry Holt & Co.

Diamond, Louise and McDonald, John (1996) *Multi-Track Diplomacy: A Systems Approach to Peace* (West Hartford, CT: Kumarian Press.

Dickinson, Andrew, Lindsay, Rae, and Loonam, James P. (2004) *State Immunity: Selected Materials and Commentary*. New York: Oxford University Press.

Dierks, Rosa Gomez (2001) *Introduction to Globalization: Political and Economic Perspectives for the New Century*. Chicago: Burham Inc. Publishers.

Dignam, Alan and Galanis, Michael (2009) *The Globalization of Corporate Governance*. Burlington, VT: Ashgate.

Dinstein, Yoran (1994) *War, Aggression and Self-Defense*, 2nd edn. New York: Cambridge University Press.

Dizard, Wilson, Jr (2001) *Digital Diplomacy: U.S. Foreign Policy in the Information Age*. Westport, CT: Praeger.

Dolgopol, Ustina (1995) "Women's Voices, Women's Pain," *Human Rights Quarterly*, 17 (1).

Dollar, David and Kraay, Aart (2002) "Spreading the Wealth," *Foreign Affairs*, 81 (1).

Donnelly, Jack (2000) *Realism and International Relations*. New York: Cambridge University Press,

Donnelly, Jack (2003a) "In Defense of the Universal Model," in Gene M. Lyons and James Mayall (eds.), *International Human Rights in the 21st Century*. Lanham, MD: Rowman & Littlefield.

Donnelly, Jack (2003b) *Universal Human Rights in Theory and Practice*, 2nd edn. Ithaca, NY: Cornell University Press.

Dover, Nigel (2003) *Introduction to Global Citizenship*. Edinburgh: Edinburgh University Press.

Dowla, Asif and Barua, Dipal (2006) *The Poor Always Pay Back: The Grameen II Story*. Bloomfield, CT: Kumarian Press.

Doyle, Michael and Sambanis, Nicholas (2006) *Making War and Building Peace: UN Peace Operations*. Princeton, NJ: Princeton University Press.

Drahos, Peter and Mayne, Ruth (eds.) (2002) *Global Intellectual Property Rights: Knowledge, Access and Development*. New York: Palgrave Macmillan/Oxfam.

Drinan, Robert F. (2001) *The Mobilization of Shame: A World View of Human Rights*. New Haven, CT: Yale University Press.

Drumbl, Mark A. (2002) "Law and Justice," in Diana Ayton-Shenker (ed), *A Global Agenda: Issues Before the 57th General Assembly of the United Nations*. Lanham, MD: Rowman & Littlefield.

Dunn, David H. (1996) "What is Summitry?" in David H. Dunn (ed.), *Diplomacy At the Highest Level: The Evolution of International Summitry*. New York: St Martin's Press.

Dunne, Tim (1995) "The Social Construction of International Society," *European Journal of International Relations*, 1 (3).

Dunne, Tim (1998) *Inventing International Society: A History of the English School*. New York: St Martin's Press.

Dunoff, Jeffrey L. and Trachtman, Joel P. (2009) *Ruling the World? Constitutionalism, International Law, and Global Governance*. New York: Cambridge University Press.

Dupuy, Pierre-Marie and Vierucci, Luisa (eds.) (2008) *NGOS in International Law: Efficiency in Flexibility?* Northampton, MA: Edward Elgar.

Eckersley, Robin (2004) "Soft Law, Hard Politics, and the Climate Change Treaty," in Christian Reus-Smith (ed.), *The Politics of International Law*. New York: Cambridge University Press.

Ehrlich, Anne H. and Ehrich, Paul R. *Earth*. New York: F. Watts.

Ehrlich, Anne and Ehrlich, Paul R. (2008) *The Dominant Animal: Human Evolution and the Environment*. Washington, DC: Island Press.

Ehrlich, Paul R. (1971) *The Population Bomb*. New York: Ballantine Books.

Eichensehr, Kristen (2003) "On the Offensive: Assassination Policy Under International Law," *Harvard International Review*, 25 (3).

Elferink, Alex G. Oude and Rothwell, Donald R. (eds.) (2001) *The Law of the Sea and Polar Maritime Delimitation and Jurisdiction*. New York: Martinus Nijhoff Publishers.

Engdahl, Ola and Wrange, Pål (2008) *Law at War: The Law as It Was and the Law as It Should Be*. Boston, MA: Martinus Nijhoff.

Epp, Roger (1998) "The English School on the Frontiers of International Society," in Tim Dunne, Michael Cox, and Ken Booth (eds.), *The Eighty Years' Crisis: International Relations 1919–1999*. New York: Cambridge University Press.

Ettinger, David J. Ettinger (1992) "The Legal Status of the International Olympic Committee," *Pace Yearbook of International Law*, 4 (97).

Evans, Malcolm D. (ed.) (2006) *International Law*, 2nd edn. New York: Oxford University Press.

Fairbanks, Charles H., Jr (with the assistance of Eli Nathans) (1982) "The British Campaign against the Slave Trade: An Example of Successful Human Rights Policy," in Fred E. Baumann (ed.), *Human Rights and American Foreign Policy*. Gambier, OH: Kenyon College.

Falk, Richard (1999) *Predatory Globalization: A Critique.* Malden, MA: Polity.

Falk, Richard (2000a) "Foreword," in Mairān Clech Lâm, *At the Edge of the State: Indigenous Peoples and Self-Determination.* Ardsley, NY: Transnational.

Falk, Richard A. (2000b) *Human Rights Horizons: The Pursuit of Justice in a Globalizing World.* New York: Routledge.

Falk, Richard A. (2008) *The Costs of War: International Law, the UN, and World Order after Iraq.* New York: Routledge.

Farmer, Paul (2003) *Pathologies of Power, Health, Human Rights and the New War on the Poor.* Berkeley, CA: University of California Press.

Fassbender, Barbo (2009) *The United Nations Charter as the Constitution of the International Community.* Boston, MA: Martinus Nijhoff.

Fawcett, Louise and Hurrell, Andrew (eds.) (1995) *Regionalism in World Politics.* New York: Oxford University Press.

Felice, William F. (1996) *Taking Suffering Seriously: The Importance of Collective Rights.* Albany, NY: State University of New York.

Felice, William F. (2003) *The Global New Deal: Economic and Social Human Rights in World Politics.* Lanham, MD: Rowman & Littlefield.

Feltham, R. G. (1980) *Diplomatic Handbook,* 3rd edn. New York: Longman.

Ferguson, Charles D. (Project Director) (2009) *U.S. Nuclear Weapons Policy.* Washington, DC: Brookings Institution Press.

Fernández-Sànchez, Pablo Antonio (ed.) (2009) *International Legal Dimension of Terrorism.* Boston, MA: Martinus Nijhoff.

Ferraro, Vincent and Rosser, Melissa (1994) "Global Debt and Third World Development," in Michael T. Klare and Daniel C. Thomas (eds.), *World Security: Challenges for a New Century,* 2nd edn. New York: St Martin's Press.

Fidler, David (1999) *International Law and Infectious Diseases.* New York: Oxford University Press.

Fidler, David (2003) "Weapons of Mass Destruction and International law," *ASIL Insights,* February.

Finnemore, Martha (1993) "International Organizations as Teachers of Norms: The United Nations Educational, Scientific, and Cultural Organization and Science Policy, *International Organization,* 47 (4).

Finnemore, Martha (1996) "Norms, Culture, and World Politics: Insights from Sociology's Institutionalism," *International Organization,* 50 (2).

Finnemore, Martha (1999) "Rules of War and Wars of Rules: The International Red Cross and the Restraint of State Violence," in John Boli and George M. Thomas (eds.), *Constructing World Culture: International Nongovernmental Organizations Since 1875.* Stanford, CA: Stanford University Press.

Fisher, Glen (1988) *Mindsets: the Role of Culture and Perception in International Relations.* Yarmouth, ME: International Press.

Flavin, Christopher and Gardner, Gardner (2005) "China, India, and the New World Order," in Sharon Guynup (ed.), *State of the World 2006: A Global Portrait of Wildlife, Wildlands, and Oceans.* Washington, DC: Island Press.

Forsythe, David and Rieffer-Flanagan, Barbara Ann J. (2007) *International Committee of the Red Cross: A Neutral Humanitarian Actor.* New York: Routledge.

Francioni, Francesco and Scheinin, Martin (eds.) (2008) *Cultural Human Rights.* Boston, MA: Martinus Nijhoff Publishers.

Franck, Thomas M. (1995) *Fairness in International Law and Institutions.* Oxford: Clarendon.

Franck, Thomas M. (1996) "Clan and Super-clan: Loyalty, Identity and Community in Law and Practice," *American Journal of International Law,* 90 (3).

Franck, Thomas M. Franck (2003) "Interpretation and Change in the Law of Humanitarian Intervention," in J. L. Holzgreffe and Robert O. Keohane (eds.), *Humanitarian Intervention: Ethical, Legal, and Political Dilemmas.* New York: Cambridge University Press.

Franda, Marcus (2001) *Governing the Internet: The Emergence of an International Regime.* Boulder, CO: Lynne Rienner.

Franda, Marcus (2002) *Launching Into Cyberspace: Internet Development and Politics in Five World Regions.* Boulder, CO: Lynne Rienner.

French, French (2000) *Vanishing Borders: Protecting the Planet in the Age of Globalization*. New York: W.W. Norton/Worldwatch Books.

Frey, Linda S. and Frey, Marsha L. (1999) *The History of Diplomatic Immunity*. Columbus, OH: Ohio State University.

Fried, John H. E. (1998) "International Law: Neither Orphan Nor Harlot, Neither Jailer Nor Never-Never Land," in Charlotte Ku and Paul F. Diehl (eds.), *International Law: Classic and Contemporary Readings* (Boulder, CO: Lynne Rienner.

Friedheim, Robert L. (ed.) (2001) *Toward a Sustainable Whaling Regime*. Seattle, WA: University Press.

Friedman, Thomas L. (1999) *The Lexus and the Olive Tree*. New York: Farrar, Straus, & Giroux.

Friedman, Thomas L. (2007) *The World is Flat: A Brief History of the Twenty-first Century*, expanded edn. New York: Picador/Farrar, Straus, & Giroux.

Friedmann, Wolfgang (1963) "The Uses of 'General Principles' in Development of International Law," *American Journal of International Law*, 57 (2).

Frowein, Jochen A. (1997) "The Implementation and Promotion of International Law Through National Courts," in *International Law as a Language for International Relations*. Boston: Brill.

Fry, Earl H. (1998) *The Expanding Role of State and Local Governments in U.S. Foreign Affairs*. New York: Council on Foreign Relations Press.

Galdorisi, George V. and Vienaa, Kevin R. (1997) *Beyond the Law of the Sea*. Westport, CT: Praeger Publishers.

Gamble, John King, Jr (1998) "The Treaty/Custom Dichotomy," in Charlotte Ku and Paul F. Diehl (eds.), *International Law: Classic and Contemporary Readings*. Boulder, CO: Lynne Rienner.

Gardam, Judith G. and Jarvis, Michelle J. Jarvis (2001) *Women, Armed Conflict and International Law*. Boston, MA: Kluwer.

Gareis, Sven Bernhard and Varwick, Johannes (2005) *The United Nations: An Introduction*. New York: Palgrave Macmillan.

Garrett, Laurie (2007) "The Challenge of Global Health," *Foreign Affairs*, 86 (1).

George, Alexander L. (1991) *Forceful Persuasion: Coercive Diplomacy as an Alternative to War*. Washington, DC: United States Institute of Peace Press.

George, Susan (1992) *The Debt Boomerang: How Third World Debt Harms Us All*. London: Pluto Press.

Gibney, Mark (2008) *International Human Rights Law: Returning to Universal Principles*. Lanham, MD: Rowman & Littlefield.

Gillespie, Alexander (2005) *Whaling Diplomacy: Defining Issues in International Environment Law*. Northampton, MA: Edward Elgar.

Gilpin, Robert (1984) *War and Change in World Politics*. New York: Cambridge University Press.

Gilpin, Robert (1987) *The Political Economy of International Relations*. Princeton, NJ: Princeton University Press.

Glennon, Michael J. (2003) "Why the Security Council Failed," *Foreign Affairs*, 82 (3).

Goldsmith, Jack and Posner, Eri A. (2005) *The Limits of International Law*. New York: Oxford University Press.

Goldsmith, Jack and Wu, Tim (2008) *Who Controls the Internet? Illusions of a Borderless World*. New York: Oxford University Press.

Goldstone, Richard J. and Smith, Adam M. (2008) *International Judicial Institutions*. Abingdon: Routledge.

Gore, Al (1992) *Earth in the Balance: Ecology and the Human Spirit*. New York: Houghton Mifflin.

Gorove, Katherine and Kamenetskaya, Elena (1995) "Tensions in the Development of the Law of Outer Space," in Lori Fisler Damrosch, Gennady M. Danilenko, and Rein Müllerson (eds.), *Beyond Confrontation: International Law for the Post-Cold War Era*. Boulder, CO: Westview Press.

Goulding, Marrack (2003) *Peacemonger*. Baltimore, MD: Johns Hopkins University Press.

Graham, Gordon (1997) *Ethics and International Relations*. Cambridge, MA: Blackwell.

Graham, Thomas, Jr (2002) *Disarmament Sketches: Three Decades of Arms Control and International Law*. Seattle, WA: Washington University Press.

Grant, Thomas D. (1999) *The Recognition of States: Law and Practice in Debate and Evolution*. Westport, CT: Praeger.

Gray, Christine (1983) "International Law: 1908–1983," *Legal Studies*, 3.

Gray, Christine (2004) *International Law and the Use of Force*, 2nd edn. New York: Oxford University Press.

Greenberg, Edward S. (1982) "In Order to Save It We Had to Destroy It: Reflections on the United States and Human Rights," in Fred A. Baumann (ed.), *Human Rights and American Foreign Policy*. Gambier, OH: Kenyon College.

Greenberg, Karen J. and Dratel, Joshua L. (2005) *The Torture Papers: The Road to Abu Ghraib*. New York: Cambridge University Press.

Greig, Alastair, Hulme, David, and Turner, Mark (2007) *Challenging Global Inequality: Development Theory and Practice in the 21st Century*. New York: Palgrave Macmillan.

Grewe, Wilhelm G. (2000) (translated by Michael Byers), *Epochs of International Law*, translated by Michael Byers. New York: Walter De Gruyter.

Grey, Stephen (2006) *Ghost Plane: The True Story of the CIA Torture Program*. New York: St Martin's Press.

Groarke, Paul (2004) *Dividing the State: Legitimacy, Secession and the Doctrine of Oppression*. Brookfield, VT: Ashgate.

Gross, Leo (1971) "The United Nations and the Role of Law," in Robert S. Wood (ed.), *The Process of International Organization*. New York: Random House.

Grosscup, Beau (2006) *Strategic Terror: The Politics and Ethics of Aerial Bombardment*. New York: Zed Books.

Grünfeld, Fred and Huijboom, Anke (2007) *The Failure to Prevent Genocide in Rwanda: The Role of Bystanders*. Boston, MA: Martinus Nijhoff.

Gualtieri, David S. (2000) "The System of Non-proliferation Export Controls," in Dinah Shelton (ed.) *Commitment and Compliance: The Role of Non-Binding Norms in the International Legal System*. New York: Oxford University Press.

Guilfoyle, Douglas (2009) *Shipping Interdiction and the Law of the Sea*. New York: Cambridge University Press.

Gulick, Eward V. (1999) *The Time Is Now: Strategy and Structure for World Governance*. Lanham, MD: Lexington.

Gurr, Ted Robert (1993) *Minorities at Risk: A Global View of Ethno-political Conflicts*. Washington, DC: United States Institute of Peace.

Gurr, Ted Robert (2000) *People Versus States: Minorities at Risk in the New Century*. Washington, DC: United States Institute of Peace.

Guthrie, Richard Guthrie, Hart, John, and Kuhlau, Frida (2005) "Chemical and Biological Warfare Developments," *SIPRI Yearbook 2005: Armaments, Disarmaments and International Security*. Stockholm: Stockholm International Peace Research Institute.

Gutman, Roy (1999) "Deportation," in Roy Gutman and David Rieff (eds.), *Crimes of War*. New York: W.W. Norton.

Guzman, Andrew T. and Sykes, Alan O. (eds.) (2007) *Research Handbook in International Economic Law*. Northampton, MA: Edward Elgar.

Hafez, Mohammed M. and Hatfield, Joseph M. (2006) "Do Targeted Assassinations Work? A Multivariate Analysis of Israel's Controversial Tactic During Al-Aqsa Uprising," *Studies in Conflict & Terrorism*, 29 (4).

Hallett, Brien (1998) *The Lost Art of Declaring War*. Urbana, IL: University of Illinois.

Handelman, Howard (2000) *The Challenge of Third World Development*, 2nd edn. Upper Saddle River, NY: Prentice-Hall.

Hannum, Hurst (2003) "Indigenous Rights," in Gene M. Lyons and James Mayall (eds.), *International Human Rights in the 21st Century*. Lanham, MD: Rowman & Littlefield.

Harris, Sheldon H. (1994) *Factories of Death: Japanese Biological Warfare 1932–45 and the American Cover-Up*. New York: Routledge.

Harvey, Robert (2003) *Global Disorder: America and the Threat of World Conflict*. New York: Carroll and Graf.

Harwell, Mark A. (1984) *Nuclear Winter: The Human and Environmental Consequences of Nuclear War*. New York: Springer-Verlag.

Hearn, Chester (2003) *Sorties into Hell: The Hidden War on Chichi Jima*. Westport, CT: Praeger.

Held, David (1995) *Democracy and the Global Order: From the Modern State to Cosmopolitan Governance*. Stanford, CA: Stanford University Press.

Henderson, Conway W. (1991) "Conditions Affecting the Use of Political Repression," *Journal of Conflict Resolution*, 35 (1).

Henderson, Conway W. (2001) "Investigating International Society," *Global Society*, 15 (4).

Henderson, Conway W. (2004) "The Political Repression of Women," *Human Rights Quarterly*, 26 (4).

Henkin, Louis (1979) *How Nations Behave: Law and Foreign Policy*, 2nd edn. New York: Columbia University Press.

Henkin, Louis (1989) "Use of Force: Law and U.S. Policy," *Right v. Might: International Law and the Use of Force*. New York: Council of Foreign Affairs.

Henkin, Louis (1995) *International Law: Politics and Values*. Boston, MA: M. Nijhoff.

Hertz, Noreena (2001) *The Silent Takeover: Global Corporations and the Death of Democracy*. New York: Free Press.

Hewson, Martin and Sinclair, Timothy J. (1999) "The Emergence of Global Governance Theory," in Martin Hewson and Timothy J. Sinclair (eds.), *Approaches to Global Governance Theory*. Albany: State University of New York Press.

Higgins, Rosalyn (1985) "Conceptual Thinking About the Individual," in Richard Falk, Friedrich Kratochwil, and Saul Mendlovitz (eds.), *International Law: A Contemporary Perspective*. Boulder, CO: Westview Press.

Higgins, Rosalyn (1994) *Problems and Prospects: International Law and How We Use It*. Oxford: Clarendon.

Hill, Stephen M. (2004) *United Nations Disarmament Processes in Intra-State Conflict*. New York: Palgrave Macmillan.

Hodder, Rupert (2007) *How Corruption Affects Social and Economic Development: The Dark Side of Political Economy*, vol. 1. Lewiston, NY: Edwin Mellen.

Hoffman, Stanley (1995) "Foreword: Revisiting 'The Anarchical Society,'" in Hedley Bull, *The Anarchical Society: A Study of Order in World Politics*, 2nd edn. New York: Columbia University Press.

Holmes, Linda Goetz (2001) *Unjust Enrichment: How Japan's Companies Built Postwar Fortunes Using American POWS*. Mechanicsburg, PA: Stackpole Books.

Homer-Dixon, Thomas (1991) "On the Threshold: Environmental Changes as Causes of Conflict," *International Security*, 16 (2).

Homer-Dixon, Thomas (1994) "Environmental Scarcities and Violent Conflict: Evidence From Cases," *International Security*, 19 (1).

Homer-Dixon, Thomas (1999) *Environment, Scarcity, and Violence*. Princeton, NJ: Princeton University Press.

Hood, Roger (2001) "Capital Punishment: A Global Perspective," *Punishment and Society: The International Journal of Penology*, 3 (1).

Hood, Roger and Hoyle, Carolyn (2008) *The Death Penalty: A Worldwide Perspective*, 4th edn. New York: Oxford University Press.

Horne, John and Kramer, Alan (2001) *German Atrocities, 1914: A History of Denial*. New Haven, CT: Yale University Press.

Horovitz, Irving Louis (1997) *Taking Lives: Genocide and State Power*, 4th edn. expanded and revised. New Brunswick, NJ: Transaction.

Howard, Michael (2002) "What's in a Name? How to Fight Terrorism," in Gideon Rose (ed.), *The War on Terrorism*. New York: Council on Foreign Relations.

Howard. Rhoda E. (1995) *Human Rights and the Search for Community*. Boulder, CO: Westview.

Hubband, Mark (1999) "Prisoners of War, Non-Repatriation of," in Roy Gutman and David Rieff (eds.), *Crimes of War*. New York: W.W. Norton.

Human Security Report 2005: War and Peace in the 21st Century. New York: Oxford University Press.

Hunt, Suzanne C. and Sawin, Janet L. (2006) "Cultivating Renewable Alternative to Oil," in Sharon Guynup (ed.), *State of the World 2006: A Global Portrait of Wildlife, Wildlands, and Oceans*. Washington, DC: Island Press.

Hurrell, Andrew (2000) "Conclusion: International Law and the Changing Constitution of International Relations," in Michael Byers (ed.), *The Role of Law in International Politics: Essays in International Relations and International Law*. New York: Oxford University Press.

Husbands, Jo Lo (2002) "Conventional Weapons," in Jeffery A. Larsen (ed.), *Arms Control: Cooperative Security in a Changing Environment*. Boulder, CO: Lynne Rienner.

ICON Group International (2009) *Arms Control and Disarmament: Webster's Timeline History, 1825–2007*. San Diego, CA: ICON Group International.

ICRC (2001) *Women Facing War: ICRC Study on the Impact of Armed Conflict on Women*. Geneva, Switzerland: International Committee of the Red Cross.

Ignatieff, Michael (2001) *Human Rights as Politics and Idolatry*. Princeton, NJ: Princeton University Press.

Iklé, Fred Charles (1964) *How Nations Negotiate*. New York: Oxford University Press.

International Law: 100 Ways It Shapes Our Lives (2006) Washington, DC: American Society of International Law.

Isbister, John (2006) *Promises Not Kept:Poverty and the Betrayal of Third World Development*, 7th edn. Bloomfield, CT: Kumarian Press.

Ishay, Micheline R. (2004) *The History of Human Rights: From Ancient Times to the Globalization Era*. Berkeley, CA: University of California Press.

Jackson, Robert H. (2001) "The Evaluation of International Society," in John Baylis and Steve Smith (eds.), *The Globalization of World Politics*, 2nd edn. New York: Oxford University Press.

Jackson-Preece, Jennifer (2003) "Human Rights and Cultural Pluralism," in Gene M. Lyons and James Mayall (eds.), *International Human Rights in the 21st Century*. Lanham, MD: Rowman & Littlefield.

Jentleson, Bruce W. (2000) "Preventive Diplomacy: A Conceptual and Analytical Framework," in Bruce W. Jentleson (ed.), *Opportunities Missed, Opportunities Seized: Preventive Diplomacy in the Post-Cold War*. Lanham, MD: Rowman & Littlefield.

Jinks, Derek and Sloss, David (eds.) (2009) *The Role of Domestic Courts in Treaty Enforcement: A Comparative Study*. New York: Cambridge University Press.

Jones, Adam (2004) "Gendercide and Genocide," in Adam Jones (ed.), *Gendercide and Genocide*. Nashville, TN: Vanderbilt University Press.

Joyner, Christopher C. (1997) "Conclusion: The United Nations As International Law-Giver," in Christopher C. Joyner (ed.), *The United Nations and International Law*. Washington, DC: American Society of International Law/Cambridge University Press.

Joyner, Christopher C. (1998) "The Reality and the Relevance of International Law in the 21st Century," in Charles W. Kegley, Jr, and Eugene R. Wittkopf (eds.) *The Global Agenda: Issues and Perspectives*, 5th edn. Boston: McGraw-Hill.

Juda, Lawerence (1996) *International Law and Ocean Use Management: The Evolution of Ocean Governance*. New York: Routledge.

Kaikobad, Kaiyan Homi (2000) *The International Court of Justice and Judicial Review: A Study of the Court's Powers with Respect to Judgments of the ILO and UN Administrative Tribunals*. The Hague: Kluwer.

Kaikobad, Kaiyan Homi and Bohlander, Michael (eds.) (2009) *International Law and Power: Perspectives on Legal Order and Justice*. Boston, MA: Martinus Nijhoff.

Kalathil, Shanthi (2003) "Dot.Com for Dictators," *Foreign Policy*, March/April.

Kalathil, Shanthi and Boas, Taylor C. (2003) *Open Networks Closed Regimes: The Impact of the Internet on Authoritarian Rule*. Washington, DC: Carnegie Endowment for International Peace.

Kane, Hal (2003) "Leaving Home: The Flow of Refugees," in Maryann Cusimano Love (ed.), *Beyond Sovereignty: Issues for a Global Agenda*, 2nd edn. Belmont, CA: Thomson/Wadsworth.

Kapstein, Ethan (2006a) "The New Global Slave Trade," *Foreign Affairs*, 85 (6).

Kapstein, Ethan (2006b) *Economic Justice in an Unfair World: Toward a Level Playing Field*. Princeton, NJ: Princeton University Press.

Kariyawasam, Rohan (2007) *International Economic Law and the Digital Divide: A New Silk Road?* Northampton, MA: Edward Elgar Publishing.

Karoubi, Mohammad Taghi (2004) *Just or Unjust War? International Law and Unilateral Use of Force by States at the Turn of the 20th Century*. Burlington, VT: Ashgate.

Keck, Margaret E. and Sikkink, Kathryn (1998) *Activists Beyond Borders*. Ithaca, NY: Cornell University Press.

Kegley, Charles W., Jr (1995a) *Controversies in International Relations Theory: Realism and the Neoliberal Challenge*. New York: St Martin's Press.

Kegley, Charles W. Jr (1995b) "Neoliberal Challenge to Realist Theories of World Politics: An Introduction," in Kegley, *Controversy in International Relations Theory*. New York: St Martin's Press.

Kegley, Charles W., Jr, and Raymond, Gregory A. (2001) *Exorcising the Ghost of Westphalia*. Upper Saddle River, NJ: Prentice-Hall.

Kelleher, Ann and Klein, Laura (2005) *Global Perspectives: A Handbook for Understanding Global Issues*, 2nd edn. Upper Saddle, NJ: Pearson/Prentice-Hall.

Kelly, Petra (2004) "The Need for Eco-Justice," in K. Conca and G. Debalko (eds.), *Green Planet Blues*. Boulder, CO: Westview.

Kenny, Charles (2006) *Overselling the Web? Development and the Internet*. CO: Lynne Rienner.

Keohane, Robert O. (2003) "Introduction," in J. L. Holzgreffe and Robert O. Keohane (eds.), *Humanitarian Intervention: Ethical, Legal, and Political Dilemmas*. New York: Cambridge University Press.

Kelsen, Hans (1966) *Principles of International Law*, 2nd edn. Revised and edited by Robert W. Tucker. New York: Holt, Rinehart, and Winston.

Kile, Shannon N. (2003) "Nuclear Arms Control, Non-Proliferation and Ballistic Missile Defense," Chapter 15, *SIPRI Yearbook, 2003 Armaments, Disarmaments, and International Security*. Stockholm: Stockholm International Peace Research Institute.

Kissinger, Henry (1994) *Diplomacy*. New York: Simon & Schuster.

Klabbers, Jan (2002) *An Introduction to International Institutional Law*. New York: Cambridge University Press.

Klabbers, Jan (2005) *International Organizations*. Burlington, VT: Ashgate/Dartmouth.

Klabbers, Jan and Sellers, M. N. S. (2008) *The Internationalization of Law and Legal Education*. London: Springer.

Klare, Michael T. (1999) "International Trade in Light Weapons," in Jeffrey Boutwell and Michael T. Klare (eds.), *Light Weapons and Civil Conflict: Controlling the Tools of Violence*. Lanham, MD: Rowman & Littlefield.

Klare, Michael T. (2002) *Resource Wars: The New Landscape of Global Conflict*. New York: Henry Holt and Co.

Klare, Michael T. and Lumpe, Lora (1998) "Fanning the Flames of War: Conventional Arms Transfers in the 1990s," in Michael T. Klare and Yodesh Chandrani (eds.), *World Security: Challenges for a New Century*, 3rd edn. New York: St Martin's Press.

Kneebone, Susan (ed.) (2009) *Refugees, Asylum Seekers and the Rule of Law*. New York: Cambridge University Press.

Kolosov, Yuri M. and Levitt, Geoffrey M. (1995) "International Cooperation Against Terrorism," in Lori Fisler Damrosch, Gennady M. Danilenko, and Rien Müllerson (eds.), *Beyond Confrontation: International Law for the Post-Cold War Era*. Boulder, CO: Westview Press.

Korten, David C. (1995) *When Corporations Rule the World*. West Hartford, CT: Kumarian Press.

Koskenniemi, Martti (2002) *The Gentle Civilizer of Nations: The Rise and Fall of International Law, 1870–1960*. New York: Cambridge University Press.

Koskenniemi, Martti (ed.) (2000) *Sources of International Law*. Burlington, VT: Ashgate/Dartmouth.

Koslowski, Rey (2003) "Challenges of International Cooperation in a World of Increasing Dual Nationality," in David A. Martin and Kay Hailbronner (eds.), *Rights and Duties of Dual Nationals: Evolution and Prospects*. New York: Kluwer.

Kouladis, Nicholas (2006) *Principles of Law Relating to International Trade*. London: Springer Press.

Krasner, Stephen D. (1991) "Global Communications and National Power: Life on the Pareto Frontier," *World Politics*, 43 (3).

Krivenko, Ekaterina Yahyaoui (2009) *Women, Islam and International Law*. Boston, MA: Martinus Nijhoff Publishers.

Ku, Charlotte and Diel, Paul F. (1991) "International Law as Operating and Normative Systems: An Overview," in Charlotte Kul and Paul F. Diehl (eds.) *International Law: Classic and Contemporary Readings*. Boulder: Lynne Rienner.

Kuper, Jenny (1997) *International Law Concerning Child Civilians in Armed Conflict*. New York: Oxford University Press.

Lambakis, Stephen (1995) "Space Control in Desert Storm," *Orbis*, 39 (3).

Lambert, June (2009) *Enforcing Intellectual Property Rights: A Concise Guide for Businesses, Innovative and Creative Individuals*. Burlington, VT: Ashgate.

Landes, David S. (1998) *The Wealth and Poverty of Nations*. New York: W.W. Norton.

Lang, Anthony F. (2003) *Just Intervention*. Washington, D.C.: Georgetown University Press.

Lang, Anthony F. and Beattie, Amanda Russell (2008) *War, Torture and Terrorism*. New York: Routledge.

Langewiesche, William (2004) *The Outlaw Sea: A World of Freedom, Chaos, and Crime*. New York: North Point Press.

Lanoszka, Anna (2009) *The World Trade Organization: Changing Dynamics in the Global Political Economy*. Boulder, CO: Lynne Rienner.

Laqueur, Walter (2001) *A History of Terrorism*. New Brunswick, NJ: Transaction.

Laqueur, Walter (2002) "Post-Modern Terrorism," in Gideon Rose (ed.), *The War on Terrorism*. New York: Council on Foreign Relations.

Larsen, Jeffrey A. (2001) "Conclusion," in James J. Wirtz and Jeffrey A. Larsen (eds.), *Rockets' Red Glare: Missile Defenses and Their Future of World Politics*. Boulder, CO: Westview Press.

Larsen, Jeffrey A. (2005) *Historical Dictionary of Arms Control and Disarmament*. Lanham, MD: Scarecrow Press.

Lauren, Paul Gordon (1998) *The Evolution of International Human Rights: Visions Seen*. Philadelphia, PA: University of Pennsylvania Press.

Lauren, Paul Gordon, Craig, Gordon A., and George, Alexander L. (1995) *Force and Statecraft: Diplomatic Problems of Our Times*, 4th edn. New York: Oxford University Press.

Lawrence, Robert Z. (1993) "Emerging Regional Arrangements: Building Blocs or Stumbling Blocs," in Jeffrey A. Frieden and David A. Lake (eds.), *International Political Economy: Perspectives on Global Power and Wealth*, 3rd edn. New York: St Martin's Press.

Lawrence, Robert Z. (2003) *Crimes & Punishment? Retaliation Under the WTO*. Washington, DC: Institute for International Economics.

Lea, David (2008) *Property Rights, Indigenous People and the Developing World*. Boston, MA: Martinus Nijhoff.

Leander, Anna (2005) "The Power to Construct International Security: Or the Significance of Private Military Companies," *Millennium: Journal of International Studies*, 33 (3).

LeBlanc, Lawrence J. (1995) *The Convention on the Rights of the Child: United Nations Lawmaking on Human Rights*. Lincoln, NE: University of Nebraska Press.

Lee Kuan Yew (2007) "United States, Iraq, and the War on Terrorism," *Foreign Affairs*, 86 (1).

Legro, Jeffrey W. and Moravcsik, Andrew (1999) "Is Anybody Still a Realist?" *International Security*, 24 (2).

Lehr, Peter (2006) *Piracy in the Age of Global Terrorism*. New York: Routledge.

Lemkin, Raphael (1944) *Axis Rule in Occupied Europe*. Washington, DC: Carnegie Endowment for International Peace

Leonard, Mark (2005). *Why Europe Will Run the 21st Century*. New York: Public Affairs.

Levi, Michael A. and O'Hanlon, Michael E. (2005) *The Future of Arms Control*. Washington, DC: Brookings Institution Press.

Levi, Werner (1974) "International Law in a Multicultural World," *International Studies Quarterly*, 18 (4).

Levi, Werner (1976) *Law and Politics in the International Society*. Beverly Hills, CA: Sage.

Li Haopei (2001) "Jus Cogens and International Law," in Sienho Yee and Wang Tieya (eds.) *International Law in the Post-Cold War World: Essays In Memory of Li Haopei*. New York: Routledge.

Li, Peter (ed.) (2003) *Japanese War Crimes*. New Brunswick, NJ: Transaction.

Lieber, Keir A. and Press, Daryl G. (2006) "The Rise of U.S. Nuclear Primacy," *Foreign Affairs*, 85 (2).

Lillich, Richard B. and Magraw, Daniel B. (eds.) (1998) *The Iran–United States Claims Tribunal: Its Contribution to the Law of State Responsibility*. Irving-on-Hudson: Transnational.

Lindsey, Charlotte (2001) *Women Facing War: ICRC Study on the Impact of Armed Conflict on Women*. Geneva: ICRC.

Lipset, Seymour Martin and Lenz, Gabriel (2000) "Corruption, Culture, and Markets, in Lawrence E. Harrison and Samuel P. Huntington (eds.), *Culture Matters: How Values Shape Human Progress*. New York: Basic Books.

Lockwood, Bert B. (ed.) (2006) *Women's Rights: A Human Rights Quarterly Reader*. Baltimore, MD: Johns Hopkins University Press.

Lomborg, Bjørn (2001) *The Skeptical Environmentalist: Measuring the Real State of the World*. New York: Cambridge University Press.

Lopez, George A. and David Cortwright, David (2004) "Containing Iraq: Sanctions Worked," *Foreign Affairs*, 83 (4).

Louka, Elli (2006) *International Environmental Law: Fairness, Effectiveness, and World Order*. New York: Cambridge University Press.

Love, Richard A. and Love, Maryann Cusimano (2003) "Multinational Corporations: Power and Responsibility," in Maryann Cusimano Love (ed.), *Beyond Sovereignty: Issues for a Global Agenda*. Belmont, CA: Wadsworth Press.

Lovelock, James (1995) *GAIA: A New Look at Life on Earth*. Oxford: Oxford University Press.

Loya, Thomas A. and Boli, John (1999) "Standardization in the World Polity: Technical Rationality over Power," in John Boli and George M. Thomas (eds.), *Constructing World Culture*. Stanford, CA: Stanford University Press.

Lumpe, Lora (2003) "Taking Aim at the Global Gun Trade," *Amnesty Now*, Winter.

Lung-chu Chen (2000) *An Introduction to Contemporary International Law: A Policy Oriented Perspective*. New Haven, CT: Yale University Press.

Lutz, Ellen L. and Reiger, Caitlin (eds.) (2009) *Prosecuting Heads of State*. New York: Cambridge University Press.

Lyall, Francis (1996) "Space Law: The Role of the United Nations," in *International Law as a Language for International Relations*. Boston, MA: United Nations/Kluwer Law International.

Lyall, Francis and Larsen, Paul B. (2009) *Space Law: A Treatise*. Burlington, VT: Ashgate.

Lyons, Gene M. and Mayall, James (2003) "Stating the Problem of Group Rights," in Lyons and Mayall (eds.), *International Human Rights in the 21st Century*. Lanham, MD: Rowman & Littlefield.

MacDonald, Ronald St F. (2001) "The Supervision of the Execution of Judgments of the European Court of Human Rights," in Sienho Yee and Wang Tieya (eds.), *International Law in the Post-Cold War World: Essays In Memory of Li Haopei*. New York: Routledge.

Magraw, Daniel Barstow and Vinogradove, Dergi (1995) "Environmental Law," in Lori Fisler Damrosch, Gennady M. Danionko (eds.), *Beyond Confrontation: International Law for the Post-Cold War Era*. Boulder, CO: Westview Press.

Mahoney, Liam and Eguren, Luis Enrique (1997) *Unarmed Bodyguards: International Accompaniment for the Protection of Human Rights*. West Hartford, CT: Kumarian Press.

Malanczuk, Peter (1997) *Akehurst's Modern Introduction to International Law*, 7th edn. New York: Routledge.

Malone, Linda (1998) *International Law*, 2nd edn. Larchmont, NY: Emanuel Publishing.

Malthus, Thomas Robert (1992) *An Essay on the Principle of Population*, edited by Donald Winch. New York: Cambridge University Press.

Mandel, Robert (2002) *Armies Without States: The Privatization of Security*. Boulder, CO: Lynne Rienner.

Mandelbaum, Michael (2006) *The Case for Goliath: How America Acts as the World's Government in the 21st Century*. Boulder, CO: Public Affairs.

Mangone, Gerard J. (1967) *The Elements of International Law* Revised ed. (Homewood, IL: Dorsey Press.

Mansfield, Edward D. and Milner, Helen V. (1999) "The New Wave of Regionalism," *International Organization*, 53 (3).

Maogot, Jackson Nyamuya (2004) *War Crimes and Realpolitik: International Justice from World War I to the 21st Century*. Boulder, CO: Lynne Rienner.

Marks, Susan and Clapham, Andrew (2005) *International Human Rights Lexicon*. New York: Oxford University Press.

Markusen, Eric and Kopf, David (1995) *The Holocaust and Strategic Bombing: Genocide and Total War in the Twentieth Century*. Boulder, CO: Westview Press.

Marlin-Bennett, Renée (2004) *Knowledge Power: Intellectual Property, Information, and Privacy*. Boulder, CO: Lynne Rienner.

Marrus, Michael R. (1997) *The Nuremberg War Crimes Trial 1945–46: A Documentary History*. New York: St Martin's Press.

Martin, David A. (2003) "Introduction: The Trend toward Dual Nationality," in David A. Martin and Kay Hailbronner (eds.), *Rights and Duties of Dual Nationals: Evolution and Prospects*. New York: Kluwer.

Martin, David A. and Aleinikoff, Alexander (2002) "Double Ties: Why Nations Should Learn to Love Dual Nationality," *Foreign Policy*, November/December.

Mastanduno, Michael (1999) *Unipolar Politics: Realism and State Strategies*. New York: Columbia University Press.

Matsuura, Jeffrey H. (2008) *Jefferson vs. the Patent Trolls: A Populist Vision of Intellectual Property Rights*. Charlottesville, VA: University of Virginia Press.

Mauro, Paolo (1997) *Why Worry about Corruption?* Washington, DC: International Monetary Fund.

May, Christopher and Sell, Susan K. *Intellectual Property Rights: A Critical History*. Boulder, CO: Lynne Rienner.

May, Larry (2008) *Aggression and Crimes against Peace*. New York: Cambridge University Press.

Mayer, Ann Elizabeth (2005) "The Islamic Declaration," in Rhona K. M. Smith and Christian van den Anker (eds.), *The Essentials of Human Rights*. New York: Oxford University Press.

McCormick, John (1999) "The Role of Environmental NGOS in International Regimes," in Norman J. Vig and Regina S. Axelrod (eds.), *The Global Environment: Institutions, Law, and Policy*. Washington, DC: CQ Press.

McCorquodale, Robert (2000) *Self-Determination in International Law*. Burlington, VT: Ashgate.

MccGwire, Michael (2005) "The Rise and Fall of the NPT: An Opportunity for Britain," *International Affairs*, 81 (1).

McShane, James P. (1999) "Weapons and International Law Enforcement," in Jeffrey Boutwell and Michael T. Klare (eds.), *Light Weapons and Civil Conflict: Controlling the Tools of Violence*. Lanham, MD: Rowman & Littlefield.

Mead, Margaret Mead (1996) [1940] "Warfare Is only an Invention – Not a Biological Necessity," in John A. Vasquez (ed.), *Classics in International Relations*, 3rd edn. Upper Saddle River, NJ: Prentice-Hall.

Meadows, Donnella (1972) *The Limits to Growth; A Report for the Club of Rome's Project on the Predicament on Mankind*. New York: Universe Books.

Meadows, Donnella et al. (2004) *The Limits to Growth: the 30-Year Update*. White River Junction, VT: Chelsea Green Publishing.

Merrills, J. G. (2005) *International Dispute Settlement*, 4th edn. New York: Cambridge University Press.

Mertus, Julie (2005) *United Nations and Human Rights: A Guide for a New Era*. New York: Routledge.

Meyer, Howard N. (2002) *The World Court in Action: Judging Among the Nations*. Lanham, MD: Rowman & Littlefield.

Meyers, Norman (ed.) (1993) *GAIA: An Atlas of Planet Management*, revised edn. New York: Anchor Books.

Miller, Alan A. (2003) *GAIA Connections*, 2nd edn. Lanham, MD: Rowman & Littlefield.

Miller, Robert Hopkins (1992) *Inside the Embassy: The Political Role of Diplomats Abroad*. Washington, DC: Congressional Quarterly.

Mau, Hans (1978) *Politics Among Nations: The Struggle for Power and Peace*, 5th edn., revised. New York: Alfred A. Knopf.

Miers, Suzanne (2003) *Slavery in the Twentieth Century: The Evolution of a Global Problem*. Walnut Grove, CA: Alta Mira Press.

Minear, Richard H. (1971) *Victor's Justice: The Tokyo War Crimes Trial*. Princeton, NJ: Princeton University Press.

Mistry, Dinshaw (2003) *Containing Missile Proliferation*. Seattle, WA: University of Washington Press.

Moore, Mike (2003) *A World Without Walls: Freedom, Development, Freedom, Development, Free Trade and Global Governance*. New York: Cambridge University Press.

Morton, Jeffrey S. and Jones, Presley (2002) "The Legal Status of Mercenaries," *Politics & Policy*, 30 (4).

Mueller, John (1989) *Retreat from Doomsday: The Obsolescence of Major War*. New York: Basic Books.

Mueller, John (2004) *The Remnants of War*. Ithaca, NY: Cornell University Press.

Muldoon, James P., Jr, Aviel, JoAnn Fagot, Reitano, Richard and Sullivan, Earl (2005) *Multilateral Diplomacy and the United Nations Today*. Boulder, CO: Westview.

Muller, A. S. and Loth, M.A. (eds.) (2009) *Highest Courts and the Internationalization of Law Challenges and Changes*. New York: Cambridge University Press.

Müllerson, Rein (2000) *Ordering Anarchy: International Law in International Society*. Boston, MA, Martinus Nijhoff.

Murphy, Craig N. (1997) "What the Third World Wants: An Interpretation of Development and Meaning of the New International Economic Order Ideology," in Paul F. Diehl (ed.), *The Politics of Global Governance: International Organizations in an Interdependent World*. Boulder, CO: Lynne Rienner.

Murphy, Craig N. (2008) *The International Organization for Standardization (ISO)*. New York: Routledge.

Murphy, John F. (1997) "International Crimes," in Christopher C. Joyner (ed.), *The United Nations and International Law*. Washington, DC: American Society of International Law/Cambridge University Press.

Naím, Moisés (2005) *Illicit: How Smugglers, Traffickers, and Copycats are Hijacking the Global Economy*. New York: Doubleday.

Nanda, Ved P. and Pring, George (2003) *International Environmental Law and Policy for the 21st Century*. Ardsley, NY: Transnational.

Nasu, Hitoshi (2009) *International Law on Peacekeeping: A Study of Article 40 of the UN Charter*. Boston, MA: Martinus Nijhoff.

Nathan, James A. (2002) *Soldiers, Statecraft, and History: Coercive Diplomacy and International Order*. Westport, CT: Praeger.

Neary, Brigitte U. and Schneider-Ricks, Holle (eds.) (2002) *Voices of Loss and Courage: German Women Recount Their Expulsion from East Central Europe, 1944–1950*. Rockport, ME: Picton Press.

Neff, Stephen C. (2005) *War and the Law of Nations: A General History*. New York: Cambridge University Press.

Neipert, David M. (2002) *Law of Global Commerce*. Upper Saddle River, NJ: Prentice-Hall

Neyer, Jürgen (2000) "Neo-Medievalism, Local Actors, and Foreign Policy: An Agenda for Research," in Mathias Albert, Lothar Brock, and Klaus Dieter Wolf (eds.), *Civilizing World Politics: Society and Community Beyond the State*. Lanham, MD: Rowman & Littlefield.

Niarchos, Catherine N. (1995) "Women, War, and Rape: Challenges Facing the International Tribunal for the Former Yugoslavia," *Human Rights Quarterly*, 17 (4).

Nicolson, Sir Harold (1964) *Diplomacy*, 3rd edn. New York: Oxford University Press.

Nye, Joseph S., Jr (2002) "Globalization's Democratic Deficit," in *Globalization: Challenge and Opportunity*. New York: Council on Foreign Relations/W.W. Norton.

Oatley, Thomas (ed.) (2005) *The Global Economy: Contemporary Debates*. New York: Pearson/Longman.

Ober, Josiah (1994) "Classical Greek Times," in Michael Howard, George J. Andreopoulos, and Mark L. Schulman (eds.), *The Laws of War*. New Haven, CT: Yale University Press.

O'Brien, John (2001) *International Law*. London: Cavendish.

O'Byrne, Darren J. (2003) *Human Rights: An Introduction*. New York: Pearson Education.

O'Connell, Mary Ellen O'Connell (2005) *International Law and the Use of Force*. New York: Foundation Press.

O'Connell, Robert L. (1989) *Of Arms and Men: A History of War, Weapons, and Aggression*. New York: Oxford University Press.

O'Keefe, Roger (2007) *The Protection of Cultural Property in Armed Conflict*. New York: Cambridge University Press.

Oeter, Stefan (2003) "Effect of Nationality and Dual Nationality on Judicial Cooperation, Including Treaty Regimes such as Extradition," in David A. Martin and Kay Hailbronner (eds.), *Rights and Duties of Dual Nationals: Evolution and Prospects*. New York: Kluwer.

Ohmae, Kenichi (1999) *The Borderless World*, revised edn. New York: Harper Business.

Onuf, Nicholas (1989) *World of Our Making: Rules and Rule in Social Theory and International Relations*. Columbia, SC: University of South Carolina Press.

Osiel, Mark (2009) *The End of Reciprocity: Terror, Torture, and the Law of War*. New York: Cambridge University Press.

O'Sullivan, Meghan L. (2003) *Shrewd Sanctions: Statecraft and State Sponsors of Terrorism*. Washington, DC: Brookings Institution.

Oxman, Bernard H. (1997) "Law of the Sea," in Christopher C. Joyner (ed.), *The United Nations and International Law*. New York: Cambridge University Press.

Papenfuß, Dieter (1998) "The Fate of the International Treaties of the GDR Within the Framework of German Unification," *American Journal of International Law*, 92 (3).

Paré, Daniel J. (2003) *Internet Governance in Transition: Who Is the Master of This Domain?* Lanham, MD: Rowman & Littlefield.

Paul, T. V., Ikenberry, G. John, and Hall, John A. Hall (eds.) (2003) *The Nation-State in Question*. Princeton, NJ: Princeton University Press.

Pauwelyn, Joost (2008) *Optimal Protection of International Law: Navigating Between European Absolutism and American Volunteerism*. New York: Cambridge University Press.

Perkovich, George (2003) "Bush's Nuclear Revolution: A Regime Change in Nonproliferation," *Foreign Affairs*, 82 (2).

Peters, Anne (2003) "International Dispute Settlement: A Network of Cooperational Duties," *European Journal of International Law*, 14 (1).

Peters, Anne (ed.) (2009) *Non-State Actors as Standard Setters*. New York: Cambridge University Press.

Peterson, M. J. (1997) "The Use of Analogies in Developing Outer Space Law," *International Organization*, 51 (2).

Pollis, Adamantia and Schwab, Peter (eds.), *Human Rights: New Perspectives, New Realities*. Boulder, CO: Lynne Rienner.

Postel, Sandra (1994) "Carrying Capacity: Earth's Bottom Line," in *State of the World 1994*. New York: W.W. Norton.

Postel, Sandra (2006) "Safeguarding Freshwater Ecosystems," in *State of the World 2006* New York: W.W. Norton.

Power, Samantha (2002) *A Problem from Hell: America and the Age of Genocide*. New York: Basic Books.

Prestowitz, Clyde V. (2003) *Rogue Nation: American Unilateralism and the Failure of Good Intentions*. New York: Basic Books.

Princeton Principles (2001) *The Princeton Principles on Universal Jurisdiction*, international chair Stephen Macedo. Princeton, NJ: Princeton University Press.

Provost, René (ed.) (2002) *State Responsibility in International Law*. Burlington, VT: Ashgate.

Pyle, Christopher (2001) *Extradition, Politics, and Human Rights*. Philadelphia, PA: Temple University Press.

Quigley, John (2006) *The Genocide Convention: An International Law Analysis*. Burlington, VT: Ashgate.

Ralph, Jason (2007) *Defending the Society of States: Why America Opposes the International Criminal Court and Its Vision of World Society*. New York: Oxford University Press.

Rana, Kishan S. (2004) *The 21st Century Ambassador: Plenipotentiary to Chief Executive*. Malta: DiploFoundation.

Ranstorp, Magnus and Wilkinson, Paul (2007). *Terrorism and Human Rights*. New York: Routledge.

Rapley, John (2006) "The New Middle Ages," *Foreign Affairs*, 85 (3).

Ratner, Steven R. and Slaughter, Anne-Marie (2004) *Methods of International Law*. Washington, DC: American Society of International Law.

Raustiala, Kal (1997) "States, NGOS, and International Environmental Institutions," *International Studies Quarterly*, 41 (4).

Rehman, Javaid (2003) *International Human Rights Law: A Practical Approach*. New York: Pearson Education/Longman.

Reisman, W. Michael (1999) *Jurisdiction in International Law*. Brookfield, VT: Ashgate/Dartmouth.

Reisman, W. Michael and Antoniou, Chris T. (eds.) (1994) *The Laws of War: A Comprehensive Collection of Primary Documents on International Laws Governing Armed Conflict*. New York: Vintage Books.

Renan, Ernest (1971) "What Is a Nation?" in Arend Lijphart (ed.), *World Politics*. Boston: Allyn & Bacon.

Renner, Michael (1994) *Budgeting for Disarmament*, Worldwatch Paper no. 122. Washington, DC: Worldwatch Institute.

Richardson, Diane and Seidman, Steven (2002) *Handbook of Lesbian and Gay Studies*. Thousand Oaks, CA: Sage.

Richardson, Louise (2005) *The Roots of Terrorism*. New York: Routledge.

Richardson, Louise (2006) *What Terrorists Want: Understanding the Enemy, Containing the Threat*. New York: Random House.

Richardson, Louise (2007) *Democracy and Counter-Terrorism: Lessons from the Past*. Washington, DC: U.S. Institute of Peace Press.

Rittner, Carol (2002) "Using Rape as a Weapon of Genocide," in Carol Rittner, John K. Roth, and James M. Smith (eds.), *Will Genocide Ever End?* St Paul, MN: Paragon House.

Riveles, Suzanne (1989) "Diplomatic Asylum as a Human Right: The Case of the Durban Six," *Human Rights Quarterly*, 11 (1).

Roberts, Adam (1993) "Humanitarian War: Military Intervention and Human Rights," *International Affairs*, 69 (3).

Roberts, Adam (1994) "Land Warfare: From Hague to Nuremberg," in Michael Howard, George J. Andreopoulos, and Mark L. Schulman (eds.), *The Laws of War*. New Haven, CT: Yale University Press.

Roberts, Guy B. (2002) "Cooperative Security Measures," in Jeffery A. Larsen (ed.), *Arms Control: Cooperative Security in a Changing Environment*. Boulder, CO: Lynne Rienner.

Rochester, J. Martin (2002) Between Two Epochs: What's Ahead for America, the World, and Global Politics in the Twenty-First Century? Upper Saddle River, NJ: Prentice-Hall.

Romano, Cesare (2000) *The Peaceful Settlement of International Environmental Disputes: A Pragmatic Approach*. Boston, MA: Kluwer Law International.

Romano, Cesare, Nolkaemper, André, and Kleffner, Jann K. (eds.) (2004) *Internationalized Criminal Courts: Sierra Leone, East Timor, Kosovo, and Cambodia*. New York: Oxford University Press.

Rothenberg, Gunther "The Age of Napoleon," in Michael Howard, George J. Andreopoulos, and Mark L. Schulman (eds.), *The Laws of War*. New Haven, CT: Yale University Press.

Rothwell, Donald R. (1996) *The Polar Regions and the Development of International Law*. New York: Cambridge University Press.

Ruggie, John Gerhard (1998) *Constructing the World Polity: Essays On International Institutionalism*. New York: Routledge.

Rummel, R. J. (1991) *Democide: Nazi Genocide and Mass Murder*. New Brunswick, NJ: Transaction.

Rummel, R. J. (1994) *Death by Government*. New Brunswick, NJ: Transaction.

Russell, Edmund (2001) *War and Nature: Fighting Humans and Insects with Chemicals from WWI to Silent Spring*. New York: Cambridge University Press.

Sachs, Aaron (1995) *Eco-Justice: Linking Human Rights and the Environment*, Worldwatch Paper no. 127. Washington, DC: Worldwatch Institute, December.

Sachs, Jeffrey D. (2005a) *The End of Poverty: Economic Possibilities for Our Time*. New York: Penguin.

Sachs, Jeffrey D. (2005b) "Resolving the Debt Crisis of Low-Income Countries," Thomas Oatley (ed.) *The Global Economy: Contemporary Debates*. New York: Pearson/Longman.

Sachs, Jeffrey D. (2008) *Common Wealth: Economics for a Crowded Planet*. New York: Penguin.

Salzman, James and Barton H. Thompson, Barton (2003) *Environmental Law and Policy*. New York: Foundation Press.

Sands, Philippe (2000) *Principles of International Environmental Law*. New York: Cambridge University Press.

Sands, Philippe (2005) *Lawless World: America and the Making and Breaking of Global Rules from FDR's Atlantic Charter to George W. Bush's Illegal War*. New York: Viking.

Sassen, Saski (ed.) (2002) *Global Network: Linked Cities*. New York: Routledge.

Schabas, William A. (1996) *The Death Penalty As Cruel Treatment and Torture: Capital Punishment Challenged in the World's Courts*. Boston, MA: Northeastern University Press.

Schabas, William A. (1997) *Abolition of the Death Penalty in International Law*, 2nd edn. New York: Cambridge University Press.

Schachter, Oscar (1994) " United Nations Law," *American Journal of International Law*, 88 (1).

Schellstede, Sangmie Choi (ed.) (2000) *Comfort Women Speak*. New York: Holmes & Meier.

Schneider, Barry R. and Davis, Jim A. (eds.) (2006) *Combating Weapons of Mass Destruction:Avoiding the Abyss*. New York: Praeger Publishing.

Schwartz, Peter and Gibb, Blair (1999) *When Good Companies Do Bad Things: Responsibility and Risk in an Age of Globalization*. New York: John Wiley & Sons, Inc.

Scott, Shirley V. (ed.) (2006) *International Law and Politics: Key Documents*. Boulder, CO: Lynne Rienner.

Segev, Tom (2006) "A Bitter Prize: Israel and the Occupied Territories," *Foreign Affairs*, 85 (3).

Sen, Amartya (1999) *Development as Freedom*. New York: Knopf Publishers.

Sewall, Sarah B. and Kaysen, Carl (eds.) (2000) *The United States and the International Criminal Court: National Security and International Law*. Lanham, MD: Rowman & Littlefield.

Shabas, William A. (2004) *An Introduction to the International Criminal Court*, 2nd edn. New York: Cambridge University Press.

Shaw, Martin (1994) *Global Society and International Relations*. Malden, MA: Polity Press.

Shaw, Martin (2007) *What Is Genocide?* Malden, MA: Polity Press.

Shue, Henry (1980) *Basic Rights: Subsistence, Affluence, and U.S. Foreign Policy*. Princeton, NJ: Princeton University Press.

Simmons, Beth A. (2000) "International Law and State Behavior: Commitment and Compliance in International Monetary Affairs," *American Political Science Review*, 94 (4).

Simon, Julian L. (1981) *The Ultimate Resources*. Princeton, NJ: Princeton University Press.

Simon, Julian L. (1990) *Population Matters: People, Resources, Environment, and Immigration*. New Brunswick, NJ: Transaction Books.

Simon, Julian L. (1992) *Population and Development in Poor Countries: Selected Essays*. Princeton, NJ: Princeton University Press.

Simpson, Gerry (2004) *Great Powers and Outlaw States: Unequal Sovereigns in the International Legal Order*. New York: Cambridge University Press.

Simpson, Gerry J. (2007) *Law, War & Crime: War Crimes, Trials and the Reinvention of International Law*. Malden, MA: Polity Press.

Simpson, Gerry (ed.) (2001) *The Nature of International Law*. Burlington, VT: Ashgate/Dartmouth.

Singer, J. David and Small, Melvin (1972) *The Wages of War, 1816–1965: A Statistical Handbook*. New York: Wiley.

Singer, P. W. (2005) "Outsourcing of War," *Foreign Affairs*, 84 (2).

Sinha, P. C. (ed.) (2005) *Encyclopedia of Arms Race, Arms Control and Disarmament*. New Delhi: Anmol Publications.

SIPRI Yearbook: Armaments, Disarmament, and International Security (annual) Stockholm: Stockholm International Peace Research Institute.

Slater, Mark B. (2003) *Rights of Passage: Passport in International Reactions*. Boulder, CO: Lynne Rienner.

Slaughter, Anne-Marie (1997) "The New Real World Order," *Foreign Affairs*, 76 (5).

Slaughter, Anne-Marie (2000) "Governing the Global Economy Through Government Networks," in Michael Byers (ed) *The Role of Law in International Relations: Essays in International Relations and International Law*. New York: Oxford University Press.

Slaughter, Anne-Marie (2003) "Mercy Killings: Why the Untied Nations Should Issue Death Warrants against Dangerous Dictators," *Foreign Policy*, May/June.

Slaughter, Anne-Marie (2004) *A New World Order.* Princeton, NJ: Princeton University Press.

Slaughter, Anne-Marie, Talumello, Andrew S., and Wood, Stepan (1998) "International Law and International Relations Theory: A New Generation of Interdisciplinary Scholarship," *American Journal of International Law*, 92 (3).

Slaughter Burley, Anne-Marie (1993) "International Law and International Relations Theory: A Dual Agenda," *American Journal of International Law*, 87 (2).

Smith, Bradley F. (1977) *Reaching Judgment at Nuremberg.* New York: Basic Books.

Smith, Fiona (2009) *Agriculture and the WTO: Towards a New Theory of International Agricultural Trade Regulation.* Northampton, MA: Edward Elgar.

Smith, Rhona K.M. Smith and van den Anker, Christian (eds.) (2005) *The Essentials of Human Rights.* New York: Oxford University Press.

Sørensen, George (2001) *Changes in Statehood: the Transformation of International Relations.* New York: Palgrave.

South Commission (1990) *The Challenge to the South: The Report of the South Commission.* Independent Commission of the South on Development Issues. New York: Oxford University Press.

Spector, Leonard (2002) "Nuclear Proliferation," in Jeffery A. Larsen (ed.), *Arms Control: Cooperative Security in a Changing Environment.* Boulder, CO: Lynne Rienner.

Speier, Richard (2000) "Can the Missile Technology Control Regime Be Repaired?" in Joseph Cirincione (ed.), *Repairing the Regime: Preventing the Spread of Weapons of Mass Destruction.* New York: Routledge.

Stacey, Robert C. "The Age of Chivalry," in Michael Howard, George J. Andreopoulos, and Mark L. Schulman (eds.), *The Laws of War.* New Haven, CT: Yale University Press, 27.

Stahn, Carsten Stahn and Sluiter, Göran (eds.) (2009) *The Emerging Practice of the International Criminal Court.* Boston, MA: Martinus Nijhoff.

Starr, Harvey Starr (1995) "International Law and International Order," in Charles W. Kegley, Jr (ed.), *Controversies in International Theories: Realism and the Neoliberal Challenge.* New York: St Martin's Press.

Steiner, Henry J. and Alston, Philip (1996) *International Human Rights in Context: Law, Politics, Morals.* New York: Oxford University Press.

Steinhardt, Ralph G. (1997) "Outer Space," in Christopher C. Joyner (ed.), *The United Nations and International Law.* Washington, DC: American Society of International Law/Cambridge University Press.

Strange, Susan (1996) *The Retreat of the State: The Diffusion of Power in the World Economy.* New York: Cambridge University Press.

Straus, Scott (2005) "Darfur and the Genocide Debate," *Foreign Affairs*, 84 (1).

Swing, John Temple (2003) "What Future for the Oceans?" *Foreign Affairs*, 82 (5).

Talbott, William J. (2005) *Which Rights Should Be Universal?* New York: Oxford University Press.

Tams, Christian J. (2005) *Enforcing Obligations Erga Omnes in International Law.* New York: Cambridge University Press.

Tanaka, Yuki (1996) *Hidden Horrors: Japanese War Crimes in World War II.* Boulder, CO: Westview.

Tanaka, Yoshifumi (2009) *A Dual Approach to Ocean Governance: The Cases of Zonal and Integrated Management in International Law of the Sea.* Burlington, VT: Ashgate.

Taylor, Charles Thomas (2002) *Toward World Sovereignty.* Lanham, MD: University Press.

Taylor, Telford (1992) *The Anatomy of the Nuremberg Trials: A Personal Memoir.* New York: Alfred A. Knopf.

Thachuk, Kimberly L. (2007) *Transnational Threats: Smuggling and Trafficking in Arms, Drugs, and Human Life.* Westport, CT: Praeger Security International.

Thayer, Charles W. (1959) *Diplomat.* New York: Harper & Brothers.

Thirlway, Hugh (1999) "The Nuclear Weapons Advisory Opinions," in Laurence Boisson de Chazournes and Philippe Sands (eds.), *International Law, the International Court of Justice and Nuclear Weapons.* New York: Cambridge University Press.

Thomson, Janice E. (1994) *Mercenaries, Pirates, and Sovereigns: State-Building and Extraterritorial Violence in Early Modern Europe.* Princeton, NJ: Princeton University Press.

Tochilovsky, Vladimir (2003) "Globalizing Criminal Justice: Challenges for the International Criminal Court," *Global Governance*, 9 (1).

Torpey, John (2000) *The Invention of the Passport: Surveillance, Citizenship and the State*. New York: Cambridge University Press.

Tremmel, Joerg Chet (ed.) (2006) *Handbook of Intergenerational Justice*. North Hampton, MA: Edward Elgar.

Trimble, Phillip R. (2002) *International Law: Foreign Relations Law*. New York: Foundation Press.

UK Ministry of Defence (ed.) (2004) *The Manual of the Law of Armed Conflict*. New York: Oxford University Press.

United Nations (1987) *Our Common Future*. New York: Oxford University Press.

United Nations (1990) *The Law of the Sea: Archipelagic States Legislative History of Part IV of the UN Convention of the Law of the Sea*. New York: United Nations.

United Nations [1997] (2008) *International Law on the Eve of the Twenty-First Century*, van Krieken, Peter J. and McKay, David (eds.), *The Hague: Legal Capital of the World*. New York: Cambridge University Press.

United Nations (1999) *World Survey on the Role of Women in Development: Globalization, Gender, and Work*. Center for Social Development and Humanitarian Affairs. Vienna: United Nations Publications.

United Nations Human Development Program (1995) *Human Development Report 1995*. New York: Oxford University Press.

United Nations Human Development Program (1998) "Unequal Human Impacts of Environmental Damage," *Human Development Report 1998*. New York: Oxford University Press.

Van De Veer, Stacey D. (2003) "Green Fatigue," *Wilson Quarterly*, 27 (4).

Van Dyke, Vernon (1970) *Human Rights, the United States, and World Community*. New York: Oxford University Press.

Väyrynen, Raimo (2003) "Regionalism Old and New," *International Studies Review*, 5 (1).

Veltmeyer, Henry (2005) "Democratic Governance and Participatory Development: The Role of Development NGOS," in the *Whitehead Journal of Diplomacy and International Relations*, 6 (2).

Verhaag, Melissa A. (2003) "It Is Not Too Late: The Need for a Comprehensive International Treaty to Protect the Arctic Environment," *Georgetown International Environmental Law Review*, Spring.

Vig, Norman J. (1999) "Introduction: Governing the International Environment," in Norman J. Vig and Regina S. Axelrod (eds.), *The Global Environment: Institutions, Law, and Policy*. Washington, DC: CQ Press.

Viikari, Lotta (2008) *The Environmental Element in Space Law: Assessing the Present and Charting the Future*. Boston, MA: Martinus Nijhoff.

van Krieken, Peter J. (ed.) (2002) *Terrorism and the International Legal Order*. The Hague, Netherlands: TMC Asser Press.

Vincent, R. J. (1986) *Human Rights and International Relations*. New York: Cambridge University Press.

Vogel, David (2006) "International Trade and Environmental Regulation," in Norman J. Vig and Michael E. Kraft (eds.), *Environmental Policy: New Directions for the Twenty-First Century*. Washington, DC: CQ Press.

von Glahn, Gerhard (1996) *Laws of Nations*, 7th edn. Boston, MA: Allyn and Bacon.

Vöneky, Silja (2003) "The Fight against Terrorism and the Rules of the Law of Warfare," in C. Walter et al. (eds.), *Terrorism as a Challenge for National and International Law: Security versus Liberty?* New York: Springer.

Waelde, Charlotte and MacQueen, Hector (eds.) (2007) *Intellectual Property: The Many Faces of the Public Domain*. Northampton, MA: Edward Elgar.

Wagner, Lynn (2003) "The Mediterranean Action Plan," in Bertram I. Spector and I. William Zartman (eds.), *Getting It Done: Postagreement Negotiation and International Regimes*. Washington, DC: United States Institute of Peace Press.

Walker, Alice (1993) *Warrior Marks: Female Genital Mutilation and the Sexual Blinding of Women*. New York: Harcourt Brace.

Waller, Forest, E, Jr (2002) "Strategic Nuclear Arms Control," in Jeffery A. Larsen (ed.), *Arms Control: Cooperative Security in a Changing Environment*. Boulder, CO: Lynne Rienner.

Walter, Christian, Vöneky, Silja, Röben, Volker, and Schorkopf, Frank (eds.) (2003) *Terrorism as a Challenge for National and International Law: Security versus Liberty?* New York: Springer.

Walters, Robert S. and Blake, David H. (1992) *The Politics of Global Economic Relations*, 4th edn. Englewood-Cliffs, NJ: Prentice-Hall.

Waltz, Kenneth N. (1979) *Theory of International Politics*. Reading, MA: Addison-Wesley.

Walzer, Michael (1992) *Just and Unjust War: A Moral Argument with Historical Illustrations*, 2nd edn. New York: Basic Books.

Walzer, Michael (2004) *Arguing about War*. New Haven, CT: Yale University Press.

Wapner, Paul (1995) "Politics Beyond the State: Environmental Activism and World Civil Politics," *World Politics*, 47 (3).

Ward, Barbara (1962) *The Rich Nations and the Poor Nations*. New York: W.W. Norton.

Ward, Barbara and Dubois, René (1972) *Only One Earth: The Care and Maintenance of a Small Planet*. New York: W. W. Norton.

Warner, Robert (2009) *Protecting the Oceans Beyond National Jurisdiction: Strengthening the International Law Framework*. Boston, MA: Martinus Nijhoff.

Warren, Mary Anne (1985) *Gendercide: The Implications of Sex Selection*. Totowa, NJ: Rowman and Allenheld.

Watkins, Michael and Rosegrant, Susan (2001) *Breakthrough International Negotiations: How Great Negotiators Transformed the World's Toughest Post-Cold War Conflicts*. San Francisco, CA: Jossey-Bass.

Watson, Adam (1992a) "Diplomacy," in John Baylis and N.J. Rengger (eds.), *Dilemmas of World Politics: International Issues in a Changing World*. Oxford: Clarendon Press.

Watson, Adam (1992b) *The Evolution of International Society*. New York: Routledge.

Watters, Lawrence (2004) *Indigenous Peoples, the Environment and Law*. Durham, NC: Carolina Academic Press.

Watts, Arthur Watts (2000) "The Importance of International Law," in Michael Byers (ed.), *The Role of Law in International Politics: Essays in International Relations and International Law*. New York: Oxford University Press.

Weiss, Edith Brown (1999) "The Emerging Structure of International Environmental Law," in Norman J. Vig and Regina S. Axelrod (eds.), *The Global Environment: Institutions, Law, and Policy*. Washington, DC: CQ Press.

Weitz, Eric D. (2003) *A Century of Genocide: Utopias of Race and Nation*. Princeton, NJ: Princeton University Press.

Wellman, Carl (1999) *The Proliferation of Rights: Moral Progress or Empty Rhetoric?* Boulder, CO: Westview Press.

Wendt, Alexander (1992) "Anarchy is What States Make of It: The Social Construction of Power Politics," *International Organization*, 46 (2).

Wesson, Robert (1990) *International Relations in Transition*. Englewood-Cliffs, NJ: Prentice-Hall.

Weston, Burns H. (2000) *International Law and World Order*, vols. 1–5. Ardsley, NY: Transnational Publishers.

Weston, Burns H. (ed.) (2005) *Child Labor and Human Rights: Making Children Matter*. Boulder, CO: Lynne Rienner.

Westra, Joel (2008) *International Law and the Use of Armed Force: The UN Charter and the Major Powers*. New York: Routledge.

Westra, Laura (2007) *Environmental Justice and the Rights of Indigenous Peoples: International and Domestic Legal Perspectives*. Sterling, VA: Stylus Publishing.

Wheeler, Michael O. (2002) "A History of Arms Control," in Jeffery A. Larsen (ed.), *Arms Control: Cooperative Security in a Changing Environment*. Boulder, CO: Lynne Rienner.

Wheeler, Nicholas J. (2000) *Saving Strangers: Humanitarian Intervention in International Society*. New York: NY: Oxford University Press.

Wheeler, Nicholas J. (2003) "The Kosovo Bombing Campaign," in Christian Reus-Smit (ed.), *The Politics of International Law*. New York: Cambridge University Press.

White, Nigel (2002) *The United Nations System: Toward International Justice*. Boulder, CO: Lynne Rienner.

White, Richard Alan (2004) *Breaking Silence: The Case that Changed the Face of Human Rights*. Washington, DC: Georgetown University Press.

Whittingham, Richard (1977) *Martial Justice: The Last Mass Execution in the United States*. Annapolis, MD: Naval Institute Press.

Wilmer, Franke (1993) *The Indigenous Voice in World Politics*. Newbury Park, CA: Sage.

Winters, Francis X. (2009) *Remembering Hiroshima: Was It Just?* Burlington, VT: Ashgate.

Wittner, Lawrence S. (2003) *Toward Nuclear Abolition: A History of the World Nuclear Disarmament Movement*. Stanford, CA: Stanford University Press.

Wolf, Martin (2004) *Why Globalization Works*. New Haven, CT: Yale University Press.

Wolf, Ronald Charles (2004) *Trade, Aid, and Arbitrate: The Globalization of Western Law*. Burlington, VT: Ashgate.

Wollstonecraft, Mary (1988) *A Vindication of the Rights of Women*. New York: W.W. Norton.

Wouters, Jan, Noellkaemper, André, and de Wet, Erika (eds.) (2008) *The Europeanization of International Law: The Status of International Law in the EU and its Member States*. New York: Cambridge University Press.

Wright, Martin (1992) *International Theory: The Three Traditions*, edited by Gabriele Wight and Brian Porter. New York: Holmes & Meier.

Wright, Quincy (1971) "The American Civil War 1861–65," in Richard A. Falk (ed.), *The International Law of Civil War*. Baltimore, MD: Johns Hopkins University Press.

Wright, Susan (2002) "Introduction," in Susan Wright (ed.) *Biological Warfare and Disarmament: New Problems/New Perspectives*. Lanham, MD: Rowman & Littlefield.

Young, Oran R. (1993) *Arctic Politics: Conflict and Cooperation in the Circumpolar North*. Hanover, NH: Dartmouth College.

Zartman, I. William (2001) "Preventive Diplomacy: Setting the Stage," In I. William Zartman (ed.), *Preventive Negotiation:Avoiding Conflict Escalation*. Lanham, MD: Rowman & Littlefield.

Zartman, I. William (2005) *Cowardly Lions: Missed Opportunities to Prevent Deadly Conflict and State Collapse*. Boulder, CO: Lynne Rienner.

Zerk, Jennifer A. Zerk (2006) *Multinationals and Corporate Social Responsibility: Limitations and Opportunities in International Law*. New York, NY: Cambridge University Press.

Index